W9-BKT-915

SHELTON STATE COMMUNITY
    COLLEGE
JUNIOR COLLEGE DIVISION
    LIBRARY

DISCARDED

H
61
.L346
1972

Lazarsfeld, Paul
    Felix, comp.

    Continuities in
the language of so-
cial research.

DATE DUE			

DISCARDED

Continuities in the Language of Social Research

Edited by

PAUL F. LAZARSFELD

ANN K. PASANELLA

MORRIS ROSENBERG

SHELTON STATE COMMUNITY
COLLEGE
JUNIOR COLLEGE DIVISION
LIBRARY

THE FREE PRESS
A Division of Macmillan Publishing Co., Inc.
New York

COLLIER MACMILLAN PUBLISHERS
London

Copyright © 1972 by The Free Press
A Division of Macmillan Publishing Co., Inc.

All rights reserved. No part of this book may be reproduced or transmitted in any form or by any means, electronic or mechanical, including photocopying, recording, or by any information storage and retrieval system, without permission in writing from the Publisher.

The Free Press
A Division of Macmillan Publishing Co., Inc.
866 Third Avenue, New York, N.Y. 10022

Collier-Macmillan Canada Ltd.

Library of Congress Catalog Card Number: 77–143525

Printed in the United States of America

printing number
    4   5   6   7   8   9   10

To
Bob Merton

SOCRATES.   Shall I propose that
we look for examples of art
and want of art, according
to our notion of them, in
the speech of Lysias which
you have in your hand, and
in my own speech?

PHAEDRUS.   Nothing could be
better; and indeed I think
that our previous argument
has been too abstract and
wanting in illustration.

—Plato, *Phaedrus*

Contents

E. Classifications and Typologies

Section II: Multivariate Analysis

A. The General Idea

B. Selected Examples

Section III: The Study of Collectives

A. Group Characteristics and Their Interrelations

B. Weight of Collective Characteristics

C. Contextual Analysis

Section IV: Panel Analysis   321

A. General Statements

B. Turnover

C. Qualified Change

D. Concurrent Change

E. Repeated Observations on Collectives

F. Relationship Between Panels and Experiments

Preface

In the first edition of this book, fifteen years ago, we tried to explain the role of methodology in the progress of the social sciences. As we described it, methodology was neither the collection of research techniques, nor a substitute for a philosophy of science. Rather, methodology was an analytical approach which examined concrete studies to make explicit the procedures that were used, the underlying assumptions that were made, and the modes of explanation that were offered. It thus involved a codification of ongoing research procedures. Actual research was the material from which methodology is built, without being identical with it.

Our basic position about methodology remains the same. We have formulated it carefully and in detail in the introduction to the first edition. Two parts of it are reproduced later, and they form an integral part of the present edition. One section deals with the nature of methodological work. It is close to two logical positions: on the one hand, to the neo-positivist idea of explication; on the other hand, to the more classical concept of critique—be it of pure reason or of literature and musical works. The other carryover section deals with the function of methodology in contemporary sociology: its educational value for disciplined thinking, its role in interdisciplinary efforts and the help it gives in the codfication and integration of empirical and theoretical work. The user of the new edition will want to scrutinize the old introduction if he wishes to compare our position with some more recent methodological discussions.*

Our selections begin and end with two metaphors which, over the years, have helped to dispel some prejudices against methodology. While our general organization remains the same, changes in the field of social research have made our task more difficult this time.

Recent Trends

For one, the scope and direction of empirical studies have greatly expanded. The empirical study of collectives has vastly grown during the last years. In terms of scope,

---

* Aaron V. Cicourel, *Method and Measurement in Sociology* (New York, The Free Press, 1964). Johan Galtung, *Theory and Methods of Social Research* (New York, Columbia University Press, 1967). Maurice R. Stein, *The Eclipse of Community*, Second Printing (New York, Harper & Row, Torchbook, 1965, originally Princeton University Press, 1960).

there are now available studies which may use as many as 100–200 organizations (colleges, hospitals, etc.) as the units of analysis. As a consequence it becomes possible to conduct an analysis at two levels: the organizations themselves and the people within them. By intertwining the two, a mode of contextual analysis is now possible which helps to integrate "holistic" ideas of classical sociology with modern empirical methods. The introduction and the selections of Section III discuss and exemplify this trend in detail.

An even more pronounced change is the emergence of the so-called panel studies which are based on repeated observations with the same people or the same collectives. These studies scarcely existed twenty-five years ago; today, they are pursued both in the United States and abroad. We can now with justice devote an entire section to this topic —as a matter of fact, Section IV is probably the most extensive systematic presentation of panel analysis available in the literature.

It was clear when we scanned the literature that not only were there a greater variety of studies, but there were more sociologists engaged in sophisticated research. The first two sections of the present volume bear witness to this. In the first section the flow from conceptual ideas to concrete research instruments can be documented in detail. Two of our selections show how indicators of class consciousness can be derived either from Marxist literature or from the observation of political movements. Another sequence exemplifies how one writer abstractly analyzes the notion of alienation; a subsequent author then converts these ideas into a manageable instrument of classification.

The increased methodological self-awareness has also encouraged us to include some more difficult material. Whereas the earlier volume assiduously avoided any selections requiring even a modest amount of mathematical knowledge, we have now included a small proportion of such material, particularly in Section II. Out of the codification of survey research grew the tradition of multivariate analysis; its purpose was to clarify the idea of causal analysis in non-experimental research. This Columbia tradition was subsequently vastly extended and enriched by other writers. Today a variety of mathematical models for formalizing empirical causal analysis are available. It was not possible to cover all these new developments adequately, but at least we have tried to convey the flavor of this new development. It is hoped that our selections communicate some of the main ideas even to those readers who still have difficulty with the use of mathematical symbols.

A trend that affected this new edition is an increased concern with methodology in undergraduate teaching. Even in the first edition we tried to go beyond the format of a conventional reader by providing detailed introductions explaining the purpose of each selection. These sectional introductions probably accounted most for the success of the volume. They have now been greatly expanded to the point where the number of interpretive pages has tripled. But all of these developments, welcome though they were, created problems for our work. The way we coped needs some comment.

The Organization of this Volume

The main question was to decide upon the relation of the new book to the earlier edition. As we stated above some of the early material could profitably have been re-used. But if we had chosen to do so, there would have been insufficient space for more recent selections. This led to an editorial policy which still managed to utilize the earlier collection without re-printing any of the readings.

In the explanatory introduction to each section in the second edition, there are two kinds of references: those to the new readings contained in the present volume and those to articles in the first edition. The old *Language* has found such general acceptance that we presume it is easily available. The purpose of the new sectional introductions is to help teacher and student to pick out exactly those points which are pertinent for a systematic methodological analysis of both new and old articles. By preserving the link with the first edition, we greatly broadened the base of our own analysis. In addition, each section contains, as before, an annotated bibliography, and the section introductions frequently allude to these works.

Even so the scarcity of space has required additional sacrifices. The first edition contained a few readings on prediction and on the use of trend data in social research. This time we built a whole section on prediction and trend research, but it turned out that this had to be omitted. We had also prepared a new section on qualitative research in order to combat a prevailing belief that only quantitative methods were susceptible to methodological clarification. It is true that quantitative procedures lend themselves more easily to explication and therefore strengthen methodological interest and skills. But fortunately this refined awareness has spilled over into the scrutiny of such procedures as participant observation on the one hand and the traditional analysis of larger social units on the other hand. (See, e.g., G. McCall and J. Simmons (eds.), *Issues in Participant Observation*, 1969.) We could not have done justice to this new methodological effort in a single section, and consequently are now preparing a second volume completely devoted to qualitative analysis on the micro- as well as the macro-level. Part of such a volume will be the empirical study of action which stands on the borderline of quantitative and qualitative research. Combined with studies on decision-making, this kind of work has also accelerated since the first edition. We have therefore eliminated the few selections which were included from this field and will give it fuller coverage in the next volume. Meantime it remains important for the student to be aware that the scope of rigorous and self-conscious procedural scrutiny now extends well beyond the areas which we are covering in the present volume.

We have maintained from the first edition the policy of not including problems of data collection such as questionnaire construction, interviewing techniques, or content analysis. The whole field of controlled experiments is excluded except for some comparisons with panel analysis in the fourth section. Altogether, we have not covered those fields where extensive methodological literature is already available.

These decisions leave for the present volume a structure which is quite straightforward and basically the same as the one we attempted in the first edition.

Section I starts with the basic question of *how units and variables are formed in the social sciences*. The flow from general conceptual ideas to the use of objective instruments is divided into four phases, and examples are given for each. At the end of Section I, some more traditional problems of classification are discussed; it is shown that the kind of material with which empirical research deals leads to some variations on an old theme.

Once the more basic units or "variates" have been dealt with, the next major problem is obviously the *interrelation of such variates in a coherent analysis*. It is here where the language of social research and the language of multivariate analysis converge. This language often serves to clarify theoretical expositions even if no empirical data are presented. But common to all our selections is the desire to derive from the manipulation of several variates, inferences regarding social phenomena. It is an open question as to what kind of problems would in principle not be susceptible to multivariate analysis, but Section II does give the floor to authors who feel that it is a restricted language.

A sociologist will be especially concerned with the question of how variate language can be applied to collectives. If we describe individuals, many distinctions are pertinent: attitudes vs. behavior; enduring dispositions vs. data which describe a state at a specific moment of time, etc. None of these distinctions were considered essential in the preparation of this volume; rather, in Section III, we concentrated upon ways of differentiating variates which pertain to an individual and *variates which refer to a collective, a group, an organization or an institution.* How can these "collective properties" be profitably classified? What is their relation to more traditional notions like "emergents"? How do they enter into propositions and especially into those where collectives and individuals are jointly taken into consideration?

All of the selections in the final section, IV, explicitly introduce the notion of time. And they do it in a very specific way: they deal with repeated observations on the same individuals or the same collectives. Such inquiries have become known as panel studies.

An astonishingly large number of new concepts can be derived from these repeated observations. The introduction to this section describes in detail how this approach is different from the analysis of trends and of prediction studies. Panel studies are the empirical language into which many discussions of processes can be translated.

Debate, discussion, and criticism flourish in any vital field, and social research methodology is no exception in this regard. At several points, then, we have given space to authors opposed to our approach, either in general or with regard to more specific areas. Thus we have included Herbert Blumer's influential presidential address to the American Sociological Association, an article which explicitly attacks the basic premises of this book. We have also selected an article by Eleanor Maccoby contending that the interpretation of panel data advanced here can be viewed in a quite different light.

The amount of search and work needed for this new edition required the addition of a third editor. Ann Pasanella bore the heaviest load of the three of us during the several years it took to do the job. The two former editors were able to infuse some of their other activities into the new edition. Morris Rosenberg published a text on *The Logic of Survey Analysis* which has provided new material for Section II. Paul Lazarsfeld has started a number of essays integrating various methodological trends; some excerpts are included in Sections I and II.

Since the pedagogical value of a work depends on how it is used, we should like to direct a word to the teacher who intends to utilize these selections. In the extended introductions to the various sections, we have often made suggestions as to what seems important in a paper from our point of view or how difficult passages might be explained or expanded. It is our experience that training in social research best proceeds along three lines. There are certain well-established techniques which are most economically presented in coherent lectures. Juxtaposed to these, the student needs clinical experience. He should be attached to a project and learn by his own experience how to sharpen his wits. Lectures remain dead without such training; but apprenticeship by itself remains provincial because it is necessarily restricted to a few topics. The bridge between doctrine and clinical work has to be provided by the careful scrutiny of concrete pieces of research, something akin to what French humanists call "explication de texte." Here the student is expected to reconstruct the path a specific author took: what considerations guided his collection of data; how, in hindsight, he might have planned better; which successes or defeats he met in the course of the analysis; and what strategies are implied in his final presentation. This technique allows an attack on a broad range of subjects and under the guidance of an expert, provides the experience of reliving a real research event.

The present book hopes to serve this challenging task of combining leadership with self-discovery.

Continuities in the
Language of Social Research

From *The Language of*

Social Research *

The Idea of Social Research Methodology

THERE IS a well known story about the centipede who lost his ability to walk when he was asked in which order he moved his feet. But other details of the story are buried in conspiratorial silence. First of all, there is no mention of the fact that the inquiry came from a methodologist who wanted to improve the walking efficiency of the centipede community. Then, little attention is paid to the other centipedes who participated in the investigation. Not all of them reacted with such disastrous effects. Some were able to give rather reasonable answers; from these the investigator worked diligently to arrive at general principles of walking behavior.

When the methodologist finally published his findings, there was a general outcry that he had only reported facts which everyone already knew. Nevertheless, by formulating this knowledge clearly, and by adding hitherto unobserved facts at various points, the average centipede in the community was eventually able to walk better. After a generation or so, this knowledge was incorporated into textbooks, and so filtered down to students on a lower level of scholarship. In retrospect this was the outstanding result. Of course, the great centipede ballet dancer and other creative walking artists continued to depend on hereditary endowments and could not be produced by the school system. But the general level of walking, characteristic of the centipede in the street, was improved. In this way, individuals endowed with great personal gifts started out at a higher level, and achieved creative performances unparalleled in the past.

Fables of this kind are often told when there does not seem to be any satisfactory way of providing a precise statement of what we have in mind. The burden of definition is shifted to the reader. He is invited to draw the implications from the fable, and to form from them his own picture of whatever is being described. It is indeed tempting to rest the definition of a methodologist upon something like this centipede story. Just as it would be difficult to elaborate a definition of an historian, so it is difficult to catalogue the interests of a methodologist or to specify his functions in any detail. But the present book is a reader on methodology in the social sciences. It is therefore incumbent on us, as the editors, to make a serious attempt to circumscribe what is meant by methodology and to consider what role it does or should play in the development of modern social research.

* Paul F. Lazarsfeld and Morris Rosenberg (eds.), *The Language of Social Research: A Reader in the Methodology of Social Research* (New York: The Free Press, 1955), pp. 1–4, 9–12.

We can facilitate our task somewhat by first recalling closely related efforts which are usually subsumed under the heading of "philosophy of science."

Explication and Critique

As a result of modern positivism, interest in clarifying the meaning of concepts and statements has become quite general. A recent monograph by Hempel [1] has been welcomed for its contributions to such clarification. He indicates what role *explication* plays in modern logic. It does not develop strict rules of thinking. Rather, it tries to narrow the gap between everyday language and scientific language, without ever claiming that this gap can be bridged completely.

> Explication aims at reducing the limitations, ambiguities, and inconsistencies of ordinary usage of language by propounding a reinterpretation intended *to enhance the clarity and precision of their meanings* as well as their ability to function in the processes and theories with explanatory and predictive force. [2]

When we transfer terms like "personality" or "law" or "cause" from everyday language into scientific usage, we must always make decisions for which we ourselves take the responsibility. We give up certain connotations which these terms have in order to make the remainder more precise and more easily amenable to verification and proof. In this sense, as Hempel points out, an explication cannot be qualified simply as true or false; but it may be judged as more or less adequate according to the extent to which it attains its objectives.

Social scientists who are interested in methodology can easily find occasion for such explication. It is instructive to examine the work of a classical writer, say, one in the field of public opinion research, and to see how his statements might be translated into the language of modern research procedures. It will be found, on the one hand, that such writings contain a great richness of ideas which could be profitably infused into current empirical work; on the other hand, it will be found that such a writer tolerates great ambiguity of expression. By proper explication, we can bring out the more precise meanings which might be imputed to him; and we would be especially interested to see which of his statements permit verification. The task of such explication is not to criticize the work, but rather to bridge a gap, in this case between an older humanistic tradition and a newer one which is more empirically oriented.

As a matter of fact, the need for such explication is particularly urgent in the social sciences. When the natural scientist makes a discovery, it usually turns out to be so different from everyday experiences that the very nature of the phenomenon forces him to develop precise and sharp terminology; the extreme example of this, of course, is mathematics. But in speaking about human affairs we are accustomed to common sense, everyday language, and we cannot avoid transferring these colloquialisms to the classroom and to the debating halls where we discuss social matters. Everyday language is notoriously vague, however, and therefore clarification and purification of discourse are very important for the social scientist. We must make deliberate efforts toward semantic analysis.

Another and related line of intellectual activity is that which has been called the *"critique of theory."* The word critique has been taken over from German philosophy, and can be easily misunderstood. When Kant wrote his *Critique of Pure Reason,* he obviously did not mean to be critical of rational thinking; by "critique" he meant an analysis of the conditions under which such thinking is possible. The same meaning is found also in the field of literary and artistic criticism; here, too, the idea is not that the critic necessarily disapproves of a piece of art, but that he analyzes its structure. In the same way, criticism of theoretical systems implies only that their foundations and tacit assumptions are clearly brought to light.

The main American representative of critical analysis is Bridgman, and a short essay of his provides what is perhaps the best introduction to critiques of this kind.[3] In his introductory statement, Bridgman puts the task quite clearly:

> The attempt to understand why it is that certain types of theory work and others do not is *the concern of the physicist as critic, as contrasted with the physicist as theorist*. The material for the physicist as critic is the body of physical theory, just as the material of the physicist as theorist is the body of empirical knowledge.

The distinction between "theory" and "critique" is important. The critic deals with empirical material—but once removed. By bringing out clearly what the theorist (or analyst) does with his primary data he contributes in his way to the progress of research. In the introduction and conclusion of his essay, Bridgman brings to the American reader an understanding of the general intellectual influences which emanated, at the turn of the century, from writers like Poincaré in France and Mach in Germany. If one were to write the intellectual history of the generation of European students who grew up during the first decades of the twentieth century, one would probably rank this kind of critique, along with psychoanalysis and Marxism, as the main intellectual influences which shaped the climate of thinking in the period.

It is interesting that Bridgman places great emphasis on the educational value of such critiques. He points out that the difficulty of assimilating the creative ideas of others is one which is greatly underrated in modern education. And he feels that if more stress were put on the development of critical faculties, the creativeness and inventiveness of the young natural scientist would be considerably enhanced.

In light of all this it was very tempting for the editors of this reader to feature it as a contribution to the philosophy of the social sciences. But a more modest terminology seemed more appropriate to the present state of the social sciences. They have a long past but a very recent history only. Yesterday's concepts are forgotten for the sake of today's notion. Who remembers Tarde's laws of imitation when he writes about reference groups? Who wonders in what respect they are different answers to the same concern, or whether they tell the same story in different words? And where is there real continuity in the formulation of theories? Has Comte's hope to understand the development of society anything to do with Parsons' efforts to analyze social systems? The danger is that we shall end up with a few logical commonplaces if we try to bring out what is common to the various ways in which scholars, say in the last century, have tried to make a science out of the more general and much older attempts to understand human society.

The term methodology seems more appropriate. It implies that concrete studies are being scrutinized as to the procedures they use, the underlying assumptions they make, the modes of explanation they consider as satisfactory. Methodological analysis in this sense provides the elements from which a future philosophy of the social sciences may be built. If our linguistic feeling is adequate, the term should convey a sense of tentativeness; the methodologist codifies ongoing research practices to bring out what is consistent about them and deserves to be taken into account the next time. Methodology and the related activities of explication and critical analysis have developed as a bent of mind rather than as a system of organized principles and procedures. The methodologist is a scholar who is above all *analytical* in his approach to his subject matter. He tells other scholars what they have done, or might do, rather than what they should do. He tells them what order of finding has emerged from their research, not what kind of result is or is not preferable.

This kind of analytical interest requires self-awareness, on the one hand, and tolerance, on the other. The methodologist knows that the same goal can be reached by alternative roads, and he realizes that instruments should be adapted to their function, and not be uselessly sharp. Thus, a reminder is needed on the ways in which methodology can *not* be defined. For example, it is probably less rigorous and more general than formal logic; on the other hand, it has less substantive content and is more formal than what has been called the psychology or sociology of knowledge. Similarly, the methodologist is not a technician; he does not tell research workers *how* to proceed, what steps to follow in the actual conduct of an investigation. And neither is it his task to indicate what problems should be selected for study. But once the topic for investigation has been chosen, he might suggest the procedures which, in the light of the stated objectives, seem most appropriate.

Enough of generalities. Further understanding will best be served by describing how and why the material in this reader has been selected.

The Role of Methodology in Development of the Social Sciences

One function of methodology is to provide formal training for young social scientists which will enable them to do better research. Every field of intellectual activity has its own ways of developing disciplined thinking among its young scholars. The natural scientist gets this training by studying mathematics and by learning the precise operations implied in experimentation. The humanist obtains formal training through intensive study of classical languages. But the kinds of formal training appropriate for the natural scientist, on the one hand, and for the humanist, on the other, are not especially suited to the needs of the modern social scientist. While mathematical models and experimental studies are coming to play an increasingly important role in the investigation of human behavior, they are not likely to become dominant modes of inquiry in the near future. And, although the social scientist might benefit from the study of Latin and Greek, his interest in contemporary materials largely limits the usefulness of these classical languages. He must therefore develop disciplined thinking in some other way. The kind of analytics called for in methodological studies *provides the required formal training*.

Methodology also increases the social scientist's ability *to cope with new and unfamiliar developments in his field*. Perhaps the best way of clarifying this idea is to elaborate the difference between technology and methodology mentioned in an earlier connection. The individual who learns how to develop certain indices or tests, or who becomes adept in the application of particular statistical techniques, masters the skills only which are available at the moment. When, in the future, new skills are proposed, he can probably learn them as well. However, will he be able to decide which of these skills are useful and which are not? Will he understand the assumptions underlying various techniques? Will he have criteria by which to appraise whether or not certain procedures are appropriate to certain problems? Obviously, the ability to make judgments of this kind is not developed merely by learning the techniques of the present or of the past. What is needed is a training which will enable the student to meet the research situations, ten or twenty years hence, which cannot possibly be foreseen now. A well trained methodologist will be able, many years after the completion of his formal education, to confront new developments in his science. He will be equipped to judge their merits, to relate them to past trends, and to make a reasoned choice as to what he wants to integrate into his own thinking, thus furthering the self-education which every responsible scholar continues most of his life.

A third way in which methodology can aid in the advancement of the social sciences is through its *contributions to interdisciplinary work*. In recent years, many scholars have expressed the hope that developments in the different social sciences could be more closely coordinated; but where such efforts at integration have been made, they have often resulted in disappointment. There are certainly many reasons to account for this. But one source is undoubtedly the fact that various disciplines put different emphases on where they place thorough scholarship and where they are satisfied with a procedural dilettantism.

> Economists who study business cycles have developed sophisticated ways of analyzing social processes; sociologists, on the other hand, often talk loosely—and with excessive complexity—about similar problems in their own field.
> Sociologists and social psychologists have become skilled in the art of questionnaire construction; economists, when they make use of such schedules, do so with little understanding of well-tested principles.
> Historians use quotations from newspapers and other documents haphazardly, without any apparent awareness of modern techniques of content analysis.
> Anthropologists, in accepting vague information and incorporating it into their work, do not seem to recognize how far historians have advanced techniques for checking and appraising evidence.
> For the past fifty years economists have given careful attention to the logic of index formation; sociometrists often put together any index which happens to come to their minds.

Such discrepancies mean that the results obtained by the several social sciences are often lacking in comparability. This, in turn, obviously interferes with interdisciplinary endeavors. Methodological analysis can help to overcome these barriers. Careful study of the basic assumptions underlying particular procedures may reveal their applicability to a broad range of problems, and may cut across the traditional lines separating different disciplines. Of course, there is no guarantee that what the economist means by the measurement of utility and what the sociologist and social psychologist mean by attitude measurement will turn out to be fundamentally similar. But whatever points of convergence exist certainly cannot be uncovered until the two areas are minutely and intensively compared. Equally detailed analysis of the way in which different disciplines formulate their problems—the explanatory models which they set up—should also give impetus to productive interdisciplinary work. By showing that two or more branches of the social sciences are concerned with the same kinds of problems however different the terminology they may use, such analysis may lead to important integrations of existing knowledge, and to significant prescriptions for future interdisciplinary efforts.

Our fourth point is derivative from the preceding ones. Methodology can make a direct contribution to the advancement of our knowledge of human affairs, inasmuch as it provides organizing *principles by which such knowledge can be integrated and codified*. Which parts of an existing body of data are worthwhile; where does there seem to be overlapping of knowledge; what is the most fruitful line of further development? These are questions whose answers are facilitated by the kinds of methodological analysis described earlier. In this connection we might consider what has sometimes appeared to be a controversy over the proper role of methodology. It is an undisputed historical fact that methodological self-criticism has served a very important function at crucial phases in the development of the natural sciences. The only question is at what point in the history of a science such methodological analysis becomes most significant. In the physical sciences it came at a rather late stage. It was only after many centuries of observation and experiment that the resulting knowledge could be systematically organized. The natural sciences thus had a long past of discovery before methodological work was introduced and was recognized as important.

If he reasons by analogy only, one might say that methodological analysis in the social sciences should wait until systematic study of human behavior has achieved a longer history. Actually, however, the position of the social sciences is quite different. Although rigorous investigation of human affairs, comparable to precise study of natural phenomena, is only quite recent, we have been accumulating knowledge about social behavior for many centuries. Interest in, and speculations about, the nature of social life have as long a history as does such life itself. Thus, before we even begin the systematic study of human behavior, we have an almost limitless store of proverbial wisdom, of introspective accounts, and of general observations about the way in which human beings behave in their societies. Indeed, this store is so vast that it is especially important to sift out the true from the untrue, and to study the conditions under which particular common sense generalizations hold. At one time or another, almost every social scientist has played a game by arraying against each other the contradictory statements about social behavior which can be found in our fund of proverbial knowledge.[4] It is at this point that methodology becomes useful. We must sort out this knowledge and organize it in some manageable form; we must reformulate common sense statements so that they can be subjected to empirical test; we must locate the gaps so that further investigations are oriented in useful directions. In other words, the embarrassment of riches with which modern social sciences start forces them to develop organizing principles at an early stage.

Emphasis on the roles which methodology can play should not lead us to overestimate its importance or to underestimate the importance of concrete substantive work. It is sometimes said that scholars who are creative do research, while those who are uncreative only talk about it. In the last analysis, it is the creative, substantive worker who really advances a science; certainly we do not want to imply otherwise. Our position is rather a sociological one. Once the creative scholar has matured and has begun his work, there is perhaps very little which he can gain from methodological reflection. At this point it is probably best to leave him to his own devices. But during the period of his training, during the time when he tries to acquire the knowledge and modes of thinking which he might use later—during this formative period a thorough grounding in methodology will be valuable. An analogy might serve to make this point clearer. It is sometimes hard to understand how it happens that sports records, like those of the Olympic Games, are continually bettered—runners run faster miles, pole vaulters clear greater heights, and so on. It is unlikely that, over the last fifty years, the capacities of *homo athleticus* have improved in any Darwinian sense. But training techniques, styles of running, and athletic equipment have steadily been refined. Great athletic stars are born; but good coaches can so raise the level of the average participant that when a star appears he starts from a higher level than did the star of a generation ago. He therefore is able to reach greater peaks of achievement, even though his individual capacities need not be superior to those of his predecessors. In the same sense, methodology, self-awareness of the field, provides a better starting background for the individual creative scholar.

Notes

1. Carl Hempel, *Fundamentals of Concept Formation in Empirical Science* (Chicago: University of Chicago Press, 1952). International Encyclopedia of Unified Science, Vol. 11, No. 7.

2. *Ibid.,* p. 12.

3. *The Nature of Physical Theory* (Princeton: Princeton University Press, 1936), p. 2.

4. See, for example, Robert S. Lynd, *Knowledge for What?* (Princeton: Princeton University Press, 1939), pp. 60–62, and H. A. Simon, "Some Further Requirements of Bureaucratic Theory" in *Reader in Bureaucracy,* R. K. Merton, A. P. Gray, B. Hockey, and H. C. Selvin (eds.) (New York: The Free Press, 1952), pp. 51–58.

Concepts, Indices, Classification, and Typologies

Introduction

THE FOUR sections of this volume deal with what might be called variate-language and its place in contemporary sociology. At first glance, this language might seem constricted or meager; we shall try to show just how rich it can be.

The first section develops the basic notion of a variate. The term has come into use to cover all devices by which people, groups, communities and other objects of sociological inquiry can be classified. For example, the dichotomy male-female is a variate; so are the ranks of students in a class, or the income of their parents. It is not difficult to express some of these in terms of numbers; thus, for example, income can be represented by quantity of dollars. Such a variate, portrayed in a quantitative way, is usually called a variable.

The General Approach

In some sociological studies, we are satisfied to deal with the variates at hand, as for instance, the birth rate in a country or the number of hours people listen to television. These are man-made variates, but simple and uncomplicated and not likely to be disputed. In other cases, we start with conceptual ideas for which we need some kind of numerical expression: we want to classify groups according to their cohesiveness, people according to their socioeconomic status, colleges according to their quality. These classificatory devices become the variates. There is no common agreement about the definition of variates nor the forms by which they are combined. Such terms as measurement, scales, indices lack precise delineation and are often used interchangeably. In the introduction to this section, we have designated "index" as the word for any empirical combination of variates. Our general theme will be the *transformation of concepts into such indices*.

What are the concepts to be discussed? For our purposes in thinking about social research, they will be *classificatory* concepts, those which permit us to take a set of people or collectives (small groups, organizations, nations) and to partition them into a number of exhaustive and mutually exclusive subsets. This meaning would, for instance, exclude the sociological concepts of role or reference group; such concepts direct the thinking of the investigator toward a broad field of observations. They enlarge his scope; they do not subdivide it. On the other hand, the cohesiveness of a group or the bureaucratization of an institution are classificatory concepts. Given a number of concrete groups, we ought to be able to decide for any pair which of the two is more cohesive (including, of course, the decision of equal cohesiveness). We are not trying to elaborate on this distinction because, from the examples presented in this section, we trust it will become quite clear what type of concepts we have in mind.

If these classificatory concepts are designed to furnish distinctions and comparisons between concrete units—people or collectives—then they have to be translated into corresponding classificatory instruments. A well-established doctrine exists for this transformation, and its various steps are exemplified in Section I. The phases are entitled dimensional clarification; choice of indicators; and index formation.

Any conceptualization originates in some observation about a number of similar concrete units which either seem to behave differentially under the same circumstances or different concrete units which appear to have a common underlying component. To give the largest leeway for these creative origins, one might talk of a first phase of imagery. The first phase is bound to be transitory as the sociologist feels impelled to communicate his imagery to others. He can do that in a variety of ways. He can cumulate verbal descriptions or he may try to give what the classical logicians call an intentional or verbal definition. If he wants to end up with concrete research instruments, he will probably specify his ideas in a second phase, what we call dimensional clarification, where the original somewhat vague construct is partitioned into components or aspects. Next, he must choose indicators of these dimensions, and finally, with this list of indicators he must make the final decision as to which to use in an

index and how to combine these indicators so that the index will serve its purposes.

Selection 1 by Paul Lazarsfeld discusses the whole process by drawing on a number of examples, the most illustrative being the history of the well known *F*-scale.

Dimensional Clarification and the Choice of Indicators

The selections in Subsection B deal with the two phases of *dimensional clarification* and the *choice of indicators* corresponding to the proposed dimensions. Note that the dimensions can be derived either from a logical analysis of the sociological concept or induced from a series of empirical findings. Selections 2 and 3 are intentionally related. Seeman identified five meanings of alienation from historical writings on the subject, thereby clarifying the diverse meanings of the term. Several years later, Middleton built upon this clarification by applying it in an empirical study.

Selection 4 is a contribution specifically written for this volume. The senior author tried out a test of class-consciousness among a sample of respondents in an upstate New York community; the test used groups of indicators, chosen on the basis of a dimensional analysis derived from observations of the European labor movement. The author shows that the same dimensions could be used in this country, although it was necessary to tap different indicators for most of them. This selection is paralleled by Selection 5, permitting an interesting comparison between the two articles. Leggett, studying class consciousness among Detroit auto workers, is also explicit about his dimensions and the way he picked his indicators. The similarity of the dimensions in the two studies is rather surprising, although Leggett draws upon the Marxist legacy rather than direct observations. The sources of some of Leggett's indicators are also more indirect. A reading of the two excerpts gives some inkling of the broad range of available techniques for the manufacture of indicators.

Index Formation

Once indicators have been selected, we face the problem of combining them into larger units which are called indices or scales or measures. It is, of course, not necessary that all indicators be combined into one such instrument. Sometimes one will be willing to represent one concept by a number of different measures. At other times, one will use the dimensional analysis mainly to make sure that, in a single instrument, no essential aspect of the original imagery has been overlooked. So many types of indices have been developed that it is impossible to provide examples for all of them. Subsection C (Index Formation) makes only one major distinction, viz., that between *itemized* and *parametric* indices. This distinction is somewhat crude, but can be described roughly along the following lines. We can take the information about each individual and characterize him by some form of more or less sophisticated "addition." On the other hand, we may take the information about a whole *group* of people and summarize the distribution of the information among the members. This latter procedure leads to parametric indices, the name being derived from the tradition that distributions are usually characterized by so-called parameters.

To give a primitive example of the distinction: An aptitude test is scored by the number of correct answers of each *individual* and gives an itemized index for each respondent. A *group* can be characterized according to whether it has a homogeneous student body with a small standard deviation of aptitude scores or a heterogeneous population with large standard deviation—a simple parametric index. We shall see in a later section that, under certain circum-

stances, collectives can be characterized by itemized indices. Inversely, an individual student might be characterized by a parametric index, as, for instance, the standard deviation of his grades in a number of subjects. Be it repeated that this dichotomy of itemized versus parametric serves to draw attention to one major distinction between indices. In other contexts, other aspects become important. Thus, in a cost of living index, two problems are raised: what items of the total budget should be considered and how should they be weighted? The experienced teacher will easily find pertinent similar problems in sociological literature.

This does not mean, of course, that mathematically based measurement models do not warrant attention. Although we cannot exemplify these models in detail here, it so happens that Samuel Stouffer has written an elementary comparison (Selection 6) between the so-called Guttman scale (an itemized index) and one type of latent structure scale where indicators are combined into mathematically based patterns. In the first edition we had an interesting article on indices from the same author on the diagnoses of mental difficulties among soldiers in several American cities. The clinical ratings provided by medical doctors varied far more than the scores derived from itemized tests. This seemed to show that, at least for comparative purposes, the latter type of instrument was preferable. Similar experiences are reported in other studies listed in the annotated bibliography.

Many parametric indices can be located in sociometric studies. The selection by Zeisel in the annotated bibliography presents the idea in its most elementary form. The basic material consists of interpersonal choices as expressed by members of a group. By putting this simple material in terms of matrices, a number of meaningful parameters can be derived: the social expansiveness of the participants, their popularity, the subgroups they form, etc.

Applying somewhat more sophisticated

operations, one is able to derive other parametric indices. The selection in the first edition by Festinger and his associates is an elementary introduction to the multiplication of matrices. This algebraic operation should, by now, be part of every sociologist's mental equipment.

The distribution of sociometric choices is not the only source of parametric indices. More unusual is the application to the description of organizational arrangements. As a simple example, Selection 7 by Hauser and Lazarsfeld reports a study of college admissions officers. Each office consists of a director and his assistant, both of whom are engaged in a series of activities. The basic material consists of the amount of time the two participants devote to these various tasks. Two of the parametric indices are easily understandable. One gives the total amount of time devoted to each activity and the other shows whether the director or the assistant is more likely to engage in the activity. A third index requires somewhat more subtle analysis. How do the interests of the director affect the assignments allocated to his assistant—both interest and assignment again expressed in terms of invested time? This selection, incidentally, provides a special opportunity to acquaint the student with the intricate structure of one of the main building blocks of social research, the fourfold table.

The question is often raised whether general rules can be established for the choice of indicators and the formation of indices. Taken in an absolute sense, the answer is certainly: No. Some claim that only after a long sequence of research can one tell whether the choice was right: indicators are combined into measures (see below) and these in turn form empirical propositions (see Section II) which one day may provide material for theoretical generalizations. Such final scientific usefulness makes for survival of the indicator base. Others, like Louis Guttman, have made a beginning toward establishing a formal procedure: it is

assumed that, for each concept there exists a "universe of items" from which a specific instrument selects a sample of items. This still leaves open the question of the source of the universe and the implicit sampling procedure.

The most concrete treatment of this problem has come from the psychologists. They have for some time been concerned with what they call *construct validity*. Can the investigator be explicit about the basis for his choice of indicators? Does he obtain from his use of a new instrument reasonable results in areas where much is known, and promising results in unexplored areas? How does his final measure based on his indicators relate to older, relatively better established classificatory instruments? Out of the large and often controversial literature we have placed several papers in the annotated bibliography. One, by Campbell and Fiske has had considerable influence on psychological test theory in raising the matter of discriminant validity—the requirement that a test not correlate too highly with measures from which it is supposed to differ. Blalock utilizes Simon's method in writing on the implication of measurement errors for making inferences.

The Theory of Indices

We have included three topics under "theory of indices." There could, of course, be many more. The first, dealing with the interchangeability of indices, raises the question of whether it makes a great difference as to what specific indicators are chosen from a larger pool of equally reasonable items. Lazarsfeld and Thielens explain in Selection 8 that in their measure of professorial prominence, it made little difference which of two indices was used. Even if the two indices were not very strongly associated, they still produced the same results when each was related to a third variate. It happened that the more prominent professors had more permissive attitudes toward their students, no matter what the index of prominence. The findings, given in detail, could be summarized by saying that the correlation between each of the two indices and the third variate was about the same.

Whereas this selection compares two cross-tabulations, an article by Horwitz and Smith in the first *Language* examines more than one hundred such pairs. Two kinds of indices of socioeconomic status are related to a number of attitudes established in several subgroups. In a two-dimensional diagram, each entry represents two correlations, that of each socioeconomic index with the attitude questionnaire items. A teacher who wants to test the ability to interpret numerical results might want to require a lengthy contrast between the Horwitz-Smith and Lazarsfeld-Thielens selections.

The doctrine of interchangeability of indices raises several issues. First, it can be shown mathematically that it is generally applicable only because, in general, the correlations in social research are rather low. Second, it leaves to individual judgment the determination of when two sets of indicators are equally plausible. How can one make this more rigorous? One way to come closer would be to study carefully the cases where two reasonably similar indices failed to turn out interchangeably. The construct validity theme we mentioned earlier reappears in this context.

Still another choice facing the social research analyst is that of unidimensionality versus multidimensionality. We alluded before to two ways in which groups or their members can be characterized. For example, with a verbal and a mathematical test score for each student, we can order the scores in two ways: either by averaging the two scores or by computing the difference between them. The two resultant indices have very different meanings. Recent literature has shown that the same formal problem

looms quite important in the measurement of socioeconomic status. Traditionally, a number of indicators of status have been accumulated in a one-dimensional scale. But conceptual analysts pointed out that the notion of status had a variety of dimensions. By comparing for the same person his standing on each of these dimensions, one reaches a measure of "status discrepancy." We offer Selection 9 by Hollingshead and Redlich as an example of a one-dimensional analysis treated with great ingenuity. It deserves special attention. In Selection 10, on the other hand, Lenski emphasizes the variations between dimensions and derives a number of interesting substantive findings which have been repeatedly pursued in subsequent literature.

The final selection in subdivision D elucidates the constant back-and-forth between a theoretical notion (scientific collaboration) and the choice of a proper index (name-ordering of authors).

Classification and Typologies

Indices, scales and similar instruments are refined devices to classify people or collectives. It should not be forgotten, however, that the problem of classification did not begin with the concern for social research methodology. It has played a great role in the early stages of every science. Some of the problems involved are perennial—the familiar rule that a system of classificatory categories should be exhaustive and mutually exclusive. But any new set of material raises its own special issues. Already in the first edition some pertinent material was presented. Since then a more systematic approach to the problem of classification in social research was developed. It is this systematics we are about to sketch.

One might describe three typical social research situations differentiated by the condition in which empirical material arrives at the analyst's doorstep. Because the first edition contains good examples of the first two research conditions we shall portray, our readings focus upon the third. But what are the situations? One is the totally unstructured, where the data reach us in one undifferentiated package. How do we condense or focus these materials in order to make some sense out of them? Think, for example, of classifying newspaper editorials commenting on a major political event. Both the event and the shape of the editorials are completely out of the researcher's control. His role comes in taking the material at hand, juxtaposing the pieces, speculating about underlying connections, and making some tentative arrangement of the contents. (The mental operations involved in this analysis would be very similar to those required in an anthropological study of family relationships or a field observation of indoctrination of new recruits in the army.) The only reason one can even attempt to classify such unstructured material is that one has the support of some preconceived ideas or hypotheses. Thus, in the Lazarsfeld-Barton article on "General Principles of Questionnaire Construction" (first edition), we saw that in order to deal with open-ended answers to a questionnaire on adolescents' problems, it was necessary to differentiate logical problem areas (work, leisure, education) before attempting to classify concrete responses.

One methodological objective is to establish a general, standard set of categories applicable to diverse but comparable bodies of material. A characteristic example can be found in the categories which Bales developed for the description of interactions between members of small groups (see annotated bibliography). His basic system has led to many interesting results in small group research.

Similarly, in asking employees what they dislike about the company that hires them, we may decide to explore four aspects of organizational identity: the system of formal roles and rules, the network of interpersonal relationships, the goals of the organization, and the rewards it bestows. This ideological framework provides some assistance in classifying the answers we receive from the employees; in the course of the analysis, there will be modifications and shifts in this framework growing out of the very material itself. To bring out the relation between the purpose for which the data were collected and the way they were ordered for presentation and interpretation is the task of the methodologist.

A second kind of classification might be termed the numerically supported variety. Here we begin with a rather arbitrary list of categories and observe the frequency with which they occur in various subgroups. Then we form a smaller number of more systematic categories, guided by our preliminary numerical findings. Usually, two columns of such initial statistical listings are needed. Thus, for instance, in a study of "The Effects of Military Rank on Various Types of Attitudes" (first edition), Hans Speier took the responses which had been tabulated separately for enlisted men and for officers and classified the items according to whether the two status groups held the same opinions or whether there were considerable differences. It turned out that the two classes of items were of very different character, and the author was able to add a convincing interpretation of what one might call a second-order difference. In an article by Lotte Radermacher and Elias Smith, also in the first edition, the basic material is a cross-tabulation between two variates: the occupation of workers who attend evening school classes and the specific courses they choose. Thus, one variate, like the Speier analysis, deals with status and the other with an expression of interest (roughly comparable to the Speier attitude variate). The cross-tabulation is more complex and is used in a different way for classificatory purposes. It is the *relation* between occupation and course content that is being classified. The resulting types of affinities again permit a more general interpretation.

There is a third situation we wish to discuss in more detail with new examples. Based either on theoretical derivation or on more extensive numerical analysis, we may have decided upon a *typology* to describe the material at hand. This is a substantive decision, and the methodologist cannot quarrel with it. But he can make a very important contribution by trying to elucidate the considerations on which the typology was based and the consequences to which it leads.

The sociological literature is rich in examples. Beginning with the Chicago school that excelled in describing types of residents in the ghetto or the Gold Coast, practically every field worker who enters a new territory strives for initial order by talking of types. At a different level, we find types of social theories, types of textbooks and, of course, our typology of the classification of empirical material. The question is whether such typological procedures can be subsumed under a more formal procedure.

The notion of attribute space as applied to typologies has received increasing attention, and we have included a condensed version of a paper by the senior editor as Selection 12. The paper erects a bridge between some developments in formal logic and their adaptation to problems of empirical social research. Lazarsfeld begins with a summary of basic work done by two German logicians who provided the formal definition of a *type*. Their starting point was the cross-tabulation of two or more variates containing any number of categories. Take their example of two variates with three categories each, a total of nine possible combinations. Under various assumptions, these nine combinations may be reduced to a smaller group which will then be called types. Some of these types can be the original combinations, others can be formed by merging several of the original cells. It is possible that some of the original combinations will not appear in the final typology because, for empirical or logical reasons,

they can be dismissed. This process of moving from combinations to types is called *reduction*. Lazarsfeld, reporting on these ideas, then proposes the reverse process, which he calls *substruction*. One moves from an intuitive typology back to underlying dimensions. Substruction raises the following question: for what combination of variates *could* the given typology have been derived by an implicit reduction? The whole procedure is of great importance in testing a typology and in applying it to new material.

Cherry (Selection 13) reports that substruction procedures play an important role in linguistics. After introducing the notion of attribute space he proceeds to a "binary description of language." The basic dimensions are 12 distinctive features of language such as nasal-oral, tense-lax, etc. No real language uses all the 12 combinations which would ensue. A specific language can be characterized by the cells it actually considers and those it neglects. Each language represents, therefore, a different reduction of the same attribute space. Thus attribute space is defined through a substruction; modern linguists have abstracted from a careful analysis of the phonemes of a large number of actual languages. Greenberg, in the paper mentioned in the annotated bibliography, has stressed how linguistics and social research use the same classificatory procedure.

A similar procedure is applied in Selection 14, where Lazarsfeld classifies the terms which we use in dealing with internal action. He has collected numerous words describing what he calls "disposition concepts": motives, plans, wishes, etc. He suggests that they all can be derived from a substruction, an attribute space based on three dimensions. It should be noticed that here all ensuing combinations are used without further reduction. The general literature has not established a clear rule about the use of the term "types" for all cells in an attribute space. Some would restrict the definition to the use of clusters of cells. (There are logicians who differentiate between "natural" and "artificial" types.) For example, think of a cross-tabulation between age and marital status. It does not make much sociological sense to distinguish between types of married men in the 30–40 age range as compared to those between 40 and 50. On the other hand, one might well study different types of bachelors, concentrating especially on those who are still unmarried after 30. If these considerations are kept in mind, then the broadest use of the word "typology" seems justified.

In the annotated bibliography we have added two papers on typologies. McKinney supplies a review of typological procedures which puts the procedure discussed here into a broader context. And Parsons provides an interesting example of how an author is led into ever greater methodological clarity by his own substantive interests. In an early book, Parsons considered what Toennies meant by his distinction between Gemeinschaft and Gesellschaft. Parsons developed a number of dichotomous criteria by which the two would be different. Later these become his famous "pattern variables." The story is an interesting convergence of social theory and the language of variates.

A. General Theory

1. Problems in Methodology

PAUL F. LAZARSFELD

The Birth and Growth of Variates

CLASSIFICATORY CONCEPTS arise from many sources. The wisdom of everyday language and experience suggests some: the honesty of a man, the exclusiveness of a school. The needs of the practitioner give birth to others: what is an efficient worker—one who works quickly, one who makes few mistakes, or the optimal combination of both? How about an efficient organization? It does not consist of efficient people only; ease of communication among its members, the absence of internal conflicts, and many other features comes to mind. On a somewhat more sophisticated level we have new kinds of conceptualization: the backslapper becomes an extrovert; the unmanageable crew has low morale. Teachers have known for many centuries that students vary in their abilities. One day two French psychologists translated this familiar observation into a program of intelligence testing, and we have not yet heard the last of it. Administrators have noticed that some colleges receive many more applications for admission than others. This raises the question of whether colleges have something resembling a qual-

ity level. Attempts to measure this level are now the object of many, often controversial, efforts.

Behind any such classificatory effort stands what we shall call an *originating observation:* variations and differences exist which are to be explained. The "explanation" consists of a vaguely conceived underlying or latent property in regard to which people or collectives differ. Four steps can usually be discerned in the translation of this imagery into empirical research instruments:

1. The original imagery, the intended classification, is put into words and communicated by examples; efforts at definition are made.

2. In the course of this verbalization, often called conceptual analysis, several indicators are mentioned, and these help to decide where a given concrete object (person or group or organization) belongs in regard to the new classificatory concept. As the discussion of the concept expands, the number of eligible indicators increases; the array of these I shall call the *universe of indicators.*[1]

Reprinted in part with permission from "Problems in Methodology," in *Sociology Today,* edited by R. K. Merton, L. Broom, and L. S. Cottrell, Jr. (copyright 1959 by Basic Books, Inc., New York).

3. Usually this universe is very large, and for practical purposes we have to select a *subset* of indicators which is then made the basis for empirical work.
4. Finally, we have to combine the indicators into some kind of index.

As I have said, the last step has been treated extensively in existing literature on measurement. We might think of very simple procedures, such as the summation of correct answers to measure the extent of knowledge of geography; or procedures which require mathematical models, which would be the case if we used paired comparisons to order pictures according to their beauty; or a combination of data which require decisions on the weighting of several indicators, such as the standard-of-living index.

In the present paper I shall not be concerned with this fourth step.[2] I want, rather, to concentrate on the earlier phases about which there has been very little systematic thinking. In particular, I shall raise two questions: How is the original universe of indicators established (steps 1 and 2)? What are the consequences of choosing one specific subset of indicators rather than another (step 3)? By scrutinizing some pertinent evidence, we shall be able to draw a few general conclusions, but it will soon become clear that much uncertainty remains.

Although we are obviously most interested in concepts appearing in sociological literature, we shall start with a psychological concept. This is advisable partly because the notion of "traits" is in many respects a paradigm for our problem and partly because we have available a case in which the authors have documented unusually well the way in which they made their decision. I am referring to the notion of an authoritarian personality and the way in which it was translated into the famous *F*-scale by a group of social scientists working at the University of California in Berkeley.[3]

The authors of *The Authoritarian Personality* deserve credit for having provided a detailed account of why they chose the items included in their instrument. They start by saying that they found, in clinical and statistical sources, many characteristics which disposed individuals to anti-Semitism. They believe that these characteristics pointed to a basic trait for which they wanted to develop a test, subsequently labeled the *F*-scale. The items of this test were required to satisfy one or both of two criteria: (1) they should be expressive of the personality structure which was surmised on the basis of previously collected material; and (2) they should make probable the presence of anti-Semitism in the tested person. The first purpose is clearly stated at the beginning of Chapter 7: "The task was to formulate scale items which, though they were statements of opinions and attitudes, would actually serve as *'giveaways' of underlying trends* in the personality" (p. 223, italics ours). At the same time, the items should be correlated with anti-Semitism: "For every item there was a hypothesis, sometimes several hypotheses, stating what might be the nature of its *connection with prejudice*" (p. 225, italics ours). . . .

The items of the test fall into two main groups. One group is supposed to indicate the "lack of integration between the moral agencies by which the subject lives and the rest of his personality" (p. 234). An example is the overemphasis on conventional values, such as good manners and hard work. The other group refers to "weakness in the ego" whereby strong impulses are repressed and displaced "because they are affect-laden and potentially anxiety-producing" (p. 236). No amount of verbal definition could make this kind of imagery really focused.[4] But the discussion of the contemplated universe of indicators gives a vivid idea of how prejudice and aggression against outgroups could be generated by a personality type, where "outside agencies are depended upon for moral decisions"

(p. 234) and where props are needed "for keeping id drives ego-alien" (p. 240).

We are not concerned here with the question of where these basic traits reside: whether they represent biochemical structures not yet discovered or whether they are to remain hypothetical constructs. For the present discussion the important thing is this: in the stream leading from basic traits to the manifestation of anti-Semitism, the indicators can be taken by dipping, so to speak, nearer to its origin or to its terminus. One item reads: "Obedience and respect for authority are the most important virtues children should learn." Agreement can indicate uneasiness in handling one's own moral problems; but the relation to anti-Semitism is certainly not obvious. Another item reads: "Most people don't realize how much our lives are controlled by plots hatched in secret by politicians"; from agreement with this statement, it is only a small step to belief in the Protocols of the Elders of Zion.

Similarly sociological authors, even if they deal with very different material and have very different goals in mind, go about forming classificatory concepts in much the same way as psychologists do when they establish a trait. The study on which our test case is based does not carry out the final index formation (step 4), but it is especially detailed on the first steps.

Two scholars assembled the strike rates of industries in eleven countries and found that a fairly stable ordering could be established among industries, from those with a consistently high to those with a consistently low propensity to strike.[5] They then raised the following question: "Is there any single theory which will largely explain the facts which we have found? Can we, at one and the same time, explain the high propensity to strike of miners, longshoremen, sailors, and loggers and the low propensity of government employees, grocery clerks, railroad employees, and garment workers?" They give this answer: "The first hypothesis is

that the *location of the worker in society* determines his propensity to strike. . . ."

Here we find clearly the idea that industries can be classified according to their "location in society." How can this notion be transformed into a classificatory device —a variate? The authors themselves give a detailed verbal elaboration of their idea which suggests how they would proceed if further empirical work were their goal. First, they give distinct names to what they themselves call the two "ends of our scale." At the strike-prone end, workers form an "isolated mass"; at the other end, an "integrated group." They then proceed to describe these two situations in correlative terms. It will suffice here to give examples for the isolated mass; the reader can easily derive the opposite characteristics of the integrated industries.

The workers who are on the isolated end of "location in society" have little social, geographical, or occupational mobility. "Just as it is hard (for miners, etc.) to move out, so also is it difficult for them to move up." There is, further, little contact with other occupational and social groups. "In these communities there are not the myriad of voluntary associations with mixed membership." Finally, they are "as detached from the employer as from the community at large" because of absentee ownership and the absence of "small-scale employing units."

In verbalizing their concept of "location in society," the authors give several good reasons why the strike rate should be affected by the presence or absence of the situational characteristics just mentioned. The lack of contact with other groups makes the isolated mass more prone to strike because "these workers don't count on public opinion to support their grievances" and "they do not aim to be more considerate of the general community than they think the general community is of them." For the integrated group, on the other hand, the "individual grievances are less likely to coalesçe into a mass grievance which is expressed on the job level . . . they are more able to escape job situations without striking than are the workers in the high propensity industries." For the latter the union also becomes more important, and this too increases the probability of strikes. (The importance of the union can be recognized by the fact that on the one hand union meetings are more adequately attended and on the other hand personal and ideological factionalism are more frequent.) The pages in which this explanatory hypothesis is developed (pp. 191–195) provide, then, a large inventory of indicators which could be used to classify industries according to their location in society.

Again, there are several varieties of indicators. Take this sequence: occupational isolation makes for a strong feeling of shared grievances; this leads to receptiveness to unionization; union leaders have a tendency to organize strikes; ergo occupational isolation is likely to lead to strikes. From this argument we can derive at least three layers of indicators: lack of contact with other elements in the community; sentiments about grievances; and attitude toward unions. As a matter of fact, in the frame of the Keer-Siegel analysis, one would probably exclude attitude toward strikes as an indicator of "location in industry" because it would be considered almost identical with the originating observation, the strike rate.

THE DRIFT OF INDICATORS

The observations made in connection with these two examples can be generalized. Almost all classificatory concepts derive in the following way: Some empirical variations are observed; they are to be explained by a more general notion, an "underlying trait." The indicators for this trait point to the new unit to be constructed, but their choice is also dictated by the originating observation.

In many measurements of this kind there is probably a secular drift toward dominance of expressive (near origin) over predictive (near terminus) indicators. Originally the same conceptual imagery—and the corresponding expressive indicators—is coupled with *different* empirical observations which it is supposed to explain. This leads to distinct subsets of predictive indicators. Finally these are fused and take on expressive functions for a *generalized* variate. Two examples should help to shed some light on this rather subtle process.

It is little known in this country that the notion of the authoritarian personality originated in another context. Around 1930 a group of sociologists at the University of Frankfurt were concerned about whether the German workers, organized largely in the Social Democratic Party, would resist the Hitler movement. Their fear was that many workers would submit to the dictatorship, despite ideological differences, because they had "authoritarian personalities." The indicators for this personality type were derived partly from a somewhat modified psycho-analytic model of the ego: the sadomasochistic character then described by Fromm and subsequently developed in his *Escape from Freedom*.[6] For all practical purposes, this imagery is not very different from the moral predicament and the weak egostructure of the authoritarian Berkeley man. Consequently, the expressive indicators in the two studies are approximately the same. Although the German sociologists never developed a formal instrument, they did carry out an empirical survey with German workers and published the elaborate questionnaire that they used.[7] The expressive indicators there are much the same as those subsequently used in the Berkeley study. Conventionalism was tested by asking the respondents how they decorated their rooms and how they felt about the then new style of short hair and lipstick for women; superstitiousness was discovered by asking about belief in prophecies;

and projectivity by questions such as "Who has the real power in the country?" and "Who is responsible for the inflation?" (a major problem in Germany at the time).

But when it comes to predictive items, the differences are as marked as the differences between the originating observations which motivated the two studies. If workers presumably differed in their willingness to defend the German republic, it was appropriate to ask such questions as "What do you think of German justice?" "Who were the greatest personalities in German history?" "What is the best constitution for a country?"—all items as closely related to the issues of the times as they could be without explicitly referring to the political Nazi program. Inversely, the questions regarding outgroups or the violation of values by alien elements which characterize the F-scale are missing. This is interesting, because Hitler's anti-Semitism was of course well known at the time, but it is never mentioned in the 600-odd pages of the German report; the all-important question was whether there would be organized resistance to Hitler.[8] Since the Berkeley study was published, the notion of the authoritarian personality has been so greatly extended that both sets of originating observations have been virtually forgotten. Current modifications of the F-scale treat it as a general variate. One day they may contain anti-Semitic and anti-democratic statements as expressive items and may be used to study the contributors of money to the Boy Scout movement.

A second example shows how a misunderstanding of this drift can lead to a confused controversy which, if our analysis is correct, can easily be resolved. I refer to the discussion between Schachter, on the one hand, and Gross and Martin, on the other, concerning the concept of group cohesiveness.[9] To pinpoint the issue we shall assume (although it is historically incorrect) that Durkheim developed his notion of integration only in order to explain vari-

ation in the suicide rate.[10] Sampling the ways in which Durkheim describes integration in a group, we find that he uses two main sets of indicators: frequency and closeness of social contact among people in a group, and the existence of norms which are accepted by the large majority of the group. Durkheim himself did not develop measures of integration; in this respect the state of his book on suicide is logically the same as that of the Kerr and Siegel paper. It contains detailed verbal descriptions of what he meant by integration, and especially by malintegration. From this imagery, indicators for a variate could easily be culled, and they would clearly be distinguishable as to their expressive and their predictive function. Consider the following passages as examples of the first type.[11]

> There is, in short, in a cohesive and animated society, a constant interchange of ideas and feelings from all to each and each to all [p. 209].
> What constitutes this [integration] . . . is the existence of a certain number of beliefs and practices common to all the faithful, traditional, and thus obligatory. The more numerous and strong these collective states of mind are, the stronger the integration of the community [p. 170].

There are other parts of the picture which are much closer to the originating observation. The man in an integrated society, where solidarity encompasses him at all points,

> . . . will no longer find the only aim of his conduct in himself and, understanding that he is the instrument of a purpose greater than himself, he will see that he is not without significance [p. 374].

And speaking of the existence of norms:

> . . . this relative limitation, and the moderation it involves, make men contented with their lot, while stimulating them moderately to improve it [p. 250].

An analogy with the history of the "authoritarian personality" leads to the following expectation. If the notion of integration were to reappear in other contexts, the expressive indicators should show greater stability than the predictive ones, which would correspond to our last two quotations and would imply greater immunity to suicide. What actually happened was that Durkheim's predictive indicators, related to moderation and freedom from anxiety, were forgotten by some students. The expressive indicators, related to social relations and dominance of values, were so extended that the ensuing variate acquired a vastly generalized character. And, in reaction, a quest for restriction and for attention to more specific originating observations was undertaken.

Group dynamics is the American heir of integration under the name of cohesion.[12] In an unpublished but recorded panel discussion, Festinger stated that the group-dynamics tradition started with the problem of why some groups have a great influence on their members while others do not. To explain this variation, it was necessary to find "a force located in the group, to provide a concept that will permit predictions to be made about the power of the group to assert influence on its members with respect to behavior and attitudes."[13] This is obviously what Durkheim meant to do in regard to a specific behavior, suicide. But in the group-dynamics tradition, the range of observations to be accounted for is so large that the whole emphasis has shifted to expressive indicators. It is as if it were forgotten that Kerr and Siegel wanted to account for strike rates, and that subsequent writers made efforts to measure "location of industry" for a large variety of purposes—for example, to predict vulnerability to fascist movements. Although the group-dynamics writers have not constructed a general index of cohesiveness, it is easy to deduce from the publications how they might have done so. Such an index would be an aggregation of the answers of group members to such questions as "Do you like

group X?" "Do you enjoy the activities of the group?" "Are most of your friends recruited from there?" "Does membership in group X increase your own prestige outside?" "Does it help you to achieve some of your goals?" (We are not concerned here, of course, with correct wording or with appropriate procedures for forming a final index or scale.)

In a variety of experiments, the group-dynamics people show how cohesion so conceived is related to opinions, to efficiency, to amount of communication, and so on. To this approach Gross and Martin object on two grounds.[14] They feel that, in each specific group-dynamics study, too small a subset of indicators is being used to measure cohesion, a point to which we shall return presently. But they also propose what they call "an alternative nominal definition of cohesiveness" (p. 553). They want to adhere more closely to the notion of "sticking-togetherness" and propose, as a definition, "resistance of a group to disruptive forces." Now, it would certainly be possible and desirable to set up "a continuum of relevant weak and strong disruptive forces and to observe at what point the group does actually begin to disintegrate." But this would be an originating observation, corresponding to variation in strike rate or anti-Semitism. Cohesiveness would be the classificatory concept developed to explain these variations, and it would have to be established independently. A clear distinction between the originating observation, the conceptual imagery, and the proposed universe of items would have shown that the two parties to the controversy are largely talking past each other.

Gross and Martin do not suggest how they would "measure" this group trait independently of their proposed experiment on resistance to break-up. But, from their discussion of the group-dynamics studies, we can make a pretty good guess: their *expressive* indicators would be about the same as the ones listed above. But they would add more *predictive* indicators, such as "What would you be willing to do to keep the group from dissolving?" "What would induce you to leave the group?" "What members would you want to take with you if you had to move to another place?" In other words, Gross and Martin want to reverse the drift which has made current cohesion measures relatively general by confining them more closely to one specific set of originating observations. Thus there is no real disagreement between them and the writers they criticize. The group-dynamics imagery of "the total field forces which act on members to remain in the group" and the supposedly opposed one of "sticking togetherness" is very much the same—even though the terminology of the latter smacks of paste and glue while that of the former is reminiscent of semi-modern physics. The choice of indicators would hardly be affected by this difference; as a matter of fact, Schachter, in his rejoinder, stresses the fact that in some studies he and his colleagues ask specific questions regarding the eagerness of group members to preserve the group against outside obstacies.[15]

Incidentally, a third point of seeming disagreement between Gross-Martin and Schachter can also be clarified if it is put in terms of methodological distinctions. A collective trait can be analytical, structural, or global. In the first case, information about individual members is aggregated; an example would be a measure of group morale based on the aggregate morale score of each member. In the second case, we aggregate some kind of information about relations between individual members; for example, groups can differ according to the number of reciprocated choices they contain in their sociograms. Finally, a global characteristic deals with a collective product irrespective of its relation to individual members; examples would be the folktales of tribes or the number of playgrounds in cities. Gross and Martin prefer

relational, or perhaps global, to analytical characteristics of groups; this is their right, and maybe even their duty, as sociologists. They object to an "additive conception, where cohesiveness of the group is regarded as an average of the attractiveness of the group for the individual members." They want more emphasis put on "the importance of the relational bonds between and among group members" (p. 554). However, the formal nature of a variate has no necessary relation either to its originating observation or to its corresponding conceptual imagery. We need not discuss this point further, because it has been clarified by numerous authors.[16]

There are limiting cases in which certain classificatory concepts begin and largely remain at one of the two extremes of the expressive-predictive continuum. An index of "ability to be a pilot" is likely to consist mainly of elements which, for all practical purposes, are tantamount to a set of predictors for a rating of pilot efficiency. In contrast are such traits as honesty, which have long been embedded in our language. We could engage in one of those evolutionary speculations of which sociologists were so fond fifty years ago: how the notion of honesty got into the language because of certain originating observations which were of practical importance for the community. Actually, however, today an index of honesty is put together as the result of contemplations of what is meant by honesty and how one could recognize an honest person; in other words, it consists of expressive indicators which are virtually tantamount to what is often called an operational definition.

One final qualification is needed. We have restricted ourselves to those variates which are empirical counterparts of conceptual imagery. Much social research starts at the other end. One finds, for example, that Catholics are more likely to vote Democratic than are Protestants; then the question arises as to what religious affiliation means in this context. Merton has called this reverse process "respecification." [17] It consists in providing a conceptual imagery by turning an incidental classifier into a variate. We do not know whether this idea of respecification is exhausted by reversing our present discussion. In any case, we must emphasize the fact that all our examples are restricted to transforming concepts into variates and not to the *post hoc* interpretation of empirical findings, a problem which has been discussed elsewhere . . .[18]

Notes

1. The term has been suggested by Louis Guttman.

2. For a review of the main procedures, see B. Green: "Attitude Measurement," in Gardner Lindzey (ed.), *Handbook of Social Psychology* (Reading, Mass.: Addison-Wesley, 1954), Vol. I. The procedures there reviewed are characteristic for all the types of indices combining itemized indicators. The restriction of Green's review to "attitudes" is quite irrelevant; the procedures he reviews apply to any of the cases we shall discuss subsequently.

3. T. W. Adorno *et al., The Authoritarian Personality* (New York: Harper, 1950).

4. The authors facilitate communication by further subdividing each of the two major groups of items. Thus such subgroups as "conventionalism," "projectivity," and "toughness" are introduced. For a first overview, see *ibid.,* p. 328.

5. Clark Kerr and Abraham Siegel, "The Interindustry Propensity to Strike—An International Comparison," in A. Kornhauser, R. Dubin, and A. M. Ross (eds.), *Industrial Conflict* (New York: McGraw-Hill, 1954), pp. 186–212.

6. Erich Fromm, *Escape from Freedom* (New York: Farrar & Rinehart, 1941).

7. M. Horkheimer *et al., Autoritaet und Familie* (Paris: Felix Alcan, 1936).

8. Characteristically, in the United States the opposite to the authoritarian personality became the democratic personality, while in Fromm's programmatic article, it is called the revolutionary. There are other, more technical, differences between the two studies. The *F*-scale contains only explicit statements, while the Frankfurt questionnaire contains more open-ended questions. "Toughness," for example, is derived from the way in which the respondent describes his favorite sport. Comparing the two studies is worthwhile because Max Horkheimer originated both and Theodore Adorno provided the staff link bridging fifteen years of crucial history. Thus the differences will shed light on the role of the originating observation, as well as on the effect of various intellectual environments upon the work of scholars.

9. N. Gross and W. E. Martin, "On Group Cohesiveness"; S. Schachter, "Comment"; Gross and Martin, "Rejoinder," *American Journal of Sociology,* 57 (1952), pp. 546–64.

10. E. Durkheim, *Suicide,* trans. G. Simpson (New York: Free Press, 1951).

11. For more details, see P. Hammond, "The Imagery of Durkheim's Concept of Integration in Suicide," a working paper written for the Columbia Project on Advanced Training in Social Research.

12. L. Festinger and A. Zander, *Group Dynamics* (New York: Row-Peterson, 1952), Section III.

13. Report on the Dartmouth Seminar on Concepts and Indices in the Social Sciences, Mimeographed, 1953, IIA, p. 3.

14. *Loc. cit.*

15. *Op. cit.,* p. 557.

16. For a recent summary, see P. F. Lazarsfeld, "Evidence and Inference in Social Research," *Daedalus* (Fall 1958), Section III.

17. R. K. Merton, *Social Theory and Social Structure,* rev. ed. (New York: The Free Press, 1957), p. 253.

18. P. Lazarsfeld, "Interpretation as a Research Operation," in *L.S.R.*

B. Dimensional Clarification and Choice of Indicators

2. On the Meaning of Alienation

MELVIN SEEMAN

At the present time, in all the social sciences, the various synonyms of alienation have a foremost place in studies of human relations. Investigations of the 'unattached,' the 'marginal,' the 'obsessive,' the 'normless,' and the 'isolated' individual all testify to the central place occupied by the hypothesis of alienation in contemporary social science.

So WRITES Robert Nisbet in *The Quest for Community;* [1] and there would seem to be little doubt that his estimate is correct. In one form or another, the concept of alienation dominates both the contemporary literature and the history of sociological thought. It is a central theme in the classics of Marx, Weber, and Durkheim; and in contemporary work, the consequences that have been said to flow from the fact of alienation have been diverse, indeed.

Ethnic prejudice, for example, has been described as a response to alienation—as an ideology which makes an incomprehensible world intelligible by imposing upon that world a simplified and categorical "answer system" (for example, the Jews cause international war). [2] In his examination of the persuasion process in the Kate Smith bond drive, Merton emphasizes the significance of pervasive distrust: "The very same society that produces this sense of alienation and estrangement generates in many a craving for reassurance, an acute need to believe, a flight into faith" [3] —in this case, faith in the sincerity of the persuader. In short, the idea of alienation is a popular vehicle for virtually every kind of analysis, from the prediction of voting behavior to the search for *The Sane Society*.[4] This inclusiveness, in both its historical and its contemporary import, is expressed in Erich Kahler's remark: "The history of

Reprinted with permission from the *American Sociological Review,* 24 (December 1959) pp. 783–91 (copyright 1959 by the American Sociological Association).

This paper is based in part on work done while the author was in attendance at the Behavioral Sciences Conference at the University of New Mexico, in the summer of 1958. The conference was supported by the Behavioral Sciences Division, Air Force Office of Scientific Research, under contract AF 49(638)-33. The work on alienation was carried out in close conjunction with Julian B. Rotter and Shephard Liverant of The Ohio State University. I gratefully acknowledge their very considerable help, while absolving them of any commitment to the viewpoints herein expressed.

man could very well be written as a history of the alienation of man." [5]

A concept that is so central in sociological work, and so clearly laden with value implications, demands special clarity. There are, it seems to me, five basic ways in which the concept of alienation has been used. The purpose of this paper is to examine these logically distinguishable usages, and to propose what seems a workable view of these five meanings of alienation. Thus, the task is a dual one: to make more organized sense of one of the great traditions in sociological thought; and to make the traditional interest in alienation more amenable to sharp empirical statement.[6]

I propose, in what follows, to treat alienation from the personal standpoint of the actor—that is, alienation is here taken from the social-psychological point of view. Presumably, a task for subsequent experimental or analytical research is to determine (a) the social conditions that produce these five variants of alienation, or (b) their behavioral consequences. In each of the five instances, I begin with a review of where and how that usage is found in traditional sociological thought; subsequently, in each case, I seek a more researchable statement of meaning. In these latter statements, I focus chiefly upon the ideas of expectation and value.[7]

Powerlessness

The first of these uses refers to alienation in the sense of *powerlessness*. This is the notion of alienation as it originated in the Marxian view of the worker's condition in capitalist society: the worker is alienated to the extent that the prerogative and means of decision are expropriated by the ruling entrepreneurs. Marx, to be sure, was interested in other alienative aspects of the industrial system; indeed, one might say that his interest in the powerlessness of the worker flowed from his interest in the con-

sequences of such alienation in the work place—for example, the alienation of man from man, and the degradation of men into commodities.

In Weber's work, we find an extension beyond the industrial sphere of the Marxian notion of powerlessness. Of this extension, Gerth and Mills remark:

> Marx's emphasis upon the wage worker as being 'separated' from the means of production becomes, in Weber's perspective, merely one special case of a universal trend. The modern soldier is equally 'separated' from the means of violence; the scientist from the means of enquiry, and the civil servant from the means of administration.[8]

The idea of alienation as powerlessness is, perhaps, the most frequent usage in current literature. The contributors to Gouldner's volume on leadership, for example, make heavy use of this idea; as does the work of C. Wright Mills—and, I suppose, any analysis of the human condition that takes the Marxist tradition with any seriousness. This variant of alienation can be conceived as *the expectancy or probability held by the individual that his own behavior cannot determine the occurrence of the outcomes, or reinforcements, he seeks.*

Let us be clear about what this conception does and does not imply. First, it is a distinctly social-psychological view. It does not treat powerlessness from the standpoint of the objective conditions in society; but this does not mean that these conditions need be ignored in research dealing with this variety of alienation. These objective conditions are relevant, for example, in determining the degree of realism involved in the individual's response to his situation. The objective features of the situations are to be handled like any other situational aspect of behavior—to be analyzed, measured, ignored, experimentally controlled or varied, as the research question demands.

Second, this construction of "powerlessness" clearly departs from the Marxian tradition by removing the critical, polemic element in the idea of of alienation. Likewise, this version of powerlessness does not take into account, as a definitional matter, the frustration an individual may feel as a consequence of the discrepancy between the control he may expect and the degree of control that he desires—that is, it takes no direct account of the value of control to the person.

In this version of alienation, then, the individual's expectancy for control of events is clearly distinguished from (a) the *objective* situation of powerlessness as some observer sees it, (b) the observer's *judgment* of that situation against some ethical standard, and (c) the individual's sense of a *discrepancy* between his expectations for control and his desire for control.

The issues in the philosophy of science, or in the history of science, on which these distinctions and decisions touch can not be debated here. Two remarks must suffice: (1) In any given research, any or all of the elements discussed above—expectancies, objective conditions, deviation from a moral standard, deviation from the actor's standards—may well be involved, and I see little profit in arguing about which is "really" alienation so long as what is going on at each point in the effort is clear. I have chosen to focus on expectancies since I believe that this is consistent with what follows, while it avoids building ethical or adjustmental features into the concept. (2) I do not think that the expectancy usage is as radical a departure from the Marxian legacy as it may appear. No one would deny the editorial character of the Marxian judgment, but it was a judgment about a state of affairs—the elimination of individual freedom and control. My version of alienation refers to the counterpart, in the individual's expectations, of that state of affairs.

Finally, the use of powerlessness as an expectancy means that this version of alienation is very closely related to the notion (developed by Rotter) of "internal versus external control of reinforcements." The latter construct refers to the individual's sense of personal control over the reinforcement situation, as contrasted with his view that the occurrence of reinforcements is dependent upon external conditions, such as chance, luck, or the manipulation of others. The congruence in these formulations leaves the way open for the development of a closer bond between two languages of analysis—that of learning theory and that of alienation—that have long histories in psychology and sociology. But the congruence also poses a problem—the problem of recognizing that these two constructs, though intimately related, are not generally used to understand the same things.[9]

In the case of alienation, I would limit the applicability of the concept to expectancies that have to do with the individual's sense of influence over sociopolitical events (control over the political system, the industrial economy, international affairs, and the like). Accordingly, I would initially limit the applicability of this first meaning of alienation to the arena for which the concept was originally intended, namely, the depiction of man's relation to the larger social order. Whether or not such an operational concept of alienation is related to expectancies for control in more intimate need areas (for example, love and affection; status-recognition) is a matter for empirical determination. The need for the restriction lies in the following convictions: First, the concept of alienation, initially, should not be so global as to make the *generality* of powerlessness a matter of fiat rather than fact. Second, the concept should not be dangerously close to merely an index of personality *adjustment*—equivalent, that is, to a statement that the individual is maladjusted in the sense that he has a generally low expectation that he can, through his own behavior, achieve any of the personal rewards he seeks.[10]

Meaninglessness

A second major usage of the alienation concept may be summarized under the idea of *meaninglessness*. The clearest contemporary examples of this usage are found in Adorno's treatment of prejudice; in Cantril's *The Psychology of Social Movements*, in which the "search for meaning" is used as part of the interpretive scheme in analyzing such diverse phenomena as lynchings, the Father Divine movement, and German fascism; and in Hoffer's portrait of the "true believer" as one who finds, and needs to find, in the doctrines of a mass movement "a master key to all the world's problems." [11]

This variant of alienation is involved in Mannheim's description of the increase of "functional rationality" and the concomitant decline of "substantial rationality." Mannheim argues that as society increasingly organizes its members with reference to the most efficent realization of ends (that is, as functional rationality increases), there is a parallel decline in the "capacity to act intelligently in a given situation on the basis of one's own insight into the interrelations of events." [12]

This second type of alienation, then, refers to the individual's sense of understanding the events in which he is engaged. We may speak of high alienation, in the meaninglessness usage, when *the individual is unclear as to what he ought to believe— when the individual's minimal standards for clarity in decision-making are not met.* Thus, the post-war German situation described by Adorno was "meaningless" in the sense that the individual could not choose with confidence among alternative explanations of the inflationary disasters of the time (and, it is argued, substituted the "Jews" as a simplified solution for this unclarity). In Mannheim's depiction, the individual cannot choose appropriately among alternative interpretations (cannot "act intelligently" or "with insight") because the increase in functional rationality, with its emphasis on specialization and production, makes such choice impossible.

It would seem, for the present at least, a matter of no consequence what the beliefs in question are. They may, as in the above instance, be simply descriptive beliefs (interpretations); or they may be beliefs involving moral standards (norms for behavior). In either case, the individual's choice among alternative beliefs has low "confidence limits": he cannot predict with confidence the consequences of acting on a given belief. One might operationalize this aspect of alienation by focusing upon the fact that it is characterized by a *low expectancy that satisfactory predictions about future outcomes of behavior can be made.* Put more simply, where the first meaning of alienation refers to the sensed ability to control outcomes, this second meaning refers essentially to the sensed ability to predict behavioral outcomes.

This second version of alienation is logically independent of the first, for, under some circumstances, expectancies for personal control of events may not coincide with the understanding of these events, as in the popular depiction of the alienation of the intellectual.[13] Still, there are obvious connections between these two forms of alienation: in some important degree, the view that one lives in an intelligible world may be a prerequisite to expectancies for control; and the unintelligibility of complex affairs is presumably conducive to the development of high expectancies for external control (that is, high powerlessness).[14]

Normlessness

The third variant of the alienation theme is derived from Durkheim's description of "anomie," and refers to a condition of *normlessness*.

In the traditional usage, anomie denotes

a situation in which the social norms regulating individual conduct have broken down or are no longer effective as rules for behavior. As noted above, Merton emphasizes this kind of rulelessness in his interpretation of the importance of the "sincerity" theme in Kate Smith's war bond drive:

> The emphasis on this theme reflects a social disorder—"anomie" is the sociological term—in which common values have been submerged in the welter of private interests seeking satisfaction by virtually any means which are effective. Drawn from a highly competitive, segmented urban society, our informants live in a climate of reciprocal distrust which, to say the least, is not conducive to stable human relationships. . . . The very same society that produces this sense of alienation and estrangement generates in many a craving for reassurance. . . .[15]

Elsewhere, in his well-known paper "Social Structure and Anomie," Merton describes the "adaptations" (the kinds of conformity and deviance) that may occur where the disciplining effect of collective standards has been weakened. He takes as his case in point the situation in which culturally prescribed goals (in America, the emphasis upon success goals) are not congruent with the available means for their attainment. In such a situation, he argues, anomie or normlessness will develop to the extent that "the technically most effective procedure, whether culturally legitimate or not, becomes typically preferred to institutionally prescribed conduct."[16]

Merton's comments on this kind of anomic situation serve to renew the discussion of the expectancy constructs developed above—the idea of meaninglessness, and the idea of powerlessness or internal-external control. For Merton notes, first, that the anomic situation leads to low predictability in behavior, and second, that the anomic situation may well lead to the belief in luck:

Whatever the sentiments of the reader concerning the moral desirability of coordinating the goals-and-means phases of the social structure, it is clear that imperfect coordination of the two leads to anomie. Insofar as one of the most general functions of the social structure is to provide a basis for predictability and regularity of social behavior, it becomes increasingly limited in effectiveness as these elements of the social structure become dissociated. . . . The victims of this contradiction between the cultural emphasis on pecuniary ambition and the social bars to full opportunity are not always aware of the structural sources of their thwarted aspirations. To be sure, they are typically aware of a discrepancy between individual worth and social rewards. But they do not necessarily see how this comes about. Those who do find its source in the social structure may become alienated from that structure and become ready candidates for Adaptation V (rebellion). But others, and this appears to include the great majority, may attribute their difficulties to more mystical and less sociological sources. . . . in such a society [a society suffering from anomie] people tend to put stress on mysticism: the workings of Fortune, Chance, Luck.[17]

It is clear that the general idea of anomie is both an integral part of the alienation literature, and that it bears upon our expectancy notions. What is not so clear is the matter of how precisely to conceptualize the events to which "anomie" is intended to point. Unfortunately, the idea of normlessness has been over-extended to include a wide variety of both social conditions and psychic states: personal disorganization, cultural breakdown, reciprocal distrust, and so on.

Those who employ the anomie version of alienation are chiefly concerned with the elaboration of the "means" emphasis in society—for example, the loss of commonly held standards and consequent individualism, or the development of instrumental, manipulative attitudes. This interest represents our third variant of alienation, the key idea of which, again, may be cast in terms of expectancies. Following Merton's lead, the anomic situation, from the individual point of view, may be defined as one in which there is a *high expectancy that socially unapproved behaviors are required to achieve given goals.* This third meaning of alienation is logically independent of the two versions discussed above. Expectancies concerning unapproved means, presumably, can vary independently of the individual's expectancy that his own behavior will determine his success in reaching a goal (what I have called "powerlessness") or his belief that he operates in an intellectually comprehensible world ("meaninglessness"). Such a view of anomie, to be sure, narrows the evocative character of the concept, but it provides a more likely way of developing its research potential. This view, I believe, makes possible the discovery of the extent to which such expectancies are held, the conditions for their development, and their consequences either for the individual or for a given social system (for example, the generation of widespread distrust).

The foregoing discussion implies that the means and goals in question have to do with such relatively broad social demands as the demand for success or for political ends. However, in his interesting essay, "Alienation from Interaction," Erving Goffman presents a more or less parallel illustration in which the focus is on the smallest of social systems, the simple conversation:

> If we take conjoint spontaneous involvement in a topic of conversation as a point of reference, we shall find that alienation from it is common indeed. Conjoint involvement appears to be a fragile thing, with standard points of weakness and decay, a precarious unsteady state that is likely at any time to lead the individual into some form of alienation. Since we are dealing with obligatory involvement, forms of alienation will constitute *misbehavior of a kind that can be called misinvolvement.*[18]

Goffman describes four such "misinvolvements" (for example, being too self-conscious in interaction), and concludes: "By looking at the ways in which individuals can be thrown out of step with the sociable moment, perhaps we can learn something about the way in which he can become alienated from things that take much more of his time."[19] In speaking of "misbehavior" or "misinvolvement," Goffman is treating the problem of alienation in terms not far removed from the anomic feature I have described, that is, the expectancy for socially unapproved behavior. His analysis of the social microcosm in these terms calls attention once more to the fact that the five variants of alienation discussed here can be applied to as broad or as narrow a range of social behavior as seems useful.

Isolation

The fourth type of alienation refers to *isolation.* This usage is most common in descriptions of the intellectual role, where writers refer to the detachment of the intellectual from popular cultural standards —one who, in Nettler's language, has become estranged from his society and the culture it carries.[20] Clearly, this usage does not refer to isolation as a lack of "social adjustment"—of the warmth, security, or intensity of an individual's social contacts.

In the present context, in which we seek to maintain a consistent focus on the individual's expectations or values, this brand of alienation may be usefully defined in terms of reward values: The alienated in the isolation sense are those who, like the intellectual, *assign low reward value to goals or beliefs that are typically highly valued in the given society.* This, in effect, is the definition of alienation in Nettler's scale, for as a measure of "apartness from society" the scale consists (largely though not exclusively) of items that reflect the individual's degree of commitment to popular culture. Included, for example, is the question "Do you read *Reader's Digest?*," a magazine that was selected "as a symbol of popular magazine appeal and folkish thoughtways." [21]

The "isolation" version of alienation clearly carries a meaning different from the three versions discussed above. Still, these alternative meanings can be profitably applied in conjunction with one another in the analysis of a given state of affairs. Thus, Merton's paper on social structure and anomie makes use of both "normlessness" and "isolation" in depicting the adaptations that individuals may make to the situation in which goals and means are not well coordinated. One of these adaptations—that of the "innovator"—is the prototype of alienation in the sense of normlessness, in which the individual innovates culturally disapproved means to achieve the goals in question. But another adjustment pattern—that of "rebellion"—more closely approximates what I have called "isolation." This adaptation [rebellion] leads men outside the environing social structure to envisage and seek to bring into being a new, that is to say, a greatly modified, social structure. It presupposes alienation from reigning goals and standards." [22]

Self-Estrangement

The final variant distinguishable in the literature is alienation in the sense of *self-estrangement*. The most extended treatment of this version of alienation is found in *The Sane Society*, where Fromm writes:

> In the following analysis I have chosen the concept of alienation as the central point from which I am going to develop the analysis of the contemporary social character. . . . By alienation is meant a mode of experience in which the person experiences himself as an alien. He has become, one might say, estranged from himself.[23]

In much the same way, C. Wright Mills comments: "In the normal course of her work, because her personality becomes the

instrument of an alien purpose, the salesgirl becomes self-alienated"; and, later, "Men are estranged from one another as each secretly tries to make an instrument of the other, and in time a full circle is made: One makes an instrument of himself and is estranged from It also." [24]

There are two interesting features of this popular doctrine of alienation as self-estrangement. The first of these is the fact that where the usage does not overlap with the other four meanings (and it often does), it is difficult to specify what the alienation is *from*. To speak of "alienation from the self" is after all simply a metaphor, in a way that "alienation from popular culture," for example, need not be. The latter can be reasonably specified, as I have tried to do above; but what is intended when Fromm, Mills, Hoffer, and the others speak of self-estrangement?

Apparently, what is being postulated here is some ideal human condition from which the individual is estranged. This is, perhaps, clearest in Fromm's treatment, for example, in his description of production and consumption excesses in capitalist society: "The *human* way of acquiring would be to make an effort qualitatively commensurate with what I acquire. . . . But our craving for consumption has lost all connection with the real needs of man." [25] To be self-alienated, in the final analysis, means to be something less than one might ideally be if the circumstances in society were otherwise—to be insecure, given to appearances, conformist. Riesman's discussion of other-direction falls within this meaning of alienation; for what is at stake is that the child learns "that nothing in his character, no possession he owns, no inheritance of name or talent, no work he has done, is valued for itself, but only for its effect on others. . . ." [26]

Riesman's comment brings us to the second feature of special interest in the idea of self-alienation. I have noted that this idea invokes some explicit or implicit human ideal. And I have implied that such comparisons of modern man with some idealized human condition should be viewed simply as rhetorical appeals to nature—an important rhetoric for some purposes, though not very useful in the nonanalytical form it generally takes. But Riesman's assertion contains, it seems to me, one of the key elements of this rhetoric—one, indeed, that not only reflects the original interest of Marx in alienation but also one that may be specifiable in a language consistent with our other uses of alienation.

I refer to that aspect of self-alienation which is generally characterized as the loss of intrinsic meaning or pride in work, a loss which Marx and others have held to be an essential feature of modern alienation. This notion of the loss of intrinsically meaningful satisfactions is embodied in a number of ways in current discussions of alienation. Glazer, for example, contrasts the alienated society with simpler societies characterized by "spontaneous acts of work and play which were their own reward." [27]

Although this meaning of alienation is difficult to specify, the basic idea contained in the rhetoric of self-estrangement—the idea of intrinsically meaningful activity—can, perhaps, be recast into more manageable social learning terms. One way to state such a meaning is to see alienation as *the degree of dependence of the given behavior upon anticipated future rewards,* that is, upon rewards that lie outside the activity itself. In these terms, the worker who works merely for his salary, the housewife who cooks simply to get it over with, or the other-directed type who acts "only for its effect on others"—all these (at different levels, again) are instances of self-estrangement. In this view, what has been called self-estrangement refers essentially to the inability of the individual to find self-rewarding—or in Dewey's phrase, self-consummatory—activities that engage him.[28]

Conclusion

I am aware that there are unclarities and difficulties of considerable importance in these five varieties of alienation (especially, I believe, in the attempted solution of "self-estrangement" and the idea of "meaninglessness"). But I have attempted, first, to distinguish the meanings that have been given to alienation, and second, to work toward a more useful conception of each of these meanings.

It may seem, at first reading, that the language employed—the language of expectations and rewards—is somewhat strange, if not misguided. But I would urge that the language is more traditional than it may seem. Nathan Glazer certainly is well within that tradition when, in a summary essay on alienation, he speaks of our modern ". . . sense of the splitting asunder of what was once together, the breaking of the seamless mold in which *values, behavior,* and *expectations* were once cast into interlocking forms." [29] These same three concepts—reward value, behavior, and expectancy—are key elements in the theory that underlies the present characterization of alienation. Perhaps, on closer inspection, the reader will find only that initial strangeness which is often experienced when we translate what was sentimentally understood into a secular question.

Notes

1. New York: Oxford, 1953, p. 15.
2. T. W. Adorno *et al., The Authoritarian Personality* (New York: Harper, 1950).
3. R. K. Merton, *Mass Persuasion* (New York: Harper, 1946), p. 143.
4. Erich Fromm, *The Sane Society* (New York: Rinehart, 1955).
5. *The Tower and the Abyss* (New York: Braziller, 1957), p. 43.
6. An effort in this direction is reported by John P. Clark in "Measuring Alienation Within a Social System," *American Sociological Review* 24 (December 1959), 849–52.

7. The concepts of expectancy and reward, or reinforcement value, are the central elements in J. B. Rotter's "social learning theory"; see *Social Learning and Clinical Psychology* (New York: Prentice-Hall, 1954). My discussion seeks to cast the various meanings of alienation in a form that is roughly consistent with this theory, though not formally expressed in terms of it.

8. H. H. Gerth and C. W. Mills, *From Max Weber: Essays in Sociology* (New York: Oxford, 1946), p. 50.

9. Cf. W. H. James and J. B. Rotter, "Partial and One Hundred Percent Reinforcement under Chance and Skill Conditions," *Journal of Experimental Psychology,* 55 (May 1958), pp. 397–403. Rotter and his students have shown that the distinction between internal and external control (a distinction which is also cast in expectancy terms) has an important bearing on learning theory. The propositions in that theory, they argue, are based too exclusively on experimental studies which simulate conditions of "external control," where the subject "is likely to perceive reinforcements as being beyond his control and primarily contingent upon external conditions" (p. 397). Compare this use of what is essentially a notion of powerlessness with, for example, Norman Podheretz's discussion of the "Beat Generation": "Being apathetic about the Cold War is to admit that you have a sense of utter helplessness in the face of forces apparently beyond the control of man." "Where is the Beat Generation Going?" *Esquire,* 50 (December 1958), p. 148.

10. It seems best, in regard to the adjustment question, to follow Gwynn Nettler's view. He points out that the concepts of alienation and anomie should not "be equated, as they so often are, with personal disorganization defined as intrapersonal goallessness, or lack of 'internal coherence' . . . [their] bearing on emotional sickness must be independently investigated." "A Measure of Alienation," *American Sociological Review,* 22 (December 1957), p. 672. For a contrasting view, see Nathan Glazer's "The Alienation of Modern Man," *Commentary,* 3 (April 1947), p. 380, in which he comments: "If we approach alienation in this way, it becomes less a description of a single specific symptom than an omnibus of psychological disturbances having a similar root cause—in this case, modern social organization."

With regard to the question of the generality of powerlessness, I assume that high or low expectancies for the control of outcomes through one's own behavior will (a) vary with the behavior involved—e.g., control over academic achievement or grades, as against control over unemployment; and (b) will be differentially realistic in different areas (it is one thing to feel powerless with regard to war and quite another, presumably, to feel powerless in making friends). My chief point is that these are matters that can be empirically rather than conceptually solved; we should not, therefore, build either "generality" or "adjustment" into our concept of alienation. This same view is applied in the discussion of the other four types of alienation.

11. See, respectively, Adorno *et al., op. cit.;* Hadley Cantril, *The Psychology of Social Movements* (New York: Wiley, 1941); and Eric Hoffer, *The True Believer* (New York: Harper, 1950), p. 90.

12. Karl Mannheim, *Man and Society in an Age of Reconstruction* (New York: Harcourt, Brace, 1940), p. 59.

13. C. Wright Mills' description reflects this view: "The intellectual who remains free may continue to learn more and more about modern society, but he finds the centers of political initiative less and less accessible. . . . He comes to feel helpless in the fundamental sense that he cannot control what he is able to foresee." *White Collar* (New York: Oxford, 1951), p. 157. The same distinction is found in F. L. Strodtbeck's empirical comparison of Italian and Jewish values affecting mobility: "For the Jew, there was always the expectation that everything could be understood, if perhaps not controlled." "Family Interaction, Values and Achievement," in D. C. McClelland *et al., Talent and Society* (New York: Van Nostrand, 1958), p. 155.

14. Thorstein Veblen argues the same point, in his own inimitable style, in a discussion of "The Belief in Luck": ". . . the extra-causal propensity or agent has a very high utility as a recourse in perplexity" [providing the individual] "a means of escape from the difficulty of accounting for phenomena in terms of causal sequences." *The Theory of the Leisure Class* (New York: Macmillan, 1899; Modern Library Edition, 1934), p. 386.

15. Merton, *op. cit.,* p. 143.

16. R. K. Merton, *Social Theory and Social Structure* (New York: The Free Press, 1957).

17. Merton, *op. cit.*

18. *Human Relations,* 10 (February 1957), p. 49 (italics added).

19. *Ibid.,* p. 59. Obviously, the distinction (discussed above under "powerlessness") between objective condition and individual expectancy applies in the case of anomie. For a recent treatment of this point, see R. K.

Merton, *Social Theory and Social Structure* (Glencoe, Ill.: Free Press, 1957, revised edition), pp. 161–94. It is clear that Srole's well-known anomie scale refers to individual experience (and that it embodies a heavy adjustment component). It is not so clear how the metaphorical language of "normative breakdown" and "structural strain" associated with the conception of anomie as a social condition is to be made empirically useful. It may be further noted that the idea of rulelessness has often been used to refer to situations in which norms are unclear as well as to those in which norms lose their regulative force. I focused on the latter case in this section; but the former aspect of anomie is contained in the idea of "meaninglessness." The idea of meaninglessness, as defined above, surely includes situations involving uncertainty resulting from obscurity of rules, the absence of clear criteria for resolving ambiguities, and the like.

20. Nettler, *op. cit.*

21. *Ibid.*, p. 675. A scale to measure social isolation (as well as powerlessness and meaninglessness) has been developed by Dean, but the meanings are not the same as those given here; the "social isolation" measure, for example, deals with the individual's friendship status. (See Dwight Dean, "Alienation and Political Apathy," Ph.D. thesis, Ohio State University, 1956.) It seems to me now, however, that this is not a very useful meaning, for two reasons. First, it comes very close to being a statement of either social adjustment or of simple differences in associational styles (i.e., some people are sociable and some are not), and as such seems irrelevant to the root historical notion of alienation. Second, the crucial part of this "social isolation" component in alienation—what Nisbet, for example, calls the "unattached" or the "isolated" —is better captured for analytical purposes, I believe, in the ideas of meaninglessness, normlessness, or isolation, as defined in expectancy or reward terms. That is to say, what remains, after sheer sociability is removed, is the kind of tenuousness of social ties that may be described as value uniqueness (isolation).

22. Merton, "Social Structure and Anomie," *op. cit.*, pp. 144–45. Merton is describing a radical estrangement from societal values (often typified in the case of the intellectual) —i.e., the alienation is from reigning *central* features of the society, and what is sought is a "greatly" modified society. Presumably, the "isolation" mode of alienation, like the other versions, can be applied on the intimate or the grand scale, as noted above in the discussion of Goffman's analysis. Clearly, the person who rejects certain commonly held values in a given society, but who values the society's tolerance for such differences, is expressing a fundamental commitment to societal values and in this degree he is not alienated in the isolation sense.

23. Fromm, *op. cit.*, pp. 110, 120.

24. Fromm, *op. cit.*, pp. 131, 134 (italics in original).

25. Fromm, *op. cit.*, pp. 131, 134 (italics in original).

26. David Riesman, *The Lonely Crowd* (New Haven: Yale University Press, 1950), p. 49. Although the idea of self-estrangement, when used in the alienation literature, usually carries the notion of a generally applicable human standard, it is sometimes the individual's standard that is at issue: to be alienated in this sense is to be aware of a discrepancy between one's ideal self and one's actual self-image.

27. Glazer, *op. cit.*, p. 379.

28. The difficulty of providing intrinsically satisfying work in industrial society, of course, has been the subject of extensive comment; see, for example, Daniel Bell, *Work and Its Discontents* (Boston: Beacon Press, 1956). A similar idea has been applied by Tumin to the definition of creativity: "I would follow Dewey's lead and view 'creativity' as the esthetic experience, which is distinguished from other experiences by the fact that it is self-consummatory in nature. This is to say, the esthetic experience is enjoyed for the actions which define and constitute the experience, whatever it may be, rather than for its instrumental results or social accompaniments in the form of social relations with others." Melvin M. Tumin, "Obstacles to Creativity," *Etc.: A Review of General Semantics*, 11 (Summer 1954), p. 261. For a more psychological view of the problem of "intrinsically" governed behavior, see S. Koch, "Behavior as 'Intrinsically' Regulated: Work Notes Toward a Pre-Theory of Phenomena Called 'Motivational,'" in M. R. Jones, editor, *Nebraska Symposium on Motivation* (Lincoln: University of Nebraska Press, 1956), pp. 42–87.

29. Glazer, *op. cit.*, p. 378 (italics added).

3. Alienation, Race, and Education *

RUSSELL MIDDLETON

ONE OF THE problems empirical studies of alienation must confront is the multiplicity of meanings attached to the concept. Seeman has suggested that there are five major meanings: powerlessness, meaninglessness, normlessness, isolation, and self-estrangement.[1] Most studies have dealt with only one of these variants of alienation—or at most two or three, singly or in combination—and there is little evidence regarding the relative frequency of different types of alienation in the population or of their differential association with various causal factors. We shall adopt, with some modifications, Seeman's variants of alienation and examine their incidence in a small southern city.

On the basis of the theoretical formulations of the classic social theorists as well as the fragmentary previous empirical research, we hypothesize that the different types of alienation are highly correlated with one another. Further, we hypothesize that each type of alienation is directly related to those disabling social conditions that limit or block the attainment of culturally valued objectives. We shall test this hypothesis with regard to two of the most important disabling conditions in American society: subordinate racial status and low educational attainment.

One possible exception to the general hypothesis is suggested by the vast literature pointing to the alienation of the intellectual from the dominant culture. Awareness of the more subtle ways in which this dominant culture may thwart human potentialities probably requires a relatively high level of education and sophistication. Cultural estrangement may therefore be inversely related to the disabling conditions specified and less highly correlated with the other types of alienation.

Method

This study was conducted in a central Florida city of 18,000 during the summer of 1962. All residents above the age of 20 were enumerated, and a simple random sample of 256 persons was drawn. Since the number of Negroes in this sample was inadequate for extensive analysis, an additional 50 Negro subjects were randomly drawn. The final sample thus consisted of 207 whites and 99 Negroes. Generalizations about the community as a whole, however, are based on the original sample of 256.

This study constituted a part of a larger cooperative survey of attitudes on a variety of subjects: civil defense, mental illness, political leadership, and the employment of married women. Since exigencies of the

Reprinted with permission from the *American Sociological Review*, 28 (December 1963) pp. 973–77 (copyright 1963 by the American Sociological Association).

* Paper read at the annual meeting of the American Sociological Association, August, 1963. This study was financed by the Research Council of Florida State University. I am indebted to Charles M. Grigg, Ivan Nye, Francis R. Allen, and Malcolm B. Parsons for their cooperation in the study. I am further indebted to the National Science Foundation and the Survey Research Center of the University of California for their support in the analysis of the data.

larger study permitted us to include only a few items dealing with alienation, a single attitude statement was formulated for each of the variants of alienation. It would have been desirable to construct scales for each type of alienation, but the single items are useful at least for exploratory analysis.[2]

The types of alienation and the attitude statements associated with each are as follows:

1. *Powerlessness.* "There is not much that I can do about most of the important problems that we face today."

2. *Meaninglessness.* "Things have become so complicated in the world today that I really don't understand just what is going on."

3. *Normlessness.* "In order to get ahead in the world today, you are almost forced to do some things which are not right." The most commonly used measure of a sense of normlessness is Srole's anomia scale.[3] The manifest content of this scale, however, appears to be a combination of cynicism and pessimism—or, as Nettler and Meier and Bell maintain, despair.[4] Although pessimism and cynicism or despair may ordinarily accompany anomia, they do not in themselves constitute it, and the degree of association is an empirical question. The concept of normlessness has also been used in several other senses,[5] but here we follow the more restricted usage of Merton and Seeman, emphasizing the expectation that illegitimate means must be employed to realize culturally prescribed goals.[6]

4. *Cultural estrangement.* "I am not much interested in the TV programs, movies, or magazines that most people seem to like." Seeman refers to this variant of alienation as "isolation," but to avoid the traditional connotation of social isolation, we use the more explicit term "cultural estrangement." Like many of the questions in Nettler's scale for alienation,[7] the present item focuses on the individual's acceptance of popular culture.

5. *Social estrangement.* "I often feel lonely."

Although Dean, working with Seeman, developed a scale to measure social isolation,[8] Seeman later decided that this was "not a very useful meaning" and abandoned social isolation as a type of alienation.[9] In doing so, however, he has abandoned a significant part of the tradition associated with the concept of alienation. Nisbet,[10] Pappenheim,[11] and Grodzins,[12] for example, follow Tönnies and Durkheim in emphasizing the loss of community in modern society as the source of alienation. On the other hand, Seeman's point that social isolation cannot readily be separated from differences in associational style—the fact that some men are sociable and some are not—makes clear the desirability of distinguishing social isolation from social estrangement. In his study of the aged, Townsend makes such a distinction: ". . . to be socially isolated is to have few contacts with family and community; to be lonely is to have an unwelcome *feeling* of lack or loss of companionship. The one is objective, the other subjective and, as we shall see, the two do not coincide." [13] Eric and Mary Josephson also comment that not all isolates are socially estranged, nor are all non-isolates free from alienation.[14] It is, then, the feeling of loneliness that is crucial to alienation, and the present item is designed to tap this subjective sense of social estrangement.

6. *Estrangement from work.* "I don't really enjoy most of the work that I do, but I feel that I must do it in order to have other things that I need and want." One of the oldest themes in the literature of alienation is that man may become estranged from himself by failing to realize his own human capacities to the fullest. Seeman suggests the absence of intrinsically meaningful activity as an indicator of self-estrangement.[15] As used by social theorists from Marx to Fromm, however, the concept of self-estrangement is considerably broader—as broad, in fact, as the concept of human nature. Fromm, for example, discusses most of the other types of alienation as aspects

of self-estrangement or as conditions leading to self-estrangement.[16] As Seeman points out, the notion of self-estrangement also begs the question in that it implies certain assumptions about human nature and the ideal human condition. Nevertheless, the notion of alienation from meaningful work has an important place in the literature and deserves separate treatment. We thus include the present item to measure estrangement from work, though one may choose to interpret it as an index of self-estrangement.

In the interviews the six items dealing with alienation were interspersed with a large number of unrelated questions. The respondents were given the following in-

association between each type of alienation and each other type is moderately strong, with Q's ranging from .46 to .81.[17] As expected, cultural estrangement is not highly correlated with the other variants of alienation; the only statistically significant relation is with normlessness, and even here the Q is a relatively low .31. The type of alienation most highly correlated with the other types is estrangement from work. This suggests that it may indeed be a useful index to self-estrangement, if, as Marx and Fromm have maintained, self-estrangement is at the core of the phenomenon of alienation.

If cultural estrangement is excluded, the five remaining items constitute a Guttman

TABLE 1.   Intercorrelations of Types of Alienation *

	Meaning-lessness	Normless-ness	Cultural Estrange-ment	Social Estrange-ment	Estrange-ment from Work
Powerlessness	.58	.61	.06	.54	.57
Meaninglessness	—	.59	.17	.46	.81
Normlessness	—	—	.31	.48	.67
Cultural estrangement	—	—	—	.08	.20
Social estrangement	—	—	—	—	.71

* The number of cases is 256; the measure of association is Yule's Q. The values of χ^2 for all relationships for which Q exceeds .30 are significant at the .05 level.

structions: "Although you may not agree or disagree completely with any of the following statements, please tell me whether you tend more to agree or disagree with each statement." Each agreement was taken as an indication of alienation.

The chi-square test of significance, with the rejection level set at .05, and Yule's coefficient of association (Q) were utilized in the statistical analysis of the data.

Findings

Intercorrelations among the types of alienation are presented in Table 1. With the exception of cultural estrangement, the

scale with a coefficient of reproducibility of .90. Although these five types of alienation may be distinct on a conceptual level, there is apparently an underlying unity. Studies employing a measure of generalized alienation thus may be feasible, though the nature of the relation of cultural estrangement to the other types of alienation perhaps needs further clarification.

Our present purpose, however, is to determine whether each of the varieties of alienation is associated with conditions of deprivation. The importance of racial status as an alienating condition is immediately apparent from the figures in Table 2. The percentage of Negroes who feel alienated is far higher than the percentage of whites for every type of alienation except cultural estrangement. Approximately two-thirds of the Negro subjects agree with most of the items indicating alienation, whereas a majority of whites disagree with every item. The racial difference is statistically significant in every instance except cultural estrangement.

The difference is largest with respect to estrangement from work. No doubt this reflects the occupational structure of the community, for 72 per cent of the employed Negroes are working in semiskilled or unskilled jobs, as compared to only 14 per cent of the whites. A marked difference between Negroes and whites also occurs in the case of normlessness. More than half the Negroes but only 16 per cent of the whites perceive a conflict between success goals and ethical means. This difference may stem in part from the Negroes' recognition that discrimination leaves few legitimate avenues to success open to them. Observation of the discrepancy between the whites' professed ideals and their actual behavior, particularly in relation to Negroes,

TABLE 2. Alienation, by Race

| Type of Alienation | PER CENT WHO FEEL ALIENATED | | |
	Negroes*	Whites	Total Community
Powerlessness	70	40	47
Meaninglessness	71	48	52
Normlessness	55	16	24
Cultural estrangement	35	34	35
Social estrangement	60	27	35
Estrangement from work	66	18	28
Number of cases	(99)	(207)	(256)

* The Negro sample is augmented by an additional 50 cases chosen randomly from the enumeration of Negro adults in the community. Figures for the total community do not include the 50 additional cases.

may also give Negroes a rather cynical perspective on society.

In Table 3 we may examine the effect of education on alienation within each racial group. Among the Negroes, those who have had 12 or more years of education are in every instance less likely to feel alienated than those with less education, though the differences are statistically significant only for social estrangement and estrangement from work. There is a similar pattern among the whites, with significant differences for powerlessness, meaninglessness, and estrangement from work.

As one would expect, the inverse relation between education and a sense of meaninglessness is particularly strong, but much more so among the whites than among the Negroes. The percentage difference between high and low educational groups among the whites is more than twice that for the Negroes. Why is education not a more significant factor in relieving Negroes of the sense that they "really don't understand just what is going on?" We might speculate that the Negroes' greater sense of powerlessness is responsible. Even educated Negroes may feel little interest in attempting to understand things they believe are beyond their control. This interpretation is supported by the fact that education has more effect on powerlessness among whites than it does among Negroes. For each of the other types of alienation, however, the percentage difference between educational groups is greater among the Negroes than among the whites.

Use of the scale for general alienation, which consists of all of the items except cultural estrangement, permits us to gain an overview of the relation between alienation and race and education. If, on the basis of this scale, the sample is divided at the median into groups of high and low alienation, the association between subordinate racial status and alienation is $Q = .79$. Approximately 6 per cent of the Negroes and 28 per cent of the whites show no

TABLE 3.   Alienation, by Race and Years of Education

| | Per Cent Who Feel Alienated | | | |
| | NEGROES* | | WHITES | |
Type of Alienation	Less Than 12 Years Education	12 or More Years of Education	Less Than 12 Years Education	12 or More Years of Education
Powerlessness	73	60	57	34
Meaninglessness	76	56	80	35
Normlessness	59	40	22	14
Cultural estrangement	39	24	42	31
Social estrangement	67	40	37	24
Estrangement from work	73	44	33	12
Number of Cases	(74)	(25)	(60)	(147)

* The Negro sample is augmented by an additional 50 cases chosen randomly from the enumeration of Negro adults in the community.

alienation with regard to any of the five types in the scale; 28 per cent of the Negroes and only 1 per cent of the whites feel alienated in every respect.

The association between education and general alienation is −.67 for the white group and −.56 among the Negroes. Thus, education appears to be of somewhat greater significance among whites than among Negroes. For Negroes in a southern community racial status is far and away the most salient fact; the whites tend to treat Negroes categorically, regardless of education, occupation, or reputation. Yet, education affects most types of alienation, even among the Negroes. On the other hand, there is no significant educational difference among Negroes in the incidence of pessimism. The highly educated Negroes are almost as likely as the poorly educated to agree with the statement, "In spite of what some people say, the lot of the average man is getting worse." Killian and Grigg report similar findings for Florida Negroes in connection with Srole's anomia scale, of which this item is a part.[18]

Conclusion

Among the adults of a small city in central Florida five types of alienation—powerlessness, meaninglessness, normlessness, social estrangement, and estrangement from work—are highly intercorrelated, but a sixth, cultural estrangement, is not closely related to the others. The hypothesis that social conditions of deprivation are related to alienation is generally supported. Subordinate racial status and limited education are strongly associated with all but one type of alienation. Several other factors, such as occupation of head of household, family income, sex, marital status, and size of community of origin, also tend to be related to alienation, but the coefficients of association are not as high as for race or education.

By far the most striking finding of the study is the pervasiveness of alienation among the Negro population, a point which is also dramatically clear in James Baldwin's essay, "Down at the Cross." In addition to each of the other types of alienation, Baldwin senses a cultural estrangement among American Negroes so extreme that "there are some wars . . . that the American Negro will not support, however many of his people may be coerced." [19] William Worthy, correspondent of the *Baltimore Afro-American,* has pointed out that the greatest amount of pro-Castro sentiment in the United States is to be found in Harlem among lower-class Negroes, and Black

Muslim publications have advocated a policy of "Hands Off Cuba!" This evidence of estrangement from American culture is not consistent with the findings of this study, which show that Negroes are no more likely to be culturally estranged than whites. The discrepancy may be due to the circumscribed nature of the item used here to determine cultural estrangement, since it deals only with attitudes toward the popular culture of the mass media. Negroes may feel a deep estrangement from basic aspects of American culture and yet turn to the soporific fare of the mass media as a means of escape from the problems and tensions of life.

Notes

1. Melvin Seeman, "On the Meaning of Alienation," *American Sociological Review,* 24 (December 1959), pp. 783–91.

2. Prior to the study the six items were presented without identification to 14 graduate students in a seminar in sociological theory who had previously read and discussed the work of Durkheim, Merton, Srole, Nettler, Meier and Bell, Seeman, and Dean on the subjects of anomie and alienation. The students, working independently, showed little hesitation in classifying the items, and they were in unanimous agreement concerning the type of alienation represented by each of the six items.

3. Leo Srole, "Social Integration and Certain Corollaries: An Exploratory Study," *American Sociological Review,* 21 (December 1956), pp. 709–16.

4. Dorothy L. Meier and Wendell Bell, "Anomia and Differential Access to the Achievement of Life Goals," *American Sociological Review,* 24 (April 1959), pp. 190–91.

5. See, for example, Dwight G. Dean, "Alienation: Its Meaning and Measurement," *American Sociological Review,* 26 (October 1961), pp. 754–55.

6. Robert K. Merton, "Social Structure and Anomie," in *Social Theory and Social Structure* (New York: The Free Press, 1957) and Seeman, *op. cit.,* pp. 787–88.

7. Gwynn Nettler, "A Measure of Alienation," *American Sociological Review,* 22 (December 1957), pp. 670–77. In addition to questions dealing with political, religious, and familial norms, Nettler asks such questions as the following: "Do you enjoy TV?" "What do you think of the new model American Automobiles?" "Do you read *Reader's Digest?*" "Do national spectator sports (football, baseball) interest you?"

8. Dean, *op. cit.,* pp. 755–56.

9. Seeman, *op. cit.,* p. 789.

10. Robert A. Nisbet, *Community and Power* (New York: Oxford University Press, 1962).

11. Fritz Pappenheim, *The Alienation of Modern Man* (New York: Monthly Review Press, 1959).

12. Morton Grodzins, *The Loyal and the Disloyal* (Chicago: University of Chicago Press, 1956), p. 134.

13. Peter Townsend, *The Family Life of Old People* (London: Routledge and Kegan Paul, 1957), p. 166.

14. Eric and Mary Josephson (eds.), *Man Alone: Alienation in Modern Society* (New York: Dell, 1962), p. 14.

15. Seeman, *op. cit.,* pp. 789–90.

16. Erich Fromm, *The Sane Society* (New York: Holt, Rinehart and Winston, 1955). See also Erich Fromm, *Marx's Concept of Man* (New York: Frederick Ungar, 1961).

17. For comparison purposes, phi coefficients (φ) were also calculated. Since φ involves a more restrictive definition of association than Q, the coefficients are uniformly lower, but the patterns of relationship among the variables are almost identical.

18. Lewis M. Killian and Charles M. Grigg, "Urbanism, Race, and Anomia," *American Journal of Sociology,* 67 (May 1962), pp. 661–65.

19. James Baldwin, *The Fire Next Time* (New York: Dial Press, 1963), p. 117. At a recent informal meeting between Attorney General Robert F. Kennedy and James Baldwin and a group of his friends, ". . . a once-injured, often-jailed young Freedom Rider waggled a finger in the astonished Kennedy's face and told him he wouldn't take up arms against Cuba. 'He was surprised to hear there were Negroes who wouldn't fight for their country,' Baldwin said later in his two-room downtown Manhattan flat. 'How many Negroes would fight to free Cuba when they can't be freed themselves?' That was precisely the message the Negroes wanted to get across—a message of anger, of quickening urgency, of deepening alienation." "Kennedy and Baldwin: The Gulf," *Newsweek,* 61 (June 3, 1968), p. 19.

4. Development of a Test for Class-consciousness

PAUL F. LAZARSFELD

[Ed. Note: In preparation for a study of decision-making during an American electoral campaign, Lazarsfeld was asked to describe the origins of his class-consciousness
scale. The following selection is the memorandum growing out of that request.]

ALTHOUGH it is well known that American
workers are not class-conscious in the
European sense, it occurred to me that it
might still be useful to try to develop an
empirical measure of class-consciousness in
Americans. Such a measure could lead to
some intriguing comparisons among different regions and occupational groups.

How to begin? I did not attempt a systematic survey of the literature on class-
consciousness though this might have
proved fruitful. Instead, I tried to base the
scale on my own recollection of a classic
example of a class-conscious worker: the
Austrian Social Democratic Party member.
In order to explain my procedure, I must
give a brief description of the Austrian
situation.

Prior to World War I, several European
countries had developed strong Social Democratic parties. When these parties dis-
sented about support of the war, they
spread into right and left wings. The Third
International capitalized upon this division
to establish strong Communist parties.
Only a few Social Democratic parties were
able to remain undivided; the Austrian
party was one of these. By 1920, it had become the proud representative of a political
labor movement which leaned neither to
the right, as the British Labor party did,
nor to the left, as the Communist party did.
"Austro-Marxism" was used to describe the
Austrian situation.

The Austrian Social Democrats earned
about 40 per cent of the electoral vote in

Austria and about 66 per cent of the vote
in Vienna. Vienna itself had a Social Democratic government which inaugurated
sweeping reforms in housing, education,
social welfare, and the taxation system.
Among the majority of the Viennese, pride
in their city and in the Social Democratic
party were almost identical. There were
continuous political meetings reverberating
with the class-conscious theme. The expression "class-conscious" was used in the same
sense as "the American way of life" in this
country or "liberty" and "equality" in the
French Revolution. I am quite sure that
no one, except a few intellectuals, gave any
thought to what class-consciousness actually meant. It was the climate in which a
member of the Austrian Labor party lived.
He did not question it.

In developing a scale for class-consciousness, I tried to reconstruct the elements of
the Austrian experience as I had lived it.
Of course, I then had to substitute American indicators for Austrian ones. I shall describe this process in the following paragraphs. There seemed to be four important
components. One was the idea that to be a
worker, or even better, a member of the
Social Democratic party, would *embrace as
many areas of one's life as possible*. There
were Social Democratic chess clubs, hiking
clubs, reading clubs. In fact, there was
practically no activity for which there did
not exist an association specifically titled
Social Democratic. I think everyone of us
would have considered it disgraceful to the

point of treason to belong to any kind of bourgeois association (buergerlich). In the American questionnaire, we tried to gauge the degree to which style of life was patterned along class lines by asking questions about clubs, story heroes, and desired professions for one's children.

The second component was an uncompromising *distrust of class enemies*. (Incidentally, the inflexibility led to the political ruin of the party fifteen years later.)

The class-conscious worker was convinced that war and peace and all institutions of the bourgeois state were maintained solely for the benefit of the bourgeois class. The class-distrust dimension was somewhat difficult to phrase in American terms, but we ended up with a question about whether city governments were business-controlled and another about whether people succeed because of ability, luck or external connections.

TABLE 1.   Elmira Workers Display Little Indication of Working-Class Consciousness
(Per Cent Who Show Class Consciousness)

AUSTRIAN DIMEN-SIONS	*THEORETICAL MANIFESTATIONS OF WORKING-CLASS CONSCIOUSNESS*	*BREADWINNER'S OCCUPATION*		
		Business, Pro-fession, Self-employed	*White Collar*	*Labor*
Symbolic or emotional	*Reactions to symbols:*			
	Favorable to "billion-dollar corporations"	74	85	75
	Favorable to "labor unions"	44	53	66
Distrust of class enemies	*Images of social institutions:*			
	Believe "most city governments make the welfare of all citizens their main concern"	63	60	50
	Believe most successful people have "gotten ahead" because of "ability"	86	88	74
All-embracing life style	*Styles of life:*			
	Prefer clubs whose members are "all of my own class"	34	36	41
	Like to read or hear stories about			
	. . . "working people"	79	86	80
	. . . "business people"	74	70	55
	If son were a lawyer, would like him to work "for himself," "in private law firm," or "for business corporation" (instead of for "labor union" or "government")	95	90	82
	If son were a doctor, would like him to be "specialist with private practice" or "head of private hospital" (instead of "head of government medical service")	96	96	92
Political militancy	*Political militancy:*			
	Believe "it would be good for country if labor unions had a political party of their own"	8	7	13
	Total no. of cases	171	106	340

These data were obtained from a mail survey conducted after the election; about 75 per cent of our original sample responded.

The third element was *political militancy*. The party member was expected to devote part of his time to political service. This meant not only canvassing and other election duties; it meant regular attendance at the local section of the party, faithful reading of the party newspapers and at least one of its periodicals, and continuous attention to party affairs. Members were expected to participate in their professional or trade union organization (the trade unions were a distinct part of the political movement). Since it was a democratic party, members were expected to vote for officers or even run for party office within the local section. Through a large network of adult worker education groups, party members were expected to give or attend speeches about many historical, economic, and social issues. On the American questionnaire, since there was no existing labor party, we simply asked whether it would be good for the nation if labor unions had a political party of their own.

The questions in the scale were designed to refer to these elements: style of life, distrust of the present system, and approval of and participation in political labor activities.

In addition, we included a fourth ingredient, a *symbolic or emotional one*. For the party member there were certain songs which quickened the heart; there was a surge of emotion at the sight of the red flag at the big demonstrations; there was pride in wearing the party button at all occasions. This element of emotional demonstrativeness about party affiliation was almost impossible to recapture in the United States, where there was no major labor movement which could elicit such reactions. Therefore, this set of items was the least satisfactory. We expressed the emotional component by items containing common, emotionally-tinged slogans about big business corporations and labor unions.

There is an interesting afterthought. Actually I do not know what the real attitudes of workers were. What I have presented is but the analysis of a participant-observer. If my class-consciousness test had been applied in Austria, it might have yielded surprising results.

But I do know what happened when the test was applied to a sample of American respondents. In 1948, in our study *Voting,*[1] we used the same dimensions of class-consciousness to see whether workers in Elmira, New York, had a set of values quite distinct from those of the business, professional, and white collar classes. As the table above shows, they did not. They do not distrust social institutions or see themselves as disadvantaged by their positions or hold deviant expectations for their children or favor a political party for labor unions. The working class seemed to adhere to the traditional middle-class ideology —the "American way of life."

Note

1. Bernard Berelson, Paul Lazarsfeld and William McPhee, *Voting: A Study of Opinion Formation in a Presidential Campaign* (Chicago: University of Chicago Press, 1954), pp. 54–9.

5. Uprootedness and Working-class Consciousness

JOHN C. LEGGETT

[Ed. Note: The working class is not all of one piece: one possible basis of division is between workers who are recent immigrants from rural areas and seasoned workers who can claim an industrial heritage. The author refers to industrial workers of recent rural origins as "the uprooted"; those workers who grew up in industrial regions are called "the prepared." In a study conducted in Detroit, Leggett examines the class consciousness and militance of these two groups of workers.]

DEGREE OF WORKING-CLASS CONSCIOUSNESS

WORKING-CLASS consciousness can be defined as a cumulative series of mental states, running from class verbalization through skepticism and militance to egalitarianism. "Class verbilization" denotes the tendency of working-class individuals to discuss topics in class terms. They need not do so consistently. In fact, only the occasional use of class symbols designates one as having some facility in their usage. "Skepticism" occurs when an individual believes that wealth is allocated within the community so as to benefit primarily the middle class. "Militance" refers to a predisposition to engage aggressively in action to advance the interests of one's class. "Egalitarianism" refers to favoring a redistribution of wealth so that each individual within the community would have (1) the same amount and (2) the material basis thereby for the full development of his natural talents.

In order to measure "class verbalization," the first aspect of class consciousness considered, a battery of eight unstructured questions was used. Each question deliberately made no reference to class, so as not to prejudice the answers of the respondent. He was asked whom he had voted for in the last election and why, who was his favorite president and why, and so forth. If the worker used class terms in just one of these instances, his comments constituted class verbalization. "Skepticism" was operationalized through the use of the following question: "When business booms in Detroit, who gets the profits?" If the respondent used categories such as "rich people," "upper class," "big business" and similar class references, he was treated as class conscious in this regard. "Militance" was measured by asking the respondent to project himself into a situation where workers were about to take action against a landlord, and to indicate whether or not he would join the group in a series of activities, including picketing. If he would take part in the *latter,* the study classified him as militant. "Egalitarianism" was determined to exist when the worker agreed with the notion that the wealth of our country should be divided up equally so that people would have an equal chance to get ahead.

These various aspects of class consciousness in turn were linked to one another so as to measure the degree to which each worker had developed class consciousness. Ideally, workers thereby fell into one of the following five categories: militant egali-

Reprinted in part with permission from the *American Journal of Sociology,* 69 (May 1963) pp. 685–88 (copyright 1963 by The University of Chicago).

tarians, militant radicals, skeptics, class verbalizers, and class indifferents. Table 1 indicates how workmen were typed.

It should be noted that approximately three-quarters of the respondents held opinions that corresponded either exactly or consistently with this model. Unfortunately, one-fourth of the workers maintained a point of view that was inconsistent with this configuration. Although they were clearly "error types," they, nevertheless, were categorized as were the rest on the basis of a point system suggested by Guttman. Thus, a total of 375 workers were classified. Of these, 38 qualified as militant egalitarians, 87 as militant radicals, 114 as skeptics, 98 as class verbalizers, and 38 as class indifferents.[1]

definition is a synthesis of several important writings. The next task is to weigh its ultility.

Expectations and Findings

It was anticipated that the uprooted should express a higher degree of class consciousness than the prepared. The data presented in Table 2 support this expectation: 52 per cent of the uprooted are either militant radicals or militant egalitarians, while only 22 per cent of the prepared can be so classified. At the other extreme, 13 per cent of the uprooted and 47 per cent of the prepared are either class verbalizers or class indifferents. The Kendall's Tau meas-

TABLE 1.   Ideal Classification of Respondents on Four Aspects of Class Consciousness

Individuals Typed According to Class Perspective	Egalitarianism*	Militance	Skepticism	Class Verbalization
Militant egalitarians	+	+	+	+
Militant radicals	−	+	+	+
Skeptics	−	−	+	+
Class verbalizers	−	−	−	+
Class indifferents	−	−	−	−

* "+" refers to class conscious; "−" refers to non-class conscious.

This treatment of class consciousness, although original, rests on several formulations found in the sociological literature. Not only the ideas of Marx and Guttman, but those of Manis and Meltzer, as well as Alfred Jones, have been used to define the various aspects of class consciousness. Marx has pointed to the utility of thinking in terms of degree of class consciousness,[2] while Guttman has suggested a suitable measurement technique.[3] Manis and Meltzer have wisely suggested that class consciousness can be treated in terms of its many aspects,[4] while the findings of Jones, in his study of the Akron sit-down strikers, have warned the researcher against ignoring its militant forms.[5] Clearly, then, this

ure of correlation is .41, while the difference between the uprooted and the prepared respondents is significant at the < .001 level.

Other relevant variables do not upset our findings. Table 3 demonstrates that, when one controls for ethnicity, the relationship still obtains. First, among Negroes, the Southern-born are more class conscious than those born in Michigan and elsewhere in the North.[6] Second, if one considers Poles and Ukranians only, those of European background are more likely to express a high degree of class consciousness than those born in the northern United States.[7] How can one explain these consistent findings?

TABLE 2.   Regional Background and Class Consciousness (Per Cent)

Regional Background	Militant Egalitarians	Militant Radicals	Skeptics	Class Verbalizers	Class Indifferents	Total
The uprooted*	17	35	35	11	2	100
The prepared**	3	19	31	37	10	100

*N = 139.
** N = 95.

TABLE 3.   Ethnicity, Regional Background, and Class Consciousness (Per Cent)

Regional Background	Militant Egalitarians	Militant Radicals	Skeptics	Class Verbalizers	Class Indifferents	Total
			Negroes			
Southern-born	21	37	32	9	1	100 (102)
Northern-born	6	29	29	24	12	100 (17)
			Poles			
European-born	6	28	44	16	6	100 (36)
Northern-born	3	17	30	40	10	100 (78)

Interpretation of Findings

Peasants and farmers transplanted from an agrarian-industrial to an industrial environment will frequently express a high degree of class consciousness partially because they are speedily injected into an economic system where their lack of formal education and urban *savoir faire* often places them in marginal occupational roles. Exploitation of these workmen, combined with their lack of skills, effectively limits the chances of the uprooted to achieve job security or to move upward into the middle class. Marginal economic position, exploitation, and lack of skills, linked to blocked mobility, in turn create grievances against the business community and sometimes generate collective protests demanding alteration of the status quo. The situation of the uprooted has these consequences, in part, because workmen are able to compare their present economi-

cally insecure positions with (1) their original optimistic expectations developed prior to movement to the industrial community and (2) the relatively high standard of living maintained by the middle class and much of the working class as well.[8]

A host of other considerations no doubt contribute to the class consciousness of the uprooted. One factor deserves particular mention. The uprooted presumably develop an antipathy toward the supraordinate classes in general because the latter, in both agrarian and industrial regions, have exploited them. In agrarian regions (such as much of Poland prior to World War II), communities have a high degree of class crystallization. Upward mobility and improvement of status among the lower classes are generally impossible. Rigid norms and legal structures backed by the landed gentry control them, to the extent that the subordinate classes find it difficult to express their grievances without being severely repressed by the upper class or its representatives. For this reason, those so adversely affected develop a marked dislike for this particular supraordinate class. This attitude is later generalized to include all supraordinate classes when the dominant class in the urban-industrial community also acts with little regard for their economic and social welfare.

The impact of past membership in a society where there is a high degree of class crystallization should not be overestimated, however. One cannot say that subordinate class membership within an agrarian industrial society (or an agrarian region) is the sole source of working-class consciousness for the uprooted. Rather, it would seem that an exploited position in an industrial community, when coupled with past membership in an agrarian region, contributes to the formation of a high degree of class consciousness among the uprooted.

The uprooted differ markedly from the prepared in previous experiences. The latter are natives of an industrial region and are thus in a much better position to acquire the occupational skills and urban values so useful in adapting successfully to the demands of the industrial community. Because of their greater sophistication, they are subject to less economic exploitation, blocked mobility, and economic insecurity. In addition, the prepared do not carry with them a strong dislike of ruling groups found in preindustrial society, for, after all, they were never members of this form of social organization. Partially because of these differences in past experiences, the prepared develop a lower degree of class consciousness than the uprooted . . .

Notes

1. In addition, it should be noted that the Menzel coefficient of reproducibility for this measure of class consciousness is .77. The formula used to compute this measure has been presented by Herbert Menzel, "A New Coefficient for Scalogram Analysis," *Public Opinion Quarterly*, XVII (September 1953), pp. 124–33.

2. Some of Marx's most provocative notions on class consciousness appear in his *The German Ideology* (New York: International Publishers, 1960).

3. Guttman's presentation of a useful measurement technique can be found in Samuel Stouffer *et al.*, *Studies in Social Psychology in World War II* (Princeton, N.J.: Princeton University Press, 1950), IV, pp. 3–90, 172–212.

4. Jerome G. Manis and Bernard N. Meltzer, "Attitudes of Textile Workers to Class Structure," *American Journal of Sociology*, LX (1954), pp. 30–55.

5. *Op. cit.*, pp. 250–80.

6. Needless to say, the relatively small number of cases of prepared workmen found among Negroes does not constitute compelling evidence.

7. In addition, it should be noted that a series of statistical controls fail to upset the relationship between uprootedness and class consciousness. Length of residence, union membership, downward mobility, generational membership, and several measures of present economic position cannot erase the importance of the uprooted hypothesis.

8. Werner Landecker has developed a quite similar interpretation of the sources of class consciousness. His explanation both achieves a higher degree of generality than the one advanced in this study and presents a point of view consistent with my own: "It seems then that in one form or another a large proportion of the population perceive their present social positions as stepping stones to higher levels. Under such conditions, one will tend to view oneself or one's family as being potentially above the transitional level occupied at the present time. Only if prospects for up-mobility seem to be dim, do people come to think of themselves as being in the same boat with others of similar status and as being part of a distinct class. It seems then that the frequency of up-mobility which is assumed to occur stands in an inverse relation to the prevalent degree of class consciousness. *The higher the apparent frequency of up-mobility is,* the lower the degree of class consciousness will tend to be" (see Ronald Freedman *et al.*, *Principles of Sociology* [New York: Henry Holt & Co., 1952], p. 426).

C. Index Formation

6. Comparison of Guttman and Latent Structure Scales

SAMUEL A. STOUFFER

VITAL to the development of social psychology and sociology as scientific disciplines is the definition and classification of the objects of study.

This requires rigorous yet economical methods for handling data which are initially *qualitative*, not quantitative. The objective of much of the Research Branch methodological endeavors . . . is to deal *with theoretical models of ordered structures or scales and with technical procedures for testing the applicability of a particular model to a particular set of qualitative data.* . . .

1. The Scalogram Theory of Establishing Rank Order

Perhaps the most drastic departure from earlier approaches is represented in the initial thinking of Louis Guttman. In 1940, just before the war, Guttman contributed a series of studies on the logic of measurement and prediction to a monograph of the Social Science Research Council.[1] This work contained the basic principle of ideas which he was to apply in the Research Branch a year later and which were to be greatly expanded theoretically and adapted for quick practical use. . . .

The scalogram model, requiring cumulative items, has at the present time been studied most thoroughly. Therefore, our attention will now be focused on it. We must keep clearly in mind the fact that the cumulative character of the items satisfying a scalogram analysis puts a restriction upon the type of data which can be used with this model. Yet the restriction is not, in practice, as severe as may at first appear.

It is often possible to find items which have an intrinsic cumulative character. The prototype is perhaps the social distance scale, with such items as the following:

1. Would you want a relative of yours to marry a Negro?
2. Would you invite a Negro to dinner at your home?
3. Would you allow a Negro to vote?

An illustration from Research Branch data of this type of intrinsic scale may be taken from a study of riflemen overseas

Reprinted in part with permission from S. A. Stouffer, E. A. Suchman, P. F. Lazarsfeld, S. A. Star, and J. A. Clausen, *Measurement and Prediction,* Chapter 1 (copyright 1950 by Princeton University Press, Princeton, N.J.).

who had recently experienced combat. . . . It was desired to see if there was a scale order in the way in which respondents reported experiencing fear. The following question was asked:

> Soldiers who have been under fire report different *physical reactions to the dangers of battle*. Some of these are given in the following list. How often have you had these reactions when you were under fire? Check one answer after each of the reactions listed to show how often you had the reaction. Please do it carefully.
> [There followed 10 items, each with a four-step check list. For example:

> Shaking or trembling all over
> _____ Often
> _____ Sometimes
> _____ Once
> _____ Never]

A scale picture . . . indicated that nine of these items formed a very satisfactory scale when ordered as follows:

1. Urinating in pants.
2. Losing control of the bowels.
3. Vomiting.
4. Feeling of weakness or feeling faint.
5. Feeling of stiffness.
6. Feeling sick at the stomach.
7. Shaking or trembling all over.
8. Sinking feeling of the stomach.
9. Violent pounding of the heart.

One item—"cold sweat"—did not fit into the scale; that is, some people who experienced less frequent fear symptoms than cold sweat also experienced cold sweat, but this was also true of some people who experienced more frequent symptoms than cold sweat. Hence "cold sweat" was shown to involve a factor or factors additional to the scale variable.

The fact that the 9 items satisfied the scalogram criteria means that if a man did not report vomiting, for example, he also did not report urinating in his pants or losing control of his bowels. If he did report vomiting, he also reported all of the other

experiences (4 through 9 on the list) which were generally more frequent than vomiting. In this case he would have a score of 7 and if the scale were perfect we would know exactly *which* seven experiences he reported. Actually, of course, the scale was not quite perfect. By an easy procedure . . . it was possible to compute a *coefficient of reproducibility,* which was .92. This means that if we knew any scale score, such as 7, and if we guessed the exact items which respondents with this scale score endorsed and did not endorse, we would guess 92 out of 100 of the items correctly and 8 out of 100 incorrectly. . . .

The possibility should be faced, however, that large areas of psychological or social behavior may not yield items which approximate the scale pattern required by scalogram analysis. For example, a short catalogue of psychosomatic symptoms which the Research Branch used in constructing a psychiatric screening test simply did not order itself in a manner satisfying the rigorous criteria set up. That is, a man who said he was bothered with shortness of breath might or might not complain of spells of dizziness, and vice versa . . . It is still possible to construct a scale—called a *quasi scale*—which lacks the property of reproducibility but which does have the valuable property of *yielding the same correlation with an outside criterion as does the multiple correlation of the individual items with that criterion.*

It is frequently possible, however, to order items cumulatively (and hence to order respondents) by constructing items with multiple check lists and choosing cutting points by combining categories such that the error of reproducibility is minimized.

Consider, for example, three items which happen to have uniform format. (Such uniformity is not at all essential—the number of response categories can vary arbitrarily from item to item and the wording of the categories can be varied):

1. How many of your officers take a personal interest in their men?
   1 _____ All of them
   2 _____ Most of them
   3 _____ About half of them
   4 _____ Some of them
   5 _____ Few or none of them

2. How many of your officers will go through anything they ask their men to go through?
   1 _____ All of them
   2 _____ Most of them
   3 _____ About half of them
   4 _____ Some of them
   5 _____ Few or none of them

3. How many of your officers are the kind you would want to serve under in combat?
   1 _____ All of them
   2 _____ Most of them
   3 _____ About half of them
   4 _____ Some of them
   5 _____ Few or none of them

If each item is dichotomized by taking the two top categories as "favorable" responses, the three items will not ordinarily form a scale by scalogram analysis. In a sense, in spite of manifest difference in content, these three particular items are more or less synonymous. Hence, the frequencies probably will not be cumulative. However, if for item 1 we take response category 1 as "positive," for item 2 response categories 1 and 2, and for item 3 response categories 1, 2, and 3, we perhaps can build a cumulative set of items. This is, of course, just one of various ways in which a cumulative set of responses might be built from these items. The procedure for selecting cutting points which will maximize scalability has been reduced to a simple routine . . . It is *not, arbitrary,* but is based upon a study of the *simultaneous distribution* of all the original responses.[2] From a practical standpoint, the operational procedures developed in the Research Branch for swiftly evaluating a large number of questions simul-

taneously may rank as one of the major contributions of the Branch to social science technique. Work which would have required hundreds of hours of elaborate machine analysis can now be done in a few hours by one semi-skilled clerk. . . .

There can be no doubt that the empirical choice of cutting points on more or less synonymous items in order to achieve a set of cumulative responses is rather crude. It needs to be studied and criticized. But it does supply an ordering of respondents with a high degree of reliability and the ultimate test will be its utility in comparison with other techniques. . . .

The greater the variety of questions, of course, the wider the generalization which can be made about the coverage of a particular scale, assuming that criteria of scalability are satisfied.

It is recommended . . . that a relatively large number of items, preferably as many as ten or twelve, be used in the initial testing of the hypothesis of scalability, and that, if possible, some of these items be trichotomized rather than dichotomized. This will ordinarily make it quite difficult to achieve high reproducibility, but protects against spurious results which might be obtained by chance with only three or four dichotomous items.

Critics of the use of only three or four items seem to have overlooked an important distinction, namely, that while it is desirable to use as many as ten or a dozen items in initial testing of scalability, a smaller number of items can be safely selected from the scalable list for practical research purposes. If a dozen items reveal a scale pattern, then a smaller number selected from these dozen will show the same pattern (though with fewer ranks). Because they belong to the same scale, according to scalogram criteria, a smaller subset of items finally selected for use—possibly comprising only three or four—will of necessity correlate very highly with other subsets of items in the same scale . . . Items comprising such a subset will have higher reliability than similar items from most other types of scales, since each response is a *definition* of the respondent's position on a single continuum and is minimally corrupted with other affective material which correlates with some items and not with others.

In fact, one of the important consequences of finding an attitude to be scalable is that one is then justified in selecting three or four items which can be used to order respondents in a limited number of ranks. It may be possible eventually to use a pretest for selecting *a single item* for practical use—such as is the staple of much conventional market research or public opinion polling. But now the item is selected *with full knowledge* as to its place in the attitude structure. . . .

In attitude research of the future, an important desideratum will be to obtain simultaneous measures on *a large number of continua* from a given respondent. Scalable attitudes lend themselves particularly well to this in practice. Why? Because each attitude can be represented by only a few items, so that a large complex of attitudes can be observed in a single study. Thus multiple factor analysis might be employed to construct a typology of these continua, and we may well be on the road to an analysis of socio-psychological problems comparable to the road which has led to progress in the study of human abilities.

When the hypothesis of the scale structure is found not to be borne out by the observed data, the attitude items may still have an ordered structure, as has been said, namely, that of the *quasi scale*. . . .

The examination of the properties of quasi scales in particular and of scalogram analysis in general, which was begun by Paul F. Lazarsfeld while a consultant in the Research Branch, led to the development of a fresh approach to the problem of ordering respondents, which will be described in the following section.

2. The Latent Structure Theory

In the last years of the war, Paul F. Lazarsfeld, while a consultant in the Research Branch, became especially concerned with these quasi scales. For several years he had been interested in the classification of attributes, and especially in the properties of partial fourfold tables, on which Yule had written many years before with much insight in the opening chapters of his *Introduction to the Theory of Statistics*. As a result of his studies, Lazarsfeld proposed a fresh attack on the fundamental conceptualization of the scaling problem.

What Lazarsfeld proposed was a return to the older concept of a *latent attitude continuum*. Guttman, before the war, had studied, perhaps more thoroughly than any other person, the possibilities of this approach but had turned for the time being in a new and different direction because he saw clearly that conventional methods of quantitative factor analysis, stemming from Spearman, were inappropriate for handling qualitative data. Lazarsfeld's primary achievement was to bring forth a new model for directly factoring qualitative data. Therefore, it would now seem to be practical to test quite rigorously the following basic hypothesis: *There exists a set of latent classes, such that the manifest relationship between any two or more items on a test can be accounted for by the existence of these basic classes and by these alone.*

This implies that any attitude item has two aspects—one which is associated with the latent classes and one which is specific to the item. The specific aspect of any item is assumed to be independent of the latent classes and also independent of the specific aspect of any other item.

The analogy with the Spearman-Thurstone approach in quantitative factor analysis and indebtedness to it is obvious. The contrast with Guttman's approach also should be clear. Guttman's model deals only with the manifest relationship among attitude items and *defines* an attitude directly as the observed responses to these items. Lazarsfeld defines an attitude as an *inference* as to latent classes, tested by fitting to the manifest data an appropriate latent structure model.

Lazarsfeld's approach is quite general as to the number of latent classes. Moreover, these classes may or may not be *ordered*. In the very important special case where they are ordered along a single dimension, Lazarsfeld has achieved further generalizations of importance. He conceives of the latent classes as segments of a continuum x. Over this latent attitude continuum, the probability, $p(x)$, of a "favorable" response to a given specific attitude item, may be described as a continuous function of x. Such a "trace line" can take any shape, but the study of relatively simple types of "trace lines," such as the straight line and polynomials of second and third degree, is proving to be of much interest.

It turns out, further, that Guttman's quasi scale can be derived analytically as a special case of latent structure analysis, Guttman's perfect scale becoming a limiting case of the quasi scale. . . .

In order to familarize the reader with the fundamental idea, let us first consider the special case where the number of latent classes is two.

This special case, which is called *latent dichotomy* analysis, to distinguish it from the more general concept of latent structure analysis, is quite simple to understand and, as will be shown, has some interesting properties.

In applying the latent dichotomy model we seek to partition the sample into two classes of respondents—those who possess the latent character and those who do not. The latent dichotomy is, of course, an inference. Whether or not a given set of items can be fitted by a latent dichotomy has to be determined from the data, which ideally must satisfy a very rigorous criterion.

This criterion requires, as already indicated, that *all* of the relationship between any two questionnaire items be accounted for by the hypothetical latent dichotomy. Suppose that all respondents had labels which permitted us to sort them into two classes—those possessing the latent character and those not possessing it. Our criterion requires that, among those possessing the latent character, there be no association or correlation between the responses to any two individual items. Similarly, among those not possessing the latent character, there be no association or correlation between the response to any two individual items. We shall make this concrete with a numerical example presently. Actually, as we shall see, the ideal criterion conditions for a latent dichotomy are not likely to be realized. But they may be *approximately* realized—at least with a close enough approximation to satisfy us that the model is appropriate for a given set of items. If so, we can then use the information obtained to order the respondents.

For each response pattern—for example, $+ - + -$, a pattern in which a person is favorable on item 1, unfavorable on item 2, favorable on item 3, and unfavorable on item 4—we can estimate how many possess the latent character and how many do not. We can therefore calculate an estimate of the *proportion* who possess the latent character. We can do this for all possible response patterns. We can then put the response patterns in rank order according to the rank order of the proportions estimated as possessing the latent character. Since the individual respondents must fall into response patterns, we have ordered the individual respondents, except that all those with the same response pattern are of course tied in rank.

It will be seen at once that the latent dichotomy concept hypothesizes a fundamentally different structure from that of the cumulative scale model.

The scalogram model considers the response to each item as providing a *definition* of the respondent's attitude on the subject of the particular attitude scale. The latent dichotomy model does not require us to call a response to a particular item a definition of the respondent's attitude. Instead, it requires that we conceive of his response as having two components—one, which is a manifestation of a latent character and the other, which is specific to the item. Thus two items endorsed by a person, such as, "The British are brave fighters" and "The British are unselfish allies" may not serve as definitions of the *same* attitude, by scalogram analysis, but may prove to possess a common latent dichotomy, as well as residual content which is *specific* for each item, respectively. But note—the residual specific content must be unrelated. That is, among all men possessing the latent character, those who say the British are brave must be no more likely to say the British are unselfish allies than do those who do not say the British are brave. All the association between these two items must be attributable to the common latent character which they possess.

Now let us look at some numerical data, from a Research Branch attitude survey, which will help the reader see concretely what goes on when the latent dichotomy model is approximately realized.

We shall take . . . four items on general attitudes toward the Army . . . using data from a sample of 1,000 noncoms, studied in October 1945. Responses are dichotomized, not as in scalogram procedure by choosing cutting points in such a way as to minimize scalogram error, but according to what seems, *a priori,* to be the manifest content of the response. We have:

1. Do you think the Army has tried its best to look out for the welfare of enlisted men?
   Proportion saying, "Yes, it has tried its best"   .254
2. In general, do you think you your-self have gotten a square deal in the Army?
   Proportion saying, "Yes, in most ways I have"   .300
3. Do you think when you are discharged you will go back to civilian life with a favorable or unfavorable attitude toward the Army?
   Proportion saying, "Very favorable" or "Fairly favorable"   .374
4. In general, how well do you think the Army is run?
   Proportion saying, "It is run very well" or "It is run pretty well"   .641

Now, after responses to each of these four items are dichotomized, there will be $2^4 = 16$ possible response patterns, determined from cross tabulation. In Table 1, column 1, the number of cases with each of the 16 response patterns is shown. For example, there are 75 cases with the response pattern $+ + + +$, favorable on all four items. There are 55 cases with the response pattern $+ - + +$, favorable on items 1, 3, and 4 and unfavorable on item 2, etc.

The reader will recognize that only 5 of these 16 response patterns would constitute perfect scale types in a scalogram analysis free of error. These, shown . . . in Table 1, are:

$+ + + +$	75 cases
$- + + +$	69 cases
$- - + +$	96 cases
$- - - +$	199 cases
$- - - -$	229 cases
Total	668 cases

The other 332 cases are distributed among the 11 response patterns which would involve error by the scalogram model. According to the latent dichotomy model, however, these 11 response patterns *do not necessarily represent error.*[3]

The problem is to determine whether or not the respondents can be partitioned into two classes, those possessing and those not possessing the latent character. We will skip

TABLE 1.   Soldiers with Various Response Patterns Ranked According to Proportions Possessing Latent Character of Favorable Attitude toward the Army

RESPONSE PATTERN Item 1 2 3 4	Observed Number of Cases (1)	Total (2) =	Possessing Latent Character (3) +	Not Possessing Latent Character (4)	Proportion Possessing Latent Character $(5) = \frac{(3)}{(2)}$	Rank (6)
+ + + +	75	72.2	71.9	0.3	.996	1
+ + − +	42	44.0	42.7	1.3	.971	2
+ − + +	55	56.8	54.2	2.6	.953	3
− + + +	69	72.8	68.4	4.4	.940	4
+ + + −	3	6.3	5.9	0.4	.938	5
+ − − +	45	43.7	32.2	11.5	.736	6
− + − +	60	59.7	40.6	19.1	.680	7
+ + − −	10	5.2	3.5	1.7	.674	8
− − + +	96	90.8	51.6	39.2	.568	9
+ − + −	8	8.0	4.5	3.5	.561	10
− + + −	16	11.4	5.6	5.8	.494	11
− − − +	199	201.0	30.6	170.4	.152	12
+ − − −	16	17.8	2.6	15.2	.148	13
− + − −	25	28.4	3.3	25.1	.117	14
− − + −	52	55.7	4.2	51.5	.076	15
− − − −	229	226.2	2.5	223.7	.011	16
Total	1,000	1,000.0	424.3	575.7		

ADJUSTED NUMBER OF CASES

now the technical details of how that determination is made and concern ourselves only with its results. Since the latent dichotomy model ordinarily will not fit quite perfectly, one can compute for each response pattern an *adjusted frequency* which will differ somewhat from the *observed frequency*. The adjusted frequencies are of such a nature that the division into latent groups can be performed with precision. The adjusted frequencies are shown in column 2. A test of the adequacy of the latent dichotomy model is the agreement between the observed frequencies in column 1 and the adjusted frequencies in column 2. In the present example, it will be seen that the agreement is rather close. For example, in response pattern + + + + the observed number is 75, the adjusted number 72.2, an error of 2.8. The sum of such errors, irrespective of sign, for the 16

response patterns is 43.6 out of a total of 1,000 cases, or less than 5 per cent.

Now let us focus our attention on the *adjusted* frequencies for the various response patterns. By technical operations whose description we shall for the present postpone, we can partition the adjusted frequencies into two components, those possessing and those not possessing the latent character. For example, take the response pattern − + + +. The 72.8 adjusted cases are patitioned into two latent classes, 68.4 who possess the latent character and 4.4 who do not. The numbers estimated as having the latent character are shown in column 3 of Table 1 and the numbers without it are shown in column 4. On any line the sum of the numbers in columns 3 and 4 add to the number in column 2.

Next, we can estimate the *proportion* in

each response pattern who possess the latent character. This is shown in column 5. For response pattern $- + + +$, for example, this proportion is $68.4 + 72.8 = .940$. Of course, we cannot pick out which *particular individual* possesses or does not possess the latent character.

With our estimate for each response pattern of the proportions possessing the latent character we can now estimate the *rank* of the response pattern as is shown in column 6. Our task is cmpleted, for we now have the respondents *ordered* in 16 rank groups according to the proportion possessing the latent character.

Now let us look again at Table 1 and see empirically what is meant by saying that there is no association between the items except that due to the latent dichotomy. Consider, for example, items 1 and 2 only. For those possessing the latent character, let us pool the results for all response patterns in which items 1 and 2 are both positive. We have, from column 3 in Table 1:

$+ + + +$	71.9
$+ + + -$	5.9
$+ + - +$	42.7
$+ + - -$	3.5
Total	124.0

Similarly, pooling the results for all response patterns in which item 1 is positive and item 2 is negative, we have:

$+ - + +$	54.2
$+ - + -$	4.5
$+ - - +$	32.2
$+ - - -$	2.6
Total	93.5

For all response patterns in which item 1 is negative and item 2 is positive we have 117.9 and for all response patterns in which both item 1 and item 2 are negative we have 88.9. Now let us form the following fourfold table:

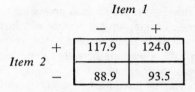

	Item 1 −	Item 1 +
Item 2 +	117.9	124.0
Item 2 −	88.9	93.5

Within the limits of error introduced by rounding, it will be seen that there is no association. In other words, the ratios of the numbers in the first row to the numbers in the second row are nearly identical. We get 1.3262 and 1.3262, identical to the fifth significant figure. Thus, among respondents possessing the latent character, there is no association between the specific components of items 1 and 2. Analogously, we can find that the same holds among respondents not possessing the latent character and it holds for any pair of items, not merely items 1 and 2.

It must be noted again that the absence of association between the specific components of any two items is achieved by basing the calculations on an adjusted number of frequencies (column 2 in Table 1). It would no longer quite hold if the percentages in column 5 were applied to the original observed frequencies in column 1. That is because the original data do not perfectly satisfy the criterion for the existence of a latent attribute. But we are making no *serious* error if we assume, say, that all the 75 cases in response pattern $(+ + + +)$ have the same proportion possessing the latent attribute (.996) as the 72.2 estimated cases after adjustment. For, as we have seen, over the whole table less than 5 per cent of the 1,000 men would be misclassified thereby.

The reader should study Table 1 and the discussion of it carefully in order to grasp the basic logic of the latent structure theory as applied in this simplest of models, namely that of a latent dichotomy. Some words of caution are now in order. In particular, the reader may ask, what sort of confidence can one place in column 5 in

Table 1—the proportions possessing the latent character among persons with a given manifest response pattern? It is necessary to issue a warning here that these proportions may be subject to several different sources of instability or sampling variability; for example:

1. The kind of variability involved in test-retest, repeating the same four items on the same population of subjects.
2. The kind of variability involved in using the same four items on two different populations of subjects.
3. The kind of variability involved in substitution of a new "parallel form" of item for each item initially used.

As the number of questions satisfying the model increases, the number of scale patterns increases and the proportions for a scale pattern converge toward zero or unity. The number of persons with scale patterns such that one cannot be pretty sure that they do or do not possess the latent character tends to become fewer and fewer.

It follows from these considerations that the ordering of persons into 16 rank groups as in Table 1 is an empirical result which is subject to several kinds of unreliability. It is possible that the 16 rank orders thus derived would be considerably more stable than the rank orders derived from, say, four items which do not satisfy the latent structure criteria. However, a rigorous analytical job on this remains to be done.

The *crucial* thing accomplished by the operations exhibited in Table 1 is that it provides evidence of the degree to which the manifest items satisfy criteria of *unidimensionality*. The need for such criteria we must keep at the forefront of our thinking. This is accomplished not perfectly in practice, but quite adequately with the latent dichotomy model in Table 1 . . .

Even if the values, in Table 1, column 5, of the proportions for a given manifest scale pattern who possess the latent character should "hop around" somewhat, under the conditions itemized above, it still seems useful to apply them in a given empirical investigation as an ordering scheme. In practice, we may wish to combine sixteen such patterns into two or three broad groups. Thus, if we inspect Table 1, we will see that the following manifest response patterns have proportions higher than .90 possessing the latent character:

Response Pattern	p
+ + + +	.996
+ + − +	.971
+ − + +	.953
− + + +	.940
+ + + −	.938

From column 1 of Table 1 it will be seen that these five response patterns include 244 of the 1,000 individuals. Moreover, it will be seen that 521 of the 1,000 individuals have one of the following response patterns with values of p lower than .20:

Response Pattern	p
− − − +	.152
+ − − −	.148
− + − −	.117
− − + −	.076
− − − −	.011

Now if we assume, provisionally, that the 244 with $p > .90$ are quite likely to have the latent character—call them group A—and the 521 cases with $p < .20$ are quite likely not to have the latent character —call them group C—we have two fairly pure extreme groups. The remaining 235 cases are indeterminate—call them group B.[4]

For practical use, either for the purpose of extracting the top or bottom class for special study or for the purpose of correlating groups A, B, and C with an outside criterion, such a combination of manifest scale patterns, guided by the p values, seems quite justifiable. Of course, taking a cutting point like $p = .90$, as in the above example, is quite arbitrary. Any other cutting points, like $p = .95$ or $p = .67$, might be chosen, depending on the degree of "purity" desired in the extreme group. Even if we took $p = .50$ we would misclassify only about an eighth of our respondents. . . .

In comparing the approaches of Guttman and Lazarsfeld to the problem of testing whether or not ordered structures apply in a given attitude region, it is important to avoid metaphysical faith in a particular model. For example, if one can dispense with the concept of a latent structure and operate effectively directly with manifest data, as Guttman does, there could be advantages of logical parsimony in the Guttman approach. The fact that a perfect Guttman scale is not obtained except approximately is not in itself a denial of the value of that model. The crucial question is whether it has ideal properties from which one may make rich and varied logical deductions—as seems to be possible in connection with the theory of principal components—and whether it leads to rapid and enlightening empirical tests of hypotheses as to the structure of concrete attitude areas. Similarly, it will be noted that Lazarsfeld's postulate of a continuous trace line $p(x)$ cannot itself be empirically demonstrated, although . . . the hypothetical latent continuum x can be cut into segments and discontinuous values of $p(x)$ determined empirically for each segment. The latent continuum is a hypothetical construct and its usefulness lies in its range of logical productivity and its effectiveness in guiding the analysis of actual data. . . .

It may be objected that the price one pays for unidimensionality is loss of generality. That can be true. But, if a given region of attitudes is not unidimensional it does no good to close our eyes to that fact and pretend that it is. Instead, if the region yields several quite specific scales, each

clearly unidimensional, we are then in a position to proceed more economically with an explicitly multiple dimensional study, testing theories of the interrelationships of the scales used. This study may require us to try eventually to reduce the number of these initial dimensions by some form of quantitative factor analysis. But the first step is analysis of the structure, in an effort to isolate clean unidimensional specific scales.

Notes

1. Louis Guttman, "The Quantification of a Class of Attributes: A Theory and Method for Scale Construction," in P. Horst *et al., The Prediction of Personal Adjustment* (Social Science Research Council. New York, 1941), pp. 319–48.

2. Two people can check different response categories and still have the same attitude, because they differ in verbal habits. For example, one person may have a general tendency toward extreme statements and say "all of them" to a given question, whereas another person may have the same attitude toward officers but express it on the same question by answering "most of them." If these two responses are treated as separate categories they could exhibit substantial error of reproducibility, which tends to vanish when the categories are combined (that is, treated as though they were the same response). The scalogram analysis shows how best to combine categories in order to reduce errors of reproducibility.

3. It must be kept in mind that the four items as here used are dichotomized quite differently from the way they were dichotomized by the scalogram analysis in which they served as items belonging to a cumulative scale.

4. It happens that group A contains all who were positive on at least three items, while group C contains all who were positive on only one item or less. Thus the grouping is the same as might have been arrived at by conventional item analysis. But we now know much more about the properties of the items than ordinary item analysis would have told us. Moreover, it is quite possible that a tabulation of the kind of Table 1 would show that *a pattern like* $- + + +$ *may actually have a smaller proportion possessing the latent character than a scale pattern like* $+ - - +$.

7. The Admissions Officer

JANE Z. HAUSER AND PAUL F. LAZARSFELD

[Ed. Note: In 1964, the authors, members of the Bureau of Applied Social Research, Columbia University, studied the careers of some eight hundred American college admissions officers and their assistants. The third chapter of the study report dealt with the division of labor among the staff of the admissions office. The purpose was to compare the young recruits to the older generation of admissions officers. An interesting set of indices was developed for this purpose.]

Admissions Activities of the Office

THE ADMISSIONS OFFICERS were given a list of possible activities and were asked how much time they and their assistants devoted to each one. The exact wording was as follows:

Following is a list of the kinds of work done by some admissions officers. Please approximate as best you can (1) the amount of time you spend on these tasks and (2) the amount of time the rest of your staff spends. If you have more than one assistant, please consider the total work assignment for all of them.

fied him as inactive. Obviously the assistants, too, can be divided into active and inactive on this task, as reported by the director. His office policy would then best be described by a fourfold table cross-tabulating the two sets of answers. Leaving out the directors who had no assistants, the following picture was obtained.

From such a table three pieces of information can be gained: one is the *total level* of activity which might be measured for instance by the average amount of activity reported for both parties in the office, column 1 plus row 1, divided by 2. Secondly

YOUR TIME				YOUR ASSISTANT'S TIME			
A great deal of time	A moderate amount of time	Little time	None	A great deal of time	A moderate amount of time	Little time	None

Before reporting the statistical results it seems useful to speculate for a moment on the kind of information that the questionnaire provides. One of the items on the list referred to is the interviewing of applicants. If the director spent "much time" or "moderate amount of time" on this activity, we considered him active on this point; if he spent "little time" or "no time," we classi-

we can compare the extent of activity the director reserves for himself with that which he assigns to his assistant; this might be called the *differential deployment*. In the present example the total level of activity is high but the director considers interviewing applicants something he prefers to do himself rather than to delegate it to an assistant (the column total for active direc-

Reprinted with permission from Jane Z. Hauser and Paul F. Lazarsfeld, *The Admissions Officer*, pp. III-6–11 (copyright 1964 by College Entrance Examination Board).

TABLE 1.   Importance of Interviewing Applicants as Indicated by the Activities of the Director and His Assistant

		DIRECTOR		
		Active	In-active	
ASSISTANT	Active	59%	9%	68%
	Inactive	23%	9%	32%
		82%	18%	100%

TABLE 1(a).   A Fictitious Case of Compensatory Policy with Marginal Activity Figures the Same as Table 3

		DIRECTOR		
		Active	In-active	
ASSISTANT	Active	53%	15%	68%
	Inactive	29%	3%	32%
		82%	18%	100%

tors is 82 per cent while the row total for active assistants is only 68 per cent).

The third item of information contained in such a table requires some elaboration. Even if the activity figures for the director and his assistant are established, two things can happen. The director could pursue a *compensatory policy:* he assigns to his assistant the activities in which he himself is not engaged. Or, he might follow a *cumulative policy:* if he himself is more active in a certain direction he also wants his assistant to do the same.

In regard to the interviewing of applicants quite obviously the cumulative policy prevails in the reported colleges. The best way to see this is to compare the two columns of Table 1. If the director is active there is almost a 3:1 chance that he will also report his assistant as active. If the director is inactive then only in half the cases will the director assign activity to his assistant. It is very important to realize that this distinction between a compensatory and a cumulative office policy is quite independent of the total level of activity as well as of the differential deployment. To make that quite clear, we are presenting a fictitious finding which would indicate a compensatory policy.

Here, the directors who are inactive in interviewing applicants are much more likely to have active assistants for this task than the active directors, although altogether the directors consider interviewing applicants very much their own domain.

When we cross-tabulate the director and the assistant's level of activity for all items on which we have collected information, *invariably a cumulative policy prevails.* If the numerical meaning of the finding is kept in mind, then it is well described by the following summary: admissions work is by and large shared within the office rather than being delegated to the assistant or retained by the director; assistants are likely to be carbon copies of their superiors and to take on a workload rather similar in character to that of the director.[1] The finding that a cumulative policy generally prevails in admissions offices does not preclude the fact that the total level of activity as well as differential deployment varies from one activity to the next. . . .

Total Level of Activity and Differential Deployment

Table 2 lists the specific activities for which the respondents had to estimate a time budget for themselves and their assistants. The figures indicate the proportion of "actives" in the sense of the previous example: persons who spend a great deal or a moderate amount of time on the listed activity. The first column pertains to the directors and the second to the assistants. The list of activities was developed in consultation with various experts who knew admissions work intimately. The numerical findings of Table 2 are best perceived if the various items are grouped somewhat differently from the way they were presented in the questionnaire. Processing applications and interviewing applicants do in essence define admissions work (items 1 and 2). The next three items are, so to say, accessory to this main activity: school visitation, research on admissions work and handling of complaints. The next two items pertain to the running of the admissions office itself—supervision of and meetings with the staff. The last two items on the list place the admissions work into the broader setting of the college: meetings with the administration or the faculty (8 and 9). The *total level of activity* is best gauged by adding the pair of figures in each row; the *differential deployment* is obtained by subtracting the second figure from the first. For easy orientation of the reader these two indices have been added in the third and fourth columns of Table 2.

The third column of Table 2 permits a quick review of the workload for the office as a whole. Its energy is, of course, most concentrated around the immediate admissions work of processing applications and interviewing applicants (items 1 and 2). It is somewhat surprising at first glance that so many report spending a good deal of time in research on admissions work (item 4); on second consideration, however, it is plausible that a comparatively new occupation is asking questions of itself and is making efforts to provide its own answers. Further exploration of the nature of the "research" and variations in topics would be interesting to investigate. Little time is given by the office as a whole to handling complaints (item 5). This suggests that either complaints are handled routinely, in which case the admissions officer would seem to have a great deal of administrative

TABLE 2.   The Admissions Director's Allocation of His Time and His Assistant's Time to Various Admissions Tasks *

ADMISSIONS TASKS	PER CENT OF RESPONDENTS WHO SPEND MUCH OR MODERATE AMOUNT OF TIME IN VARIOUS ADMISSIONS TASKS AND THE AMOUNT OF TIME FOR TASKS ALLOCATED TO THEIR ASSISTANT			
	Directors**	Assistants	Sum	Difference
1. Processing Applications	81%	74%	155	7
2. Interviewing Applicants in the Office	82%	67%	149	15
3. School Visitations	51%	62%	113	−11
4. Research on Evaluation of Admissions Work	57%	36%	93	21
5. Handling Complaints	37%	20%	57	17
6. Supervision and Conferences with People Working in Admissions	58%	37%	95	21
7. Admissions Office Staff Meetings	39%	34%	73	5
8. College Administrative Staff Meetings	61%	8%	69	53
9. Faculty Administrative Meetings	49%	8%	57	41

* The order is from the tasks receiving the most response to those receiving the least by the director.

** The directors without assistants report their admissions activities in a similar manner. They vary from the other directors by no more than two per cent for any task, with the exception of time spent in admissions office staff meetings. In this instance only 32 per cent of them report spending much time in this activity. It is interesting that those without assistants report as much time in supervision and conferences with people working in admissions as do those with assistants. Apparently the time required for supervision of the work of subordinates is relatively constant whether those subordinates are clerks or assistants.

support and clear policies governing his relations with the public, or that complaints not covered by policy are referred, at the initiative of the admissions officer, to an administrative superior.

Meetings within the office (items 6 and 7) show a somewhat higher level of activity than meetings with other groups in the college (items 8 and 9). Within these two groups of meetings one more distinction can be made. The office has somewhat more contact with the college administration than with the faculty; and within the office, individual contacts (item 6) occur more frequently than meetings of the office as a whole (item 7). To elaborate on this last statement, let us look at these items more closely. It is first clear that director and assistant spend about the same amount of time on admissions office staff meetings. These, in contrast to the supervisory conferences, probably concern immediate affairs of the office and are dealt with in sessions with the entire office force. Supervision and conferences, however, require more time from the director than from his assistant. This can be interpreted if one considers that there is no training program for admissions officers. The director must train his assistants in apprentice fashion. He could train them on the one hand as salesmen are usually trained—in group sessions; or he could train them as social workers are trained—with individual conferences with the supervisor. In the admissions office, it would seem that the individual conference is a preferred technique.

Much more revealing than the total level of activities is an inspection of the fourth column which pictures the way the director divides the workload between himself and his assistant, We notice first a negative figure related to school visitation (item 3). This is the only one where the assistants spend more time than the directors—which incidentally also explains the high total level of activity. This task occurs too frequently for both the director and his assistant to say that it is delegated by the director. It is most frequently shared, but the assistant seems to take over a somewhat greater load than the director.

Two tasks are likely to be the exclusive domain of the director—college administrative meetings and faculty administrative meetings (items 8 and 9). Meeting the public and looking for recruits, the assistant is most likely to take on the excess workload, but meeting with other members of the college in policy matters, the director takes on the excess workload. The director seems to feel that he can risk the subordinate's judgment in dealing with individual applicants but not in dealing with other institutionalized power groups in the college. The remaining differences are small, and the pattern is self-explanatory. One should notice, however, that 8 out of 9 are positive. In the view of the director, he spends more time than his assistants at everything but school visits.

Note

1. In statistical terms the result is as follows: the association in Table 1, and in all similar tables which have been analyzed, is markedly positive. The degree of the positive association can be measured by a number of coefficients which are conveniently attached to fourfold tables. No additional finding seems to emerge from such greater precision.

D. The Theory of Indices

8. Comments on the Nature of Classification in Social Research

PAUL F. LAZARSFELD
AND WAGNER THIELENS, JR.

[Ed. Note: In the 1950's a study was undertaken to examine the impact of the "McCarthy scare" on freedom of expression among social science teachers. Faculty rank was shown to have a bearing upon reaction to the threat. In the following selection, Lazarsfeld and Thielens show how two indicators of professional "eminence," though imperfectly related to one another, nevertheless show very similar relationships to faculty rank.]

. . . In our study of "the academic mind," we wished to classify social scientists according to something which might be called their "eminence." Such an intended classification is necessarily vague. A concept like "eminence," taken over from everyday language, can be translated into a research instrument in many ways. We can think of a long list of items which would serve as indicators; but for practical purposes we usually want to settle on a small number of them. A heated debate over which items to include in the final index often occurs. But what difference would various choices actually make? To clarify the issue the following experiment was undertaken. . . .

We constructed two indices, both based on the external achievements of university teachers. The indices were as follows:

Honors Index

1a. Has a Ph.D.
2a. Has published three or more papers
3a. Has held office in a professional society
4a. Has worked as a consultant

Productivity Index

1b. Has written a dissertation
2b. Has published at least one paper
3b. Has read three or more papers at meetings
4b. Has published at least one book

By intention the indices have two partially overlapping items: 1a and 1b differ only to the extent that there are respondents who have finished a dissertation but not fulfilled other Ph.D. requirements; we have 271 such cases.[1] 2b has a lower requirement than 2a: 363 respondents have published either one paper or two. The remaining pairs of items differ in manifest

Reprinted in part with permission from *The Academic Mind: Social Scientists in a Time of Crisis*, pp. 402–06 (copyright 1958 by The Free Press, Division of the Macmillan Company, New York).

content. These deal with honors, rather than with other kinds of publications, as indicators of eminence.

Table 1 classifies all respondents in two ways: according to their productivity scores and to their scores on the honors index.

TABLE 1.   Interrelation between Two
Indices of Eminence

PRODUC-TIVITY SCORE	HONORS SCORE			
	4.3 (High)	2 (Me-dium)	0.1 (Low)	Total
4.3 (High)	789	261	64	1114
2 (Medium)	196	214	201	611
0.1 (Low)	20	134	535	689
Total	1005	609	800	2414*

* The remaining thirty-seven respondents did not answer all of the questions on which the two scores are based.

In the main diagonal, reading from upper left to lower right, we find all the people (789 + 214 + 535) who have the same level of eminence on either index. The remainder, 36 per cent of the total, are classified differently by the two indices. At first sight this looks like a discouraging result; the "eminence" measured by one index is quite often not the same as that measured by another.

This outcome, however, is both unavoidable and of limited consequence. It is unavoidable because indicators can at best have only an inferential relation to the underlying factor sought after. Whether a man is liberal, whether he has status in the community, whether an armed unit has morale, or whether an educational system is a success—all these questions can never be answered explicitly, because one cannot measure morale or status with the kind of agreement and precision that one can measure weight or length of an object. This has nothing to do with the fact that some of the things we might want to clas-

sify are mental or psychological intangibles. Whether two men are friends is indeed often a matter of external observation, but friendship itself is not a concrete object to be perceived directly. Indicators are still needed to make an inference of its existence. One might tag the whole procedure "diagnostic process."

Indicators will of course vary in how well they reveal the characteristics we seek. To study a person's anxiety, we might show him a set of pictures which are somewhat ambiguous in content and ask him to interpret them. If his answers repeatedly refer to dangerous situations, we could conclude that the person is quite anxiety-ridden. Such an inference from a Thematic Apperception Test undoubtedly seems more complex and less certain than, say, an inference of mathematical ability based on a test of mathematical performance.

The certainty of the inference from manifest data to latent characteristics depends upon many factors. One of these is the degree to which an indicator question permits varied interpretation. It is not possible to formulate a question whose answers allow of only one interpretation. Respondents' experiences immediately prior to the interview may enter in. A man who belongs, by and large, in the middle range of permissiveness might give very restrictive answers one particular morning when his children have irked him a great deal, and unusually permissive ones another time just after an excellent dinner. In short, indicators are only related to an intended underlying classification with a certain probability. The latent characteristic can never, therefore, be reached with certainty. All classifications of this kind in social research have to be "impure."

The consequences of this fact are twofold. One of these is encouraging. If we have a reasonable collection of indicator items, then it does not matter much for most purposes which subset we use to form our index. This is true so long as we are aiming at finding statistical relations between a number of variables, not at the correct classification of each individual person. The idea is best explained by a concrete example. We shall raise a problem in which "eminence" is one of the characteristics involved. We shall then look at the actual data twice: first using the productivity index and then the honors index as a measure of eminence. The purpose of the comparison will be to see what difference this makes in the final result.

Our problem will be to weigh the relative importance of eminence and age in a teacher's chances for reaching success in the professional hierarchy by becoming a full professor. How do age and eminence together affect promotion? Table 2 gives the answer we get if we use our productivity index as the measure of eminence.

the age of 41 and 50, whereas in the middle productivity range the same proportion is reached only in the oldest age group. On the other hand, even in the lowest productivity group almost half the respondents past the age of fifty have become full professors. Many of these men and women doubtless earn their promotion to top rank by their excellent service as teachers.

What would have happened if we had used the honors index as a measure of eminence? Table 3 gives the answer. The result is much like the one before. Again age is more important than eminence. Only in the second row is there a noticeable difference between Tables 2 and 3. Productivity seems to be more helpful in the 41–50 age group; honors play more of a role among the oldest people.

In spite of the fact that, as shown by

TABLE 2. Percentages Who Are Full Professors According to Age and Eminence (Productivity Index) *

	AGE		
EMINENCE IN TERMS OF PRODUCTIVITY SCORE	Under 40	41–50	51 or More
4.3 (High)	15% (324)	63% (358)	87% (421)
2 (Medium)	7% (349)	39% (131)	65% (122)
0.1 (Low)	2% (439)	23% (126)	45% (108)

* In this and all following tables in the Appendices, the total numbers of cases on which percentages are based are given in parentheses. For example, 15 per cent of the 324 teachers under forty and with high productivity were full professors.

In Tables 2 and 3, lecturers and respondents saying they have no formal rank are not included.

Table 2 tells a rather interesting story. Reading across each row, we see that regardless of their eminence the proportion of full professors increases sharply with age. Within the columns, we then learn that teachers who are more eminent in terms of productivity have more often been made full professors. The table also suggests that age and productivity can compensate for each other. On the highest productivity level about two-thirds have already become full professors . . . between

Table 1, the two indices are far from perfectly correlated with one another, when they are related to an outside variable they produce much the same result. This "interchangeability of indices" reappears again and again in empirical social research. Studies have shown, for instance, that different social strata have sharply contrasting attitudes on economic and political matters. But what are "social strata," and how should they be measured? We could use as indicators such things as peoples' possessions, their income, or their education. In most such studies it has turned out that whichever index is used, the correlation between strata and any given attitude is about the same. In other words, the findings of empirical social research are to a considerable extent invariant when reasonable substitutions from one index to another are made.

2. The two indices will usually lead to very similar empirical results if they are separately cross-tabulated against a third outside variable.

While this rule of the "interchangeability of indices" is one of the foundations of empirical social research, its beneficial consequences are paid for by a serious but unavoidable price. Because we can never

TABLE 3.   Table 2 Repeated Using the Honors Index of Eminence

EMINENCE IN TERMS OF HONORS SCORE	AGE		
	Under 40	41–50	51 or More
4.3 (High)	18% (312)	65% (308)	88% (368)
2 (Medium)	6% (298)	28% (149)	73% (148)
0.1 (Low)	2% (488)	22% (150)	44% (132)

This then is the general rule based on very diversified research practice. To translate a rather broad but nonconcrete concept into an empirical research instrument, there will always be a large number of indicators eligible for a classificatory index. A relatively small number of such items is practicably more manageable. If we choose two sets of reasonable items to form two alternative indices, the following two facts will usually be found:

1. The two indices will be related, but they will not classify all the people in a study in precisely the same way.

reach "pure" classifications, a certain number of cases must always be misclassified, and therefore the empirical findings are less clear than if we could somehow have precise measures for the variables with which a study is concerned. . . .

Note

1. Another six are recorded as having a Ph.D. without a dissertation—probably a result of interviewing and coding mistakes. Some respondents may have written a "dissertation" for the Masters degree.

9. The Index of Social Position

AUGUST B. HOLLINGSHEAD AND FREDRICK C. REDLICH

[Ed. Note: In the early 1950's, August B. Hollingshead, a sociologist, and Fredrick C. Redlich, a psychiatrist, undertook an investigation of the connection between the social system and psychiatric practice. The central objective was to understand the bearing of social class on modes of referral and commitment, prevalence of disorders, types of mental illness, kinds of treatment, and treatment expenditures. The selection below describes the procedure employed in this study to locate people within the social class structure.]

THE INDEX of Social Position was developed to meet the need for an objective, easily applicable procedure to estimate positions individuals occupy in the status structure of the community. Its development was dependent both upon detailed knowledge of the community's social structure and procedures social scientists have used to delineate class status positions in other studies. It is premised upon three assumptions: (1) the existence of a class status structure in the community, (2) that class status positions are determined mainly by a few commonly accepted symbolic characteristics, and (3) that characteristics symbolic of class status may be scaled and combined by the use of statistical procedures so that a researcher can quickly, reliably, and meaningfully stratify the population.

Phases in the Development of the Index of Social Position

BACKGROUND KNOWLEDGE OF THE COMMUNITY

New Haven has been studied by historians, psychologists, and sociologists for many years. Although there is general agreement among these social scientists that the community's social structure is differentiated both horizontally and vertically, we were faced with the problem of determining how to place a given individual or family in this social system in an objective and reliable manner.

This situation is not peculiar to New Haven. Numerous studies have reported stratification in American communities, but there is little agreement among research workers as to how individuals may be placed in the status structure that impinges upon them.

Before the plethora of facts accumulated from diverse studies can have meaning they have to be conceptualized in some systematic way. Careful analysis of the discrete data on the social structure of the community indicated three things about it: First, the community's social structure is differentiated *vertically* by racial, ethnic, and religious factors, and *horizontally* by a series of strata or classes. Second, each stratum or class in a vertical division is similar in its cultural characteristics to the corresponding stratum in other vertical divisions. Third, the primary status system of each racial, ethnic, and religious group is

Reprinted with permission from August B. Hollingshead and Fredrick C. Redlich, *Social Class and Mental Illness,* pp. 387–97 (copyright 1958 by John Wiley and Sons, Inc., New York).

patterned after the one prevailing in the old Yankee segment of the community, because the old Yankees provided the master cultural mold that has shaped the acculturation of each ethnic and racial subgroup in the community. For example, Italians, Jews, and Poles, in a given class, have cultural characteristics similar to Yankees in the same class and aspire to similar status positions. However, these groups are separated into different vertical divisions by religious and ethnic factors.

CROSS SECTIONAL SAMPLE OF HOUSEHOLDS

General knowledge of the community's class structure was supplemented by a study of a cross sectional random sample of 552 households. Each household drawn in the sample was interviewed in the home with a 200-question schedule designed to furnish detailed data on the family's ethnic, religious, economic, educational, social, and residential backgrounds in the New Haven community, elsewhere in the United States, and other countries. The interview lasted from two to three hours. In addition to the answers to the semistructured and structured questions, each interviewer wrote a detailed statement of his impressions of the family and how he believed the family was adjusted to the community and to one another. This study provided detailed data on the size of the family, participation in economic, religious, educational, and leisure-time institutions, as well as the members' values, attitudes, aspirations, standards of living, ideas of the future, and their frustrations, desires, hopes, and fears.

ESTIMATES OF CLASS POSITION

Two sociologists familiar with the community's social structure, August B. Hollingshead and Jerome K. Myers, studied each family's schedule in detail and the interviewer's discussion of the family. On the basis of the detailed schedule data and the interviewer's impression, Hollingshead and Myers, working independently, made judgments as to where they believed each family belonged in the stratification system of the community. Previous to the independent judgment of each family's position in the community's stratificational system, Myers and Hollingshead agreed that functionally the horizontal strata in the New Haven community could well be divided into five class or social levels.

When the process of individual estimation of class position had been completed, the tentative class positions assigned to a family by Hollingshead and Myers were compared. They were in agreement on where they thought 96 per cent of the families belonged in the stratificational system of the community. On the 4 per cent where there was disagreement, Hollingshead and Myers re-examined the evidence, and assigned the family to a class by mutual agreement. Their agreements and disagreements were distributed unevenly in the status structure. They agreed on thirty-five families who they judged to be in the two top classes. They disagreed on the class positions of two families immediately below these strata. Myers placed one family in the second class, and the other in the third class; Hollingshead placed these families in the opposite positions. They disagreed on the placement of ten families in the third and fourth class areas of the social structure and nineteen families in the fourth and fifth class areas. In each instance, one judge placed the family in a different class from that of the other judge. However, in no instance was the discrepancy of one judge more than one class position away from the other, and there was no consistent tendency for one judge to overplace or underplace families compared with the placements made by the second judge.

Characteristics Symbolic of Status

When the work on the judgment of class positions was completed, Hollingshead and

Myers discussed the criteria they thought they had followed to make their judgments. Although a number of different criteria were followed by each man, they were in general agreement that most consideration was given to (a) where a family lived, (b) the way it made its living, and (c) its tastes, its cultural orientation, and the way it spent its leisure time. After considerable additional discussion, the conclusion was reached that the educational level of the head of the household was probably a good single index to the general area of cultural and social values exhibited in the answers the respondents had given to questions about their associations and leisure time activities.

SCALING OF SYMBOLIC CHARACTERISTICS

The next step was to abstract from the interview schedules, as specific indicators of class position, the family's address, the occupation of its head, and the years of school he had completed. These data were placed on tabulation sheets, along with the agreed estimate of the family's position in the status system. After this step was completed, the address, occupation, and years of school completed were scaled.

1. *The Residential Scale*. The residential scale was based upon ecological research carried on by Maurice R. Davie and his associates in the New Haven community over a 25-year span. In the early 1930's, Davie mapped the city of New Haven ecologically, and ranked residential areas on a six-position scale that ranged from the finest homes to the poorest tenements. Jerome K. Myers brought Davie's data up to date as of 1950, within the city of New Haven, and mapped the suburban towns in the same way that Davie had mapped New Haven in earlier years. This work provided a uniform scale for the evaluation of addresses.

2. *The Occupational Scale*. The occupational scale is a modification of the Alba Edwards system of classifying occupations into socioeconomic groups used by the United States Bureau of the Census. The essential differences between the Edwards system and the one used is that Edwards does not differentiate among kinds of professionals or the sizes and economic strengths of businesses. The scale used in the Index of Social Position ranks professions into different groups and businesses by their size and value. Without further discussion of similarities and differences between the Edwards system and ours, we will proceed to characterize each of the seven positions on the scale we used: (1) executives and proprietors of large concerns and major professionals, (2) managers and proprietors of medium-sized businesses and lesser professionals, (3) administrative personnel of large concerns, owners of small independent businesses, and semiprofessionals, (4) owners of little businesses, clerical and sales workers, and technicians, (5) skilled workers, (6) semiskilled workers, and (7) unskilled workers.

This scale is premised upon the assumption that occupations have different values attached to them by the members of our society. The hierarchy ranges from the low evaluation of unskilled physical labor toward the more prestigeful use of skill, through the creative talents, ideas, and the management of men. The ranking of occupational functions implies that some men exercise control over the occupational pursuits of other men. Normally, a person who possesses highly trained skills has control over several other people. This is exemplified in a highly developed form by an executive in a large business enterprise who may be responsible for decisions affecting thousands of employees.

3. *The Educational Scale*. The educational scale is premised upon the assumption that men and women who possess similar educations will tend to have similar tastes and

similar attitudes, and they will also tend to exhibit similar behavior patterns.

The educational scale was divided into seven positions:

1. *Graduate professional training.* (Persons who completed a recognized professional course which led to the receipt of a graduate degree were given scores of 1.)
2. *Standard college or university graduation.* (All individuals who had completed a four-year college or university course leading to a recognized college degree were assigned the same scores. No differentiation was made between state universities or private colleges.)
3. *Partial college training.* (Individuals who had completed at least one year but not a full college course were assigned this position.)
4. *High school graduation.* (All secondary school graduates whether from a private preparatory school, public high school, trade school, or parochial high school were given this score.)
5. *Partial high school.* (Individuals who had completed the tenth or eleventh grades, but had not completed high school were given this score.)
6. *Junior high school.* (Individuals who had completed the seventh grade through the ninth grade were given this position.)
7. *Less than seven years of school.* (Individuals who had not completed the seventh grade were given the same scores irrespective of the amount of education they had received.)

THE MATRIX OF SCALE PATTERNS

The exact scores a family head received on each of the four variables—judged class position, address, occupation, and education—were placed in a matrix, and the families were ranked from high to low on the basis of the scale patterns. Families who were judged to belong in the top social class in the community, and had a scale score of 1 on ecological area, 1 on occupation, and 1 on education were placed at the top of the listing. Families with a combination of different, but high scores on the four variables, were listed immediately below this group. For example, a family may have been judged to be in the top class if it lived in the best residential area and its head was a vice-president of a large industry and had a B.A. degree. The score pattern would be 1, 1, 1, 2. Another family head was judged to be in the top class, but he lived in an area that was graded ecologically as second class; however, he was a partner in a large brokerage firm, and had a degree from the Harvard Business School. His score pattern was, thus: 1, 2, 1, 1.

As the listing of the different scores proceeded from higher to lower sequences, the combinations of ones and two faded out and a few cases entered the matrix where a family's score was 1 on class, 1 on occupation, 2 on address, but 3 on education. This process was carried succesively lower until all the families were listed and all the score combinations were available for examination.

The listing of families by their score patterns enabled us to delineate areas of complete agreement between our clinical judgments of class position and the objective scores of a family on the three criterion scales, as well as variations between the judgments and the achieved scale scores of the family. It indicated also where there were "pure" patterns of scores, such as 2 on class, 2 on address, 2 on occupation, and 2 on education, and "mixed" patterns where the four scale values showed a range of two or three points. For example, one family is given a class judgment of 3, but its address is scored as 1, its occupational score is 4, and its educational score is 3. The head of the family is a bank teller, who completed two years of college. His home was purchased by an inheritance, and it is maintained, in part, by income from the residue of his legacy and the man's own "do-it-yourself" efforts on weekends and evenings.

Score patterns such as these revealed heterogeneity in the different facets of social reality which we were using to measure the indirect quality of social status. They also gave us a clue as to where we might cut the continuum of scores in a meaningful way to produce operational classes we could work with in later phases of our research.

Homogeneous score patterns, at the top and the bottom of the continuum, were believed to be indicative of the existence of two clearcut classes—an "upper" one and a "lower" one. But how were we to differentiate among the combinations of scale scores of the intervening patterns to give us the most meaningful index of an individual family's position in the community's status system? The tentative answer was to cut the continuum at the points where the greatest amount of variation existed between the four variables. We inferred these points were indicative of meaningful discontinuities in the social hierarchy of the community.

Multiple Correlation and Regression

MULTIPLE CORRELATIONS

The next analytical problem was to determine how the three variables, address, occupation, and years of school completed, were combined and weighted in our judgments of class position. The answer to this problem was sought by intercorrelating the four variables of judged class position, address, occupation, and years of school completed by the family's head. The essential findings on the intercorrelations of the four variables are summarized in Table 1.

Examination of the intercorrelations will show that the highest association is obtained when a combination of area of residence, education, and occupation is correlated with judged class position as would be expected in view of the high correlation of each of these variables with the criterion. Slightly lower r's are obtained when judged class position is correlated with a combination of any two of the three variables. In general, lower r's appear when judged class position is correlated with the individual factors in the matrix. However, the lowest associations appear when the criterion factors are correlated with one another.

MULTIPLE REGRESSION EQUATION

The mulitple regression analysis of these data indicated the weights appropriate for

TABLE 1. Intercorrelations between Judged Class Position, Ecological Area of Residence, Education, and Occupation of Sample Families in New Haven, 1948

A. INTERCORRELATIONS OF SCALE VARIABLES

	Correlation
Education with residence	.451
Occupation with residence	.505
Occupation with education	.721

B. CRITERION PREDICTED FROM ONE VARIABLE

Judged class with residence	.692
Judged class with education	.782
Judged class with occupation	.881

C. CRITERION PREDICTED FROM TWO VARIABLES

	Multiple Correlation
Judged class with residence and education	.870
Judged class with residence and occupation	.926
Judged class with education and occupation	.906

D. CRITERION PREDICTED FROM THREE VARIABLES

Judged class with residence, education, and occupation	.942

each factor when estimating the class position of families in the sample.

These multiple regression weights could then be applied to families other than those in the present sample, and thus estimates of their class positions could be obtained. The computed multiple equation was:

$$X_1 \text{ (Estimated class pasition)} = .183X_2$$
$$\text{(Residence)} + .154X_3 \text{ (Education)} +$$
$$.269X_4 \text{ (Occupation)} + .884$$

Use of this multiple regression equation will give a distribution of estimated class positions ranging from approximately 1 to 5. For simplicity of computation, however, the constant (.884) can be omitted and the *approximate* weights of 6, 5, 9, respectively, can be used to weight the factors X_2, X_3, X_4 appropriately. This will yield a distribution of scores ranging from a theoretical low of 20 to a theoretical high of 134, and representing a continuum from the very highest class to the very lowest. The distribution can then be broken into segments or ranges of scores indicative of meaningful social positions in the class structure.

Estimation of Class Position

INDEX OF SOCIAL POSITION SCORES AND CLASS

The computation of an Index of Social Position score is only one phase of the problem of determining class. The determination of the points where the continuum of scores should be cut to differentiate among the classes of the community's social system is crucial. This problem is handled by computing Index of Social Position scores for each of the families included in the multiple correlation and multiple regression procedures discussed above.

In this operation, the factor weights of 6, 5, and 9 respectively established through the multiple regression equation were used in combination with the scale position scores (1 to 6 on residence, 1 to 7 on occupation, and 1 to 7 on education) to compute the Index of Social Position scores. When these scores were computed, each family's weighted score was compared with its position on the continuum of raw scale scores and judged class position. This comparison indicated where there was homogeneity and heterogeneity between the raw scores and the weighted scores. Where there was homogeneity in the patterns of the raw scale scores, and congruity of these scores with judged class position, we assumed that the cluster was indicative of a functional segment of the community's status system. Where there was heterogeneity in the score clusters, we assumed there was indeterminacy in the status system. Thus the inference was made that Index of Social Position scores should cut at the point of most heterogeneity in the scale score patterns. By the use of this procedure, the range of scores of each "class" was decided to be shown as follows:

Class	Range of Scores	Percentage of Total Number of Families
I	20–31	2.7
II	32–55	9.8
III	56–86	18.9
IV	87–115	48.4
V	116–134	20.2

This procedure compresses the continuum of scores into score groups. It assumes that the differences *between* the score groups are greater than the differences *within* each score group in terms of class status characteristics. Within each group differences in individual scores are ignored, and each score is treated as a unit in a cluster. This procedure assumes there are differences between the score groups. Families with scores that fall into a given segment of the range of scores assigned to a particular class position are presumed to belong to the class the Index of Social Position score predicts for it.

DETERMINATION OF A FAMILY'S INDEX OF SOCIAL POSITION SCORE

To obtain a family's score on the Index of Social Position, the researcher needs to know three things: (1) its address, (2) its head's exact occupational pursuit, and (3) the years of school he has completed. The next step is to assign the appropriate scale scores for address, occupation, and education. Once the scale scores are determined, each factor is multiplied by the appropriate weight. For example, the score of a family whose head works at a clerical job, is a high school graduate, and lives in a middle-rank residential area would be computed thus:

This definition of class position is based on three assumptions: First, a family's mode of living is mirrored in its home; second, the occupation of its head reflects the skill and power associated with maintenance functions in the society; and third, the amount of formal education the head has received reflects the tastes of the family. The combination of these factors enables a researcher to determine within approximate limits the position a family occupies in the status structure of such an industrialized community as New Haven.

The operationally determined hierachy of scores which emerges is presumed to be an estimation of the status hierarchy which exists in the community. In short, the Index of Social Position attempts to delineate op-

Factor	Scale Value $\times$	Factor Weight $=$	Partial Score
Residence	3	6	18
Occupation	4	9	36
Education	4	5	20
Index of Social Position Score $=$			74

The computations for a family whose head is a semiskilled factory worker who attended high school for two years and lives in an area of two family houses would be:

erationally the socially discriminating comparisons people make of each other in their day-to-day behaviors.

Factor	Scale Value $\times$	Factor Weight $=$	Partial Score
Residence	5	6	30
Occupation	6	9	54
Education	5	5	25
Index of Social Position Score $=$			109

10. Status Crystallization: A Nonvertical Dimension of Social Status

GERHARD E. LENSKI

IN RECENT YEARS there have been numerous indications that, in the analysis of social stratification, sociology is rapidly outgrowing the classical conceptual schemes inherited from the past. Critically inclined students have come increasingly to recognize the inability of the older schemes to incorporate many of the findings of present day research, or to adapt themselves to newer theoretical concerns.

This trend is evident even with respect to such a basic matter as the manner in which the vertical structure of groups is conceived. From Aristotle to Marx to Warner, most social philosophers and social scientists have described the vertical structure of human groups in terms of a single hierarchy in which each member occupies a single position. Different exponents of this traditional scheme have not always agreed regarding the nature or characteristics of this hierarchical structure. Nevertheless, all have shared the common conception of a unidimensional structure.

Since Max Weber's day, however, this traditional approach has come to be criticized by a growing number of sociologists, who have argued that the unidimensional view is inadequate to describe the complexities of group structure. These critics have maintained that the structure of human groups normally involves the coexistence of a number of parallel vertical hierarchies which usually are imperfectly correlated with one another.

If this newer approach is sound, the traditional conception of individual or family status will require radical revision. Instead of being a single position in a unidimensional hierarchy, it becomes a series of positions in a series of related vertical hierarchies.

An important question which is raised immediately by such a view is the question of how these several positions are interrelated. Theoretically it becomes possible to conceive of a nonvertical dimension to individual or family status—that is, a consistency dimension. In this dimension units may be compared with respect to the degree of consistency of their positions in the several vertical hierarchies. In other words, certain units may be consistently high or consistently low, while others may combine high standing with respect to certain status variables with low standing with respect to others.[1]

While it is one thing to conceive of new theoretical models, it is another matter to demonstrate their utility. This article reports the results of an empirical study designed to test the significance and utility of this nonvertical dimension of status. More specifically, this study was designed to discover whether an analysis employing this new dimension would be capable of accounting for some of the variance in political behavior which is left unexplained by traditional methods of stratification analysis.

Reprinted with permission from the *American Sociological Review*, 19 (August 1954), pp. 405–13 (copyright 1954 by the American Sociological Society).

The Research Design

The basic hypothesis tested in this study is as follows: *individuals characterized by a low degree of status crystallization* [2] *differ significantly in their political attitudes and behavior from individuals characterized by a high degree of status crystallization, when status differences in the vertical dimensions are controlled.*

The data were gathered in the first Detroit Area Study.[3] In the spring of 1952, a random sample of the residents of the metropolitan Detroit area was interviewed.[4] A total of 749 interviews was obtained. Comparisons with 1950 census data indicated that the sample obtained was highly representative of the total population of the metropolitan area.[5]

Two basic variables employed in the present study require operational definition. These are (1) social status, and (2) status crystallization.

SOCIAL STATUS

For operational purposes, the statuses of respondents were defined in terms of their relative positions in four vertical hierarchies: the income hierarchy; the occupation hierarchy; the education hierarchy; and the ethnic hierarchy. These four were chosen both because of their great importance and also because of the relative ease with which necessary information relating to them could be obtained.

With respect to income and education, there was no problem in defining the structure of the hierarchy. Both hierarchies are quantitative in nature. With respect to occupation and ethnic background there was, unfortunately, no such built-in scale. Thus, the construction of scales of relative rank had to be undertaken.

In ranking occupations, the Edwards classificatory scheme was considered and rejected on the grounds that it does not constitute a sufficiently precise scale of status. Top business executives, for example, enjoy greater prestige than many professional men. At the same time, very small proprietors (who are classified with top executives in the Edwards scheme) may enjoy no more prestige than skilled workers. Furthermore, recent empirical studies indicate that skilled workers today enjoy greater prestige than many clerical and sales workers.[6] In short, the overlap between occupational categories when judged by the criterion of relative prestige seemed too great in the Edwards scheme.

The best empirical basis for constructing a scale of occupational rank seemed to have been provided by the National Opinion Research Center's study of occupational prestige.[7] Using the occupations evaluated in that study as a basis, five occupational prestige levels were defined, and an attempt was made to extrapolate from the rated occupations to others not rated in that study. Slightly over 50 per cent of the occupations of the family heads in the Detroit sample required such extrapolation. Coding reliability in these cases was better than 90 per cent.[8]

No national sample of public opinion was available for the construction of the ethnic scale. In the circumstances, the best solution seemed to be an evaluation of the various ethnic groups by Detroit-area residents. For this purpose a sample of 195 Detroit area students enrolled in introductory sociology courses at the University of Michigan was obtained during the academic year 1951–52. These students were asked to rate all of the major ethnic groups found in the Detroit area on the basis of what they thought to be the general community evaluation, as distinguished from their own personal evaluation.[9] As was expected, the northwest European groups were ranked ahead of the south and east European groups, and these in turn were generally ranked ahead of the colored group.[10]

For respondents who were not themselves the family head, the status characteristics of the head were used to define their position in the four hierarchies. This procedure was followed for two reasons. First, current literature, both theory and research, indicates that the family is normally a status unit and that the social attributes of the family head are the chief determinants of status for all dependent relatives in the domicile.[11] Second, this procedure rendered the data collected from wives and other dependent relatives comparable with that for individuals who were themselves family heads.[12] This latter consideration was quite important due to the relatively small size of the sample.

STATUS CRYSTALLIZATION

Having established the structure of these vertical hierarchies, the next problem was to establish common scales for all of them, so that the relative position of respondents in the several hierarchies might be compared. Without common scales, a measure of status crystallization would be impossible.

To this end, frequency distributions were established for each hierarchy. Using these distributions as a basis, scores were assigned for each of the various positions (or intervals) in each hierarchy on the basis of the midpoint of the percentile range for that position (or interval). Table 1 below illustrates the procedure as it was employed in assigning scores to the various income intervals.[13]

Having obtained comparable scores for the four hierarchies, the last remaining step was to establish the quantitative measure of status crystallization. This was accomplished by taking the square root of the sum of the squared deviations from the mean of the four hierarchy scores of the individual and subtracting the resulting figure from one hundred.[14] The more highly consistent or crystallized an individual's status, the more nearly his crystallization score approached one hundred; the less consistent or crystallized his status, the more nearly his crystallization score approached zero.

TABLE 1. Frequency Distribution of Respondents by Income of Family Head, and Assigned Percentile Scores for Each Income Range

Annual Income of Family Head	Number of Respondents	Cumulative Percentile Range	Assigned Score
$10,000 or more	29	95.4–100.0	98
8,000–9,999	15	93.0– 95.3	94
7,000–7,999	19	90.0– 92.9	91
6,000–6,999	58	80.7– 89.9	85
5,000–5,999	82	67.6– 80.6	74
4,000–4,999	137	45.6– 67.5	57
3,000–3,999	191	15.0– 45.5	30
2,000–2,999	57	5.9– 14.9	10
1,000–1,999	21	2.5– 5.8	4
1– 999	10	0.9– 2.4	2
No income	5	0.0– 0.8	0
Total	624*		

* This figure includes only those who were themselves currently in the labor force or respondents who were members of families in which the head was in the labor force and for whom income data were available.

THE STUDY GROUP

Of the original 749 respondents, it was necessary to eliminate 136 from the study group, either because of incomplete or inadequate data on one of the four key status variables, or because the family head was not in the labor force.[15] Due to the small number of cases, it seemed advisable to divide the study group into only two crystallization categories—a high crystallization category and a low crystallization category. Those with crystallization scores of 53 or more were placed in the former category ($N = 439$) while those with scores of 52 or less were placed in the latter category ($N = 174$). This line of division was selected because in the course of the analysis it was discovered that something roughly approximating a natural breaking point was discernible here.

Findings

As a first test of the basic hypothesis, the voting behavior and preferences of the two categories of respondents were compared. Data relating to three elections were used: (1) the 1948 presidential election; (2) the 1950 Michigan gubernatorial election; and (3) the 1952 presidential election. For the first two elections comparisons were made on the basis of the respondents' reports of their behavior. For the 1952 election, it was necessary to make the comparison on the basis of the respondents' indications of their party preferences, since the interviews were conducted eight to ten months before the election.

In each election, the proportion of respondents supporting the Democratic party was substantially greater in the low crystallization category than in the high crystallization category. As may be seen from Table 2, below, these differences were significant at the five per cent level in all

TABLE 2. Voting Behavior and Preferences in the 1948, 1950, and 1952 Elections, by Degree of Status Crystallization

	PER CENT OF VOTERS SUPPORTING DEMOCRATS		
ELECTION YEAR	Low Crystal- lization	High Crystal- lization	Prob- ability Less Than
1948	81.3*	69.0*	.03
1950	84.0	68.4	.01
1952	73.2	64.7**	.11

* Includes supporters of the Progressive party, since 70 per cent of these individuals ($N = 10$) were normally Democratic voters; none gave any indication of ever having supported a Republican candidate.
** Refers to the percentage expressing a *preference* for the Democratic party.

but the 1952 election.[16]

Although the data in Table 2 suggest that the basic hypothesis is sound, no conclusions can be drawn until controls are established for status differences in the four vertical dimensions. This is necessary in the present problem because of the well established fact that variations in these four dimensions are closely associated with variations in political behavior and attitudes. Thus, the variations between the two crystallization categories observed in Table 2 might be due simply to failure to control vertical status differences between the two categories.

A check of the mean scores of the two categories of respondents in the four vertical dimensions revealed, as shown in the upper half of Table 3, that low crystallization respondents had higher *mean* education and ethnic scores than high crystallization respondents. At the same time, however, high crystallization respondents had higher *mean* income and occupation scores.

This latter fact is important, since it

TABLE 3.   Mean Income, Occupation, Ethnic, and Education Scores by
Crystallization Categories, Before and After Correction to Control
Status Differences in the Vertical Dimensions

Crystallization Category	N	Mean Income Score	Mean Occupation Score	Mean Ethnic Score	Mean Education Score
Uncorrected:					
Low crystallization	174	46.6	49.5	50.1	54.1
High crystallization	439	51.3	50.2	50.0	46.1
Corrected:					
Low crystallization	166	48.6	50.0	49.7	53.7
High crystallization	413	48.4	48.2	48.4	44.1

might be argued that income and occupation are the chief determinants of political behavior, while education and ethnic background are of negligible importance. If this were so, the tendency of high crystallization respondents to favor the Republican party might then be simply a function of their higher average income and superior occupational status.

To test this alternative hypothesis, 26 respondents with the *highest* incomes in the high crystallization category and eight respondents with the *lowest* incomes in the low crystallization category were dropped from the study group. The elimination of these respondents had the effect of controlling status differences simultaneously in *all* of the four vertical dimensions as shown in the lower half of Table 3. In other words, after the elimination of these 34 cases, respondents in the low crystallization category had a higher mean score than respondents in the high crystallization category with respect to *each* of the four status variables. Thus, any Democratic bias remaining after the elimination of these respondents could not be attributed to a failure to control status differences in these vertical dimensions. On the contrary, whatever differences might remain after this control was applied would remain *in spite of the fact* that respondents in the low crystallization category had slightly higher mean scores than respondents in the high

TABLE 4.   Voting Behavior and
Preferences in the 1948, 1950, and
1952 Elections, by Degree of Status
Crystallization, After Correction

PER CENT OF VOTERS
SUPPORTING
DEMOCRATS

ELECTION YEAR	Low Crystallization	High Crystallization	Probability Less Than
1948	82.2*	71.4*	.05
1950	83.5	71.3	.04
1952	72.2**	68.0**	.46

* Includes supporters of the Progressive party.
** Refers to the percentage expressing a *preference* for the Democratic party.

crystallization category. As may be seen by an inspection of Table 4, the application of this rigorous control tended to reduce the margin of difference in political behavior between the two crystallization categories. With the exception of the 1952 election, however, a statistically significant margin of difference remained. Even in the 1952 election, the direction of the difference was consistent with the pattern observed in the other two elections.

The significance of the differences between the two crystallization categories became more apparent when a further test of the basic hypothesis was made, using other data. A 50 per cent subsample of the respondents ($N = 311$) were asked their views on (a) a government-sponsored health insurance program, (b) price controls, and (c) a general extension of governmental powers. As shown in Table 5 below, respondents in the low crystallization category took a more liberal (i.e., leftist) stand on each of these questions than did respondents in the high crystallization category. In two of the three cases, the difference was significant at the 2 per cent level.

TABLE 5.   Frequency of Strongly Liberal Responses on Controversial Issues, by Degree of Status Crystallization

	PERCENT STRONGLY LIBERAL		
ISSUE	Low Crystal- lization	High Crystal- lization	Prob- ability Less Than
Government health insurance	26.7	14.9	.02
Price controls	31.1	25.8	.35
Extension of government powers	40.0	25.8	.02

As in the analysis of the data on voting behavior and preferences, the application of controls for differences in the four status hierarchies reduced slightly the margin of differences between the two crystallization categories. It should be noted, however, that even with the application of these controls, the difference between the two categories was still significant at the five per cent level for both the health insurance question and the question regarding the extension of governmental powers.

On the basis of the data described above, it would therefore appear that a definite association existed between low crystallization and political liberalism among respondents in this cross-section sample of metropolitan Detroit. Before such a relationship could be asserted with confidence, one further problem required examination. Briefly stated, the problem was whether the differences observed between the two crystallization categories were due to the lack of status crystallization *per se,* or rather were a function of particular patterns of status inconsistency which were present in large numbers in the low crystallization category. Thus, for example, it might be argued that the combination of extensive education and limited income is associated with strong liberal biases, while the reverse combination is not, and that the differences observed in Tables 4 and 5 were due to the fact that persons possessing the former combination were extremely numerous in the low crystallization category, giving the category as a whole a liberal bias which was not due to lack of status crystallization *per se.*

To test this alternative hypothesis, a detailed analysis of the low crystallization category was made. All of the respondents in this category were classified on the basis of the various relationships between the income, occupation, education, and ethnic hierarchies. Thus, for example, respondents whose income score was markedly higher than their education score (i.e., 30 or more points higher) were placed in one category, while those whose education score was markedly higher than their income score were placed in a second category. Each of the twelve resulting categories of low crystallization respondents were then compared with high crystallization respondents in terms of their voting record and their views on the three controversial issues.[17] The results of this analysis are shown in Table 6.

Two tentative conclusions may be drawn from a careful analysis of Table 6. First, *liberal political tendencies are associated*

TABLE 6. Summary Comparison of Voting Records and Attitudes on Controversial Issues of Twelve Categories of Low Crystallization Respondents with High Crystallization Respondents

PAIRED VARIABLES*		COMPLETE SAMPLE		SUBSAMPLE	
High	Low	N	Per Cent Strongly Democratic**	N	Per Cent Strongly Liberal***
Income	—Ethnic	53	56.6	23	34.8
Occupation—Ethnic		53	50.9	28	39.3
Education	—Ethnic	68	50.0	34	32.4
Occupation—Education		36	47.2	16	25.0
Education	—Occupation	56	42.8	28	17.8
Income	—Occupation	28	39.6	21	4.8
Education	—Income	67	38.8	31	25.8
Income	—Education	41	36.6	21	28.6
Ethnic	—Occupation	53	35.8	29	17.2
Ethnic	—Education	48	35.4	26	19.2
Ethnic	—Income	63	34.9	32	21.9
Occupation—Income		32	34.4	17	29.4
All high crystallization		413	34.2	207	15.5

* In the case of each comparison respondents had an assigned percentile score 30 or more points higher for the high variable than for the low variable.

** Includes all those who supported Democratic (or Progressive) candidates at least twice between 1948 and 1952.

*** Includes all those who took strongly liberal stand on at least two of the three controversial issues.

with a low degree of status crystallization regardless of the specific relationship of the status variables. This conclusion seems justified in view of the fact that despite the relatively small number of cases involved, 23 out of 24 of the comparisons made yielded differences in the predicted direction. In short, regardless of whether income rank was high and educational rank low, or the reverse, or what the particular nature of the status inconsistency was, the fact of imperfect status crystallization *per se* seems to have been related to political liberalism.

The data in Table 6 also suggest the tentative conclusion that *certain types of status inconsistencies are more closely related to political liberalism than others.* For example, relatively low ethnic status in combination with relatively high income, occupational, or educational status was more closely associated with liberal tendencies than the reverse. Also, the data suggest

that status inconsistencies involving high occupational rank and low educational rank are more closely associated with liberal tendencies that the reverse. However, in view of the small number of cases in each cell, it is necessary to use considerable caution in drawing conclusions from the present data regarding which patterns of relationships are most closely associated with political liberalism.

Discussion

Not only do the findings in the preceding section suggest that a recognition of this nonvertical dimension of social status may help account for some of the previously unexplained variance in political behavior, but also they hint at a more basic relationship between social structure and social change. Extrapolating from these findings, one might predict that the more frequently acute status inconsistencies occur within a population the greater would be the proportion of that population willing to support programs of social change.[18]

Apparently the individual with a poorly crystallized status is a particular type of marginal man, and is subjected to certain pressures by the social order which are not felt (at least to the same degree) by individuals with a more highly crystallized status. Conceivably a society with a relatively large proportion of persons whose status is poorly crystallized is a society which is in an unstable condition. In brief, under such conditions the social system itself generates its own pressures for change.

Some insight into the manner in which such pressures for change may be generated by status inconsistencies has been supplied by Hughes in this excellent discussion of "Dilemmas and Contradictions of Status." [19] The Negro doctor, by virtue of the fact that in his person he combines two roles of grossly discrepant status, is apt to be subjected with some frequency to social experiences of an unpleasant or frustrating nature. The same will tend to be true of the highly educated man with limited income, or the business executive with a grammar school education.

Not all such individuals would be expected to react against the social order which produces such unpleasant experiences in their lives. For various reasons the individual may develop other reactions. For example, the individual may react by blaming other individuals *as individuals* rather than as agents of the social order. Such a reaction might be common among persons raised in an individualistic tradition or who, because of limited educational opportunities, have not learned to relate individual experiences to the social order. Another possibility open to the individual with a poorly crystallized status is that he will react to resulting unpleasant experiences by blaming himself. Finally, there is the possibility that the individual may withdraw in such a manner as to diminish the frequency and the seriousness of the socially disturbing experiences which arise as a result of his status inconsistencies. Such alternative types of reactions may very well explain a part of the variance in responses among individuals in the poorly crystallized category in the present study. It should be noted, however, that the tendency to react by advocating change in the social order seems to have been a frequent type of reaction in the present sample.

Building on this foundation, the political liberalism of several diverse groups in American society begins to appear as a common expression of a common social experience. In recent years political observers have reported relatively strong support for liberal political programs from such diverse groups as college professors, Jewish businessmen, Hollywood actors, and the Protestant clergy. All four of these categories of persons, it must be noted, are characterized by a relatively low degree of status crystallization. Professors and clergymen enjoy high occupational and educational rank, yet their income is sometimes less than that of skilled manual workers. Screen stars frequently combine high income rank with low educational rank, and sometimes with low ethnic rank as well. Jewish businessmen combine high income and occupational rank (and often high educational rank) with low ethnic rank. If the foregoing analysis is sound, one would be led to expect a relatively high frequency of liberal biases among the members of such groups, and for the same fundamental reason.

Building on the present foundation, it also becomes possible to predict one of the sources of leadership of successful revolutionary movements. Years ago Marx and Engels noted that successful revolutionary movements are usually characterized by the combination of broad support from the masses or lower strata, and leadership recruited from the higher strata in the old order.[20] The present study suggests that persons of poorly crystallized status may be an important source from which such leadership is recruited. Quite often such persons combine the personal skills necessary for effective leadership with the equally necessary motivation.

Finally, it may be noted that if the conception of social status presented in this paper is as fruitful as the findings of this pilot study would seem to indicate, some considerable modification of the traditional conception of social class will also be required. This point will be developed more fully in subsequent papers based on the present project.

One methodological implication of the present study remains to be discussed. During the past two decades it has become fashionable in social science circles to construct indices of socioeconomic status by averaging up in some manner several status variables.[21] The findings of this present study indicate that such constructions are seriously deficient in characterizing the social status of a significant minority of the population. Such techniques for classifying individuals fail to take into account what appears to be an important dimension of status, and thus may frequently fail to account for an important part of the variance in the phenomena under investigation.

Conclusions

The conclusions which are drawn from a pilot study such as the present one should be concerned primarily with questions of the advisability of pursuing further the projected line of research, and the methods appropriate to further research, if such is warranted. Conclusions concerning the validity of given hypotheses about social relationships are hardly warranted, except

insofar as they relate to the question of the advisability of further research.

In the present case the writer feels that the findings fully warrant further exploration of the crystallization dimension of status. This view seems justified not only on the ground that status crystallization seems a useful tool for reducing the range of unexplained variation in American political behavior, but also because of the broader theoretical and methodological implications which were outlined in the preceding section.

Future research in this area should be directed not only to the checking and rechecking of the relationship of status crystallization and political liberalism, but also to the exploration of the relationship of status crystallization to variations in other areas of behavior, and in personality development as well. Possibly fruitful new discoveries will result.

Notes

1. This possibility has also been noted in recent years by Emile Benoit-Smullyan, "Status, Status Types and Status Interrelationships," *American Sociological Review,* 9 (1944), pp. 151–61; Pitirim A. Sorokin, *Society, Culture, and Personality,* New York: Harper & Brothers, 1947, pp. 289–94; Harold F. Kaufman *et al.,* "Problems of Theory and Method in the Study of Social Stratification in Rural Society," *Rural Sociology,* 18 (1953), p. 15; and Stuart Adams, "Status Congruency as a Variable in Small Group Performance," *Social Forces,* 32 (1953), pp. 16–22.
2. The term "status crystallization" will be used throughout the remainder of the article as a synonym for "status consistency."
3. For details regarding the Detroit Area Study, see Ronald Freedman, "The Detroit Area Study: A Training and Research Laboratory in the Community," *American Journal of Sociology,* 59 (1953), pp. 30–33.
4. Respondents were selected by the area sampling method. In general, the sampling procedure involved: (1) random selection of a sample of blocks in the community; (2) within these blocks a random selection of households; and (3) within each household a

random selection of persons to be interviewed. For a more detailed description of the methods employed, see Leslie Kish, "A Two-Stage Sample of a City," *American Sociological Review*, 17 (1952), pp. 761–69, and Kish, "A Procedure for Objective Respondent Selection Within the Household," *Journal of the American Statistical Association*, 44 (1949), pp. 380–87.

5. For detailed comparisons with census data, see *A Social Profile of Detroit: 1952* (Ann Arbor: Michigan University Press, 1952), pp. 34–37.

6. See "Jobs and Occupations: A Popular Evaluation," *Opinion News*, 9 (1947), pp. 3 ff.

7. *Op. cit.*

8. Admittedly this technique was not wholly satisfactory. It seemed, however, the most satisfactory approximation which could be achieved within the financial and temporal limitations of this project.

9. Student evaluations of their own ethnic group were not included, in order to minimize personal biases which might not be consistent with community biases.

10. Separate ranks were determined for each of the specific groups within these general categories. In the case of respondents of mixed ethnic backgrounds, the scores of the several ethnic groups (see below) were averaged.

11. See, for example, Talcott Parsons, "A Revised Analytical Approach to the Theory of Social Stratification," in *Class, Status and Power*, edited by Reinhard Bendix and Seymour Lipset (New York: The Free Press, 1953), pp. 166–67; Kingsley Davis, *Human Society* (New York: The Macmillan Company, 1949), p. 364; W. Lloyd Warner and Paul S. Lunt, *The Social Life of a Modern Community* (New Haven: Yale University Press, 1941), p. 90.

12. If this were not done, comparisons of nonemployed dependent relatives would be most difficult.

13. In computing the educational scores of the respondents, one variation was introduced. Respondents forty years of age and over were separated from those younger. This was considered necessary in view of the rapid changes in educational expectations and attainments in American society in recent times. Direct comparisons of older persons with younger persons in terms of educational attainments would be unrealisitc, since failure to complete high school, for example, is a far more serious handicap for members of the younger generation than for members of the older. Some allowance for this difference is usually made in the evaluative process in contemporary society.

14. The use of squared deviations from the mean rather than simple deviations was employed to emphasize effect of larger deviations and to minimize the effect of smaller deviations. This was considered desirable since the techniques employed in quantifying positions (or intervals) in the several hierarchies were sufficiently crude so that no great importance could be attached to small deviations.

The technique of subtracting the resulting figure from one hundred was employed so that respondents whose status was highly crystallized would have numerically higher crystallization scores than those whose status was poorly crystallized. This was done solely to avoid semantic difficulties.

15. It seemed desirable to remove those respondents in families in which the family head was not currently in the labor force due to retirement, prolonged illness, or extended unemployment, since serious difficulties arose in any attempt to compare them with the remainder of the sample with respect to their position in the occupational hierarchy.

16. It will be noted in Table 2 that the proportion of persons supporting the Democratic party is far above the national average in all three elections. Some difference in this direction was to be expected, since the sample was drawn from the metropolitan Detroit area, which is the stronghold of the Democratic party in Michigan. This, however, does not entirely account for the preponderance of Democratic voters. In the 1948 election, for example, slightly less than 60 per cent of the major party vote in the metropolitan Detroit area went to the Democratic party. However, slightly more than 70 per cent of the respondents in the study group reported that they voted for the Democratic party that year. This discrepancy seems to be due to the fact observed by polling organizations that many persons report on interviews that they voted in a previous election, when careful checking of the voting lists reveal they did not. This seems to be more frequently a characteristic of Democrats than of Republicans of the larger cities.

Some evidence of this tendency was discovered in the present study. In cases where the respondent resided at the same address in 1948 or 1950, the accuracy of his response was checked. Such checks revealed that at least 13 per cent of those who claimed to have voted in 1948, had not, in fact, voted. Eighty-five per cent of those who erroneously claimed to have voted reported voting for either the

Democratic or Progressive parties, while only 15 per cent reported voting for the Republican party. While these respondents were not counted as voters in Table 2, others undoubtedly remained who gave erroneous reports, but for whom no check was possible due to a change in residence during the intervening period.

Among the erroneous reports discovered, the proportion of erroneous Democratic reports was somewhat greater in the high crystallization category while the proportion of erroneous Republican reports was somewhat greater in the low crystallization category. If it is assumed that comparable proportions of Republican and Democratic voters would be found in the undiscovered erroneous reports, this would mean that the present uncorrected error in the data works *against* the basic hypothesis, since it tends to make the difference in voting behavior between the two categories of respondents appear less than it actually was.

17. This comparison was made *after* the correction to control for status differences in the four hierarchies.

18. It might be argued that conservatives advocate programs of social change just as do liberals, especially in periods of liberal control. Strictly speaking, this is true, but it must be noted that such changes are usually put forward as a program of return to former conditions. Although experts might challenge this claim in many respects, it is a claim which is accepted by the general public. Thus, in the public mind the liberal or left-wing parties are usually thought of as the parties advocating change, while the conservative parties are thought of as the supporters of the present order (or the old order).

19. *American Journal of Sociology,* 50 (1944), pp. 353–57. It should be noted that Hughes uses the term "status" differently from the use made in this article. It is not difficult, however, to relate his discussion to the present problem if this fact is kept in mind.

20. *Manifesto of the Communist Party* (New York: International Publishers, 1932), p. 19.

21. See, for example, W. Lloyd Warner, *et al., Social Class in America* (Chicago: Science Research Associates, 1949), Part 3; or Clyde V. Kiser and P. K. Whelpton, "Social and Psychological Factors Affecting Fertility, IX. Fertility Planning and Fertility Rates by Socio-Economic Status," *Milbank Memorial Fund Quarterly,* 27 (1949), pp. 214–16.

11. Patterns of Name Ordering among Authors of Scientific Papers: A Study of Social Symbolism and Its Ambiguity [1]

HARRIET A. ZUCKERMAN

IN SCIENCE, as in every other social activity, assessments are made of individual role performance; the most crucial aspect of a scientist's role performance is, of course, his published contributions to knowledge. This is nothing new. What is new is the profound increase in the extent of collaborative investigation [2] which, in many cases, reduces the visibility of role-performance of individual investigators.[3] In the past, there were, as now, discrepant judgments about the quality of a scientist's work, but rarely was there any ambiguity about who had done what. A scientist may have had

Reprinted in part with permission from the *American Journal of Sociology,* 74 (November 1968), pp. 276–91 (copyright 1968 by the University of Chicago).

technical assistants working with him, but he was unambiguously *the* investigator, not merely the "principal investigator." When he put his findings into print, he was, with few exceptions, the sole author. There could be no doubt whose scientific performance was being assessed.

But the considerable increase in the incidence of collaborative research only exacerbates an old problem for scientists: will their own contributions be recognized and judged significant by their colleagues? Some assert that the matter of recognition is altogether trivial but others openly admit their concern with it. Even Nobel laureates [4] who presumably have had substantial response from the scientific community find the matter of recognition and its place in a scientist's work discomfiting. When the issue of recognition is complicated by the need to allocate it among co-workers, it becomes all the more disconcerting. For one thing, decisions have to be made about whose contribution was greatest, and for another, some means of conveying the outcomes of these decisions must be found. Finally, attention must be given to how each of these will be perceived by scientist-readers of the publication.

The laureates report embarrassment at taking senior authorship as a matter of course, and they report having been concerned that others might think their role in research was minor. As one physicist with a name in the latter part of the alphabet observed:

> Alphabetical ordering of names is quite unfair, especially when the two people who are doing the work are very different in their reputations—and the junior man naturally comes second . . . [because] there is a general tendency to assume that all is due to the senior author.

Not only are there problems when co-workers are distinctly unequal in rank, work with scientific peers creates some difficulties as well. How does one convey precisely and unequivocally that contributions are equal? Another physicist answered:

> . . . we used alternation of names on the several papers to show we were both involved . . . if we had listed them aphabetically, the problem would have been with my name. I would have had an advantage . . . we alternated to show definitely that we were both at least equally involved.

And finally it is not surprising that there are times when scientists want some way of making it clear who really made the major contribution to the work being reported. Such was the case reported by a chemist-laureate:

> In this series of papers—there are three of them—I am the first author in each because they involved a lot of theoretical analysis and I felt that I was really the important part of the papers. I had carried out the theoretical analysis and I had developed the methods required.

The fact is that the matter of allocating credit among co-workers produces tension, embarrassment, anxiety and, in some, firm denial that the issue is important at all.

As collaborative research became more frequent and as the number of co-authors (what I call the author-set) increased, new practices were introduced to lessen the ambiguity about the distinctive roles of co-authors in doing research and in preparing published papers. Various patterns of name ordering of co-authors were evolved for this purpose.[5]

This is just the sort of device that produces ambivalence. Intrinsically, it seems trivial or humiliating to be concerned with the order in which the names of authors appear; for scientists to be as interested in the order of their billing as actors or business partners. But symbolically, name ordering is an adaptive device that facilitates the allocation of responsibility and credit among co-workers in otherwise ambiguous situations induced by the new structures of scientific research. It is designed to have the reward system operate with a degree of equity and adequacy. The ambivalence toward name ordering is only one more instance of scientists' ambivalence toward recognition for their work and the means used to achieve it.[6]

Beyond this, two aspects of the ordering of authors' names need only be mentioned here. First, name orders convey ambiguous information about the relative contributions of co-workers since, as we shall see, customary practices differ among disciplines and within them, and since name orders, like other symbols, are sometimes adapted to serve purposes other than their manifest ones. As a result of this ambiguity, circles of scientists ascribe their own meanings to sequences of authors' names, meanings that often diverge from those intended by the authors themselves. For example, textual references to scientist "X and his collaborators" when scientist X is listed third or fourth in a long list of names are indicators that scientist readers sometimes ignore name orders in seeking to allocate credit and responsibility among coworkers. In the process, it is not unusual for scientists to request and to receive information about "who did what" through informal channels of communication.

Little is known about actual patterns of name ordering employed by scientists of varying degrees of eminence and in various fields. To get some leverage on these questions, patterns of name ordering found on the scientific papers of forty-one of the fifty-five Nobel laureates living in the United States are compared to those on a random sample of articles listed in the abstracts of physics, chemistry, and the biological sciences from 1920 to 1964—the period corresponding to the dates of the laureates' publications.[7] Although the author of a particular article appearing in the abstracts may be as eminent as a laureate, on the average, randomly selected authors are, of course, far less distinguished and represent the average scientists publishing in these fields.

Using these data, I can systematically compare name-ordering practices among scientists of varying eminence in different fields. Later on, I shall consider the practices of men at different stages of the scientific career.

Patterns of Name Ordering

Three principal patterns of name ordering are used in multi-authored papers. The first may be described as the "equality pattern" since it is designed to put all co-authors on a plane and, so far as possible, not to distinguish their respective contributions. This type consists of alphabetized and reverse alphabetical sequences according to the initial letters of authors' last names. A classically literal case of alphabetizing was contrived not long ago by the trio of physicists who signed their paper Alpher, Bethe, and Gamow.[8]

The second consists of patterns which enhance the visibility of one or another member of the set of authors. These also take two principal forms: the first-author-out-of-sequence followed by an alphabetized group (thus: ZABC), and the last-author-out-of-sequence preceded by an alphabetized list (thus: XYZA). In both forms, the out-of-sequence author appears as a figure against a ground. He stands in contrast to the others who appear as mere elements of an alphabetical pattern.[9]

The third major type of ordering usually gives prime visibility to the first-author and smaller increments of visibility to each succeeding author. This is the alphabetically random pattern. As we shall see, names are arranged according to definite criteria other than the arbitrary one of alphabetical order. Each pattern requires separate consideration.

TABLE 1.   Percentage of Papers with Alphabetized Name Orders by Laureates and a Sample of Authors Listed in Abstracts according to Field and Size of Author-Set

| | SIZE OF AUTHOR-SET | | | | | | | | | | |
	2		3		4		5		6+		All	
Physics:												
Laureates	71	(398)	55	(147)	63	(58)	54	(46)	83	(46)	67	(695)
Abstracts	64	(1,410)	38	(643)	35	(142)	39	(38)	26	(34)	57	(2,267)
Chemistry:												
Laureates	52	(638)	17	(337)	12	(119)	6	(49)	11	(35)	35	(1,178)
Abstracts	55	(3,519)	25	(1,162)	14	(305)	14	(81)	12	(58)	45	(5,125)
Biological sciences:												
Laureates	47	(750)	19	(380)	4	(186)	1	(100)	1	(78)	29	(1,494)
Abstracts	55	(2,802)	22	(1,061)	10	(347)	2	(112)	6	(63)	41	(4,385)
All:												
Laureates	54	(1,786)	24	(864)	16	(363)	15	(195)	27	(159)	39	(3,367)
Abstracts	57	(7,731)	27	(2,866)	16	(794)	12	(231)	13	(155)	46	(11,777)

Differential Use of Name-Order Patterns

ALPHABETICAL SEQUENCES

At first appearance, Table 1 seems to indicate that laureates are a little less apt to use the alphabetical equality pattern than their less distinguished counterparts: 39 per cent of papers by prize winners and 46 per cent of the others carry alphabetic orders. What we actually find are greater differences in the use of the pattern among different disciplines. Alphabetizing is more frequently used in physics than in chemistry or the biological sciences, and it is much more often used by physicist laureates than by rank-and-file physicists. In chemistry and biology, by contrast, laureates are slightly less apt to signal equality of contributions by using alphabetical listings. As I shall show, Nobelists in these fields attempt to confer credit upon their co-workers in other ways.[10]

Obviously, alphabetical sequences do not always symbolize equality of contribution. In some cases, the alphabetical order will coincide by chance with the order of differential contributions. A chemist laureate reported this familiar type of case from his own experience. "This paper I was co-author of did not have this authorship question in it . . . because . . . the sequence of authors in terms of contribution was identical with the alphabetical order and this put me first which is unusual [considering that] my name begins with T."

Scientists are abundantly aware of this type of ambiguity. In many cases, the manifest "equality" pattern supplies misinformation. One of the several laureates who collaborated with Enrico Fermi emphasized the frequency of this symbolically inept sequence when working with the great physicist: "Anytime I did something . . . with Fermi [and the group], although we always co-authored these things . . . in alphabetical order . . . [it] has to be understood that Fermi did the lion's share of the work."

A second artifact that makes for ambiguity in the meaning of alphabetical orders is their increasingly preferred use as the number of co-authors increases, since the task of ranking the contributions of many authors, say, the laureates, is then especially difficult, unpleasant, and apt to induce conflict. A physicist put it this way: "When a lot of people are involved . . .

the alphabetical order . . . certainly simplifies matters. And I just don't like this weighing of each person's contribution. It is almost impossible to do." In these cases too, the reader of scientific papers is confronted with alphabetical orders which do not convey the unequal contributions of co-authors.[11]

Table 1 cannot tell us whether there is a preference for alphabetical name orders. This is evident in the case of papers by two authors. In these papers, if no preference for name ordering were being exercised, names on about half of the papers would be alphabetized and the other half would be reverse alphabetical. With three-author papers, in the absence of choice, about one-sixth would have alphabetized orders, another sixth, reverse alphabetical, and so on as summarized in Table 2. A measure of preference for alphabetized orders—or any one of the other name-order patterns—is therefore provided by the ratios of observed frequencies of papers to the number of papers that would be expected if no preferences were being exercised.

In Table 3, we see that preference for alphabetized name orders becomes noticeable among laureates and the sample of authors listed in the abstracts when papers have four or more co-authors. The tendency to choose alphabetical orders as the size of the author-set increases is much the same among both groups. With four-author papers, both choose to alphabetize about four times as often as would be expected if this were not a matter of deliberate decision. The ratios rise rapidly for five-author papers to nineteen times as many papers by the laureates and sixteen times among the others. Finally, when papers have six or more authors, alphabetizing occurs 270 times as often as would be expected (if it were random rather than preferential) for the laureates and 133 times for other scientists. Ratios based on small expected frequencies tend to be inflated, of course, but it is clear that alphabetizing is

preferred as the size of the author-set increases beyond four.[12]

There is also an increase, though less marked, in preference ratios for patterns which heighten the visibility of first- and last-authors. These will be examined later. The alphabetically random sequence of names—presumably reflecting deliberate sequences gauged in terms of relative contribution—occur somewhat less often in successively larger author-sets than would be expected if no preferences were being exercised.[13]

So much for the comparison of actual authorship practices with patterns which would occur if authors were not deliberately choosing some sequences rather than others. We still must deal with the question of whether laureates' selections of name-order patterns are different from those of rank-and-file scientists. Taking all multi-authored papers by both groups and classifying them according to patterns of name ordering, we find that these distributions differ significantly from one another.[14] Table 3 shows that the differences between eminent scientists and their less celebrated colleagues are concentrated in papers with at least five authors,[15] and in particular in the choice of alphabetical orders.[16] Although available data do not permit us to test the validity of any explanation of differences, it is, as we shall see, consistent with other evidence we have, to assume that these differences can be accounted for in two ways. First of all, the laureates' names are so familiar to the scientific audience that they sacrifice relatively little by having their names alphabetized along with those of several other scientists. Wherever their names come in these sequences, they are visible. In this respect, and as we shall see in others as well, adopting conventions which do not signal their pre-eminence is nearly cost-free. And second, the chances are that laureates, even when they are very young or very old, contributed enough to particular researches to

TABLE 2. Probabilities That Particular Patterns of Name Ordering Will Appear on Multi-Authored Papers in the Absence of Exercised Preferences

	NUMBER OF AUTHORS				
ORDERING PATTERNS	2	3	4	5	6
Alphabetical	.500	.167	.042	.008	.001
Reverse alphabetical	.500	.167	.042	.008	.001
Alphabetical except for first name	—	.333	.125	.033	.007
Alphabetical except for last name	—	.333	.125	.033	.007
Alphabetically random	—	—	.667	.917	.983

TABLE 3. Ratios of Observed to Expected Frequencies of Papers with Different Name-Order Patterns by Laureates and a Sample of Authors of Papers Listed in Abstracts

	NUMBER OF AUTHORS				
NAME-ORDER PATTERNS	2	3	4	5	6+ *
Alphabetical:					
Laureates	1.1	1.5	3.9	19.3	270.4
Abstracts	1.1	1.6	3.9	15.6	133.3
Reverse alphabetical					
Laureates	0.9	0.9	0.7	4.0	‡
Abstracts	0.9	0.9	0.9	0.6	‡
X + Alphabetical: †					
Laureates	—	0.9	1.0	2.3	8.1
Abstracts	—	0.9	1.1	1.7	8.2
Alphabetical + X: †					
Laureates	—	0.8	0.9	1.2	3.6
Abstracts	—	0.8	1.2	0.8	‡
Alphabetically random:					
Laureates	—	—	0.8	0.8	0.7
Abstracts	—	—	0.8	0.8	0.8
Number of papers:					
Laureates	(1,786)	(864)	(363)	(195)	(159)
Abstracts	(7,731)	(2,866)	(794)	(231)	(155)

* The incremental probabilities governing the expected frequencies of papers with seven or more authors are so small that we used the probabilities of a six-author paper as the base for computing the number of expected papers.

† These refer, respectively, to the pattern of first-author-out-of-sequence followed by an alphabetical sequence and the last-author-out-of-sequence preceded by an alphabetical sequence.

‡ No cases appeared in these cells.

be considered by their co-workers as equals. In any case, we find that laureates are no more apt to have their names in sequences which emphasize the contributions of particular authors than are rank-and-file scientists—with the exception of the laureates' greater use of the last-author-out-of-sequence pattern on papers with many authors. In this sense, the elite has much the same preferences with regard to name ordering as other scientists on the majority of their published papers. But as we shall see, laureates differ from their colleagues in the positions they occupy in name orders rather than in their preferences for particular sequences as such.

SPECIAL SITUATIONS AFFECTING THE AMBIGUITY OF ALPHABETICAL NAME ORDERS

When alphabetized name orders are adopted as a matter of custom,[17] scientists whose names begin with letters late in the alphabet and those who collaborate with distinguished men are consistently penalized.[18] One physicist laureate spoke out of his own experience about the consequences of persistent alphabetizing for men whose names come at the end of the alphabet: "Since publication is such an important source of judgment of the individual's work . . . if a given person is always put [late in lists] . . . there is a tendency for people to think that he is just a subsidiary all the time."

The laureates imply that the allocation of credit to well-known scientists for particular contributions—at the expense of subordinates—is especially problematic in the case of alphabetical sequences. This is one version of the Matthew Effect described by Merton as "the accruing of greater increments of recognition for particular scientific contributions to men of considerable repute and the withholding of such recognition from men who have not yet made their mark.[19] When the name of an eminent man happens to come first in an alphabetical sequence, the scientific community, which tends to credit him with the work in any case, is all the more likely to do so. One physicist who has been listed first for this alphabetical reason confessed that it "was just embarrassing."

To prevent injustices that would be perpetrated by consistently alphabetizing authors' names on a series of joint papers, scientists have seized upon the expedient of rotating names through lists. A geneticist reported: "With F, it was not at all clear [how we should order our names] because we did everything together . . . So we tended to alternate . . . I had a general feeling of 'Gosh, we're equal; let's just alternate and give the [correct] impression that it's an equal partnership.' "

When only a pair of collaborators is involved, rotation of names on a series of papers—to equalize credit—is easy to arrange. As the number of co-workers increases, the number of papers they must publish to give every man first-authorship must, of course, equal the number of authors—and if every author is to be given an equal chance to occupy every position in the list, the number of papers required would obviously be *n!*. To put the matter simply, six co-authors would have to publish a mere 720 papers to rotate every author through the sequence. Such precisely mathematized allocations of credit would scarcely be visible to the scientific community and would reveal little more than an obsessive concern with the problem.

Rotation of names is not the only expedient tried and discarded in the search for an equitable ordering pattern. One laureate expressed his dissatisfaction with all the alternatives in these words: "It has been tried to rotate the alphabetical order; it

TABLE 4. Percentage of Papers by Laureates and a Matched Sample of Scientists on Which They Are First-Authors, by Age at Publication *

Age	Laureates		Matched Sample	
20–29	49	(103)	38	(34)
30–39	40	(304)	38	(130)
40–49	26	(578)	56	(80)
50–59	20	(374)	37	(131)
60+	18	(222)	25	(64)
All	27	(1,581)	39	(439)

* Papers here refer to those having three or more authors.

has been tried to put [only] the institution [as author] and none of these has worked out . . . When you say, 'We will go alphabetical,' and you get a student whose name begins with 'A'; after a while, you get fed up . . . No perfectly standard and uniform practice has been established nor can it be."

We find that alphabetical ordering patterns designed to symbolize equality of contribution have their own share of ambiguity. How do things stand for other name-order patterns?

Non-Alphabetic Orders

Lists of authors appearing out of alphabetical order are presumably intended to indicate unequal contributions to the research. In practice, such ordering is determined both by this criterion and by the relative ranks of authors.

FIRST-AUTHORSHIP

With these two criteria for name ordering, we would expect the laureates to be first-authors more often than those whose contributions to science have been less substantial. When the laureates are compared not to a sample of authors in the abstracts but to a sample matched to them for age, field of specialization, organizational affiliation, and initial letter of last name, as in Table 4, we find that this is not the case.[20] The laureates are listed first on 27 per cent of their multi-authored [21] papers and the matched sample on 39 per cent of their papers. This is consistent with the Coles' finding that the correlation between the visibility of physicists and their propensity toward first-authorship is insignificant.[22] Laureates are, of course, highly visible but not given to placing their names first on scientific papers. The difference between laureates and the rank and file holds in all three fields of science. But though the laureates are less often first-authors on all their

collaborative papers, it might still be that they earmark their contributions by electing to be first in the name order that especially heightens the visibility of first-author. This is, as we noted earlier, the "first-author-out-of-sequence" pattern (ZABC). Yet here too the laureates are first-authors less often than the matched sample; they occupy first place on 34 per cent of these papers as against their less eminent colleagues who are first 41 per cent of the time.

Why do the laureates take the first position less often than those in the matched sample? Laureates' contributions to collaborative investigations are scarcely apt to be less significant than those of the matched sample, and we know that they are highly ranked. Their name-order practices and the interview data, taken together, suggest that they often abide by the standard of *noblesse oblige*: their rank imposes special obligations. Precisely because the Nobel prize—or the other symbols of recognition received before it—confers high rank upon them, they are expected not to exercise their authority and power to the limit. And so they, more often than the less distinguished sample, are moved to give co-workers an enlarged share of the credit. A biochemist explained it this way: "If I publish my name first, then everyone thinks the others are just technicians . . . if my name is last, people will credit me anyway for the whole thing, so I want them to have a bit more glory."

This remark and others like it signal that the laureates are well aware that they are not penalized by their distinctive name-order practices. The Matthew Effect, which enhances the standing of eminent men at the expense of their less distinguished co-workers, assures them of recognition wherever they are placed on author lists. To this extent, their generosity is cost-free.

This interpretation, in terms of *noblesse oblige,* is at least consistent with a more detailed review of the data in Table 4 where laureates' publication patterns at various ages are compared to those of the matched sample. In their twenties, the laureates-to-be were first-authors on half of their collaborative papers. Both motive and opportunity structure joined to produce this result. First of all, they were intent upon establishing their distinctive contributions to joint entreprises. Recalling those days, a biochemist mused: "When you are young and not really very far advanced, you are much more excited about [being first-author] than you are later on. It's not very important now."

And second, when the laureates were young, they worked with eminent scientists. In fact, twenty-six of the forty-one laureates who were interviewed worked under men who were, themselves, Nobel prize-winners. And of the total of fifty-five Nobel laureates at work in the United States, thirty-four worked under older laureates. Their mentors often made decisions to put young men first just as the present laureates now do. As one laureate remembered: "When I worked with T [an older prize-winner] it usually turned out that I was listed first." His experience is not unique. When the laureates-to-be co-authored papers with their laureate masters, it turns out that the junior men were first-authors 60 per cent of the time and the seniors only 16 per cent of the time.[23] Simultaneously, the young laureates-to-be were recipients of the generosity of their mentors and socialized into the pattern of *noblesse oblige*. We can identify anticipatory socialization in the case of a chemist who engaged in name-order practices associated with eminence and seniority early in his career:

INTERVIEWER: From the earliest times, when you published with students, I notice your name appeared last.

LAUREATE: Oh, that was just an affectation . . . I suppose. But there are two customs . . . either you put the students' names first or else it's alphabetical.

This combination of having made significant contributions—none of the laureates was a "late bloomer"—and generosity on the part of their seniors makes for a high proportion of first-author listings among the laureates' papers published when they were young. Different values of the same two variables are tentatively taken to account for the lower percentage of first-authors among the matched sample. Their contributions to collaborative research were probably less significant and their own mentors probably less generous than those of the laureates.

As both the laureates and the matched sample take control over name-order decisions—and the interviews indicate that these decisions are generally made by senior investigators—the laureates place themselves first less often than they did earlier and the matched sample more often. By their forties, most of the laureates are distinguished men, and half of them have already received the Nobel prize. They are, by this time, aware that their visibility and eminence are not diminished by their name-order practices.

Finally, as the scientists become older, the issue of name ordering, in particular, and competition for recognition, in general, declines in importance for both groups. Furthermore, the contributions of older men to particular investigations are probably less significant. Again, in the interviews, older laureates say with regret that research is tiring and that, increasingly, they now serve in a supervisory capacity.

Up to now, I have ascribed the inverse relationship between first-authorship of papers and age at publication among laureates to their growing eminence and visibility. Some additional data support this interpretation. First of all, rates of first-authorship should decrease quite considerably following the Nobel prize which, after all, confers much prestige upon its recipients. Table 5 shows that the laureates' rates of first-authored papers, already low, decline some 9 per cent following the award; the publication practices of the matched sample do not change at all in the same period.

This change, following the Nobel prize, is not as great as we would have expected, given the very substantial prestige bestowed

TABLE 5. Percentage of Multi-Authored Papers on Which Laureates and a Matched Sample of Scientists Are First-Authors according to Time of Publication

	DATE OF PUBLICATION RELATIVE TO THE AWARD*		
	6 or More Years before the Award	0–5 Years before Award	1 or More Years after the Award
Laureates	39 (688)	22 (477)	13 (416)
Matched sample	43 (153)	35 (82)	36 (204)

* Time of publication of papers of the men in the matched sample was determined by using the date of the prize of the laureate in each matched pair. A paper by a member of the matched sample published in 1952, for example, was classified as being in the category 0–5 years before the award if his laureate twin received the prize between 1952 and 1956.

by the award. My analysis, however, disregards the fact that not all Nobel laureates were equally distinguished *before* receiving the prize. Some were already uncrowned laureates; they were members of their own national academies and foreign ones, recipients of major scientific awards, and holders of multiple honorary degrees. For these men, the Nobel prize only caps distinguished research careers. Others, however, were neither academicians, recipients of important awards, nor holders of honorary degrees before they were named laureates. The Nobel prize confers very considerable increments of prestige upon these men. I want, then, to compare the authorship practices of men who achieved substantial eminence before receiving the prize to those of men who had not, in order to see whether the exercise of *noblesse oblige* is indeed more characteristic of eminent men.

As Figure 1 indicates, men who were eminent before receiving the prize began to transfer first-authorship to their co-workers before their less eminent colleagues did so.[24] In the period just before the award, laureates who were already distinguished scientists took first place in author lists only 17 per cent of the time, but men who had not yet made their mark did so twice as often. Differences between the two groups of laureates, moreover, cannot be attributed to variations in name-order practices with aging. Taking those who received the prize before they were fifty, for example, we find that the previously eminent were first-authors on only 15 per cent of their papers published just before the award, but the less eminent laureates-to-be were listed first 48 per cent of the time. After the award, first-authorship is far less frequent—10 per cent of the already eminent and 19 per cent of the newly eminent larueates' papers carried their names first.[25] In this respect, future laureates—young and old—who had not yet become members of the scientific elite are much like the rank-and-file scientists in the matched sample. These laureates-to-be presumably felt obliged to earmark their contributions to collaborative efforts to an extent that their eminent colleagues did not. After the award, the practices of the previously eminent and the newly eminent—regardless of age—converge: they are first-authors 12 per cent and 16 per cent of the time, respectively. The Nobel prize apparently goes far toward equalizing earlier differences in prestige among laureates. It also minimizes the tendency among prize-winners to highlight their own contributions to joint research through symbols of authorship.

These data are consistent with the sug-

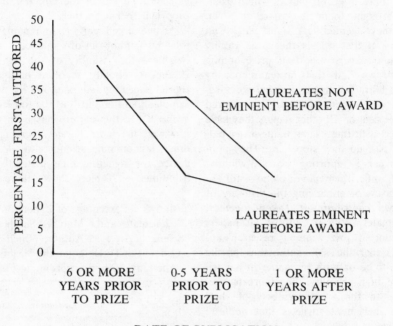

FIGURE 1.   Percentage of multi-authored papers by laureates on which they are first-authors, according to date of publication and eminence at time of the award.

gestion that *noblesse oblige* is exercised more frequently as the eminence of individual scientists increases. It does not imply, however, that laureates are entirely selfless or wholly unconcerned with recognition; they "stake their claims" without hesitation to work to which they believe they made signal contributions. Two laureates emphasized this consideration when describing name-ordering patterns on papers reporting research for which each received the prize: "I think both Joe and Jim [his two co-workers] regarded me as the originator of the idea and the main promoter of the experiments. I have never felt with either of them, the slightest awkwardness as to whose idea it was or anything like

that . . . And this was why I was first . . . But I would also like to say that without any one of us, it would not have been carried through." Just as directly, the other laureate reported: "Why was my name first? . . . I suppose one should publish in alphabetical order . . . [but] it was really my job that I had been working on and then he came in. So I don't think it was unfair to him. He did supply a key piece of the thing [but] his time on it was small compared to mine anyway."

These laureates suggest that they adopt some symbolic device for earmarking significant contributions as their own. We would expect these distinguished scientists to use one or another of the high visibility positions in name orders—either the first-author- or the last-author-out-of-sequence or first place in the alphabetically random pattern more often on papers which eventually brought them the prize than on others they deemed less significant. And it turns out that this is the case. Taking only those papers reporting prizewinning research, we find that laureates occupy high visibility positions in name-order sequences 46 per cent of the time compared to 30 per cent on all other papers they have published with these same name-order patterns.[26] Nor do they stop here. They publish papers reporting award-winning research under their names alone—still another means of enhancing the visibility of their own contributions. Taken together, approximately 60 per cent of all papers that reported prizewinning research appeared under the sole authorship of the laureate-to-be or with his name in a position of high visibility. The laureates' reluctance to forego all symbols of their prime achievement suggests that *noblesse oblige* has its limits.

LAST-AUTHORSHIP

It might be assumed that the normative criteria for last place in author lists are reciprocals to those for first place; that authors who contribute least and rank lowest should come last. Yet the laureates are last-authors more often than the members of the matched sample; in 53 per cent of their papers as against 33 per cent for the others.[27]

The practice of these laureates again expresses the norm of *noblesse oblige*. A laureate in medicine said: "My name *always* comes last . . . I did receive quite a bit of recognition for the work I did on X compound [not the work for which he won the prize]. Just so long as my name was there, it didn't make any difference where it appeared. Don't you think that's true? So why not put it last?" And another even described it as a matter of etiquette:

"You'll find in recent years that my name is always last. This isn't because I think I have contributed least. But I think that, as senior person in the lab, it's more appropriate that it be there."

As we noted earlier, one name order, the last-author-out-of-sequence, actually heightens the visibility of the last-author. It appears equally as often on multi-authored papers by laureates and the matched sample, about one-fifth of the time for each group. Once this pattern has been chosen, however, the laureates *are* more apt than other, less eminent scientists to use it as a device for signaling their distinctive contributions. As Table 6 shows, laureates are

TABLE 6. Percentage of Papers on Which Laureates and a Matched Sample of Scientists Are Last-Author, Which Are so Ordered as To Heighten the Visibility of the Last-Author, according to Field *

Field	Laureates	Matched Sample
Physics	52 (21)	41 (27)
Chemistry	63 (125)	10 (10)
Biological sciences	59 (143)	35 (55)
All	61 (289)	34 (92)

* The last-author in this pattern is alphabetically out of phase and is preceded by an alphabetical sequence (XYZA).

last-authors almost twice as often on this high visibility pattern than are men in the matched sample, 61 per cent of the time as against 34 per cent.[28] Here again, *noblesse oblige* apparently is exercised to a point and no further. Moreover, the laureates adopt this pattern of visibility increasingly often as they get older, thereby earmarking their contributions without demanding first-authorship. In the biological sciences and in chemistry, for example, the laureates tell us, last-authorship has prestige, even when name orders do not call attention to it. A medical researcher remarked: "In our field, the last name of a group is the 'father' of the effort. . . . This has become a pattern in medicine so that the last name does have a certain position." Our data bear this out; laureates in the biological sciences and in chemistry are more often "fathers" of investigations; they are last on 62 and 59 per cent of the papers, respectively, with names listed in the alphabetically random pattern, compared to laureates in physics who were last authors only 28 per cent of the time on papers of the same type.

I have shown that patterns of name ordering have been devised as adaptive mechanisms to heighten the visibility of role-performance of individual investigators working in collaboration. The various patterns which, at first, seem to have unequivocal meanings for scientists do convey varying degrees of ambiguity and, to this extent, fail to serve their intended functions. However, it is also the case that such ambiguity in the meaning of name orders reduces the stress of collaboration. As in other departments of social life, making things explicit often introduces strain into social relations.

Laureates, having been faced with decisions on name ordering and their consequences, are well aware of the tensions which accompany emphasis on strict weighting of contributions. They agree that some measure of ambiguity in this delicate matter of allocating credit and responsibility helps to maintain peace in collaborative situations. A physicist's remarks are representative of general feelings:

I think [a standard system for distinguishing the contributions of co-authors] would tend to produce a great deal of interference. . . . If a system were set up to try to dispense credit with complete justice, I think we'd end up with almost everyone . . . disappointed, in general, with what they've gotten —feeling that other people have perhaps gotten more than their share. . . . So I would be opposed to trying to cut this very fine. It seems to me that the decision as to whether somebody should be senior author or should appear simply alphabetically is perhaps as fine as it should be reasonably cut.

It appears that, in the long run, the functional requirements of the evaluation system and of collaborative groups are incompatible and so call for different and sometimes conflicting procedures for making role-performance visible.

One matter remains for discussion. Until now, we have assumed that position in name-order sequences enhances the visibility of individual role-performance and thereby makes it possible to allocate credit among co-workers. Whether this is so or not, the fact is that scientists believe that it does. As with other definitions of the situation, consequences are apt to reflect such beliefs. It seems to be the case that eminence and name-order positions jointly affect visibility in such a way that occupying visible positions in name-order sequences is important for the young and unknown but less so for scientists whose names are familiar to their colleagues. If so, then there is some isomorphism between the consequences of name ordering and differential concern with the matter. Finally, if name-order positions do not affect visibility in any consistent fashion, they have latent functions for co-workers. Individual collaborators often want symbolic recognition of their unequal contributions, if only to "keep the record straight" and to maintain equity within the group. This may explain why discussions of name ordering are anything but affectively neutral, even when co-workers believe that the published papers are routine.

I have noted that certain patterns of name ordering are variously adopted by eminent men more often than by others, that preferences for name orders differ among fields and among men at different stages of the scientific career.[29]

Since this device serves its purpose only partially, we should expect continuing attempts to modify existing name-order practices—as well as continuing dissatisfaction with them—until other arrangements are devised which integrate more effectively the functional requirements of research groups and of the evaluation system in science.[30]

Notes

1. Revision of a paper read at the Annual Meeting of the American Sociological Association, August 1967. This research was supported by a grant from the National Science Foundation (GS 960) to the Program in the Sociology of Science, Columbia University. I want to thank Robert K. Merton for his guidance and criticism; and Orville G. Brim, Jr., and Norman Storer for their suggestions. An earlier draft of this paper was read at the Laboratory for Socio-Environmental Studies, National Institute of Mental Health. This may be identified as Publication No. A-489 of the Bureau of Applied Social Research, Columbia University.

2. This change in the social organization of scientific work is reflected in the rapid increase of multi-authored publications. About 80 per cent of papers in chemistry are now multi-authored (a four-fold increase since the turn of the century), 60 per cent in physics, and 40 per cent in the biological sciences, in contrast to the one per cent of papers in such humanistic subjects as philosophy, literature and language. See Derek J. deS. Price, *Little Science, Big Science* (New York: Columbia University Press, 1963), pp. 88 ff.; Bernard Berelson, *Graduate Education in the United States* (New York: McGraw-Hill Book Co., 1960), p. 55; Harriet Zuckerman, "Nobel Laureates in the United States: A Sociological Study of Scientific Collaboration" (unpublished Ph.D. dissertation, Columbia University, 1965).

3. For a systematic discussion of the relations between visibility of role-performance, evaluation, and social control, see R. K. Merton, *Social Theory and Social Structure* (New York: The Free Press, 1957), pp. 320 ff.

4. These data are drawn from interviews with 41 of the 55 laureates at work in the United States in 1963. See Zuckerman, *op. cit.*

5. It may be of interest that this study was under way at the very time that Norman Kaplan was observing with regret that "there has been no known systematic study of the norms pertaining to . . . the arrangement of names in multiple-authored papers" ("Sociology of Science," p. 857 in R. E. L. Faris, [ed.], *Handbook of Modern Sociology* [Chicago: Rand McNally & Co., 1964], pp. 852–81).

6. See R. K. Merton, "Priorities in Scientific Discovery: A Chapter in the Sociology of Science," *American Sociological Review,* XXII (December 1957), pp. 635–59, for his analysis of the tension between institutional norms requiring humility and the emphasis placed on making a distinctive contribution to science.

7. Articles listed in *Science Abstracts* (physics), *Chemical Abstracts,* and *Biological Abstracts* were randomly sampled for two years of each decade from 1920 to 1959 and for two years in the period 1960–64. Since multi-authored papers were comparatively rare in the first two decades, these were oversampled. Absolute numbers of papers do not represent actual distributions of multi-authored papers.

8. R. Alpher, H. Bethe, and G. Gamow, "The Origin of Chemical Elements," *Physical Review,* LXXIII (1948), p. 803.

9. There are, of course, variations on this theme. A group consisting of two senior investigators and several junior colleagues may list the names of the senior men first or last and then alphabetize names of the juniors. To simplify coding, these were treated as alphabetically random sequences.

10. Although differences between fields are significant, we are not yet in a position to explain them satisfactorily. Data on the types of collaboration in which laureates have been involved suggest that the rank structure of research groups may account for them. Physicist laureates, for example, are more apt to have worked with peers than are chemists and bioscientists whose groups tend to be comprised of one senior scientist and a number of juniors. Data on the distribution of types of collaborative groups in the fields being considered are needed to test this hypothesis.

11. At the same time, the intent of authors becomes more visible as the number of authors increases. A two-author paper may indeed be alphabetized without this being unambiguously identified as the principle governing the two-item sequence. With three authors, alphabetizing becomes perceptible, and this increases with the number of authors up to a point after which the addition of items does not add extra information. This, of course, is simply a special instance of the Weber-Fechner principle of perception of patterns.

12. Both laureates and the sample of authors listed in abstracts choose the alphabetical order significantly more often than would be expected. $\chi^2 = 50.6$ for laureates, $\chi^2 = 54.6$ for sample, 1 d.f., $p < .001$ for both groups.

13. These are nonetheless the most numerous in absolute terms.

14. $\chi^2 = 163.7$, 4 d.f., $p < .01$. The χ^2

value is inflated by the absolute size of the samples being considered.

15. Differences between the two groups on selection of name-order patterns on papers with fewer than five authors are not significant. χ^2 for four-author papers $= 2.54$, 4 d.f., $p > .10$. For papers with five authors, $\chi^2 = 8.65$, 4 d.f., $p < .10$; and for papers with six or more authors, $\chi^2 = 14.63$, 4 d.f., $p < .01$.

16. Examination of χ^2 computations indicates that the bulk of the difference between the two groups of scientists on papers with five or more authors is concentrated in the differences between them in their tendency to alphabetize; more than 60 per cent of the χ^2 value is due to this difference.

17. In some circles, this convention has become normative; one investigator remarked: "Gentlemen publish with names in alphabetical order" (G. R. Wendt, *Science*, CXLV [July 10, 1964], 110–12).

18. This has become more acute as automated information retrieval systems are designed to keep track of the names of the first two or three authors and to anonymize the others in the category of *et al.*—"that club of scientific unmentionables whom the world is too busy to notice" (Editorial, *Journal of the American Medical Association* [May 11, 1963], p. 497).

19. R. K. Merton, "The Matthew Effect in Science," *Science*, CLIX (January 5, 1968), 56–63.

20. Bibliographies were received from fifty-five of the 123 scientists drawn from *American Men of Science* from whom they were requested, permitting comparison of forty matched pairs of scientists. These pairs were matched in the following respects: (1) Age: Within five years of the laureate's birth date. When more than one bibliography was returned for a particular match, the one closest to the laureate in age was chosen. (2) Field of Specialization as listed in *American Men of Science*. Although the numbers of men in each specialty are the same for the laureates and the matched sample, the proportion of papers are not, since men were not matched for productivity. (3) Type of Organizational Affiliation: classified according to whether they had worked in independent research laboratories, industrial laboratories, or universities. . . . (4) Initial Letter of Last Name: In order to avoid variations in positions in author lists attributable to place in the alphabetical sequence, men in the matched sample were matched to the laureates in this respect. Taking various criteria of eminence, such as receipt of scientific awards, prestige of depart-

ments, or holding editorships or elected positions in scientific organizations, the laureates are, as a group, substantially more eminent than men in the matched sample. However, these men whose names were drawn from *American Men of Science* are probably more distinguished than most scientists, since that directory lists only about a fourth of all scientific workers. Finally, there is no reason to suppose that men who returned their bibliographies differed from those who did not, with respect to name-order practices.

21. Multi-authored papers refer to those having at least three authors, unless otherwise specified. . . .

22. J. Cole and S. Cole, "Visibility and the Structural Bases of Awareness in Science," *American Sociological Review*, XXXIII (June 1968), 387–413.

23. Neither laureates-to-be nor their laureate masters were first-authors on the remaining 24 per cent of papers. This situation is a marked contrast to papers co-authored by scientist peers, both of whom later became laureates. On these papers, one future laureate is just as apt as the other to be first-author in papers having at least three authors. In two-author papers—those with one laureate mentor and one young scientist and later prizewinner—the junior man is first-author 68 per cent of the time, more often than would be expected if no preferences were being exercised.

24. Differences between the two groups cannot be attributed to differences in time elapsed between publication of prizewinning research and the receipt of the prize. Scientists, already eminent at the time of the award, received it nine years on the average after publication, and the others waited more than seven years for the prize to be given.

25. Analysis of eminence and authorship practices of men who received the prize before the age of fifty and after it suggests that eminence is more important than age in shaping authorship decisions. There are a few papers by the very few men who were more than fifty at the time of the prize and not yet eminent. The reward system in science appears to be sufficiently effective to minimize the number of men who have done significant work but have not achieved eminence by the age of fifty.

26. Laureates symbolize their distinctive contributions to prizewinning work more often than on other papers. First, they are slightly less apt to use alphabetical orders in these papers than on other publications—19 per cent as against 26 per cent. More important, they place themselves in highly visible positions on

those papers with name orders which enhance the visibility of a particular author.

27. The difference between the two groups is concentrated in chemistry and the biological sciences for reasons that remain obscure.

28. Although we know that the laureates are, more often than not, the most eminent members of their research groups, we do not know whether this is the case for men in the matched sample. It may be that the most distinguished co-workers of the sample members are last-authors on papers of this type as often as the laureates are. The reported differences in last-authorship are then suggestive, not decisive.

29. Cross-cultural comparisons will show whether these patterns have uniform meanings for the world community of scientists and, in particular, whether the distribution of patterns differs between socialist and other societies.

30. Resistance by physicists to the use of "institutional authorship"—that is, the listing of laboratories rather than individual investigators—suggests that more visibility, rather than less, is desired by scientists. For the comments of one distinguished psysicist on this matter, see S. A. Goudsmit, *Physical Review Letters,* VIII (March 15, 1962), 229–30.

E. Classifications and Typologies

12. Some Remarks on Typological Procedures in Social Research *

PAUL F. LAZARSFELD

EMPIRICAL SOCIAL research produces daily crops of problems which students attempt to solve with out-of-pocket measures. After some time, a body of procedures accumulates; these techniques are handed down until they form a well established methodological tradition. However, it often takes years before these techniques are systematically reviewed with an eye to their logical underpinnings.

A book by Carl G. Hempel and P. Oppenheim "Der Typusbegriff im Licthe der Neuen Logik" (The Concept of Types in the Light of the New Logic) [1] offers such an opportunity. This book attempts to analyze the logic of typological procedures where these procedures are used in the social and natural sciences. Since the establishment of types is one of the recent developments of social research, a systematic discussion of the problems involved is very appropriate. The following discussion attempts to present and to enlarge upon the ideas of Hempel and Oppenheim, applying them to the practical problems of social research. As a result, these remarks are less than a summary, inasmuch as they do not report the whole book, and more than a review, inasmuch as they introduce additional experiences and considerations.

One is safe in saying that the concept of type is always used in referring to special compounds of attributes. In speaking of the midwestern type of American, one may have in mind certain physical features, certain attitudes and habits, certain affiliations and talents attributed to the inhabitants of this region. In speaking of types of books or of types of governments, a special combination of attributes is thrown into relief. Sometimes not all the attributes entering a typological combination can be enumerated. When the psychologist describes the extrovert type, he hopes that subsequent research will find more and more attributes which enter into this particular combination. There can and will be much discussion on how such a special combination of attributes is found, delineated and justified.

* Condensation by Ann Pasanella.

Taken from *Zeitschrift für Sozialforschung,* 6 (1937), pp. 119–39.

First it is necessary to introduce the concept of attribute space. Suppose that for a number of objects, several attributes are taken into consideration. Let it be these three: size, beauty, and the possession of a college degree. It is possible to visualize something very similar to the frame of reference in analytic geometry. The X-axis, for instance, may correspond to size; in this direction, the object can really be measured in inches. The Y-axis may correspond to beauty; in this direction the objects can be arranged in a serial order, so that each object gets a rank designation, rank No. 1 being the most beautiful. The Z-axis may correspond to the academic degree; here each object has or has not a degree. Those two possibilities shall be designated by plus and minus, and shall be represented arbitrarily by two points on the Z-axis on the two opposite sides of the center of the system. Each object is then represented by a certain point in this attribute space, for instance, by the following symbolism: (66; 87; plus;). If the objects to be grouped are the women in a certain sample, then this particular woman would be 5½ feet tall, would rank rather low in a beauty contest, and would have a college degree. To each individual would correspond a certain point in the space (though not every point would correspond to an individual). The reader is invited to familiarize himself by examples of his own with this very useful concept of attribute space; each space will, of course, have as many dimensions as there are attributes in the classifying scheme.

In the frame of an attribute space, the operation of *reduction* can be defined and explained. In order to have a simple example, the case of three characteristics will be discussed first. They might be this: To have $(+)$ or not to have $(-)$ a college degree, to be of white $(+)$ or colored $(-)$ race, and to be native $(+)$ or foreign-born $(-)$ resident of the United States. Evidently only the following eight combinations are possible:

Combination Number	College Degree	White	Native Born
1	+	+	+
2	+	+	−
3	+	−	+
4	+	−	−
5	−	+	+
6	−	+	−
7	−	−	+
8	−	−	−

(thus combination 6 is, for example, the white, foreign-born without a college degree). By reduction is understood any classification as a result of which different combinations fall into one class.

Suppose that one tries to estimate the social advantages which correspond to these eight combinations of college degree, race, and nativity. It is possible (no question of the actual facts shall be implied here) to argue in the following way: To be a Negro is such a disadvantage in this country that college degree and nativity make little difference. Therefore, the combinations 3, 4 and 7, 8 fall into one class of greatest discrimination. For the whites, nativity is much more important than education, because one can substitute self-education for formal training, but one cannot amend foreign birth. Therefore, the combinations 2 and 6 form the next class—the foreign-born white—which is presumably less discriminated against than the Negroes. Among the native-born whites, education may be an important factor. Therefore, a special distinction is introduced between the combinations 1 and 5. Thus an order of social advantage is established: the native white with college degree, the native white without college degree, the foreign-born white irrespective of education, and the Negro irrespective of nativity and education.

By merging some of our original eight combinations, we now have four classes. We have reduced the attribute space.

There are at least three kinds of reduction which should be distinguished:

1. The functional;
2. The arbitrary numerical;
3. The pragmatic.

1. In a functional reduction there exists an actual relationship between two of the attributes which reduces the number of combinations. If, for instance, Negroes cannot acquire college degrees, or if tall girls are always judged more beautiful, certain combinations of variables will not occur in actuality. In this way, the system of combinations is reduced. The elimination of certain combinations can either be complete or these combinations may occur so infrequently that no special class need be established for them.

2. Arbitrary numerical reduction is best exemplified by index numbers. In the analysis of housing conditions, for instance, the following procedure is frequently used: Several items, such as plumbing, central heating, refrigeration, etc., are selected as especially indicative, and each is given a certain weight. Central heating and ownership of a refrigerator, without plumbing, might be equivalent to plumbing without the other two items, and, therefore, both cases get the same index number.

The weights for such a procedure can originate in different ways, of course.

3. In the case of functional reduction, certain combinations are eliminated in view of relationships existing between the variables themselves. In the case of pragmatic reduction, certain groups of combinations are assigned to one class in view of the research purpose. The example of degree-race-nativity, given above, offers such a pragmatic reduction. In considering the concrete problem of discrimination, no distinction was made between the other qualifications of the Negroes, and all were regarded as one class. . . .

Reduction [2] is a grouping of attribute combinations involving more than one attribute. To make the matter quite clear, we can examine the simplest case, two attributes, x and y, both of which might be visualized as ranks. Take, for example, the situation in which a large sample of married couples are studied with respect to two variables: (1) the attitude of the wives toward their husbands and (2) the economic success of the husband. y, the attitude of the wife, is ranked from very favorable to distinctly unfavorable and x, the success of the husband, is ranked from very great to very little. It would be possible to set up three grades for each variable, designated as high, medium, and low. As a result, there would be nine possible combinations of attitude and success. As yet, no reductions have taken place. Suppose, however, that as a result of a further analysis, we find that if the wife's attitude toward the husband is favorable, then the economic success will not influence marital relations, whereas, if the wife has only a medium attitude toward him, he needs at least medium success to make the marriage a success, and only great success can save the marriage if the wife's attitude is altogether unfavorable. If the problem is to classify all the marriages in two groups—one for which the attitude-success combinations are favorable for good marital relations, and one for which the combinations are unfavorable—the diagram of a reduction on p. 102 would ensue.

If one keeps to the more geometrical representation of these combinations he would say that the combinations resulting from a reduction always "turn the corner," because they involve more than one axis. . . .

It is by no means alleged that typological systems ought to originate in such a combination procedure as has been exemplified

X: Economic success of husband

so far. Quite the contrary, it would be very worthwhile to analyze the different ways and means by which types have been established in different fields of research. The only claim made here is that once a system of types has been established by a research expert, it can always be proved that, in its logical structure, it could be the result of a reduction of an attribute space.

This procedure of finding, for a given system of types, the attribute space in which it belongs and the reduction that has been implicitly used is of such practical importance that it should have a special name; the term *substruction* is suggested.

When substructing to a given system of types the attribute space from which, and the reduction through which it could be deduced, it is never assumed that the creator of the types really had such a procedure in mind. It is only claimed that, no matter how he actually found the types, he could have found them logically by such a substruction. . . .

The most common use of types is made when a writer gives an impressionistic classification of the material he has at hand. Here is a student who groups different types of criminals, another who classifies reasons for marital discord, a third one who deals with types of radio programs, and so on. These types are conceived as expedient tools and serve the study if they yield a

valuable numerical distribution or correlation with other factors. . . .

Whenever a writer uses such a typological classification, he should substruct to it a corresponding attribute space and the reduction connected therewith, in order to be aware of what is logically implied in his enumeration of types. There would be many advantages in this discipline. The writer would see whether he has overlooked certain cases, he could make sure that some of his types are not overlapping, and he would probably make the classification more valuable for actual empirical research. This practical value of a substruction deserves special attention. If a student invents types of family discord, his contribution is valuable only if in any concrete case it is possible to say whether the given discord belongs to a certain type or not. For this purpose, criteria have to be worked out. These criteria, in general, point directly to the attribute space from which the type was reduced. Therefore, the substruction of the adequate attribute combinations to a given system of types adapts them better to actual research purposes.

As an example, there is reported here an adventure in substruction which summarizes once more all the points made so far. For a study of the structure of authority in the family, conducted by the International Institute of Social Research, a questionnaire was devised pertaining to authoritarian relations between parents and children. E. Fromm, the director of the study, suggested as a theoretical basis in outlining the study, four types of authoritarian situations:

> Complete authority;
> Simple authority;
> Lack of authority;
> Rebellion.

By using the procedures of reduction and substruction, it was possible to attain a thorough research procedure, and at the same time to exhaust all possible significance of Fromm's types.

An authoritarian situation in a family is determined by the way the parents exercise their authority, by the way in which the children accept it, and by the interrelations between exercise and acceptance. Two main categories in the questionnaire covered the matter of exercise: Questions were asked to discover whether parents used corporal punishment and whether they interfered with such activities as recreation, church attendance, etc. Two groups of indices were used in regard to acceptance: The children were asked if they had confidence in their parents, and whether conflicts with them in various fields of activity were frequent. Each index had two possible scores: high $(+)$ and low $(-)$. By this means, the following four combinations were reached:

Corporal Punishment

Interference	$+$	$-$
$+$	1	2
$-$	3	4

It was then possible to reduce this scheme to a rough one-dimensional order of intensity of exercise. The combination No. 1 (corporal punishment is used and interference is frequent) is apparently the strongest form and No. 4, the weakest. The type in which corporal punishment is used but no interference in the child's activities was attempted (No. 3) can be eliminated as practically contradictory. The combination No. 2 was left to describe a moderate degree of exercise. These three combinations, plus-plus, minus-minus, and minus-plus, can then be reduced to a one-dimensional order, X, Y and Z, with X as the strongest degree.

The same procedure may be applied to the indices pertaining to acceptance of authority:

Conflicts

Confidence	$+$	$-$
$+$	1	2
$-$	3	4

Combination No. 2 (absence of conflicts and existence of confidence) is readily seen to be the highest degree of acceptance. The inverse combination, No. 3, is the weakest. The combination No. 1 can practically be disregarded as confidence will hardly co-exist with persistent conflicts.[3] The combination minus-minus (no conflicts and no confidence) is roughly a median grade. The three grades of acceptance are then labeled A, B, and C, with A as the highest degree.

Here two separate reductions have been carried through: The two-dimensional space consisting of corporal punishment and interference has been reduced to one dimension "exercise of authority." In the same way, conflict and confidence were reduced to "acceptance of authority."

A further step leads to the drawing of a chart which constitutes the attribute space into which the four initial types of authority will have to be placed. It turns out that nine combinations are logically possible, while Fromm suggested only four types. By the procedure of substruction, the last scheme will have to be matched with Fromm's types (which were, of course, conceived in a wholly different way).

Exercise	*Acceptance*		
	A	B	C
X	1	2	3
Y	4	5	6
Z	7	8	9

It may be assumed that Fromm's type "complete authority" is covered by the combinations 1 and 2. Simple authority is covered by combinations 4 and 5. The lack of authority is represented by combination 8 and rebellion by 3 and 6. For greater clarity the substruction is repeated in another form:

in concrete applications which lie beyond the scope of the present exemplification.

It may again be stressed strongly that this whole analysis does not limit the research man in the actual sequence of his work. It is by no means postulated that he should start by deciding what attributes he wants to use, then proceed with the reduction, and so finally get his system of types. Often, especially if many attributes are at stake, it might be much better for the student to become deeply acquainted with his material and then bring order into it by first blocking out a few main types on a completely impressionistic basis. Only

Combination	Type	Exercise	Acceptance
1 and 2	Complete authority	Strong (*X*)	Voluntarily accepted (A) or just accepted (B)
4 and 5	Simple authority	Medium (*Y*)	Voluntarily accepted (A) or just accepted (B)
8	Lack of authority	Weak (*Z*)	Just accepted (B)
3 and 6	Rebellion	Strong (*X*) or medium (*Y*)	Refused (C)

Combinations 7 and 9 are not covered. Apparently it was assumed that neither voluntary acceptance nor rebellion against an authority which is scarcely exercised is possible. The substruction, however, may be used as a tool for discovery. It discloses the possibility that children might long for an authority which no one offers them. These discovered combinations suggest further research.

The reader may disagree with the above substruction and may think that other combinations should be matched with Fromm's types. Then he may try to improve the types on the basis of the general scheme suggested above. He will see for himself that the procedure of substruction can lead to improvements in typologies which have been construed on the basis of theoretical considerations or intuitions. The proof of the success of the procedure lies, of course,

thereafter would he reconsider the matter and substruct to his own typological intuitions an adequate attribute space and bring into relief the reduction which he has used implicitly. The best results probably will be gained in just this combination of a first general survey and a subsequent systematic analysis. The elaborate example just given provides a good illustration.

The problem comes up whether to every given system of types there corresponds only one attribute space and one mode of reduction. The answer is probably "no." The typological classifications used in current social research are somewhat vague and, therefore, more than one logical substruction can usually be provided for them. The different attribute spaces originating from these substructions can be transformed one into another, however. The procedure of transformation is very important because it is the logical background of what is generally termed "an interpretation of a statistical result." It could be shown that such an interpretation is often nothing more than transforming a system of types from one attribute space into another with different coordinates, and therewith changing simultaneously one reduction into another. There is no opportunity here to discuss this question beyond giving one example.

Several hundred pupils were grouped in a rough way, according to their physical development and according to their scholastic achievements. Combinations of these two attributes yielded five rather distinct empirical types. The physically underdeveloped children were either especially bright or especially unsuccessful. The same was true for well developed children; most of them also appeared among the two scholastic extremes. The children of medium physical development were, on the whole, medium in their scholastic achievement as well. Relatively few children were of medium physical development and especially good or bad in their school work; and relatively few children of unusually good or bad physical condition were medium in their ability in school.

The result was interpreted in the following terms. Among the physically underdeveloped children there are two types: those who were too handicapped to be successful in school; those who overcompensated for their physical weakness and did especially well in school. Every teacher knows those two types from his own experience. Among the especially well developed children, one group was the all-around type, combining mental with physical maturity. The other group was the "hoodlum" type which, on the basis of strength, has such a good position in class that it does not consider it necessary to make an effort in school work. If this interpretation is analyzed in the light of the previous considerations, it turns out that these types can be described in two completely different

sets of dimensions. Instead of the original attributes of physical and mental developments, new terms are used. These are overcompensations, parallelism between physical and mental activity, and peer recognition versus peer neglect. Such an interpretation consists logically of substructing to a system of types an attribute space different from the one in which it was derived by reduction, and of looking for the reductions which would lead to the system of types in this new space. That is what transformation means.

The operations of reduction, substruction, and transformation could be called "typological operations," because their application links any system of types with an attribute space. (We use the word "type" for those systems where more than one attribute is at stake and where the reductions cut across the axis of the attribute space.) The logic of these typological operations has not been given enough attention so far; its careful study could improve considerably the use of types in practical research.

These remarks have been mainly concerned with illustrating those typological operations. The focus was the reduction of an attribute space to a system of types. Three kinds of reduction were distinguished: the functional, the arbitrary numerical, and the pragmatic. The latter is the most important in empirical research; its inversion is called substruction. Substruction consists of matching a given system of types with that attribute space and that reduction from which it could have originated logically. This substruction of an attribute combination to a given system of types permits one to check the omissions or overlappings in this system and points the way to its practical applications.

Notes

1. A. W. Siythoff, W. V. Leiden, 1936.

2. The first two procedures of reduction and the concept of reduction itself are clearly dis-

cussed by Hempel and Oppenheim. They lay much less stress upon them, however, than is given in these remarks. In a logical analysis of typological operations, the process of reduction ought to have a commanding place.

When it comes to empirical social research, pragmatic reduction overshadows the other two kinds. Hempel and Oppenheim have not included it in their analysis. The desire to discuss the method of pragmatic reduction has given rise to the present paper.

3. If a few such cases come up, they might first be eliminated or else lumped together with the moderate degree of acceptance. Later, they might be studied separately.

13. Binary Attributes of Phonemes

COLIN CHERRY

[Ed. Note: The following selection is drawn from an essay on language by a professor of telecommunication. His concern here is with the classification of speech sounds. Cherry notes that any sound may be pictorially represented in an attribute space, treating each sound as binary (present or absent). The author selects the distinctive features of speech sounds, indicates how each sound can potentially be located in a multidimensional attribute space, and suggests how reduction can occur through elimination of logically contradictory types.]

Distinctive Feature; Binary Attributes of Phonemes

MUSIC HAS BOTH a melodic and an harmonic structure, the melody being a time sequence of sounds and the harmony a set of simultaneous sounds. By analogy, speech may be regarded as a stream of sound, segmented into a time sequence of phonemes for purposes of linguistic analysis; or it may well be viewed as a series of concurrent activities corresponding to muscular control of the vocal cavities, the larynx, lips, tongue, and teeth. The linguist's transcription then has some likeness to a musical score; the phonemes represented by a sequence of chords, conveying not a single melodic line but a four-, six-, or greater, part "harmony." Such analogy is little more than simile but, to continue with the comparison, the notes of a chord are like the attributes of a phoneme. A phoneme may be regarded as a chord, or bundle, of attributes.

Human speech is produced by a living apparatus of extraordinary complexity, flexibility, and effectiveness; it is surpassed in delicacy and precision only by the ear. Both are, as "engineering products," built of the most unpromising materials—tissue and bone! When we speak, a complex musculature comes into play, operated by neural controls, which mold and move the cavities of the mouth, the lips, and tongue, set the chords of the larynx buzzing, open the nasal cavity to the throat by raising the velum, and adjust the parting of the teeth— all with the greatest precision. Speech is

Reprinted in part with permission from "On Signs, Language, and Communication," in *On Human Communication: A Review, A Survey, and a Criticism,* 2nd Ed. (Cambridge, Mass.: The M.I.T. Press, 1966), pp. 92–96 (copyright 1957, 1966 by the Massachusetts Institute of Technology).

then formed by a number of concurrent activities.

We intuitively detect certain attributes of speech sounds with readiness; the buzzing vibrations of the chords of the larynx, called *voicing,* heard during all English vowels (h*a*rd, m*oo*n, s*ee,* etc.) and in certain consonants (z, v, etc.); the hissing breath sounds (as in h*a*rd, *sh*ort, *th*ink, etc.); the explosive sounds like *b*oy, *d*ay, *p*ink, etc.); the nasal quality (which appears in *m*ore, *n*ew, si*ng,* etc.). Other characteristics of speech sounds are less prominent, but still important.

Classification of the various sounds, based upon such evident characteristics, was carried out by the Hindus as early as 300 B.C. Modern phonetics owes the greatest debt to ancient Indian inquiry into the nature of speech—work carried out to a great extent prior to Greek science, which itself accomplished very little in this field. In particular, the Hindus had identified certain phonetic elements such as vowels, fricatives, continuants, and stops; furthermore they had achieved some measure of classification into characteristic forms of articulation—*closure, opening, constriction, voicing, aspiration, nasality*—and to some extent they had the notion of binary oppositions.

The interesting feature of this description is that it was in part binary, though not quite. The first linguists to present a fully binary description of phonemes were Roman Jakobson and his collaborators.

It is not our business here to discuss or even to comment upon the particular set of attributes of phonemes which were in fact chosen for this binary classification; many different sets might have been used, but this one has advantages in two respects: it is correlated fairly closely to the articulatory process and, as a logical description, it is quite efficient. There is no question of a *unique* set; the problem is a practical one, that of describing and distinguishing between the phonemic stocks of the various languages.

The attributes chosen by Jakobson and his associates [1] have been called *distinctive features;* they distinguish 12 such features, or binary oppositions, which "we may detect in the languages of the world and which underlie their entire lexical and morphological stock. . . . " They name them: (1) vocalic/nonvocalic, (2) consonantal/nonconsonantal, (3) interrupted/continuant, (4) checked/unchecked, (5) strident/mellow, (6) voiced/unvoiced, (7) compact/diffuse, (8) grave/acute, (9) flat/plain, (10) sharp/plain, (11) tense/lax, (12) nasal/oral. Such features may be regarded as forming a set of orthogonal axes of an attribute space (phonemic feature space) . . . the various phonemes are then representable by cubic cells lying in a hyperspace of 12 dimensions. Of course, we cannot visualize such a space, but the idea may be illustrated by a three-dimensional projection, as in Figure 1. But we may calculate the number of cubic cells contained in a twelve-dimensional space and thus the number of phonemes which may be represented distinguishably in such a space. Each attribute (or feature) has two possible states, so that N features may have $2N$ states. In our present case, $N = 12$, and a set of 12 features could serve to distinguish 4096 different phonemes, if called upon to do so. Such a complete system of features enables us, in principle, to describe the phonemes of any language; but when restricted to one particular language, the full freedom of choices is not employed. Most languages use only a few dozen phonemes. English may be considered to contain 28, if the prosodic features are excluded (or about 40 otherwise). For describing the phonemes of any one language then, the 12 feature oppositions offer a highly redundant set of attributes.

As a useful alternative to the hyperspace model, the feature system may be illustrated in tabular form. Figure 2 represents

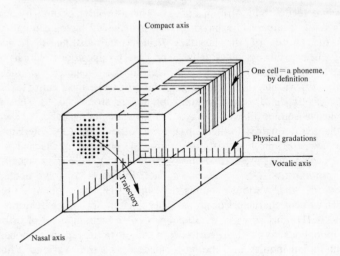

FIGURE 1. "Features" as "general coordinates." Phonemes as quantal cells, and speech as trajectory of system points. Only three features can, of course, be illustrated.

a phoneme feature pattern of English (Received Pronunciation); in this diagram the binary signs, $+$, $-$, relate to the various oppositions: vocalic/nonvocalic, consonantal/nonconsonantal, interrupted/continuant, and so on. It will be seen that a number of spaces are left blank; these correspond to *redundant* features, to questions which do not have to be answered. It is important to appreciate that such a table does not tell us precise *sounds;* rather it represents a cipher which describes the minimal distinctions between the various phonemes. Just because one feature opposition is left blank, such as the nasal-oral feature of all the vowel phonemes, this does not mean that English speakers necessarily differ in their nasalizing of their vowel sounds. It implies rather that we do not need to know whether or not they do, to be able to identify the vowels, provided that we know certain other features (numbers 1 to 5 in the example). The table as shown represents a cipher of *minimal distinctive*

features; examination will quickly show that each phoneme is distinguished from every other by its binary chain of $+$, $-$ feature oppositions, and that the distinction is everywhere at least one feature opposition. For example, /b/ and /d/ differ only in the grave/acute feature; similarly /s/ and /z/ correspond to the single opposition tense/lax. On the other hand, /b/ and /t/ differ by two feature oppositions; /t/ and /v/ by three.

The minimal distinctions between words may also be defined in terms of these oppositions. If we take the word *bill* and commute the initial phoneme /b/ with various others to form different words in the English language, we could draw up the list: bill, pill, vill, fill, mill, dill, till, thill, sill, nil, gill/gil/, kill, gill/zil/, chill, hill, ill, rill, will. The minimal distinction between any pair is then expressible in terms of feature oppositions.

This "logical" feature description of phonemes may be interpreted as a set of rules

	o	a	e	u	ə	i	l	ŋ	ʃ	ʧ	k	ʒ	ʤ	g	m	f	p	v	b	n	s	θ	t	z	ð	d	h
1. Vocalic/nonvocalic	+	+	+	+	+	+	+	−	−	−	−	−	−	−	−	−	−	−	−	−	−	−	−	−	−	−	−
2. Consonantal/nonconsonantal	−	−	−	−	−	−	+	+	+	+	+	+	+	+	+	+	+	+	+	+	+	+	+	+	+	+	+
3. Compact/diffuse	+	+	+	−	−	−		+	+	+	+	+	+	+	−	−	−	−	−	−	−	−	−	−	−	−	+
4. Grave/acute	+	−	−	+	−	−		+	−	−	+	−	−	+	+	+	+	+	+	−	−	−	−	−	−	−	+
5. Flat/plain	+	−	−	+		−			+			+															
6. Nasal/oral								+							+					+							
7. Tense/lax	+	−	+	+	−	+			+	+	+	−	−	−		+	+	−	−		+	+	+	−	−	−	+
8. Continuant/interrupted									+	−	−	+	−	−		+	−	+	−		+	+	−	+	+	−	+
9. Strident/mellow									+	+	−	+	+	−		+	−	+	−		+	−		+	−		

FIGURE 2.   The phoneme pattern of English (Received Pronunciation) after Jakobson, Fant, and Halle. Key to phonemic transcription: /o/-pot, /a/-pat, /e/-pet, /u/-putt, /i/-pit, /ə/-putt, /l/-lull, /ŋ/-lung, /ʃ/-ship, /ʧ/-chip, /k/-kip, /ʒ/-azure, /ʤ/-juice, /g/-goose, /m/-mill, /f/-fill, /p/-pill, /v/-vim, /b/-bill, /n/-nill, /s/-sill, /θ/-thill, /t/-till, /z/-zip, /ð/-this, /d/-dill, /h/-hill. The prosodic opposition, stressed vs. unstressed, splits each of the vowel phonemes into two.

—linguistic rules, which a speaker must obey if he is to conform to the language. Of course, he is not normally aware of such rules of language. Rules are expressed in meta-language; the speaker may be described *as though* he obeys such rules.

It may be of interest to note that the blank spaces in Figure 2, corresponding to redundant feature questions, do not really make this cipher a three-valued one, because these questions need not be given +, − (yes-no) answers; consequently the feature description is strictly a binary one. It can be shown that all these blank spaces may be eliminated by a simple transformation of the ordering of the feature oppositions.

Of course, the whole success and value of this distinctive-feature concept depends upon the choice of the features, the attributes of phonemes, and the possibility of basing these on some kind of physical measurements. As they have been set out here, they are derived essentially from the linguist's accumulated experience of the world's languages and their phonetic structures. Such experience may well be correlated eventually with physical acoustic measurements, and specifications; this work is still proceeding. As stressed at the commencement of this section, the list of feature oppositions is chosen empirically, to serve an essentially practical purpose in as simple a manner as possible; the features or attributes of phonemes are no more unique or absolute than are the attributes chosen for other descriptions—such as the height, weight, age, girth and so on which we choose for distinguishing between men. The attributes are chosen in both cases to bear some correlation with "natural" physical data which have been singled out for other purposes in the past.

Note

1. A full treatment of the "distinctive feature" theory of Professor Roman Jakobson is to be presented in his forthcoming book in this series, *Sound and Meaning*.

14. A Typology of Disposition Concepts

PAUL F. LAZARSFELD

[Ed. Note: The following excerpt is taken from an article in which the author proposes empirical studies of economic behavior as a fruitful way of studying the relationships between individuals and their social environment. The author states that before such an analysis can be undertaken, a classification of individual "disposition concepts" is needed. His suggestion for such a typology is included below.]

A Digression on Disposition Concepts

BEFORE GOING further, the role of dispositions in empirical action analysis has to be clarified. . . . No general classification of disposition concepts exists. An author is usually interested in one of them; he tries to define it carefully and then gives a list of comparisons with "related concepts." . . . The literature along this line is practically endless.

But, by starting from shifting linguistic usages, one misses just those distinctions which lead to essential variations in research procedures and in interpretations. It is more fruitful to bring out the dimensions along which distinctions have been proposed so that the intent of various authors becomes more comparable and the terminology loses its importance. A scrutiny of various texts shows that three dimensions dominate the discussion. One is generality and specificity (e.g., a personality trait that can be exhibited in many substantive spheres versus an interest usually directed toward a limited object). Another may be described as degree of directiveness (e.g., an attitude toward versus a desire for something, the former being more of the passive, the second more of the driving kind). A third dimension relates to the time perspective (e.g., a plan or an expectation spans the future; an urge or a perceptual bias focuses on the present). If we dichotomize these three dimensions of substantive scope, dynamics, and time range, we get eight combinations which can serve classificatory purposes and at the same time show what other aspects are involved in the linguistic tradition of these disposition concepts (Figure 1). (In a more detailed discussion the three dimensions would be treated as continuous, so that finer distinctions could be made).

Most terms have been used differently by various authors, and most readers will attach their own private associations to them. This should be remembered in reading a few examples that illustrate the relatively simple three-dimensional scheme, which for our purpose seems useful.

1. *Preferences* as for specific foods and *opinions* on specific issues are specific, passive, and current.
2. *Traits* like broad-mindedness, more general *attitudes* like economic liberalism, as well as such "frames of reference" as looking at issues from a "businessman's point of view" are general, passive, and current.
3. What are usually called *wants* or *needs,* like being hungry or looking

Reprinted in part with permission from "Reflections on Business," the *American Journal of Sociology,* 65 (July 1959) pp. 8–10.

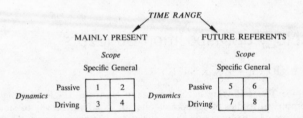

for a new car to replace a worn-out one, are specific, driving, and current.

4. More *directional traits* like vitality and energy or aggressiveness may be described as general, driving, and current.

5. *Expectations* as to future prices and customer demands that are important in modern economic analysis are typical examples of the specific, passive, and future-oriented dispositions.

6. *Tendencies* to consider longer chains of possible consequences and *inclinations* like optimism come to mind as examples of the more general, passive, and future-oriented dispositions.

7. Investment *intentions,* occupational *plans,* and schemes for getting promoted to an impending executive vacancy may be described as specific, driving, and future-oriented.

8. The ubiquitous term "motivation" should become less ambiguous here. In the present paper I shall restrict the term "motivation" to a disposition of rather *general scope* and with the implication that it *directs* its bearer toward activities that bridge the present and the *future.*

Type 8 is the one most relevant for many purposes, but, as a by-product, a number of worthwhile distinctions can be suggested. Types 2, 4, and 6 are usually lumped together as traits. We can assume that businessmen are more conservative

(type 2) than, say, university professors and more energetic (type 4). Whether the businessmen are more optimistic as to future events (type 6) than professors is hard to guess and might change according to circumstances. The specific (odd-numbered) dispositions are more pertinent in the present context. Types 5 and 7, expectations and plans, have acquired importance in econometric studies of business intentions. They can both be introduced as variables in time-series studies. There the double role of time becomes especially clear. For any expectation we have to know at what time it is held and to what future period it refers. The relation between the "passive" expectation and the "driving" plan is complex. While plans lead to action, expectations affect plans; we know from voting studies that intentions often color expectations. Type 3, wants or needs, are traditional in consumer studies. Types 5 and 7 often seem more accessible to simple interviews than type 3; the latter were the entering wedge for projective techniques. Type 1 includes the typical objects of polls.

Thus we see that even this simple classification of dispositions leads to differences in problems and research techniques which can be derived from the position of the types in the dimensional scheme. Additional variations can be handled more casually because they do not seem to be of much consequence for our subject matter; this holds for the means-end relation, for instance, and the separation of a state (angry) from a trait (irascible). The distinction between physiological and culturally induced wants hardly applies to a modern business analysis. But one other complication has to be introduced. It came about when anthropologists and sociologists began to scan these concepts of disposition. A goal may be pursued or a selection made with or without the feeling that doing so is morally desirable or will be socially rewarded. This leads to the notion of norm or value. All the categories listed above can take on a normative element, although some may do so more easily than others. Intentions (type 7) and wants (type 3) seem to be more often "affected by public interest" than expectations (type 5) and frames of reference (type 2). For most purposes it is enough to refer to the normative element when needed, without doubling the terminology.

Every one of the eight types of dispositions can become a motive in the study of specific acts. One finds in the literature statements to the effect that people are motivated by optimism, by a specific goal, by a cultural orientation, by an expectation, etc. Inasmuch as these refer to concrete acts where the causal role of any of the dispositions is assessed, the phrasing is consistent with our terminology. The term "motivation," on the other hand, should be reserved for a rather broad, driving, and future-oriented disposition of type 8 in our scheme. Often it is used in a much broader and looser sense, sometimes being applied to all dispositions, sometimes to all those of great scope or all those with strong directive implications. . . . We use the term to refer to a described disposition which at best has a good probability of becoming a motive in a specific act.

Auxiliary Readings

A. General Theory

P. F. Lazarsfeld, "Evidence and Inference in Social Research," *Daedalus*, 87 (1958), No. 4, pp. 100–105.

Traces the flow from concepts to empirical indices. Specifies and exemplifies four stages: imagery; concept specification; selection of indicators; and formation of indices. These stages form the foundation for development of variate language.

B. Dimensional Clarification and Choice of Indicators

C. Y. Glock, "The religious revival in America?" pp. 25–42 in The University of California, *Religion and the Face of America* (Berkeley: University of California University extension).

Notes that the question of whether religiousness has increased, declined, or remained stable since World War II is unanswerable without prior clarification of the concept. Differentiates four dimensions of religiousness—the experiential, the ritualistic, the ideological, and the consequential. Suggests appropriate indicators for each dimension, distinguishing between indicators of degree and indicators of kind, and suggesting types of indicators appropriate for collectives, as distinguished from individuals. The data relevant to these dimensions are then evaluated.

E. J. Webb, D. T. Campbell, R. D. Schwartz, and L. Sechrest, *Unobtrusive Measures: Nonreactive Research in the Social Sciences* (Chicago: Rand McNally and Co.), 1966.

While social psychological indicators are typically based upon individual responses, the authors draw attention to a wide range of other types of social science indicators, often from unexpected sources. Ingenious indicators may be found in physical traces, archives (running records and episodic and private records), simple observations, and contrived observations.

L. J. Cronbach and P. E. Meehl, "Construct Validity in Psychological Tests," *Psychological Bulletin*, 52 (May 1955), pp. 281–302.

Holds the view that construct validity is employed when no criterion measure is available. Other kinds of evidence are then brought to bear to assess the validity of the concept, such as studies of group differences, factor analysis, studies of internal structure, studies of change, and studies of process. Construct validity rests on a theoretical base; the authors explicate the logic through the concept of the "nomological net."

R. Blauner, *Alienation and Freedom* (Chicago: University of Chicago Press), 1964.

Blauner's main thesis is that a worker's feeling of alienation depends very much upon the kind of organization within which he works. It is not correct to assume that all factory conditions automatically give rise to the same levels of dissatisfaction. Empirical data from four industries showed that assembly line automobile workers felt most alienated, printers, least so. Alienation itself was conceived of as a four-dimensional concept: powerlessness to control the work process; meaninglessness of one's own job in relation to the total; isolation from fellow workers; and lack of self-fulfillment through work. Blauner does not develop specific scales for these; he uses the dimensions skillfully to organize a great diversity of indicators that characterize typical work situations in the four industries he selected.

D. T. Campbell and D. W. Fiske, "Convergent and Discriminant Validation by the Multitrait-Multimethod Matrix," *Psychological Bulletin,* 56 (March 1959), pp. 81–105.
Convergent validation refers to the validation of a new measure of a concept by examining its association with another measure of the same concept. The authors propose the additional requirement of *discriminant* validation. It is argued that the measure should correlate more highly with another measure of the same concept using a different method than with a measure of a different concept using the same method. Typical examples from the literature are presented, showing that they frequently fall short of these requirements.

C. Index Formation

L. A. Free and H. Cantril, *The Political Beliefs of Americans: A Study of Public Opinion* (New Brunswick, N. J.: Rutgers University Press, 1967), pp. 13–58.
Two nationwide studies of attitudes toward a variety of national and international issues were conducted in the fall of 1964. The salience of liberalism and conservatism was heightened at the time by the Johnson-Goldwater election campaign. In the section cited, two itemized indices are developed: an "Operational Spectrum," based on six items dealing with the use of Federal power and resources for the public welfare, and an "Ideological Spectrum," a five-item index dealing with acceptance of the conservative ideology. The relationship of these itemized indices to one another and to certain demographic characteristics is presented.

H. Zeisel, *Say It With Figures,* 4th ed. (New York: Harper and Row, 1957), pp. 110–14.
Describes the surprisingly large number and variety of parametric indices that can be developed from simple sociometric data using measures of central tendency, dispersion, and association. Seven group members are asked to indicate their acceptance or rejection of one another. From these data it is possible to index group acceptance of each member (mean score received); degree of unanimity in group attitudes (average deviation from mean score received); "active sociability" of each member (mean score expressed); discrimination in acceptance of others (average deviation from mean score expressed); reciprocation of others' feelings (correlation between scores expressed and scores received); and many other indices.

S. A. Stouffer, *Communism, Conformity and Civil Liberties* (Garden City, N. Y.: Doubleday and Co.), 1955, pp. 262–66.
A nationwide study of attitudes toward civil liberties was undertaken during the McCarthy era. A variety of indicators of "willingness to tolerate noncomformists" was found to have a cumulative property, such that acceptance of a position on "stronger" items was predictive of acceptance of that position on "weaker" items. The author employed the device of "contrived items" to improve the Guttman scale.

P. M. Blau, "Operationalizing a Conceptual Scheme: The Universalism-Particularism Pattern Variable," *American Sociological Review,* 27 (April 1962), pp. 159–69.
A standard is particularistic if persons select others who share their own characteristics; if choices are made regardless of one's own characteristics, the standard is universalistic. The measurement of universalism-particularism within a collective is thus based on a "who-to-whom" matrix of choices based on the characteristics of chooser and chosen.

D. The Theory of Indices

H. Jacob, "The Consequences of Malapportionment: A Note of Caution," *Social Forces,* 43, No. 2 (1964), pp. 256–61.

Various weaknesses and defects of state governments have been attributed to legislative malapportionment. The author has selected three reasonable indices of malapportionment; the Spearman Rank Order Correlation Coefficients among them range from .63–.69. Each index, however, shows similar relationships to a number of alleged consequences of malapportionment.

E. P. Hollander and W. B. Webb, 1964. "Comparison of Three Morale Measures: A Survey, Pooled Group Judgments, and Self-Evaluations," pp. 139–47 in E. P. Hollander (ed.), *Leaders, Groups, and Influence* (New York: Oxford University Press, 1964).

The concept of "morale" has been indexed in a wide variety of ways by social scientists. The authors compare three measures of morale in the same sample, examine the relationships among the three measures, and relate each to the behavioral criterion of morale. Although the correlations among the morale measures are not high, two of the measures are "interchangeable," i.e., predict almost identically to the criterion; the third does not.

E. F. Jackson, "Status Consistency and Symptoms of Stress," *American Sociological Review,* 19 (August 1962), pp. 469–80.

Challenging the assumption that social status is a unidimensional continuum, the author specifies three status dimensions on which people can be ranked: occupation, education, and racial-ethnic background. The similarity or dissimilarity of rank among these three dimensions generates a new unidimensional continuum, viz., degree of "status consistency."

E. Classifications and Typologies

R. F. Bales, 1951. *Interaction Process Analysis* (Cambridge, Massachusetts: Addison-Wesley, 1951), Chapter 1, Appendix.

Interaction Process Analysis represents an ambitious attempt to develop a *general* set of categories which will appropriately encompass the highly complex interaction that takes place in discussion groups. In this book the author provides a detailed discussion of mechanical procedures for recording interaction, the theoretical rationale for the categories, problems of observer reliability and training, index formation, analysis, etc. The recommended sections discuss the nature of the 12 interaction categories and provide detailed coding instructions for the data.

D. McClelland, J. Atkinson, R. A. Clark, and E. L. Lovell, "Scoring of the Thematic Apperception Test," Chapter 4 in *The Achievement Motive* (New York: Appleton-Century-Crofts, 1953).

Indicators of the concept "achievement motivation" are sought in reactions to semi-structured stimuli. The subject is asked to make up a story in response to a vaguely adumbrated picture. When appropriately classified, the stories serve as indicators of the underlying motive of achievement.

J. K. Hemphill, Griffiths, D. E., and N. Fredericksen, "Scoring the in-baskets," Chapter 6 in *Administrative Performance and Personality: A Study of the Principal in a Simulated Elementary School* (New York: Teachers College, Columbia University, 1962).

The basic material to be classified was a large number of handwritten documents, such as letters, memoranda, agenda, calendars, and self-reminders. Two general categories were distinguished: *content* of performance (*what* is done) and *style* of performance (*how* it is done). The procedure involved working back and forth between theoretical concepts and empirical materials to produce the most parsimonious, complete, and theoretically meaningful coding categories.

I. L. Child, E. H. Potter, and E. M. Levine, "Children's Textbooks and Personality Development: An Exploration in the Social Psychology of Education," *Psychological Monographs,* 60, No. 3 (1946).

A content analysis of third grade readers, classified according to character, behavior, circumstances, consequences, and types of stories. The investigators are able to specify which types of behavior (using Murray's categories), engaged in by characters (boys, girls, men, women, animals, supernatural creatures), have certain consequences (reward or punishment). A powerful example of role socialization and normative indoctrination.

B. Berelson and P. J. Salter, 1946. "Majority and Minority Americans: An Analysis of Magazine Fiction," *Public Opinion Quarterly,* 10 (Summer 1946), pp. 168–90.

A content analysis of popular magazine fiction during the 1937–1943 period reveals the implicit ethnic prejudice of the stories. Story characters are classified according to their roles (e.g., major, minor; hero, villain); status (occupation, education, etc.); social origin (nationality, race, religion); plus-minus position (approval-disapproval, sympathy-hostility, etc.); and other qualities. The majority group appears as more important, attractive, likeable, possessing superior status and values, etc. Implicitly, ethnic stereotypes are perpetuated in this fiction.

C. Hempel, "Fundamentals of Taxonomy," pp. 137–54 in *Aspects of Scientific Explanation* (New York: The Free Press, 1965).

A philosopher of science discusses current taxonomy of mental disorders. Noting that most scientific classification evolves from the descriptive to the theoretical, Hempel sees a similar development in medical science from the symptomatological to the etiological. Notes certain problems in psychiatric classification, such as concepts with valuational overtones, need for interpretation of instruments, and subjectivity in classification. Hempel predicts two future developments in the classification of mental disorders: a shift from systems defined by reference to observable characteristics to systems based on theoretical concepts, and a shift from *classificatory* concepts and methods to *ordering* concepts.

B. Kass, 1949. "Overlapping Magazine Reading: A New Method of Determining the Cultural Levels of Magazines," in P. F. Lazarsfeld and F. M. Stanton (eds.), *Communications Research, 1948–1949* (New York: Harper and Brothers).

An ingenious device for measuring the cultural level of magazines through the study of overlapping magazine reading. The assumption is made that magazines read in combination will tend to be culturally proximate. A procedure for analyzing the correlation matrix is presented which enables one to rank the magazines along the cultural level continuum.

M. Rosenberg, *Occupations and Values* (New York: The Free Press, 1957), pp. 10–15.

In a study of occupational values, the findings indicate that the values can be ordered on a continuum of "psychological distance" or "contiguity." The numerical results afford a basis for classifying values as "people-oriented," "self-expression oriented," and "extrinsic-reward oriented."

J. H. Greenberg, 1957. "The Nature and Uses of Linguistic Typologies," *International Journal of American Linguistics,* 23 (April 1957), pp. 68–77.

In the author's view, every descriptive scheme is typological. He discusses a wide range of modes of linguistic classification and typological criteria which have been employed in the literature. Suggests that the location of language elements within a multidimensional property space can produce more general and comprehensive linguistic typologies. The empirical rarity of possible types might be explained by psychological, logical, or other non-linguistic factors.

R. Dubin, "Parsons' Actor: Continuities in Social Theory," *American Sociological Review,* 25 (August 1960), pp. 457–66.

An explication and critique of Parsons' paradigm of the social act. A logical analysis demonstrates that there are 1,024 types of possible acts that connect person and object. Since so large a number of types is conceptually unmanageable, the author suggests certain procedures for the functional reduction of this complex property space. Through discarding categories and eliminating vacuous types based on logical tautologies, Dubin reduces the possible types of social acts to 640; the assumption of an "affectivity" choice further reduces the number to 160.

T. Parsons, 1937. *The Structure of Social Action* (New York: McGraw-Hill, 1937), pp. 668–673.

On these pages the author discusses Toennies' classical distinction between Gesellschaft and Gemeinschaft. Parsons singles out the aspects in which these two forms of society differ; later, these aspects became the famous pattern variables. Toennies' typology was revived by American anthropologists in terms of the spectrum from "folk society" to modern urban forms of life. The problems involved in these concepts were discussed in the selection by Horace Miner that was included in the first edition of the *Language*.

J. McKinney, *Constructive Typology and Social Theory* (New York: Appleton-Century-Crofts, 1966).

This is a thorough review of typological efforts. It includes the position taken in our Section I, as well as typologies of broader social systems which necessarily require more intuitive procedures. The large number of examples lead easily to a comparative discussion of the two approaches and their interrelation.

Multivariate Analysis

Introduction

THE FIRST SECTION of this reader has dealt with establishing the nature of variates. In actual research, it is certainly not sufficient to classify a population according to one such variate. It is the combination of a large number of variates into meaningful structures that becomes the essence of empirical analysis. Just as in everyday language we distinguish between words and sentences, so in multivariate analysis, the variates provide the basic vocabulary and the propositions are the sentences we can form to describe the interrelationship among variates. These propositions are enunciated by cross-tabulating the variates; this is what is usually called multivariate analysis.

Most studies based on statistical material collected for a specific purpose proceed in a sequence of steps. First, one tabulates what is called the "marginals." If questionnaires are used—and this will frequently be the case—the marginals show the distribution of answers to each individual item. Though such distributions might appear to provide rather low-level information, quite a number of important leads can be acquired at this point. We can, for example, examine what the psychometrician would call the discrimination of the items. Are there questions which would be virtually

useless in any further analysis because all the answers fall into one category? If we want to divide the sample into two approximately equal subsets (as may often be the case), what would be the best cutting point? For what questions will it be impossible to form dichotomies, because the frequencies are highest in middle category with about equal numbers above and below.

The Role of Cross-Tabulation

Once we have pored over the marginals, the next step is to cross-tabulate some of the questions pairwise. These cross-tabulations are of different types, according to the purpose they are meant to serve. With some of these cross-tabulations, we search for differences between significant subgroups in the study sample. Do men and women answer differently? Does age or income or amount of schooling affect the way people answer items? Such a *descriptive cross-tabulation* should reveal the role of what are usually called demographic characteristics, an admittedly vague term whose exact nature depends upon the specific content of the inquiry. In a political study, for instance, a classification by party affiliation will play the role of a demographic variate; in a consumer research study, comparison between the users and nonusers of a certain product might have a similar function.

The descriptive function of cross-tabulation remains unchanged, no matter how many additional demographic variates are brought into play. For instance, it is known that in most Western countries, there is a marked relation between age and education: due to the rapid spread of education, younger people are likely to have gone to school longer than older ones. Knowing this, we might immediately carry out our cross-tabulations simultaneously for age and education. In another situation, we might use age and marital status of women as simultaneous independent variates; we know in advance that being unmarried at the age of 40 means something different from being unmarried at the age of 18, and we look at responses in terms of these age-marital groups.

In many cases, instead of introducing demographic variates, we *cross-tabulate some of the main questions of the study against one another.* Our aim is to probe the meaning of the answers. We can see how respondents interpret the wording of the items by looking for consistencies or inconsistencies among responses to pairs of items. General questions about interest or preference might immediately be cross-tabulated against more concrete behavioral indicators to check whether a term such as "interest" was interpreted differently from one respondent to the next. Such cross-tabulations of questions are especially necessary when we have a large proportion of "don't knows." In one German study, for instance, an extraordinary number of people claimed that they did not remember whether or not their parents had spanked them as children. It turned out that these youngsters expressed unusual hostility to their parents on other questions, thus leading to the suspicion that the lack of memory had special significance.

These two types of cross-tabulation belong to the elementary tradition of survey work and are not further pursued in the present section. Instead, we focus upon a third type, for which we have employed the term *elaboration.*

The Process of Elaboration

Whatever relation between two variates we do find in a cross-tabulation, we will want to understand it. We begin to speculate in a general way about the underlying dynamics, we touch upon ideas of cause and effect, we are tantalized and want to know more. But within the framework of a nonexperimental, empirical study, we are forced to rely upon statistical manipulations in order to try out and verify ideas. The only way to proceed is to add further variates to our cross-tabulations. The general procedure of adding variates is properly called multivariate analysis. (The expression is also used in mathematical statistics with a somewhat broader meaning, but no confusion need be feared.) In the special case we are discussing in this section, the main purpose is to understand an initial relationship between two variates. What do we mean by "understand"? We might as well have used terms like "explain" or "interpret." But because these terms have been discussed in a more philosophical literature, we shall employ a completely neutral word, "*elaboration.*" By this will be meant nothing more than the introduction of additional variates into an analysis where the cross-tabulation between two variates is used as the starting point.

The purpose of the selections in Subsection A is to infuse this bland term with life. It may sound as if elaboration is an endless process where the results of the new cross-tabulations will vary infinitely, according to the substantive relation between the new variates and the old ones. This is true. But there is a way of formalizing these substantive relations in terms of three types of operations: explanation, interpretation, and specification. These names are only labels to facilitate communication; the operations underlying them have been described by various authors.[1]

The logic is the same whether the necessary operations are actually carried through or simply considered abstractly. Of course, we can always think of additional factors to introduce, and empirically, we will never definitely establish a causal relation. It will only seem increasingly plausible as it survives one after another of the relevant test factors. To put it another way: a bivariate relation is causal if it is nonspurious, a fact which can only be explored by an ever longer series of elaborations.

This definition has a special bearing on the following kind of discussion. Suppose it is found that in densely populated areas, the crime rate is higher than in sparsely populated areas. Some authors state that this could not be considered a true causal relation, but such a remark is often used in two different ways. It could mean: crowded areas have cheaper rents and, therefore, attract less desirable inhabitants. Here the character of the inhabitants is antecedent to the characteristics of the area. In this case, the original relationship is indeed explained as a spurious one and should not be called causal. But it might also be that the critic refuses to accept a relation as causal if he can point to an intervening variate: the crowded cities increase nervous irritation which in turn leads to more frequent crises. Such a sequence, if correct, does not detract from the causal character of the original relationship, according to the definition suggested here. The original interest in elaboration procedures was focused on the clarification of valid causal inferences. But gradually the formalization described above directed interest more and more to the type called above "conditional relations" rather than those that focused upon the disappearance

of contingent relations with the introduction of a test factor. At first, the question was not much more than a byproduct of the statistical procedure: what if the two contingent four-fold tables were clearly different? Slowly it appeared that this would be a type of finding with special characteristics, particularly interesting to empirical social research. The following artificial example will, we hope, convey the general idea.

The Meaning of Conditional Relations

It is well known that the occupation of a father affects the occupational intentions of his son at the beginning of college. This plan, in turn, will obviously be related to the son's occupational choice at the end of college. But what if the occupation of the father affects the *interrelation* between intention and choice? To exemplify the problem, suppose we deal with a sample of professional fathers, divided into medical doctors and other professions. The intentions and the final choices of the sons are divided into a medical, nonmedical dichotomy. The results could be as in Figure 1. The figure shows that father's profession greatly affects the *relation* between early intention and final choices. If the father is an M.D., the son carries out his intention —on the left side $(xy: z)$ is positive. But on the right side $(xy: \bar{z})$ is negative: if the father is not a medical doctor, then an early intention is easily corroded, perhaps because the father as a role model and persuader counteracts his son's deviant choice. On the other hand, if this same son has not expressed an early intention, new influences can reach him and in the end he will be more likely to become a doctor than if he had made an early choice. The essence of the example is that the difference between the two contingent associations as shown above can be as revealing as the mean of the

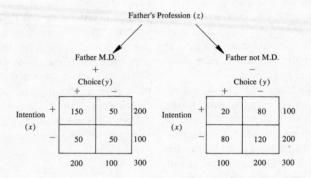

Father's Profession (z)

	Father M.D.					Father not M.D.			

FIGURE 1.

two contingent associations that is expressed by the partial correlation coefficient.

This formal idea permits a rather surprisingly large number of substantive variations. Selection 16 by Rosenberg offers an abundance of pertinent examples. We will see the same general theme reexpressed in Section III where the differences in contingent associations are related to the social context and in Section IV where moderator variables are introduced.

The role of contingent relations permits us to describe another development to the student. Some time ago Herbert Simon raised the question of whether the distinction between a spurious and a truly causal correlation could be transferred to quantitative variables. He agreed with the conclusion that the time order of the variates was crucial but showed that much could be gained by expressing this idea in the language of linear equations. His approach has been greatly extended by Hubert Blalock, Jr. whose ideas and their various applications to the research problem are presented in his book on *Causal Inferences in Non-Experimental Research,* included in the auxiliary readings. We have selected a paper of his, Selection 17, which provides a good sketch of the major tools of analysis in the Simon-Blalock tradition. The usually vague idea of causal connection

between a number of factors is replaced by the model of a set of recursive equations. Blalock shows how the coefficients of this equation can be found by connecting them with known correlations between observed variables. The conclusions drawn from this model permit one to study the causal links between many pieces of observed data. Recently, the identical ideas have been brought to the attention of sociologists under the name of path analysis. In the annotated bibliography we give a number of additional references. But the basic notion can be found in the Blalock selection included here.

How is the method of recursive linear equations related to the elaboration procedures on which this section focuses? The main advantages of path analysis are two: the number of variates utilized can be very large, and the causal imagery introduced is easy to follow. However, all of the contingent relations get lost, and the rich complexity of many sociological relations is obscured.

It is only fair to stress that not all sociologists will agree that the interrelation between variates is the proper language of social research. Herbert Blumer in a presidential address to the American Sociological Association has voiced eloquent dissent. It would be unfair for the editors to argue with Blumer. The reader of Selection 18 will want to form his own opinion on a controversy which probably has more connection to the opinion one holds about the future than about the present state of empirical inquiry.

Now that we have conveyed the general idea of multivariate analysis, it should be helpful to include a number of concrete examples.

Selected Examples

Selvin's article (Selection 19) has both methodological and historical interest. It is generally accepted that the first great sociological work of multivariate analysis was Durkheim's *Suicide*. The formalization of the principles of his analysis enables today's reader to bring a new perspective to bear on this study. One is able to point to those principles of which Durkheim, even in this early work, was implicitly or explicitly aware. Selvin demonstrates that, fundamentally, all of Durkheim's procedures can be subsumed under the major types of elaboration. As often happens in such cases, the formal approach is able to illuminate certain gaps in the reasoning of an early pioneer.

In Selection 20 Suchman examines ethnic variations in responses to illness or medical care. He finds, for instance, that Puerto-Rican-born New Yorkers behave in a specific way. Is being Puerto-Rican a meaningful sociological category? Not necessarily so, but it can be converted into one by using additional information. A person of Puerto-Rican descent might or might not prefer Puerto-Rican friends, old-time traditions, etc. The author investigates differences in the amount of ethnic identification (as measured by a cosmopolitan-parochialism index) for several groups living in New York and traces the ways in which health orientation can be linked to the degree of "ethnicity" *within* the population groups.

Selection 21 by Stouffer and DeVinney shows multivariate analysis in an unexpected role. The authors had asked a large sample of soldiers in World War II whether they thought it was fair that they were drafted or whether they should have been deferred. The authors cross-tabulated the answers against age, level of education, and marital status. It turned out that consistently, the younger, the better educated, and the unmarried were more willing to accept the draft status. In their interpretation Stouffer and DeVinney point out that in each of these three demographic groups deferments were least frequent. If the soldiers compared themselves with others of their group, they had least basis for what the authors call a feeling of relative deprivation. Each demographic variate is treated as an indicator of expectation relative to a group of others similar to the respondents. The function of the analysis is to show that each of these indicators has some cumulative effect upon the dependent variate, "satisfaction." In a formal way this is akin to a multiple regression. But the numerical results are used to postulate a hypothetical intervening variate which interprets the multitude of associations. Here, multivariate analysis serves as an heuristic procedure which has similiarity to the idea of numerically supported classifications discussed in Section I. *The American Soldier* provides several examples of this kind. Merton later linked up the concept of relative deprivation to the old idea of reference groups, partly by using more detailed case studies provided by Stouffer (see annotated bibliography).

It has to be kept in mind that, for simplicity's sake, we have concentrated upon the introduction of one additional variate in the cross-tabulation of two original ones. To track down complicated relationships in the course of an actual study, of course, requires a much larger system of elaboration. But this would only consist of more complex combinations of the elementary forms.

Blau, Selection 22, has formulated a challenging inversion of the elaboration procedure. The standard' method is first to establish the time order of variates and then to inspect numerical results. Blau proposes to reverse this sequence. His starting point is the observation that the way people feel about their age and the way they believe others think of them is strongly associated. Do they project their own feelings onto others, or does other peoples' treatment affect their self-assessment? Blau brings in the variate of chronological age. Feeling old and believing that others consider one old both increase in frequency with actual age, and age is, of course, antecedent to both variates. It could be that the original relation would disappear if age is introduced as a test factor. But this is not the case. A rather intricate argument is derived from the actual figures, leading the author to the conclusion that self-image precedes the reaction of others.

Blau's method is not quite so esoteric as it may sound. In many market research studies, it is important to try to discover whether exposure to a product or medium determines consumer opinions or whether the opinions are prior to the fact of exposure. Questions such as these can become more manageable through panel studies (see Section IV), a special breed of multivariate analysis.

Formalization

The level of training in undergraduate sociology has made rapid progress in recent years. Fifteen years ago we had to avoid any mention of formulas in the volume. But today, it does not seem too dangerous to give students a feeling of how the interrelation between dichotomous variates can be treated more abstractly. We are including as Selection 23 an excerpt from Lazarsfeld's essay on dichotomous algebra. A student who makes some effort to follow this quite elementary derivation will be pleased to see how many consequences can

be traced out if an adequate symbolism is introduced.

Once the reader is acquainted with dichotomous algebra and presumably able to read linear equations, he will then have no difficulty in following Selection 24. In the tradition now called path analysis, Pearsonian correlation coefficients are applied to fourfold tables, an arbitrary procedure which also requires unnecessary computations. Actually the idea of linearity, wherever it is substantively justified, can be directly adapted to the dichotomies which are so basic in social research. Coleman and Boudon have developed important ideas along this line. Selection 24 summarizes and develops their approach starting with the core of all recursive equation systems—regression analysis.

Somewhere during this section, the teacher might be sure that the students realize how multivariate material can be presented in a condensed form which takes advantage of percent figures. Thus, any eight-fold table may be presented in the following form:

	Test Factor	
	+	−
Attribute (1) +	.75	.50
Attribute (1) −	.60	.10

If the "base figures" are as follows:

	Test Factor	
	+	−
Attribute (1) +	200	100
Attribute (1) −	100	200

the figures would take the following familiar form:

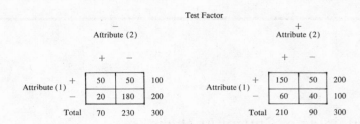

FIGURE 2.   Proportion of Respondents Positive on Attribute (2).

Multivariate analysis in one form or another is probably the core of all empirical research. We could only carve out the primary elements; it was impossible to elucidate that combination of a lucky supply of pivotal variates, a creative imagination to play with their interconnections, and a disciplined mind to test speculations against empirical elements. The skill is only slowly acquired and the careful scrutiny of successful examples helps greatly to develop it.

We have no space to add examples where the formalism of multivariate analysis succeeds in clarifying the meaning of solely verbal statements. Some pertinent cases will be found in Lazarsfeld's paper on "Public Opinion and the Classical Tradition." [2]

Notes

1. Among them, H. Hyman, "The Introduction of Additional Variables and the Elaboration of the Analysis," *Survey Design and Analysis* (New York: The Free Press, 1955). Also Charles Y. Glock, "Survey Design and Analysis in Sociology," *Survey Research in the Social Sciences* (New York: Russell Sage, 1967), pp. 1–62.

The original presentation was put forth by Paul F. Lazarsfeld at the American Sociological Convention in 1946. At that time, there was little interest in methodological discussion so the paper was not submitted to any journal. The first publication of the elaboration formula was in a chapter by Patricia L. Kendall and Paul F. Lazarsfeld in *Continuities in Social Research,* edited by R. K. Merton and P. F. Lazarsfeld (New York: The Free Press, 1950). The convention paper itself was published in the first edition of *The Language of Social Research* under the title "Interpretation of Statistical Relations as a Research Operation."

2. *Public Opinion Quarterly,* 21 (1957), pp. 39–53.

15. Principles of Causal Analysis

TRAVIS HIRSCHI AND HANAN C. SELVIN

[Ed. Note: The following selection is drawn from a book devoted to an analysis and critique of research in the field of delinquency. The authors show how the criteria for causal interpretations would be applied to this substantive area.]

To SAY that an analysis is adequate or inadequate requires some criterion or set of principles against which it can be judged. . . . We present here some of the principles on which we shall base our judgments. We shall also use this discussion to define technical terms and to show the kinds of statistical configurations we have in mind when these terms are used.[1]

The Logical Bases of Causal Inference

We begin by accepting the idea that it is possible and meaningful to discuss such propositions as, inadequate supervision is a cause of delinqency, and, assigning street workers to gangs causes a reduction in the rate of serious delinquency.[2] Both of these proportions are of the form A causes B; we shall speak of A as the independent variable and B as the dependent variable. The typical question that the empirical investigator faces is how to test such propositions, i.e., how to collect and treat empirical data so as to make reasonable statements about causal hypotheses.

In the empirical social sciences there is general agreement on the criteria for evaluating such statements. Our central task, then, is to apply these criteria to the analysis of empirical data. We shall have very little to say about the sources of hypotheses, the nature of abstract theory, and such broad philosophical problems as inductive inference.[3]

CRITERIA OF CAUSILITY

In Hyman's account [4] there are three principal requirements that an empirical investigator must meet in order to be able to say that A causes B:

1. A and B are statistically associated.
2. A is causally prior to B.
3. The association between A and B does not disappear when the effects of other variables causally prior to both of the original variables are removed.

Reprinted with permission from *Delinquency Research: An Appraisal of Analytic Methods*, pp. 37–51 (copyright 1967 by The Free Press, a division of the Macmillan Company, New York).

We shall consider A a cause of B if all three of these criteria are satisfied; it follows that demonstrating any one of the three to be false is enough to show that A is not a cause of B. For simplicity we shall refer to these three criteria as association, causal order, and lack of spuriousness.

Hyman also advocates another criterion: that one or more intervening variables link the independent and dependent variables. This criterion is psychologically, substantively, and even aesthetically desirable; knowing the process through which A affects B is more rewarding to the investigator than the bare statement that A causes B. Nevertheless, this criterion is not part of the minimum requirements for demonstrating causality. Holding a match to a pile of leaves is a cause of their bursting into flame, even if one cannot describe the intervening chemical reactions.

EXPERIMENTATION AND OBSERVATION

Consider once again the two propositions: Inadequate supervision is a cause of delinquency, and, Assigning street workers to gangs causes a reduction in the rate of serious delinquency. Although these two propositions are formally similar in having an independent and a dependent variable, they differ fundamentally in the kinds of studies that may be used to test them. The investigator of inadequate supervision must take children as he finds them; he cannot decide that this child's mother shall adequately supervise him and that that child's mother shall not. In other words, he cannot manipulate the values of his independent variable. The investigator of juvenile gangs can, however, decide which gangs will receive street workers and which will not. It is this ability to manipulate the values of the independent variable that makes experiments possible.

One additional ingredient is necessary for a genuine experiment.[5] The investigator must use some chance mechanism to determine which gangs get a street worker

and which do not. For example, he might toss a coin for each gang, assigning a street worker if the coin falls heads. This randomization allows the experimenter to deal with unwanted or extraneous causal variables and thus to satisfy our third requirement for making a causal inference: that the association between the independent and dependent variables does not result from their having a common cause.

To see why this is so, consider two procedures that the investigator might use instead of randomization in assigning street workers to gangs: (1) allow the gangs to decide for themselves whether or not they will get a worker; or (2) make the decision himself on any basis that he chooses. The objection to the first procedure is clear. If he lets the gangs decide for themselves, the more law-abiding gangs may choose to have workers; any subsequent difference in the rates of serious delinquency may be the result of such differences in the gangs themselves rather than the effects of the street workers. The objection to the second procedure is less obvious but equally cogent. Even with the best of intentions the investigator may unknowingly assign street workers to groups that are less predisposed to serious delinquency. No matter what basis of choice is used, any purposive assignment is open to a similar objection.

Randomization, however, meets this objection. If the decision to assign a street worker is made at random, the presence of street workers cannot be associated with any other characteristic of the gangs, such as their predisposition to violence. At least this is what will happen on the average: The number of gangs predisposed to violence among those getting a street worker will be approximately equal to the number predisposed to violence among those not getting a street worker, so that there will usually be a small or zero association between a gang's predisposition to violence and the presence of a street worker.

It is always possible, however, that the

process of randomization does not completely remove the associated between the extraneous variable and the independent variable. Just as one may get ten heads in ten tosses of an unbiased coin, so randomization may occasionally give more street workers to docile gangs than to violent gangs. With the techniques of statistical inference, it is possible to calculate the probability of such an occurrence. That is, in advance of gathering his data, an experimenter can decide how strong his results must be in order to be reasonably confident that they are not simply the accidental outcomes of randomization.

Although randomization is necessary for a good experiment, it is not sufficient. The field known as the statistical design of experiments is largely devoted to ways of making randomized experiments more powerful and more precise. Here, however, we need pursue this line of thought no further, for there are few areas of research on the causes of delinquency in which one can legitimately experiment. As our proposition about street workers illustrates, experimental research usually deals with the treatment of delinquency rather than its causes. In the far larger number of studies represented by our proposition about supervision the investigator must look to other ways of ensuring that extraneous variables have not produced the observed association between his independent and dependent variables.

Suppose that an investigator has found a relation between inadequate supervision and delinquency. He might then reason:

Inadequately supervised children are likely to come from broken homes, and broken homes are known to be associated with delinquency. Since broken homes are causally prior to both variables of the original relation, could the apparent meaning of the original relation be spurious, i.e., could it have come about through the associations of broken homes with both of the original variables rather than through the effect of inadequate supervision on delinquency?

Unlike the experimenter, the nonexperimental investigator cannot use randomization to remove the association between his extraneous variable and the independent variable. Instead of controlling extraneous variables in the design of the study, he relies on statistical manipulation of the data after they have been gathered.

This statistical analysis can take many forms, including partial correlation, standardization, analysis of variance, and the construction of multivariate tables (cross-classification or cross-tabulation). Although there are reasons to believe that more powerful statistical methods will eventually replace cross-classification as a tool of investigation, most empirical studies of delinquency have relied on tabular analysis. Moreover, tables remain the clearest and simplest way to present the conclusions of an analysis. For these reasons both our examples and our methodological analyses will rely on tables.

Statistical Configurations in Analysis

Consider once again the proposition: "Inadequate supervision is a cause of delinquency." The first task of the analyst who wants to test this proposition is to see whether or not the two variables, supervision and delinquency, are associated— that is, whether or not there is a difference in the proportion of delinquents between adequately supervised boys and inadequately supervised boys.

In Table 1, the proportion delinquent among the suitably supervised boys is 30 per cent, while the proportion delinquent among the unsuitably supervised boys is 83 per cent, a difference of 53 percentage points.

We are using percentage comparisons to describe the association between two variables; we might have used one or another summary measures of association, such as a correlation coefficient, Yule's Q, Cramér's

TABLE 1. Delinquency by Suitability
of Supervision *

| | SUPERVISION | |
	Suitable	Unsuitable
Per cent delinquent	30	83
Number of cases	(607)	(382)

* This table is adapted from Sheldon and Eleanor Glueck, *Unraveling Juvenile Delinquency* (Cambridge: Harvard University Press, 1950), p. 113.

T, or the more modern measures developed by Goodman and Kruskal.[6] The numerical measure of the association would have differed according to the coefficient used, but all would have led to the same interpretation: that there is a moderate association between supervision and delinquency.

After measuring the association, the analyst must demonstrate that his independent variable, supervision in our example, is causally prior to his dependent variable, delinquency. There are serious problems in this demonstration . . . however, these problems are not tabular or even statistical in the usual sense of that term.[7]

In demonstrating lack of spuriousness, the third criterion of causality, the analyst goes beyond the two-variable table to examine three-variable relations, or even more complicated configurations. It will suffice here to consider only the simplest form, the three-variable table.

Table 2 permits reexamination of the re-lation between the suitability of supervision and delinquency, with mother's employment held constant.[8] In this case, the proposed antecedent variable, mother's employment, does not affect the relation between suitability of supervision and delinquency: The relation is as strong within categories of mother's employment as it is when mother's employment is left free to vary (see Table 1). The analyst can thus conclude that the observed relation is not spurious, at least with respect to mother's employment. (Following Lazarsfeld, we shall refer to the disappearance of a relation as *explanation* when the third variable is causally prior to the independent variable and as *interpretation* when the third variable intervenes between the independent and dependent variables.)

This, then, is the basic procedure for demonstrating causality: Starting with an association between a causally prior independent variable and a dependent variable, the analyst considers possible antecedent variables that might account for the observed relation. If he finds such a variable, he declares that the apparent causal relation is spurious, and he moves on to a different independent variable. If he fails to find the original relation spurious, he tentatively concludes that his independent variable is a cause of his dependent variable.

This conclusion must be tentative, for it is always possible that another antecedent variable may do what those already ex-

TABLE 2. Delinquency and Suitability of Supervision by Mother's Employment *

| | Mother's Employment | | | | | |
| | HOUSEWIFE | | REGULARLY EMPLOYED | | OCCASIONALLY EMPLOYED | |
Supervision:	Suitable	Unsuitable	Suitable	Unsuitable	Suitable	Unsuitable
Per cent delinquent	32	84	20	77	33	88
Number of cases	(442)	(149)	(80)	(110)	(85)	(116)

* This table is adapted from Sheldon and Eleanor Glueck, "Working mothers and delinquency," *Mental Hygiene,* 41 (1957), p. 331.

amined have not done. Logically, then, the demonstration of causality is never complete.[9] In practice, however, analysts become increasingly confident of their provisional causal interpretation as they fail to find it spurious.

Noncausal Analysis

The reader familiar with delinquency research may find this account of causal analysis too austere. Surely there is more to analysis than association, causal order, and lack of spuriousness. We agree wholeheartedly; in the foregoing we have deliberately restricted ourselves to the elements of *causal* analysis, but there is indeed more to research than the demonstration of causality.

INTERVENING VARIABLES

One may think of research as a linking together of apparently different things. Thus the theorist frames propositions relating independent variables to dependent variables, and the empirical researcher shows how the indicators of these concepts are related (the two roles meet within a single person in the processes of conceptualization and operationalization). The theorist links concepts verbally; for example, Cohen ties status frustration to gang delinquency through the mechanism of reaction formation, and Miller joins social class and delinquency through a system of values.[10] Gold advances the following three-variable hypothesis:

> . . . the higher the quality of recreational and educational facilities, the more attractive the community will be to its youngsters, and consequently, the less likely they will be delinquent.[11]

In empirical research, there is a range of complexity in the demonstration of links between variables. At one extreme, the researcher, like the theorist, provides a con-

jectural link; he speculates about the intervening variable, but he does not look at the appropriate three-variable relation. At the other extreme, Blalock and Boudon have shown how to fit relatively complex mathematical models of causal linkages to empirical data.[12] Most analysts work between these two extremes, using three-variable tables to link an independent variable and a dependent variable. The statistical configuration of the three-variable table showing that C links A and B is the same as that of the three-variable table used to show that D makes the relation between E and F spurious. In both cases the original two-variable relation disappears in the three-variable table. The only difference is in the causal order of the independent variable and the additional variable: In demonstrating spuriousness the new variable is causally prior to the independent variable, but in demonstrating a causal link the new variable intervenes between the independent variable and the dependent variable.

Table 2, which was previously used to show that the relation between adequency of supervision and delinquency did not disappear when the effects of an antecedent variable (mother's employment) were removed, can also be used to illustrate the disappearance of the relation between mother's employment and delinquency when the effects of an intervening variable (adequacy of supervision) are removed. In actual practice, of course, one would examine the three-variable relation of Table 2 for only one of these purposes, depending on which of the two-variable relations had appeared first, the relation between supervision and delinquency (Table 1) or the relation between mother's employment and delinquency.

It is necessary to construct this latter relation in order to show what happens when the effects of supervision are removed. This construction does not require returning to the punched cards. . . It is possible to construct this table from the data given in

Table 2, and it is a useful exercise for the reader to do so. We shall outline the procedure here and leave the details to the reader:

1. Multiply the percentage in each column of Table 2 by the number of cases at the bottom of the column, to get the numerator of each percentage (e.g., in the first column, 32 per cent of 442 is 141, the number of boys who were delinquent, suitably supervised, and sons of housewives).

2. Subtract these numbers from the figures at the bottoms of the columns to get the number in each column who were *not* delinquent (c.g., $442 - 141 = 301$ boys who were nondelinquent, suitably supervised, and sons of housewives).

3. Combine figures from appropriate columns to get the number of delinquents whose mothers were housewives, the number of nondelinquents whose mothers were housewives, and so on (e.g., the number of delinquents whose mothers were housewives is the sum of 141 and the corresponding figure of 125 obtained in the same way in the second column of Table 2).

4. Compute the percentages for the table showing delinquency by mother's employment.

This undoubtedly seems more complicated than it is. We could easily have given the recomputed table, but we believe the reader will learn more by working it out for himself. A comparison of this recomputed table with Table 2 shows how a large association between mother's employment and delinquency essentially disappears when the effects of supervision are removed; in other words, supervision is the link between mother's employment and delinquency.

EXAMINING CONDITIONAL RELATIONS

The most common outcome of introducing a third variable into a two-variable relation is neither the persistence of the original relation, as in demonstrating lack of spuriousness, nor the vanishing of the re-

lation, as in demonstrating spuriousness or showing a link between two variables; instead, the analyst finds that the new variable interacts with the original independent variable, so that the effects of the independent variable differ from one value of the new variable to another.

In Table 3 the proportion of delinquents rises as the strictness of the discipline exercised by the mother falls. It is almost automatic in such cases to ask whether the effect of discipline is the same for boys as for girls—in other words, to look at the three-variable relation in Table 4. In the left hand half of Table 4 there is virtually no relation between discipline and delinquency among the boys, but in the right hand half there is a larger relation among the girls than was true for the original relation in Table 3. This outcome, which Lazarsfeld has called *specification,* may lead the analyst to redefine his problem. Attempts to show how laxity of discipline by the mother produces delinquent behavior would henceforth be restricted to girls.

DESCRIPTION OF VARIATION

Locating intervening variables and studying interaction are operations that grow out of causal analysis. Other operations may not involve causation at all. Even before examining the association of delinquency with some independent variable, the analyst

TABLE 3. Delinquency by Strictness of Mother's Discipline *

| | STRICTNESS OF DISCIPLINE | | |
	Strict	Fairly Easy	Very Easy
Per cent delinquent	25	30	37
Number of cases	(220)	(332)	(195)

* This table is adapted from F. Ivan Nye, *Family Relationships and Delinquent Behavior* (New York: Wiley, 1959), p. 82.

may want to show how delinquency is distributed in his sample—say, how many are seriously delinquent, moderately delinquent, and not delinquent at all. He might do this, for example, in order to compare the rates of delinquency in his sample with those in other studies.

A table may have both dependent and independent variables and still serve a descriptive function rather than be part of a causal analysis. Thus an investigator may report arrest rates by sex and then go on to analyze the causes of delinquency in each sex separately, rather than try to show that sex is a cause of delinquency. In short, what determines whether a table serves a descriptive or an analytic purpose is not the nature of the variables included in it but what the analyst does with them.

DETERMINATION OF MEANING

Finding out what variables mean is an important part of most empirical studies. Answers to questions on sex or age make sense to everyone, but answers to questions on social class or delinquency are something else. What meaning does one attach to empirical data that purport to measure these variables? The methodological problem here is the relation between a theoretical concept and its empirical indicator: how to operationalize a theoretical concept and how to conceptualize an empirical indicator. The statistical problems in these procedures may be fully as complex as those of causal analysis.

Causal analysis, then, is only part of the overall task of the empirical analyst. Depending on his interests and his data, it can become the major part of his work, or it can be reduced to nothing, as in descriptive accounts of life in delinquent gangs. Even in these studies, however, the idea of causal analysis is always implicit in the analyst's thinking, for what, after all, is the purpose of a description that does not lead to greater understanding of causal relations?

Notes

1. Some of the general treatments of causal analysis that we have found most useful in our own research and teaching include: Herbert H. Hyman, *Survey Design and Analysis* (New York: The Free Press, 1955; Hans Zeisel, *Say it with Figures* (New York: Harper, 1957); W. Allen Wallis and Harry V. Roberts, *The Nature of Statistics* (New York: The Free Press, 1965); C. A. Moser, *Survey Methods in Social Investigation* (New York: Macmillan 1958); Claire Selltiz *et al.*, *Research Methods in Social Relations* (New York: Holt, Rinehart and Winston, 1959); Matilda White Riley, *Sociological Research* (New York: Harcourt, Brace & World, 1963).

2. On the meaning of such propositions, see Robert R. Brown, *Explanation in Social Science* (London: Routledge and Kegan Paul, 1963).

3. Our position is essentially Karl Popper's: that the task of science is to formulate universal propositions; that it is impossible to prove the truth of a universal proposition, but it is possible to disprove or "falsify" it; that the best strategy for a scientist is to formulate each proposition so that it will survive the

TABLE 4.   Delinquency and Strictness of Mother's Discipline by Sex *

	Boys			Girls		
	STRICTNESS OF DISCIPLINE					
	Strict	Fairly Easy	Very Easy	Strict	Fairly Easy	Very Easy
Per cent delinquent	32	32	38	18	27	37
Number of cases	(104)	(158)	(97)	(116)	(174)	(98)

* Source: same as for Table 3.

most stringent tests he can devise; and that, when this proposition fails, he formulates a new proposition that passes all of the previous tests, and thus begins anew the cycle of "conjecture and refutation." Karl R. Popper, *The Logic of Scientific Discovery* (New York: Basic Books, 1959). See also his *Conjectures and Refutations: The Growth of Scientific Knowledge* (New York: Basic Books, 1963).

4. *Op. cit.*, Chapters 5–7.

5. We are using *experiment* in the sense it has had among statisticians ever since the pioneering work of R. A. Fisher. See his *Design of Experiments* (New York: Hafner, 1953 first published in 1935).

6. Leo A. Goodman and William H. Kruskal, "Measures of association for cross classifications," *Journal of the American Statistical Association,* 49 (1954), pp. 732–64. See also Herbert Costner, "Criteria for measures of association," *American Sociological Review,* 30 (1965), pp. 341–353.

7. For a formal treatment of the intuitive notion of causal order, see Hubert M. Blalock, Jr., *Causal Inferences in Nonexperimental Research* (Chapel Hill: University of North Carolina Press, 1964).

8. Although it is almost always logically incorrect to speak of holding a variable constant, the usage is so common as to defy attempts to change it. The danger of this usage is that the analyst may believe the words rather than look at what he is actually doing.

To divide boys into two groups—say, those under twelve and those twelve or more—is not to hold age constant. A better statement is that age is held more nearly constant. A correct, if cumbersome formulation is: The relation between X and Y is reexamined in groups in which the variation of X is reduced from what it was in the original relation. Since the purpose of such control is to remove the effects of the test factor, i.e., to produce a zero relation between the test factor and the independent variable, the possibility of spuriousness remains to the extent that there is residual variation in the test factor.

9. To avoid awkward constructions we shall often refer in the text to the demonstration of causality, but the reader should bear in mind the limitations of such demonstrations discussed here.

10. Albert K. Cohen, *Delinquent Boys* (New York: The Free Press, 1955). Walter B. Miller, "Lower class culture as a generating milieu of gang delinquency," *Journal of Social Issues,* 14 (1958), pp. 5–19.

11. Martin Gold, *Status Forces in Delinquent Boys* (Ann Arbor: Institute for Social Research, University of Michigan, 1963), p. 39.

12. Blalock, *op. cit.*, and Raymond Boudon, "A method of linear causal analysis: dependence analysis," *American Sociological Review,* 30 (1965), pp. 365–74.

16. Conditional Relationships

MORRIS ROSENBERG

WHILE CONDITIONAL relationships are widely reported in social research today, it may be suggested that their full theoretical potential has yet to be realized. The purpose of this paper is to point to certain contributions to analysis, interpretation, or theory which conditional relationships may make.

Kendall and Lazarsfeld note that, in the study of conditional relationships, "we focus our attention on the relative size of the partial relationships. We want to see whether the original relationship is more pronounced in one subgroup than in the other when the total sample is divided by

This paper is drawn from a longer exposition of the subject in *The Logic of Survey Analysis,* Chapters 5–6 (copyright 1968 by Basic Books, New York).

the test factor. Thus, we try to specify the conditions of the original result." [1] For example a relationship between political interest and voting would be an *original relationship*, but if the strength of the relationship differed for men and women, these would be *conditional relationships*.[2]

Technically the examination of such relationships is called *specification*: one wishes to specify the conditions under which the original relationship is strengthened or weakened.

Such conditional relationships are not invariably greeted with enthusiasm by the survey analyst. For a science avidly in search of invariant social laws or general relationships between social variables, such conditional relationships are often felt to be an embarrassment, a digression, or simply an irritant. Physical scientists would be extremely uneasy if Newton's law stipulating that every action has an equal and opposite reaction held true in Missouri but not in Nebraska. Similarly, if the physical principle of inertia differed in middle class homes and in working class homes, then the scientific value of the law would be seriously impaired.

In social science, however, there is no escaping the fact that conditional relationships are often an accurate reflection of social reality. While the descriptive value of conditional relationships is generally recognized in social research, less attention seems to have been paid to their analytic, interpretive, or theoretical potentialities. In this paper, we wish to suggest certain contributions to analysis or theory which may emerge from the focus on conditional relationships.

1. Conditional Relationships May Call into Question the Interpretation of an Original Relationship

The serious challenge to an existing interpretation of data is often an important first step in the development of theory. For example, in a study of students in the later stages of adolescence, the original relationship showed that adolescents from higher social classes had higher levels of self-esteem than students from lower classes.[3] A respectable and easily available body of theory was at hand to explain this relationship. George Herbert Mead had shown that the self is a product of reflected appraisals,[4] and Cooley had described how the individual's self-concept was influenced by his imagination of what others think of him.[5] Since social class is fundamentally a reflection of prestige in the society, it would follow that those experiencing favorable social regard would tend to develop favorable self-attitudes, and *vice versa*.

When conditional relationships were examined, however, it was found that the relationship of class to self-esteem was strong among boys but weak among girls [6] (Table 1). This finding called into question the interpretation offered above since there is no obvious reason why the principle of reflected appraisals (as determined by social prestige) should not operate in the same way for both sexes. Subsequent analysis revealed that the major reason upper class boys had higher self-esteem was not their greater social prestige but their closeness to their fathers.

Conditional relationships may thus demand a re-thinking of the interpretation, and this re-thinking may often redound to the advantage of theory. In disturbing the condition of "closure," the conditional relationship is no doubt an irritant, but it is only by breaking such closure that theoretical advance is likely to come.

2. Conditional Relationships May Support or Strengthen the Original Interpretation

This theoretical contribution may appear surprising, since one would assume that if the interpretation were adequate for the original relationship, then it should also

TABLE 1.   Social Class and Self-Esteem, by Sex *

SELF-ESTEEM	Boys			Girls		
	SOCIAL CLASS					
	Upper	Middle	Lower	Upper	Middle	Lower
High	55%	47%	36%	47%	46%	41%
Medium	17	25	26	28	25	27
Low	28	28	39	24	29	32
Total per cent	100	100	100	100	100	100
(Number)	(89)	(1383)	(168)	(106)	(1311)	(172)

* Morris Rosenberg, *Society and the Adolescent Self-Image* (Princeton: Princeton University Press, 1965), p. 41, Table 2.

explain the relationship in different population subgroups. In fact, however, *different* results in various groups may *strengthen* the interpretation, whereas *similar* results in different groups would *weaken* it.

In the study cited above, it was found that adolescents whose parents had been divorced showed somewhat more psychological disturbance than others.[7] It was suggested that this was due to the *social definition* of divorce in the society. Since divorce is generally disapproved in the society, one could assume that (1) parents who have been divorced have experienced more tension and conflict than others, and (2) the social stigma of divorce would make the child feel different and inadequate.

If this were so, however, then it would follow that in those groups in which the cultural resistance to divorce was strongest, the child's self-esteem would be most affected. The data suggested that the social pressure against divorce was stronger among Catholics and Jews than among Protestants. Further analysis revealed that among Catholics and Jews, the association between divorce and self-esteem in the child was relatively strong, whereas among Protestants it was weaker (Table 2). Rather than calling into question the original interpretation, then, these *conditional relationships made the original interpretation more compelling.* Had the relationships been the same in all religious groups, the adequacy of the interpretation would have been called into question.

In other words, when a survey analyst interprets a relationship, he is obliged to confront the further question: *if* this interpretation is correct, then what conse-

TABLE 2.   Divorce and Self-Esteem, by Religion *

SELF-ESTEEM	CATHOLICS		JEWS		PROTESTANTS	
	Divorced	Intact	Divorced	Intact	Divorced	Intact
High	36%	44%	44%	54%	40%	44%
Medium	24	26	17	24	26	25
Low	40	30	39	21	34	32
Total per cent	100	100	100	100	100	100
(Number)	(90)	(1583)	(18)	(514)	(112)	(1391)

* Morris Rosenberg, *Society and the Adolescent Self-Image* (Princeton: Princeton University Press, 1965), p. 89, Table 2.

quences should follow? In some cases, the logical consequences require differential patterns of association in different groups. Conditional relationships may thus represent a vital basis for confirmation in social science.

3. Conditional Relationships May Modify the Interpretation by Making It More Exact

It is often the case that the interpretation of a relationship may be correct but at the same time incomplete, oversimplified, or inexact. An interesting example appears in a study of child-rearing practices conducted by Sears, Maccoby, and Levin. The investigators were interested in learning whether severe toilet training produced emotional upset in the child. The data showed that this was in fact the case: "over half of the most severely trained children showed some disturbance, while not more than a sixth of the least severely trained showed it ($p < .01$; $r = .47$)." [8]

The authors, however, went on to inquire what the *meaning* of severe pressure is to the mother and child.

> We reasoned that if the mother's punishment was an expression of an underlying hostility or rejection, we might expect it to be more upsetting to the child than punishment which occurred in a context of emotional security. In a sense, the child punished by a hostile mother was in double jeopardy; there was the physical pain of the punishment, plus the anxiety produced by the loss of love implied in the mother's manner while punishing. To the child of the cold and hostile mother, punishment may have meant, "I don't like *you*," while to the child of the warm mother, it may have meant, "I don't like *what you did*."
>
> This reasoning led us to expect that severe toilet training would be more anxiety-provoking, and hence more upsetting, for the children of cold mothers than for the children of warm mothers. This proved to be true, as Table 3 shows. Severe training produced far more upset in the children of

relatively cold mothers, but it had no differential effect whatsoever on the children of warm mothers. This finding requires us to qualify the generalization, made before, that severity of training produced emotional upset. The statement can now be amended and made more precise: *severe toilet training increased the amount of upset in children whose mothers were relatively cold and undemonstrative.*[9]

TABLE 3.   Percentage of Children Who Showed Emotional Upset Over Toilet Training, in Relation to Severity of Toilet Training and Warmth of the Mother *

Severity of Toilet Training	Mother Warm	Mother Relatively Cold	Horizontal Differences
Mild toilet training	21% (112)	11% (101)	N. S.
Severe toilet training	23% (48)	48% (98)	$p = .01$
Vertical differences	N. S.	$p = .01$	

* Robert R. Sears, Eleanor E. Maccoby, and Harry Levin, *Patterns of Child Rearing* (Evanston, Ill.: Row, Peterson, 1957), p. 125, Table IV:7.

4. Conditional Relationships May Lead to a Radical Revision of the Original Interpretation

The usefulness of conditional relationships is most dramatically illustrated when this occurs. Let us return to an example cited earlier. Analysis of conditional relationships had shown that the relationship between social class and self-esteem was fairly strong for boys but quite weak for girls. On the basis of further examination of the literature, it was found that social classes tended to differ in their social norms regarding father-son and father-daughter relationships. Apparently, middle class fathers were much more supportive of, encouraging, and helpful to their *sons* than working class fathers, but middle and working class fathers differed little in supportive attitudes toward *daughters*. It was further found that paternal supportiveness was associated with high self-esteem. It was thus hypothesized that if one eliminated the effect of degree of father's supportiveness of the son, the relationship of social class to self-esteem should substantially decrease.

Table 4 shows that when one eliminates the effect of father's supportiveness, the difference in the proportion of upper and lower class boys with high self-esteem decreases and the difference in the proportions with low self-esteem completely disappears. An important reason for the different self-esteem levels of upper and lower class boys is thus shown to be the different father-son relationships in the various social classes.

Note how radically different this interpretation is from the original one. Originally, it seemed reasonable to assume that the self was largely the product of reflected appraisals, that different social classes vary in prestige, and that the individual's self-attitude was a reflection of the broader society's evaluation of him. Now it is suggested that social classes differ in certain family norms; that one of these norms deals with father's attitude toward his children and, in particular, father's supportiveness of sons and of daughters. The data have produced a shift from a social prestige hypothesis (which was called into question by the conditional relationships) to an interpretation based on social class norms. The data are clearly consistent with the latter interpretation.

TABLE 4.   Social Class and Self-Esteem:
(A) Original Relationship and
(B) Relationship Standardized on
Closeness of Relationship with Father
(Boys) *

A. Original Relationship

SELF-ESTEEM	SOCIAL CLASS		
	Upper	Middle	Lower
High	54.2%	50.1%	40.8%
Medium	12.5	22.0	18.4
Low	33.3	27.8	40.8
Total per cent	100.0	100.0	100.0
(Number)	(24)	(345)	(49)

B. Standardized Relationship

SELF-ESTEEM	SOCIAL CLASS		
	Upper	Middle	Lower
High	52.3%	50.1%	44.3%
Medium	7.5	21.9	19.5
Low	40.2	27.9	36.3
Total per cent	100.0	100.0	100.0
(Number)	(24)	(345)	(49)

* Morris Rosenberg, *Society and the Adolescent Self-Image* (Princeton: Princeton University Press, 1965), p. 46, Table 6.

5. Conditional Relationships May Enable the Analyst to Choose Between Alternative Interpretations of a Relationship

Everyone engaged in survey research knows that while his data may be clear, the *meaning* of the data often is not. It is commonplace to find two equally plausible or compelling interpretations which neatly fit the results. Conditional relationships sometimes enable one to resolve the issue. If one of the possible interpretations is sound, then it follows that the relationship should be strong under one condition, whereas if the other interpretation is correct, then the relationship should be strong under a different condition.

In studying adolescents whose parents had been divorced or widowed, it was found, surprisingly, that children whose parents remarried had *lower* self-esteem than children whose parents had not re-married.[10] (In almost all cases of divorce, and in most cases of death, the child was with the mother, and it was therefore the mother who did or did not remarry.) Two interpretations were considered: (1) Freudian theory might suggest that the individual's basic personality is formed in early childhood and that the reinstitution of the Œdipus complex might produce low self-esteem, e.g., through the development of a strong and punishing superego (which comes from the father) or through fear of the father which would sap the child's self-confidence. (2) An alternative theoretical interpretation would be phrased in terms of role theory and social integration. Here the argument might run that the absence of the father requires the mother and children to take over the father's roles. In addition, the extra burdens tend to bind mother and children more closely together, since they must face the problems of doing without the aid of the man in the house. When the mother remarries, life becomes easier for mother and child, but the mother may now turn part of her attention to her new husband and possibly stepchildren. As a result, the child is deprived of the self-confidence he had gained from successfully assuming paternal responsibility and at the same time loses his position as the object of central, if not exclusive, interest of his mother.

One way to deal with this problem is to consider the child's *age* at the time of the family rupture. The data show that the relationship of maternal remarriage to the child's self-esteem is stronger among children who were *older* at the time of the family breakup than among children who were *younger* (Table 5). In other words, if the child was young at the time (3 years or less), then his mother's remarriage has no deleterious effect upon his self-esteem. If, on the other hand, the child was 10 years or older, then the maternal remarrige is strongly associated with lower self-esteem.

The social role interpretation thus seems more consistent with these data. By the age of 10 or more, the child has undoubtedly assumed some of the paternal responsibility and has for a long time been united with his mother in dealing with the problems of life. To be thrust out of the center of his mother's stage could thus have deleterious consequences for his self-esteem. On the other hand, self-esteem is not lowered among younger children. Hence, the notion of newly developed fear of the father and internalization of a strong superego as a

TABLE 5. Divorce or Widowhood, Remarriage and Child's Self-Esteem by Child's Age at Time of Family Break-up *

| | *Child's Age at Time of Divorce or Death* | | | | | |
| | *3 YEARS OR LESS* | | *4–9 YEARS* | | *10 YEARS OR MORE* | |
Self-Esteem	Remarried	*Not* Remarried	Remarried	*Not* Remarried	Remarried	*Not* Remarried
High	32%	37%	33%	46%	32%	49%
Medium	32	27	19	21	27	26
Low	35	37	48	32	41	26
Total per cent	100	100	100	100	100	100
(Number)	(71)	(41)	(64)	(56)	(37)	(78)

* Morris Rosenberg, *Society and the Adolescent Self-Image* (Princeton: Princeton University Press, 1965), p. 104, Table 14.

result of this fear—a consequence to be expected in early years—is not supported by the data. We thus see that the examination of conditional relationships at times affords a basis for selection between reasonable alternative interpretations of the original relationship.

6. Conditional Relationships May Reveal Contrasting Trends

The phenomenon of counteracting trends is one of the most widely recognized types of conditional relationships. The term "spurious noncorrelation" is sometimes applied to this type of relationship.[11] A spurious noncorrelation is one in which the contingent associations have opposite signs (some of the contingent associations are positive and others negative). As a result, the contingent associations cancel one another, producing a total relationship between the original two variables which is low or completely absent.

The danger of misleading interpretations is particularly acute when the analyst is confronted with no relationship—a zero correlation—between his variables. He is disposed to conclude that his hypothesis has been in error and to move toward more fruitful lines of inquiry. But this approach

may lead to serious theoretical impoverishment.

Assuming that the analyst does pursue the noncorrelation further and discovers that it derives from a positive association in one of the contingent relationships and a negative association in the other, he may explain his results in two ways: (1) he may offer one explanation of why the relationship is positive under one condition and a different explanation of why it is negative under another condition: we will call these *separate interpretations;* (2) he may offer a single explanation which, at a higher level of abstraction, accommodates the two contradictory findings; these are *integrated interpretations.* Since separate interpretations are commonplace, let us consider an example of an integrated interpretation.

A striking illustration of how contradictory trends in contingent associations may be encompassed within a single theoretical framework is provided in a study of rural work patterns by Goldstein and Eichhorn.[12] The authors were interested in the Protestant Ethic value of work as an end in itself in relation to the use of farm machinery. The high work-oriented farmers, they found, were somewhat more likely than the low work-oriented farmers to use a 2-row rather than a 4-row corn planter on their farms. The interesting

TABLE 6.   Work-Orientation and Type of Corn Planter Used, by Size of Farm *

TYPE OF CORN PLANTER USED	SIZE OF FARM					
	< 60 acres			60 + acres		
	WORK-ORIENTATION					
	High Work	Middle Work	Low Work	High Work	Middle Work	Low Work
2-row planter	62%	71%	87%	50%	34%	14%
4-row planter	38	29	13	50	66	86
(Number)	(37)	(55)	(24)	(30)	(74)	(29)

* Bernice Goldstein and Robert L. Eichhorn, "The Changing Protestant Ethic: Rural Patterns in Health, Work, and Leisure," *American Sociological Review,* 26 (August 1961), p. 562, Table 1 (abridged and adapted).

point, however, is that when one stratifies by size of farm, the relationships between work-orientation and type of farm machinery go in opposite directions (Table 6).

But a single explanation easily covers these opposite results, viz., *the lesser rationality of the highly work-oriented men.* Two-row corn planters are more appropriate for small farms and 4-row planters are better suited for large farms. On small farms, we see, men with high work-orientation are *less* likely than others to use two-row planters, whereas on large farms they are *more* likely to do so. According to Goldstein and Eichhorn, ". . . the high work-oriented men are less likely to have the machine best suited to the size of their enterprise . . ." [13] This single explanation satisfactorily accommodates these opposite results.

In sum, the spurious noncorrelation, or spuriously low correlation, represents one of the theoretically most fruitful types of conditional relationships. It shows that the absence of a relationship between two variables does not necessarily mean that there is no causal connection between them. The connection may be of a complex sort—positive under one test factor condition and negative under another. These contradictory results may be subject to separate interpretations, or they may be embraced by a single integrated interpretation which satisfactorily includes the opposite results. Where such integrated interpretations are found—and they are not so rare as might be assumed—they hold promise of yielding theoretical principles of great elegance and power.

7. *Conditional Relationships May Shed Light on Trends or Processes*

Since social life consists of change, development, and movement, the sociologist is interested in describing and understanding such change. The matter is complex, and diverse techniques have been applied to the study of change. The examination of conditional relationships is one useful procedure for studying trends or processes; characteristically, this involves the introduction of some aspect of time as a test factor.

For example, it is a well documented finding that both religious affiliation and socioeconomic status are important determinants of voting behavior. But what is the trend in recent generations? Has secularization reduced the influence of religion on vote, or has the "religious revival" increased it? Does the new generation vote in a more or less class-conscious way than its forebears? Or are people voting more "independently," i.e., less in accord with either of these groups? Although these questions deal with social dynamics, the examination of conditional relationships within a single survey enables one to deal with them.

Table 7 shows that while religious affiliation still plays an important role in voting behavior, its influence has declined substantially in more recent generations. [14] The difference in proportion of Republicans between Protestants and Catholics in the older age group is 70 per cent, whereas in the younger age group this difference is only 28 per cent. As Berelson *et al.* note: "The succession of generations seems to be softening the religious differences. . ." [15] Younger people are deviating more from the political norms of their religious groups; religion is declining in importance as a basis for political behavior.

Quite the reverse is true of class, which seems to be *increasing* as a determinant of political decisions. In the oldest age group, as seen in Table 7-A, the difference between the extreme classes is 18 per cent, whereas in the youngest group it is 37 per cent. Indeed, one can even specify when this class crystallization began; there is a sharp rise in class-based voting in the 35–44 age group, i.e., the generation growing up in the New Deal.

TABLE 7.   Religion and Vote, by Age *

	Age					
	55 AND OVER		35–54		UNDER 35	
	Protestant	Catholic	Protestant	Catholic	Protestant	Catholic
Per cent Republican	88	18	82	41	66	38
Difference		70		41		28

* Bernard R. Berelson, Paul F. Lazarsfeld, and William N. McPhee, *Voting* (Chicago: University of Chicago Press, 1954), p. 70, Chart XXVIII (adapted).

TABLE 7(a).   Socioeconomic Status and Political Affiliation, by Age

	Age											
	55 AND OVER			45–54			35–44			21–34		
	Socioeconomic Status											
	Higher	Mid-dle	Lower	Higher	Mid-dle	Lower	Higher	Mid-dle	Lower	Higher	Mid-dle	Lower
Per cent Republican	83	71	65	80	75	63	83	74	52	81	56	44
Difference between high and low		18			17			31			37	

* Bernard R. Berelson, Paul F. Lazarsfeld, and William N. McPhee, *Voting* (Chicago: University of Chicago Press, 1954), p. 60, Chart XXII (adapted).

If one were simply to compare the influence of religion and socioeconomic status on vote, the data would indicate that religion is a more powerful influence. What conditional relationships reveal, however, is that these two influences are moving in opposite directions—religion declining in influence in the younger generation while social class is increasing in influence. Since most surveys are conducted at one point in time, the ability of such studies to deal with social change, movement, or development is regrettably limited. To the extent that conditional relationships, using some aspect of time as a test factor, do shed light on such dynamic processes, their contribution is especially to be valued.

8. Conditional Relationships May "Purify," or Reduce Contamination in, the Original Relationship

The size of a relationship between two variables reflects the degree to which an inherent link exists between two variables plus the influence of factors irrelevant to that inherent link. To the extent that one is able to filter out irrelevant conditions, one is able to see the purer and clearer impact of the independent upon the dependent variable.

Assume, for example, that one wished to investigate the relationship of personality to behavior. One might hypothesize that people with "authoritarian" personalities would be more likely than those with "democratic" personalities to discriminate against minority groups. But one would not expect the effect of the personality factor to be the same under all conditions. In the Deep South, for example, one would expect the impact of personality to be less significant because discrimination is a more accepted cultural practice. In this region of the country, a White would probably not invite a Negro to his home irrespective of whether he had an authoritarian or a democratic personality. In the North, on the other hand, the authoritarian would be less likely than the democratic personality to issue such an invitation. Hence, if one examined the relationship of authoritarianism to discrimination in regions outside the South, the relationship would be "purer" and stronger.

Consider the finding that the lower the adolescent's level of self-esteem, the less likely is he to engage in discussions of political affairs with his high school companions.[16] Here we see the bearing of a particular personality quality on a certain type of social interaction. Adolescents with low self-esteem tend to be self-conscious about expressing their views, are afraid that they will say something stupid, tend to be awkward in their relationships with others, etc. It is thus understandable that they tend to be shy and retiring in expressing their political views.

But the relationship between self-esteem and political discussion is purified if one takes account of the factor of *political interest*. One would not, after all, expect such a relationship among those who are *not* politically interested.[17] If a youth with high self-esteem is not interested in politics, why should he talk about it? The analyst studying the influence of personality factors is thus really concerned with knowing why, among people who *are* politically interested, low self-esteem should lead to low participation in political discussion.

Table 8 indicates that among those who

are *not* interested, there is little relationship between self-esteem and "intensity of political discussion." (Indeed, those with high self-esteem are somewhat *less* likely to talk politics, which is a rational response in light of their low interest.) This enables one to focus more sharply on the relevant relationship, i.e., the relationship between self-esteem and political discussion among those who *are* politically interested. This relationship is purer, stronger, and less contaminated than the original relationship. The inclusion of low-interest people in the original relationship was simply blurring the clarity of the influence of the personality variable upon the behavior.

The issue of establishing "pure" conditions is, of course, familiar in the physical sciences. The law of falling bodies, for example, is assumed to hold true only in a vacuum. Other physical principles may be dependent on temperature. The empirical operation of physical laws are usually meant to apply in the absence of interfering factors. In social science, any generalization is implicitly assumed to obtain, or to obtain most clearly, under specified conditions. Usually this specification remains implicit. We suggest that it may be of value to the analyst to be explicit in stating those conditions under which the interpretation is assumed to be true, and to examine this assumption empirically.

9. Conditional Relationships May Specify Conditions Facilitating the Relationship

It is by now apparent that any relationship between two variables is the result of many currents and cross-currents, often operating differentially—sometimes with differential strength, sometimes in contrary directions—to produce the final result. Some conditions "facilitate" the relationship, whereas others "inhibit" it. Let us consider the issue of facilitating conditions—what

TABLE 8. Self-Esteem and Intensity of Political Discussion, Among Those Interested in Public Affairs *

INTENSITY OF DISCUSSION	Interested						Not Interested					
	SELF-ESTEEM											
	High 0	1	2	3	4	Low 5–6	High 0	1	2	3	4	Low 5–6
High	63%	56%	46%	53%	44%	43%	5%	5%	11%	8%	12%	4%
Medium	26	32	37	32	30	30	34	38	37	34	42	48
Low	11	12	17	15	25	27	60	57	52	58	46	48
Total per cent	100	100	100	100	100	100	100	100	100	100	100	100
(Number)	(182)	(254)	(226)	(123)	(63)	(44)	(38)	(58)	(65)	(50)	(26)	(25)

*Morris Rosenberg, "Self-Esteem and Concern with Public Affairs," *Public Opinion Quarterly*, XXVI (Summer 1962), p. 205.

might be called, from the viewpoint of the relationship, "propitious circumstances."

Arnold and Gold's "The Facilitation Effect of the Social Environment" [18] is a good case in point. This study dealt with the campaign and voting for a constitutional convention in Iowa to reapportion state legislative districts. Since the large counties were expected to benefit from such reapportionment and the small counties to lose, it was anticipated that favorableness of response would vary with county size; this hypothesis was strikingly supported by a .87 correlation between population size and vote.

One would, of course, interpret this finding as a simple reflection of self-interest. On the basis of other theory and research, however, the authors interpreted this relationship as also reflecting "social facilitation." It was not simply that each individual privately pursued his self-interest, but that this self-interest was stimulated by impersonal and interpersonal communications which made the issue salient to him, and which activated his latent self-interest. The behavior was not merely a private rational decision but also a consequence of interpersonal forces.

If this interpretation were correct, however, then one would expect the relationship between population size and vote to be strongest in those counties in which the issue was most socially salient, i.e., where there was heightened general awareness of the issue.

Two forces making for heightened awareness were considered. One was the activity of a citizen's committee (the CCCC) in support of the convention. This group was active in 41 counties and inactive in the remaining 58. In the counties in which the CCCC was active, the correlation between county size and vote was .92, whereas in the other counties it was only .59.

The other factor presumably increasing awareness of the issue was the presence of a daily newspaper in the county; the assumption was that the newspaper would stimulate interest in the issue. In the 38 counties with a local daily paper, the association between population size and vote was .92, whereas in the 61 counties without a paper, the correlation was only .56.[19]

Indeed, if the two indices of facilitation are combined, the results are still sharper. In the 28 counties with both a local paper and CCCC activity, the relationship of population size to vote was .92; when one of these was present, the correlation was .40; and when neither was present, the correlation was only .21.

We thus see that the simple explanation of self-interest is insufficient to account for the relationship. The influence of self-interest is strong where the issue has been made salient through press and organizational activity; under other circumstances, self-interest turns out to be a relatively weak determinant of vote.

There is thus patent value in specifying —in "pointing to"—those conditions, such as environmental influences, group affiliations, or subjective states, under which the relationship appears with special sharpness. Social science has been justly criticized for its neglect of situational factors. One may know that general principles obtain, but one does not know whether these principles have predictive value in specific circumstances because of special situational factors. The specification of facilitating conditions affords some aid in dealing with this problem.

10. Conditional Relationships May Specify Conditions Inhibiting or Blurring the Relationship

In many cases it is of value to the survey analyst to specify those conditions under which a relationship is particularly *weak*. One purpose of separating the weak relationship, as noted, is to "purify" or reduce contamination in the relationship. The purpose we wish to stress here, however, is the inherent interest in the inhibiting condition itself. Otherwise expressed, the fact that a relationship is weak under a particular condition may tell us a great deal about that condition.

An investigation of the relationship between faith in people and success-orientation affords an illustration of this point. College students with low faith in people, it was found, were more likely to stress the importance of getting ahead in life.[20] The interpretation offered was that those with low faith in people tended to view the world as a jungle in which only the fittest could survive. Hence, the striving for success was to them a means of gaining power (money, prestige, etc.), which was the prime objective in the struggle for survival.

The investigator suggested, however, that the general cultural pressure to succeed would tend to "mute" or "inhibit" the relationship between faith in people and success-orientation. In other words, one would expect that the impact of faith in people upon one's desire to get ahead would tend to be strongest upon those who are not under strong cultural pressure to be successful. One simple fact which is overlooked surprisingly often in discussions of success is that the value is considered much

more appropriate for men than for women. Women are much more likely to attain higher status through the success of their husbands than through their own achievements. This certainly tends to be the case among these college students; only 29 per cent of the women, compared with 51 per cent of the men, considered it "very important" to get ahead in life. One would thus expect the influence of the individual's degree of faith in people on his success-orientation to be greater among the women than among the men since, in the former case, this relationship is less likely to be adulterated by a general social pressure to succeed.

The results in Table 9 confirm this expectation. Among the men, 59 per cent of those with low faith in people considered it "very important" for them to get ahead, compared with 52 per cent of those with medium faith and 48 per cent of those with high faith. The male's basic interpersonal attitude thus has *some* influence on his desire for success, but it is not a very strong one. Even men with high faith in people often accept the cultural value of success quite completely. Among the women, on the other hand, fully 51 per cent of those with low faith in people were particularly anxious to be successful compared with only 19 per cent of those with high faith, a difference of 32 per cent, or nearly three

TABLE 9.   Faith in People and Desire to Get Ahead, by Sex *

	Men			Women		
	FAITH IN PEOPLE					
Important to Get Ahead	High	Medium	Low	High	Medium	Low
Very important	48%	52%	59%	19%	34%	51%
Not very important	52	48	41	81	66	49
Total per cent	100	100	100	100	100	100
(Number)	(444)	(491)	(200)	(229)	(137)	(51)

* Morris Rosenberg, "Faith in People and Success-Orientation," in P. F. Lazarsfeld and M. Rosenberg (eds.), *The Language of Social Research* (New York: The Free Press, 1955), p. 161, Table 3.

times as great as that obtaining among the men. Many men in American society, irrespective of their attitudes toward humanity, accept the idea that they should do their best to get ahead. Consequently, the relationship between these two variables in this population subgroup is considerably smaller than that among women, who are not exposed to the same amount of cultural pressure to get ahead.

11. Conditional Relationships May Stipulate Necessary Conditions

The survey analyst examining an asymmetrical relationship does so on the basis of some theoretical assumption concerning the impact of the independent upon the dependent variable. But implicit in virtually every such relationship is the assumption that certain necessary conditions obtain which render the observed effect possible. In a sense, virtually every relationship is a conditional one, i.e., is assumed to hold under certain conditions but not others. Ordinarily, these necessary conditions are implicit, but it is often of value to make them explicit.

Consider Sewell's finding that, among high school graduates, boys are more likely to plan to go to college than girls.[21] The stronger male emphasis upon college attendance, however, is not basically assumed to operate under all conditions; it is assumed to operate *chiefly among those who are college material*. This is evident when one examines the relationship of sex to college plans, stratifying by intelligence. Among those low in intelligence, there is little difference (2 per cent) between boys and girls in plans to attend college, whereas in the high intelligence group the difference is greater (14 per cent). It is only when the necessary condition of a superior level of intelligence is satisfied that the male norm of college attendance makes its influence felt.

Discussion

The purpose of this paper has been to alert and sensitize the reader to some of the potential contributions of conditional relationships to theoretical understanding. All survey analysis involves conditional relationships, but too often only the descriptive, rather than the explanatory, value of these data is appreciated.

Where an interpretation succeeds in encompassing, or satisfactorily accommodating, divergent contingent associations simultaneously, we speak of *integrated* interpretations. At their best, these integrated interpretations not only have great elegance but also raise the original interpretation to a higher level of abstraction, thus generating broader, more comprehensive, or even new theories. In other cases, of course, one is obliged to apply *separate* interpretations to the several contingent associations. But whether one uses integrated or separate interpretations, one is able to make more exact or more refined statements about the nature of social life. To the extent that conditional relationships are fruitful in generating new insights, either with regard to the meaning of a relationship, the meaning of a variable, or the existence of unconsidered variables, they deserve the attention of the social investigator.

It is true that we often find something discomforting about conditional relationships, for they seem to violate our sense of order and parsimony. Admittedly, with the glittering model of physical science, with its universal laws, dangling invitingly before our eyes, it is much more tempting to search for universals. But, as noted, conditional relationships may show "inconsistent" findings in various groups which produce a consistent interpretation; indeed, they may strengthen rather than weaken the interpretation. In other cases, they may modify the interpretation or lead to a completely new theoretical formulation. In these ways, conditional relationships deepen, enrich, and strengthen survey data analysis.

Notes

1. Patricia L. Kendall and Paul F. Lazarsfeld, "Problems of Survey Analysis," in R. K. Merton and P. F. Lazarsfeld (eds.), *Continuities in Social Research: Studies in the Scope and Method of "The American Soldier"* (New York: The Free Press, 1950), p. 163.

2. There is still no standard terminology to describe this type of relationship. Hanan C. Selvin, "Durkheim's *Suicide* and Problems of Empirical Research," *American Journal of Sociology,* LXIII (May 1958), p. 610, notes: "The phenomenon of statistical interaction has been given many different names (e.g., specification, conditional relationship, differential impact, differential sensitivity, and nonadditivity of effects." The test factor is sometimes referred to as the qualifier variable. Lazarsfeld has distinguished two types of qualifier variables: he describes a test factor as a "condition" if it is antecedent to the independent variable, and as a "contingency" if it intervenes between the independent and dependent variables (Paul F. Lazarsfeld, "Evidence and Inference in Social Research," *Daedalus,* 87 (1958), pp. 120–21). In the present discussion, we will use the term *specification* to refer to the process of establishing different degrees of association, *conditional relationships* to the contingent associations which emerge, and *test factor* to the variable upon which the relationship is stratified.

3. Morris Rosenberg, *Society and the Adolescent Self-Image* (Princeton: Princeton University Press, 1965), p. 40.

4. *Mind, Self and Society* (Chicago: University of Chicago Press), 1934.

5. Charles Horton Cooley, *Human Nature and the Social Order* (New York: Scribner's, 1912), p. 152.

6. Rosenberg, *op. cit.,* p. 41.

7. *Ibid.,* p. 86.

8. Robert R. Sears, Eleanor E. Maccoby, and Harry Levin, *Patterns of Child Rearing* (Evanston, Ill.: Row, Peterson, 1957), pp. 122–23.

9. *Ibid.,* pp. 124–25.

10. Rosenberg, *op. cit.,* p. 99.

11. Hans Zeisel, *Say It With Figures* (New York: Harper, 1947), pp. 198–99.

12. Bernice Goldstein and Robert L. Eichhorn, "The Changing Protestant Ethic: Rural Patterns in Health, Work, and Leisure," *American Sociological Review,* 26 (August 1961), pp. 557–65.

13. *Ibid.,* p. 563.

14. Bernard R. Berelson, Paul F. Lazarsfeld, and William N. McPhee, *Voting* (Chicago: University of Chicago Press, 1954), p. 70.

15. *Ibid.*

16. Morris Rosenberg, "Self-Esteem and Concern with Public Affairs," *Public Opinion Quarterly,* XXVI (Summer 1962), pp. 201–11.

17. To be sure, personality factors may influence the level of political interest, but that is an issue for separate examination.

18. David O. Arnold and David Gold, "The Facilitation Effect of Social Environment," *Public Opinion Quarterly,* XXVIII (Fall 1964), pp. 513–16.

19. *Ibid.,* p. 515.

20. Morris Rosenberg, "Faith in People and Success-Orientation," in P. F. Lazarsfeld and M. Rosenberg (eds.), *The Language of Social Research* (New York: The Free Press, 1955), pp. 158–61.

21. William H. Sewell, "Community of Residence and College Plans," *American Sociological Review,* 29 February 1964), p. 28, Table 2.

17. Evaluating the Relative Importance of Variables *

HUBERT M. BLALOCK, JR.

IT HAS become almost a truism to say that the social scientist must deal with large numbers of variables. In the exploratory phases of any given discipline, one of the most difficult tasks is that of merely locating those variables which seem to be most important in accounting for the variation in some dependent variable. At later stages, however, it becomes increasingly necessary to attempt to evaluate the relative importance of such variables, if only for the practical reason that both theorists and empiricists must limit themselves to a reasonable number of explanatory variables.

The purpose of the present paper is to raise certain questions about the criteria used to determine the relative importance of a number of "independent" variables and to suggest that the indiscriminate use of multiple regression and partial correlational techniques to evaluate importance can, on occasion, yield highly misleading conclusions.[1] It will be argued that a technique proposed by H. A. Simon for making causal inferences from correlational data offers certain potentialities for overcoming these difficulties.[2]

Two Criteria for Evaluating Importance

There are at least two very different sorts of criteria used in evaluating importance. To oversimplify somewhat, the first cri-

terion is usually applied when the social scientist is dealing with actual numerical data, whereas the second seems to be implied in certain types of theoretical discussions. Unfortunately, the two criteria do not necessarily lead to similar decisions; at least as often as not, they can be expected to yield exactly opposite conclusions.

THE QUANTITATIVE CRITERION

The first type of criterion seems to be purely empirical. Some sort of measure of association between an independent and dependent variable is computed. If there are several independent variables, their relative importance is assessed by comparing measures of association of each independent variable with the dependent variable, usually controlling for all of the remaining independent variables. The measure of association may be some sort of correlation coefficient, in which case the respective partials are compared. Or the measure may involve a prediction equation in which slopes are used to measure the change in the dependent variable produced by a given change in an independent variable. In the case of multiple regression analysis, one can compute beta weights which indicate the change in the dependent variable produced by standardized changes in each independent variable controlling for all the remaining variables. Usually, although not always, the conclusions reached using par-

Reprinted with permission from the *American Sociological Review,* 26 (December 1961) pp. 866–74 (copyright 1961 by the American Sociological Association).

*This research was conducted while the writer was supported by a Social Science Research Council Post-doctoral Research Training Fellowship.

tial correlations will be essentially similar to those arrived at using beta weights.[3] For our purposes we shall therefore consider these various measures of association as involving a single type of criterion which, for convenience, we shall refer to as the *quantitative criterion* for evaluating the importance of variables.

One extremely significant point about this quantitative criterion deserves special emphasis. The importance of a given independent variable is always a function of the amount of variation in that variable. This is perhaps most obvious in the case of regression coefficients, where we are interested in the amount of change in the dependent variable produced by a given change in an independent variable. But the magnitude of a correlation coefficient also depends on the extent of variation in the independent variable, though this fact is sometimes not explicitly recognized.

The same argument would apply to purely theoretical attempts to assess importance. For example, in explaining minority discrimination it would seem to be meaningless to claim that economic variables are more important than religious ideologies, or even that a plantation economy is more important than Catholic ideology in explaining the position of Negroes in Brazil. Some basis for comparison must always be made. Thus one might argue that the *differences* between the economies of Brazil and the American South were more important than *differences* between Catholic and Protestant ideologies in accounting for differences in discrimination. Similarly, one would not ask whether temperature is more important than volume in determining the pressure of a gas in an enclosed space. But one could assess the change produced in pressure by a given change in either temperature or volume, and one might then answer the question as to which of these specific changes had the greatest effect on pressure.[4] The quantitative criterion of importance can be applied only

to *specific* cases and not to abstract relationships among variables.

THE CAUSAL CRITERION

Let us now turn to a second criterion of importance, one which does not appear explicitly in discussions in the literature but which nevertheless seems to be used in various theoretical arguments. This criterion involves the causal ordering among variables and will be labeled the *causal criterion*. Briefly put, if A causes B and B in turn causes C, it may be argued that A is more important than B in determining C since A is a more ultimate cause, whereas B is merely an immediate cause. Thus if the nature of the economy is seen to determine in part the details of the socialization process, which in turn affect specific beliefs concerning the nature of God, then economic variables are considered the more important of the two. Similarly, if the Northward migration of Negroes makes possible a more vigorous protest movement which, in turn, leads to lesser discrimination, then it is this migration rather than any social psychological leadership variables which is conceived to be most important. Or in Linton's discussion of social change among the Tanala-Betsileo the most important factor in determining a change in mental outlook and personality would be taken to be the change from dry to wet rice, since it was presumably this change which set in motion a chain reaction ultimately resulting in changes in personality.[5]

It can immediately be seen that this type of causal criterion is both sensible, in some sense, and yet capable of leading to endless debate. If pushed to the extreme, it would lead to absurd conclusions since if

$$A \rightarrow B \rightarrow C \rightarrow \ldots \rightarrow K \rightarrow L$$

then A is a more important factor than K in determining L regardless of the weaknesses in any part of the causal chain and regardless of the strength of the relationship between K and L. It can be shown for such a simple causal chain that intercorrelations among various pairs of variables become weaker and weaker the further removed the variables are from one another in the chain.[6] Thus

$$| r_{AL} | \leq | r_{BL} | \leq | r_{KL} |$$

and in this particular case the quantitative and causal criteria lead to opposite conclusions.

Perhaps the adherent of the quantitative criterion would argue that it is theoretically meaningless or at least unwise to become involved with the problem of evaluating the relative importances of variables which stand in some sort of causal relationship to each other. It might be claimed that we must recognize that some causes are more immediate than others and that one can legitimately compare only those variables which have the same degree of immediacy. The contrary argument, however, would obviously be that such an ideal is neither practically nor theoretically possible. Since, in reality, most variables with which the social scientist deals are linked in a rather complex causal network, the criterion one uses must reflect this fact and cannot ignore completely the problem of causation. To say that an immediate cause is the most important factor, merely because it is most highly associated with the dependent variable, is to take an absurdly extreme position.

Ideally, it might be desirable to develop a single criterion for evaluating importance which, somehow or another, would combine the desirable features of both the quantitative and causal criteria. It would also be advantageous if this single criterion could be stated with sufficient precision that it could be applied unambiguously to relatively complicated multivariate causal networks. For the present, we can only indicate the direction in which a fruitful search for a combined criterion might be made. A quantitative technique is needed which can take into consideration the various causal relationships among "independent" variables. Before discussing such a technique, however, we shall first consider the kinds of questions that can and cannot be answered by ordinary multiple regression methods.

Single Multiple Regression Equations Versus Simon's Method

The contrast between laboratory experiments and real life situations is of course well known. In the laboratory, the scientist raises a series of hypothetical questions concerning the covariation among several variables with other relevant variables remaining constant or, at least, with the supposed effects of these other variables somehow being taken into consideration. The multiple regression equation has been designed with this ideal in mind. In multiple regression we can investigate the amount of change produced in a single dependent variable Y by a given change in any particular independent variable X_1 with the effects of the remaining variables controlled. If beta weights are used, we may compare the relative changes in the dependent variable for standardized changes in the various independent variables, each time with the effects of the other variables controlled. Likewise, one may use the square of the partial correlation coefficient to give the proportion of variation in the dependent variable associated with any given independent variable after adjusting for the effects of the remaining variables.[7]

The use of such beta weights or partial correlations enables one to answer the hypothetical question as to what would happen to the dependent variable *if* all but one of the independent variables were to remain fixed. If we cannot conceive of a laboratory situation in which all but one of the independent variables were literally held constant, we can at least imagine survey data for which there are some cases having identical values for all but one of these independent variables. Within each of these sets of cases, we could then investigate the relationship between the dependent variable and the remaining independent variable.[8] Actually, in using a regression equation we conceive of a distribution of Y's for *fixed* values of X_i. In other words, the various values of X_i are taken as givens and the Y's are predicted from these values.[9] For example, if we thought of a student as having certain abilities and certain motivational tendencies which would remain constant during his four years of college, we then might use scores on various tests designed to measure these traits in order to predict his performance. The predicted performance would be the mean performance level for all students having exactly his combination of abilities and motivation. Or we might ask questions of the following type: "If a student's abilities were to remain the same, how will his performance be affected by a given change in his motivation?"

But we can also ask a very different type of question, one which at first glance seems to be similar to the above question. We may ask, "What is the change, or expected change, produced in Y by a given change in a particular X_i, given the fact that certain of the other supposedly independent variables also may be affected by this change in X_i?" The single regression equation with Y as the dependent variable takes into consideration the *correlations* among the various X's, but it begs the question of the *direction of causality* among these variables. Presumably, they are merely thought not to be causally dependent on Y, although there is nothing in the mathematical formula for the regression equation to prevent one from interchanging Y with any of the X's. Such a single equation does not permit one to distinguish between situations in which X_1 causes X_2 and those where X_2 causes X_1.

In raising this second kind of question we seem to be coming closer to real-life situations in which there is a complex causal network where not only is Y causally dependent on the various X's, but some of these X's in turn are causally dependent on certain of the others. Thus if a particular change in one X occurs, not only may there be a direct effect on Y, but there may be effects on some of the remaining X's and therefore an additional indirect effect on Y. In fact, there may be no direct effect on Y at all but only a series of indirect effects. For example, we may have a causal pattern as indicated in Figure 1.

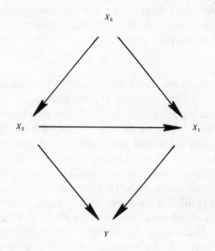

Figure 1.

To represent such a causal network we need not one but a number of separate equations which, when taken simultaneously, can be used to predict changes in Y. For example, assuming linearity, the network in Figure 1 can be represented by the following set of equations:

$$Y = a_1 + b_{11}X_1 + b_{12}X_2 + e_1$$
$$X_1 = a_2 + b_{22}X_2 + b_{23}X_3 + e_2$$
$$X_2 = a_3 + b_{33}X_3 + e_3$$

where the e's represent the effects of all variables not taken into consideration in the causal model.[10]

If X_3 were to change there would be direct effects on X_1 and X_2 but only an indirect effect on Y. If X_2 were to change there would be no effect on X_3 but both X_1 and Y would be changed, and furthermore the total effect on Y would stem not only from the direct effect of X_2 but from the change in X_1 as well. In any given case we could estimate the change in Y by making use of the complete set of equations. Thus if X_3 changes by one unit, X_2 will change b_{33} units. The change in X_1 will then be $b_{22}b_{33} + b_{23}$, the second term being due to X_3 directly and the first to the indirect effect through X_2. We can now predict a change in Y in a similar manner. This change will be

$$b_{11}(b_{22}b_{33} + b_{23}) + b_{12}b_{33}$$

Suppose, however, that we had asked about the change in Y for a change in X_3, presupposing that X_1 and X_2 remained constant. It can be shown that in such an instance we would have reached the conclusion that Y would not change.[11] This is both correct and misleading unless we clearly understand that we have raised an hypothetical question which may, in real life, be absurd. At least if we are to produce a change in X_3 without corresponding changes in X_1 and X_2, we must introduce certain *other* variables in the laboratory situation which exactly counteract the effects of X_3. The major point is that although the use of a single prediction equation may be useful in answering the type of hypothetical question which can be answered in laboratory experiments, we must not be tempted to use such a method in answering more complex questions in which we take into consideration the causal relationships among the variables which have been treated as independent. In this latter instance, which we recognize as being perhaps more realistic for most problems with which the social scientist deals, we need to work with an entire set of equa-

tions rather than with a single equation and a single dependent variable.

A method proposed by H. A. Simon for making causal inferences from correlational data makes use of such a set of simultaneous equations.[12] In the present paper it will be sufficient merely to outline the essentials of Simon's method since the procedure has been discussed at greater length elsewhere.[13] Simon restricts himself to linear models, but in principle his argument is quite general. Basically, the method involves writing an equation for each variable in the system taken as a possible dependent variable. Some of the regression coefficients can then be set equal to zero if there is no *direct* link between the two variables concerned. If certain assumptions can be made about outside variables which may possibly have disturbing effects, one can then make use of this set of equations rather than the single regression equation. A series of prediction equations can be derived which can be used to test the adequacy of any given causal model. Once a given model has been decided upon, the method can then be used to enable one to estimate not only the direct effects of a change in one variable but the indirect effects as well.

Direction of Causality and the Use of Controls

If we wish to combine the quantitative and causal criteria of importance, we must decide upon the conditions under which we should or should not control for other "independent" variables. Such a decision will presumably depend upon the assumed causal ordering among these variables. Let us suppose that Simon's method, or perhaps some other technique of a similar nature, has been used to test the goodness of fit of a particular causal model to the empirical data. We are then in a position to commit ourselves on a particular causal model and can next raise questions as to the use of controls.

The question of when and when not to control for a given variable seems to be considerably more complex than is often recognized. Here, it will be sufficient to point out that the answer depends on whether one is primarily interested in determining the relative importance of certain variables or whether one's concern is with problems of interpretation or specification.[14] Where one is attempting to as-

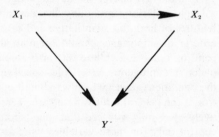

FIGURE 2.

sess importance, and interest centers therefore on indirect as well as direct effects of some independent variable, it would seem to make little sense to control for intervening variables. But can any really general rules be established enabling one to decide when to control? Before such rules can be laid down, we would have to know considerably more about the behavior of both the correlation and regression coefficients under various assumptions about causal models and outside variables. In the present paper, the best we can do is to indicate the direction in which the answer would seem to lie.

Suppose we had only three variables related causally as in Figure 2. According to the causal criterion of importance, X_1 would automatically be more important than X_2. At first glance, it might seem as though the quantitative criterion would point to the same conclusion, but we must remember that the direct relationship between X_2 and Y might be much stronger than those between X_1 and X_2, on the one hand, and X_1 and Y on the other. How, then, would we compare the relative importance of X_1 and X_2? Would we compare $r_{y1\cdot2}$ with $r_{y2\cdot1}$?[15] Or would we use r_{y1} versus $r_{y2\cdot1}$? Probably the latter if we reasoned that the relationship between X_2 and Y is partly spurious and if we wished to take into consideration both the direct and indirect effects of X_1. We see, however, that when decisions must be made about controls, the quantitative criterion of importance is by no means unambiguous. Also, our decision as to controls may depend on whether our measure of importance involves correlation or regression coefficients. For instance under the assumptions required for Simon's method, it can be shown that if the arrow between X_1 and Y were erased the magnitude of $r_{y2\cdot1}$ would be less than that of r_{y2}. But the comparable betas would be identical, indicating no change in the slope of the relationship between X_2 and Y when X_1 is controlled.

In the case of the three variable chain $X_1 \rightarrow X_2 \rightarrow Y$, a control for the intervening variable X_2 will produce a zero value for both the partial correlation and beta between X_1 and Y if the assumptions for Simon's method are met. In this very simple case we have a rather obvious and dramatic instance in which the automatic use of multiple regression might lead to absurd conclusions. In more complex situations, however, it may be much more difficult to keep track of what is happening.

Suppose we had a situation involving five variables, with the causal model as indicated in Figure 3. In another paper, the author concluded, using Simon's method, that this particular causal model represented a better fit to certain empirical data than several other models.[16] To discuss the particular variables concerned would introduce considerations which are extrane-

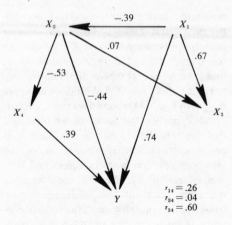

$r_{14} = .26$
$r_{34} = .04$
$r_{34} = .60$

FIGURE 3.

ous to the present argument. Instead, let us assume the causal model to be correct and focus attention on the numerical values of the various correlation coefficients which are also given in Figure 3. In this particular instance both causal and quantitative criteria for importance would seem to point to X_1 as the most important variable in determining Y. Not only is the zero-order coefficient between X_1 and Y larger than any other correlation, but X_1 is taken as either a direct or an indirect cause of all the other variables.

What if we had more or less indiscriminately related Y to each of these independent variables, with controls on each of the remaining variables? Of course with a best-fitting causal model in front of us, there would be little reason for carrying out such an operation. Among other things, we would perhaps argue that controlling for X_3 makes little sense in that the relationship between X_3 and Y is spurious.[17] This is, in fact, the major argument in favor of some such attempt to assess the causal interrelationships among variables. For if we were to relate X_1 to Y, controlling for X_2, X_3, and X_4, we would find that the correlation would be reduced from .74 to .33. Furthermore with controls on the other

three variables, the correlation between X_3 and Y would be changed from .60 to .38, and we might be led to the conclusion that with "all relevant variables controlled," X_3 is slightly more important than X_1. Using the figure, however, and admitting the possibility of a direct causal link between X_3 and Y, it would undoubtedly seem more reasonable to compare $r_{y3.12}$ with r_{y1} rather than $r_{y1.234}$. Likewise, r_{y1} might also be compared with $r_{y2.1}$ and with $r_{y4.12}$ if one wished to combine the quantitative and causal criteria.

As indicated above, the development of a single criterion combining the desirable features of both the quantitative and causal criteria of importance would seem to depend on our being able to set forth a completely unambiguous set of rules specifying the conditions under which we should control in the general multivariate case. Tentatively, we may suggest that one should control only for those variables which are assumed to be causally prior to the independent variable in question.[18] Note, however, that in the case of Figure 3 there is a possible ambiguity as to whether to control for X_4 in relating X_3 to Y, though such a control would probably make little sense in this instance. Once the mathematical implications of Simon's method have been more thoroughly worked out it is hoped that such issues can be satisfactorily resolved. It may also be possible to see more clearly the relative advantages and disadvantages of using slopes as contrasted with correlation coefficients as measures of relative importaince.

A NOTE ON RECIPROCAL CAUSATION

We have completely ignored thus far the problem of reciprocal causation. Ideally, we must always allow for the possibility of two-way causation and also for the fact that a causal relationship may be stronger in one direction than in the other. If we raise the hypothetical question as to how much change we would expect in one variable given a change in the other, we may reach the theoretical conclusion that a change in either variable would affect the other. For example it might be argued that not only would certain types of changes in the economy lead to changes in the socialization process, but, likewise, if changes in the latter type of variable were to occur, the economy would also be affected. If, for some reason, all children in America were brought up in Gandhian fashion and taught to scorn material goods, there would undoubtedly be certain major changes in the American economy.

In raising such hypothetical questions we are not attempting to assess the *likelihood* of a given initial change in one or the other of these variables. We have simply asked what would happen to the economy *if* certain changes were made in the socialization process. When we pose the question of the likelihood of such a change, we immediately run into the problem of the relationship of each of these two variables to *other* factors. In real-life situations it may turn out that we practically always find changes in the economy followed by changes in socialization, rather than the other way around. This does not invalidate the assumption that there is reciprocal causation involved; it may merely indicate that initial changes in the one variable are easier to achieve or are more likely than changes in the other variable. In some other type of social system, perhaps one in which children are trained at a very early age by agents of the state, a consciously developed plan to modify socialization may have important effects on the economy. Again we need to distinguish the hypothetical question involving presumed changes from the kind of question we are apt to ask about an actual situation occurring outside the laboratory of the scientist. This does not mean that the answers to the scientist's hypothetical questions may not ultimately provide answers to more complex problems. For our purposes it is sufficient to emphasize that the two types of questions need to be clearly distinguished.

If two-way causation is assumed, the problems of evaluating relative importance and of deciding on the use of control variables become much more complex. Also, Simon's method yields results which have not as yet been systematically investigated by the writer. Considerably more attention needs to be given to the question of reciprocal causation before the various issues raised in the present paper can be resolved.

Concluding Remarks

Two criteria for evaluating the importance of variables, a quantitative and a causal criterion, have been discussed. Also, the distinction has been made between the kinds of questions that may be answered by ordinary regression analysis and those requiring the use of an entire set of simultaneous equations which allow for possible causal relationships among the supposedly independent variables. If one wants to make use of the purely quantitative criterion for evaluating importance, thereby begging the question of the causal interrelationships among independent variables, one may legitimately make use of beta weights or partial correlations. In so doing, one will obtain answers to the hypothetical question, "What is the relationship between the dependent variable and any given independent variable, assuming fixed values for the remaining independent variables?"

If one wishes to combine the two criteria for importance by somehow assessing the indirect as well as the direct effects of changes in any of the independent variables, one must first commit oneself to an appropriate causal model. Simon's method for making causal inferences from correlational data provides us with a procedure for evaluating the degree to which a given set of data actually fits such a causal model. The next step is to decide whether or not to control for a particular variable when relating some other factor to the dependent variable. Ultimately, it may prove possible to provide a completely unambiguous set of rules for making such a decision.

It may turn out that rather than searching for such a single combined criterion of importance, it will be more fruitful to think in terms of an orderly sequence of specific questions, each of which permits a relatively simple answer. A list of such questions might be as follows:

1. What is the *causal ordering* among all of the variables included in the system? (Simon's method provides a goodness-of-fit test for evaluating the adequacy of any given causal model.)

2. Given these assumptions about the causal network, what is the relative magnitude of each *direct* relationship? (Here, some rules for controlling for remaining variables would be required.)

3. Given these assumptions about the causal network and given the measures of each direct relationship, what is the *total effect*, direct and indirect, of a change in one variable on any other variable in the system? (Here, if we are using slopes to measure effects, we would need to make use of an entire set of simultaneous equations as was done illustratively above.)

4. Given the answers to the above three questions, which variables are *most likely* to change under given circumstances? (Answers to this question may involve variables not included in the causal system but may also help to resolve debates over reciprocal causation.)

5. Given answers to the first three questions, what is the *easiest* way to produce a given change in a dependent variable? (This is the practical question involved in social engineering.)

The kind of program of specific questions outlined above may seem to require a degree of knowledge which is completely unrealistic to expect of the social sciences in the near future. Perhaps, however, the explicit statement of an ideal will make it less tempting for an individual social scientist to assess the relative importance of variables by merely shrugging off the question of causal relationships among independent variables. Nor will he be as likely to go ahead more or less blindly controlling for all relevant variables without stopping to ask himself what kinds of questions he can hope to answer in such a manner or whether he is actually posing the kinds of questions he really wishes to have answered.

Notes

1. This general point is not new, of course. See especially Arnold M. Rose, "A Weakness of Partial Correlation in Sociological Studies," *American Sociological Review,* 14 (August 1949), pp. 536–39.

2. Herbert A. Simon, "Spurious Correlation: A Causal Interpretation," *Journal of the American Statistical Association,* 49 (September 1954), pp. 467–79.

3. For example, if a relationship is nonlinear or if the dispersion about the regression equation does not remain constant from one point of the curve to the next, certain peculiar results may be obtained. For an excellent discussion of the use of beta weights as an alternative to partial correlation see Donald J. Bogue and D. L. Harris, *Comparative Population and Urban Research via Multiple Regression and Covariance Analysis* (Oxford, Ohio: Scripps Foundation, 1954), pp. 3–18.

4. The scientist could also attempt to answer the practical question whether it would be *easier* to produce a given change in pressure by changing the volume or temperature. Several persons have pointed out to the writer that the ease with which a change can be made in a given variable may somehow affect one's evaluation of its importance. This suggests a possible third criterion of importance, but one which will not be discussed in the present paper.

5. See Ralph Linton, "The Tanala of Madagascar," in Abram Kardiner, *The Individual and His Society* (New York: Columbia University, 1939), pp. 251–90.

6. See Simon, *op. cit.*

7. Actually, controlling by means of partial correlations involves an adjusting operation which is somewhat different from literally

holding the control variables constant. But the actual method of controlling is not of concern to us in the present discussion.

8. The criticism of the indiscriminate use of controls also applies to controls involving contingency tables as well as to partial correlations. Our discussion is in terms of correlation coefficients primarily for purposes of clarity of presentation.

9. The usual distinction is being made here between the regression equation and the least squares equation used for purposes of estimation.

10. For a discussion of the rationale for describing causal relationships in terms of a set of simultaneous equations see Herbert A. Simon, "Causal Ordering and Identifiability," Chapter 3 in *Studies in Econometric Methods* (Cowles Commission Monograph 14).

11. This can be shown by making use of Simon's method which is described in the following paragraph. This method requires the assumption that the various *e's* are uncorrelated, i.e., that possible outside disturbing influences have essentially random effects on the relationships among the variables included in the causal system. Some such assumptions about outside variables are of course always necessary if one is to make causal inferences.

12. See Herbert A. Simon, "Spurious Correlation: A Causal Interpretation," *loc. cit.*

13. *Ibid.* See also Hubert M. Blalock, Jr., *Social Statistics* (New York: McGraw-Hill,

1960), pp. 337–43, and Hubert M. Blalock, Jr., "Correlation and Causality: The Multivariate Case," *Social Forces,* 39 (March 1961), pp. 246–51.

14. For an excellent discussion of these other types of controlling situations see Herbert Hyman, *Survey Design and Analysis* (New York: The Free Press, 1955), pp. 275–329. Where interpretation is the goal, a control for an intervening variable may legitimately be made in order to see whether or not the partial reduces to zero. If such a partial is zero in the three-variable case, and if certain assumptions can be made both about the causal ordering among the three variables and also about variables not included in the system, it may then be concluded that there is no *direct* link between the independent and dependent variables.

15. We are using this somewhat unconventional notation to emphasize that Y has been taken as the single dependent variable. The symbol $r_{y1.2}$ means the correlation between Y and X_1, controlling for X_2.

16. Blalock, "Correlation and Causality: the Multivariate Case," *loc. cit.*

17. Actually, the data indicate that it may be reasonable to draw an additional arrow from X_3 to Y, in which case this relationship— as measured by r_{y3}—is only partly spurious.

18. This proposal is certainly not original. See Rose, *op. cit.*

18. Sociological Analysis and the "Variable" *

HERBERT BLUMER

My AIM in this paper is to examine critically the scheme of sociological analysis which seeks to reduce human group life to variables and their relations. I shall refer to this scheme, henceforth, as "variable analysis." This scheme is widespread and is growing in acceptance. It seems to be becoming the norm of proper sociological analysis. Its sophisticated forms are becoming the model of correct research proce-

Reprinted with permission from the *American Sociological Review,* 21 (December 1956) pp. 683–90 (copyright 1956 by the American Sociological Society).

* Presidential address read at the annual meeting of the American Sociological Society, September 1956.

dure. Because of the influence which it is exercising in our discipline, I think that it is desirable to note the more serious of its shortcomings in actual use and to consider certain limits to its effective application. The first part of my paper will deal with the current shortcomings that I have in mind and the second part with the more serious question of the limits to its adequacy.

Shortcomings in Contemporary Variable Analysis

The first shortcoming I wish to note in current variable analysis in our field is the rather chaotic condition that prevails in the selection of variables. There seems to be little limit to what may be chosen or designated as a variable. One may select something as simple as a sex distribution or as complex as a depression; something as specific as a birth rate or as vague as social cohesion; something as evident as residential change or as imputed as a collective unconscious; something as generally recognized as hatred or as doctrinaire as the Œdipus complex; something as immediately given as a rate of newspaper circulation to something as elaborately fabricated as an index of anomie. Variables may be selected on the basis of a specious impression of what is important, on the basis of conventional usage, on the basis of what can be secured through a given instrument or technique, on the basis of the demands of some doctrine, or on the basis of an imaginative ingenuity in devising a new term.

Obviously the study of human group life calls for a wide range of variables. However, there is a conspicuous absence of rules, guides, limitations and prohibitions to govern the choice of variables. Relevant rules are not provided even in the thoughtful regulations that accompany sophisticated schemes of variable analysis. For example, the rule that variables should be quantitative does not help, because with ingenuity one can impart a quantitative dimension to almost any qualitative item. One can usually construct some kind of a measure or index of it or develop a rating scheme for judges. The proper insistence that a variable have a quantitative dimension does little to lessen the range or variety of items that may be set up as variables. In a comparable manner, the use of experimental design does not seemingly exercise much restriction on the number and kind of variables which may be brought within the framework of the design. Nor, finally, does careful work with variables, such as establishing tests of reliability, or inserting "test variables," exercise much restraint on what may be put into the pool of sociological variables.

In short, there is a great deal of laxity in choosing variables in our field. This laxity is due chiefly to a neglect of the careful reduction of problems that should properly precede the application of the techniques of variable analysis. This prior task requires thorough and careful reflection on the problem to make reasonably sure that one has identified its genuine parts. It requires intensive and extensive familiarity with the empirical area to which the problem refers. It requires a careful and thoughtful assessment of the theoretical schemes that might apply to the problem. Current variable analysis in our field is inclined to slight these requirements both in practice and in the training of students for that practice. The scheme of variable analysis has become for too many just a handy tool to be put to immediate use.

A second shortcoming in variable analysis in our field is the disconcerting absence of generic variables, that is, variables that stand for abstract categories. Generic variables are essential, of course, to an empirical science—they become the key points of its analytical structure. Without generic variables, variable analysis yields only separate and disconnected findings.

There are three kinds of variables in our discipline which are generally regarded as generic variables. None of them, in my judgment, is generic. The first kind is the typical and frequent variable which stands for a class of objects that is tied down to a given historical and cultural situation. Convenient examples are: attitudes toward the Supreme Court, intention to vote Republican, interest in the United Nations, a college education, army draftees and factory unemployment. Each of these variables, even though a class term, has substance only in a given historical context. The variables do not stand directly for items of abstract human group life; their application to human groups around the world, to human groups in the past, and to conceivable human groups in the future is definitely restricted. While their use may yield propositions that hold in given cultural settings, they do not yield the abstract knowledge that is the core of an empirical science.

The second apparent kind of generic variable in current use in our discipline is represented by unquestionably abstract sociological categories, such as "social cohesion," "social integration," "assimilation," "authority," and "group morale." In actual use these do not turn out to be the generic variables that their labels would suggest. The difficulty is that such terms, as I sought to point out in an earlier article on sensitizing concepts,[1] have no fixed or uniform indicators. Instead, indicators are constructed to fit the particular problem on which one is working. Thus, certain features are chosen to represent the social integration of cities, but other features are used to represent the social integration of boys' gangs. The indicators chosen to represent morale in a small group of school children are very different from those used to stand for morale in a labor movement. The indicators used in studying attitudes of prejudice show a wide range of variation. It seems clear that indicators are tailored

and used to meet the peculiar character of the local problem under study. In my judgment, the abstract categories used as variables in our work turn out with rare exception to be something other than generic categories. They are localized in terms of their content. Some measure of support is given to this assertion by the fact that the use of such abstract categories in variable research adds little to generic knowledge of them. The thousands of "variable" studies of attitudes, for instance, have not contributed to our knowledge of the abstract nature of an attitude; in a similar way the studies of "social cohesion," "social integration," "authority," or "group morale" have done nothing, so far as I can detect, to clarify or augment generic knowledge of these categories.

The third form of apparent generic variable in our work is represented by a special set of class terms like "sex," "age," "birth rate," and "time period." These would seem to be unquestionably generic. Each can be applied universally to human group life; each has the same clear and common meaning in its application. Yet, it appears that in their use in our field they do not function as generic variables. Each has a content that is given by its particular instance of application, e.g., the birth rate in Ceylon, or the sex distribution in the State of Nebraska, or the age distribution in the City of St. Louis. The kind of variable relations that result from their use will be found to be localized and non-generic.

These observations on these three specious kinds of generic variables point, of course, to the fact that variables in sociological research are predominantly disparate and localized in nature. Rarely do they refer satisfactorily to a dimension or property of abstract human group life. With little exception they are bound temporally, spatially, and culturally and are inadequately cast to serve as clear instances of generic sociological categories. Many would contend that this is because variable research and analysis are in a beginning state in our discipline. They believe that with the benefit of wider coverage, replication, and the coordination of separate studies disparate variable relations may be welded into generic relations. So far there has been little achievement along these lines. Although we already have appreciable accumulations of findings from variable studies, little has been done to convert the findings into generic relations. Such conversion is not an easy task. The difficulty should serve both as a challenge to the effort and an occasion to reflect on the use and limitations of variable analyses.

As a background for noting a third major shortcoming I wish to dwell on the fact that current variable analysis in our field is operating predominantly with disparate and not generic variables and yielding predominantly disparate and not generic relations. With little exception its data and its findings are "here and now," wherever the "here" be located and whenever the "now" be timed. Its analyses, accordingly, are of localized and concrete matters. Yet, as I think logicians would agree, to understand adequately a "here and now" relation it is necessary to understand the "here and now" context. This latter understanding is not provided by variable analysis. The variable relation is a single relation, necessarily stripped bare of the complex of things that sustain it in a "here and now" context. Accordingly, our understanding of it as a "here and now" matter suffers. Let me give one example. A variable relation states that reasonably staunch Erie County Republicans become confirmed in their attachment to their candidate as a result of listening to the campaign materials of the rival party. This bare and interesting finding gives us no picture of them as human beings in their particular world. We do not know the run of their experiences which induced an organization of their sentiments and views, nor do we know what this organization is; we do not know the social

atmosphere or codes in their social circles; we do not know the reinforcements and rationalizations that come from their fellows; we do not know the defining process in their circles; we do not know the pressures, the incitants, and the models that came from their niches in the social structure; we do not know how their ethical sensitivities are organized and so what they would tolerate in the way of shocking behavior on the part of their candidate. In short, we do not have the picture to size up and understand what their confirmed attachment to a political candidate means in terms of their experience and their social context. This fuller picture of the "here and now" context is not given by variable relations. This, I believe, is a major shortcoming in variable analysis, insofar as variable analysis seeks to explain meaningfully the disparate and local situations with which it seems to be primarily concerned.

The three shortcomings which I have noted in current variable research in our field are serious but perhaps not crucial. With increasing experience and maturity they will probably be successfully overcome. They suggest, however, the advisability of inquiring more deeply into the interesting and important question of how well variable analysis is suited to the study of human group life in its fuller dimensions.

Limits of Variable Analysis

In my judgment, the crucial limit to the successful application of variable analysis to human group life is set by the process of interpretation or definition that goes on in human groups. This process, which I believe to be the core of human action, gives a character to human group life that seems to be at variance with the logical premises of variable analysis. I wish to explain at some length what I have in mind.

All sociologists—unless I presume too much—recognize that human group activity is carried on, in the main, through a process of interpretation or definition. As human beings we act singly, collectively, and societally on the basis of the meanings which things have for us. Our world consists of innumerable objects—home, church, job, college education, a political election, a friend, an enemy nation, a tooth brush, or what not—each of which has a meaning on the basis of which we act toward it. In our activities we wend our way by recognizing an object to be such and such, by defining the situations with which we are presented, by attaching a meaning to this or that event, and where need be, by devising a new meaning to cover something new or different. This is done by the individual in his personal action, it is done by a group of individuals acting together in concert, it is done in each of the manifold activities which together constitute an institution in operation, and it is done in each of the diversified acts which fit into and make up the patterned activity of a social structure or a society. We can and, I think, must look upon human group life as chiefly a vast interpretative process in which people, singly and collectively, guide themselves by defining the objects, events, and situations which they encounter. Regularized activity inside this process results from the application of stabilized definitions. Thus, an institution carries on its complicated activity through an articulated complex of such stabilized meanings. In the face of new situations or new experiences individuals, groups, institutions and societies find it necessary to form new definitions. These new definitions may enter into the repertoire of stable meanings. This seems to be the characteristic way in which new activities, new relations, and new social structures are formed. The process of interpretation may be viewed as a vast digestive process through which the confrontations of experience are transformed into activity. While the process of interpretation does not embrace everything that leads to the formation of human group activity and structure, it is, I think, the chief means through which human group life goes on and takes shape.

Any scheme designed to analyze human group life in its general character has to fit this process of interpretation. This is the test that I propose to apply to variable analysis. The variables which designate matters which either directly or indirectly confront people and thus enter into human group life would have to operate through this process of interpretation. The variables which designate the results or effects of the happenings which play upon the experience of people would be the outcome of the process of interpretation. Present-day variable analysis in our field is dealing predominantly with such kinds of variables.

There can be no doubt that, when current variable analysis deals with matters or areas of human group life which involve the process of interpretation, it is markedly disposed to ignore the process. The conventional procedure is to identify something which is presumed to operate on group life and treat it as an independent variable, and then to select some form of group activity as the dependent variable. The independent variable is put at the beginning part of the process of interpretation and the dependent variable at the terminal part of the process. The intervening process is ignored or, what amounts to the same thing, taken for granted as something that need not be considered. Let me cite a few typical examples: the presentation of political programs on the radio and the resulting expression of intention to vote; the entrance of Negro residents into a white neighborhood and the resulting attitudes of the white inhabitants toward Negroes; the occurrence of a business depression and the resulting rate of divorce. In such instances—so common to variable analysis in our field—one's concern is with the two variables and not with what lies between them. If one has neutralized other factors which are regarded as possibly exercising influence on the dependent variable, one is content with the conclusion that the observed change in the dependent variable is the necessary result of the independent variable.

This idea that in such areas of group life the independent variable automatically exercises its influence on the dependent variable is, it seems to me, a basic fallacy. There is a process of definition intervening between the events of experience presupposed by the independent variable and the formed behavior represented by the dependent variable. The political programs on the radio are interpreted by the listeners; the Negro invasion into the white neighborhood must be defined by the whites to have any effect on their attitudes; the many events and happenings which together constitute the business depression must be interpreted at their many points by husbands and wives to have any influence on marital relations. This intervening interpretation is essential to the outcome. It gives the meaning to the presentation that sets the response. Because of the integral position of the defining process between the two variables, it becomes necessary, it seems to me, to incorporate the process in the account of the relationship. Little effort is made in variable analysis to do this. Usually the process is completely ignored. Where the process is recognized, its study is regarded as a problem that is independent of the relation between the variables.

The indifference of variable analysis to the process of interpretation is based apparently on the tacit assumption that the independent variable predetermines its interpretation. This assumption has no foundation. The interpretation is not predetermined by the variable as if the variable emanated its own meaning. If there is anything we do know, it is that an object, event or situation in human experience does not carry its own meaning; the meaning is conferred on it.

Now, it is true that in many instances the interpretation of the object, event or situation may be fixed, since the person or people may have an already constructed meaning which is immediately applied to the item. Where such stabilized interpretation occurs and recurs, variable analysis would have no need to consider the interpretation. One could merely say that as a matter of fact under given conditions the independent variable is followed by such and such a change in the dependent variable. The only necessary precaution would be not to assume that the stated relation between the variables was necessarily intrinsic and universal. Since anything that is defined may be redefined, the relation has no intrinsic fixity.

Alongside the instances where interpretation is made by merely applying stabilized meanings there are the many instances where the interpretation has to be constructed. These instances are obviously increasing in our changing society. It is imperative in the case of such instances for variable analysis to include the act of interpretation in its analytic scheme. As far as I can see, variable analysis shuns such inclusion.

Now the question arises, how can variable analysis include the process of interpretation? Presumably the answer would be to treat the act of interpretation as an "intervening variable." But, what does this mean? If it means that interpretation is merely an intervening neutral medium through which the independent variable exercises its influence, then, of course, this would be no answer. Interpretation is a formative or creative process in its own right. It constructs meanings which, as I have said, are not predetermined or determined by the independent variable.

If one accepts this fact and proposes to treat the act of interpretation as a formative process, then the question arises how one is to characterize it as a variable. What quality is one to assign to it, what property or set of properties? One cannot, with any sense, characterize this act of interpretation in terms of the interpretation which it constructs; one cannot take the product to stand for the process. Nor can one characterize the act of interpretation in terms of what enters into it—the objects perceived, the evaluations and assessments made of them, the cues that are suggested, the possible definitions proposed by oneself or by others. These vary from one instance of interpretation to another and, further, shift from point to point in the development of the act. This varying and shifting content offers no basis for making the act of interpretation into a variable.

Nor, it seems to me, is the problem met by proposing to reduce the act of interpretation into component parts and work with these parts as variables. These parts would presumably have to be processual parts—such as perception, cognition, analysis, evaluation, and decision-making in the individual; and discussion, definition of one another's responses and other forms of social interaction in the group. The same difficulty exists in making any of the processual parts into variables that exists in the case of the complete act of interpretation.

The question of how the act of interpretation can be given the qualitative constancy that is logically required in a variable has so far not been answered. While one can devise some kind of a "more or less" dimension for it, the need is to catch it as a variable, or set of variables, in a manner which reflects its functioning in transforming experience into activity. This is the problem, indeed dilemma, which confronts variable analysis in our field. I see no answer to it inside the logical framework of variable analysis. The process of interpretation is not inconsequential or pedantic. It operates too centrally in group and individual experience to be put aside as being of incidental interest.

In addition to the bypassing of the process of interpretation there is, in my judgment, another profound deficiency in variable analysis as a scheme for analyzing human group life. The deficiency stems from the inevitable tendency to work with truncated factors and, as a result, to conceal or misrepresent the actual operations in human group life. The deficiency stems from the logical need of variable analysis to work with discrete, clean-cut and unitary variables. Let me spell this out.

As a working procedure variable analysis seeks necessarily to achieve a clean identification of the relation between two variables. Irrespective of how one may subsequently combine a number of such identified relations—in an additive manner, a clustering, a chainlike arrangement, or a "feedback" scheme—the objective of variable research is initially to isolate a simple and fixed relation between two variables. For this to be done each of the two variables must be set up as a distinct item with a unitary qualitative make-up. This is accomplished first by giving each variable, where needed, a simple quality or dimension, and second by separating the variable from its connection with other variables through their exclusion or neutralization.

A difficulty with this scheme is that the empirical reference of a true sociological variable is not unitary or distinct. When caught in its actual social character, it turns out to be an intricate and inner-moving complex. To illustrate, let me take what seems ostensibly to be a fairly clean-cut variable relation, namely between a birth control program and the birth rate of a given people. Each of these two variables—the program of birth control and the birth rate—can be given a simple discrete and unitary character. For the program of birth control one may choose merely its time period, or select some reasonable measure such as the number of people visiting birth control clinics. For the birth rate, one merely takes it as it is. Apparently, these indications are sufficient to enable the investigator to ascertain the relations between the two variables.

Yet, a scrutiny of what the two variables stand for in the life of the group gives us a different picture. Thus, viewing the program of birth control in terms of *how it enters into the lives of the people,* we need to note many things such as the literacy of the people, the clarity of the printed information, the manner and extent of its distribution, the social position of the directors of the program and of the personnel, how the personnel act, the character of their instructional talks, the way in which people define attendance at birth control clinics, the expressed views of influential personages with reference to the program, how such personages are regarded, and the nature of the discussions among people with regard to the clinics. These are only a few of the matters which relate to how the birth control program might enter into the experience of the people. The number is sufficient, however, to show the complex and inner-moving character of what otherwise might seem to be a simple variable.

A similar picture is given in the case of the other variable—the birth rate. A birth rate of a people seems to be a very simple and unitary matter. Yet, in terms of what it expresses and stands for in group activity it is exceedingly complex and diversified. We need consider only the variety of social factors that impinge on and affect the sex act, even though the sex act is only one of the activities that set the birth rate. The self-conceptions held by men and by women, the conceptions of family life, the values placed on children, accessibility of men and women to each other, physical arrangements in the home, the sanctions given by established institutions, the code of manliness, the pressures from relatives and neighbors, and ideas of what is proper, convenient and tolerable in the sex act— these are a few of the operating factors in the experience of the group that play upon the sex act. They suffice to indicate something of the complex body of actual experience and practice that is represented in and expressed by the birth rate of a human group.

I think it will be found that, when converted into the actual group activity for which it stands, a sociological variable turns out to be an intricate and inner-moving complex. There are, of course, wide ranges of difference between sociological variables in terms of the extent of such complexity. Still, I believe one will generally find that the discrete and unitary character which the labeling of the variable suggests vanishes.

The failure to recognize this is a source of trouble. In variable analysis one is likely to accept the two variables as the simple and unitary items that they seem to be, and to believe that the relation found between them is a realistic analysis of the given area of group life. Actually, in group life the relation is far more likely to be between complex, diversified and moving bodies of activity. The operation of one of these complexes on the other, or the interaction between them, is both concealed and misrepresented by the statement of the relation between the two variables. The statement of the variable relation merely asserts a connection between abbreviated terms of reference. It leaves out the actual complexes of activity and the actual processes of interaction in which human group life has its being. We are here faced, it seems to me, by the fact that the very features which give variable analysis its high merit—the qualitative constancy of the variables, their clean-cut simplicity, their ease of manipulation as a sort of free counter, their ability to be brought into decisive relation—are the features that lead variable analysis to gloss over the character of the real operating factors in group life, and the real interaction and relations between such factors.

The two major difficulties faced by variable analysis point clearly to the need for a markedly different scheme of sociological analysis for the areas in which these difficulties arise. This is not the occasion to spell out the nature of this scheme. I shall merely mention a few of its rudiments to suggest how its character differs fundamentally from that of variable analysis. The scheme would be based on the premise that the chief means through which human group life operates and is formed is a vast, diversified process of definition. The scheme respects the empirical existence of this process. It devotes itself to the analysis of the operation and formation of human group life as these occur through this process. In doing so it seeks to trace the lines of defining experience through which ways of living, patterns of relations, and social forms are developed, rather than to relate these formations to a set of selected items. It views items of social life as articulated inside moving structures and believes that they have to be understood in terms of this articulation. Thus, it handles these items not as discrete things disengaged from their connections but, instead, as signs of a supporting context which gives them their social character. In its effort to ferret out lines of definition and networks of moving relation, it relies on a distinctive form of procedure. This procedure is to approach the study of group activity through the eyes and experience of the people who have developed the activity. Hence, it necessarily requires an intimate familiarity with this experience and with the scenes of its operation. It uses broad and interlacing observations and not narrow and disjunctive observations. And, may I add, that like variable analysis, it yields empirical findings

and "here-and-now" propositions, although in a different form. Finally, it is no worse off than variable analysis in developing generic knowledge out of its findings and propositions.

In closing, I express a hope that my critical remarks about variable analysis are not misinterpreted to mean that variable analysis is useless or makes no contribution to sociological analysis. The contrary is true. Variable analysis is a fit procedure for those areas of social life and formation that are not mediated by an interpretative process. Such areas exist and are important. Further, in the area of interpretative life variable analysis can be an effective means of unearthing stabilized patterns of interpretation which are not likely to be detected through the direct study of the experience of people. Knowledge of such patterns, or rather of the relations between variables which reflect such patterns, is of great value for understanding group life in its "here-and-now" character and indeed may have significant practical value. All of these appropriate uses give variable analysis a worthy status in our field.

In view, however, of the current tendency of variable analysis to become the norm and model for sociological analysis, I believe it important to recognize its shortcomings and its limitations.

Note

1. "What is Wrong with Social Theory?" *American Sociological Review,* 19 (February 1954), pp. 3–10.

B. Selected Examples

19. Durkheim's *Suicide* and Problems of Empirical Research

HANAN C. SELVIN[1]

SIXTY-EIGHT years after it first appeared in print, Émile Durkheim's *Suicide* [2] is still a model of sociological research. Few, if any, later works can match the clarity and power with which Durkheim marshaled his facts to test and refine his theory. The stature of this work is even more impressive when one remembers that Durkheim lacked even so rudimentary a tool as the correlation coefficient. Yet the methodology of *Suicide* is important to those now engaged in empirical research, not merely to historians of sociology. Durkheim recognized and solved many of the problems that beset present-day research. Others he formulated so lucidly—perhaps because he did not exile his methodology to appendixes—that their solution is relatively simple with the tools now available.

"Methodology" has several meanings to sociologists. To some it means questionnaires, interviews, punched cards—the hand tools of research. To others, such as Durkheim himself and Parsons,[3] it is the assumptions and concepts used in constructing a theory. Here it will be used to mean the systematic examination of the procedures, assumptions, and modes of explanation in the analysis of empirical data.[4] This focus on Durkheim's methodology is not meant to minimize the importance of his theoretical insights; the value of methodological investigations, after all, is that they lead to more effective theorizing about social behavior. But Durkheim's theoretical development has been discussed by many authors, . . . while his analytical procedures have not received the attention they deserve.

Multivariate Analysis

Central to Durkheim's methodology is his use of what has been called *multivariate analysis:* "the study and interpretation of complex interrelationships among a multiplicity of characteristics." [5] Much of the empirical analysis in *Suicide* can be viewed as the progressive introduction of additional variables. It will be useful to examine one of these analyses in detail, for it includes several of the procedures to be considered in this paper.

Reprinted from the *American Journal of Sociology*, 63 (1958), pp. 607–613. This paper can also be found reprinted in *Émile Durkheim,* R. A. Nisbet, ed. (Englewood Cliffs, N. J.: Prentice-Hall, 1965).

The first chapter on egoistic suicide (Book II, Chapter ii) begins with the relation between religion and suicide rates for three groups of countries—the predominantly Protestant, the mixed Protestant and Catholic, and the predominantly Catholic.[6] But, as Durkheim points out, this comparison includes countries with radically different social conditions and requires consideration of the relation between religion and suicide *within* each country. Bavaria, the German state with the lowest proportion of Protestants, has the lowest proportion of suicides. And, in what may seem a mere piling-up of instances, the provinces within Bavaria also exhibit this same relationship: "Suicides are found in direct proportion to the number of Protestants and in inverse proportion to that of Catholics." Prussia and the Prussian provinces are the site of a similar analysis. Then the analysis is repeated for a third country: Switzerland. Here Durkheim takes advantage of the fact that both French- and German-speaking areas contain some cantons that are largely Catholic and others that are largely Protestant. This allows him to hold constant the effect of language as well as nationality ("race") while examining the effect of religion on suicide.

All the preceding analyses are based on data for nations or other large aggregations; thus the discussion of Bavaria cites the relatively high rate of suicides in provinces with high proportion of Protestants and the low rate in provinces with many Catholics. The implications of this procedure will be considered later; here it is important to note only that Durkheim recognized the difference between relationships based on aggregate data and those based on individual data, for he goes on to say that "in a fairly large number of cases the number of suicides per million inhabitants of the population of each confession has been directly determined." And he presents data on the suicide rates by religion for twelve periods of time in five

countries, as well as some fragmentary data for France.

After disposing of the "deviant case" of Norway and Sweden, Durkheim considers the low suicide rate among Jews. As compared with Protestants and Catholics, Jews are more likely to live in cities and to pursue intellectual occupations—both conditions that are associated with higher suicide rates. Therefore, Durkheim reasons, if the reported rate of suicide among Jews is lower, despite these conditions, the "true" Jewish rate must be even lower than the figures reveal it to be.

As this passage makes plain, multivariate analysis meant more to Durkheim than simply considering the separate relationships between suicide and the several independent variables—religion, nationality, and language. Each new variable is progressively incorporated into the preceding analyses, so that several variables are considered jointly. The methodology of multivariate analysis is most clearly seen in the case where a relationship between one independent variable (say, religion) and the dependent variable (suicide) is "elaborated" by the introduction of a third variable or "test factor" (say, nationality). Lazarsfeld, Kendall, and Hyman have defined three major types of elaboration: explanation, interpretation, and specification.[7] Explanation is the attempt to "explain away" the apparent meaning of an observed relationship. For example, the association between religion and suicide might have been a manifestation of nationality, since countries like Germany have both a high suicide rate and many Protestants. Looking into this possibility, Durkheim finds that the original association between religion and suicide persists when national differences are taken into account; nationality is therefore not an explanation of this relationship.

Once convinced that nationality and language do not explain away the association between religion and suicide, Durkheim turns to the interpretation of this relationship: what is the chain of variables connecting two such disparate phenomena as Protestantism and a high suicide rate? A spirit of free inquiry, according to Durkheim, is the most important link in this chain: Protestantism fosters free inquiry and free inquiry in turn leads to a higher rate of suicide.

Although Durkheim lacked the statistical techniques to develop these ideas rigorously, he saw their central place in theoretically oriented research. The relationship between two variables ". . . may not be due to the fact that one phenomenon is the cause of the other but to the fact that they are both the effects of the same cause, or, again, that there exists between them a third phenomenon, interposed but unperceived, which is the effect of the first and the cause of the second." [8]

Specification, the third mode of elaboration, identifies the conditions under which a relationship holds true in greater or less degree. For example, the effect of religion on suicide is less in the German cantons of Switzerland than in the French. Since specification appears in many forms in *Suicide* and since its role in the development of sociological theory differs from the other modes of elaboration, it will be considered at some length.

Specification leads to the development of multivariate theories of behavior in a way that is not true of explanation and interpretation. The aim of specification is to construct three-variable relationships—to say that, as in the example just cited, the effect of religion on suicide is greater in one place than in another. Note that this statement cannot be decomposed into a set of two-variable relationships. Explanation, on the other hand, involves a three-variable association only as an intermediate step, either toward rejecting the apparent finding or toward affirming its provisional meaning; in either case, the result is not a three-variable relationship. Interpretation, like-

wise, uses the three-variable association only to produce a series of two-variable relationships, to show that these relationships are linked by the variables they have in common.

This greater complexity of specification, its essential three-variable nature, leads to more complex problems in analysis. Durkheim's successes and failures in coping with some of these problems are instructive. . . .

Contextual Analysis

The variety of analyses that come under the heading of specification is suggested by Hyman's classification; among other ways, one can specify a relationship according to the interest and concern of respondents, the time and place at which it occurs, or the conditions and contingencies on which it depends.[9] Durkheim's analysis provides still another type based on the "units of analysis." This type of specification of which there are several varieties, has been called "contextual analysis": it involves the joint effects of an individual characteristic and a group characteristic on rates of individual behavior. In discussing the lower suicide rate among married people, Durkheim points out that in France the difference between the married and the single (his "coefficient of preservation") is greater among the men, while in the Grand-Duchy of Oldenburg it is greater among the women.[10] That is, the social and cultural differences between France and Oldenburg are manifested in two essentially different ways: (1) They exert a *direct* effect; the over-all suicide rate is noticeably higher in France than in Oldenburg. (2) They exert an *indirect* effect; the *relationship* between sex and suicide is different in France and in Oldenburg. In other words, national characteristics have a differential impact on the sex-suicide association in the two countries, the difference between the sexes

being greater in France than in Oldenburg.

Statistical Interaction

Methodological devices like contextual
analysis are more than ingenious ways to
manipulate data. As Merton has emphasized, they are important in opening new
directions for theory.[11] Durkheim's contextual analysis raises questions about the
ways in which group and individual characteristics interact to affect behavior. For
example, under what conditions do national
characteristics produce such a marked reversal in the association between individual attributes and behavior?

The negative side of this case can also
be found in *Suicide:* where Durkheim
lacked adequate statistical techniques, he
was occasionally led into theoretical contradictions. At one point he asserts that
"the relation between the aptitude for suicide of married persons and that of widowers and widows is identically the same
in widely different social groups, from the
simple fact that the moral condition of
widowhood everywhere bears the same relation to the moral constitution characteristic of marriage." [12] But Durkheim's data
on Oldenburg and France lead to the opposite conclusion—that the relation between the suicide rates of married persons
and widows and widowers was *not* the
same in the two countries. What Durkheim
lacked and what has since become available is a precise conception of statistical
interaction, the ways in which the association between two variables depends on the
values of a third variable.[13]

Durkheim's treatment of statistical interaction and of the theoretical relationships
that it measures is notably inconsistent.
Sometimes, as here, he ignores the presence of interaction in his data. Elsewhere,
he correctly notes its presence, remarking,
for example, that seasonal differences in
suicide are less pronounced in cities than
in rural areas.[14] And in another place he
assumes, without any evidence for or
against his assumption, that the interaction
of temperature and location is zero: ". . .
if the temperature had the supposed influence, it should be felt equally in the geographical distribution of suicides." [15]

One possible reason for Durkheim's inconsistency is that he had not formalized
his analytical procedures. In effect, each
time he came to a case of specification, it
had to be reasoned through from the beginning. Formalizations such as the Lazars-
feld-Kendall-Hyman types of elaboration
enable the analyst to recognize the same
principle at work in different instances and
therefore to treat them similarly.

When to Stop an Empirical Analysis

The idea of elaboration also illuminates
the seemingly unrelated problem of deciding when further analysis is needed. Durkheim's treatment of "race" and suicide provides a case in point.[16] Arguing that the
high rate of suicide in Germany "might
be due to the special nature of German
civilization," he decides to "see whether
the German retains this sad primacy outside of Germany." To this end he examines
the suicide rates in the provinces of Austria-
Hungary, in which German-speaking people range from 1.9 to 100 per cent, and
finds "not the least trace of German influence" on the suicide rate.[17] However, a
close examination of Durkheim's data, particularly of the five provinces that have
high proportions of Germans and disproportionately few suicides, leads to quite
different conclusions. These provinces—
Upper Austria, Salzburg, Transalpine
Tyrol, Carinthia, and Styria—comprise the
western part of present-day Austria. If these
five contiguous provinces are removed, the
Spearman rank correlation for the remain-

ing ten provinces is .95, indicating an almost perfect relationship between the suicide rate and the proportion of German-speaking people.

The important point here is not substantive but methodological. Durkheim stopped his analysis as soon as he found a "zero" relationship. This procedure is perhaps more common in research today. Small associations are considered a signal to turn to other matters, especially when the associations are not statistically significant. The reasoning behind this assumption is never made explicit, but it would seem to be that, if two variables are not associated when other items are left free to vary, they will not be associated when these other items are "held constant." That is, if the total association between two variables is zero, the partial associations will be zero. Sometimes this is true; often it is not. Hyman's passage on the "elaboration of a zero relationship" [18] indicates that this may happen when the two partial relations are approximately equal in size and opposite in sign. For example, a surprisingly small association between job satisfaction and participation in community organizations resulted from a positive association between participation and satisfaction among members of the working class and a negative association of approximately the same size in the white-collar class.

To my knowledge, Hyman's is the only published discussion of this problem. It may be useful, therefore, to make two further points suggested by Hyman's brief treatment. First, he implies that this kind of relationship is uncommon and even accidental. Actually, it may occur frequently under certain conditions—for example, in the kind of contextual analysis discussed above, where people are assigned to groups instead of being born into them or choosing them themselves. A study of leisure-time behavior in army training companies found that many small or zero associations between behavior and an individual characteristic, such as marital status, resulted from opposite and approximately equal associations in companies with different "leadership climates." [19]

Second, still another type of elaboration of a zero relationship may be ranged alongside the two identified by Hyman. A zero association between two variables may occur even when both partial associations are in the same direction. The hypothetical example in Table 1 shows that this case would interest the student of political behavior. At both levels of education, the people with more information tend to choose the Democratic party, yet the "collapsed" table of information and party affiliation without regard to education will show that, among both the more-informed and the less-informed, 50 per cent are Democrats. The two partial associations are positive (and about the same size); the total association is zero. Unrealistic as this example may be (although it could describe a university town with a Democratic newspaper), it does demonstrate the importance of looking into those zero associations that theory or previous research suggests should not have been zero. A zero association between two variables may therefore result from any one of three different conditions in the partial relationships: zero associations in both partials, equal and opposite associations, or associations in the same direction. Only the first of these is a signal to stop the analysis.

TABLE 1. Information and Party Affiliation Education Held Constant (Hypothetical Data)

	LESS EDUCATED		MORE EDUCATED	
	Much Infor- mation	*Little Infor- mation*	*Much Infor- mation*	*Little Infor- mation*
Per cent Democratic	38	24	74	63
N	(200)	(100)	(100)	(200)

Notes

1. An earlier version of this paper appeared in the *American Journal of Sociology,* Vol. LXIII (1958), pp. 607–19.

2. Émile Durkheim, *Suicide,* trans. John A. Spaulding and George Simpson (New York: The Free Press, 1951).

3. Émile Durkheim, *The Rules of Sociological Method,* trans. Sarah A. Solvay and John H. Mueller (Glencoe, Ill.: Free Press, 1938); Talcott Parsons, *The Structure of Social Action* (New York: The Free Press, 1949), pp. 20–27 and Chapter ix.

4. Paul F. Lazarsfeld and Morris Rosenberg (eds.), *The Language of Social Research* (New York: The Free Press, 1955), p. 4.

Parsons, *op. cit.*; Harry Alpert, *Émile Durkheim and His Sociology* (New York: Columbia University Press, 1939), Parts II and III; Émile Benoit-Smullyan, "The Sociologism of Émile Durkheim and His School," in Henry Elmer Barnes (ed.), *An Introduction to the History of Sociology* (Chicago: University of Chicago Press, 1948), Chapter xxvii. His chapter contains a considerable bibliography.

5. Lazarsfeld and Rosenberg, *op. cit.,* p. 11.

6. This and the following two paragraphs are taken from *Suicide,* pp. 152–56.

7. Paul F. Lazarsfeld, "Interpretation of Statistical Relations as a Research Operation," in Lazarsfeld and Rosenberg, *op. cit.,* pp. 115–25; Patricia L. Kendall and Paul F. Lazarsfeld, "Problems of Survey Analysis," in Robert K. Merton and Paul F. Lazarsfeld (eds.), *Continuities in Social Research: Studies in the Scope and Method of "The American Soldier"* (New York: The Free Press, 1950), pp. 133–96, esp. pp. 135–67; Herbert H. Hyman, *Survey Design and Analysis* (New York: The Free Press, 1955), Chapters vi and vii.

8. *Rules,* p. 131.

9. Hyman, *op. cit.,* pp. 295–311.

10. *Suicide,* pp. 177–80.

11. Robert K. Merton, *Social Theory and Social Structure* (Glencoe, Ill.: Free Press, 1949), Chapter iii.

12. *Suicide,* p. 307.

13. The phenomenon of statistical interaction has been given many different names (e.g., specification, conditional relationship, differential impact, differential sensitivity, and nonadditivity of effects).

14. *Suicide,* p. 120.

15. *Ibid.,* p. 113.

16. *Ibid.,* pp. 86–87.

17. By today's standards Durkheim's table shows a moderately high degree of association. The Spearman rank correlation is .57. In general, Durkheim regarded anything much less than perfect rank correlation as "independent." The reason why he could demand and find such high levels of association, while survey researchers are content with much less impressive relationships, has to do with the differences in the numbers of cases on which the associations are based. See the discussion of "grouping" in G. Udny Yule and M. G. Kendall, *An Introduction to the Theory of Statistics* (14th ed.; New York: Hafner, 1950), pp. 313–14.

18. *Op. cit.,* pp. 307–10.

19. Hanan C. Selvin, *The Effects of Leadership Climate on the Nonduty Behavior of Army Trainees* ("University Microfilms Publications," No. 19.250 [microfilmed Ph.D. dissertation, Columbia University, 1956]), Appendix F.

20. Sociomedical Variations among Ethnic Groups [1]

EDWARD A. SUCHMAN

THE INFLUENCE of cultural background upon a society's definition of illness and appropriate illness behavior has been well documented by numerous social and anthropological field studies.[2] In general, these studies have shown that the perception and definition of illness, the functions it serves, the medical care sought, and the adjustments made are rooted in social-group factors—religious beliefs, group values, family organization, and child-rearing practices. Zborowski, for example, studied variations in reactions to pain among Jewish and Italian patients and found that Jewish patients were more concerned with the meaning and consequence of their symptoms, while Italian patients primarily sought relief from pain.[3] This preoccupation of the Jewish group with symptoms of illness is supported in a study by Croog, who, in a comparison of army inductees, found that Jews at all educational levels reported the greatest number of symptoms.[4] While explanations for these observed differences in illness-related attitudes and behavior are usually offered in terms of an ethnic group's traditional cultural patterns,[5] very few studies have actually attempted to control for such factors in comparing variations in illness responses among ethnic groups. In one of the few studies utilizing such controls, Mechanic found little support for the hypothesis that differences in illness behavior between Jewish and Catholic students could be ex-

plained in terms of varying degrees of religiosity.[6]

The purpose of this report is to examine ethnic variations in health-related knowledge, attitudes, and behavior in terms of the different forms of social organization found among the different ethnic groups in an urban community. While anthropological surveys have amply documented crosscultural variations in relation to health and illness, much less is known about such differences within a single community.[7] "Society," especially complex, modern, mass society, is not a single homogeneous group of people but is compounded of many varieties of overlapping subgroups with different attributes and intensities of cohesion. It is our major hypothesis that, within a community with as heterogeneous an ethnic composition as New York City, significant differences will be found among ethnic subgroups in responses to illness and medical care and that, furthermore, these differences will be associated with variations in the form of social organization of the ethnic groups.

To test this hypothesis, we propose (1) to determine how ethnic groups vary in their responses to illness and medical care, (2) to analyze these ethnic groups for differences in form of social organization, and (3) to relate any significant differences in social organization to the observed variations in sociomedical factors in an attempt to determine the extent to which such eth-

Reprinted with permission from *The American Journal of Sociology,* LXX (November 1964) pp. 319–31 (copyright 1964 by The University of Chicago Press).

nic variation can be attributed to underlying differences in social organization.

Method of Procedure

This study is based upon information obtained by personal interviews with a representative cross-section of adults, twenty-one years of age or over, living in the Washington Heights community of New York City. Data were obtained for a probability sample of 5,340 persons comprising some 2,215 families by means of household interviews conducted from November, 1960, through April, 1961.

The first interview was conducted with an adult member of the family, usually the female head of the household. This interview obtained the basic demographic data, including ethnicity, for all members of the household, an inventory of all chronic conditions and impairments, and a record of all medically attended illnesses experienced by any family member during the past year. All adult members of this initial sample were then listed, and a random sample of 1,883 respondents was selected for a more detailed interview on medical knowledge, attitudes, and behavior. This is the sample upon which the current report is based. A weighted completion rate of over 90 per cent was obtained from all eligible respondents.[8]

According to the 1960 Census, the Washington Heights community contains about 100,000 dwelling units comprising approximately 270,000 people. Because there is a great deal of ethnic variation within the community, it was possible to study sizable samples of several different ethnic groups. The per cent nonwhite in the community has increased rapidly since 1930 until nonwhites now constitute about a quarter of the total population. Foreign-born whites represent another quarter of the population. This proportion has stayed fairly constant since 1930, when the predominant foreign country of birth was Russia. The predominant foreign country of birth in 1950 was Germany. Today, the influx of Puerto Rican migrants to New York City has resulted in a sizable number of Puerto Ricans in the community. The increase in the nonwhite population is complemented by a decrease in the native-born white population, which currently makes up about one-half the population of the district.[9]

FORMATION OF ETHNIC GROUPINGS

The three major ethnic characteristics chosen for comparison were race, religion, and country of origin. At first these were to be analyzed separately, but it immediately became apparent that they were so closely interrelated as to make a separate analysis meaningless. Negroes were predominantly native-born Protestants, while Puerto Ricans were "foreign"-born Catholics. Because of this inherent overlap of race, religion, and country of birth, we have formulated the following six categories as representing the major ethnic subgroups in our study community.[10]

Ethnic Group	No.	Per Cent
Negro	442	25
Puerto Rican-born	170	9
White:		
Jewish	490	27
Protestant	165	9
Catholic	354	20
Irish-born Catholic	174	10
Total	1,795*	100

* Ethnicity could not be determined accurately in eight cases of the total sample of 1,883.

The above classification eliminates overlapping categories between race, religion, and country of birth and permits a comparison of the six major ethnic groups residing in the study community. These six subgroups, in our opinion, constitute meaningful sociocultural entities with diverse cultural traditions and social structures and among which we may expect to find differences in health-related knowledge, attitudes, and behavior.

Findings

The ethnic groups included in our sample were asked a series of questions dealing with various aspects of health, illness, and medical care. These questions tapped three major areas of medical concern: (1) knowledge of disease and its prevention; (2) attitudes toward medical care; and (3) responses to illness. In each area, two indexes were developed using Guttman scale analysis techniques as follows:

Knowledge of disease and its prevention:
Knowledge about disease
Preventive medical behavior
Attitudes to medical care:
Skepticism of medical care
Physician's interest in patient's welfare

Responses to illness:
Acceptance of sick role
Dependency in illness.[11]

The observed differences are presented in Table 1 and show quite conclusively that ethnic differences do occur in relation to each of these sociomedical factors.

To summarize, we find that in regard to "knowledge about disease," Puerto Ricans are least informed (48.2 per cent receiving a "low" score), while white Protestants are best informed (only 18.1 per cent scoring "low"). On a measure of "preventive medical behavior," the Puerto Ricans again score lowest, with the Jews and Protestants scoring highest (20.1 versus 10.5 per cent and 14.6 per cent "low," respectively). In regard to attitudes toward medical care, the Puerto Ricans score highest on "skepticism of medical care," while Protestants score lowest (38.2 versus 12.7 per cent "high skepticism," respectively). However, only slight differences occur in relation to an index of "physician's interest in patient's welfare" with all ethnic groups being quite

TABLE 1. Relationship between Ethnicity and Health-Related Indexes (Per Cent)

| | | | WHITE | | | | |
	NEGRO	PUERTO RICAN	Protes-tant	Cath-olic	Jewish	Irish	TOTAL
Knowledge about disease:							
Low score	29.5	48.2	18.1	26.4	26.2	28.3	28.6
Preventive medical behavior:							
Low	12.8	20.1	14.6	21.2	10.5	15.6	15.0
Skepticism of medical care:							
High	23.1	38.2	12.7	23.2	16.9	17.2	21.3
Physician's interest in patient's welfare:							
Low interest	18.1	18.2	18.8	16.7	26.5	13.2	19.7
Acceptance of sick role:							
Low	40.5	50.0	42.4	44.9	37.4	50.6	42.6
Dependency in illness:							
High	26.2	37.7	17.0	31.1	20.0	34.5	26.5
Total cases*	(442)	(170)	(165)	(354)	(490)	(174)	(1,795)

* Total no. of cases in each table may vary slightly depending upon frequency of "no answer" category.

similar except for the Jewish group, which has a significantly negative attitude in this respect. An analysis of responses to illness shows the Puerto Rican group having the greatest difficulty in "acceptance of sick role," while the Irish-Catholic group shows the highest "dependency in illness."

In general, it would seem that the greatest ethnic-group contrast in regard to sociomedical factors occurs between the Puerto Ricans on the one hand and the white Protestants and Jews on the other. In most aspects of health knowledge, attitudes, and behavior, the Puerto Rican group stands out as most divorced from the objectives and methods of modern medicine and public health, while the Protestants and Jews are most in accord with them. This finding would help explain why the Puerto Ricans, and to a lesser extent the Negroes, constitute the core of the "hard-to-reach" groups in public health and medical care.[12]

The interpretation of the meaning and significance of the above differences in ethnic responses to illness has been discussed in a separate report and need not concern us further.[13] Suffice it to say that, in the present study, ethnic groups have been found to vary significantly on a series of measures indicative of health knowledge, attitudes, and behavior. Our problem now is to try to determine to what extent the observed ethnic differences in sociomedical factors are due to variations in the social organization of these groups. We hypothesize that the more ethnocentric and cohesive the social group, the more isolated and alienated it will be from the larger society and the less likely it will be to accept the objectives and methods of the formal medical care system.

In this study, we have developed five main indexes of social organization based upon degree of "in-group" identification. These indexes deal with the individual's friendship groups, his family, and his community relationship and may be identified as (1) ethnic exclusivity, (2) friendship solidarity, (3) social-group cohesiveness, (4) family tradition and authority orientation, (5) religious attendance.[14]

Table 2 shows the differences among ethnic groups for these specific indexes of social organization. In regard to "ethnic exclusivity" and "religious attendance," the Jewish and Protestant groups show the least amount of ethnic solidarity, while the Puerto Ricans and Catholics show the most, with Negroes falling in between. When we turn to the closeness of the individual's relationship with his own particular friendship group, we again find that the Puerto Ricans and Irish tend to belong to friendship groups which may be characterized as highly cohesive while the Protestants, Jews, and Negroes belong to rather loose friendship groups. Finally, in regard to the authority structure of the family, the Puerto Ricans and Irish also show the strongest "orientation toward tradition and authority" as compared to the Protestants and the Jews.

From what we know of the social organization of the various ethnic groups in New York City, the differences observed above in the degree and type of social integration appear valid. Other studies have noted the strong ethnocentric ties of the Puerto Rican migrants to New York City and their relative "isolation" from the mainstream of American affairs.[15] Their high degree of social integration probably reflects both this isolation and the less cosmopolitan nature of the Puerto Rican society from which they have migrated. Similarly, the lower religiosity of the Protestant and Jewish groups reflect basic differences in the values and norms of these groups as compared to the Catholics, both native and foreign-born.

The ambivalent position of the Negro in American society is also documented by our findings.[16] While the members of the Negro group tend to be isolated from the majority group, they have not developed

TABLE 2.   Relationship between Ethnicity and Indexes of Social-Group Organization (Per Cent)

| | NEGRO | PUERTO RICAN | WHITE | | | | TOTAL |
			Protes-tant	Cath-olic	Jewish	Irish	
Ethnic exclusivity:							
High	18.1	36.5	9.7	12.4	6.9	15.5	14.7
Friendship solidarity:							
High	29.2	56.5	15.2	42.6	33.1	56.9	36.8
Social-group cohesiveness:							
High	27.5	37.6	29.3	32.7	19.6	33.7	27.7
Family orientation to tradi-tion and authority:							
High	24.0	43.4	16.9	32.9	20.2	42.4	27.8
Religious attendance:							
High	23.2	43.5	16.0	48.9	11.1	80.8	32.1
Total cases	(442)	(170)	(165)	(354)	(490)	(174)	(1,795)

the strong sense of ethnic identity of the Puerto Ricans. Their social-group ties are also weaker than the other minority groups as are their attachments to the family. Thus they appear to live as members of the larger American society but lack many of its social supports.

Given these findings: (1) ethnic groups vary on health knowledge, attitudes, and behavior, and (2) ethnic groups vary in social organization, we may now proceed to test the extent to which ethnic variations in health-related variables are due to underlying differences in social organization. For purposes of this analysis, we have developed combined scores of social organization and of sociomedical responses. A multivariate analysis of the five indexes of social organization and the six indexes of sociomedical responses indicated that reliable and valid combinations could be made of the following sets of indexes:

SOCIAL ORGANIZATION

1. Ethnic exclusivity
2. Friendship solidarity
3. Family orientation to tradition and authority

SOCIOMEDICAL RESPONSES:

1. Knowledge about disease
2. Skepticism of medical care
3. Dependency in illness [17]

The combined index of social organization indicates the degree to which the individual comes from a social group that may be characterized as homogeneous and highly cohesive. We have labeled this dimension as "cosmopolitanism-parochialism," with the cosmopolitan end of the scale indicating heterogeneous and loosely knit interpersonal relationships while the parochial end indicates homogeneous and closely knit interpersonal relationships.[18] This measure may be taken to indicate the degree of identification of an individual with a parochial or limited, traditional, narrowly confined, and closely knit "ingroup" point of view, as opposed to a cosmopolitan or more worldly, progressive, "urban" or less personal way of life.

The combined index of sociomedical varables indicates the degree to which the individual maintains an informed, favorable, and independent approach to illness and medical care. This dimension we have

TABLE 3.   Relationship between Ethnicity, Social Organization, and Health Orientation

ETHNICITY	NO.	PER CENT "PARO-CHIAL" SOCIAL ORGAN-IZATION	PER CENT "POPU-LAR" HEALTH ORIEN-TATION	PER CENT "POPULAR" HEALTH ORIENTATION BY SOCIAL ORGANIZATION		
				Cosmopolitan	Mixed	Parochial
Puerto Rican	170	60.6	51.8	24.0 (25)	35.7 (42)	65.0 (103)
Black	442	29.0	27.0	18.0 (128)	23.2 (185)	41.4 (128)
White:						
Catholic	354	33.3	27.1	13.7 (80)	23.1 (156)	41.5 (118)
Irish	174	48.9	24.7	12.9 (31)	20.7 (58)	31.8 (85)
Protestant	165	12.7	15.2	7.5 (80)	15.6 (64)	42.9 (21)
Jewish	490	24.5	16.5	9.1 (186)	17.4 (184)	26.7 (120)

labeled as a "scientific-popular" health orientation with the scientific end of the scale indicating an objective, formal, professional, independent approach while the popular end indicates a subjective, informal, lay, dependent health orientation.[19] It is our hypothesis that a cosmopolitan form of social organization will be more highly related to a scientific approach to illness and medical care than a parochial social organization, which will be more highly related to a popular health orientation. Thus we would predict that the more parochial an ethnic group is, the more likely it is that its members will adhere to a popular or nonscientific health orientation.

Table 3 reveals highly significant differences in both social organization and health orientation among the various ethnic groups. The Puerto Rican group is highly parochial while the white Protestant and Jewish groups are highly cosmopolitan. The Irish-Catholic group is also highly parochial, as are other Catholics, while the Negro group is more inclined toward cosmopolitanism than parochialism. As hypothesized, differences in health orientation parallel these differences in social organization with the Puerto Ricans, the most highly parochial group, being twice as likely to have a popular health orientation

as any of the other ethnic groups. Probably this high combination of parocialism and popular health orientation among Puerto Ricans reflects both the social structure and health culture of their country of origin reinforced by their currently low socioeconomic status and minority-group treatment in the United States. White Protestants and Jews, the most cosmopolitan of the ethnic groups, are also the most scientific in their approach to health and medical care.

Looking at the effect of social organization on health orientation within each ethnic group, we find that in each case higher parochialism is associated with a more popular or nonscientific health orientation.[20] This relationship is highest among white Protestants and Jews and lowest among the Puerto Ricans. Thus we conclude that the relationship between social organization and health orientation is independent of ethnic-group membership. Both ethnicity and form of social organization contribute independently and cumulatively to health orientation with the popular approach being followed least by the cosmopolitan Protestants (7.5 per cent) and most adhered to by the parochial Puerto Ricans (65 per cent).

A final comparison may be made combining both the demographic variables of socioeconomic status and ethnicity. Ethnicity is, of course, related to social class, with the Puerto Ricans and Negroes belonging predominantly to the lower socioeconomic level, while the white Protestants and Jews come from the upper socioeconomic level. Looking at socioeconomic status [21] and ethnicity simultaneously in Table 4 only serves to increase the social-group differences, with both social class and ethnicity being independently related to social organization and health orientation. Lower-class Puerto Ricans are both most parochial and most popular-health oriented while upper-class white Protestants and Jews are most cosmopolitan and scientific in their approach to health and medical care.

When we look at the relationship between social organization and health orientation for the combined ethnic and social class groups, we see (Table 5) that within each ethnic and socioeconomic group parochialism continues to be associated with a popular or nonscientific health orientation. Thus, for example, at the same time that Puerto Ricans *as a group* are more parochial and more popular-health oriented than Protestants and Jews, within each of these groups the more parochial an individual is, the more likely is he to be popular-health oriented. Our extreme contrasting groups now become lower-class, parochial Puerto Ricans, 71.2 per cent of whom hold a popular-health orientation, and upper-class, cosmopolitan Protestants, only 5.4 per cent of whom have a popular-health orientation.

Looking at Table 5, we note a possible interaction effect, with social-class differences being quite pronounced among the parochial groups but small and irregular among the cosmopolitan groups. It would appear that social-class variations in health orientation are, in part, a function of the

TABLE 4. Social Organization and Health According to Socioeconomic Status and Ethnicity

		Socioeconomic Status		
ETHNICITY	*UPPER*	*UPPER MIDDLE*	*LOWER MIDDLE*	*LOWER*
		Per Cent "Parochial" Social Organization		
Puerto Rican	*	59.0 (39)	55.4 (83)	73.0 (37)
Negro	16.2 (37)	23.6 (123)	26.9 (171)	40.5 (84)
White:				
Catholic	17.2 (29)	17.9 (123)	43.7 (128)	55.7 (61)
Protestant	2.9 (35)	9.8 (61)	21.6 (51)	*
Jewish	20.8 (101)	16.7 (210)	34.5 (110)	43.2 (44)
Irish	40.0 (20)	36.9 (65)	50.0 (60)	71.8 (27)
		Per Cent "Popular" Health Orientation		
Puerto Rican	*	33.3 (39)	53.0 (83)	70.3 (37)
Negro	13.5 (37)	21.1 (123)	24.7 (170)	47.6 (84)
White:				
Catholic	27.6 (29)	20.3 (123)	25.0 (128)	44.3 (61)
Protestant	2.9 (35)	13.1 (61)	27.5 (51)	*
Jewish	8.9 (101)	13.8 (210)	24.5 (110)	29.5 (44)
Irish	5.0 (20)	20.0 (65)	31.7 (60)	37.0 (27)

* Less than 15 cases.

type of social organization of the group. Ethnic differences decrease greatly in importance once social class and parochial-cosmopolitanism are controlled. With the single exception of the Puerto Rican group, which represents a rather special case of relatively recent removal from a folk culture, only minor ethnic variations occur within the separate social-class and parochial-cosmopolitan groups.

On the basis of these findings, we may now reformulate our initial hypotheses as follows:

1. Ethnic groups differ in regard to sociomedical variables of knowledge about disease, attitudes to medical care, and responses to illness.
2. But (a) ethnic groups also differ in form of social organization; and (b) social organization also relates to the sociomedical variables.
3. Therefore, we now determine the way in which ethnicity and social organization are interrelated in their effect upon the sociomedical factors. We test two possible models of "causation": (a) Ethnicity leads to sociocultural differences which in turn lead to sociomedical variations, or (b) both ethnicity and sociocultural factors independently (and hence cumulatively) affect sociomedical variations.

In general, it would appear that form of social organization transcends the mere fact of ethnic-group membership in determining sociomedical variations. While ethnicity and social class are both independent contributing factors to parochial-cosmopolitanism, it is this latter variable which continues to show the highest and most consistent relationships to health orientation. Thus, our findings would point toward alternative (a) as more closely fitting the available data.

In the above analysis we have dealt with two combined indexes of social organization and health orientation. We now return to a brief discussion of the specific variables included in these general indexes since each one does tap a somewhat different and significant aspect of of social organization and health orientation. Space limitations will require us to touch only on the main findings and to forego any detailed statistical presentation.

In regard to knowledge about disease, we find that, for all ethnic groups in general, a lack of information is associated with higher ethnic exclusivity, friendship-group solidarity, and family orientation to tradition and authority. It would thus appear that the stronger the individual's social

TABLE 5.   Relationship between Social Organization and Health Orientation According to Socioeconomic Status and Ethnicity

| | Per Cent "Popular" Health Orientation | | | | | |
| | UPPER SOCIOECONOMIC GROUPS | | | LOWER SOCIOECONOMIC GROUPS | | |
ETHNICITY	Cosmopolitan	Mixed	Parochial	Cosmopolitan	Mixed	Parochial
Puerto Rican	*	*	46.4 (28)	28.6 (14)	42.4 (33)	71.2 (73)
Negro	18.5 (54)	15.5 (71)	28.6 (35)	18.1 (72)	30.4 (102)	47.5 (80)
White:						
Catholic	16.1 (56)	20.3 (69)	37.0 (27)	9.1 (22)	24.7 (77)	42.2 (90)
Protestant	5.4 (56)	9.1 (33)	*	15.0 (20)	23.3 (30)	42.9 (14)
Jewish	8.5 (142)	12.4 (113)	21.4 (56)	13.5 (37)	26.7 (60)	33.3 (57)
Irish	14.3 (21)	15.6 (32)	18.7 (32)	10.0 (10)	26.9 (26)	41.2 (51)

* Less than 10 cases.

ties, the lower his level of health knowledge. We can only speculate that such
group support tends to decrease the need
for a cognitive understanding of disease.
It is as if the search for facts about disease
provided an alternative form of security for
those individuals with weak community,
social, and family ties. On the other hand,
it is also possible that high social-group
integration and low health knowledge are
both reflections of a common low level of
acceptance of modern social change. Support for this explanation may be seen in
the particularly large differences in health
knowledge among those individuals who
are highly parochial as compared to those
who are highly cosmopolitan.

In general, strong in-group allegiances
are also associated with a higher degree of
skepticism toward medical care. Again it
would seem that the stronger the social ties
of an individual, the greater his distrust of
outside influences, including medical care.
It would appear that the individual's support from and dependence upon his social
group acts somewhat as a barrier to seeking
professional medical care outside the group.

The above skepticism does not seem to
extend in the same manner to an evaluation of the individual physician's interest
in the welfare of his patients. Among all
groups, more favorable evaluations of the
physician-patient relationship are registered
by those individuals who belong to social
groups with high solidarity and who come
from families with a high orientation to
tradition and authority. This is the opposite direction from the previous finding on
skepticism of medical care. It would seem
that stronger in-group identification becomes associated with greater distrust of
the medical-care system at the same time
that it becomes more favorable toward the
individual physician. This could be a reflection of differing attitudes toward im-
personalized, official medical organization
contrasted to personalized, private care.
Strong social-group allegiances appear to
oppose the former and favor the latter,
perhaps indicating the greater value placed
upon close interpersonal relationships by
those individuals who belong to the more
highly integrated social groups.

It is in relation to family orientation to
tradition and authority that we find the
most significant relationship between social
organization and acceptance of the sick
role. The higher the degree of family orientation to tradition and authority, the greater
the difficulty in assuming the sick role. This
is particularly true for the Irish, Puerto
Ricans, and Negroes. It would seem that,
in general, strong family authority acts
against giving in to illness. It may be that
the obligations of a family member to carry
on his normal activities in the face of illness is felt most strongly within families
with a high orientation toward tradition
and authority.[22]

Significant, and consistent, relationships
are found between illness dependency and
social organization for all ethnic groups.
In all cases lower dependency in illness is
associated with lower ethnic exclusivity,
friendship-group solidarity, and family orientation to tradition and authority. Regardless of ethnic-group membership, it would
seem that the degree of support one seeks
and secures from one's social group is influenced by the degree of social integration
of the group. The more cohesive the group,
the greater the dependency of the individual upon it for support during illness.

There is an interesting reversal, however,
between social-group support and family
support. We find, for each ethnic group,
that strong social-group integration seems
to make it easier for one to turn to one's
group for help, while strong family authority seems to make it more difficult to seek
help within the family. As a possible explanation of this reversal, we suggest that
the relinquishing of one's normal respon-
sibilities in illness constitutes more of a
threat and disruption to one's family than
to one's social group. The individual usu-

ally is more necessary to the functioning of the family than to his social group, and hence the family may make it more difficult for him to assume a dependency in illness than does the social group. In other words, the reversal may reflect the fact that a close-knit family is more likely to *demand* support from the adult individual while a close-knit social group is more likely to *give* support to the individual.

The independent and cumulative nature of the contribution of both ethnicity and social organization to health orientation noted previously in regard to the combined cosmopolitan-parochial and scientific-popular indexes is supported by each of the individual measures. In all cases, ethnicity and the specific index of social organization continue to be related separately to each of the specific indexes of health orientation. The cumulative differences produced by both factors are illustrated, for example, in Table 6 which contrasts Puerto Ricans in highly cohesive social groups with white Protestants in weakly integrated groups according to knowledge about disease, skepticism of medical care, and dependency in illness.

This comparison of sociomedical responses between Puerto Ricans and Protestants belonging to groups with contrasting forms of social organization highlights one of the main implications of this study for the field of medical sociology. Of all the so-called ethnic "minorities" (a term which requires a special interpretation in New York City where such sociological "minorities" often constitute numerical majorities), Puerto Ricans show the greatest deviation from what might be evaluated as "desirable" sociomedical knowledge, attitudes, and responses to illness. The Puerto Rican-born individual lies on one end of a continuum of ethnic variations in relation to health and medical care while we find the native-born white Protestant at the other. The Negro group tends to resemble the Puerto Ricans, while the Jewish group is closer to the Protestants.

Thus, it would seem that individuals and groups ranking high in parochialism find it more difficult to accept the type of highly organized and formal medical-care system to be found in New York City. A conflict exists between a highly bureaucratic administrative system of medical care and a large segment of the population more at home with personalized care.[23] Puerto Ricans, being in general more parochial than other ethnic groups, appear to have the greatest difficulty in adapting themselves to the modern "scientific" as opposed to a "folk" approach to medical care. In a sense, social isolation seems to breed "medical" isolation. The generally restricted outlook and lower expectations of the socially withdrawn groups find expression in narrower health horizons.

TABLE 6.   Comparison of Sociomedical Variations between Puerto Ricans and White Protestants of Contrasting Social Organization (Per Cent)

	PUERTO RICANS ("HIGH")			WHITE PROTESTANTS ("LOW")		
	Ethnic Exclusivity	Friendship Solidarity	Family Authority	Ethnic Exclusivity	Friendship Solidarity	Family Authority
Low knowledge about disease	66.1	57.3	64.6	15.8	14.1	10.8
High skepticism of medical care	48.4	41.7	44.6	5.3	7.1	7.7
Low dependency in illness	9.7	8.3	9.2	47.4	45.5	49.2
No. of cases	(62)	(96)	(65)	(95)	(99)	(65)

This statement of the problem of providing medical care for the minority groups in our large cities—groups, incidentally, most in need of such care—may help to explain the resistance of such groups to health programs in terms of their general alienation from the dominant American society.[24] Their under-utilization of modern medical facilities and their lack of cooperation in community health programs may be simply one more expression of their general estrangement from the mainstream of middle-class American society. In this respect, "medical" disorganization among these groups becomes another form of social disorganization. Health problems constitute an inherent aspect of the larger social problem of poverty and social deprivation. It is doubtful that the barriers that now interfere with effective medical care for this "second America" can be removed except as barriers to full participation in other aspects of American society are also removed.

Notes

1. This investigation was supported in whole by Public Health Service Grant CH00015 from the Division of Community Health Services. Field work was done in cooperation with the Washington Heights Master Sample Survey, Columbia University School of Public Health and Administrative Medicine, supported by the Health Research Council of the City of New York under contract U-1053, Jack Elinson, principal investigator. Lois Alksne, Edward Wellin, Margaret C. Klem, and Sylvia Gilliam (deceased) played a major role in the planning of this project, while field work and analysis were aided by Marvin Belkin, Martin Goldman, Martin Smolin, Raymond Maurice, and Daniel Rosenblatt. John Colombotos and Annette Perrin O'Hare were in charge of interviewing, with Regina Loewenstein responsible for sampling and data-processing.

2. See, e.g., Benjamin D. Paul (ed.), *Health, Culture and Community* (New York: Russell Sage Foundation, 1955); George M. Foster, *Problems in Intercultural Health Programs* (Social Science Research Council Pamphlet 12 [New York: Social Science Research Council,

1958]); Steven Polgar, "Health and Human Behavior: Areas of Interest Common to the Social and Medical Sciences," *Current Anthropology,* III (April 1962), pp. 159–205.

3. Mark Zborowski, "Cultural Components in Responses to Pain," in E. Gartly Jaco (ed.), *Patients, Physicians, and Illness* (New York: The Free Press, 1958), pp. 256–68.

4. Sydney H. Croog, "Ethnic Origins, Educational Level, and Responses to a Health Questionnaire," *Human Organization,* XX (Summer 1961), pp. 65–69.

5. Mark Zborowski and E. Herzog, *Life Is with People* (New York: International Universities Press, 1952); Lyle Saunders, *Cultural Differences and Medical Care* (New York: Russell Sage Foundation, 1954).

6. David Mechanic, "Religion, Religiosity, and Illness Behavior: The Special Case of the Jews," *Human Organization,* XXII (Fall 1963), pp. 202–8.

7. Examples of several such studies would include Beatrice Berle, *Eighty Puerto Rican Families in New York City* (New York: Columbia University Press, 1958); Earl C. Koos, *The Health of Regionville* (New York: Columbia University Press, 1954); Leo Srole *et al., Mental Health in the Metropolis* (New York: McGraw-Hill Book Co., 1962).

8. The first round of interviewing yielded a return of 73 per cent from the eligible dwelling units. A random subsample of one-third of the remaining dwelling units was then selected, and the responses of the interviewers was given triple weight. A detailed comparison of the final sample with the 1960 Census on all available demographic characteristics revealed no major category differing by more than 3 per cent. For details of sampling and census comparisons, see Jack Elinson and Regina Loewenstein, *Community Fact Book for Washington Heights* (New York: School of Public Health and Administrative Medicine, 1963).

9. Lee A. Lendt, *A Social History of Washington Heights, New York City* (New York: Columbia-Washington Heights Community Mental Health Project, February 1960).

10. The meaning of ethnicity in a society with a "melting-pot" tradition such as the United States has is, of course, complex. Lines of racial and national origin are apt to be crossed, and it is extremely doubtful that we can speak of ethnic-group membership in any biological sense. This is of little consequence for a study of responses to illness, since we view these ethnic-group labels mainly as indicative of sociocultural differences, and by "Black" or "Puerto Rican" we mean, for the

most part, a tendency for individuals who hold these characteristics in different degrees also to share common sets of values, norms, attitudes, etc., and to be more or less subject to similar living conditions and social experiences. It is our supposition that, as these shared values and common experiences change, so will the responses of the ethnic individuals to illness and medical care.

11. These indexes were based upon the following specific items:

The "knowledge about disease" score was compiled by scoring 1 point for each right answer to thirteen questions on etiology, treatment, and prognosis of different diseases. The "preventive medical behavior" index was based upon the number of "yes" responses to the following three questions: (1) "Do you get periodical medical checkups when you are not ill?" (2) "Have you had any polio shots yet?" (3) "Are you very careful to see that you eat a balanced diet?" The "skepticism of medical care" index was based on responses (agree = "high" skepticism) to (1) "I believe in trying out different doctors to find which one I think will give me the best care," (2) "When I am ill, I demand to know all the details of what is being done to me," (3) "I have my doubts about some things doctors say they can do for you." The index of "physician's interest in patient's welfare" asked for responses to (1) "Most doctors charge too much money" (agree = negative), (2) "Most doctors are more interested in the welfare of their patients than in anything else" (disagree = negative). The index of "acceptance of sick role" was based on responses (disagree = "high" acceptance) to (1) "I find it very hard to give in and go to bed when I am sick," (2) "I usually try to get up too soon after I have been sick." The "dependency in illness" index asked for responses (agree = "high" dependency) to (1) "When I think I am getting sick, I find it comforting to talk to someone about it," (2) "When a person starts getting well, it is hard to give up having people do things for him."

12. Berle, *op. cit.;* Paul B. Cornely and Stanley K. Bigman, "Some Considerations in Changing Health Attitudes," *Children,* X (January–February 1963), pp. 23–28.

13. Edward A. Suchman, *Socio-Cultural Variations in Illness and Medical Care* (New York: New York City Health Department, 1963).

14. Each of these indexes is based upon combined scores for the following items:

Index of "ethnic exclusivity" is based on responses (agree = "high" exclusivity) to (1) "The parents of most of my friends come from the same country as my parents come from," (2) "I prefer to deal in stores where clerks are the same kind of people as we are." The index of "friendship solidarity" asked for responses (agree = "high" solidarity) to (1) "Almost all my friends are people I grew up with," (2) "Most of my close friends are also friends with each other," (3) "Most of my friends have the same religion as I do," (4) "Most of my friends come from families who know each other well." The "social-group cohesiveness" index is based on reactions to (1) "We are interested in how different people organize their social lives. I am going to ask you to tell me about your friends; you don't have to give me their full names, just the first name or nickname will do, so that we can keep them straight. Would you tell me the first names or nicknames of the people you see most often socially? Start with the person closest to you"; (2) "Are any of these people related to you?" (3) "Do all these people know one another well? Which ones do *not* know which others?" (Enter two "*X*'s" in the proper places in the matrix); (4) "Now about No. 1 . . . does he like No. 2 *very much,* does he like him only *somewhat,* or is he *indifferent* to him?" (Enter "*V*," very much, "*S*," somewhat, or "*I*," indifferent, in matrix. Continue for all relationships.) The "family tradition and authority orientation" index is based on responses (agree = "high" orientation) to (1) "Everybody in my family usually does what the head of the house says without question," (2) "My family usually waits until the head of the house is present before we have dinner," (3) "In my family we think the old-time customs and traditions are important." The index for "religious attendance" asked (1) "About how often do you go to (church) (synagogue) (services)?" (2) "Did you happen to go to (church) (synagogue) (services) last week?"

15. Nathan Glazer and Daniel M. Moynihan, *Beyond the Melting Pot* (Cambridge, Mass.: M.I.T. Press and Harvard University Press, 1963).

16. Gunnar Myrdal, *An American Dilemma* (New York: Harper & Bros., 1944).

17. Matrix tables presenting the intercorrelations of all indexes are given in Edward A. Suchman, *Social Patterns of Health and Medical Care* (New York: New York City Department of Health, 1963).

18. Similar characterizations of social structure may be found in Eliot Freidson, *Patients' Views of Medical Practice* (New York: Russell Sage Foundation, 1961); Alvin W. Gouldner, "Cosmopolitans and Locals: Toward an Analysis of Latent Social Roles—I," *Admin-*

istrative Science Quarterly, II (December 1957), pp. 281–306; Robert Merton, "Patterns of Influence and of Communications Behavior in a Local Community," in Paul Lazarsfeld and Frank Stanton (eds.), *Communications Research, 1948–1949* (New York: Harper & Bros., 1949), pp. 180–219.

19. Discussions of the difference between a scientific and popular health orientation may be found in Stanley King, *Perceptions of Illness and Medical Practice* (New York: Russell Sage Foundation, 1962), pp. 91–120; Lyle Saunders and Gordon W. Howes, "Folk Medicine and Medical Practice," *Journal of Medical Education,* XXVIII (September 1953), pp. 43–46.

20. It has been suggested that this relationship may be an artifact of an "acquiescent response set." The use of scale score instead of individual item correlations decreases this possibility. More important, the observed ethnic-group variations and the relationship between social organization and health orientation holds for such non-attitudinal indexes as social-group cohesion based on number of close friends in one's friendship group, religious attendance, knowledge of illness based on informational questions, and preventive medical behavior based on actual behavioral items.

21. The socioeconomic status index was formed from the person's education, occupation, and total family income as follows. Education was divided into five categories: some college, high-school graduate, some high school, grammar-school graduate, and some grammar school. Occupation was divided into four categories: professional and managerial; clerical and sales; craftsmen and operators; and household, service workers, etc. Total family income was divided into four categories: $7,500 plus, $5,000–$7,500, $3,000–$5,000 and less than $3,000. These were scored and distributed on an index which ranged from a score of 13 for highest SES to 3 for lowest SES. Where information was not ascertained for one of the three index components, the score was based upon a linear interpolation of the remaining two components. Ethnic differences in socioeconomic status were as follows: Per cent "upper" and "upper middle"—Jews (66.8 per cent); Protestants (60.0 per cent); Irish (49.4 per cent); Catholics (44.6 per cent); (Negroes (38.6 per cent); and Puerto Ricans (27.3).

22. To some extent, the presence of a sick individual in the family presents a threat to the harmony of the family (see Talcott Parsons and Renee Fox, "Illness, Therapy, and the Modern Urban American Family," *Journal of Social Issues,* VIII [1952], pp. 31–44; see also Clark E. Vincent, "The Family in Health and Illness: Some Neglected Areas," *Annals of the American Academy of Political and Social Science,* CCCXLVI (March 1963), pp. 109–16).

23. Herbert Gans, *The Urban Villagers* (New York: The Free Press, 1962), p. 277; Ozzie Simmons, *Social Status and Public Health* (New York: Social Science Research Council, 1958), pp. 23–29.

24. See Daniel Rosenblatt and Edward A. Suchman, "The Under-utilization of Medical Care Services by Blue Collarites," and "Blue Collar Attitudes and Information toward Health and Illness," *Blue Collar World,* ed. A. Shostak and W. Gomberg (Englewood Cliffs, N.J.: Prentice-Hall, Inc., 1964).

21. Willingness for Military Service

SAMUEL A. STOUFFER

[Ed. Note: The *American Soldier* was a four-volume account of research on the American Army in World War II by the Research Branch, Information and Education Division of the War Department. The concept of relative deprivation was introduced in these volumes, and the following selection is one of the empirical investigations contributing to the development of the concept.]

PREVIOUSLY in this work we have found that on items reflecting personal *esprit* and personal commitment the following relations held:

The better educated tended to be *more* favorable than the less educated.

The married tended to be *less* favorable than the unmarried.

The men twenty-five and over tended to be *less* favorable than the men under twenty-five in personal commitment, and the age differences on personal *esprit* were inconsistent.

In order to study such patterns more intensively, let us look at a cross-section of soldiers in the United States in February 1944, and focus on one query: namely, how did men feel about being drafted when they entered the Army?

First, we shall see that responses to a question about the fairness of induction distinguished between the cross-section of soldiers and two groups of deviants— AWOL's and psychoneurotics.

Second, we shall see that when the cross-section is broken down, it also reveals consistent differences in attitudes toward induction by education, age, and marital condition.

The question, with its check-list categories, is as follows:

At the time you came into the Army did you think you should have been deferred?
□ I was not drafted, the question does not apply to me.
□ No, I did not think I should have been deferred.
□ Yes, because of dependents who needed my support.
□ Yes, because of the importance of my job.
□ Yes, because of my health or physical condition.
□ Yes, because of some other reason.

In evaluating responses to this question, one must remember that volunteering, in many instances, meant merely entering the Army one step ahead of draft-board action. Nevertheless, Table 1 shows that, if we combine the proportions who said they volunteered and who said they should not have been deferred, we find 74 per cent among the cross-section, 53 per cent among the psychoneurotics, and 41 per cent among the AWOL's. Among the psychoneurotics, 35 per cent gave health as a "reason" that they should have been deferred; the AWOL's "reasons," on the other hand, divided mainly between "dependents who need my support" (26 per cent) and "health" (20 per cent).

While this question belongs primarily in the general area of personal commitment, responses to it also reflect personal *esprit*

Reprinted in part with permission from Chapter 4, pp. 122–27 of *The American Soldier: Adjustment during Army Life,* Vol. I, by Stouffer, Suchman, De Vinney, Star, and Williams (copyright 1949 by the Princeton University Press).

TABLE 1.   Attitudes toward Being Drafted and "Reasons" Given Why One Should Not
Have Been Drafted (United States, September 1943, and January 1944)

QUESTION: "AT THE TIME YOU CAME INTO THE ARMY DID YOU THINK YOU SHOULD HAVE BEEN DEFERRED?"	PERCENTAGE GIVING INDICATED RESPONSE		
	Cross-Section*	Psychoneurotics	AWOL's**
I was not drafted—this question does not apply to me.	25	17	25
No, I did not think I should have been deferred	49	36	16
Yes, because of:			
Dependents who needed my support.	7	5	26
The importance of my job.	5	3	4
My health or physical condition.	9	35	20
Some other reason. (Includes no answer.)	5	4	9
	100	100	100
Number of cases	3,729	613	218

* Cross-section and PN's from S-99, January 1944.
** AWOL's from S-74, September 1943.

at the time of response. This is shown by the fact that among men in the cross section who were highest in personal *esprit* as determined by a cross-tabulation of the "good spirits" item and two other related items, 90 per cent said either that they volunteered or that they should not have been deferred. The responses to this question are not, however, *merely* a reflection of state of mind at the time of response. When asked of new recruits, whose report on their feelings about induction could not be colored by months or years of subsequent Army experience, the question discriminated significantly between recruits who *later* become psychoneurotics and other men. For example, in Volume II, Chapter 9, of *The American Soldier*, it is shown that among seventy-three new recruits studied soon after they entered the Army and found later to have been diagnosed as psychoneurotics within a period of six months *after* the attitude survey, 32 per cent gave reasons why they should not have been drafted. This was a response to a question worded somewhat differently from that in Table 1. By contrast, in a sample of 730 "normal" recruits—equated

with the psychoneurotics for education, age, and marital condition—who were part of the original sample to which the subsequently diagnosed psychoneurotics belonged, only 12 per cent gave reasons why they should not have been drafted. As with the psychoneurotics in Table 1, health was the predominant "reason" for deferment given by the pre-psychoneurotics.

Attitudes toward induction among new recruits also were positively associated with *subsequent* promotion, although this relationship, discussion of which is found in Section V, Chapter 4, Volume I, of *The American Soldier*, is complicated by a countervailing tendency of older men to have the worst attitude toward induction but better objective chances of advancement.

Now let us see how willingness for service varied by education, age, and marital condition. The results, for the same Army cross-section shown in Table 1, are given in Table 2. The range in proportions saying either that they volunteered or that they should not have been deferred was from 59 per cent among the married men

TABLE 2. Willingness for Service, by Marital Condition on Entering the Army, Education, and Age *

| | *Percentage in Cross-Section Who Said They Volunteered or Should Not Have Been Deferred* | | | |
| | *UNMARRIED WHEN ENTERED ARMY* | | *MARRIED WHEN ENTERED ARMY* | |
	Not H.S. Graduates	*H.S. Graduates*	*Not H.S. Graduates*	*H.S. Graduates*
30 and over	68 *(320)*	77 *(157)*	59 *(193)*	64 *(128)*
25 to 29	72 *(323)*	89 *(289)*	60 *(124)*	70 *(146)*
20 to 24	73 *(572)*	85 *(719)*	67 *(144)*	76 *(105)*
Under 20	79 *(200)*	90 *(217)*		

* Number of cases is shown in parentheses. For source of data see Table 1.

over thirty years old who had not gone through high school to 90 per cent among the unmarried high school graduates under twenty years of age. Quite consistently, Table 2 shows, the favorable responses go up as age goes down, are higher for the unmarried than married in corresponding age and educational groups, and are higher for high school graduates than others in each age group by marital condition. This table—which can be replicated from other studies—makes it quite unmistakable that the older married men and the less educated were more inclined to express reluctance about being in the Army than were other soldiers and thus more nearly resembled the AWOL's and psychoneurotics in their responses.

To help explain such variations in attitude, by education, age, and marital condition, a general concept would be useful. Such a concept may be that of relative deprivation, which, as we shall see, is to prove quite helpful in ordering a rather disparate collection of data. . . . The idea is simple, almost obvious, but its utility comes in reconciling data, . . . where its applicability is not at first too apparent. The idea would seem to have a kinship to and in part include such well-known sociological concepts as "social frame of reference," "patterns of expectation," or "definitions of the situation."

Becoming a soldier meant to many men a very real deprivation. But the felt sacrifice was greater for some than for others, *depending on their standards of comparison.*

Take one of the clearest examples: marital condition. The drafted married man, and especially the father, was making the same sacrifices as others plus the additional one of leaving his family behind. This was officially recognized by draft boards and eventually by the point system in the Army which gave demobilization credit for fatherhood. Reluctance of married men to leave their families would have been reinforced in many instances by extremely reluctant wives whose pressures on the husband to seek deferment were not always easy to resist. A further element must have been important psychologically to those married men who were drafted. The very fact that draft boards were more liberal with married than with single men provided numerous examples to the drafted married man of others in his shoes who got relatively better breaks than he did. Comparing himself with his unmarried associates in the Army, he could feel that induction demanded greater sacrifice from him than from them; and comparing himself with his married civilian friends, he could feel that he had been called on for sacrifices that they were escaping altogether. Hence, the married man, on the average, was more likely than others to come into the Army, with reluctance and, possibly, a sense of injustice.

Or take age. Compared with younger men—apart now from marital condition—the older man had at least three stronger grounds for feeling relatively greater deprivation. One had to do with his job—he was likely to be giving up more than, say, a boy just out of high school. Until the defense boom started wheels turning, many men in their late twenties and early thirties had never known steady employment at high wages. Just as they began to taste the joys of a fat pay check, the draft caught up with them. Or else they had been struggling and sacrificing over a period of years to build up a business or profession. The war stopped that. Second, the older men, in all probability, had more physical defects on the average than younger men. These defects, though not severe enough to satisfy the draft board or induction station doctors that they justified deferment, nevertheless could provide a good rationalization for the soldier trying to defend his sense of injustice about being drafted. Both of these factors, job and health, would be aggravated in that a larger proportion of older men than of younger men got deferment in the draft on these grounds—thus providing the older soldiers, like the married soldiers, with ready-made examples of men with comparable backgrounds who were experiencing less deprivation. Third, on the average, older men—particularly those over thirty—would be more likely than youngsters to have a dependent or semi-dependent father or mother—and if, in spite of this fact, the man was drafted, he had further grounds for a sense of injustice.

The concept of relative deprivation may seem, at first glance, not to be applicable to the educational differentials in attitude toward being drafted, as it is to differentials by age and marital condition. Indeed, it is plausible that differentials in comprehension of the nation's military requirements and feelings of personal responsibility concerning them may have accounted for some part of the educational differentials in all attitudes reflecting personal commitment. Some evidence supporting this view is presented in Chapter 9, Volume I, of *The American Soldier,* on "The Orientation of Soldiers toward the War." However, the same types of factors that would seem to vary with age may also have varied with education, age and marital condition constant.

Take health. It would not be unreasonable to surmise that the better educated, *on the average,* were healthier than the less educated. Education and income are quite highly correlated, and it is likely that men from homes of relatively higher income were more likely to have had better nutrition as children, better medical and dental care, less venereal disease, and better protection against the hazards of insanitation. Consequently, such men, on the average, would be less likely to have real physical grounds for feeling that an injustice had been done in inducting them and also would have, on the average, relatively fewer friends who were classified 4-F.

Or take jobs. The less educated soldiers may have made no greater sacrifice on this score than the better educated, but when they compared themselves with their civilian friends, they may have been more likely to feel that they were required to make sacrifices which others like them were excused from making. The two great classes of work which accounted for most exemptions on occupational grounds were farming and skilled labor, predominantly work done by men who have not finished high school. The great mass of professional, trade, and white-collar occupations were not deferable, although there were important exceptions in some managerial and engineering fields. The average high school graduate or college man was a clear-cut candidate for induction; marginal cases on occupational grounds probably occurred much more often in groups with less educational attainment. On the average, the non-high school man who was inducted could point to more acquaintances conceivably no more entitled to deferment than himself, who nonetheless had been deferred on occupational grounds. As Research Branch data show, the soldier who was a non-high school graduate was more likely than the better educated to report that he actually tried to get deferred and was turned down. Finally, the better educated (still keeping age and marital condition constant) would on the average have somewhat less anxiety about dependent fathers or mothers, since their parents would on the average be in relatively more secure income groups.

As is discussed in detail in Chapter 9, Volume I, of *The American Soldier,* "The Orientation of Soldiers toward the War," the informal as well as formal social pressures in the civilian community demanded military service where deferment was not clearly indicated. It is likely, too, that the positive social pressures were felt more keenly by some classes of the population than others. Thus, the healthy youngster, the man without a family, and especially the man who was concerned about his future civilian status in his community or in the larger society, would be most vulnerable to these social pressures. The man with future status aspirations, in particular, could not afford to jeopardize them. This situation could serve to counteract, to some extent, feelings of deprivation which might otherwise have been stronger, particularly among the better educated, who, by and large, would represent the majority of those with high social aspirations.

22. Determining the Dependent Variable in Certain Correlations

PETER M. BLAU

THE INTERPRETATION of a correlation between two variables is a common problem in the analysis of research findings. Even if the persistence of the relationship when relevant conditions are controlled indicates that it is not a spurious one, the distinction between independent and dependent variable still has to be made. Does A affect B, or does B affect A, or is a combination of these influences responsible for their correlations?

Various procedures exist to solve this problem when a controlled experiment is not feasible. In all of them, an attempt is made to ascertain the time sequence of the occurrence of the two variables. Sometimes,

Reprinted with permission from the *Public Opinion Quarterly*, XIX (Spring 1955) pp. 100–05 (copyright 1955 by the Princeton University Press).

this can be done on logical grounds. It is evident that a relationship between sex and voting behavior cannot be due to the fact that going into an election booth affects a person's sex, but only to the influence of the sex role on voting. Retrospective questions are another means of establishing the order of precedence of related variables. This technique, however, is not suitable for the study of attitudes and other psychological states, since reliable information can hardly be expected in answer to questions such as whether the respondent had felt twenty years ago that he had to struggle for everything in life. Finally, the panel design—repeated interviews with the same sample of respondents—provides evidence of the existence of certain attitudes prior to the emergence of others, but the cost of this procedure and the difficulty presented by the loss of cases, particularly when long time periods are involved, have limited its use in social research. Often, therefore, the chronological order of related phenomena is unknown.

A method for determining the direction of influence between two related variables in the absence of information about the time sequence of their development is here suggested. This method consists of a new application of Lazarsfeld's schema for testing the validity of theoretical interpretations.[1] He shows that the confirmation of an explanatory hypothesis—the correlation between X and Y is due to Z—requires evidence that the partial relationships between X and Y disappear when Z is held constant. Thus, Durkheim's interpretation of the relationship between religion and suicide rates in terms of differences in social integration between religious groups can be tested by classifying communities on the basis of social integration and demonstrating that, within each class of equally integrated ones, the suicide rates of Protestant and Catholic communities do not differ. Partial relations disappear, however, not only when the intervening variable that

accounts for the influence of the independent on the dependent variable is held constant, but also when the antecedent variable responsible for a spurious relationship between two factors is held constant. For example, if a correlation between height and vocabulary of children were to vanish when age differences are controlled, this would indicate that both height and extent of vocabulary increase with age without affecting one another, and not that height determines age and thereby vocabulary. Since the same statistical result is obtained whether the process by which one factor influences another has been discovered or a spurious correlation has been uncovered, Lazarsfeld stresses that use of this test presupposes knowledge about the time order of the variables under consideration.[2] By implying that the test cannot serve to determine the direction of influence in a relationship between two factors, he underestimates the potentialities of his own analytical tool. It can serve this purpose provided that one condition is met, namely, data on a common antecedent variable is available.

A recent study of elderly people found that an individual's self-image in respect to age is related to his idea of how his close associates conceive of him.[3] Table 1 shows that people who consider themselves old or elderly are more than five times as likely as those who consider themselves middle-aged to believe that others think of them as old.

Two opposite hypotheses can be advanced to explain this correlation. First, if an individual with advancing years starts to conceive of himself as old and to act as an old person, others will treat him as such, but if he continues to identify himself with middle-aged people, his associates will usually not think of him as old, and even when they do, he is not likely to perceive it. Second, if, and only if, his significant others begin to treat an individual who is getting old as an old man or woman,

TABLE 1.   Self-Image and Idea of Significant Others' Conception of One's Age

Idea of Conception of Others**	Old or Elderly (Per Cent)	Self-Image* Middle-Aged (Per Cent)	Qualified Response (Per Cent)
Yes, old	49	9	20
No, not old	32	82	66
Don't know	19	9	14
Total	100	100	100
Number of cases	119	279	65

* "We'd like to know how you think of yourself as far as age goes—do you think of yourself as: elderly—middle-aged—old—or what?"
** "Do you think that the people that you see and care most about think of you as an old man (woman)?"

his self-image will change from that of a middle-aged to that of an old person.

The crucial distinction between these two hypotheses is the direction of influence between the two variables. If it were known whether the change in self-image preceded the realization that others treat one as an old person, or whether this realization antedated the change in self-image, one could immediately decide which hypothesis is correct. Conversely, if evidence for accepting one hypothesis and rejecting the other can be furnished, the direction of influence would be simultaneously established, even though the time sequence of the two variables is not known.

The existence of data on a common antecedent variable, namely chronological age, makes it possible to supply this evidence. Nearly half (47 per cent) of the people seventy years or older define themselves as old or elderly, in contrast to only 11 per cent of those in their sixties. Older people are also more likely to find that their associates think of them as old than younger ones (32 per cent, as compared with 13 per cent). Since it is logically evident that, in either relationship, actual age is the independent variable, the two alternative hypotheses can be schematically presented in the following form:

Hypothesis 1: Age—self-image—conception of significant others.
Hypothesis 2: Age—conception of significant others—self-image.

A third possibility, however, must be considered first. The relationship between self-image and idea of associates' conception may be a spurious one, due to the simultaneous effect of chronological age on both factors, which would mean that neither hypothesis is acceptable. If this were the case, there would be no relationship between the two variables among respondents in the same age group. But actually, the magnitude of the original relationship is hardly affected by controlling for age; whether a person is under seventy or older, if he thinks of himself as old he is more prone to believe that others do so.[4] This shows that the observed relationship is not simply the result of concomitant changes that occur with increasing chronological age. Either a person's self-image influences his experience of being treated as an old man or woman by associates, or this experience influences his self-image.

To test the second hypothesis, respondents are classified in Table 2 by the conception their significant others have of them, as far as they know. The partial relationships between actual age and self-image have not disappeared in this table;

TABLE 2. Age as Related to Self-Image When Idea of Significant Others' Conception of One's Age is Controlled *

	Idea of Conception of Others					
	YES, OLD		NO, NOT OLD		DON'T KNOW	
AGE:	60–69	70 and Over	60–69	70 and Over	60–69	70 and Over
SELF-IMAGE	(Per Cent)	(Per Cent)	(Per Cent)	(Per Cent)	(Per Cent)	(Per Cent)
Old or elderly	39	75	5	29	25	50
Middle-aged	39	17	81	13	75	24
Qualified response	22	8	14	58	0	27
Total	100	100	100	100	100	101
Number of cases	36	59	216	94	24	34

* Note: The differences between the first two and the second two columns are significant on the .01 level.

indeed, they are larger than the original relationship.[5] Regardless of whether a person feels that others consider him old or not, he is more likely to think of himself as old once he passes 70. Hence, Hypothesis 2 must be rejected.

If respondents are divided on the basis of their self-image, on the other hand, the partial relationships between actual age and idea of the conception of significant others, although they do not completely disappear, become insignificantly small, as Table

3 shows. This confirms Hypothesis 1; self-image is the intervening variable. People in their sixties are less apt than older ones to experience being treated as old by their associates only because they are more likely to continue to identify themselves with the middle aged.

The acceptance of Hypothesis 1 and the rejection of Hypothesis 2 make the direction of influence between the two original variables evident, and thereby indicate the time sequence of their development, about

TABLE 3. Age as Related to Idea of Significant Others' Conception of One's Age When Self-Image is Controlled *

	Self-Image—Age					
	OLD OR ELDERLY		MIDDLE-AGED		QUALIFIED RESPONSE	
	60–69	70 and Over	60–69	70 and Over	60–69	70 and Over
	(Per Cent)	(Per Cent)	(Per Cent)	(Per Cent)	(Per Cent)	(Per Cent)
Yes, old	45	50	7	14	21	19
No, not old	36	31	85	75	79	46
Don't know	19	19	8	11	0	35
Total	100	100	100	100	100	100
Number of cases	31	88	206	73	39	26

* Note: None of the differences between values in adjacent columns of the first row are significant on the .05 level.

which no direct data existed. Changes in self-image among elderly persons tend to produce the realization that others think of them as old men or women, and not vice versa. The general principle is that the dependent variable in a correlation can be determined by establishing that the partial relations between it and a common antecedent factor disappear when the other variable in the original correlation is held constant.[6] In attitude surveys and other studies where it is impossible to date crucial variables, it is often possible to obtain information about common antecedents. The method presented is intended for use in such situations.

Notes

1. Patricia L. Kendall and Paul F. Lazarsfeld, "Problems of Survey Analysis," in *Continuities in Social Research,* edited by Robert K. Merton and Paul F. Lazarsfeld (New York: The Free Press, 1950), esp. pp. 147–58. For the statistical equations used, see G. Udny Yule

and M. G. Kendall, *An Introduction to the Theory of Statistics* (New York: Hafner Publishing Company, 14 ed., 1950), pp. 31–41, esp. p. 36.

2. *Ibid.,* pp. 141–43, 156–57.

3. Zena S. Blau, *Old Age: A Study of Change in Status,* unpublished Ph.D. dissertation (Columbia University, 1955). The data on which this study is based were collected in Elmira, N.Y., under the direction of John P. Dean, and are part of a larger study on aging being conducted by the Department of Sociology and Anthropology, Cornell University. Permission to use these data is gratefully acknowledged.

4. Compare *alternate* columns in Table 3.

5. In the entire sample, 32 per cent of the older respondents and 13 per cent of the younger ones defined themselves as old, a difference of 19 per cent. The corresponding differences in Table 2, where idea of associates' conception is controlled, are 36 (75 − 39), 24 (29 − 5) and 25 (50 − 25) per cent respectively.

6. To be sure, there may be some feedback effect. Proof that B is dependent on A without affecting it at all would require evidence that the partial relations between A and all relevant antecedent variables vanish when B is controlled.

23. The Algebra of Dichotomous Systems

PAUL F. LAZARSFELD

1. Observations on Dichotomous Systems

THE STATISTICS of attributes has made little progress since Yule [1] gave it a standard form in the first chapters of his famous textbook. Investigators have concentrated on problems that required the use of continuous variables. Only in recent

years has the development of social research focused attention on dichotomies, like yes-no answers to questionnaires, or classification of sex. Survey analysis has to take into account so many variables that a reverse process has set in; even continuous variables, like age and income, are often treated as dichotomies: old-young and rich-poor.

Reprinted in part with permission of Stanford University Press from *Studies in Item Analysis and Prediction,* H. Solomon (ed.) (copyright 1961 by the Board of Trustees of the Leland Stanford, Jr. University.)

As a result, it seemed worthwhile to develop new ideas on the treatment of what might be called "dichotomous systems": the set of relative frequencies by which a sample of people is partitioned into 2^m classes which come about if they are classified by m dichotomous observations. The following sections develop a number of significant theorems that exist between three dichotomies, and then extend some of them to more general systems. (These extensions are omitted from the present condensation.)

2. The Cross Product

Two dichotomies lead to the well-known fourfold table:

Attribute j

		+	−	
	+	p_{ij}	$p_{i\bar{j}}$	p_i
Attribute i	−	$p_{\bar{i}j}$	$p_{\bar{i}\bar{j}}$	$p_{\bar{i}}$
		p_j	$p_{\bar{j}}$	1

$$(2.1)$$

The symbolism is obvious. For any dichotomy one of the two observations or "responses" is arbitrarily designated as positive $(+)$, the other as negative $(-)$. The corresponding frequencies will be designated as p_i and $p_{\bar{i}}$, respectively,[1] and $p_i + p_{\bar{i}} = 1$. For the response pattern $+ +$ the joint frequency is p_{ij}, for the response pattern $+ -$ it is $p_{i\bar{j}}$, etc. The items are listed and numbered in an arbitrary sequence, which remains fixed in the course of one investigation.

The association between the two attributes in (2.1) can be "measured" by a variety of coefficients. They all have in common that they compare the association with statistical independence, which is characterized by the vanishing of the so-called cross product

$$|ij| = \begin{vmatrix} p_{ij} & p_{i\bar{j}} \\ p_{\bar{i}j} & p_{\bar{i}\bar{j}} \end{vmatrix} = \begin{vmatrix} p_{ij} & p_i \\ p_j & 1 \end{vmatrix} = p_{ij} - p_i p_j \tag{2.2}$$

The three well-known indices of association all have the cross product as a nucleus. They differ only by the way they introduce the marginal frequency of the two dichotomies; i.e.,

$$\phi = \frac{|ij|}{\sqrt{p_i p_{\bar{i}} p_j p_{\bar{j}}}} \qquad \chi^2 = N\phi^2 \qquad f_{ij} = \frac{|ij|}{p_i p_{\bar{i}}} \tag{2.3}$$

A word may be added about the third coefficient, which is often used in connection with controlled experiments. People are divided into two groups, one of which is exposed to some stimulus (i). Then some reaction of theirs (j) is ascertained. The effect of the stimulus is measured by comparing the relative frequencies in which the response appears in the two groups; i.e.,

$$f_{ij} = \frac{p_{ij}}{p_i} - \frac{p_{\bar{i}j}}{p_{\bar{i}}} = \frac{1}{p_i p_{\bar{i}}} \begin{vmatrix} p_{ij} & p_{\bar{i}j} \\ p_i & p_{\bar{i}} \end{vmatrix} = \frac{|ij|}{p_i p_{\bar{i}}} \tag{2.4}$$

It should be noted that $f_{ji} = |ij| / p_j p_{\bar{j}}$, and therefore differs from f_{ij}. The product $f_{ij} \times f_{ji}$ obviously equals ϕ^2.

The frequencies can be ordered by their "level," that is, p_i is of first-level, p_{ij} of second-level. When we consider three attributes at a time, there are eight third-level class proportions. These eight elements can be thought of as occupying the eight positions formed by cutting a cube by three normal planes, just as the four cells of the fourfold table were formed by cutting a square from two directions. This *dichotomous cube,* the extension of the fourfold table to three dimensions, will be discussed in some detail.

For convenience of language we shall often talk as if the cross product itself were the measure of association. However, none of the formulas we shall develop will prejudice what measure of association should actually be used.

3. The Dichotomous Cube

The relation between two dichotomous attributes was summarized in the fourfold table, a two-dimensional array with four cells, one for each of the four second-level class proportions. Such a dichotomous cube consists of eight smaller cubes, each corresponding to one of the third-level proportions. We shall arrange these proportions in such a way that the four proportions having the subscript 1 in common, p_{123}, $p_{1\bar{2}3}$, $p_{12\bar{3}}$, and $p_{1\bar{2}\bar{3}}$, are in the left section of the cube, while those proportions having the subscript $\bar{1}$ in common lie in the right section of the cube. Similarly, the four proportions with the subscript 2 in common are in the upper layer, and those with $\bar{2}$ in common are in the lower layer. The front sheet contains the four proportions having the subscript 3 in common; the back sheet, those with $\bar{3}$ in common.

The dichotomous cube and the relative position of the third-level frequencies are shown in Figure 1.

A second-level frequency can be *expanded* in terms of its third-level compo-

nent. Thus, e.g., $p_{1\bar{2}} = p_{1\bar{2}3} + p_{1\bar{2}\bar{3}}$. No frequency can be negative. Therefore *if a second-level frequency vanishes, so do its components.* If, e.g., $p_{1\bar{2}} = 0$, then it follows that $p_{1\bar{2}3} = p_{1\bar{2}\bar{3}} = 0$.

If we deal with $m > 3$ dichotomies, we could talk of a cube of m dimensions; but little is gained from such a terminology. The rules of handling indices, however, apply quite directly to such an extension. A word may be added about an alternative possibility and why it has been discarded. Some authors use the symbols 1 and 2 for positive and negative responses, respectively; and they assign to each item a fixed position in the frequency symbol. Thus $p_{1.2}$ would be the frequency of a positive response to the first item and a negative to the third, irrespective of the response to the second item. In our symbolism this would be $p_{1\bar{3}}$, because we take the order of the item from a numbered list, fixed for the whole study. With a larger number of dichotomies this makes for considerable saving in space. Furthermore, as the reader will see, the use of bars for negative responses puts better into relief a number of basic theorems.

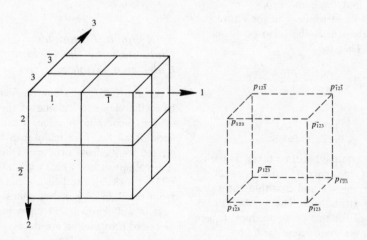

FIGURE 1.

4. Stratified Fourfold Tables

Consider now the elements that lie in the front sheet of the dichotomous cube. Keeping them in their same relative position, they are

	1	$\bar{1}$	
2	p_{123}	$p_{\bar{1}23}$	p_{23}
$\bar{2}$	$p_{1\bar{2}3}$	$p_{\bar{1}\bar{2}3}$	$p_{\bar{2}3}$
	p_{13}	$p_{\bar{1}3}$	p_3

This is a fourfold table that summarizes the relation between attributes 1 and 2 within only a part of the complete set of individuals—within only that subset of individuals who possess attribute 3. Such a table will be called a *conditional or stratified fourfold table*.[2]

As with the fourfold table, the conditional table can be bordered by marginal entries, which are the sums of the respective rows and columns as indicated in the margins of the preceding schema.

If within the subset of individuals who possess attribute 3 there is no relation between attributes 1 and 2, then we would expect to find the same proportion of individuals with attribute 1 in the entire subset as in the subset that also possesses attribute 2. That is,

$$\frac{p_{13}}{p_3} = \frac{p_{123}}{p_{23}}$$

or

$$\begin{vmatrix} p_{123} & p_{23} \\ p_{13} & p_3 \end{vmatrix} = 0$$

This determinant will be taken as the definition of the partial cross product between attributes 1 and 2 within the subset possessing attribute 3. The symbol $|\,12;3\,|$ will be used for this cross product. In general, then, we shall define $|\,ij;k\,|$ by

$$|\,ij;k\,| = \begin{vmatrix} p_{ijk} & p_{jk} \\ p_{ik} & p_k \end{vmatrix} \qquad (4.1)$$

Suppose now we consider the elements in the back sheet of the dichotomous cube. They make up the following conditional fourfold table:

	1	$\bar{1}$	
2	$p_{12\bar{3}}$	$p_{\bar{1}2\bar{3}}$	$p_{2\bar{3}}$
$\bar{2}$	$p_{1\bar{2}\bar{3}}$	$p_{\bar{1}\bar{2}\bar{3}}$	$p_{\bar{2}\bar{3}}$
	$p_{1\bar{3}}$	$p_{\bar{1}\bar{3}}$	$p_{\bar{3}}$

This table summarizes the relation between attributes 1 and 2 within the subset of individuals lacking attribute 3. The cross product of this stratified fourfold table will be denoted by $|\,12;\bar{3}\,|$, where

$$|\,12;\bar{3}\,| = \begin{vmatrix} p_{12\bar{3}} & p_{2\bar{3}} \\ p_{1\bar{3}} & p_{\bar{3}} \end{vmatrix} = \begin{vmatrix} p_{12\bar{3}} & p_{\bar{1}2\bar{3}} \\ p_{1\bar{2}\bar{3}} & p_{\bar{1}\bar{2}\bar{3}} \end{vmatrix}$$

in general we shall define $|\,ij;\bar{k}\,|$ by

$$|\,ij;\bar{k}\,| = \begin{vmatrix} p_{ij\bar{k}} & p_{j\bar{k}} \\ p_{i\bar{k}} & p_{\bar{k}} \end{vmatrix} \qquad (4.2)$$

It should be noted that Equation (4.1) suffices to define both $|\,ij;k\,|$ and $|\,ij;\bar{k}\,|$ if in (4.1) we allow the index k to range through both barred and unbarred integers designating particular attributes.[3]

5. A Single Parameter Characterizing the Dichotomous Cube as a Whole

Six fourfold tables can be formed, each from the elements on one of the six faces of the dichotomous cube. Each of these conditional fourfold tables can be characterized by its cross product. Thus, six partial cross products, $|\,12;3\,|$, $|\,12;\bar{3}\,|$, $|\,23;1\,|$, $|\,23;\bar{1}\,|$, $|\,13;2\,|$, and $|\,13;\bar{2}\,|$, can be formed from the data of a dichotomous cube.

It is well known that eight independent pieces of information are necessary to form a *fundamental set* for a system of three dichotomies. The eight ultimate frequencies form one such set. The frequencies on all levels that have no barred indices, together with the size of the sample, form another. (These are the two investigated by Yule.) Another could be formed from the following elements: let n be the total number of individuals; let p_1, p_2, p_3 be the first-level proportions; and let $|\,12\,|$, $|\,23\,|$, $|\,13\,|$ be the three possible cross products. But these are only seven elements, and so far we have utilized no third-level data. The eighth element must be of the third level, somehow characterizing the dichotomous cube as a whole.

We might choose our eighth element from among the six conditional cross products, but there is no good reason for choosing one in preference to another. Also, any one of these would lack the symmetry that one can reasonably require of a parameter representing the whole cube.

Our choice of the eighth parameter will be determined by three criteria:

a) The parameter should be *symmetric*, i.e., its value should not be affected by the numbering of the three attributes from which it is formed. The cross product, characterizing the fourfold table as a whole, has the following property of symmetry: the value assigned to the symbol $|\,12\,|$, i.e., $|\,12\,| = p_{12} - p_1 p_2$, is not changed by an interchange of the subscripts.

b) The parameter should be *homogeneous* of the third level, i.e., each of its terms should involve three subscripts. What is meant by this requirement is best seen by examining the cross product, which is homogeneous of the second level. The cross product between attributes 1 and 2, as shown above, has two terms on the right, each of which involves two subscripts. In this sense each of these terms is of the second level.

c) The parameter should be such that we can use it, together with lower level class proportions, to evaluate any third-level class proportion. That the cross product has the corresponding property can be easily shown.

$$p_{12} = p_1 p_2 + |\,12\,| \qquad p_{1\bar{2}} = p_1 p_{\bar{2}} - |\,12\,|$$
$$p_{\bar{1}2} = p_1 p_2 - |\,12\,| \qquad p_{\bar{1}\bar{2}} = p_1 p_{\bar{2}} + |\,12\,|$$

$$(5.1)$$

These four equations can be condensed into a single equation if in the equation $p_{ij} = p_i p_j + |\,ij\,|$ we allow the indices i and j to range over both unbarred and barred numbers. This equation thus defines the new symbols $|\,i\bar{j}\,|$, $|\,\bar{i}j\,|$, and $|\,\bar{i}\bar{j}\,|$. That this is true is easily seen when we recognize that the definition $|\,ij\,| = p_{ij} - p_i p_j$ implies that

$$|\,i\bar{j}\,| = -\,|\,ij\,| \qquad |\,\bar{i}j\,| = -\,|\,ij\,|$$
$$|\,\bar{i}\bar{j}\,| = |\,ij\,|$$

$$(5.2)$$

For example, by letting $i = 1$ and $j = \bar{2}$, we obtain

$$p_{1\bar{2}} = p_1 p_{\bar{2}} + |\,1\bar{2}\,| = p_1 p_{\bar{2}} - |\,12\,|$$

A homogeneous, symmetric parameter of the third level can be built up from lower-level data as follows:

$$p_{ijk} = p_i p_j p_k + p_i\,|\,jk\,| + p_j\,|\,ik\,| + p_k\,|\,ij\,| + |\,ijk\,| \quad (5.3)$$

The quantity $|\,ijk\,|$, implicitly defined by this equation, quite evidently satisfies the criteria of homogeneity and symmetry; that it can be used together with lower-level data to compute any third-level class proportion will be shown in Section 7.

6. *The Intuitive Meaning of the Symmetric Parameter in a Dichotomous Cube*

It is possible to give the symmetric parameter a first intuitive meaning by looking at the case where zero-order cross products vanish. Then the parameter is the difference between an actual third-level frequency and its chance value. From Equation (5.3) we find in this case that

$$p_{ijk} - p_i p_j p_k = |\,ijk\,|$$

It is not too difficult to think of a concrete example. Suppose we are dealing with a community in which the educational system is fairly stabilized. Among the adult population we shall then find educational differences due to ability and social background; but the probability that a person went beyond high school would not be related to age as it is now in the United States, where the high-school system is still expanding from year to year. In such an adult population there would be no association between age (1) and education (2). Consider now the relation between age and interest in serious music (3). Empirical studies indicate that people who never go beyond high school reach the peak of their cultural taste right after they leave school because from then on their tastes become corroded by their work and their environment. College graduates, on the other hand, who live and work in a middle-class environment develop further cultural taste as they grow older and lose the vitality of their youth. These two trends may compensate each other, and in a mixed population we therefore have no relation between age and interest in serious music, for $| 13 | = 0$.

To this we have to add one more assumption, which is considerably less realistic: no relation exists between education (2) and interest in serious music (3). This could be approximated in an ethnically mixed community, i.e., one in which the poorly educated Italians are mainly interested in opera while the more highly educated Germans are mainly interested in classical symphony. In this kind of situation all three zero-order cross products would vanish. But because of the differential age trend for the two educational groups, the third-order symmetric parameter would still have a positive value.

It is possible to represent this situation by a coin-throwing experiment. We represent education by a regular penny (1) and

age by a regular nickel (2). Interest in serious music (3) is represented by a biased coin with the probability of .8 to fall heads. In the case of the two regular coins, a showing of heads is considered equivalent to a positive response; in the case of age, this will signify "old"; and in the case of education, it will signify having gone beyond high school. For the third coin we have a conditional scoring.

If (1) and (2) are either $(+ +)$ or $(- -)$, then heads for the third coin scores $(+)$; if (1) and (2) are either $(+ -)$ or $(- +)$, then heads for the third coin scores $(-)$. If the three coins are thrown often enough, the distribution of scores will approach the following scheme:

	1 +				1 −		
	3 +	3 −			3 +	3 −	
2 +	.20	.05	.25	2 +	.05	.20	.25
2 −	.05	.20	.25	2 −	.20	.05	.25
	.25	.25	.5		.25	.25	.5

The reader can easily satisfy himself that in this scheme $| 12 | = | 13 | = | 23 | = 0$. However, $p_{123} = .20$, and therefore

$$| 123 | = p_{123} - p_1 p_2 p_3$$
$$= .20 - (\tfrac{1}{2})^3 = .075$$

In our example the two sides of the scheme would correspond to educated and uneducated people, respectively. The left (educated) side shows a positive association of age and interest in serious music. The right (uneducated) side shows a negative association. The vanishing of the cross products $| 13 |$ and $| 23 |$ can be seen from the fact that the two fourfold tables have the same distribution in corresponding marginal rows and columns. That $| 12 | = 0$ can be seen from adding the two tables cell by cell.

We shall presently find additional interpretations of the third-order symmetric parameter.[4]

7. *Use of the Parameter* (ijk) *to Compute Third-Level Class Proportions*

If we again allow the indices i, j, and k to range through any three different barred or unbarred numbers, it is easily shown that the symbols $|\,ij\bar{k}\,|$, $|\,i\bar{j}k\,|$, etc., thus defined are not independent but are related as follows:

$$|\,ij\bar{k}\,| = -\,|\,ij\bar{k}\,|\quad |\,\overline{ij}k\,| = \,|\,ijk\,|$$
$$|\,i\bar{j}\bar{k}\,| = -\,|\,ij\bar{k}\,| \tag{7.1}$$

In words: if in $|\,ijk\,|$ an odd number of indices is barred, the symmetric parameter changes its sign; if an even number is barred, the value of $|\,ijk\,|$ remains unchanged. As an example we show that $|\,ijk\,| + |\,ij\bar{k}\,| = 0$.

The index k in this equation appears in each term and only either inside or outside a symmetric parameter. If inside, the bar causes a change in sign, and the addition cancels (e.g., $p_k\,|\,ij\,| + p_k\,|\,i\bar{j}\,| = 0$). The bar outside the symmetric parameter causes (after addition) the index to disappear (e.g., $p_k\,|\,ij\,| + p_{\bar{k}}\,|\,ij\,| = \,|\,ij\,|$).

To choose a specific case:

$$|\,123\,| = p_{123} - p_1 p_2 p_3 - p_1\,|\,23\,|$$
$$- p_2\,|\,13\,| - p_3\,|\,12\,|$$
$$|\,12\bar{3}\,| = p_{12\bar{3}} - p_1 p_2 p_{\bar{3}} + p_1\,|\,23\,|$$
$$+ p_2\,|\,13\,| - p_{\bar{3}}\,|\,12\,|$$

If we add the two equations, the third and the fourth terms on the righthand side cancel because the bar *inside* the cross products makes for a change in sign. The first, second, and last terms have the bar *outside* the cross products; by adding the corresponding terms in the two equations, we see that the coefficients add up to unity. As a result

$$|\,123\,| + |\,12\bar{3}\,| =$$
$$p_{12} - p_1 p_2 - |\,12\,| = p_{12} - p_{12} = 0$$

Thus $|\,123\,| = -\,|\,12\bar{3}\,|$. This mode of computation will presently turn out to have very general applications, which is the main advantage of symmetric parameters.

Once we define and compute a symmetric parameter by Equation (5.3), we can compute any desired third-level class proportion. For example,

$$p_{\bar{1}2\bar{3}} = p_{\bar{1}} p_2 p_{\bar{3}} + p_{\bar{1}}\,|\,2\bar{3}\,| + p_2\,|\,\overline{13}\,|$$
$$+ p_{\bar{3}}\,|\,\overline{12}\,| + |\,\overline{123}\,|$$
$$= p_{\bar{1}} p_2 p_{\bar{3}} - p_{\bar{1}}\,|\,23\,| + p_2\,|\,13\,|$$
$$- p_{\bar{3}}\,|\,12\,| + |\,123\,| \tag{7.2}$$

We note in passing that subtracting (7.2) from (5.3) yields

$$p_{123} - p_{\bar{1}2\bar{3}} = p_2 (p_1 p_3 - p_{\bar{1}} p_{\bar{3}}) + |\,23\,|$$
$$+ |\,12\,|$$
$$= p_2 (p_1 - p_{\bar{3}}) + |\,23\,| + |\,12\,|$$
$$= p_2 (p_3 - p_{\bar{1}}) + |\,23\,| + |\,12\,| \tag{7.3}$$

Actually a general formula, which we shall find useful later, can be derived without the use of the third-order symmetric parameters; i.e.,

$$p_{ijk} - p_{i\bar{j}k} = p_{ijk} - p_{ij} + p_{i\bar{j}k} = p_{ik} - p_{i\bar{j}}$$
$$= p_i (p_k - p_{\bar{j}}) + |\,ik\,| + |\,ij\,| \tag{7.4}$$

But the parameter enters into another important relation, i.e.,

$$p_{ijk} - p_k p_{ij} = p_i\,|\,jk\,| + p_j\,|\,ik\,| + |\,ijk\,| \tag{7.5}$$

The computation is straightforward. (The reader is invited to carry it out as an exercise.)

With the introduction of the third-order symmetric parameter a three-attribute dichotomous system can now be completely summarized by the fundamental set of eight parameters:

$$n, p_1, p_2, p_3, |\,12\,|, |\,13\,|, |\,23\,|, |\,123\,|$$

8. *The Transformation of Stratified Cross Products*

We introduce symmetric parameters into the form

$$| ij;k | = \begin{vmatrix} p_{ijk} & p_{ik} \\ p_{jk} & p_k \end{vmatrix} \quad (8.1)$$

We subtract in the last determinant the second *row* multiplied by p_i from the first row; then we subtract the second *column* multiplied by p_j from the first column. This leaves us on the right-hand side of Equation 8.1 with

$$| ij;k | = \begin{vmatrix} | ijk | + p_k\,| ij | & | ik | \\ | jk | & p_k \end{vmatrix}$$

Thus

$$| ij;k | = p_k\,| ijk | + p_k^2\,| ij | - | ik |\,| jk | \quad (8.2)$$

By a similar computation we arrive at

$$| ij;\bar{k} | = - p_{\bar{k}}\,| ijk | + p_{\bar{k}}^2\,| ij | - | ik |\,| jk | \quad (8.3)$$

The last two formulas are of course related to each other by the general rule of barred indices expressed above.

It is worth while to give intuitive meaning to Equations (8.2) and (8.3). Suppose we study the relation between political interest (i) and voting (j), computed separately for men and women (k). The cross product for voting and interest as it prevails among men alone is $| ij;k |$. According to Equation (8.2), this conditional interrelation is the cross product $| ij |$ as it prevails in the total population, corrected for relation of sex to both voting and interest, that is, the product $| ik |\,| jk |$. But an additional correction has to be considered, the triple interaction between all three attributes, to wit, $| ijk |$.

9. The Sum of Two Conditional Cross Products—"Partial Association"

By dividing (8.2) and (8.3) by p_k and $p_{\bar{k}}$, respectively, we obtain

THEOREM 1.

$$\frac{| ij;k |}{p_k} + \frac{| ij;\bar{k} |}{p_{\bar{k}}} = | ij | - \frac{| ik |\,| jk |}{p_k p_{\bar{k}}} \quad (9.1)$$

The formula on the left-hand side is analogous to the traditional notion of partial correlation: a weighted average of the two conditional cross products. We may call it the partial association between (i) and (j) with (k) partialed out.

It is very important to *distinguish between the partial and conditional associations*. A partial association, for instance, can be zero, whereas the two conditional ones can have numerical values, one positive and one negative. This is exactly what happened in our example in Section 6, which should be reread in the present context.

Equation (9.1) is of considerable importance in the theory of survey analysis. It can be made the basis for systematic analysis of what is usually called interpretation.

We are now in a position to answer a question raised in Section 2. Suppose someone likes to express associations between dichotomies in terms of the ϕ-coefficient. How would we use the theorem just derived? The ϕ-coefficient between two attributes is

$$\phi_{12} = \frac{| 12 |}{\sqrt{p_1 p_{\bar{1}} p_2 p_{\bar{2}}}}$$

The coefficient for a conditional association, for example, would be

$$\phi_{12.3} = \frac{| 12;3 |}{\sqrt{p_{13} p_{\bar{1}3} p_{23} p_{\bar{2}3}}}$$

Theorem 1 can be restated in the following form:

$$\phi_{12} = \frac{\phi_{12.3}}{p_3} \sqrt{\frac{p_{13}p_{1\bar{3}}p_{23}p_{\bar{2}3}}{p_1 p_{\bar{1}} p_2 p_{\bar{2}}}}$$

$$+ \frac{\phi_{12.\bar{3}}}{p_{\bar{3}}} \sqrt{\frac{p_{1\bar{3}}p_{\overline{13}}p_{2\bar{3}}p_{\overline{23}}}{p_1 p_{\bar{1}} p_2 p_{\bar{2}}}} + \phi_{13}\phi_{23}$$

$$(9.2)$$

The only change that occurred affects the weights of the algebraic sum on the right-hand side. Similar adjustments can be made in all other theorems and formulas we shall subsequently derive. It is doubtful whether anything is gained by introducing these conventional coefficients.[5]

Theorem 1 has an important *corollary*, which was pointed out by David Gold of the University of Iowa (personal communication). Let us introduce for the left side of (9.1) the symbol $|ij;\hat{k}|$. It can be shown that if in a dichotomous cube $|12;3| = 0$, then neither $|13;\hat{2}|$ nor $|23;\hat{1}|$ can vanish as long as none of the zero-order cross products $|ij|$ vanish. Take, e.g.,

$$|23;\hat{1}| = |23| - \frac{|12||13|}{p_1 p_{\bar{1}}}$$

$$(9.3)$$

Because of the original assumption

$$|12| = \frac{|13||23|}{p_3 p_{\bar{3}}} \qquad (9.4)$$

Substituting (9.4) in (9.3), we obtain

$$|23;\hat{1}| = |23| - \frac{|13|^2|23|}{p_1 p_{\bar{1}} p_3 p_{\bar{3}}}$$

$$= |23| \{ 1 - \phi_{13}^2 \}$$

$$(9.5)$$

Except if items (1) and (3) are identical, we will always have $\phi_{13} < 1$, which proves the corollary. Let it be noticed that ϕ_{13} in (9.5) is not a "coefficient" invented to "measure" something, but is shorthand for a term that evolved from the general algebraic relation just demonstrated.

10. The Difference between Two Conditional Cross Products— the Meaning of $|ijk|$

Subtracting Equation (8.3) from Equation (8.2) and rearranging terms, we obtain

THEOREM 2.

$$|ijk| = |ij;k| - |ij;\bar{k}| - |ij| (p_k - p_{\bar{k}})$$

$$(10.1)$$

The symmetric parameter thus "measures" in a way the difference in the degree of association between $|ij|$, under the condition of k, and $\bar{k}$. This would be especially true of $p_k = p_{\bar{k}}$, that is, if the two conditions are represented equally often. Thus in the example given in Section 7, if we had an equal number of men and women, $|ijk|$ would tell how different the association between vote and interest is, comparing the two sex groups. The conditional relations concealed by (9.1) are brought into focus by (10.1). The numerical scheme of Section 5 permits a check on (10.1). The cross products for the two conditional fourfold tables are .0375 and −.0375, respectively. Their difference is .075, a value for $|123|$ that we had found previously in a different way. (In this example $p_3 = p_{\bar{3}} = .5$.)

Such an intuitive interpretation of the symmetric parameter can be put still in another way. Let us think of a controlled experiment where item (i) is the stimulus applied under conditions k and $\bar{k}$ with the purpose of measuring the effect on item (j). In such an experiment the experimental and the control groups are matched, which means that by definition the stimulus (i) is uncorrelated with any other factor, and therefore $|ik| = 0$. Consequently, $p_{ik}p_{\bar{i}k} = p_{i\bar{k}}p_{\bar{i}\bar{k}} = c$. (We maintain the presumption that $p_k = p_{\bar{k}}$, which means that the two groups are alike in size.) In this situation the coefficients $f_{ij.k}$ and $f_{ij.\bar{k}}$ mentioned early in the chapter are appropriate measures of the effect of (i) on (j) under the two specified conditions. Theorem 2 tells us that

$$f_{ij.k} - f_{ij.\bar{k}} = \frac{|ijk|}{c} \qquad (10.2)$$

and thus $|ijk|$ expresses the difference it makes whether the effect of (i) on (j) is studied under condition k or $\bar{k}$.[6]

This is a good place to say a word about the relation between the Yule tradition and the tenor of the present paper. The original objective of Yule's attribute statistics was very similar to a logician's presentation of Boolean algebra; to this he added the study of joint frequencies and their deviation from chance values. In a later edition Yule added one page on "relations between partial association." He did not attach much importance to this approach:

The existence of these relations is of little or no value. They are so complex that lengthy algebraic manipulation is necessary to express those which are not known in terms of those which are.

The few computations Yule presented were indeed rather clumsy. It is easy to see what brought about improvement: the use of determinants, an index notation, and most of all the symmetric parameters. Still it has to be aknowledged that Yule drew attention to the program that is here being carried out to a certain extent. Incidentally, Yule reported the theorem on the weighted sum of stratified cross products. It did not appear until after the tenth edition and was later called "the one result which has important theoretical consequences." The consequences he had in mind were the roles of spurious factors in causal analysis, which he called "illusory associations."

11. Application to Panel Analysis

Theorem 2 has various applications to the type of studies in which a sample of

people is repeatedly interviewed. One question of interest is the stability of responses. Suppose a first response (1) and a second one (2) to the same question is recorded separately for men and women (3). The stability of their responses is well indicated by the conditional cross products $|12;3|$ and $|12;\bar{3}|$. Theorem 2 shows that difference in their stability depends essentially upon the parameter $|123|$.

The panel idea—the analysis of repeated responses—requires the notion of trend, i.e., the ratio between the frequency of the first and the second responses.

In the case of propaganda studies the notion of differential trend becomes especially important. Suppose we classify people according to whether they are interested or not in an election, say in August (1). Then we watch whether they were contacted or not by a party worker (2). Finally, we repeat the question on interest, say in October (3). We first compare the people who were contacted (p_2) with those who were not ($p_{\bar{2}}$). Their interest in October relative to their interest in August is p_{32}/p_{12} and $p_{3\bar{2}}/p_{1\bar{2}}$, respectively. If intervening contact is effective, we should find that $p_{32}/p_{12} > p_{3\bar{2}}/p_{1\bar{2}}$. This is tantamount to saying that

$$D = \begin{vmatrix} p_{32} & p_{3\bar{2}} \\ p_{12} & p_{1\bar{2}} \end{vmatrix} = \begin{vmatrix} p_{32} & p_3 \\ p_{12} & p_1 \end{vmatrix} > 0$$
$$(11.1)$$

It can now happen that $D = 0$, i.e., the trend for the two groups is the same. From this one might conclude that contact with party workers had no effect on interest. This, however, could be a mistake. We develop

$$D = \begin{vmatrix} p_3 p_2 + |23| & p_3 \\ p_1 p_2 + |12| & p_1 \end{vmatrix} = \begin{vmatrix} |23| & p_3 \\ |12| & p_1 \end{vmatrix}$$

or

$$|23| = \frac{D + p_3|12|}{p_1}$$

On the left-hand side we substitute for $| 23 |$ the stratified cross products according to Theorem 1. This give us

$$\frac{| 23;1 |}{p_1} + \frac{| 23;\bar{1} |}{p_{\bar{1}}} = \frac{D + p_3 | 12 |}{p_1}$$
$$- \frac{| 12 | | 13 |}{p_1 p_{\bar{1}}}$$

and finally

THEOREM 3.

$$\frac{| 23;1 |}{p_1} + \frac{| 23;\bar{1} |}{p_{\bar{1}}} = \frac{p_{\bar{1}} D + | 12 | p_{3\bar{1}}}{p_1 p_{\bar{1}}}$$

(11.2)

with D, the differential trend, defined in Equation (11.1).

Specific indices are used to remind the reader that the notion of a differential trend D hinges on the idea that items (1) and (3) are comparable observations made at different times and that item (2) occurs between (1) and (3). But even so, Theorem 3 needs further discussion before its utility becomes evident.

What is the meaning of $| 23;1 |$? It refers to the people who had a positive interest in the beginning. It reports their responses at the second interview, which establishes whether or not they have meanwhile been exposed to the party workers. It will usually be found that some defection has occurred from the positive position, but this happens less often among the exposed people. We might loosely talk of a *preserving effect* of the exposure. Numerically this is represented by $p_{1\bar{2}3}/p_{13} < p_{1\bar{2}\bar{3}}/p_{1\bar{3}}$, which is tantamount to saying that

$$\begin{vmatrix} p_{1\bar{2}3} & p_{1\bar{2}\bar{3}} \\ p_{13} & p_{1\bar{3}} \end{vmatrix} < 0$$

or that $| 23;1 | > 0$. (The reader is urged to carry out the details as an exercise.)

How about $| 23;\bar{1} |$? Here we deal with the subset of people who originally had a negative response. Some of them will have changed to a positive interest the second time. In the same way as before it can be shown that if such conversions are more frequent among exposed people, $| 23;1 |$ will be positive. In this case we shall talk of a *generating effect* of the exposure.

Now Equation (11.2) can be properly interpreted. The two conditional "effects" on the left-hand side depend upon the differential trend D and a term that is positive if $| 12 | > 0$ and $p_{3\bar{1}} > 0$. The latter is necessarily the case. No frequency can be negative. The frequently observed case of *selective exposure* is signified by $| 12 | > 0$; people tend to expose themselves to the propaganda with which they tend to agree anyhow.

If the last term in (11.2) is positive, then D can vanish, and the conditional effects on the left-hand side of (11.2) still exist. This is an interesting result. The trend in people's attitude might be the same whether or not they are exposed to a certain piece of propaganda; and yet the latter might have a generating and preserving effect. This however is only the case if the exposure to the propaganda is selective, and is found more frequently among the people who favor its side to begin with; i.e., $| 12 | > 0$. Obviously the two differential effects are needed to maintain this positive association between the respondent's attitude and his exposure to propaganda.

The following numerical scheme illustrates the situation:

		Contacted (2) October Interest (3)		
		High	Low	
August Interest (1)	High	40	10	50
	Low	20	30	50
		60	40	100

	Not Contacted ($\bar{2}$) October Interest (3)		
	High	Low	
High	30	10	40
Low	18	42	60
	48	52	100

In both fourfold tables high interest increases by twenty per cent from August to October, as can be seen from comparing the marginals. The trend is the same for contacted and uncontacted people. And, therefore, $D = 0$. But if we compare the first line of four figures in the above scheme with the second line, we find the following *conditional effects* of contact: Among people with high initial interest, contact *preserves* interest, i.e., there are relatively fewer losses on the left- than on the right-hand side; among people of initially low interest, contact *generates* interest, i.e., there are relatively more gains on the left- than on the right-hand side. For full understanding, the reader is urged to insert the figures of this scheme into Equation (11.2) and consider its separate terms numerically.

Theorem 3 is of interest in still another context. Suppose that (1) is an intended action (e.g., the intention to become a physician); (3) is the action actually carried out some time later; (2) is a condition favorable to the intention (e.g., the father's being a physician). Then $| 12 | > 0$, and Theorem 3 predicts that most often the following proposition will be found: if a condition favors a certain intention, then this intention is also more likely actually to be carried out if the same condition prevails. To stay with our example: sons of doctors have a tendency toward wanting to be doctors too; among all the people who want to become doctors the sons of doctors will more often carry this intention to a successful end. Findings of this kind are very frequent in social research, and their implications are much discussed. Theorem 3 specifies when they are bound to occur and under what condition exceptions will be found.

12. The Simultaneous "Effect" of Two Attributes on a Third

So far we have examined the effect of stratification by one dichotomy on the as-

sociation of two others. But the dichotomous cube permits still another application. Often one wants to study a problem like this: How does a certain attitude (1) differ if we compare people of high education (2) and high income (3) with people of low education and low income. Here we deal with two stratifiers and their effect upon presence or absence of a third attribute, in this case sometimes called the criterion. Essentially this comes down to a study of the determinant

$$E = \begin{vmatrix} p_{123} & p_{1\overline{23}} \\ p_{\overline{1}23} & p_{\overline{1}\,\overline{23}} \end{vmatrix} = \begin{vmatrix} p_{123} & p_{1\overline{23}} \\ p_{23} & p_{\overline{23}} \end{vmatrix} \quad (12.1)$$

We now subtract in (12.1) the first column from the second, applying Equation (7.4). This gives

$$E = \begin{vmatrix} p_{123} - p_1(p_2 - p_{\overline{3}}) - | 13 | - | 12 | \\ p_{23} \qquad\qquad - (p_2 - p_{\overline{3}}) \end{vmatrix} \quad (12.2)$$

(The reader should confirm that $p_{\overline{23}} - p_{23} = p_{\overline{2}}p_{\overline{3}} - p_2 p_3 = p_{\overline{3}} - p_2$.) Now in (12.2) we multiply the second row by p_1 and subtract it from the first row. Using Equation (7.5) we obtain

$$E = - | 123 | (p_2 - p_{\overline{3}}) - E_1 \quad (12.3)$$

where

$$E_1 = \begin{vmatrix} p_2 | 13 | + p_3 | 12 | & | 13 | + | 12 | \\ p_{23} & (p_2 - p_{\overline{3}}) \end{vmatrix} \quad (12.4)$$

Now E_1 can be looked upon as a third-order determinant expanded along its third row (or by pivotal condensation around $| 13 |$), i.e.,

$$E_1 = \begin{vmatrix} | 13 | & p_3 & 1 \\ - | 12 | & p_2 & 1 \\ 0 & p_{23} & (p_2 - p_{\overline{3}}) \end{vmatrix} \quad (12.5)$$

But E_1 can also be expanded along its first column. The unsigned cofactor of $| 13 |$ is

$$\begin{vmatrix} p_2 & 1 \\ p_2 p_3 + \mid 23 \mid & (p_2 - p_{\bar{3}}) \end{vmatrix}$$

$$= \begin{vmatrix} p_2 & 1 \\ \mid 23 \mid & p_2 - 1 \end{vmatrix} = - (p_2 p_{\bar{2}} + \mid 23 \mid)$$

The unsigned cofactor of $- \mid 12 \mid$ in (12.5) is

$$\begin{vmatrix} p_3 & 1 \\ p_{23} & p_2 - p_{\bar{3}} \end{vmatrix} = \begin{vmatrix} p_3 & 1 \\ \mid 23 \mid & - p_{\bar{3}} \end{vmatrix}$$

$$= - (p_3 p_{\bar{3}} + \mid 23 \mid)$$

therefore (12.5) becomes

$$E_1 = \begin{vmatrix} p_3 p_{\bar{3}} + \mid 23 \mid & \mid 13 \mid \\ p_2 p_{\bar{2}} + \mid 23 \mid & - \mid 12 \mid \end{vmatrix}$$
$$(12.6)$$

We obtain

THEOREM 4.

$$\begin{vmatrix} p_{123} & p_{1\overline{23}} \\ p_{\bar{1}23} & p_{\overline{123}} \end{vmatrix} = \mid 123 \mid (p_{\bar{3}} - p_2) - E_1$$

where E_1 is given by Equation (12.6).

The third-order symmetric parameter does not enter the theorem if $p_2 = p_{\bar{3}}$. This can often be achieved by making $p_2 = p_3 = .5$; this means choosing an equal number of people with, say, high and low income (2) and with high and low education (3) in the original sample. Then the joint effect of these two attributes upon the attitude (3) under study would be measured by an index, the nucleus of which would be $\{.25 + \mid 23 \mid \} \{\mid 12 \mid + \mid 13 \mid \}$. The joint effect is the greater the stronger two stratifiers are associated among themselves and each singly with the "criterion" (3).

The use of third-order determinants also facilitates greatly the computation of another form:

$$G = \begin{vmatrix} p_{12\bar{3}} & p_{1\bar{2}3} \\ p_{\bar{1}2\bar{3}} & p_{\bar{1}\bar{2}3} \end{vmatrix}$$

This form comes up when we ask which of two attributes has a stronger effect on a third. For the record we present the appropriate expression of G in terms of symmetric parameters, leaving it to the reader to carry out the proof as a very useful exercise. The necessary computations are completely parallel to those carried out in this section, i.e.,

$$G = \mid 123 \mid (p_2 - p_3) + G_1,$$

$$G_1 = \begin{vmatrix} p_3 p_{\bar{3}} - \mid 23 \mid & \mid 13 \mid \\ p_2 p_{\bar{2}} - \mid 23 \mid & \mid 12 \mid \end{vmatrix}$$

It is important to see the difference between Theorem 4 and Theorem 2, especially in the derived form of Equation (9.2). The "both-or-neither effect" of, say, income and education does not essentially depend on $\mid 123 \mid$ as shown by E_1 in Theorem 4. What is it then that the third-order parameter describes according to Theorem 2? Staying with the same substantive example, the answer is as follows. The two attributes of education (2) and income (3) divide the whole group into four subsets, to wit, $(--)$, $(-+)$, $(+-)$, and $(++)$. Suppose that the proportion of people in each subset who have attitude (3) increases in the direction just indicated: the proportion is lowest in subset $(--)$, highest in subset $(++)$, and somewhere in between in the other two subsets. This means that both education and income increase the probability of attitude (3). This still leaves the question of whether the effect of one of these factors as compared to none is the same as the effect of two of the factors as compared to one. If the two factors are "linearly additive" in this sense, then $\mid 123 \mid$ will vanish. If the symmetric parameter does not vanish, then the "jump" in the attitude between $(--)$ and $(-+)$ is greater (or smaller) than the "jump" between $(+-)$ and $(++)$. The sign of $\mid 123 \mid$ decides whether "greater" or "smaller" applies. An exact computation shows that the result is the same whether we start with the order $(-+)$ $(+-)$ or with the order $(+-)$ $(-+)$. The reader can easily formalize the general argument by restudying Equation (9.2) in the light of this new interpretation of $\mid 123 \mid$. The matter becomes practically obvious if we assume the weak restriction that $p_2 = p_3$ and $| 23 | = 0$.

In the light of all this, Theorem 4 then states that the joint effect of two attributes is essentially the same, irrespective of whether they are linearly additive or not.

13. Hybrid Stratification

For certain problems it is necessary to substitute into $| ij |$ one after another the corresponding columns of $| ij;k |$. This leads to the *compound,* which is defined as

$$C = \begin{vmatrix} p_{ijk} & p_j \\ p_{ik} & 1 \end{vmatrix} + \begin{vmatrix} p_{ij} & p_{kj} \\ p_i & p_k \end{vmatrix}$$

Each of these determinants can be derived from $| ij |$ by stratifying one column at a time, i.e., by adding the index k. This is why we talk here of hybrid stratification.

Inserting the symmetric parameters and using Equation (7.5), we obtain

$$C = | ijk | + p_i | jk | + p_k | ij | + p_k | ij | \\ - p_i | jk | = | ijk | + 2p_k | ij |$$

From (10.1) we can express $| ijk |$ in terms of two stratified cross products and obtain

$$C = | ij;k | - | ij;\bar{k} | + | ij |$$

This result is interesting because it shows that C is dependent upon cross products only, and not upon p_k; this is not the case for $| ijk |$ if it is expressed in terms of cross products.

The compound C appears in the determinantal equation

$$\begin{vmatrix} p_{ijk} - tp_{ij} & p_{jk} - tp_j \\ p_{ik} - tp_i & p_k - t \end{vmatrix} = 0$$

which plays an important role in latent-structure analysis. The equation has the form

$$| ij;k | - Ct + | ij | t^2 = 0 \quad (13.1)$$

The reader can easily verify this result by expanding the determinantal equation.

14. Symmetric Parameters in General

We have discussed so far symmetric parameters of the second order—the familiar cross products—and symmetric parameters of the third order. The criteria by which the third-order symmetric parameter was chosen suggest the form of a fourth-order parameter. The symbol $| ijkl |$ will be used to denote the fourth-order symmetric parameter, which will be defined implicitly by

$$\begin{aligned} p_{ijkl} = {} & p_i p_j p_k p_l + p_i p_j | kl | + p_i p_k |jl| \\ & + p_i p_l | jk | + p_j p_k | il | + p_j p_l | ik | \\ & + p_k p_l | ij | + p_i | jkl | + p_j | ikl | \\ & + p_k | ijl | + p_l | ijk | + | ijkl | \end{aligned}$$
$$(14.1)$$

This equation can be written more concisely in the form

$$\begin{aligned} p_{ijkl} = {} & p_i p_j p_k p_l + \Sigma p_i p_j | kl | \\ & + \Sigma p_i | jkl | + | ijkl | \end{aligned}$$

where the summation sign indicates summation over all possible permutations of the four indices. In general the symmetric parameter of order m will be defined implicitly by

$$\begin{aligned} p_{12\cdots m} = {} & p_1 p_2 \cdots p_m \\ & + \Sigma p_1 p_2 \cdots p_{m-2} | (m-1)m | \\ & + \Sigma p_1 p_2 \cdots p_{m-3} | (m-2)(m-1)m | + \cdots \\ & + \Sigma p_1 | 23 \ldots (m-1) | + | 12 \ldots m | \end{aligned}$$
$$(14.2)$$

A dichotomous system of m attributes can be completely summarized by 2^m independent pieces of data. The *fundamental set* using symmetric parameters consists of the data presented on the next page.

The numbers of terms of the various orders below are the coefficients of the binomial expansion of $(a + b)^m$. If we let $a = b = 1$, it then follows that the total number of such parameters of all orders is 2^m.

It can be seen easily that these higher-order symmetric parameters can be used to compute simply all ultimate frequencies. *Thus, e.g., a formula for p_{ijkl} can be ob-*

Order of term	Number of terms	Parameters of given order
0	1	n
1	m	$p_1, p_2, \ldots, p_m$
2	$\dfrac{m}{2!(m-2)!}$	$\mid 12 \mid, \mid 13 \mid, \ldots, \mid (m-1)m \mid$
3	$\dfrac{m}{3!(m-3)!}$	$\mid 123 \mid, \ldots, \mid (m-2)(m-1)m \mid$
$\vdots$	$\vdots$	
$m-1$	m	$\mid 12 \mid \ldots (m-1) \mid, \ldots, \mid 23 \ldots m \mid$
m	1	$\mid 12 \ldots m \mid$

tained by changing in (14.1) *any p_i into $p_{\bar{i}}$ and by changing the sign of any symmetric paramter in which a barred index appears.* The proof from frequency level 3 to level 4 is exactly the same that was given above for frequency level 3. The general rule is obvious, and can be obtained by induction from any level to the next.

Notes

1. For brevity's sake, the word "relative" will be omitted. We shall always deal with proportion of the total sample and not with absolute frequencies.

2. The term "conditional" emphasizes the fact that we are concerned with the relation between two attributes under the condition that a third attribute is present (or absent). "Stratified" emphasizes the fact that all entries in such a table carry the index of the attribute by which the population has first been sorted; the role of this "stratifier" is very important for many purposes. We shall use the two terms interchangeably.

3. It is difficult to decide how the symbol introduced by Equation (4.1) should be used. The stratified cross product pertains to a subset of the total sample. To make it comparable with the unstratified cross product, it should really be standardized for the size of the subset, and therefore be divided by $(p_k{}^2)$. This, however, yields a very clumsy notation. The standardization, as will be seen, can always be introduced after a theorem has been developed. Only occasionally will we use the standardized conditional cross product and then indicate it by a prime, i.e.,

$$\mid ij; k \mid' = \frac{\mid ij; k \mid}{p_k{}^2}$$

There is also a problem of terminology. Cross products can have levels of stratification. We shall designate the level by reference to the level of the subset. Thus, a zero-order cross product pertains to the total sample; a first-order cross product pertains to a subset, which is a result of partitioning the original sample by one dichotomy; and so on. Thus, the cross product appearing in Equation (4.1) is called of first order although it comprises frequencies up ot the third level.

4. Again a terminological issue has to be clarified. The level of cross products is determined by the level of the subset to which they belong (see footnote 3). Symmetric parameters are better described by the number of items they feature. This makes $[ij]$ a zero-order cross product but a second-order symmetric parameter. The anomaly is due to the desire to keep in tune with corresponding terminology in correlation analysis. Maybe after a while it will be advisable to agree on a more consistent terminology, which systematically starts with the idea of stratification levels.

5. If one likes to carry out analogies, the following observation may be made: $p_{i2}p_{\bar{i}3}/p_3$ is the variance of item (i) in the subset of people who give a positive response to item (3) and may be symbolized by $\sigma^2{}_{i.3}$. In the same way $\sigma^2{}_{i.\bar{3}}$ may be defined for the subset whose response to item (3) is negative. The variance of item (i) for the whole sample is $\sigma^2{}_i = p_i p_{\bar{i}}$. The coefficient of $\phi_{12.3}$ in Equation (9.2) is therefore $\sigma_{1.3}\sigma_{2.3} \mid \sigma_1 \sigma_2$. A corresponding reinterpretation can be made for the coefficient of $\phi_{12.\bar{3}}$.

6. It is hoped that by now the introduction of conventional indices of association into the formulas developed here has become familiar. We shall not continue this line of argument for the rest of this chapter.

24. Regression Analysis with Dichotomous Attributes

PAUL F. LAZARSFELD

IN RECENT YEARS sociologists have become interested in mathematical models which are based on systems of recursive linear equations between a set of variables. The movement started with an article by Herbert Simon who translated certain findings of dichotomous algebra into quantitative terms.[1] The idea was then extended by Hubert Blalock.[2] Raymond Boudon pointed out that path analysis introduced 40 years earlier by the biometrician, Wright, was really representing the same approach.[3] Following his lead Otis Duncan then published a series of examples in which path analysis was applied to social data.[4] Path analysis has considerable attraction for social scientists because its ideas can be graphically represented by the now well-known arrow scheme and because its algebra can be extended to any number of variables. But like any linear system it cannot reproduce conditional relations.[5]

In many cases the advantage of dealing economically with many variates outweighs the loss of higher level information. For this reason Coleman[6] developed in 1964 a formalism by which we can translate the idea of linearity into dichotomous terms. In 1968 Boudon[7] simplified considerably the computational aspect of his approach. The following paper recasts the Coleman-Boudon model in terms of dichotomous algebra. Leaving the main ideas of the two authors unchanged, the present approach seems to provide further simplification. The paper is part of a larger presentation which shows that its theorems can be extended to apply the idea of path analysis to dichotomous systems. This generalization will be found in the proceedings of the 1970 UNESCO Seminar on mathematical social sciences.

The Contribution Rule

The general problem of regression analysis is best symbolized by the scheme of Fig. 1, where, to simplify matters, we can just think of three independent attributes (with odd indices) and one dependent attribute (with even index).

FIGURE 1.

The problem of regression analysis can be expressed verbally in a variety of forms. How do the independent attributes affect the dependent one? What do they contribute to it? If the odd items "jointly cause" item 2, what weight should be given to the effect of each item in isolation?

Algebraically the Coleman-Boudon procedure proposes the following formulation. We subdivide a given population into eight subsets by a full cross-tabulation of the three independent items. For each subset we then compute the proportion of positive responses to item 2. These properties can be stated in the following obvious symbolism.

$$\frac{p_{1235}}{p_{135}} = \pi_{2,135} \quad \frac{p_{123\bar{5}}}{p_{13\bar{5}}} = \pi_{2,13\bar{5}} \text{ etc.} \dots \frac{p_{2,x}}{p_x}$$

$$= \pi_{2,x}$$

The eight subsets are characterized by the presence or absence of positive responses to the three independent items. Now three assumptions are made:

1. The conditional positive response to item 3 is determined by the signature of each of the subsets.

2. A subset makes a *contribution* a_{i2} to p_2 according to whether the response to item i was positive or not.

3. These contributions are additive.

These three assumptions can be summarized in the following schema:

Schema A

LAYER 1 SIGNA- TURE			FRE- QUENCY	CONDITIONAL PROBABILITY OF $2(\pi_{2,x})$
1	*3*	*5*	p_x	
+	+	+	p_{135}	$a_{12} + a_{32} + a_{52} + e_2$
+	+	−	$p_{13\overline{5}}$	$a_{12} + a_{32} \qquad + e_2$
+	−	+	$p_{1\overline{3}5}$	$a_{12} \qquad + a_{52} + e_2$
+	−	−	$p_{1\overline{3}\overline{5}}$	$a_{12} \qquad\qquad + e_2$
−	+	+	$p_{\overline{1}35}$	$a_{32} + a_{52} + e_2$
−	+	−	$p_{\overline{1}3\overline{5}}$	$a_{32} \qquad + e_2$
−	−	+	$p_{\overline{1}\overline{3}5}$	$a_{52} + e_2$
−	−	−	$p_{\overline{1}\overline{3}\overline{5}}$	e_2

The symbol e_2 is self-explanatory. It is the conditional probability of positive responses for item 2 in the sub-group where none of the independent items elicits a positive response. The schema is a mathematical model in the sense that it has fewer unknown parameters than observed data. Schema A exhibits seven independent equations. But there are only four unknown parameters in the model. We therefore have to remember what the main steps in model analysis are:

Step 1: What are the restrictions which this model puts on empirical data which are supposed to satisfy it?

Step 2: What combination of empirical data lead to equations suitable for the computation of the model parameters?

Step 3: How do we compute algebraically these parameters under the assumption of perfect data?

Step 4: How can we test the adequacy of the model if we deal with concrete and therefore imperfect data?

The answer to the *first step* can be seen immediately from the main Schema A. If we subtract the second from the first line we immediately get a_{52}, the contribution of item 5 to item 2. But the same is the case if we subtract the next three pairs of lines. We therefore get four determinations of a_{52} which the model requires to be equal. The same is obviously true for the other two contribution parameters.

What does this mean in terms of empirical data? The following equations are expected to hold true:

$$a_{52} = \pi_{2,135} - \pi_{2,13\overline{5}} = \pi_{2,1\overline{3}5}$$
$$-\pi_{2,1\overline{3}\overline{5}} \cdots \text{etc.} = f_{52,\overline{13}}$$

Similar equations apply to the other two contribution parameters. The finding can be put into the words of Theorem A.

Theorem A: *If we divide the population into eight ($= 2^3$) subsets by cross-classifying three independent items; if we then compute for each subset the conditional f-coefficient [8] between the remaining dependent and the independent items: then those four f-coefficients have to be numerically alike.*

It will soon be seen that this type of condition characterizes all asymmetric systems which we are now investigating.

In a way we have already implicitly touched on Step 4. With concrete data we would get for each contribution parameter four estimates, and by some additional assumptions we could get the most desirable estimate. This is actually how Coleman proceeded. But as usual it was soon shown that a variety of estimation procedures would lead to slightly different numerical results. It is therefore fortunate that this model permits a direct determination of the contribution parameters which moves the problem of statistical significance to a later and more convenient step. It is at this point that the present text introduces new ideas.

The Unique Determination of the Contribution Parameters

We now move to the *second step* in the preceding list. In many models the original equations can be recombined in order to simplify the algebraic computation. In the present case this can be done in an especially advantageous way. In order to show this we will recast the model in a somewhat different way. In Schema B the first column contains the ultimate frequencies for all four items, including item 2. The second column reproduces these frequencies in terms of the contribution parameters.

SCHEMA B

(A)	(B)
$p_{123\overline{5}}$	$(a_{12} + a_{32} + a_{52} + e_2)p_{135}$
$p_{12\overline{3}5}$	$(a_{12} + a_{32} \quad\quad + e_2)p_{13\overline{5}}$
$p_{1\overline{2}3\overline{5}}$	$(a_{12} \quad\quad + a_{52} + e_2)p_{1\overline{3}5}$
$p_{1\overline{2}3\overline{5}}$	$(a_{12} \quad\quad\quad\quad + e_2)p_{1\overline{3}\overline{5}}$
$p_{\overline{1}235}$	$(\quad\quad a_{32} + a_{52} + e_2)p_{\overline{1}35}$
$p_{\overline{1}23\overline{5}}$	$(\quad\quad a_{32} \quad\quad + e_2)p_{\overline{1}3\overline{5}}$
$p_{\overline{1}235}$	$(\quad\quad\quad\quad a_{52} + e_2)p_{\overline{1}\overline{3}5}$
$p_{\overline{1}2\overline{3}\overline{5}}$	$(\quad\quad\quad\quad\quad + e_2)p_{\overline{1}3\overline{5}}$

Four items permit the formation of sixteen ultimate frequencies but it will turn out that we shall need only the eight subsets where the response to the dependent item 2 is always positive. The pertinent relative proportions are given in column (A). The second column (B) reports the proportion of all people who make a positive response to item 2 computed in terms of the whole population. These are now not conditional probabilities but the actual frequencies of people who in each subset are positive on item 2—divided, of course, by the size of the whole sample. Therefore if we add up the eight terms in column (B) we have p_2, the relative frequency of all positive re-

sponses to 2 irrespective of the responses to the independent items. We can collect in this sum all the items which contain the same contribution parameter. The reader can easily check that we then get the following result:

$$p_2 = p_1 a_{12} + p_3 a_{32} + p_5 a_{52} + e_2 \quad (1)$$

The symmetry of all these equations suggests the following strategy. We shall read off from Schema B directly the values for p_{i2}; these are of course the positive joint frequencies between the dependent and each independent attribute. The hope is that the cross-products $(p_{i2} - p_i p_2)$ will turn out especially simple. This is indeed the case. Taking item 1, for instance, we get the joint frequency of items 1 and 2 by adding the first four lines of column (B). The result is clearly

$$p_{12} = p_1(a_{12} + e_2) + p_{13}p_{32} + p_{15}p_{52} \quad (2)$$

(We get similar equations for p_{32} and p_{52} by simply exchanging the index 1 for the index of each of the other two independent items.) We now form the cross-product [12] by subtracting from the last equation (2) the preceding one multiplied by p_1. We collect again terms which refer to the same contribution parameter and we end up with the following equation:

$$[12] = p_1 p_{\overline{1}} a_{12} + [13]a_{32} + [15]a_{52} \quad (3)$$

Two corresponding equations can be derived for [32] and [52].

These equations permit a drastic visual interpretation by returning to the graph with which we started. The cross-product between an independent and the dependent item [i2] is the weighted sum of all three contribution parameters. The contribution of item i is weighted by its split $p_i p_{\overline{i}}$. The other contributions are weighted by the cross-products which can be formed between item i and the other items on the independent layer I; for item 5, for instance, this would be cross-product [51] and cross-product [53].

Because of the importance of these equations we shall give them a special name. They will hereafter be called the *contribution equations*. We have three such linear contribution equations which contain as the three unknowns the contribution parameters.

The third step in our list is now easily answered. We have to solve the three contribution equations. We shall of course use Kramer's rule and for this purpose it is useful to put the whole result into the language of vectors and matrices. We first define a matrix C_I which in the case of three independent attributes would read as follows:

$$C_I = \begin{pmatrix} p_1 p_{\bar{1}} & [13] & [15] \\ [31] & p_3 p_{\bar{3}} & [35] \\ [51] & [53] & p_5 p_{\bar{5}} \end{pmatrix} \quad (4)$$

This matrix is symmetric because in a cross-product the order of the indices does not make any difference. C_I contains three possible cross-products which can be formed between all the items in layer I. The main diagonal contains the split of the three items.[9]

The cross-products between the independent and the one dependent item from a column vector which we shall call $\{C_{12}\}$; the three contribution parameters form another column vector which we shall call $\{A_{12}\}$. Our inspection of the original Coleman-Boudon schema then leads us to the general equation 5:

$$C_{Ii} = C_I A_{Ii} \quad (5)$$

(In Coleman's terminology this would be called the regression equation for attributes.)

By writing it in terms of matrices and vectors, we see immediately that it applies to any number of independent attributes.

Cross-products are never meant to be a "measure" of anything. They are an indispensable statistic if one wants to see the implications of the Coleman-Boudon schema. Often it is desirable to have a more intuitively meaningful index with some conventional characteristics like varying between minus 1 and plus 1. Because of the asymmetric nature of the regression equation the f-coefficient is a natural candidate. Equation 3 can easily be transformed by dividing each side by $s_i = p_1 p_{\bar{1}}$. We then obtain the following form:

$$f_{12} = a_{12} + f_{13} a_{32} + f_{15} a_{52} \quad (6)$$

In the corresponding equation for cross-product [32] and [52] we would divide by $p_3 p_{\bar{3}}$ and $p_5 p_{\bar{5}}$ respectively. For the whole system that changes the matrix C_I into another which we shall for obvious reasons now call F_I. The definition is

$$F_I = \begin{pmatrix} 1 & f_{13} & f_{15} \\ f_{31} & 1 & f_{35} \\ f_{51} & f_{53} & 1 \end{pmatrix} \quad (7)$$

We have now unity in the major diagonal. But this matrix is not really symmetrical because the f-coefficients can have different numerical values according to the sequence of the indices. In terms of f-coefficients the regression equations then read

$$\{F_{Ii}\} = F_I \{A_{Ii}\} \quad (8)$$

The solution for the contribution parameters would of course be identical whatever form we use. One may choose the cross-product form or the f-coefficient form, whichever facilitates the mathematical argument or the reader's intuition.

A Numerical Example

Because the regression equations apply to any number of independent attributes, we can be satisfied with a very simple example. Coleman has reported a study in which high school students were asked two questions: whether they felt that they were members of the leading crowd (item 1); and whether they felt it morally all right to belong (item 3). This latter attitude question was repeated with the same students several months later (item 4). In terms of our preceding analysis the question can be raised what the replies to the two questions at the first interview contribute to the attitude question repeated at the second interview. These two contributions have intuitively two different meanings. The contribution of item 3 to item 4 corresponds vaguely to the notion of attitude stability. The contribution of item 1 to item 4 tells whether membership in a group later affects the attitude toward it. The empirical numerical data are as follows:

TABLE 1.

		(4)		
(1)	(3)	+	–	
+	+	591	125	716
+	–	142	156	298
–	+	897	361	1258
–	–	377	611	988
		2007	1253	3260

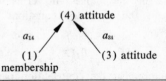

(4) attitude

a_{14} a_{34}

(1)   (3) attitude
membership

We want to evaluate a_{14} and a_{34} with the help of equation 5. From the preceding

table we compute the following set of empirical data:

$$[14] = .033 \quad p_1 = .311 \quad p_1 p_{\bar{1}} = .214$$
$$[13] = .031 \quad p_3 = .606 \quad p_3 p_{\bar{3}} = .239$$
$$[34] = .084 \quad p_4 = .616$$

Thus we have two equations in two unknowns:

$$.033 = .214 a_{14} + .031 a_{34}$$
$$.084 = .031 a_{14} + .239 a_{34}$$

By conventional methods, we may solve for the parameters:

$$a_{14} = .109 \qquad a_{34} = .337$$

Evaluating e_4:

$$p_4 = e_4 + p_1 a_{14} + p_3 a_{34}$$
$$.616 = e_4 + .331 \times .109 + .606 \times .337$$
$$e_4 = .378$$

Testing the fit by comparing expected and observed values of the proportions, we have Table 2 below. For immediate inspection we compare proportions line by line. A defensible test would be to apply a chi-square computation to the eight raw frequencies.

Let us highlight the main feature of this numerical example.

1. We first compute the contribution parameters with the help of the regression equation. In this example we use the cross-products because the f-coefficients would have required additional computations.

TABLE 2.

	Expected	Observed
$\pi_{4,13}$	$a_{14} + a_{34} + e_4$ $= .109 + .337 + .378 = \underline{.824}$	$\dfrac{591}{716} = .825$
$\pi_{4,1\bar{3}}$	$a_{14} + e_4 = .109 + .378 = \underline{.487}$	$\dfrac{142}{298} = .477$
$\pi_{4,\bar{1}3}$	$a_{34} + e_4 = .337 + .378 = \underline{.715}$	$\dfrac{897}{1258} = .713$
$\pi_{4,\bar{1}\bar{3}}$	$e_4 = \underline{.378}$	$\dfrac{377}{488} = .382$

2. We then compute the proportion of people who have an approving attitude the second time even if they were neither members nor friendly the first time. We have stressed that this is not the empirical proportion which we would have gotten by just inspecting line 4 in our numerical table. It is derived from the model equation for p_4 after the contribution parameters have been computed.

3. Having computed all the parameters of the model we can now compute third-order frequencies which were not used in the computation of the parameters. The result is indicated in the "expected" column of Table 2. Those figures can now be compared with the observed proportions. On inspection the differences seem quite small. But there are tests available to find out whether a linear model is indeed appropriate for these empirical data.

This example implicitly answers the question raised in the *fourth step* which is needed in a model analysis.

A Generalization to Several Dependent Attributes

The situation which we want to analyze is easily described by the following graph:

to the use of f-indices we make the following observations:

What we called the F_I matrix remains the same irrespective of the index of the dependent attribute. It is a characteristic of Layer I.

The column vectors on the left side of the equation can now be put side by side and form a new matrix, which we shall call for obvious reasons $F_{I\,II}$. In the case of three attributes on each layer the definition is as follows:

$$F_{I\,II} = \begin{pmatrix} f_{12} & f_{14} & f_{16} \\ f_{32} & f_{34} & f_{36} \\ f_{52} & f_{54} & f_{56} \end{pmatrix} \qquad (9)$$

$$\{f_{12}\}\{f_{14}\}\{f_{16}\}$$

The column vector formed of a_{i2} now also repeats itself twice more with shift in index number for the dependent attribute. This results in a new matrix:

$$A_{I\,II} = \begin{pmatrix} a_{12} & a_{14} & a_{16} \\ a_{32} & a_{34} & a_{36} \\ a_{52} & a_{54} & a_{56} \end{pmatrix} \qquad (10)$$

$$\{A_{12}\}\{A_{14}\}\{A_{16}\}$$

All the information depicted in Figure 2

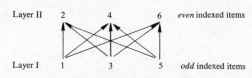

| Layer II | 2 | 4 | 6 | *even* indexed items |

| Layer I | 1 | 3 | 5 | *odd* indexed items |

FIGURE 2.

With the formulae established so far we can go one step further.

The algebrac translation of this graph presents no new problem but suggests a more economic symbolism. For each separate item on Layer II we have the contribution equation 3. The three sets of equations are alike except for the index of the dependent attribute which changes from 2 to 4 to 6, respectively. Turning directly

can then be summarized in the following: Theorem B:

> If a Coleman-Boudon model links a Layer I of independent and a Layer II of dependent attributes, then the contribution parameters can be computed from the matrix equation

$$F_{I\,II} = F_I A_{I\,II} \qquad (11)$$

where the empirically observed F-matrices are defined respectively by equation 9 and equation 7 and the parameter matrix A is defined by equation 10. (Of course we can also use the equivalent form $C_{I\ II} = C_I A_{I\ II}$.)

The theorem is especially important in so-called panel analysis. There the same questions are asked twice corresponding to Layer I and Layer II respectively. Theorem B can be considered as panel analysis under the assumption of the linear model and therefore in disregard of empirical information beyond the second stratification level. In a different way Theorem B can be considered a generalization of Donald Campbell's cross-lagged correlation applied to dichotomies and taking into consideration their stability.

Clearly two new problems arise. For one we would have to explore what relation *within* Layer II exists as a result of the Coleman-Boudon model. And secondly, what happens if additional layers of attributes are added? The answers lie beyond the scope of this paper. But they are available and form the basis of a path analysis for dichotomous attributes.

Notes

1. Herbert A. Simon, "Spurious Correlation: A Causal Interpretation," *Journal of the American Statistical Association,* 49 (September, 1954), 467–479.

2. Hubert M. Blalock, *Causal Inferences in Nonexperimental Research* (Chapel Hill, N.C.: University of North Carolina Press, 1964).

3. Raymond Boudon, "A Method of Linear Causal Analysis: Dependence Analysis," *American Sociological Review,* 30 (June, 1965), 365–374.

4. Otis Duncan, "Path Analysis: Sociological Examples,"*American Journal of Sociology,* 72 (July, 1967), 1–16.

5. See, for example, this author's entry on analysis of attribute data in the *International Encyclopedia of the Social Sciences,* 1968. Vol. 15, pp. 418 ff.

6. James S. Coleman, *Introduction to Mathematical Sociology* (New York: The Free Press, 1964), Chapter 6.

7. Raymond Boudon, "A New Look at Correlation Analysis," in H. M. Blalock, Jr. and A. Blalock (eds.), *Methodology in Social Research* (New York: McGraw-Hill, 1958).

8. The reader who refers back to the preceding selection can notice that the symmetric parameters and third or higher level cannot be reproduced in the linear system.

9. The split S_i-$p_i p_{\bar\imath}$ has a maximum if the item i splits 50–50. The more asymmetric the split, the smaller is S.

Auxiliary Readings

A. The General Idea

H. H. Hyman, *Survey Design and Analysis* (New York: The Free Press, 1955), Chapter VII.

A product of extensive research experience, this book introduces a fundamental distinction between descriptive surveys (concerned with the precise measurement of variables in a sample) and explanatory surveys (concerned with inferences about causation). Chapter VII provides a detailed treatment of the theme of "elaboration." Through formalization, the logical and arithmetic bases for distinguishing interpretation, explanation, and specification are presented. Excellent examples of each procedure make the points vivid.

C. Y. Glock, "Survey Design and Analysis in Sociology," pp. 1–62 in C. Y. Glock (ed.) *Survey Research in the Social Sciences* (New York: Russell Sage, 1967), pp. 1–62.

The first two-thirds of this article is an excellent presentation of the principles of elaboration. The author suggests what can be learned by the examination of marginals (frequency distributions), time-bound (symmetrical) associations, and time-ordered (asymmetrical or causal) associations. The author makes an important distinction between "differentiated description" and "explanation." Good illustrations of explanation, interpretation, and specification are presented. Studies are classified as those which focus on the dependent variable ("accounting studies"), on the independent variable ("implications studies"), and on a variable which is first treated as independent and then as dependent ("phenomenon studies").

M. Rosenberg, *The Logic of Survey Analysis* (New York: Basic Books, 1968).

An extension of the principle of elaboration, distinguishing additional types of test factors and contributions of conditional relationships. An abundance of empirical examples seeks to alert the reader to a wide range of potential substantive and theoretical contributions inherent in survey data.

H. Zeisel, *Say It With Figures* (New York: Harper and Brothers, 1970), 5th ed.

A clear and concise discussion of conditional relationships, independent effects, spurious non-correlations, explanation, interpretation, etc. Numerous simple examples bring out the points sharply.

B. Selected Examples of Elaboration

L. I. Pearlin and M. L. Kohn, "Social Class, Occupation, and Parental Values: A Cross-National Study," *American Sociological Review*, 31 (August 1966), pp. 466–79.

While Italian and American parents differ in their child-rearing values, this study shows that the *relationship* of social class to parental values is similar in both countries. But what is the decisive component of social class that produces these different values? The authors seek the answer in the occupational realm, specifically, the degree of self-direction or external control in work. Controlling on the self-direction aspect of work activity, the class differences in child-rearing values largely disappear.

H. Goldhamer and A. W. Marshall, *Psychosis and Civilization* (New York: The Free Press, 1949).

The authors examine the widely held assumption that rates of psychosis have increased during the past century. Rates of hospitalization for psychosis in Massachusetts are examined for 1845 and 1945, and the results in fact indicate such an increase. If, however, one looks at the rates within each *age* category, then one finds (with the exception of the over 50 group) virtually no change. The increased rates of mental illness are largely due to the great increase in length of life, introducing a much larger proportion of senile dementia cases.

P. F. Lazarsfeld, B. Berelson, and H. Gaudet, *The People's Choice* (New York: Columbia University Press 1948), p. 19, Chart 4.

This monograph contains many examples of elaboration. Thus, Catholics more often vote the Democratic ticket than Protestants; but the difference is less marked among younger than older people. (Chart 7) Less educated people are more likely not to vote; but this difference is fully accounted for by an index of interest. (Chart 15) In general, less educated people prefer the radio to the newspaper, but in the 1940 campaign, on each educational level, Democrats found the radio more congenial and Republicans liked the newspaper. (Chart 37) For other examples see especially chapters V and XV.

R. K. Merton and A. S. Kitt, "Contributions to the Theory of Reference Group Behavior," *Continuities in Social Research:* Studies in the Scope and Method of "The American Soldier," R. K. Merton and P. F. Lazarsfeld, eds. (Glencoe, Ill.: The Free Press), 1950.

The authors show that the cases reported by Stouffer permit distinctions between various kinds of reference groups according to whether one is actually a member, aspires to be one, competes with present members, etc. This discussion shares with Stouffer's original data the merit of having made the notion of reference groups a firm tool of modern social research.

L. D. Haber, "Age and Integration Setting: A Re-appraisal of "The Changing American Parent," *American Sociological Review,* 27 (October 1962), pp. 682–89.

In an influential work, *The Changing American Parent,* Miller and Swanson had shown that "entrepreneurial" families were more likely to use a rigid, disciplinary approach to childrearing whereas "bureaucratic" families tended toward a permissive, self-regulatory approach. Occupational activity was thus seen as relevant to values. A careful re-examination of the data, however, showed that entrepreneurial families were older, and were more likely to have reared their children at an historical period when rigid, disciplinary practices were in vogue. It is thus highly possible that it is the spurious factor of historical epoch (reflected by age) rather than the occupational structure which is the effective influence.

D. O. Arnold and D. Gold, 1964. "The Facilitation Effect of Social Environment," *Public Opinion Quarterly,* XXVIII (Fall 1964), pp. 513–16.

In a campaign and vote to reapportion state legislative districts, there was a high correlation between county size and support of reapportionment. The investigators hypothesized, however, that this correlation would be stronger where the issue was made more salient by the presence of newspapers or by the activity of interested citizens' committees; the results clearly supported the expectation. This illustration of conditional relationships specifies the conditions which facilitate or inhibit the relationship between the variables.

P. Blau and R. Schoenherr, *The Structure of Organizations* (New York: Basic Books, 1971), Chapter 10.

The authors show that supervisors in large organizations have more people working for them than supervisors in small agencies. But this positive correlation between size of organization and "span of control" is quite different according to the authority level of the supervisor himself. At the lowest level (foreman), the correlation is very high indeed. But top managers have only small groups of assistants, and these groups take approximately the same size no matter what the size of the total organization. The chapter actually contains a double specification: the effects of the supervisor's level upon the basic relation varies among different functional departments of the organizations.

B. Goldstein and R. L. Eichhorn, "The Changing Protestant Ethic: Rural Patterns in Health, Work, and Leisure," *American Sociological Review*, XXVI (August 1961), pp. 557–65.

How does the "Protestant Ethic work value" influence the type of farm machinery employed? Overall, the authors find a modest relationship. But on small farms the high-work oriented people are much *more* likely than others to use large machines, whereas on large farms they are much *less* likely to do so. In both cases the high work-oriented men are less likely to use the machinery most appropriate for the farm size.

H. H. Hyman, 1953. "The Value Systems of Different Classes: A Social Psychological Contribution to the Analysis of Stratification," pp. 426–42 in R. Bendix and S. M. Lipset (eds.), *Class, Status and Power* (New York: The Free Press, 1953).

While social class differences in mobility have characteristically been attributed to unequal opportunity, Hyman suggests that an important intervening variable between low position and lack of upward mobility may be a system of beliefs and values. Drawing upon a number of surveys conducted over the years, he shows how social classes differ in the value placed on formal education, the motivation to advance in the economic structure, the belief in the opportunity structure, the forms of success striving, etc. A highly sophisticated secondary analysis.

C. Formalization

An elementary introduction to path analysis was contributed by Kenneth Land to *Sociological Methodology* (R. Hill, ed.), San Francisco: Jossey Bass, 1969. The point of view of the present section is easily available in the two entries on "Survey Analysis" in the *Encyclopedia of the Social Sciences*. Hanan Selvin, one of the two authors, stresses the need for a bridge to regression analysis. Raymond Boudon, in his contribution to *Methodology in Social Research* (H. M. Blalock, Jr. and A. Blalock, eds.), New York: McGraw-Hill, 1958, shows that certain rather simple transformations actually link regression analysis, path analysis, and dichotomous algebra.

The Study of Collectives

Introduction

EVERY SOCIOLOGIST is keenly sensitive to the distinction between the individual and the group. From a mere analytical point of view, however, this distinction is not so fundamental; whether the individual or the group is the unit of analysis, the principles are basically the same. The development of variates, described in Section I, and the examination of the interrelation among these variates, discussed in Section II, apply equally to groups and to individuals. A multivariate tabulation, the units of which are cities, would not look any different from one based on people. When we move to the group level, however, new methodological issues arise. The present section seeks to map out this unfamiliar territory.

First consider a terminological matter. The term "group" has a certain ambiguity, sometimes being reserved for people who interact with one another in accord with established patterns, but at other times being extended to include masses or even social categories. To bypass this debate, we shall use the term collective to refer to any combination of individuals, whether it be small integrated informal groups, formal organizations, cities, nations, etc. When such a collective is characterized by some variate, we shall give brevity precedence over grammar and speak of a *collective characteristic* (rather than a characteristic of a collective or even a collective's characteristic). In earlier sections, we have primarily dealt with *individual characteristics*. While we have not codified individual characteristics, some classification of collective characteristics is advisable. If one thinks of a collective as composed of individuals, the collective characteristic can originate from an aggregation of discrete individual characteristics. The wealth of a city can be measured by the average income of its citizens; the homogeneity of the urban economy might be indicated by the standard deviation of the distribution of individual incomes. The process of aggregation, however, is not always a matter of simple addition. It would be possible to propose, for example, that a group be characterized according to whether the men get along better with each other than women do.

A collective characteristic which is not based on aggregation will be called global. Global properties characterize the collective as a whole, and do not derive from the accumulations of individual characteristics. It is easy to give specific examples. Instead of averaging individual incomes to characterize the wealth of a city, we could ascertain the space allotted to such cultural activities as museums, concert halls, libraries. The social distance between professors and students in a specific country could be measured by aggregated observations on the way the two behave toward one another; one also might employ global characteristics such as whether the professors have campus office hours or whether their home telephones are listed, etc. Certain global characteristics, though not labeled as such, occupy a traditional position in the sociological literature. One recalls, for example, Durkheim's distinction between societies with restitutive and repressive laws. The analysis of documents for certain linguistic features (the number of words the Arabs are supposed to have for "camel") is another use of global characteristics.

The distinction between aggregative and global characteristics is not always unequivocal. The divorce rate compiled from a sampling survey would have to be an aggregate characteristic because it is computed from discrete data. But sometimes we are inclined to think of rates as global measures. Abstract rates derived from public records have this character. Suicide rates, birth rates, strike rates, crime rates, all have the flavor of global characteristics. But such borderline cases should not erode the very special character of global characteristics (CC's). For example, the historical sociologist has little else but such global measures, and accordingly, global CC's play a dominant role in national comparisons.

Group Characteristics and Their Interrelations

The problems of clarifying one's concepts, specifying their aspects or dimensions, selecting indicators, and joining them into indices are common both to the study of individuals and of collectives. In Selection 25 Lazarsfeld and Menzel classify various types of aggregative properties of collectives according to the operations involved in their measurement. The Hemphill and Westie and the Landecker articles in

the first edition illustrate some of the steps in the process of developing measures of group characteristics.

But once we turn to global CC's, the territory is relatively uncharted. Barton has made a start by an inventory of the characteristics actually used in empirical studies of organizations, and Selection 26, an excerpt from this book, contains numerous examples of global characteristics. Another way of approaching global CC's would be through the social anthropologist's speculations about national characteristics. The annotated bibliography contains some references; unfortunately, no systematic classification of global characteristics yet exists.

A word should be inserted here regarding the role of so-called demographic variates. Is being male or female, or foreman or farmer, a collective property or an individual characteristic? The answer probably depends upon the interpretation of the variate. Sex might indicate the world of differing norms within which American boys and girls are raised. In this case, it could be considered collective rather than individual. In general, the "truer" social units relate individuals to one another through rules, laws or institutions. Once again, the matter of definition must necessarily be left unresolved. Methodology tries to carve out major types of research procedures; there will always be concrete situations where the borderlines are uncertain.

Once the researcher has succeeded in classifying his collective units in terms of relevant variates, he will want to see how they are combined into propositions. The task before him is, once again, multivariate analysis. Though obvious, this practice is a surprisingly recent development. In the previous edition it was mentioned that we were unable to locate any studies where more than two collective characteristcs were analyzed simultaneously; true multivariate analyses did not come to light. The situation has changed radically in the ensuing years. Partly because of the availability of funds for research and partly because of a spurt of interest in the study of organizations, it is now possible to cite complex propositions based on the study of a large number of collectives. An example of the analysis of the interrelationships of group characteristics is Kendall's paper, Selection 27, comparing the environments of various types of hospitals in terms of three dimensions of the setting: observability of house staff performance; relations of interns and residents; orientation, whether local or cosmopolitan. The author allows us to see how she moves from these dimensions to their indicators. She then examines variations among hospitals of differing size and affiliation.

Selection 28 points to specific procedures by which collective characteristics can be developed irrespective of their more formal nature. Coleman allows us to see the possibilities of using traditional survey research methods, hitherto exclusively reserved for the study of individuals, for the examination of social structure and the relations among individuals.

Weight of Collective Characteristics

The findings exemplified in the studies of the interrelations of group attributes could satisfy Durkheim's definition of social facts. If Durkheim had indeed been looking for interrelations between collective characteristics, he would have had to think in terms of global CC's. Had he known about sampling surveys, he would probably have accepted aggregate CC's as sociological facts, too. He maintained that social facts possessed a coercive power over the behavior of individuals; today, it is possible to show empirically that he was correct. The attitudes and behavior of people *are* affected by the contexts in which they live. If we adopt this perspective, a number of interesting new questions arise: which of two collective characteristics has the greater

impact in affecting some outcome, say, behavior or attitudes? Does a collective characteristic have an effect independent of an individual characteristic, even when the collective characteristic is an aggregate of these self-same individual characteristics? In a particular investigation, which has the greater influence: the collective or the individual characteristic?

The selections in Subdivision B show various ways in which the effect of broader contexts can be demonstrated. In Selection 29, Coleman shows that in schools where athletic achievement is highly valued, young athletes have more self-confidence than in schools with a more academic tradition (Table A). Here the climate of the school was established from the responses of students to a questionnnaire about their activities, interests, and values. In Table 3 the result is further refined; Coleman introduces an additional subdivision as to whether the student is characterized by others as a member of the leading crowd. In all schools, the popular boys have less desire than the total student body to be regarded as brilliant students. But in schools which are not academically oriented, this desire is especially low and especially distinct from the total student attitude. Thus Coleman demonstrates how general school orientation and membership in specific groups jointly affect the attitudes of the students toward academic work.

A typical example of a collective characteristic is the well-known notion "climate of opinion." In 1961, the *Public Opinion Quarterly* published a symposium on this topic. The statements by David Sills as moderator and James Coleman as commentator could well be read as part of the present introduction. It is known that children from families with higher economic status score higher on aptitude tests and are more inclined to go to college. But superimposed on the effect of family background is the role of what Michael calls the school climate, in Selection 30. This climate affects test performance and, even more so, college aspirations.

This and similar studies have led to an interesting controversy. While not denying the weight of such characteristics, Sewell and Armer in Selection 31 raise interesting problems and make the point that a more refined analysis shows that the effect of these variables could be overrated. Does it really show that the social context is not as weighty as other authors assume or does it rather expose the "mechanisms" by which the environment could exercise its influence? Students and teachers could benefit from a discussion of these varying interpretations.

Another interesting contribution to this debate is Campbell and Alexander's paper, Selection 32. Once again, data on college aspirations is related to socioeconomic indicators. But here, there are two contexts for individual plans. One is the aggregate of the socioeconomic backgrounds of the seniors in the school. The other is the aggregate status of the student's friends at the school. When thirty schools were compared, school status had a positive relationship to the individual student's college plans; so did the status of his friends. These are not surprising results to us. But by contrast, when the relationship of school status to college desires was examined within each socioeconomic level of friends, the relationship was negligible. The authors suggest that they are identifying the mechanism by which the environment affects plans such that the larger and more remote con-

text works through the smaller and closer one.

Contextual Analysis

The most important application of collective characteristics occurs in what has become known as contextual analysis. One way to explain the matter is through the utilization of a simple scheme. Suppose we have studied people in two different social contexts and have concentrated on the interrelation between two individual characteristics. By thinking only of dichotomies, all the empirical findings can be entered into the cells of Table 1.

The fictitious data can be interpreted in two steps. First we might ignore the inside cells of the two contingent 4-fold tables and just look at their marginals. We would then see that attribute (1) is more frequent in context A as compared to context B (600 to 400); attribute (2) shows no difference whatsoever in the two contexts (500 to 500). Studies which concentrate on this effect we shall call comparative studies; they compare the impact of different contexts on certain dependent variables.

But we can also look at the inside of the two contingent tables. We then see that the two attributes are not related in context A, while they are markedly related in B. It is this latter approach for which we propose to reserve the notion of "contextual propositions." These are conditional relation-

TABLE 1. Interpreting Two Individual Characteristics and One Collective Characteristic

| | | Context A | | | | | Context B | | |
| | | IC (2) | | | | | IC (2) | | |
		+	−	Total			+	−	Total
IC (1)	+	300	300	600	IC (1)	+	300	100	400
	−	200	200	400		−	200	400	600
Total		500	500	1000	Total		500	500	1000

ships involving a collective variate as the test factor. Selection 33 serves as a typical example. Nasatir relates individual orientation to their failure at college. The relation is different according to the type of dormitory in which the student lives. Rosenberg, in the reference in the annotated bibliography, relates religion to self-esteem of high school students. It turns out that this relation differs according to whether the young people live in a neighborhood where the families belong to the religious minority or religious majority.

The difference between the examples of Subdivision B and those in C can be linked up with a well known statistical terminology. When we talked about the weight of collective characteristics, we implied they had an *additive* role in the whole analysis. Take a fictitious example where one would compare the mathematical performance of boys and girls in coeducational schools and in schools where the sexes are separate. It might be that a 10 point superiority of boys is the same if we compare test scores in both types of schools. But it might also be that the difference in mathematical performance between, for example, Columbia boys and Vassar College girls is much greater than between boys and girls at Swarthmore. There would then be what statisticians call *interaction* between the school context and the sex of the individual student.

Two fictitious tables will make the difference numerically clear. The example compels us at the same time to bring to the attention of the teacher a difficulty in the presentation of such data which is often found among novices.

TABLE 2. Proportion of People with Individual Attribute (2)

		Context A	Context B
Individual	+	50%	75%
Attribute (1)	−	50%	33%

In this table we have taken the figures of Table 1 and rearranged them. The entries are now proportions rather than absolute frequencies. What we see once we have done this is that not only does context B add to the effect of attribute (1) as compared to context A, but the relationship between (1) and (2) is different in the two contexts. In A, the proportion of people with attribute (2) was not related to the proportion of people with attribute (1). In context B, those with attribute (1) were far more likely to display attribute (2) than those without attribute (1). This is a contextual table.

Compare these findings to the hypothetical ones of Table 3.

TABLE 3. Proportion of People with Individual Attribute (2)

		Context A	Context B
Individual	+	35%	50%
Attribute (1)	−	10%	25%

Once again, the context adds to the effect of attribute (1). But here, the relationship between attribute (1) and (2) is not affected by the context. In each context there is a difference of 25 per cent in attribute (2) between those who do and do not have attribute (1). We call this an additive effect of the context.

As usual the collective characteristics entering a multivariate analysis can be of two kinds: global or aggregative. Certain statistical problems can come up in the latter case but a discussion would go beyond the scope of this book. The student, however, might get a general feeling for the difference through Selection 34 (Lazarsfeld and Thielens) where colleges are characterized in a variety of ways. Sometimes the authors distinguish turbulent and quiet colleges according to the number of academic freedom incidents that occurred, a global characteristic. At other points, the authors talk of liberal and conservative colleges, an index aggregated from the attitude of the faculty members. In both types of cases, the effect of the college on the interrelation between two individual characteristics is studied. Davis and his associates have developed a collective characteristic which is an aggregate of two individual ones. Here, they manage to distinguish subtypes (see annotated bibliography).

Finally, a terminological distinction deserves attention. We know now what a contextual *proposition* is. But sometimes (for instance in Lazarsfeld-Menzel, selection 25) an author talks of a contextual *property*. By this is meant a way of characterizing an individual by his membership in a collective. Thus, for instance, the I.Q. of a student is a conventional individual property. Whether he goes to a coeducational college or not is an individual property which characterizes the student through a context, and may thus be called a contextual property. In some cases one has to make arbitrary decisions. Thus the ethnic character of a student could be considered an individual property, but also a contextual one if his race is used as an indicator of the socal background in which he grew up. How to decide such matters is partly a convention and partly may depend upon the general tenor of a specific inquiry.

Contextual propositions are important because they help to bridge different research traditions. Some sociologists have criticized survey research as atomistic, as focusing on the parts rather than the whole. Such critics tend to prefer studies of single communities where a perceptive investigator can trace the effect of the total community upon the pattern of individual behavior. But as the cases in Subdivision C show, the role of the "whole" can very well be traced by the type of finding where collective as well as individual characteristics appear simultaneously.

In the next section, time itself will serve as the context for the analysis.

A. Group Characteristics and Their Interrelations

25. On The Relation Between Individual and Collective Properties *

PAUL F. LAZARSFELD AND HERBERT MENZEL

Introductory Considerations

1. PURPOSE

SOCIAL SCIENTISTS often make use of variables to describe not only individual persons but also groups, communities, organizations, or other "collectives." [1] Thus one reads, for example, of "racially mixed census tracts," of "highly bureaucratized voluntary organizations," or of a "centrally located rooming-house district." At other times the variables, although describing individuals, are based on data about certain collectives, as in a comparison of "graduates of top-ranking medical schools" with "graduates of other medical schools." This paper attempts to clarify some of the operations involved in the construction and use of such variables in empirical research, and provides a nomenclature for the different ways in which information about individuals and about collectives may be interwoven in these properties. The properties will be classified according to the measurement operations involved in their construction.

2. SOME FEATURES OF GENERALIZING PROPOSITIONS

The intended meaning of the variables often remains ambiguous if they are not examined in the context of the propositions in which they are used. It is therefore necessary at the outset to highlight certain features which are common to all generalizing propositions, whether or not they involve collectives. (As an illustration, reference is made to the proposition "Children of rich parents go to college in greater proportion than do children of poor parents.")

a. Generalizing propositions assert something about a set of *elements* (children).
b. For the research purposes at hand, these elements are considered *comparable*. In

* This article is one of a series sponsored by the Documentation Project for Advanced Training in Social Research, Columbia University. It may be cited as Publication A-322 of the Bureau of Applied Social Research, Columbia University.
Reprinted with permission from A. Etzioni (ed.), *Complex Organizations: A Sociological Reader* (Copyright 1961 by Holt, Rinehart, and Winston, Inc.).

other words, the same set of *properties* (wealth of parents; going to college) is used to describe each element.

c. Each element has a certain *value* on each property. The values (rich parents, poor parents; going to college, not going to college) may be quantitative or qualitative.

d. The propositions assert interrelationships between the properties of the elements.

3. PRESENT CONCERN

The propositions with which the present discussion is concerned have the additional characteristic that their elements are dealt with either as collectives or as members of collectives. An example of the first kind is "There is a negative correlation between the rate of juvenile delinquency of American cities and the proportion of their budget given over to education." An example of the second kind is "Those recognized as leaders do not deviate very far from the norms of their group."

4. SPECIAL MEANING OF "COLLECTIVE" AND "MEMBER"

The terms "collective" and "member" are used here in a specific sense which needs clarification. A collective may be an element of a proposition; that is, it is one of a set of units which are regarded as *comparable* in the sense specified above: the same set of properties is used to describe all the elements. These elements are *collectives* if each is considered to be composed of constituent parts, called *members,* which are regarded as comparable in their turn. "Comparable is used in the same sense as before: all members are described by a single set of properties. (This is usually not the same set as that used to describe the collectives.)

In other instances members are the elements of the propositions. Elements will be called "members" if they are considered to be constituent parts of larger units, called "collectives," which are regarded as comparable in the same sense as before.

Thus one set of properties is always used to describe or classify all the members, and another single set of properties is used to characterize all the collectives. It is clear that under these definitions one can speak of "collectives" only when their "members" are also being referred to, and of "members" only when their "collectives" are also involved. Furthermore, there must be a multiplicity of members if the term "collective" is to be meaningful. It is perhaps less obvious but will be seen later that there must also be a multiplicity of collectives, i.e., the members of more than one collective must be referred to, if the distinctions between properties to be described below are to be relevant. . . .

5. DISTINCTION BETWEEN INDIVIDUALS AND MEMBERS

In the examples that come to mind most easily, the members of collectives are individual persons. Thus, for example, cities are the collectives and people are the members in the following two propositions:

(1) "The oldest settlers of cities are most likely to hold political office," or (2) "The more industry there is in a city, the higher the proportion of Democratic voters." The first proposition has members and the second has collectives as elements. In the same sense, a precinct can be treated as a collective, with the inhabitants as members. However, the members of a collective are not necessarily individual persons. A city, for example, can be described as a collective with the voting precincts as members. It follows that what appears as a collective in one context (e.g., precincts), can appear as a member in another. In any analysis of a piece of writing in which some of the elements are collectives, it is always necessary to specify clearly of what members the collectives are composed (for the purposes at hand).[2]

The following graph will help to keep this terminology in mind:

The circles symbolize the collectives, the crosses within it their members. The dots indicate that we are dealing with collectives as elements of a proposition. This is the situation with which we deal in the first part of this paper. In paragraphs 10 and 11 we discuss research where members are the focus of attention. They are then the elements of propositions, but their membership in one of a series of collectives is one of their characteristics.

6. POSSIBILITY OF "THREE-LEVEL" PROPOSITIONS

In some studies, more than two levels appear: for example, inhabitants, precincts, and cities may all be elements of the same study. This whole matter could, therefore, be elaborated by pointing out the various relationships which can exist between inhabitants, precincts, and cities. The next few pages are restricted to collectives which have only one kind of member; the members in most illustrations will be individual persons, but we will also present some examples in which the members themselves are larger units. Only much later (in paragraph 16) will examples of "three-level" propositions be taken up, in which units, e.g., "union shops," are simultaneously considered to be both members of their locals *and* collectives of individual workers.

7. PROPOSITIONS ABOUT COLLECTIVES AS SUBSTITUTES IN THEIR OWN RIGHT

Propositions about collectives are sometimes made as substitutes for propositions about individual persons, simply because the necessary data about individual persons are not available. For example, a high Republican vote in "silk-stocking" districts is sometimes accepted to show that wealthy people are likely to vote Republican, when no records about individual votes and individual incomes are available.[3] For this reason it is often not realized that a large number of sociologically meaningful empirical propositions can be made of which only collectives are intended to be the elements. Thus, for example, an anthropologist may show that the political independence of communities is correlated with their pattern of settlement. A student of social disorganization may ask whether city zones with a high incidence of juvenile delinquency also show a high incidence of commitments for senile dementia. A small-group experimenter may hypothesize that "the probability of effective utilization of the insights that occur is greater in certain communication patterns than in others."[4] Much discursive writing also consists, in a hidden way, of such propositions.

A Typology of Properties Describing "Collectives" and "Members"

8. PROPERTIES OF COLLECTIVES

It is often useful to distinguish three types of properties which describe collectives: analytical properties based on data about each member; structural properties based on data about the relations among members; and global properties, not based on information about the properties of individual members.[5] The following examples may clarify these distinctions:

a. *Analytical.* These are properties òf collectives which are obtained by performing some mathematical operation upon some property of each single member.[6]

The average rental paid in a precinct and the proportion of its inhabitants who have

"Old Immigrant" (English, German, Scottish, Scandinavian) names are analytical properties of a collective (precinct) composed of individuals.[7] The proportion of the communities of a given state that have their own high school is an analytical property of a collective (state) the members of which are communities. The diffusion of a message in a city, defined as the per cent of the target population knowing the message, is an analytical property of the city.[8]

The standard deviation of incomes in a nation appears as an analytical property in the following example. The effect of postwar legislation in Great Britain was to make the income distribution much narrower. Economists have predicted that under these conditions people will save more, because they will spend less money on display consumption which might help them be socially acceptable in the higher strata.

Correlations are sometimes used to characterize collectives and then also constitute analytical properties. The correlation of age and prestige in a given community, for example, has been used as a measure of its norms regarding old age. Sometimes more indirect inferences are involved. MacRae shows that in urban areas voting is highly correlated with occupation, while this is not the case in rural districts. He concludes from this vote that in rural districts there is a stronger spirit of community and cohesion.[9]

b. *Structural.* These are properties of collectives which are obtained by performing some operation on data about the relations of each member to some or all of the others.

Assume, for example, that a sociometrist has recorded the "best-liked classmate" of each student in a number of classes. He can then describe the classes by the degree to which all choices are concentrated upon a few "stars." Or he might, alternately, classify them according to their cliquishness, the latter being defined as the number of subgroups into which a class can be divided so that no choices cut across subgroup lines. In these examples the collective is the school class, and the members are the individual students; "concentration of choices" and "cliquishness" are structural properties of the classes.

For an example in which the members are larger units, consider a map of the precincts of a city, which indicates the number of Negroes residing in each. Let a "Negro enclave" be defined as a precinct in which some Negroes live, but which is completely surrounded by precincts without Negroes. The proportion of the precincts of a city which are Negro enclaves would then be a structural property of the city.

c. *Global.* Often collectives are characterized by properties which are not based on information about the properties of individual members.

American Indian tribes have been characterized by the frequency with which themes of "achievement motive" make their appearance in their folk tales.[10] Societies have been classified as to the presence of money as a medium of exchange, of a written language, etc.[11] Nations may be characterized by the ratio of the national budget allotted to education and to armaments. Army companies may be characterized by the cleanliness of their mess equipment.

Voting precincts have been classified according to the activities and attitudes of their Republican and Democratic captains, including hours spent on party duties, number of persons known to the captain personally, and his expressed commitment to the party.[12] In experiments in message diffusion by leaflets dropped from airplanes, cities have been treated to different degrees of "stimulus intensity," defined as the per capita ratio of leaflets dropped.[13] All these are global properties.

The density of settlement is a global property of a district. Having a city manager form of government is a global property of a city. The insistence on specified initiation rites as a prerequisite to membership is a global property of a religious cult or of a college fraternity. Accessibility from the nearest big city is a global property of a village. A scale score assigned to each state according to the combination of duties assigned to the state board of education (rather than left to local authorities) is a global property of each state.[14]

"Emergent," "integral," "syntalic" and other terms have been used in meanings very similar to that of our term "global."

It is not at all certain which term is most useful.[15]

Notice that all three of the above types of properties—analytical, structural, and global—describe collectives.

9. A SUBSIDIARY DISTINCTION AMONG ANALYTICAL PROPERTIES OF COLLECTIVES

An interesting distinction may be made among the analytical properties. The first two examples given above were the average income of a city, and the proportion of the communities of a given state that have their own high school. These properties of collectives have what one might call a similarity of meaning to the properties of members on which they are based. The wealth of a city seems to be the same sort of thing as the wealth of an inhabitant. The endowment of a community with a high school and the rate of high-school endowed communities in a state have a parallel meaning. This is not true for the remaining examples of analytical properties given above—the standard deviation of incomes in a nation, or correlations like that between age and prestige in a given community. Correlations and standard deviations can apply only to collectives and have no parallel on the level of members. The standard deviation of incomes in a city, for example, denotes something quite different—lack of homogeneity, perhaps—from individual income, the datum from which it is computed.

Another variable of this sort is "degree of consensus." When a Democrat and a Republican are competing for the mayoralty, the degree of political consensus in a particular club might be measured by the extent of the club's deviation from a fifty-fifty split. In this instance the analytic property is measured by a proportion, but it is not the simple proportion of adherents of either party; clubs which are 80 per cent Democratic and those which are 20 per cent Democratic are regarded as equal in consensus.

Whereas correlations, standard deviations, and similar measures always have a meaning peculiar to the group level, averages and proportions may or may not have a parallel meaning on the individual and collective levels.[16] Lack of parallel meaning is perhaps most clearly illustrated in the concept of a "hung jury," that is, a jury rendered indecisive by its inability to reach the required unanimity. Such a state of affairs is most likely when the individual jurors are most decisive and unyielding in their convictions.

10. PROPERTIES OF MEMBERS

Another set of distinctions can be made between properties describing members in context where collectives have also been defined.

a. *Absolute* properties are characteristics of members which are obtained without making any use either of information about the characteristics of the collective, or of information about the relationships of the member being described to other members. They thus include most of the characteristics commonly used to describe individuals.

> In the proposition, "Graduates of large law schools are more likely to earn high incomes at age 40 than graduates of small law schools," income is an absolute property of the members (the individual students).

b. *Relational* properties of members are computed [17] from information about the substantive relationships between the member described and other members.

> Sociometric popularity-isolation (number of choices received) is a relational property. Many other sociometric indices fall into this category. For example, if each member of a small group has rated each other member on a five-point scale of acceptance-rejection, each member can be characterized by the total score he received (popularity), by the total score he expressed (active sociability), by the average deviation of the scores he

accorded the others (discrimination in his acceptance of other members), etc.[18] In a study of the diffusion of the use of a new drug through a community of doctors, the physicians were classified according to whether or not they had a friend who had already used the new drug on a certain date.[19]

Some investigators have clarified the structure of relational properties by the use of matrices.[20] This new device can be fruitfully applied to some older papers.[21]

The distinction between relational properties of individuals and structural properties of collectives deserves emphasis. The former characterize members of collectives in their relations to one another. The latter characterize collectives and are aggregates over the relational properties of their members.

c. *Comparative* properties characterize a member by a comparison between his value on some (absolute or relational) property and the distribution of this property over the entire collective of which he is a member.

Sibling order is a comparative property of individuals in the proposition, "First-born children are more often maladjusted than intermediate and last-born children." Note that each individual is characterized by comparison with the age of the other individuals in his family; in the resulting classification, many of the "last-born" will be older in years than many of the "first-born." Being a "deviate" from the majority opinion in one's housing project unit is a comparative property.[22]

Another example is contained in the following proposition: "Students who had the highest I.Q. in their respective high school classes have greater difficulty in adjusting in college than students who are not quite at the top in high school, even when their actual I.Q. score is equally high." Here the comparative property (being at the top in high school or not) is established in terms of the I.Q. distribution in each student's respective high school; the proposition pertains to a set of college students which includes boys from several high schools (collectives).

d. *Contextual* properties describe a member by a property of his collective.

Consider an example cited previously: "Graduates of large law schools are more likely to earn high incomes at age 40 than graduates of small law schools." In this proposition, "being a member of a large law school" is a contextual property of individuals.

Contextual properties are also used in the following propositions: "Union members in closed shops are less militant than union members in open shops." "Residents of racially mixed districts show more racial prejudice than those of racially homogeneous districts." "The less the promotion opportunity afforded by a branch (of the army), the more favorable the opinion (of soldiers) tends to be toward promotion opportunity."[23] In these propositions, being a member of closed shop, residing in a mixed district, or being a soldier in a branch with frequent promotions are all examples of contextual properties.

Contextual properties are really characteristics of collectives applied to their members. Thus the classification of "collective properties" developed above could be repeated here as a subdivision of contextual "individual properties."[24] Note also that a contextual property, unlike a comparative property, has the same value for all members of a given collective.

11. CONTEXTUAL AND COMPARATIVE PROPERTIES MEANINGFUL ONLY WHERE MORE THAN ONE COLLECTIVE IS INVOLVED

It is not meaningful to speak of contextual or comparative properties when the elements under study are all members of the same collective—for instance, when only graduates of one law school are being studied—for the following reasons. Any *contextual* property would, in that case, have the same value for all the elements; hence nothing could be said about the interrelationship of this property and any other property. Any *comparative* property would, under these circumstances, classify the elements in exactly the same way as the absolute property from which it was derived, except that the calibration may be grosser. (If only children of one family are considered, the classification into "first-born," "intermediate," and "last-born" differs from that by age only in the grosser calibration. Similarly, if I.Q. scores of graduates of one law school are replaced by classification into lowest, second, third, and highest I.Q. quartile within their school, nothing will change except that the number of categories is reduced.)

12. SPECIAL CASE WHERE THE TYPOLOGY CAN BE APPLIED IN TWO ALTERNATE WAYS

A difficulty comes about when all the members of a set of collectives (or a representative sample of the members of each) constitute the elements of a proposition which includes a contextual property. Suppose, for instance, that the income ten years after graduation is recorded for all who graduate from fifty law schools in a certain year. A possible finding might be, "The income of law school graduates is correlated with the size of the school they graduated from." This is a proposition about students, relating their income (an absolute property) to the size of their law school (a contextual property). The same proposition could be interpreted also as one where the elements are the law schools; the average income of the students would then be an analytical property of each law school; its size would be a global property of these collectives.

13. THE PRESENT CLASSIFICATION IS FORMAL RATHER THAN SUBSTANTIVE

As stated at the outset, the scheme suggested above is intended for the classification of properties according to the operations involved in their measurement. Although a classification by the underlying concepts or forces that the properties may

be intended to represent might have numerous parallels to the present classification, it would not be the same.[25] In the present methodological context, for example, "number of libraries in a community" and "occurrence of aggressiveness themes in folk tales current in a tribe" are classified as global properties because they are not based on information about the properties of individual members. Yet it would be convincing to argue that these properties are relevant to the behavioral sciences only because properties of individuals, of the relations among individuals, or of the resulting social structures are inferred from them. Similarly, the title of office held by a person in a hierarchy would here be classified as an "absolute" property, even when the researcher is actually interested in the incumbent's power over subordinates which the title implies.

At some points arbitrary decisions have to be made. On an intuitive basis we decided to consider the number of members in a collective (e.g., population size) as a global property, although one might argue that it is analytical, obtained by counting the "existence" of each member. Even more ambiguous is the classification of rates, based on the behavior of ex-members, e.g., suicide rates. No definitive practice is proposed for such borderline cases.

Combinations of Types of Properties

The types of properties which have been defined can appear in various forms of combinations.

14. SEVERAL TYPES IN THE SAME PROPOSITION

Very commonly, as many of the above examples have shown, one proposition will make use of properties of several types. An additional illustration of this can be drawn from a study of political processes within the International Typographical Union, which has been operating under an internal two-party system for many decades. The shops of this union were classified according to their degree of "political consensus"; shops in which 67 per cent or more of the members favored the same party were regarded as high in consensus, the remainder as low. Individual members were graded according to the amount of union political activity they engaged in. It was expected that men in shops where political consensus was high would be more active in politics than those in shops where consensus was low. The hypothesis, however, was borne out only in small shops (i.e., those with thirty men or less). The finding could therefore be expressed in the following proposition: "For workers in small shops, there is a correlation between consensus of the shop and degree of political activity of the men; for workers in large shops, there is no such correlation." In this proposition there appear two contextual properties (size and consensus of each man's shop) and an absolute property (political activity.)[26]

The following hypothetical example again shows the use of several types of variables in one proposition—in fact, in each of several propositions. Ten preliterate tribes living in a certain country are classified according to the number of wars they have fought during the last hundred years. This characteristic, in the present terminology, is a global property of each tribe. A representative sample of one hundred men from each tribe is given a test of "aggressiveness"—an absolute property, from which a summary score for each tribe is computed, as an analytical property. At this point, the correlation between average aggressiveness and the number of wars can be computed. One may regard this computation as either a correlation between an analytical and a global property of ten collectives, or a correlation between an absolute and a contextual property of one thousand individual persons.

Now a factory is opened in the district, and some men from each of the ten tribes find employment there as laborers. Each is given the test of "aggressiveness"; each is also observed for a period of one month, and the number of fights he starts with other employees is recorded. Then the following two correlations can be computed:

a. The correlation between the score on the aggressiveness test and the number of fights. This is a proposition the elements of which are people and the properties of of which are conventional psychological characteristics—absolute properties, in the present terminology.

b. The correlation between the number of fights and the number of wars reported for the tribe from which each individual came. This is again a proposition the elements of which are people. But one of the variables (number of wars) now is a contextual property.

The comparison between these two propositions is interesting. In proposition (a) actual fighting is related to the psychological trait of aggressiveness. In proposition (b) actual fighting is related to something that one might call the normative background of each person.

15. PROPERTIES OF ONE TYPE CONSTRUCTED FROM PROPERTIES OF ANOTHER TYPE

The types of properties outlined can also be compounded in that a property of one type may be constructed from properties of another. Contextual properties, for example, have been defined as properties describing a member by a property of his collective. But what property of his collective is to be used? In most of the examples given, contextual properties of members were based on global properties of their collectives, as in the phrase "men from tribes that have engaged in many wars." But contextual properties can equally well be based on any other kind of property of a collective—for example, on a structural property, as when doctors are classified according to whether or not they ever practiced in cities ridden by medical cliques. One might test whether those who formerly practiced in cliqueless cities have less tendency to form cliques in their new location.

This compounding is also illustrated by examples, cited earlier in another connection: "being a worker in a big shop" and "being a worker in a shop with high consensus." The first of these is a contextual property constructed from a global property; the second is a contextual property constructed from an analytical property.

16. SEVERAL TYPES FROM THE SAME
DATA

In some instances one body of research will construct properties of several different types from the same data, as in the following excerpts from a report on the adoption of modern farming practices by Kentucky farmers.

393 farm operators . . . in thirteen neighborhoods were interviewed. . . . Information was obtained on the extent to which each of the operators had tried and was following 21 farm practices recommended by the agricultural agencies. For each respondent, an adoption score was calculated. This score is the percentage of applicable practices which the operator had adopted. For example, if 18 of the practices applied to the farm operations being carried on and the operator had adopted 9, his score was 50. Neighborhoods varied widely in the mean adoption scores of residents, which range from a low of 25 in one neighborhood to a high of 57 in another. . . . The neighborhoods were combined . . . into three types of neighborhoods: "low adoption areas," "medium adoption areas," and "high adoption areas.". . .

The following operational hypothesis . . . is suggested: In areas of high adoption, those from whom other farmers obtain farming information have higher adoption rates than farmers in general; but, in areas of low adoption, the adoption rates of leaders are similar to adoption rates of farmers in general . . . the hypothesis is supported by data. In the "low adoption areas" the mean score of all farmers was 32 and that of the

leaders 37, while in the "high adoption areas" the mean score of all farmers was 48 and that of the leaders 66.[27]

Here the farm operator's "adoption score" is used as an absolute property of information leaders and of farmers in general. It is also used as the datum from which the classification of neighborhoods into "high adoption areas" and "low adoption areas" is computed. This classification is an analytical property of the neighborhoods; when used, as in the proposition quoted, to characterize the farmers resident in the neighborhoods, it becomes a contextual property of the farmers.

17. SIMULTANEOUS CHARACTERIZATION
OF THE SAME ELEMENTS AS COLLECTIVES
AND AS MEMBERS

Complexity of another sort arises when one set of elements appears both as members and as collectives in the same proposition. Up to this point examples of such "three-level propositions" have deliberately been excluded. It is now appropriate to introduce such examples. Consider, for instance, the following assertion: "Women's clubs which are internally divided into cliques have less easy-going relationships with other women's clubs than have clubs which are not so divided." Here the elements (women's clubs) are first categorized according to a structural variable (internal division into cliques) and then an assertion is made about a relational property (relationship with other clubs) of the elements in each structural category.

In the study of political processes within the International Typographcal Union, which was cited earlier, each printer's vote in a union election was recorded. A liberal and a conservative candidate competed for union office. Each printer's vote was compared with his own conservative-liberal predisposition, determined by an attitude scale. The individuals could thus be classified as voting according to or contrary to their own predisposition. Up to this point, no collective is involved; there is merely a combination of two absolute properties into one. This combined absolute property of each printer was then compared with two contextual properties: the majority vote in his shop, and the majority vote in the local to which his shop belonged. The question was whether the climate of opinion in a man's shop or that in his entire local is more important in affecting his decisions. The answer could be determined only by examining cases where the shop and the local were in conflict. It was found that more people voted contrary to their own predisposition when it was in conflict with the majority of their shop (but not of their local) than when it was in conflict with the majority of their local (but not of their shop). In this instance each person is first characterized as voting according to or contrary to his predisposition. This absolute variable is then correlated with two contextual variables, both describing the same members (persons), but each having reference to a different level of collectives (shops or locals).[28]

18. OUTLOOK

The preceding analysis can be extended in many directions; three of them shall be briefly sketched. For one we can introduce status differences among the members of the collectives. Colleges have professors and administrators, factory teams have workers and foremen, platoons have soldiers and noncoms. This may call for extending the notion of structural properties if, e.g., we distinguish various types of supervision; or analytical properties may be generalized if we classify colleges according to the degree to which the administration and the faculty share the same values. Stouffer has made ingenious use of such status differences by developing what one could call partitioned analytical properties. He wanted to know whether the food provided for army units had an effect on soldiers' morale. If he had asked the

soldiers to rate the food he would not have known whether their morale did not affect their rating of the food. So he asked the noncommissioned officers to judge the food and correlated their average rating with the average morale score of the soldiers; the elements of the correlation were of course the army units studied.[29]

A second line of analysis opens up if the elements of a proposition are pairs of individuals: people who are friends tend to vote the same way; egalitaran relationships are more enduring than those which are hierarchic. It would be artificial to call such notions "propositions about collectives." Obviously dyads can be characterized in an even more complex way: pairs of doctors who commonly discuss cases with each other as equals are more likely to use the same type of drug than are pairs of doctors who stand in an advisor-advisee relationship to each other.[30] A scrutiny of recent sociometric literature is likely to provide distinctions going beyond those offered in this paper.

Finally, the utility of the present approach deserves argument. Obviously no one wants to make methodological classifications for their own sake. They are, however, useful in reminding us of the variety of research operations that are possible, and in clearing up misunderstandings. It can, for example, be shown that many arguments about atomistic versus "holistic" approaches in current sociological literature can be clarified by an explication of the formal types of properties which enter into speculative or empirical propositions. In another publication, the senior author has summarized passages from several recent works of social research which relate, often in quite complex ways, the characteristics and attitudes of individuals, their propensity to choose friends inside and outside of variously overlapping collectives, the composition of these collectives in terms of members' background and perceptions, and the recent occurrence of certain events in the history of the collectives. He attempted to show that such "contextual propositions" go a long way toward satisfying the frequently heard demand that social research should "consider structures" or "take the total situation into account." [31]

Notes

1. Individuals and collectives made up of individuals do not, of course, exhaust the matters which social scientists describe. Social-science propositions may, instead, have various other units for their subjects. Not infrequently the subjects are acts, behavior patterns, customs, norms, "items of culture," and the like, as in the assertion that "items of culture that are . . . not much woven into a pattern . . . are least likely to encounter resistance to their diffusion."—Ralph Linton, *The Study of Man* (New York: Appleton, 1936), pp. 341–42. "Beliefs and practices" have been sorted into four classes according to the pattern of their differential distribution among mobile and nonmobile holders of high and low positions in a stratification system."—Peter M. Blau, "Social Mobility and Interpersonal Relations," *American Sociological Review*, 21 (1956), pp. 290–95.

2. It is, of course, also possible to make propositions about cities without reference to any members at all, just as it is possible to make propositions about individuals without reference to any collectives. Thus one may, e.g., correlate city size with number of churches, or location with building materials used, just as one can correlate individual income and education. In neither case are the distinctions made in the present paper relevant, because the individuals are not treated as "members" and the cities are not treated as "collectives" as here defined (i.e., as composed of "members"—constituent units described by their values on some one set of properties). It is thus clear that the typology of properties here presented is not always pertinent.

3. This procedure can lead to very misleading statistics, as pointed out by W. S. Robinson in "Ecological Correlations and the Behavior of Individuals," *American Sociological Review*, 15 (1950), pp. 351–57. Sounder methods for inferring individual correlations from ecological data are proposed by Leo A. Goodman, "Ecological Regressions and Be-

havior of Individuals," *American Sociological Review*, 18 (1953), pp. 663–64, and by Otis Dudley Duncan and Beverly Davis, "An Alternate to Ecological Correlation," *ibid.*, pp. 665–66.

4. For details on these and additional examples, see Paul F. Lazarsfeld and Morris Rosenberg (eds.), *The Language of Social Research* (New York: The Free Press, 1955), pp. 302–22. Compare also Herbert Menzel, "Comment," *American Sociological Review*, 15 (1950), p. 674.

5. This classification of properties of collectives corresponds closely to the classifications presented earlier by Cattell and by Kendall and Lazarsfeld and reprinted in Lazarsfeld and Rosenberg (eds.), *op. cit.*, pp. 291–301. Analytical properties are Cattell's population variables and Kendall and Lazarsfeld's Types I, II, and III. Structural properties are Cattell's structural variables and Kendall and Lazarsfeld's Type IV. Our global properties are Cattell's syntality variables and Kendall and Lazarsfeld's Type V. See also n. 25.

6. It should be understood that the distinctions here proposed do not depend on who performs the operations involved. For example, "average income of a city" would be classified as an analytical property regardless of whether the investigator (a) obtains individual income data from all inhabitants directly and then computes the average, (b) obtains individual income data from the files of the tax collector and then computes the average, or (c) looks up the average income in the published census reports. Compare also n. 17.

7. Phillips Cutright and Peter H. Rossi, "Grass Roots Politicians and the Vote," *American Sociological Review*, 23 (1958), pp. 171–79.

8. Melvin L. DeFleur and Otto N. Larsen, *The Flow of Information* (New York: Harper, 1958).

9. Duncan MacRae, Jr., "Occupations and the Congressional Vote, 1940–1950," *American Sociological Review*, 20 (1955), pp. 332–40.

10. See David C. McClelland and G. A. Friedman, "A Cross-cultural Study of the Relationship between Child Training Practices and Achievement Motivation Appearing in Folk Tales," in Guy E. Swanson, Theodore M. Newcomb, and Eugene L. Hartley (eds.), *Readings in Social Psychology* (New York: Holt, Rinehart and Winston, 1952), pp. 243–49.

11. See, e.g., Linton C. Freeman and Robert F. Winch, "Societal Complexity: An Em-

pirical Test of a Typology of Societies," *American Journal of Sociology,* 62 (1957), pp. 461–66.

12. Cutright and Rossi, *loc. cit.*

13. DeFleur and Larsen, *loc. cit.*

14. Robert Redfield, *The Folk Culture of Yucatan* (Chicago: University of Chicago Press, 1941); and Margaret J. Hagood, and Daniel O. Price, *Statistics for Sociologists* (rev. ed., New York: Henry Holt and Company, 1952), pp. 141–52.

15. Although global properties of collectives are not based on information about members, the above examples are, of course, listed here on the assumption that assertions about the members are made somewhere in the same proposition or at least in the same body of work; otherwise the distinction between "global" and "absolute" properties would become pointless (cf. n. 2). It may also bear repeating here that any discussion of a "collective" requires clear specification of what its members are considered to be. The proportion of the buildings of a city which are devoted to cultural activities was given as an example of a "global property" of a city on the assumption that the city is treated as a collective of inhabitants; i.e., that statements involving the inhabitants are made in some connection with this measure of "cultural level." It is, of course, also possible to treat a city as a collective of buildings; then the proportion of buildings devoted to cultural activities would become an analytical property. Which of these two types of property it is can be judged only from the context. (See also paragraph 13.)

16. Compare the notion of "counterpart" in Edgar F. Borgatta, Leonard Cottrell, Jr., and Henry J. Meyer, "On the Dimensions of Group Behavior," *Sociometry,* 19 (1965), p. 233.

17. It may be worth repeating here that the distinctions proposed are independent of who performs the operations involved. Thus, e.g., "sociometric popularity" would be classified as a relational property when measured in any of the following three ways: (a) the investigator counts the number of choices accorded to a member by his colleagues in answer to a sociometric questionnaire; (b) the investigator observes the frequency of interactions between the member and his colleagues; (c) the member is asked, "How many visits did you receive from colleagues during the last week?" These distinctions are, of course, important in themselves but not relevant to the present typology (cf. n. 6).

18. Some sociometric indices are listed in Hans Zeisel, *Say It with Figures,* 4th ed. (New York: Harper, 1957), pp. 110–14, 148–53. The list includes indices not only of relational properties but of comparative and structural properties as well.

19. Herbert Menzel and Elihu Katz, "Social Relations and Innovation in the Medical Profession: The Epidemiology of a New Drug," *Public Opinion Quarterly,* 19 (1956), pp. 337–52.

20. See Zeisel, *loc. cit.,* and Leon Festinger, Stanley Schachter, and Kurt Back, "Matrix Analysis of Group Structures," in Lazarsfeld and Rosenberg, *op. cit.,* pp. 358–67. In both instances matrices are also used to develop indices for structural properties of groups.

21. See, e.g., Robert R. Sears, "Experimental Studies of Projection," *Journal of Social Psychology,* 7 (1936), pp. 151–63.

22. Festinger, Schachter, and Back, *op. cit.,* pp. 367–82.

23. S. A. Stouffer, *et al., The American Soldier* (Princeton, N.J.: Princeton University Press, 1949), I, p. 256.

24. It is sometimes helpful to talk of "collective properties" instead of the cumbersome "properties of collectives"; the same holds for "individual properties." It is important, however, not to be misled by this linguistic condensation.

25. Cattell's classification of population, structural, and syntality variables (cf. n. 5 above), which is closely paralleled in form by our analytical-structural-global distinction, seems to be based on a mixture of measurement criteria and considerations of causality. The latter gain the upper hand in the critique of Cattell's scheme by Borgatta, Cottrell, and Meyer: e.g., "Aggregate measures, to the extent that they cannot be accounted for as population variables (in direct parallel measures), may be considered syntality variables. . . . Further, changes in population variables attributable to social interaction should be regarded as syntality variables."—Borgatta, Cottrell, and Meyer, *op. cit.,* p. 234. Peter M. Blau's "Formal Organization: Dimensions of Analysis," *American Journal of Sociology,* 63 (1957), pp. 58–69, contains an analysis in terms of intended underlying concepts which parallels the present discussion of measurement operations in certain respects.

In addition, the literature contains, of course, classifications of group properties which are based on quite different criteria. See, e.g., John K. Hemphill and Charles M. Westie, "The Measurement of Group Dimensions," in Lazarsfeld and Rosenberg, *op. cit.,* pp. 323–24; and Robert K. Merton, "Provisional List of Group Properties," in his *Social Theory and Social Structure* (rev. ed.; New York: The Free Press, 1957), pp. 310–26. The Hemphill–Westie categories are subjected to a factor analysis and compared with certain other schemes in Borgatta, Cottrell, and Meyer, *op. cit.*, pp. 223–40.

26. See S. M. Lipset, Martin Trow, and James Coleman, *Union Democracy: The Inside Politics of the International Typographical Union* (New York: Free Press, 1956).

27. C. Paul Marsh and A. Lee Coleman, "Group Influences and Agricultural Innovations: Some Tentative Findings and Hypotheses," *American Journal of Sociology*, 61 (1956), pp. 588–94. Other varying examples

of the use of properties describing or referring to collectives will be found in Lazarsfeld and Rosenberg, *op. cit.*, pp. 287–386.

28. Adapted from Lipset, Trow, and Coleman, *op. cit.*

29. Stouffer, *et al.*, *op. cit.*, I, pp. 353–58.

30. James Coleman, Herbert Menzel, and Elihu Katz, "Social Processes in Physicians' Adoption of a New Drug," *Journal of Chronic Diseases*, 9 (1959), p. 18.

31. Paul F. Lazarsfeld, "Problems in Methodology," in Robert K. Merton, Leonard Broom, and Leonard S. Cottrell, Jr. (eds.), *Sociology Today* (New York: Basic Books, 1959), pp. 69–73.

26. Organizational Measurement

ALLEN H. BARTON

[Ed. Note: The following chapter is excerpted from a book that classifies measurements of organizations developed by researchers in many fields. Along with chapters on "inputs" and "outputs," environmental variables are characterized as external attributes of organizations. This chapter shows many ways in which environments have been defined and measured.]

Environmental Variables

BY ENVIRONMENTAL variables we mean characteristics of the larger social units in which the organization is located—community, region, industry, and so forth; or information on the *relationships* between the organization and its environment—its "public relations," its "interorganizational relations," and perhaps its relations with other units or levels within some larger-scale organization of which it is a part.

COMMUNITY OR REGIONAL CONTEXTS

A study of local chapters of the National Foundation for Infantile Paralysis used or-

ganizational and official records to measure two salient features of the environment of local chapters: the polio rate of the county (a measure of the need for the organization's services), and the income level of the county (a measure of available community resources). It was found that the local chapter's organizational achievement in fund-raising, as measured by per capita contributions, was strongly influenced by both of these environmental features, as seen in Table 1 (Sills, p. 194).

In a study of local unions, the relevant context was the region, which was described by its degree of unionization. The locals themselves were classified by their degree

Reprinted in part with permission from *Organizational Measurement and Its Bearing on the Study of College Environments*, pp. 20–39 (copyright 1961 by the College Entrance Examination Board).

TABLE 1. Per Cent of Polio Chapters Raising Over 34¢ Per Capita

MEDIAN FAMILY INCOME OF COUNTY	POLIO INCIDENCE RATE OF COUNTY*		
	High	Medium	Low
High	75%₂₅₃	57%₃₈₄	54%₈₃
Medium	64%₄₈₄	35%₇₉₃	25%₂₉₈
Low	29%₅₄	4%₄₀₆	3%₃₁₈

* Smaller size figures indicate total number of counties on which percentages are based.

of militancy as revealed in their voting on referenda concerning union policies. Working entirely with available institutional statistics, the investigator was able to find strong evidence for the proposition that union members in less organized industries are more militant (Alexander).

There is a large body of studies of local school systems which relate school system attributes to community characteristics. From available census and other governmental data it is possible to measure the educational level, taxable wealth, per cent foreign born, population density, occupational distribution, population growth, and economic trends of a community; some of the factors are assumed to be related to the values of the community members, and some to their resources. It was found that the wealth and the educational level of the local population were the factors most highly related to a measure of educational innovation, as well as to school expenditures, training of school staff, and other organizational features (Mort and Cornell, 1941; Ross). Public attitudes toward modern educational practices, measured by surveys of parents, were also found to be related to the practices used in the schools. However it was not clear from the analysis whether they exerted any independent effect when community background factors were held constant, or indeed whether they were

not the product of the school system practices.

For colleges, the importance of community and regional contexts is presumably less striking since they typically draw students, resources, and boards of control from a wider area and a more limited segment of the public. Yet these factors should be worth investigating. The growth of local community colleges may create a class of institutions much more subject to these local influences (Riesman, pp. 135–36), while the degree of discrepancy between the personnel of a high-quality college and the surrounding community may have its own special effect on campus life. A study of regional effects made in the early 1930's related attitude toward the Negro to years in college, for northern college students at Ohio State University, southern college students at the University of Alabama, and students of northern origin attending a southern college (see Table 2).

TABLE 2. Mean Score on Scale of Attitude toward Negro *

Year in College	Northern Students in Northern Colleges	Northern Students in Southern Colleges	Southern Students in Southern Colleges
Freshman	6.4	6.2	5.0
Sophomore	6.7	5.8	4.9
Junior and Senior	6.8	5.2	5.0

* Scale ranged from 1 (least favorable) to 11 (most favorable).

The results suggest that college attendance in the North may have had some liberalizing influence on students of northern origin, but that the southern colleges had no such influence on its students; and that going to college in the South effectively changed the attitudes of students of northern origin to conform to the southern norm.

How much of this effect derived from the faculty and the program, how much from contact with fellow students, and how much from general contact with the population and institutions off the campus was not distinguishable (Sims and Patrick).

PUBLIC RELATIONS

Public relations refers to the attitudes and beliefs of the community or regional public toward the organization, as distinct from their sociological attributes or their opinions in general. In spite of the enormous amount of attention (and money) devoted to public relations, there is very little empirical data on the relationship of public opinion about an organization to other organizational characteristics. There is much common sense support for the notion that an organization will do better in a friendly rather than a hostile environment but community power structures and decision processes are complicated and do not usually reflect public opinion, as known through surveys, in any direct way.

One study which has tried to correlate public opinion of organizations with other organizational characteristics is a study of eight industrial firms and the five local unions which represented their workers in a midwestern city (Chalmers *et al.*). The

study produced a number of results which were not entirely obvious. Generally the public liked companies and unions which the workers liked. Public approval was much less closely related to management's satisfaction with its labor relations, and it was downright negatively related to management's satisfaction with the union. This suggests that either the workers are communicating their opinions effectively to other community members by informal contacts, or that the community in general has the same impressions and is using the same standards to evaluate organizations as do the workers. It also suggests that management tends to like weak and ineffectual unions, and that their standards for judging labor relations differ widely from the public's and the workers' (Table 3).

Lazarsfeld's and Thielens' study of 165 colleges obtained measures of public relations at least in the negative form of community pressures and attacks. The percentage of the faculty reporting "pressure to avoid controversy" from the community was one of a set of "pressure" ratings used in an over-all index. Another measure was a count of the number of specific "incidents of attempts to interfere with civil liberties or academic freedom of faculty members" that were reported by at least two faculty respondents, which included a category of

TABLE 3. Public Attitude Toward Unions in Relations to Worker and Management Attitudes

COMPANIES IN WHICH UNIONS ARE LOCATED	PERCENTAGE FAVORABLE TOWARD UNION		
	Community Public	Management	Workers
Grain processing company	96%	59%	60%
Metal product company	88	45	58
Trucking company A ⎫	78	46	70
Trucking company B ⎭		19	57
Garment company X ⎫	75	49	42
Garment company A ⎭		61	58.7
Construction company A ⎫	48	71	59.2
Construction company B ⎭		57	35

Rank-order correlation of public attitude with management attitude: −.46
Rank-order correlation of public attitude with worker attitude: +.43

incidents originating in the local community. The researchers found that community pressures on colleges applied mainly to higher-quality schools, suggesting that it was the inherent characteristics of free and searching inquiry with the attendant toleration of nonconformist political and social thought that aroused the hostility. They report in qualitative terms, however, that within the lower-quality group of schools, the locally supported, locally attended "streetcar colleges" were also subject to much community pressure despite their relative lack of intellectual daring (Lazarsfeld and Thielens, 165–166).

INTERORGANIZATIONAL RELATIONS

. . . Unions and business firms have a special form of pair relationship which has been much studied on a case basis, and on which systematic comparative and even correlational studies are coming to be available. We have earlier given a table showing the correlation between labor-management relations as viewed by each side and public approval of the union and company, based on eight company-union pairs in one city (Chalmers *et al.*). A study of four union locals in another city suggests that the degree of union conflict with the company, as measured by ratings of informed officials, is positively related to the members' loyalty to the union, measured by an attitude survey (Tannenbaum) . . .

A recent study of organizations in the health field has attempted directly to obtain data on the entire matrix of interorganizational relations of health organizations within one community. The findings take the form of "sociometric" matrices showing the amount of communication, referrals, joint activities, and transfer of resources between different types of organizations (Levine and White). This type of data makes it possible to characterize organizations by the same kinds of sociometric indices as those developed for relational analysis of individuals. . . .

One of the few pieces of quantitative data on the relation between sources of economic support and other college attributes is found in a study by the North Central Association which aimed to validate criteria for accreditation. Budgetary data were obtained from colleges concerning the breakdown of income between student fees, endowment, taxation, "continuing gifts and grants," and borrowing.

These forms of support were then correlated with indices of student performance, faculty quality, and administration quality. Interestingly enough the "stable" factor of endowment was less favorable for quality than the "unstable" factor of student fees. Reliance on "continuing gifts and grants" and on borrowing were negatively related to quality (Russell and Reeves).

LARGER ORGANIZATIONAL CONTEXT AND RELATIONSHIPS

We have been considering all kinds of organizational units which may be studied comparatively as objects of measurement; this has included work groups within a factory, small army and air force units, government agencies, and research groups within industry, as well as formally independent organizations. For any such subordinate unit within a larger organization, the characteristics of that larger organizational setting are of the highest importance. . . .

Besides classifying the "part" by attributes of the whole to which it belongs, we may classify it by information on the actual *relationships* between part and whole.

A study of 100 League of Women Voters locals included measures of the relationship of each local to the national organization in terms of degree of conflict. The investigators found that conflict with higher levels was related to relatively poor performance, at least as measured by a rating scale which included opinions of the higher level officers (Kahn, Tannenbaum, and Weiss). . . . .

One of the simplest versions of the organizational context variable is whether in fact the unit studied is part of a larger organization or independent. Newspapers can be classified as independent or part of a chain or local monopoly. There are trend

TABLE 4. School Practices in 16 Independent and 16 Centrally Controlled School Systems

School Practices	Independent Schools	Centrally Controlled Schools
Movable classroom furniture used	11	0
Teacher experimentation encouraged by superintendency	12	6
Course of study developed co-operatively by local teachers	14	2
Adequate provision for vocational education	6	16
Provision for pupils with special disabilities	8	16
Adequate tenure provisions	2	16
Total schools studied	16	16

studies of the share of the newspaper market held by independent and chains over time (Lee). One study compared the content of the press in cities with two independent dailies with that where both papers were owned by one company and found very little difference (Bigman).

Thirty-two "community" school systems were compared, of which 16 were in independent suburban towns, and 16 were in informally defined "neighborhood communities" within New York City, and thus controlled by one centralized Board of Education. The general population characteristics were matched, so as to isolate the effects of independence versus centralized control on local schools. A large number

of relationships were found, as seen in Table 4 (Cillié).

The locally controlled schools were more flexible in a number of ways; the schools which were part of the New York City system excelled in bureaucratic virtues like tenure, pensions, and presence of highly specialized services. . . .

Lazarsfeld and Thielens tried to create a measure of church control using those indicators which were available in the published sources: whether *any* church representation is required on the board, and whether chapel attendance or courses in religion are compulsory. The latter two are of course measures of the program of activities of the institution, which are presumed to be *consequences* of strong church control (Lazarsfeld and Thielens, pp. 407–409). . . .

Even the crude classification of control as public, private nonsectarian, Protestant, and Catholic shows significant relationships with other organizational characteristics. As shown in Table 5, it was related to the attitude-climate of the faculty, as measured on a scale of permissiveness toward Communist, Socialist, and "radical" political activities (Lazarsfeld and Thielens, p. 128).

Type of control was naturally related quite directly to the relationships between the college and political leaders. The aspect of these which was measured was the amount of "pressure to avoid controversy" from the legislature and local politicians, as shown in Table 6 (Lazarsfeld and Thielens, p. 181).

The behavior of the colleges trustees under different conditions of political pressure is markedly different for the public and private colleges. See Table 7 (Lazarsfeld and Thielens, p. 182).

In these last examples the measure of "pressure" is an aggregative measure based on individual perceptions: the per cent of faculty members who report pressure from a given source. It should be noted that this is quite different from using the proportion

TABLE 5. Political Permissiveness of Faculty by Type of Control and Size

| TYPE OF CONTROL | MEAN PER CENT OF FACULTY WHO ARE "CLEARLY PERMISSIVE"* | |
	Large Institutions	Small Institutions
Private	57%₄₉₇	53%₃₂₆
Public	49%₈₂₁	23%₁₁₃
Protestant	—	32%₂₉₁†
Catholic	12%₉₃	3%₁₁₅

* Smaller size figures indicate total number of professors on which percentage is based.

† Includes 28 respondents from large Protestant institutions.

of liberals or of Ph.D.'s among the faculty to characterize that group; here we are using them as informants about the behavior of *other* groups. The behavior of the politicians would ideally be measured by interviewing or observing or analyzing records of the behavior of the politicians themselves. The professors' perceptions of their behavior are used only as a readily available substitute. Such a measure obviously presents problems; if pressures are

TABLE 6. Level of Pressure from Politicians on Public and Private Colleges

Degree of Pressure Reported*	Per Cent of Public Colleges under Various Degrees of Pressure	Per Cent of Private Colleges under Various Degrees of Pressure
Low	29%	57%
Medium	32	18
High	39	25
	100%₃₁	100%₂₈

* Here colleges were classified as under low pressure if less than 20 per cent of the respondents report increased pressure; medium if 20 to 39 per cent report pressure; high if 40 per cent or more report it.

TABLE 7. Trustee Behavior Under Low and High Political Pressure at Public and Private Colleges *

| TRUSTEE PRESSURE ON ADMINIS- TRATION | PUBLIC COLLEGES | | PRIVATE COLLEGES | |
	Political Pressure High	Political Pressure Low	Political Pressure High	Political Pressure Low
High	11	1	6	4
Low	5	14	6	12
Total colleges	16	15	12	16

* Dividing line between high and low is 20 per cent of faculty reporting pressure for privately controlled colleges, but 30 per cent for public colleges.

really present, why doesn't everyone report them? Is a college where 50 per cent report pressures under "twice as much pressure" as one where only 25 per cent report them? Perhaps they just have better internal communications. The assumptions underlying the use of such "rates of perception of others' behavior" need to be closely examined.

Social Structure Variables

We now come to variables characterizing the inner workings of the organization. The term "social structure" actually covers a wide range of attributes, which will be considered in turn.

FORMAL AUTHORITY STRUCTURE

Some gross aspects of the formal authority structure can be indicated by simple *rates*. The degree of bureaucratization of schools has been measured by the proportion of total personnel in administrative jobs (Terrien and Mills); that of voluntary organizations by the proportion of paid staff to volunteers (Sills, pp. 70, 204–06;

Tsouderos). Speculation about the growth of bureaucracy in business firms is abundant, but actual data over time are scarce. Haire presents a staff/line ratio over time on several cases, and concludes that:

"In the early years, while the line grows linearly, the staff grows by some exponential function (though no single one seems to describe the curve well). Later, in another period of growth, they grow at quite similar rates" (Haire, p. 292).

The overall closeness of supervision in a plant might be indicated by the average length of time a worker can go without intervention by his supervisor (Jacques, 1956).

Another aspect of the formal authority structure is the average span of control of all officers, or of officers at each given level (March and Simon; Evan; Worthy; Urwick). The basic data for such a measure is a simple question, observation, or count from the formal organization chart, of the number of people to whom each official is supposed to give orders routinely. This is a kind of average based on counting *relationships* of a certain type in which an individual is engaged, or is supposed to be engaged. If we make our count simply from the formal organization chart or the book of rules, we are not characterizing people by what they actually do but by what the formal rules say they should do. We are aggregating data on "formally defined statuses" which may represent no more than the ideas of some long-dead writer or chartmaker; if we aggregated data based on the actual people occupying these formal statuses the results might be quite different. These two kinds of aggregative measures should be clearly distinguished: those based on actual people and their behavior or beliefs; and those based on written rules or charts, or on the testimony of people who simply assume that the formal rules are followed. The term "formal" in our category of authority structure has a somewhat ambiguous meaning—on the one hand implying what has been formalized in written rules, on the other implying what the participants consider *legitimate,* which may differ from the written rules because of ignorance, differences in interpretation, or because an orally transmitted revision has supplanted the written rules which are now considered "dead" and legitimately ignored. Both of these notions of formal authority are distinct from the question of who holds actual power or influence. . . .

A case study of a national health organization informally compared it with other large voluntary associations and suggested that the official decentralization of authority over spending the funds raised was a major factor in maintaining the vitality of the local units and avoiding bureaucratic deviations from the official goals (Sills, pp. 44–46, 72–75). . . .

A well-known experiment in industrial sociology manipulated the degree of centralization of formal authority in several units within a business firm by changing the rules and giving new training to the first and second-line supervisors. In two offices the supervisors were given training in how to delegate and decentralize; in two similar offices the supervisors were trained to exercise closer supervision over subordinates. Effects were measured both for productivity and for job satisfaction. Over a year's time the more centralized offices had higher production, but lower worker satisfaction (Morse and Reimer).

A series of surveys by the American Association of University Professors has tried to measure the formal authority of the faculty in college and university government (A.A.U.P.). A long checklist of powers and organizational forms was filled out by the informants in each of several hundred colleges; it included such items as whether the faculty was consulted in various appointments and in various budget matters, whether there was an academic senate, whether there was definite plan for exchange of opinion with the trustees, and so on. A crude scale of "faculty self-government" was created by giving numerical weights to various possible answers to each question, and the results were compared for a group of 173 institutions surveyed both in 1939 and 1953 (Table 8).

Such a repeated study of the same units could of course give rise to turnover tables, showing the extent to which there had been both gains and losses, and the extent of

TABLE 8.   Faculty Authority in
173 Colleges

FACULTY SELF-GOVERNMENT INDEX	DISTRIBUTION OF COLLEGES		
	1939	1953	Change
0–4	38.7%	17.3%	−21.4%
5–9	31.8	32.4	+ .6
10–14	16.8	31.8	+15.0
15–28	12.7	18.5	+ 5.8
Total	100.0%	100.0%	

gradual versus drastic shift in scale position. By dividing the sample in terms of information on possible causes or conditioners of organizational change, one might be able to trace the influence of such factors on faculty self-government in college. This would have represented the first panel analysis of organizations as subjects.

INFLUENCE STRUCTURE

By influence structure we mean who actually determines what goes on in an organization; this need not correspond to the formal authority structure. The purest determinant of influence would be to observe whose desires prevail in a series of conflicts. A fairly close approximation of this method is found in a study of eight industrial firms in a midwestern community (Chalmers *et al.*). The influence of the union was rated by the researchers, on the basis of both formal documents and interviews with par-

ticipants, within each of 12 problem areas such as hiring and firing, grievance procedures, setting piece rates, efficiency and technical change, and so on. All eight plants were ranked by combining these into a single index of union influence, and the researchers tried (within the limits of their eight cases) to assess the effects of union influence. One highly plausible finding was that union influence correlated −.57 with management satisfaction with labor-management relations, while it correlated +.64 with union leader satisfaction.

In *The Academic Mind* the relative influence of different groups with respect to academic freedom problems was rated by samples of faculty members, responding to the following question:

"If you had to choose one, who would you say has the most powerful voice here on this campus, in determining the degree of academic freedom that exists here—the trustees, the president, the deans, the heads of departments, the faculty, the students, or who?" (Lazarsfeld and Thielens, p. 170).

A score for each school was constructed by summing up all individual professors' responses, with faculty having a value of 2, the president and deans a score value of 1, and trustees, 0. (This assumed that the administrators were somewhat more accessible or responsive to faculty desires than the trustees.) The resulting measure of faculty influence correlated highly with academic quality, as shown in Table 9 (Lazarsfeld and Thielens, pp. 170–72).

Similar ratings by samples of respondents have been used to measure the influence of the members, executive board, bargaining committee, and president in union locals (Tannenbaum). We have already quoted one result of the study of League of Women Voters which used member ratings to measure the relative power of the membership and of the president (Kahn, Tannenbaum, and Weiss). With this measure obtained from 100 locals, the researchers were able

TABLE 9.   Relationship of Faculty
Influence in Academic Freedom
Matters to Quality of College

FACULTY INFLUENCE	QUALITY SCORE OF COLLEGE		
	Low and Medium Low	Medium High	High
Low (under 1.1)	15	18	8
High (1.1 or more)	4	13	19
Total colleges studied	19	31	27

to show that the greater the relative influence of the membership, the more widely known the organization was in the community, the more active were the members, the more the officers were aware of member desires, the more the officers attended discussion group meetings, and—interestingly enough—the more frequently there was conflict among the members, as reported by the sample. . . .

COMMUNICATION AND JOB CONTACT STRUCTURE

The communication structure of organizations has been studied in various ways, both directly by asking about or observing the flow of information, and indirectly by seeing who has what information. The study of 100 local civic organizations found that where the members had more power, the officers rated themselves as more highly informed about the members' wishes, and actually attended more discussion group meetings (Kahn, Tannenbaum, and Weiss). A case study of organizational change within a prison observed that increased communications between the rehabilitation staff and the administration led to a change in the power position of the guard staff and of the inmate elite of "fixers" (McCleery). A quantitative measure of frequency of communications was used in the study of

two Air Force wings (Thompson). Despite the fact that the formal authority structure was identical, it was found that in Wing B the assistant to the director of materials played a major role in the communications structure, while his opposite number in Wing A did not. Communications frequency was measured by work-contact questionnaires and from contact diaries kept by the major executives during a sample week. In the wing where he had a higher communications frequency and scope, this assistant was rated as having considerably more "say about how the wing gets its work done," on a questionnaire of all higher officers. Furthermore, in Wing B the maintenance officers generally occupied a higher position of communications and power. The author's qualitative observations as to the consequences were:

"In Wing A the director of operations dominated maintenance executives. . . . On several occasions he planned major operations on the basis of his own inadequate estimates of maintenance capabilities and later, to the general confusion, was forced to change his plans. The director of material was handicapped, in staff meetings, by the fact that he had to transact business with operations executives without the help of his chief assistant, the maintenance control officer, whose position gave him detailed information about maintenance schedules and capacities. . . .

"In Wing B the directors of operations —and material worked more closely together, checking on each other's needs and capacities at several stages of their planning."

In this Air Force study we see the use of both power ratings and direct measures of communications frequency between individuals and status groups, along with a qualitative characterization of effectiveness of output; if more than two cases of "identical" organization had been available, statistical measures of the relationships among these variables could have been used.

The basic form of measures of communication in organizations is that of a who-to-whom matrix. Such a matrix gives us scores on individual frequencies of originating or receiving communications; as in the Air Force study, organizations can then be classified by whether a given status-position or status-group has a high or low communications score. It is also possible to derive indices from the matrix as a whole as well as from its marginal totals. Consider for instance the data in Table 10 which was produced by a hospital study which asked nurses, technicians, and attendants how often they discussed each of eight topics with members of their own or other hierarchical or functional groups (Mishler and Tropp).

Such a matrix sums up numerical estimates made for the researcher by the respondent; it would also be possible to have asked directly about each pair relationship in the organization and then had the researcher do the addition from the raw data. In any case once we have such a matrix we have a measure of the mean communications on the topics covered

TABLE 10.   Amount of Discussion Between Members of Hospital Status Groups

GROUPS REPORT-ING DIS-CUSSIONS*	MEAN NUMBER OF TOPICS DISCUSSED WITH GROUP MEMBERS			
	Doc-tors	Nurses	Tech-ni-cians	At-tend-ants
Nurses	4.5	6.4	5.0	4.5
Technicians	3.5	5.0	6.1	5.2
Attendants	3.2	4.0	5.6	6.1

* Questions not asked of doctors.

between any two status groups, as well as within each. Summary measures could be made by comparing within-status to between-status communications; this would

tell us how "status-centric" an organization was. We could also compare the separate matrices for each of the eight topics of discussion, and see which were more status-centric than others. These are all examples of what we have called *relational pattern* measurements.

Pace and Stern have developed a 300-item College Characteristics Index by which student or faculty samples can report on various aspects of the college. In their own analysis the items have been classified in terms of Henry Murray's list of personality needs—achievement, aggression, nurturance, play, and so forth. Student needs are to be measured by a personality test (the Activities Index), while the extent to which the college provides resources for meeting these needs is measured by the College Characteristics Index.

It is quite possible however to reclassify the items according to *sociological* categories and construct our own indices from them. For example, in the College Characteristics Index we find several items which ask for respondent ratings of faculty-student (Pace and Stern):

"The professors seem to have little time for conversation with students."

TABLE 11.   Faculty-Student Contact at Five Colleges

COLLEGE	MEAN PER CENT PERCEIVING CONTACTS*	
	Student Respond-ents	Faculty Respond-ents
Midwestern state college	37_{100}	(No data)
Private eastern men's college	50_{100}	67_{20}
Private university	41_{68}	47_{11}
Municipal college	23_{111}	31_{15}
University of Chicago	65_{44}	62_{25}

* Smaller size figures indicate total number of respondents on which percentages are based.

"Faculty members seldom visit informally with students in dormitories or residences."

"Faculty members and administrators will see students only during their regularly scheduled office hours."

"The professors really talk *with* the students, not just *at* them."

From seven such items we can form a crude index of faculty-student contact by adding up the per cent who indicate that there is considerable contact. From Pace and Stern's pretest data on five colleges the above results can be computed using our index (Table 11).

Bibliography

American Association of University Professors, "The Place and Function of Faculties in College and University Government," *41 A.A.U.P. Bulletin* (1955), 62–81.

Alexander, K. J. W., "Membership Participation in a Printing Trade Union," *Sociological Review,* 2 (1954), p. 161.

Bigman, Stanley, "Rivals in Conformity," *Journalism Quarterly,* 25 (1948), pp. 127–31.

Chalmers, W. E., M. K. Chandler, L. L. McQuitty, R. Stagner, D. E. Wray, and M. Durber, *Labor-Management Relations in Illini City,* Vol. 2, *Studies in Comparative Analysis* (Champaign, Illinois: Institute of Labor and Industrial Relations, University of Illinois, 1954).

Cillié, Francis S., *Centralization or Decentralization?* (New York: Bureau of Publications, Teachers College, Columbia University, 1940).

Evan, William M., "Indices of the Hierarchical Structure of Industrial Organizations," paper delivered at Fourth World Congress of Sociology, Stresa, Italy, 1959.

Haire, Mason, "Biological Models and Empirical Histories of the Growth of Organizations," in Mason Haire (ed.), *Modern Organization Theory* (New York: John Wiley & Sons, 1959), Chapter 10.

Jaques, Elliot, *The Measurement of Responsibility* (Cambridge: Harvard University Press, 1956).

Kahn, Robert, Arnold Tannenbaum, Robert Weiss, *et al., A Study of the League of Women Voters of the United States,* 5 mimeo (Ann Arbor: Survey Research Center, University of Michigan, 1956).

Lazarsfeld, Paul F. and Wagner Thielens, Jr. *The Academic Mind* (New York: The Free Press, 1958).

Lee, Alfred McClung, *The Daily Newspaper in America* (New York: The Macmillan Company, 1947).

Levine, Sol and Paul E. White, "Exchange as a Conceptual Framework for the Study of Interorganizational Relationships," (unpublished report, Harvard School of Public Health, 1960).

Lipset, Seymour Martin, Martin A. Trow, and James S. Coleman, *Union Democracy* (New York: The Free Press, 1956).

March, James G. and Herbert A. Simon, *Organizations* (New York: John Wiley & Sons, 1958).

McCleery, Richard H., *Policy Change in Prison Management* (East Lansing: Governmental Research Bureau, Michigan State University, 1957).

McGrath, Earl, "The Control of Higher Education in America," *Educational Record,* 17 (1936), pp. 259–72.

Mishler, Elliot G. and Asher Tropp, "Status Interaction in a Psychiatric Hospital," *Human Relations,* 9 (1956), pp. 187–203.

Morse, Nancy and E. Reimer, "The Experimental Change of a Major Organizational Variable," *Journal of Abnormal and Social Psychology,* 52 (1955), pp. 120–29.

Mort, Paul R. and Francis G. Cornell, *American Schools in Transition* (New York: Bureau of Publications, Teachers College, Columbia University, 1941).

Pace, C. Robert, "Five college environments," *College Board Review,* 41 (1958), pp. 24–28.

Pace, C. Robert and George G. Stern, *A Criterion Study of College Environment* (Syracuse University Research Institute, Psychological Research Center, 1958).

Riesman, David, *Constraint and Variety in American Education* (New York: Doubleday, 1958).

Ross, Donald (ed.), *Administration for Adaptability* (New York: Institute of Administrative Research, Teachers College, Columbia University, 1958).

Russell, John D. and Floyd W. Reeves, *Finance,* Vol. 7 of *The Evaluation of Higher Institutions* (North Central Association of Colleges and Secondary Schools, 1936).

Sills, David, *The Volunteers* (New York: The Free Press, 1958).

Sims, V. M. and J. R. Patrick, "Attitude Toward the Negro of Northern and Southern College Students," *Journal of Social Psychology,* 7 (1936), pp. 192–204.

Tannenbaum, Arnold S., "Control Structure and Union Functions," *American Journal of Sociology,* 61 (1956), pp. 536–45.

Terrien, Frederick W. and Donald L. Mills, "The Effect of Changing Size Upon the Internal Structure of Organizations," *American Sociological Review,* 20 (1955), pp. 11–13.

Thompson, James D., "Authority and Power in 'Identical' Organizations," *American Journal of Sociology,* 62 (1956), pp. 290–301.

Tsouderos, John E., "Organizational Change in Terms of a Series of Selected Variables," *American Sociological Review,* 20 (1955), pp. 206–10.

Urwick, Lyndall F., "The Manager's Span of Control," *Harvard Business Review,* 34 (1956), pp. 39–97.

Worthy, J. C., "Organizational Structure and Employee Morale," *American Sociological Review,* 15 (1950), pp. 169–79.

27. The Learning Environments of Hospitals

PATRICIA KENDALL

THIS PAPER examines variations of hospital environments along several dimensions held to be significant in sociological theory. This is subject to two major restrictions. First, I do not characterize the entire hospital environment, but only the portion that constitutes the learning environment for interns and residents. Every hospital that offers training to house officers provides them with more or less routinized occasions for carrying out different activities, with a set of expectations about what they should get from their year of training, and with standards regarding the levels of performance they should achieve. These several and interrelated elements form the learning environment for the house staff.

The other restriction leads us to deal with only three dimensions of variability in these learning environments. The first of these is the *observability* of the house staff's performance by its superiors in the hospital hierarchy. As Merton has pointed out, observability of a group's behavior is a precondition for exercising social control over that group. To gain some impression of the extent to which a hospital exerts controls over its house officers, we must therefore find out how visible their behavior is—and how much it is observed. Second, we examine one part of the total *role-set* of interns and residents, namely, their relations with each other. These peer-group relations are assumed to have various effects on the behavior of the house staff. For example, they may affect the probability that house

officers select one another as reference individuals. Third is a focus on the *local or cosmopolitan* orientation of different types of hospitals. This is assumed to be related to the kinds of men who are attracted to the hospitals, and also to the kinds of doctors they ultimately turn out. . . .

Plan of the Study

The study was based on questionnaires and interviews with house officers and chiefs of staff in a sample of 167 hospitals, stratified by size and degree of affiliation with medical schools—these characteristics were intended to differentiate the learning environments of hospitals. . . .

Dimensions of Learning Environments in Hospitals

With this broad range of data, we could characterize the learning environments provided by different types of hospitals in many ways. We could, for example, focus on the kinds of available facilities. In how many and in which types of hospitals is there a library that is adequately stocked and open to qualified users at convenient times? In how many and, again, in which types of hospitals are there facilities for carrying out both laboratory and clinical investigations? Or, turning to the personnel available in different kinds of hospitals, we

Reprinted in part with permission from Chapter 7 of *The Hospital in Modern Society,* edited by Eliot Freidson (copyright 1963 by The Free Press, a Division of the Macmillan Company New York).

can ask in how many, and, once more, in which types of hospitals, the chiefs of service hold full-time or part-time appointments.

These learning environments of different types of hospitals can also be compared along other lines which are at once more subtle and less tangible than that of available facilities and personnel. We shall study the kinds of "atmospheres" found in different hospital settings. . . .

RELATION OF HOUSE STAFF TO
AUTHORITIES: OBSERVABILITY AND
SUPERVISION

Interns and residents are members of a hierarchy. As physicians, they occupy positions of authority over the so-called "ancillary personnel" in the hospital—nurses, aides, laboratory technicians, and so on. But the positions they occupy are definitely subordinate to those of chiefs of service, attending physicians, the director of medical education, and other senior physicians. And, as subordinates, the behavior of interns and residents is, to a greater or lesser extent, controlled by those in authority. This control, which takes the form of supervision in graduate medical training, presupposes the visibility of the house staff's performance. . . .

Before studying variations in such visibility according to the type of hospital, we might consider briefly the reactions of interns and residents to supervision, or the exercise of controls over their behavior. In many fields of graduate education, notably the humanities and social sciences, the notion that a graduate student needs to be supervised in his daily activities is often viewed with disapproval. Independence in scholarship and research activities is the ideal, and acknowledgment of need for more than occasional supervision is taken as an admission that the student is incapable of such independence. This is not at all the case in graduate medical education. Most house officers welcome having

their work closely supervised by accomplished physicians, for without this they cannot readily increase their knowledge or improve their skills. . . . Consider, for example, the comments made by a third-year resident in obstetrics-gynecology in a small community hospital:

> I am a spotted cow. I was never eligible to become chief resident. I fully expected, however, to be fully a part of the residency program and I expected the professors to see to it that I was well trained. This was not done. *None of them has ever watched me deliver a baby!* (#6580) [Emphasis supplied.]

Another man was also critical because he had not received enough supervision:

> As a first-year resident in OB–Gyn, I am in charge of all ward deliveries when I am on duty. The intern *only* assists the attending for deliveries. This results in no advice or supervision of techniques. If all goes smoothly, all is well. If serious complications arise we only receive criticism and abuse, but never guidance as to how to avoid such a complication again (#5734). [Emphasis in original.]

Comments from others also underscore the importance attached to adequate supervision. . . .

House officers reporting that their work had been sufficiently supervised were more apt to judge the educational program favorably. They did not regard this as limiting their independence of action. . . .

It seems generally agreed that a good program in graduate medical education is one that, among other things, provides for "helpful supervision" of the house staff. But, as we have noted, effective supervision presupposes that the performance of the house staff is easily visible. We therefore want to find out whether there are systematic variations in visibility. With this in mind, we presented the house officers with two statements, and asked them to indicate "how much of the time, if ever" these applied to "this hospital." The statements read as follows:

"Evaluation of the house staff goes on. . . . "

"Work of the house staff is reviewed by other doctors. . . . "

The interns and residents in the sample could answer "almost always," "fairly often," "occasionally," or "almost never."

Table 1 shows that constant evaluation of the house staff is more common in closely affiliated than in unaffiliated hospitals, particularly in the smaller hospitals.

TABLE 1. Frequency of Evaluation of House Staff

Degree of Affiliation with Medical School	Per Cent of House Officers Saying Evaluation Takes Place "Almost Always"	
	LARGE	SMALL
Close	41	40
Some	39	31
None	35	20

The small, unaffiliated hospitals probably have fewer occasions on which the performance of house officers *could* be evaluated: the chiefs of service are almost all part-time men who spend only a limited part of the workday or work week directing their services, and the attending physicians are primarily practitioners who take time out from seeing their private patients to make brief visits to the hospital. And since, on the average, there are far fewer interns and residents in these small, unaffiliated institutions than in any other type of hospital, each house officer is apt to work alone rather than in a group. Thus, even were the *motivation* to evaluate the house staff equally strong in all hospital types, the *opportunities* for doing so in small, unaffiliated hospitals are limited: the potential evaluators are not often on the scene, and, even when they are, it may be

difficult to find the few house officers who are to be evaluated.

The second question—that concerned with reviews of the house staff's work—deals with a similar matter and exhibits the same kinds of variations by [degree of affiliation] as were observed in Table 1. . . . However, size of hospital does not play any role. The explanation for the relatively greater freedom from review that house officers in the unaffiliated hospitals enjoy is probably very much the same as that offered previously: there are fewer staff resources for carrying out such reviews.

In sum, then, the work of house officers in closely affiliated hospitals tends to be supervised more fully than is the case in hospitals with some or no affiliation. The comments quoted earlier suggest that close supervision is welcomed. But the high degree of observability on which it is based can, of course, result in almost intolerable pressures. . . . If this alone operated, we should expect the existence of pressures to parallel the existence of close supervision; in the light of some earlier findings, we should expect more tensions in closely affiliated than in unaffiliated hospitals. But we know, of course, that there are other sources of tensions for the house staff. For example, we can assume that the pressures experienced by interns and residents will be affected by such conditions as the ratio of patients to staff. The higher this ratio, the more probable it is that house officers will experience pressures. And, according to general information about the different types of hospitals, this ratio should be more favorable in closely affiliated than in unaffiliated hospitals. It is not entirely clear, therefore, just how the experience of pressures will be related to type of hospital.

To explore this, the respondents were presented with a third statement—"Demands are so great they're almost impossible to meet"—and were asked to indicate how generally this applied to their hospitals. . . . The possible parallel between closeness of supervision and experience of pressures was not found. . . . Is the existence of tensions related to the work load of the house staff? To study this more directly, we used data pertaining to each of the participating hospitals—the average daily census of inpatients and the total number of house officers working in the hospital. These two items of information made it possible to construct an index, based on the ratio of patients to interns and residents; for the sake of simplicity, we can call this an "index of work pressures" in the hospital. Table 2 shows a fairly strong relationship between the work pressures present in the hospital and its characterization as a place in which it is difficult to fulfill all demands made on the house officers:

TABLE 2.   Experience of Pressures According to Index of Work Pressures

Ratio of Patients to House Officers	Per Cent of House Officers saying it is impossible to meet demands "ALMOST ALWAYS" or "FAIRLY OFTEN"	Total Cases
1–5	17	(862)
6–10	20	(598)
11–20	27	(472)
21 or more	33	(104)

About a third of the straight interns and residents working in hospitals with the highest ratio of patients to house officers (twenty-one or more) reported frequent difficulties in meeting the demands made on them; this was true for only half as many of the men working in the hospitals with the lowest ratio of patients to house officers. . . .

RECIPROCAL RELATIONS OF HOUSE OFFICERS: GENERATING SOCIAL ATMOSPHERES

When we set out to study the relations house officers have with their superiors in their role-set, it seemed evident that we should think in terms of subordination-superordination. When we begin to examine the relations house officers have with their peers in their role-set, it seems equally evident to think in terms of competition-cooperation. We consider, then, this aspect of atmosphere prevailing in the several types of hospitals.

As before, the respondents were asked to serve as informants about their hospitals. . . . But in the case of competition-cooperation it was more useful to distinguish between the atmosphere prevailing among interns and among residents in the hospital. Accordingly, the straight interns and residents were given another set of descriptive statements, and were asked, first, to how many of the interns in the hospital each statement applied, and, then, to how many of the residents. Two of these statements dealt with professional cooperativeness:

[They] are open and free about exchanging information.
[They] are willing to help out when a fellow intern or resident has a lot of work to do.

It is not easy to guess how this sort of cooperativeness will vary by hospital type. From the previous section we know that the work of interns and residents is more frequently evaluated and reviewed in closely affiliated than in unaffiliated hospitals. We might suppose that, because house officers in closely affiliated hospitals know that they are under fairly constant scrutiny and that, in some sense, their future careers depend on how well they perform, they will be "cagey" with each other. On this assumption, we should expect house officers in closely affiliated hospitals to be *less* open and free in the exchange of information and *less* willing to help each other out. This finds support in the words of a third-year resident in a hospital closely affiliated with a medical school; he wrote:

In teaching hospitals the residents are competing for hospital appointments and frequently sacrifice their opinions, integrity, and loyalty toward their subordinate house officers in order to gain favor with the attending staff and administration.

But we also know that many in the medical profession place high value on the "team approach" to patient care. And we can assume that such teamwork, which obviously requires cooperation among house officers as well as with other members of the hospital staff, is more likely to be emphasized in closely affiliated hospitals where the larger numbers of full-time personnel make it more readily feasible.

In other words, there is reason to believe that the atmosphere in closely affiliated hospitals will be characterized by *less* cooperation than is the case in unaffiliated hospitals; and there is also reason to believe that the atmosphere of these university teaching centers will be characterized by *more* cooperation. The net result may be a product of these countervailing forces. But the data suggest the greater effectiveness of the second tendency, although not with complete consistency. Let us review the questions one at a time.

The results in Table 3 are quite clear cut. From the closely affiliated to the unaffiliated hospitals, the proportion saying that almost all interns exchange information freely declines steadily. And, although the differences are not so large when residents are being described, they exhibit the same general trend.

Although the size of the hospital is less important than degree of affiliation in

producing differences in cooperativeness, it does play some slight role. In general, house officers in the larger institutions are more likely to say that almost all of their colleagues exchange information freely. . . .

Responses to the second statement show less clear-cut differences between hospital types. Closely affiliated hospitals appear to be more likely than unaffiliated hospitals to have almost all *interns* willing to help one another out; but there are no consistent differences when the cooperativeness of *residents* is examined.

We found that, as affiliation with a medical school declines, so does the proportion of house officers saying that almost all interns are willing to help a colleague when he is under pressure. . . .

Of course, there can be barriers to interactions. One of these is imposed by the structure of the hospital. The division of the hospital into different departments, and the assignment of straight interns and residents to only one of these departments, may make it difficult for them to become acquainted with and to interact with men in other departments.

Another barrier may exist when members of the house staff come from different cultural backgrounds. This is especially apt to be the case when there are differences in their native languages. To study this, we separated the straight interns and residents who were citizens of the United States and then classified them according to the proportion of foreign-trained and generally, therefore, foreign-speaking house officers in their hospitals. Table 4 shows how the sociability of residents is related to the

TABLE 3.   Freedom in Exchanging Information *

	Large Hospitals			Small Hospitals		
	CLOSE AFFIL.	*SOME AFFIL.*	*NO AFFIL.*	*CLOSE AFFIL.*	*SOME AFFIL.*	*NO AFFIL.*
Per cent saying "almost all" Interns are open and free	80	73	66	81	63	60

* Data from original table about residents not included here.

proportion of foreign-trained residents in the hospital. The results suggest that cultural homogeneity affects close social interaction between members of the house staff. (Had there been enough cases, we could have made the corresponding comparison for foreign nationals. In that instance, we would have expected that, the larger the proportion of, say, Spanish-speaking residents, the *more* sociability there would be among them.)

TABLE 4.   Sociability of Residents According to Proportion of Foreign-Trained Residents (United States citizens)

Per Cent of Residents Who Are Foreign-trained	Per Cent Saying "Almost All" Residents Get Along	Total Cases
Less than 25	63	(1157)
25–50	57	(216)
51 or more	42	(59)

So far we have seen that relations between house officers in closely affiliated hospitals are somewhat more friendly than is true in unaffiliated institutions. But since the results are not clearcut, we look for other factors that might make for differences in the extent of friendly and cooperative relations between members of the house staff. An obvious possibility, again, is department. We have seen elsewhere in this chapter that departments of surgery are more tense than departments of medicine. Do they also have less amicability? To answer this, we shall . . . call on the rotating interns who . . . were asked to evaluate the relations between residents on the medical and surgical services. Rather than consider their answers to the separate questions, we have combined them into an index of cooperativeness. To do so, we counted the number of times each rotating intern said that the medical residents in his hospital displayed friendly behavior; we repeated this count separately for the re-

sponses of rotating interns regarding residents on the surgical service. The indices have values from 0 to 4, and, the higher the value, the greater the amount of amicability attributed to the residents. . . . The rotating interns report more friendliness among medical residents than among surgical residents.

A structural factor also seems to make for differences in the degree of cooperative relations between members of the house staff. This is the "shape" of the residency system. Some residency programs offer the same number of positions in each year of residency training; for example, they may have three positions for first-year residents, three for second-year residents, and three for third-year residents. This kind of system we shall describe as a "parallelogram." Other hospitals (or other departments in the same hospital) may have what is called a "pyramidal" system, offering progressively fewer positions to the higher levels of residents. Such a pyramidal system, for example, may have six first-year positions, three second-year positions, and one third-year position.

It is generally recognized that pyramidal systems operate on the basis of competition among the advancing residents. Some look on such competition as promoting a high level of medical care. . . . Others are more critical of the competition a pyramidal system is assumed to create. . . .

The competition created by a pyramidal system can be seen as a healthy spur to excellence and as a source of demoralization. But, in either case, a higher level of competitiveness is associated with the presence of pyramidal systems. To examine the extent of this, we first classified each of the departments offering a residency program (of more than one year). In the case of a pure parallelogram or a pure pyramid, this classification did not offer any problems. But there were, as there always are in empirical reality, intermediate cases that did not conform to either of these polar types. For example, some departments offer three first-year positions, three second-year positions, and one third-year position. Others offer, let us say, ten first-year positions, six second-year positions, six third-year residencies, and two fourth-year positions. These intermediate cases, combining features of both the parallel and pyramidal types, were designated "semipyramids."

The next step was to classify the respondents, in this case the straight interns and residents, according to the "shape" of the service on which they were working. Finally, using an index similar to that constructed for rotating interns, we examined how much cooperativeness these several groups attributed to the residents in their hospital. The results are shown in Table 5.

Bearing in mind that the higher the score-value of the index, the greater the degree of cooperativeness, we find that interns and residents working on services or-

TABLE 5.   Cooperativeness of Residents According to "Shape" of Residency Programs

DEPARTMENT	AVERAGE SCORE ON INDEX*		
	Pyramid	Semi-pyramid	Parallel-ogram
Medicine	2.66	2.78	2.86
Obstetrics-gynecology	2.36	2.50	2.55
Pediatrics	2.47	2.55	2.51
Surgery	2.03	2.44	2.57

* The totals on which these average score values are based are as follows:

Department	Pyramid	Semi-pyramid	Parallel-ogram
Medicine	387	202	160
Obstetrics-gynecology	22	100	211
Pediatrics	108	49	83
Surgery	86	488	164

ganized as pyramidal systems perceive more competitiveness among their colleagues than do those working in departments with an equal number of positions on each level of residency training. The single exception is in departments of pediatrics; but this is only a slight deviation from the basic tendency.

RELATIONS OF HOUSE STAFF WITH PRACTITIONERS AND THE SCIENTIFIC COMMUNITY: LOCAL AND COSMOPOLITAN ORIENTATIONS

We have dealt so far with the relations of house officers to their superiors and to each other. In this final section, we consider the relations of the house staff in different types of hospitals to the broader medical community. We now take them out of the hospital, but we do so only to characterize the learning environments within different kinds of hospitals. In describing these relations of house officers to the larger medical community, we shall draw on concepts of "local" and "cosmopolitan" orientations that had their origin in a quite different context.

The distinction was originally developed in R. K. Merton's community study of people who influenced the decisions, tastes, and behavior of others.[1] These influentials were found to be of two types, depending on their orientation to the community. The "local influentials" were found to be primarily oriented to the community, to be more concerned about its problems than about national or international situations, to have a wide network of friends and acquaintances in the community, to belong to a variety of local organizations, and so on. The "cosmopolitan influentials," in contrast, were found to be more interested in what was going on outside the community, to be less loyal and devoted to the community, to have fewer friends among their neighbors, and the like. . . .

To put it most succinctly, we define a local orientation as one in which the physician is primarily concerned with patients and problems of practice, and a cosmopolitan orientation as one in which he is primarily concerned with scientific medicine and research. From all this, we should of course expect that closely affiliated hospitals are characterized by greater cosmopolitanism than unaffiliated hospitals.

Here, as in previous sections, we are not interested in finding out *which* interns and residents in our sample have a local and which a cosmopolitan orientation. Rather, as before, we want to determine how the climates or atmospheres of different hospitals vary. Once more, therefore, we asked our respondents to serve as informants about the hospitals in which they were working. We did so in several ways.

A first indicator of whether a hospital is primarily cosmopolitan or local is the orientation of the attending physicians with whom house officers work most closely. With this in mind, we asked a direct question:

> During this year, have you actually worked mostly with attending physicians who are scientifically oriented, or who are patient and practice oriented?

The great majority of the house officers in our sample reported that they had worked mostly with attendings who, according to our definition, were locally oriented. But . . . the size of these majorities depends greatly on the extent to which a hospital is or is not affiliated with a medical school.

Almost two-thirds of the interns and residents in closely affiliated hospitals reported that most of the attending physicians who supervised their work were primarily oriented to patients and problems of practice; the other third told us that their attendings were scientifically oriented. However, in hospitals with some, but not close, affiliation, nine out of every ten respondents said that their attendings were primarily patient-oriented; and in hospitals with no affiliation

this is almost universal, with such reports being given by 95 per cent of the house staff. In this respect, then, expectations are borne out: university teaching hospitals are more cosmopolitan in their orientation.

A second measure of this orientation was based on a semi-projective question. With the help of a medical educator, we devised a list of six titles of lectures. Two of these dealt quite obviously with questions about the practice of medicine: "Group Practice —Pros and Cons" and "How to Avoid Malpractice Suits"; these were intended as measures of a local orientation. Two others dealt with topics in basic medical science: "Lipid Metabolism" and "The Role of Serotonin in Disorders of the Gut"; they were intended to indicate a cosmopolitan orientation. The two remaining titles were meant to suggest practical applications of medical knowledge: "Office Treatment of Thyroid Disorders" and "Stimulants and Sedatives."

The titles were arranged so that these pairs were not grouped. The respondents were then asked: "Suppose the following lectures were offered in your hospital. In your opinion, which two lectures would bring out the largest audience in this hospital?" We expected, first of all, that interns and residents in unaffiliated community hospitals would more often say that lectures dealing with problems of practice would be popular in their institutions, thereby indicating the primarily local orientation of these hospitals. Table 6 indicates that this is the case, especially in connection with the question of how to avoid malpractice suits.

Conversely, we expected that when lectures dealing with topics of basic medical science were considered, they would be selected more frequently by interns and residents in closely affiliated hospitals, indicating the more cosmopolitan orientation of such hospitals. As Table 7 shows, neither of these lectures seems likely to attract a large audience. But, according to the in-

TABLE 6.   Selection of Practice-Oriented Lecture Titles

	Large Hospitals			Small Hospitals		
	CLOSE AFFIL.	SOME AFFIL.	NO AFFIL.	CLOSE AFFIL.	SOME AFFIL.	NO AFFIL.
Per cent selecting "How to Avoid Malpractice Suits"	43	57	68	43	62	66
Per cent selecting "Group Practice—Pros and Cons"	31	38	39	31	39	37

terns and residents in our sample, they would be considerably more popular in closely affiliated than in unaffiliated hospitals. . . .

All of our findings point to the conclusion that a cosmopolitan orientation is typical of closely affiliated hospitals, while a local orientation is typical of those institutions that do not have any formal association with a medical school. However, it is not clear whether a hospital with a cosmopolitan orientation offers an environment more favorable to learning medicine than does one with a local orientation. . . .

Summary

Hospitals that offer graduate training programs for interns and residents differ in the kinds of learning environments they provide. These can be variously described. They can be characterized in terms of the physical facilities or the categories of personnel that are available, and in terms of the atmospheres that prevail. For the present purposes, we adopted the second approach.

To describe the learning environments found in different types of hospitals, we selected three sociological variables bearing on the relations of house officers to others in their role-set and to the broader medical community. We saw, first of all, that the visibility of the house staff's performance significantly affects their relations with superiors in the hospital structure. Only when the behavior of interns and residents is observable can they receive the kind of supervision they generally report as helpful. Conditions making for such observability were more often found in closely affiliated than in unaffiliated hospitals, and, therefore, adequate supervision is more general in the former rather than the latter. We did not find that such observability resulted in tensions or pressures on the house staff. Instead, the degree of tension seems

TABLE 7.   Selection of Basic Science Lecture Titles

	Large Hospitals			Small Hospitals		
	CLOSE AFFIL.	SOME AFFIL.	NO AFFIL.	CLOSE AFFIL.	SOME AFFIL.	NO AFFIL.
Per cent selecting "Lipid Metabolism"	38	21	13	38	25	10
Per cent selecting "The Role of Serotonin in Disorders of the Gut"	30	23	8	32	11	10

to follow departmental lines, and to be more directly related to the work load of the house officers.

Next we investigated how the relations that interns and residents have with their colleagues vary from one kind of hospital to another. House officers tend to have more amicable relations with their peers in closely affiliated rather than in unaffiliated hospitals. But the absence of clear-cut differences by size of hospital or degree of affiliation led us to look for other structural factors that might account for variations in these interpersonal relations. Cultural homogeneity was found to be a condition for close interaction between house officers; in the eyes of rotating interns, at least, there is more cooperativeness among medical than among surgical residents; and the degree to which residents cooperate with one another is influenced by structural arrangements of the residency program in their hospital.

A final section examined the local-cosmopolitan orientation of different types of hospitals, and considered the implications this might have for the adequacy of educational programs in these hospitals. It was found, as we expected, that closely affiliated hospitals have more of a cosmopolitan orientation than do hospitals of other types. There are some who assume that such an orientation, with its emphasis on scientifically based medicine and research findings, automatically makes for a superior learning environment. To clarify this assumption, we examined opposing arguments set forth by medical educators, as well as by the house staff in the study. These generally stated that what is missing in the scientifically and research-oriented (cosmopolitan) hospital is a proper concern for the practical problems of medical practice.

Notes

1. See Robert K. Merton, "Patterns of Influence: A Study of Interpersonal Influence and of Communications Behavior in a Local Community," in P. F. Lazarsfeld and F. N. Stanton, eds., *Communications Research, 1948–1949* (New York: Harper & Brothers, 1949).

28. Relational Analysis: A Study of Social Organization with Survey Methods

JAMES S. COLEMAN

SURVEY RESEARCH methods have often led to the neglect of social structure and of the relations among individuals. On the other hand, survey methods are highly efficient in bringing in a large volume of data —amenable to statistical treatment—at a relatively low cost in time and effort. Can the student of social structure enjoy the advantages of the survey without neglecting the relationships which make up that structure? In other words, can he use a method which ordinarily treats each in-

Reprinted in part with permission from *Human Organization,* 17 (1958–1959), pp. 28–36 (copyright 1959 by the Society for Applied Anthropology).

dividual as an isolated unit in order to study social structure?

The purpose of this paper is to describe some important developments in survey research which are giving us a new way of studying social organization.

It is useful to trace briefly the history of survey research, to indicate how it has grown from "polling" to the point where it can now study problems involving complex human organization. A look at this history indicates two definite stages. The first was a polling stage which was concerned with the *distribution* of responses on any one item: What proportion favored Roosevelt in 1936? What proportion was in favor of labor unions? This type of concern continues even today among pollsters, and to the lay public it is still the function of surveys to "find out what people think" or to see just how many feel thus and so.

Among sociologists, however, this purely descriptive use of survey research was soon supplanted by an *analytical* one. First there began to be a concern with how different subgroups in the population felt or behaved. From this, the analysts moved on to further cross-tabulations. Finally, some survey analysts began, through cross-tabulations and correlations, to study complicated questions of why people behaved as they did. By relating one opinion item to another, attitude configurations and clusters of attitudes emerged; by relating background information to these attitudes, some insight was gained into the *determinants* of attitudes. It was in this analytical stage, then, beyond the simple description of a population, that survey research began to be of real use to social science.

But throughout all this one fact remained, a very disturbing one to the student of social organization. The *individual* remained the unit of analysis. No matter how complex the analysis, how numerous the correlations, the studies focused on individuals as separate and independent units. The very techniques mirrored this

well: samples were random, never including (except by accident) two persons who were friends; interviews were with one individual, as an atomistic entity, and responses were coded onto separate IBM cards, one for each person. As a result, the kinds of substantive problems on which such research focused tended to be problems of "aggregate psychology," that is, *within*-individual problems, and never problems concerned with relations between people.

Now, very recently, this focus on the individual has shown signs of changing, with a shift to groups as the units of analysis, or to networks of relations among individuals. The shift is quite a difficult one to make, both conceptually and technically, and the specific methods used to date are only halting steps toward a full-fledged methodology. Nevertheless, some of these methods are outlined below, to indicate just how, taken together, they can even now provide us with an extremely fruitful research tool. This tool has sometimes been used for the study of formal organization but more often for the study of the informal organization which springs up within a formal structure. In both cases, it shows promise of opening to research, problems which have been heretofore the province of speculation.

Problems of Design and Sampling

The break from the atomistic concerns of ordinary survey analysis requires taking a different perspective toward the individual interview. In usual survey research and statistical analysis, this interview is regarded as *independent* of others, as an entity in itself. All cross-tabulations and analyses relate one item in that questionnaire to another item in the same questionnaire. But, in this different approach, an individual interview is seen as a *part* of some larger structure in which the respondent finds himself: his network of friends, the shop or office where he works, the bowling team he belongs to, and so on. Thus, as a part of a larger structure, the individual is *not* treated independently. The analysis must somehow tie together and interrelate the attributes of these different parts of the structure.

So much for the basic change in perspective—away from the atomistic treatment of the individual interview, and toward the treatment of each interview as a part of some larger whole. This basic perspective has several implications for the kind of data collected and for the sample design. Perhaps the most important innovation in the kind of data collected is sociometric-type data in the interview, that is, explicit questions about the respondent's relation to other specific individuals. Each person may be asked the names of his best friends, or the names of his subordinates in the shop upon whom he depends most, or any one of a multitude of *relational* questions. For example, in a study of two housing projects by Merton, Jahoda, and West,[1] one way to map out the informal social structure in the community was to ask people who their best friends were. Having obtained such data from all the families in the project, so that each family could be located in the network of social relations in the community, it was then possible to examine the relation between this social structure, on the one hand, and various values and statuses on the other. Specifically, this information allowed these authors to show that in one housing project social ties were based very largely on similarities in background and religion; in the other, social relations were more often built around common leisure interests and participation in community organizations. More generally, the incorporation of sociometric-type data into survey research allows the investigator to *locate* each interviewed individual within the networks of voluntary relations which surround him. In some cases, these networks of voluntary

relations will be superimposed on a highly articulated formal structure. In a department of a business, for example, there are numerous hierarchical levels and there are numerous work relations which are imposed by the job itself. In such cases, sociometric-type questions can be asked relative to these formal relations, e.g.: "Which supervisor do you turn to most often?" or, "Which of the men in your own workgroup do you see most often outside of work?" or, "When you want X type of job done in a hurry to whom do you go to get it done?" or, "When you need advice on such-and-such a problem, whom do you usually turn to?"

Another kind of data is that which refers to some larger social unit. For example, in some research on high schools currently being carried out at the University of Chicago, it is necessary to find the paths to prestige within a school, so that the boys are asked: "What does it take to be important and looked up to by the other fellows here at school?" Then the responses to this question—aggregated over each school separately—can be used to characterize the *school* as well as the individual. Because of this, the question itself makes explicit reference to the school.

But apart from the kinds of data collected, there are also important *sampling* considerations. In this kind of research, it is no longer possible to pull each individual out of his social context and interview him as an independent entity. It is necessary to sample parts of that context as well or, to say it differently, to sample explicitly with reference to the social structure. There are numerous ways of doing this; only a few, which have been successfully tried, are mentioned below.

a. SNOWBALL SAMPLING

One method of interviewing a man's immediate social environment is to use the sociometric questions in the interview for sampling purposes. For example, in a study of political attitudes in a New England community, Martin Trow has used this approach: first interviewing a small sample of persons, then asking these persons who their best friends are, interviewing these friends, then asking *them* their friends, interviewing these, and so on.[2] In this way, the sampling plan follows out the chains of sociometric relations in the community. In many respects, this sampling technique is like that of a good reporter who tracks down "leads" from one person to another. The difference, of course, is that snowball sampling in survey research is amenable to the same scientific sampling procedures as ordinary samples. Where the population in ordinary samples is a population of individuals, here it is two populations: one of individuals and one of *relations* among individuals.

b. SATURATION SAMPLING

Perhaps a more obvious approach is to interview *everyone* within the relevant social structure. In a study of doctors in four communities, *all* the doctors in these communities were interviewed.[3] Sociometric type questions were then used to lay out the professional and social relations existing among these doctors. This "saturation" method or complete census was feasible there, because the total number of doctors in these communities was small—less than three hundred. But in the study mentioned earlier which used snowball sampling, such an approach would have been practically impossible, for the community was about 15,000 in size. Thus this "saturation sampling" is only feasible under rather special circumstances. A borderline case is the study of high schools mentioned earlier. There are 9,000 students in the ten schools being studied. Only because these students are given self-administered questionnaires, rather than interviews, is it possible to use a saturation sample, and thereby characterize the complete social structure.

c. DENSE SAMPLING

Another approach is to sample "densely." This is a compromise between the usual thinly dispersed random sample and the saturation sample. An illustration will indicate how this may be useful. In a study of pressure upon the academic freedom of college social science teachers, carried out by Paul Lazarsfeld, at least *half* of the social science faculty in every college in the sample was interviewed.[4] Thus, by sampling densely, enough men were interviewed in each college so that the climate of the college could be characterized, as well as the attitudes of the individual respondent.

d. MULTI-STAGE SAMPLING

Any of the above approaches to sampling can be combined with an element found in many sample designs: the multistage sample. For example, in the academic freedom study referred to above, it would have been impossible to have a dense sample of social science teachers in *all* the colleges in the United States, so a two-stage sample was used: first sampling colleges, and then teachers within colleges. In doing this, of course, the crucial question is what balance to maintain between the sampling of colleges and the sampling of teachers within colleges. Enough colleges are needed to have representativity, yet few enough so that the sampling within each one can be dense. In a study of union politics, reported in *Union Democracy,*[5] we perhaps made a wrong decision: we interviewed in ninety printing shops, spreading the interviews so thinly that only one man out of three— at most—was interviewed within the shop. This meant that we had only a very few interviews in each shop, and could not use the interview material to characterize the climate or atmosphere of the shops, except in the very largest ones.

These sampling procedures are, of course, not the only possible ones. An infinite degree of variation is possible, depending upon the problem and upon the kind of social structure involved. The most important point is that the individual interview can no longer be treated as an independent entity, but must be considered as a part of some larger whole: in the sampling, in the questions asked, and in the subsequent analysis.

Analytical Methods

The real innovations in this new kind of research are in the techniques of analysis. I will mention several of these with which I am most familiar, to give an indication of the kinds of problems this research examines and the way it examines them.

a. CONTEXTUAL ANALYSIS

The first, and the one closest to usual survey research, might be termed contextual analysis. In essence, it consists of relating a characteristic of the respondent's social context—and the independent variable—to a characteristic of the individual himself.[6] A good example of this occurred in *The American Soldier*, where the attitudes of inexperienced men, in companies where most others were inexperienced, were compared to attitudes of similarly inexperienced men in companies where most others were veterans. It was found that inexperienced men in green companies felt very differently about themselves, and about combat, than their counterparts in veteran companies. That is, when men were characterized by both individual characteristics and by their social surroundings, the latter were found to have an important effect on their attitudes.

In the union politics study mentioned above, one of the major elements in the analysis was an examination of the effect of the shop context on the men within the shop. We had access to voting records in union political elections for these shops,

and these made it possible to characterize the shop as politically radical or politically conservative and as high or low in political consensus. Then we could examine the different behavior or attitudes of men in different kinds of shops and compute a "shop effect." An example is given in Table 1. Each man is in a shop of high or

TABLE 1.

	Shops of High Political Consensus	Shops of Low Political Consensus
Percent of men active in union politics	29%	7%
N	(125)	(28)

low political consensus, depending on whether the men in the shop vote alike or are evenly split between the radical and conservative parties. And each man has a certain degree of political activity. In this table, the shop's political consensus and the man's political activity are related. The table indicates that in shops of high consensus, men are politically more active than in shops of low consensus. The inference might be that high consensus provides a kind of resonance of political beliefs which generates a greater interest in politics. In any case, the table exemplifies the use of an attribute of a *shop* related to an attribute of a *man* in the shop. This general kind of analysis, which bridges the gap between two levels of sociological units—the individual and his social context—seems to be a very basic one for this "structural" approach to survey research.

b. BOUNDARIES OF HOMOGENEITY

A second kind of analysis attempts to answer the question: How homogeneous are various groups in some belief or attitude? In a medical school, for example, are a student's attitudes toward medicine more like those of his fraternity brothers or more like those of his laboratory partners? This question, incidentally, has been posed in a study of medical students presently being carried out at Columbia University.[7] The answer is, in the particular medical school being studied, that his attitudes are far more like those of his fraternity brothers. In other words, in this medical school, the "boundaries of homogeneity" of certain attitudes about medicine coincide very largely with fraternity boundaries.

The major problems in answering questions of group homogeneity are problems of index construction. Consider the above example: each student has twenty or thirty fraternity brothers, but only three laboratory partners in anatomy lab. How can the effects of variability between groups, due to small numbers in a group, be separated out from the actual tendency toward homogeneity of attitude? It can be done, and indices have been developed to do so. The indices, incidentally, are much like the formulas by which the statisticians measure the effects of clustering in a random sample. . . .

An example of group homogeneity may indicate more concretely how this approach can be useful in research. In the study of doctors in four communities mentioned earlier, we were interested in the social processes affecting the physician's introduction of a new drug into their practices. Through interviewing all doctors and asking sociometric questions in the interview, we were able to delineate seven "cliques" of doctors who were sociometrically linked together. (How to reconstruct such cliques is another problem, which will be considered shortly.) The question, then, became this: At each point in time after the drug was marketed, were cliques homogeneous or not in their members' use or nonuse of the drug? If they were homogeneous, then this was evidence that some kind of social influence or diffusion was going on in relation to the measured sociometric ties. If not, this indicated that the cliques delineated on the basis of questions in the interview had little relevance to drug adoption. Table 2 shows, for several time periods, just how much homogeneity there was in the cliques, beyond that which would arise by chance. An index value of 1.0 means each clique is completely homogeneous in its use or nonuse of the drug. An index value of 0 means there is no more homogeneity than would arise through chance variation between groups.

TABLE 2.

Months After Drug Was Marketed	Amount of Clique Homogeneity	Per Cent of Doctors Who Had Used the Drug
1	no homogeneity	14%
3	no homogeneity	32
5	no homogeneity	49
7	.07	66
9	.12	71
11	.18	76
13	.03	83
15	no homogeneity	86

Table 2 shows that there was no homogeneity until around seven months after the drug was introduced, that is, until over 50 per cent of the doctors had used the drug. The maximum homogeneity was reached at about eleven months, when three-fourths of the doctors had begun to use the drug. Then after that, the homogeneity receded to zero again.

This result helped to reinforce a conclusion derived from other findings in the study: that the social networks measured in the study were effective as paths of diffusion at certain times but not at others. However, apart from the substantive results of the study, this example indicates how such analysis of the boundaries of homogeneity may be useful for the study of the functioning of various social organizations.

c. PAIR ANALYSIS

Neither of the above kinds of analysis has required the use of sociometric-type data. An important kind of analysis which does use such direct data on relationships is the analysis of *pairs*. Here, the pair formed by A's choosing B becomes the unit of analysis. Speaking technically, "pair cards" may be constructed for each sociometric choice, and then these cards used for cross-tabulations. In other words, instead of cross-tabulating a man's attitude toward Russia with his attitude toward the United Nations, we can cross-tabulate the man's attitude toward Russia with the attitude toward Russia of the man he eats lunch with at the cafeteria.

One of the most important problems which has been studied in this way is the similarity or difference in attitudes or backgrounds between the two members of a pair. That is, do people have friendship relations with those who are like them politically, with people of the same age, with persons in the same occupation?

This kind of problem can be illustrated by Table 3, which contains hypothetical data. This table, which looks very much like an ordinary contingency table, must

TABLE 3.

		CHOSEN		
		boy	girl	
CHOOSER	boy	45	15	60
	girl	20	20	40
				100

be treated in a slightly different fashion. It allows us to raise the question: do boys tend to choose boys more than would be expected by chance? and, do girls tend to choose girls more than would be expected by chance? The answer, of course, depends upon what we take as chance. However, chance models have been worked out, so that one can assign measures of the tendency to choose others of one's own

kind. . . . For the above example, one measure (varying between 0 and 1) says that the tendency to in-choice for boys is .38 and that for girls is .7. By comparing such indices for numerous attributes, one could get a good glimpse into the informal social organization of the group. For example, in the medical study mentioned earlier which is being carried out at Columbia University, the values of in-choice tendency for friends shown in Table 4 were found:

TABLE 4.

Subgroups	Tendencies Toward In-Choice
Class in school	.92
Fraternity	.52
Sex	.33
Marital status	.20
Attitudes toward national health insurance	.37

By looking at the relative sizes of these index values, we get an idea of just how the informal social relations—that is, the friendship choices—at this medical school mesh with the formal structure, and with the distribution of attitudes.

In the study mentioned above of drug introduction by doctors, these pair relations were used as the major aspect of the analysis: by examining how close in time a doctor's first use of a new drug was to the first use of the doctor he mentioned as a friend, it was possible to infer the functioning of friendship networks in the introduction of this drug.

These examples of pair analysis give only a crude picture of the kinds of problems which can be studied in this fashion. The important matter is to break away from the analysis of *individuals* as units to the study of *pairs* of individuals. To be sure, this involves technical IBM problems and problems of index construction along with conceptual problems, but the difficulties are not great.

d. PARTITIONING INTO CLIQUES

Another important kind of problem is the partitioning of a larger group into cliques by use of sociometric choices. This problem is a thorny one, for it involves not only the delineation of cliques, but, even prior to this, the *definition* of what is to constitute a clique. Are cliques to be mutually exclusive in membership, or can they have overlapping memberships? Are they to consist of people who all name one another, or of people who are tied together by more tenuous connections? Such questions must be answered before the group can be partitioned into cliques.

A good review of some of the methods by which cliques and subgroups can be treated is presented in Lindzey and Borgatta.[8] The two most feasible of these are the method of matrix multiplication [9] and the method of shifting rows and columns in the sociometric choice matrix until the choices are clustered around the diagonal.[10] This last technique is by far the more feasible of the two if the groups are more than about twenty in size. When the groups are on the order of a hundred, even this method becomes clumsy. An IBM technique was successfully used in the study of doctors and the study of medical students, both mentioned above, in which the groups were 200–400 in size. At the University of Chicago, a program has been developed for Univac, using a method of shifting rows and columns in a matrix, which can handle groups up to a thousand in size.[11] The necessity for some such method becomes great when, for example, one wants to map out systematically the informal organization of a high school of a thousand students.

Conclusion

These four kinds of analysis, contextual analysis, boundaries of homogeneity, pair analysis, and partitioning into cliques, are only four of many possibilities. Several other approaches have been used, but these four give some idea of the way in which survey analysis can come to treat problems which involve social structure. In the long run, these modes of analysis will probably represent only the initial halting steps in the development of a kind of structural research which will represent a truly sociological methodology. In any case, these developments spell an important milestone in social research, for they help open up for systematic research those problems which have heretofore been the province of the theorist or of purely qualitative methods. . . .

Unfortunately, it has not been possible here to present any of the tools discussed above fully enough to show precisely how it is used. In giving a broad overview of a number of developments, my aim has been to point to an important new direction in social research, one which may aid significantly in the systematic study of social organization. . . .

Notes

1. Robert K. Merton, Patricia S. West, and Marie Jahoda, *"Patterns of Social Life: Explorations in the Sociology of Housing,"* unpublished manuscript, 1947.

2. Martin A. Trow, "Right Wing Radicalism and Political Intolerance: A Study of Support for McCarthy in a New England Town," unpublished Ph.D. dissertation, Columbia University, 1957.

3. J. S. Coleman, E. Katz, and H. M. Menzel, "Diffusion of an Innovation among Physicians," *Sociometry*, XX (December 1957).

4. P. F. Lazarsfeld and Wagner Thielens, *The Academic Mind: Social Scientists in a Time of Crisis* (New York: The Free Press, 1956).

5. S. M. Lipset, M. A. Trow, and J. S. Coleman, *Union Democracy* (New York: The Free Press, 1956).

6. Peter Blau has emphasized the importance of such analysis in formal organizations for locating the "structural effects" of a situation upon the individuals in it. See his "For-

mal Organization: Dimensions of Analysis," *American Journal of Sociology*, LXIII (1957), pp. 58–69.

7. Some of the work in this study (though not the work mentioned here) is reported in P. L. Kendall, R. K. Merton, and G. S. Reader (eds.), *The Student Physician* (New York: Commonwealth Fund, 1957).

8. G. Lindzey (ed.), *Handbook of Social Psychology* (Cambridge: Addison-Wesley, 1956), Chapter II.

9. See L. Festinger, "The Analysis of Sociograms Using Matrix Algebra," *Human Rela-tions,* II, No. 2 (1949), pp. 153–58; and R. D. Luce, "Connectivity and Generalized Cliques in Sociometric Group Structure," *Psycho-metrika,* XV (1950), pp. 169–90.

10. C. O. Beum and E. G. Brundage, "A Method for Analyzing the Sociomatrix," *Soci-ometry,* XIII (1950), pp. 141–45.

11. A description of this program, written by the author and Duncan McRae, is available upon request from the author and the program itself is available for copying, for those who have access to a Univac I or II.

B. Weight of Collective Characteristics

29. Scholastic Effects of the Social System

JAMES S. COLEMAN

[Ed. Note: The preceding chapter of this study of high school life examined some indicators of the psychological effects of adolescent social systems on their members. Among these effects were the differences in self-evaluation among students who achieved in various status systems. Some schools rewarded academic achievement, some athletic accomplishment, some social success. Table A gives an example of the approach.]

TABLE A. Negative Self-evaluations of Boys Named Only As Best
Athletes in Schools Where the Rewards for Athletic Achievement
Are High and in Those Where the Rewards Are Lower

	High (4, 5, 6, 7, 9)	Low (0, 1, 2, 3, 8)
Per cent wanting to be someone different	9.1	15.4
Number of cases	(132)	(91)

SOME OF the most explicit goals of high schools are those having to do with matters of the mind: transmission of knowledge, development of mental skills, and inculcation of positive attitudes toward learning. Effects of the adolescent system of some of these matters are the concern of this chapter. . . . The effects shown will be mere indications of broader effects of these social systems.

Effects Upon the Image of Intellectual Activity

. . . The leading crowds of boys want more to be remembered as star athletes, less as brilliant students, than do the student bodies as a whole. Similarly, the leading crowds of girls were oriented away from thinking of themselves as brilliant students, and were oriented toward, in some schools, the image of activities leader, and in others, the image of most popular. . . .

This means that the social elites of these high schools are less willing to see themselves as engaging in intellectual activity, and find the idea of being seen as "intellectuals" more repugnant, than do those who are outside the leading crowds. By extrapolation to adulthood, these same social elites will be similarly oriented away from anything with a strong stamp of intellectual

Reprinted in part with permission from Chapter IX of *The Adolescent Society: The Social Life of the Teenager and Its Impact on Education* (copyright 1961 by the Free Press, a Division of the Macmillan Company, New York).

activity upon it. Such extrapolation is perhaps not too far-fetched, because this research includes not only small-town schools, part of whose leading crowds will remain in the town, and not only working-class schools, whose leading crowds will be a social elite only to their working-class constituency, but also urban middle-class schools—and, with Executive Heights, an upper-middle-class school that trains the children of some of the larger society's social elite. . . . The leading crowds in this last school are even more oriented away from the "brilliant student" image than are the leading crowds of other schools, with less than 10 per cent of the boys and 1 per cent of the girls in the leading crowd wanting to be remembered as brilliant students.[1]

Even if this study included only leading crowds that would never become the social elite of the larger society, the matter would still be important. For they nevertheless come to be the elites of the towns and cities in which they remain, and thus become the "grassroots" leaders of attitudes toward intellectual activities.

Most of the post-high-school consequences of the leading crowd's wanting to be remembered as brilliant students can only be conjectured, but from one outside source has come evidence of an important consequence. In a study of graduate students in American universities [2] a question was asked of each graduate student in the sample: "Were you a member of the leading crowd when you were in high school?" He could classify himself as a member of a leading crowd, as a member of another crowd but not a leading crowd, as a member of no crowd, or as an "outsider." These students were also asked whether they regarded themselves as intellectuals. Table 1 below shows the proportion who considered themselves intellectuals as a function of the crowd they were in—or not in.

The result is clear: even among the highly select group of high-school students who end up in graduate school studying for an advanced degree, those who were in the leading crowd in high school are slightly less likely to consider themselves intellectuals, although, by any definition, they are surely engaging in intellectual activity.

One might dismiss this result with the notion that anyone in a leading crowd, whatever the school's values, will less likely think of himself as an intellectual than someone on the outside. However, foreign students, who had attended high school in Europe or somewhere else outside this country, were included in this same graduate-student study.[3] Table 2 shows their self-images as a function of whether or not they were in the leading crowd.

Among students who had attended foreign high schools, there are two differences from the Americans: the average level of considering themselves intellectuals is higher; but most crucial to our analysis, those who were members of the leading crowd in their high school were slightly *more* likely to consider themselves intel-

TABLE 1.   Self-image as an Intellectual Among American Graduate Students, in Relation to Their Social Location in High School

	Members of Leading Crowd	Members of Other Crowd	Not Members of Any Crowd, or Outsider
Per cent who consider themselves definitely or in many ways an intellectual	43	48	49
Number of cases	(859)	(725)	(570)

TABLE 2.   Self-image as an Intellectual Among Foreign Graduate Students in American Universities, in Relation to Their Social Location in High School

	Members of Leading Crowd	Members of Other Crowd	Not Members of Any Crowd, or Outsider
Per cent who consider themselves definitely or in many ways an intellectual	63	42	59
Number of cases	(126)	(114)	(125)

lectuals than those who were not members of the leading crowd—exactly opposite to the result for graduates of American high schools.

To go back to the high-school level, are there any differences in the intellectual images—wanting to be remembered as a brilliant student—among those schools where the adolescent culture rewards such activity and those where it does not? Table 3 shows, for boys, the proportions wanting to be remembered as a brilliant student among all students, and among those mentioned ten or more times as members of the leading crowd; in the schools where schol-

arship is more rewarded and in those where it is less rewarded.

The boys as a whole more often want to be remembered as brilliant students in "high" schools; and the boys in the leading crowds in these schools do also. Although, in both sets of schools, the members of the leading crowd less often want to be remembered as brilliant students than the school as a whole, this decrease is far less for the schools where there are more rewards for academic achievement. . . . [4]

Notes

1. This almost complete absence of wanting to be remembered as a brilliant student is both more surprising and more disconcerting than in the other schools. For this leading crowd is about 50 per cent Jewish (56 per cent for boys, 62 per cent for girls, if only those with 10 or more choices are included; 41 per cent for boys, 49 per cent for girls if all with 2 or more choices are included); in view of the traditional Jewish cultural emphasis on education and learning, one would not expect this. These results strongly suggest the decay of this tradition, and its replacement by the values of the dominant Protestant social elite, among those Jews whose mobility brings them into this elite. It is very likely that the parents of these Jewish children, many of whom had lower-middle-class origins, themselves wanted to be thought of as brilliant students when in school, rather than as star athletes or activities leaders, as their sons and daughters now do.

2. This study is being conducted by James A. Davis, at the National Opinion Research Center of the University of Chicago. I am

TABLE 3.   Per cent of Boys Wanting To Be Remembered as a Brilliant Student, in Schools Where the Rewards for Academic Achievement Are Higher and in Those Where These Rewards Are Lower

Boys	All Boys	Those Mentioned 10 Times or More as Members of Leading Crowd
"High" schools (1, 2, 3, 5, 7, 8)	35.1%	24.0%
Number of cases	(2,781)	(108)
"Low" schools (0, 4, 6, 9)	27.2%	9.5%
Number of cases	(1,578)	(74)

grateful to NORC, to Professor Davis, and to Professor Jan Hajda, who carried out the analysis reported here, for permission to use these data.

3. The analysis was done by a sociologist, Jan Hajda, who had himself attended a high school in Czechoslovakia. He was puzzled at the results of Table 1 when he found them, for, on the basis of his own high school experience, he had expected those from the lead-ing crowds to more often think of themselves as intellectuals.

4. The difference still exists, though it is attenuated, when Executive Heights, where so few in the leading crowd want to be remembered as brilliant students, is excluded. Excluding Executive Heights, the percentages are 29.7 and 15.8 for the student bodies, and leading crowd groups, respectively, in the "low" group of schools.

30. High School Climates and Plans for Entering College

JOHN A. MICHAEL*

EACH YEAR America's high school seniors decide whether or not they will continue their education by attending college. Scholastic ability and family background together form the traditional foundation for analyses of college attendance. The National High School Study directed by Natalie Rogoff at the Bureau of Applied Social Research confirms the usual finding that a youngster's decision to attend college is determined to a large extent by his ability and family background.

But the amount of college attendance varies radically from one high school to another. Some schools seldom produce a college-bound senior, while others contribute a disproportionately large number of seniors to the college rolls. The fluctuation of college-entrance rates from school to school is not adequately explained by inspecting variations in the individual attributes, ability and family background.

Rather, the amount of college attendance is related to the high school's characteristics, which are independent of the attributes of any senior attending that school.

In this paper we shall focus on the larger social milieu in which the high schools and their seniors are located, since we hypothesize that the milieu influences the decision to go to college, in addition to any personal factors connected with a youngster. It is not enough to locate differences in the larger social environment: these differences must be patterned so that different social environs, which we term "high school climates," exhibit distinctive college attendance rates. We start by comparing seniors of similar abilities and family backgrounds but of differing high school climates. For each climate we shall observe their propensities for attending college. If their propensities vary from one climate to another, we shall have discovered another

* The author is with the Research Center of the New York School of Social Work, Columbia University. This paper may be identified as publication No. A-315 of the Bureau of Applied Social Research, Columbia University.

Reprinted with permission from the *Public Opinion Quarterly,* 25 (1961), pp. 585–95 (copyright 1961 by Princeton University Press).

determinant of college attendance in addition to ability and family background.

At the same time, let us consider a second type of analysis. This approach points to the differential efficacy with which ability or family background operates in predicting college attendance.[1] For example, Kahl's study in the suburbs of Boston shows the family to be almost twice as important as ability, yet Sewell's Wisconsin data suggest ability to be three times as important as family background.[2] The seemingly contradictory findings of Kahl and Sewell may be understood if, instead of asking whether family background or ability is more important, we ask in what high school climates is one more important than the other. Here our emphasis shifts from our first approach—locating different high school climates to account for varying propensities for going to college among similarly circumstanced seniors—to an investigation of the relative importance of ability and family background from one climate to another.

Thus, by simultaneously inspecting the different combinations of individual characteristics in varying high school climates, we shall illustrate the impact of the larger social milieu on seniors' college plans. For each climate, we shall measure the contributions made by family background and scholastic ability in order to locate those social conditions under which both individual characteristics exert great or little influence, or under which one plays the major, the other a minor, role. In doing this, we not only achieve greater power in predicting the educational future of high school seniors, but we also identify those social contexts in which individuals with given characteristics are advantaged or disadvantaged.

In a nationally representative sample of over 500 public high schools, information on the career and college plans of more than 35,000 seniors was collected in 1955 by the Educational Testing Service.[3] At the same time the Educational Testing Service administered a twenty-item scholastic aptitude test. The quartile score on this test is used to represent ability.[4] In addition, seniors provided family-background data such as their fathers' occupation and education and whether their older siblings attended college. From this information we constructed an index of the socio-educational status of the family and classified students by five family types. Furthermore, from the principals of these schools Educational Testing Service also collected descriptive materials concerning school size, location, personnel, course offerings, and consulting services.[5] To depict the school setting more fully, we abstracted supplementary data from national and state school directories, other published surveys, and census sources describing the towns and countries in which the schools are located.

The Definition and Description of the High School Climate

What indicator would most accurately portray the educational milieu? High schools can be classified in many ways. Classroom size; the number of pupils enrolled; the quality and size of the teaching and professional staff; and differential emphasis on a general, academic (college preparatory), or vocational curriculum are only a few of many possible characterizations of a high school. Each of these educational features contributes to the high school climate and either enhances or depresses the college-entrance rate of the seniors.

The community context is also a relevant aspect of the high school climate. The larger independent cities and suburbs have proportionately more well-educated families of higher occupational standing than do small towns, villages, and rural areas. The distribution of such characteristics in the community determines the social-class composition of the high schools. Libraries, museums, and other cultural facilities, as well as financial resources, are also differentially present in various types of communities.

Although the precise nature of the relationship between the school and its community is still under investigation, there can be no doubt that school and community characteristics are highly correlated. Schools with desirable educational features are located in communities with more cultural facilities.

One of the criteria for choosing an indicator of the high school climate is that it be related to both high school and community attributes. More specifically, our indicator should reflect the structural conditions under which a high school operates. The proportion of the senior class in the top two family-status quintiles satisfies our stated criteria and is the indicator selected.

Our sample of high schools is classified into five climates, as follows: schools with less than 20 per cent of the senior class in the top two family-status quintiles are designated the first (I) high school climate; schools with 20 to 29 per cent of their seniors from such homes are the second (II) high school climate; schools with 30 to 39 per cent and 40 to 49 per cent of their senior classes in the top two family-status quintiles are called the third (III) and fourth (IV) climates, respectively; and, finally, schools with a majority of their senior class coming from privileged homes represent the fifth (V) high school climate.

First let us examine the high schools in each setting to see in what relevant ways they differ. After this, we shall determine the effect that the high school climate has on youngsters' scholastic abilities and college plans. Last, we shall discuss the relative importance of scholastic ability and family background in each of the five school contexts.

The characteristics of high schools, their

communities, and their senior classes are presented in Table 1. The attributes selected for this table are all highly correlated with going to college. They include the presence of a community library with 5,000 or more volumes, school accreditation, and the presence of one or more guidance counselors. College attendance is also higher as the proportion of the senior class enrolled in an academic (college-preparatory) curriculum increases, as the proportion of the senior class cognizant of major scholarship programs increases, and as the proportion of the senior class stating his best friend plans college increases. Finally, the more seniors there are with at least six semesters of mathematics, the higher the propensity to go to college.

The five high school climates display great differences in all these attributes. Schools are most likely to have the characteristics associated with college attendance if they have a majority of the senior class in the top two family-status quintiles, the fifth context. In contrast, those schools with less than 20 per cent of their senior class coming from such privileged backgrounds exhibit a consistent lack of such characteristics. With few exceptions, the fourth, third, and second high school climates stand in an intermediary position between the two extremes, in the expected order.

High School Climates and Ability

A school possessing or lacking characteristics of the type shown in Table 1 would certainly influence its pupils' selection of vocational and educational goals. One direct way in which a school affects its student body is to inflate or depress the level of scholastic ability. Schools in the fifth context, for example, have two-thirds (67 per cent) of their students scoring in the top half of the scholastic aptitude test. In successive climates the proportion of

TABLE 1.   Characteristics of High Schools, Their Communities, and Senior Classes, According to High School Climate

	HIGH SCHOOL CLIMATE					
	V	*IV*	*III*	*II*	*I*	*All Climates*
Family status quintile:						
5 (high)	2,711	1,783	1,351	520	204	6,569
4	1,715	1,827	1,842	964	444	6,792
3	1,219	1,637	1,842	1,179	679	6,556
2	1,053	1,805	2,449	1,795	1,228	8,330
1 (low)	539	1,222	1,938	1,542	1,948	7,189
All family-status quintiles	7,237	8,274	9,422	6,000	4,503	35,436
Percentage of schools:						
With a community library of 5,000 or more volumes	76	75	65	50	32	56
Which are accredited*	61	70	44	26	13	38
With 1 or more guidance counselors	45	43	32	20	14	28
With a majority of the senior class:						
Enrolled in the academic curriculum	35	13	7	8	7	12
Hearing of 1 or more major scholarship programs	79	77	70	44	29	55
Saying their best friend plans to attend college	89	84	72	46	47	63
With at least ⅓ of senior class with 6 or more semesters of math	71	67	57	47	41	54
Number of schools	62	79	122	123	132	518

* For the six New England states and California we have used state accreditation; for all other states it was possible to use regional accreditation.

seniors scoring in the top half of this twenty-item test drops to 55, 48, 41, and 29 per cent. Although this is quite a substantial difference between the fifth and first setting (38 per cent), we cannot attribute all this difference to the impact of the school milieu. It is well known that scholastic ability is highly correlated with family background, so that the proportions above may merely be reflecting the fact that the fifth climate is comprised of many more seniors from privileged homes. Indeed, 72 per cent of the youngsters in our highest family-status quintile did score in the top half of the scholastic aptitude test. This proportion drops to 56, 48, 44, and 33 per cent for each successive family-status quintile. The range between the highest and lowest family status quintile is 39 per cent, a difference almost identical to that produced by high school climate.

To determine the effect of both the senior's family background and his high school on his ability, we present both variables simultaneously in Table 2. Here we see that the percentage scoring in the top half of the aptitude test ranges from 78 to 22. Within each high school climate, a larger percentage of the high-family-status seniors achieve scores above the median than do low-family-status seniors. But for any particular family-status quintile, a larger percentage of the high-family-status high school climate achieve high scores than do their counterparts in the first climate. The high school markedly shapes the talents of children from all backgrounds. But the increase in the percentage scoring

TABLE 2.   Percentage of Seniors Scoring in the Top Half of the Scholastic Aptitude Test, According to Socioeducational Status of the Family and High School Climate

| | HIGH SCHOOL CLIMATE | | | | | |
FAMILY STATUS QUINTILE	V	IV	III	II	I	All Climates
5 (high)	78	74	66	57	44	72
4	67	59	51	47	37	56
3	62	51	45	46	32	48
2	58	48	46	38	31	44
1 (low)	47	39	37	32	22	33
All quintiles	67	55	48	41	29	50

above the median is disproportionately favorable to the highest-family-status seniors: their proportion scoring high is elevated from 44 to 78 per cent, an improvement of 34 per cent, while the lowest family-status quintile is raised only 25 per cent.

Thus far this seems to tell a story of the rich getting richer. But one other aspect of this table should be considered. The lowest-family-status seniors in the fifth high school climate benefit from their superior educational environment, with 47 per cent of them scoring in the top half. Compare this with only 44 per cent of the highest-family-status youngsters in the first high school climate scoring above the median. Even though more seniors from the higher family statuses attain better scores within any single social context, the differences between the high school climates is sufficiently great that even the lowest-socioeducational-status youngsters in the most favorable social setting surpass the performance of the highest-socioeducational-status seniors in the least favorable context.

Using this evidence, we tentatively conclude that the educational milieu has at least as great an effect on a youngster's ability as does his own social background. We have taken the precaution of dividing both family-status quintiles and high school climates into five groups, with roughly the same number of seniors in each, so that we give neither family status nor school climate an advantage.[6] But there may still be some doubt as to whether the two cells in our table (44 and 47 per cent) are truly representative of a pattern which exists in all other cells of Table 2. How do we know that these two proportions don't just *happen* to reflect a margin of superiority on behalf of the school climate over family background? Perhaps by considering the amount of variation in ability which is attributable to class and context, using a measure based on the entire table, we would find a contradictory pattern, with family background being given the edge over the social setting in shaping ability.

To explore this notion, we employ a measure of association that will express the relations to ability in terms of a single value for family status and a single value for high school context. The statistical technique used here is called "effect parameters," a measure developed by James Coleman.[7] Computing this measure, we find that .284 of the variation in ability is attributable to the senior's family background, .292 to high school climate. Although the margin of difference between the two is small, it corroborates our original statement that the high school climate is at least as influential as a senior's family background for his scoring in the top half of the scholastic aptitude test.

Since this finding is at odds with the hundreds of others in the literature dealing with the relationship between family background and ability, we shall investigate it even further. Remember that we have been examining the distribution of those seniors who scored in the top *half* of the aptitude test. For college purposes, it is more realistic to consider the distribution of only those seniors who scored in the top *quarter* of the aptitude test. This is presented as Table 3.

Again there are vast differences between family backgrounds and high school climates, with the percentages ranging from 51 to only 5. In many respects the pattern is similar to that shown in Table 2, except that this time only 17 per cent of the lowest-family-status seniors in the fifth high school climate score in the top quarter, whereas 22 per cent of the highest-socioeducational-status seniors from the first climate do as well. Now the pattern of influence on ability is reversed, with class having a 5 percentage point edge over the high school context. Again, to ensure that this is a general pattern throughout the entire table and not just idiosyncratic to these two particular cells, we compute the effect parameters. The amount of variation in ability which is attributable to class is .252, while the amount for the school climate is only .180. This confirms our finding that a senior's socioeducational status is more important than the high school climate in

shaping ability at the top quartile level of the nation.

In conclusion, what can be said about ability is this: A youngster's family background and his educational milieu are equally determinate of above-average aptitudes. One shapes ability as much as the other. But very high aptitudes are determined more by a youngster's family background than by his larger social setting. Although the length of time a child spends in a high school climate would refine this discussion even further (in that those low-family-status youngsters attending schools of a superior educational quality for a longer period of time would be expected to overcome the top-quartile barrier), we have no data on the length of residence and school attendance and hence cannot explore this problem further.

Family Background, Ability and College Plans

Now we are prepared to investigate the determinants of college attendance. Earlier we stated that class and ability are the traditional predictors of whether or not a senior will continue his education beyond the high school level. Our data confirm this, with 71 per cent of the highest socioeducational-status seniors planning to attend college. In successive family-status quintiles,

TABLE 3.   Percentage of Seniors Scoring in the Top Quarter of the Scholastic Aptitude Test, According to Socioeducational Status of the Family and High School Climate

FAMILY STATUS QUINTILE	HIGH SCHOOL CLIMATE					
	V	IV	III	II	I	All Climates
5 (high)	51	45	39	31	22	44
4	33	30	24	22	15	27
3	31	23	19	17	13	22
2	25	20	19	16	12	18
1 (low)	17	15	14	11	5	11
All quintiles	37	27	22	17	10	24

this percentage drops to 48, 35, 27, and 26. Ability percentages display a similar trend: from the top to bottom aptitude levels, the percentages of college-bound seniors are 65, 43, 32, and 24. Although it might seem relevant now to show the college propensities of every family status for each ability level, we shall not do this here. Our investigation differs from previous college analyses in that we are also concerned with the contribution that the educational setting makes to college planning. And, indeed, the high-school climate does have an impact: from the fifth to first context the college attendance rates are 57, 43, 38, 29 and 30 per cent. Table 4 shows the proportion of those seniors scoring in the top quarter of the aptitude test who plan to go to college, by family status and high school climate.[8]

As can be seen in this table, equally talented youngsters exhibit diverse educational futures. The proportions planning to attend college in this most talented group range from 86 to 38 per cent. For any given family status, the fifth high school climate displays a consistently higher propensity to go to college than any other. But the differences between climates are relatively small when compared with the strik-ing differences in the ability picture seen in Tables 2 and 3. The college rates of the highest socioeducational-status seniors vary only 9 per cent from the fifth to the second high school climate, with any of their proportions being greater than that of the youngsters in the fourth family-status category. Although the differences between climates are small, the differences within any one climate are quite marked. Propensities to enter college in the fifth high school climate vary 29 per cent, and in the first climate, 36 per cent. Evidently, the financial ability to procure a college education suppresses any significant effects the educational milieu might have on going to college.

Table 4 leaves little doubt that college attendance is heavily determined by social class. But since we have looked at only one ability level, the true force of ability remains unstated in Table 4. Abiding by our earlier decision, we will not present the effect of aptitude and family status simultaneously for each of the five high school contexts, but, instead, for each climate, we will present a single value for ability and a single value for family status, using the effect-parameters measure. This has the virtue of being less cumbersome, although

TABLE 4.   Percentage of Seniors Scoring in the Top Quarter of the Scholastic Aptitude Test Who Plan to Attend College, According to Socioeconomic Status of the Family and High-School Climate

	HIGH SCHOOL CLIMATE					
FAMILY STATUS QUINTILE	V	IV	III	II	I	All Climates
5 (high)	86	81	82	77	80*	83
4	74	67	68	54	72*	68
3	63	57	53	48	48*	56
2	57	46	49	40	38	47
1 (low)	57*	48	46	45	44	47
All quintiles	77	65	62	51	50	65

* With such a large sample, most of the proportions are based on 100 or more cases. There are four exceptions to this, however, since aptitude scores, family status, and high school climate are interrelated. The 80%, 72%, 48%, and 57% are the exceptions: the number of cases for these cells are 45, 67, 90, and 94, respectively.

TABLE 5. Average Percentage Differences in College Rates between All
Socioeducational Statuses and All Scholastic Ability Levels, According to
High School Climate

AVERAGE PERCENTAGE DIFFERENCES IN COLLEGE RATES	*HIGH SCHOOL CLIMATE*					
	V	*IV*	*III*	*II*	*I*	*All Climates*
Between all socioeducational statuses	.350	.320	.350	.322	.312	.358
Between all scholastic ability levels	.380	.336	.336	.294	.238	.326
Total differences	.730	.656	.686	.616	.550	.684

some of the richness of the data is lost. The average percentage differences in college rates are shown in Table 5.

For the entire sample of seniors, the average percentage difference for family status is .358, while that for ability is .326. For the national sample, then, a senior's family background is slightly more influential in his college plans than his ability. Even so, the influence of class is greater in some climates than others. Socioeducational status plays the least effective role in that high school climate comprised largely of youngsters from less privileged homes. Here the amount of variation is only .312, whereas it is .350 in the high school context having a majority of seniors from professional and businessmen's homes.

Ability similarly shows an average percentage difference of only .238 in college rates in the first high school climate, whereas it increases to .380 in the fifth climate. Interestingly enough, that social context most influential in shaping youngster's talents is the same climate which exacts the most importance from their ability standing. (Remember that the fifth high school climate had the highest median ability level for all students, no matter what their social origins.) At the same time, ability plays the more volatile role in college attendance in that it varies more than does family background. In the first three high school climates, social class is more predictive of one's educational future than

is one's talent. But the fourth and fifth climates reverse this pattern, with ability more predictive than class.

Finally, Table 5 reveals the total amount of variation in college attendance that can be accounted for by both ability and social class. These two personal attributes are strongest in the fifth climate and, combined, they play a much greater role than they play together in the first climate. Seventy-three per cent of the variation in college attendance is accounted for by the two personal characteristics in the fifth climate; contrast this with only 55 per cent of the variation accounted for in the first climate. The strength of our independent predictors, class and ability, vary considerably, not only in relation to each other, but in relation to themselves from context to context.[9]

Summary

We have seen that college attendance rates are best predicted by taking into account the individual characteristics, ability and family background, although the educational milieu does exert some influence. When we consider the top half of the aptitude distribution only, the high school climate has as much impact in shaping its seniors' ability as has family background. On the other hand, class is still the dominant predictor of whether or not a youngster will score in the top quarter of the aptitude distribution.

While considering the factors affecting college attendance rates, we cited Kahl's study, in which social background showed twice as much influence as ability, and Sewell's data, which showed ability as being three times as important as social background. Our own national sample falls squarely between these two earlier studies, with these individual attributes playing a roughly equal role.

The efficacy of the combined individual attributes as a predictor of college attendance is altered by the social context, however. The senior's social class and ability are much more predictive of his educational future in the superior educational milieu than in any other social context. In that fifth high school climate, which shapes proportionately more capable youngsters, ability accounts for the greatest portion of variation in college attendance. Conversely, a senior's social class is more predictive of his educational future in the first climate, the social context which develops fewest talented youths. By taking both the high school climate and individual attributes into account, we increase our ability to predict whether a senior will decide to go to college and, at the same time, understand more fully why similar individuals in different environments arrive at different decisions.

Notes

1. In her article, "Public Schools and Equality of Opportunity," *Journal of Educational Sociology,* 33 (1960), pp. 252–59, Natalie Rogoff has formalized this explanation into three types of patterns: the *radical* pattern, in which ability alone predicts college attendance; the *conservative* pattern, in which class alone predicts college attendance; and the *moderate* pattern, in which class and ability equally predict college attendance.

2. See Joseph A. Kahl, "Educational and Occupational Aspirations of 'Common Man'

Boys," *Harvard Educational Review,* 23 (1953), pp. 186–203; and William H. Sewell, Archie O. Haller, and Murray A. Straus, "Social Status and Educational and Occupational Aspirations," *American Sociological Review,* 22 (1957), pp. 67–73.

3. The self-administered questionnaire elicited seniors' college intentions; a followup study indicates a high correlation between their plans and actually going to college.

4. Since seniors' test scores are highly correlated with their academic standing, we have used ability and aptitude interchangeably throughout this paper.

5. The following reports have been prepared by the Educational Testing Service: Charles C. Cole, Jr., *Encouraging Scientific Talent* (College Entrance Examination Board, 1956); Glen Stice, W. G. Mollenkopf, and W. S. Torgerson, "Background Factors and College-going Plans among High Aptitude Public High School Seniors" (Educational Testing Service, 1956); and "Background Factors Relating to College Plans and College Enrollment among Public High School Students" (Educational Testing Service, 1957).

6. The draft of this paper presented at the AAPOR Conference contained three contexts and two social classes, giving high school climate an even greater influence, but doing so at an unfair advantage. I am indebted to Natalie Rogoff for her incisive remarks on this matter.

7. That portion of effect parameters in which we are interested here turns out to be the average percentage difference. A short example from Table 2 will show how it is computed. Within each high school climate starting with the fifth, to obtain a single value for the effect of family status, we subtract 47 from 78, 39 from 74, 37 from 66, 32 from 57, and 22 from 44. This gives us percentage differences of 31, 35, 29, 25, and 22 respectively. Summing these percentage differences and dividing by 5 (N), we obtain an average percentage difference of 28.4 per cent (or .284) attributable to socioeducational status. Similarly, to compute the amount of variation attributable to high school context, we subtract the percentage for each class across climates, like this: 44 from 78, 37 from 67, 32 from 62, 31 from 58, and 22 from 47. This results in an average percentage difference of 29.2 (or .292) attributable to social context. The sum of the average percentage differences (.284 and .292) gives the total amount of variation within ability scores that is attributable to both socioeducational status and context. In our sample this constitutes over half the variation,

being .576. For a full discussion on the computation and logic of this technique, which is parallel in nature to multiple regression coefficients for continuous variables, see James Coleman, "Multivariate Analysis" (Baltimore: Johns Hopkins University, September 1958, mimeographed).

8. The patterns of college attendance in other quartile levels are similar to that found in the top quartile.

9. In the calculations of average percentage differences, we have used four ability groupings and five class groupings. This means that family background has been given a slight advantage over ability. Had the same number of groupings for both variables been used to calculate the effect parameters, we would expect the influence of ability to be somewhat greater than it is here.

31. Neighborhood Context and College Plans *

WILLIAM H. SEWELL AND J. MICHAEL ARMER

NUMEROUS studies have appeared in recent years attempting to account for educational aspirations of high school seniors. To date, most research effort has been concentrated upon individual and family background attributes. Of all the factors studied, sex, intelligence, and socioeconomic status have been most frequently, consistently and clearly associated with educational aspirations.[1] More recently the social environments or contexts in which individuals live have been examined for their bearing on educational aspirations. Such specific social context variables as rural-urban residence, peer group associations, the socioeconomic composition of the high schools, and the socioeconomic composition of the community or neighborhood have been sug-

gested by a number of investigators.[2] The present paper reports an empirical examination of the influence of one of these social contexts, neighborhood socioeconomic status, on the college plans of high school youth.

Speculation regarding the influence of residential segregation on the educational aspirations of youth has gained considerable currency within recent years. Much of the stimulus for the view may be traced to popular assessments of American education by various educational authorities. Especially noteworthy among these assessments is James Bryant Conant's *Slums and Suburbs,* in which he draws a striking contrast between the educational aspirations of public high school students in prosperous sub-

* This research program is currently financed by a grant (M-6275) from the National Institutes of Health, U.S. Public Health Service. The basic survey from which the original data were obtained was conducted by J. Kenneth Little under a contract with the U.S. Office of Education. (See J. Kenneth Little, *A Statewide Inquiry into Decisions of Youth about Education beyond High School* [Madison, Wis.: School of Education, University of Wisconsin, 1958].) For the present paper, data for the Milwaukee public high schools were recoded, and new indexes were constructed. The writers wish to acknowledge the assistance of Vimal P. Shah, the critical suggestions of Archie O. Haller, and the computational services of the Numerical Analysis Laboratory of the University of Wisconsin.
Reprinted with permission from the *American Sociological Review,* 31 (April 1966), pp. 159–68 (copyright 1966 by the American Sociological Association).

urbs and in city slums.[3] Natalie Rogoff (Ramsoy) has provided the most explicit and succinct statement of the community context thesis in the following passage.

> . . . let it be granted that the various social classes are not randomly distributed among the diverse sizes and types of communities in the United States today. . . . It follows that each of the social classes will be more heavily concentrated in some kinds of community environments than in others, and that communities will vary in the predominant or average social-class affiliation of their residents. Such structural differences may set in motion both formal arrangements —such as school, library, and general cultural facilities in the community—and informal mechanisms, such as normative climates or model levels of social aspiration, which are likely to affect *all* members of the community to some extent—parents and children, upper, middle, and working classes.[4]

Although Rogoff's point of reference is communities, the argument applies equally well to school districts, neighborhoods, and other subcommunity areas which are also differentiated by ecological segregation. Despite the intuitive and authoritative evidence in behalf of these ideas, little empirical research attention has been paid to the problem at either the community or neighborhood level.

The most direct test of the thesis that community context influences the aspirations of youth comes from studies by the senior author.[5] This research, based on a large random sample of Wisconsin high school seniors, indicates that the community context, as measured by size of community (Rogoff's measure), is clearly associated with the educational and occupational plans of youth. However, when sex, family socioeconomic status, and measured intelligence are controlled, the original relationship between community size and educational aspiration is greatly reduced. This permits the tentative conclusion that differences in aspirations may be due more to differences in the sex, socioeconomic, and ability composition of high schools than to normative differences in community contexts. Of course, tests employing more direct indices of community socioeconomic status and normative climates are necessary before more definitive conclusions can be drawn regarding the viability of the thesis as applied to communities.

On the neighborhood level, Alan B. Wilson, in a study of high school boys in the San Francisco Bay-Oakland area, reported a positive relationship between residential segregation, as measured by social class composition of schools, and educational aspirations.[6] This relationship was not eliminated when either family socioeconomic status or measured intelligence was controlled. Since he did not control for these variables simultaneously, it is not known whether their joint effects would have been sufficient to eliminate the association between school status and educational aspirations. Moreover, the nonrandom nature of the sample of students and the purposive selection of high and low status schools further reduce the dependability and generality of his findings.

Similar sampling limitations also handicap Ralph Turner's study of Los Angeles area high schools in regard to the influence of neighborhood environments on ambition. Turner indexed ambition by means of a composite score on occupational, educational, and material aspirations, and based his measurement of neighborhood environment on the socioeconomic status composition of the high school class. Using these measures he obtained correlations between neighborhood context and ambition of $+0.16$ and $+0.12$, for males and females respectively, when the effects of family socioeconomic status and intelligence were simultaneously partialed.[7] Unfortunately, since correlations using educational aspiration as the dependent variable were not presented, the relevance of his findings to the present problem is limited.

John A. Michael, in an article based on a national study of high schools, focused directly on educational aspiration, but his data are limited in other ways.[8] He argued that college plans of high school seniors are related to school climate (also indexed by the socioeconomic composition of the senior class) independently of the socioeconomic status of the student's family or his ability. However, his data showing the relationship of school socioeconomic status to college plans with family status controlled, using only students in the top quarter in scholastic aptitude, fail to provide clear support for the assertion. The differences in college plans for schools of different status levels are realtively small and suggest that the socioeconomic status and intelligence of students may account for most of the relationship. Michael's evidence is also limited by the fact that the only relevant data presented in his article are based on the top ability group and consequently do not indicate the influence that school status has on the aspirations of other less able students.

The dependability of the evidence in the studies by Wilson, Turner, and Michael is further weakened by the fact that there is an element of contamination in the neighborhood or school environment variable measured by school socioeconomic status because both the school status and the family status indexes are based on the same information. Carolyn Sherif's study of the association of educational aspiration with the social rank of three urban areas in Oklahoma City avoids this problem, but the author fails to describe her social rank index of urban areas or to control for the effects of sex, intelligence, or socioeconomic status of the teenagers in her study.[9]

Because of limitations in the research reported by these investigators, the question of the influence of residential segregation within large and complex communities on the educational aspiration of students, over and above the influence of the other

known sources, remains largely unanswered.[10]

The essential arguments and expectations of the thesis may be summarized as follows. Much evidence has accumulated to indicate that ecological processes in large cities result in socioeconomic segregation. It has also been shown that school segregation is in large part a consequence of residential segregation.[11] Since high school enrollment areas represent functioning subcommunities for high school youth within larger urban complexes, it may be expected that informal mechanisms, such as normative climates or modal levels of aspiration, would emerge and would have some pervasive influence on the aspirations of all youth residing in the neighborhood, regardless of the socioeconomic status or ability levels of the youth. In other words, the prediction would be that the socioeconomic status of the high school district—since it presumably reflects the shared norms and aspirations of its members—would have an important effect on the educational aspirations of its youth over and above that of family socioeconomic status or individual ability. It is the purpose of this study to test this hypothesis using elaboration techniques and correlation analysis.[12]

The Data

The principal source of the data on which this study is based is a survey of all high school seniors in public and private schools in Wisconsin in 1957.[13] The total universe of public high school seniors in the Milwaukee metropolitan area (3,999 students) is included in this analysis. Data pertaining to school district boundaries and school district socioeconomic status were obtained from the Wisconsin Department of Education and from census tract information in the 1960 Census for Milwaukee. Only public high school seniors are included in the analysis since there are no parochial high school districts strictly comparable with the public high school districts. Information was gathered from the students on a number of matters, including educational and vocational plans, socioeconomic status, and measured intelligence.

The County of Milwaukee was selected for study because it is the largest and most diverse metropolitan area in Wisconsin; its 1960 population was 1,036,041. It contains twenty public high schools: thirteen in the central city and seven in independent suburbs. The high school enrollment districts were selected as the basic unit for analysis of neighborhood context because they may be considered functional social areas within the larger community. This is true in the sense that a community of shared interests among students tends to form around the high school; students identify themselves with the school and its many curricular and noncurricular activities.

The index of socioeconomic status for each neighborhood (school enrollment district) is the proportion of males fourteen years and older living in the area who are employed in white-collar occupations. Since census figures are not reported for these areas, it was necessary to combine census tracts to fit as closely as possible the neighborhood boundaries as defined in this study. The neighborhood status for each student attending a given school is the percentage of white-collar workers in the area. The range in status was from 13 to 83 per cent for the twenty neighborhoods. For the cross-tabular analysis, these neighborhoods were divided into three neighborhood context categories: High, 41–83 per cent white-collar; Middle, 31–40 per cent white-collar; and Low, 13–30 per cent white-collar. The high category consists of four high status suburbs located on the northern and western borders of the city and two high status neighborhoods adjacent to them but within the city limits of Milwaukee. The low category includes five low status neighborhoods located in and surrounding the central business and lake-shore industrial district and two industrial suburbs. The seven middle status neighborhoods are scattered throughout the metropolitan area. Each of these three neighborhood categories is distinct from the others not only in occupational distribution but also in such other relevant criteria as the percentage of adults with one or more years of college education, the average value of homes, and the percentage of nonwhites. However, it should also be noted that the distinctions are not exaggerated in this study, as in much previous research, by purposely selecting only neighborhoods which differ widely in socioeconomic status.

The college plans variable is based on the senior student's statement that he definitely plans to enroll in a degree-granting college or university (or one whose credits are acceptable for advanced standing at the University of Wisconsin) upon graduation from high school.

The control variables in the analysis are sex, intelligence, and socioeconomic status. The intelligence variable is based on scores on the Henmon-Nelson Test of Mental Ability which is administered annually in

TABLE 1.   Percentage with College Plans by Neighborhood Status, for Male and Female Milwaukee Public High School Seniors

Neighborhood Status	Males		Females		Total	
Low	30.5	(524)	20.3	(743)	24.6	(1267)
Middle	39.7	(658)	21.1	(833)	29.3	(1491)
High	62.2	(572)	53.2	(669)	57.4	(1241)
Total	44.3	(1754)	30.4	(2245)	36.5	(3999)

all high schools in Wisconsin.[14] Students were divided into approximately equal thirds in measured intelligence: High (67 per cent percentile and above), Middle (38 per cent to 66 per cent percentile), and Low (37 per cent percentile and below). The socioeconomic status classification is based on a factor-weighted score of father's educational level, mother's educational level, an estimate of the funds the family could provide if the student were to attend college, the degree of sacrifice this would entail for the family, and the approximate wealth and income status of the student's family.[15] The students were divided into three categories of approximately equal size, labeled High, Middle, and Low in socioeconomic status.

Results

The central hypothesis of this study is that the neighborhood in which the student resides has an important influence on his educational plans in addition to that of his sex, measured intelligence, and the socioeconomic status of his family. To test this hypothesis the following questions should be considered: First, is neighborhood status associated with college plans? Second, does the association persist when the effects of sex, socioeconomic status, and intelligence are separately controlled? Third, does the relationship persist when these variables are simultaneously controlled? Fourth, how much variance does neighborhood status account for over and above that accounted for by sex, socioeconomic status, and intelligence?

The data bearing on the first question are given in summary form in Table 1. Less than one-fourth of the students in low-status neighborhoods plan on attending college, but more than one half of those in high-status neighborhoods have plans to attend college. Partialling out the effects of sex does not disturb the relationship except to reduce the difference between the low- and middle-status neighborhoods for girls and to increase the difference for boys.

Table 2 shows the influence of intelligence and socioeconomic status on college plans. It is apparent that each of these variables is related to college plans. (In terms of the percentage differences, *either* variable is more closely related to college plans than is the neighborhood context.) Those from high socioeconomic status families or of high intelligence are approximately three times as likely to plan on college as those of low socioeconomic status or of low intelligence. The same relationships hold for both boys and girls.

In Table 3, it will be noted that the lower status neighborhoods have a disproportion of females, students from lower socioeconomic status families, and students of lower

TABLE 2. Percentage with College Plans by Intelligence and Socioeconomic Status, for Male and Female Milwaukee Public High School Seniors

	Males		Females		Total	
Intelligence						
Low	24.0	(516)	13.1	(863)	17.2	(1379)
Middle	42.1	(620)	34.6	(741)	38.0	(1361)
High	63.4	(618)	49.0	(641)	56.1	(1259)
Socioeconomic Status						
Low	24.6	(561)	14.1	(799)	18.5	(1360)
Middle	41.2	(610)	28.2	(791)	33.8	(1401)
High	66.6	(583)	53.0	(655)	59.4	(1238)
Total	44.3	(1754)	30.4	(2245)	36.5	(3999)

measured intelligence—each of these would tend to reduce the proportion of those planning on college. Because sex, intelligence, and socioeconomic status—all of which are related to college plans—are also all related to neighborhood context, these variables must be controlled in assessing the influence of neighborhood context on college plans.

The effects of the control of sex and socioeconomic status, and of sex and intelligence, on the relationship between neighborhood context and college plans are given in Tables 4 and 5. Control of intelligence reduces the original relationship between neighborhood context and college plans for boys—but not greatly—and in no case is there a single reversal in the ordering. For girls, the control of intelligence results in the virtual elimination of differences between the low and middle neighborhood status groups, but there are still large differences between the college plans of girls in these two categories and those in the high-status neighborhoods—for all three intelligence levels. Thus controlling for intelligence does not explain the original differences either for boys or for girls.

Control for socioeconomic status (Table 5) greatly reduces the neighborhood differences in college plans for boys from low socioeconomic status families, but large neighborhood differences persist for middle and high socioeconomic status groups. For girls, the partialling tends to eliminate the differences between the low and middle status neighborhoods, but the differences between these two neighborhood categor-

TABLE 3.   Percentage Distribution of Sex, Intelligence, and Socioeconomic Status by Neighborhood Status, for Milwaukee Public High School Seniors

NEIGHBORHOOD STATUS	A. SEX		
	Male	Female	Total
Low	41.4	58.6	100.0 (1267)
Middle	44.1	55.9	100.0 (1491)
High	46.1	53.9	100.0 (1241)
Total	43.9	56.1	100.0 (3999)

	B. INTELLIGENCE		
	Low Third	Middle Third	High Third
Low	41.3	36.5	22.2	100.0 (1267)
Middle	37.5	28.9	33.6	100.0 (1491)
High	23.9	37.6	38.5	100.0 (1241)
Total	34.5	34.0	31.5	100.0 (3999)

	C. SOCIOECONOMIC STATUS		
	Low Third	Middle Third	High Third
Low	43.8	35.3	20.9	100.0 (1267)
Middle	37.4	38.6	24.0	100.0 (1491)
High	20.0	30.5	49.5	100.0 (1241)
Total	34.0	35.0	31.0	100.0 (3999)

TABLE 4.   Percentage with College Plans by Neighborhood Status and Intelligence, for Male and Female Milwaukee Public High School Seniors

NEIGHBORHOOD STATUS	INTELLIGENCE			
	Low	Middle	High	Total
Males				
Low	15.9 (195)	31.4 (207)	52.5 (122)	30.5 (524)
Middle	24.5 (212)	35.6 (191)	55.3 (255)	39.7 (658)
High	37.6 (109)	57.7 (222)	77.6 (241)	62.2 (572)
Total	24.0 (516)	42.1 (620)	63.4 (618)	44.3 (1754)
Females				
Low	8.8 (328)	26.6 (256)	34.0 (159)	20.3 (743)
Middle	8.1 (347)	21.7 (240)	39.0 (246)	21.1 (833)
High	29.8 (188)	55.5 (245)	69.5 (236)	53.2 (669)
Total	13.1 (863)	34.6 (741)	49.0 (641)	30.4 (2245)

ies and the high-status neighborhoods are marked—especially for girls from high socioeconomic status families. Thus, controlling for socioeconomic status does not explain the neighborhood differences in college plans either for boys or for girls.

Since the results of the partialling thus far leaves large unexplained differences in college plans of students from neighborhoods of varying status, the next step is to determine the effects of controlling sex, socioeconomic status, and intelligence simultaneously. The results of this operation produce, in effect, eighteen tables showing the percentage of students with college plans according to neighborhood context in all of the possible combinations of sex, socioeconomic status, and intelligence categories. These results are summarized in Table 6. For the boys, all but one of the subpopulations show marked reduction in the association of neighborhood status with college plans, and in several subpopulations there are reversals in the low and middle categories. The only remaining comparatively large difference between the high and low neighborhood contexts is for boys in the middle intelligence, high socioeconomic

TABLE 5.   Percentage with College Plans by Neighborhood Status and Socioeconomic Status, for Male and Female Milwaukee Public High School Seniors

NEIGHBORHOOD STATUS	SOCIOECONOMIC STATUS			
	Low	Middle	High	Total
Males				
Low	22.6 (217)	29.3 (188)	47.1 (119)	30.5 (524)
Middle	21.1 (232)	40.9 (259)	63.5 (167)	39.7 (658)
High	35.7 (112)	55.2 (163)	76.1 (297)	62.2 (572)
Total	24.6 (561)	41.2 (610)	66.6 (583)	44.3 (1754)
Females				
Low	11.8 (338)	22.8 (259)	35.6 (146)	20.3 (743)
Middle	11.7 (325)	20.8 (317)	37.7 (191)	21.1 (833)
High	25.7 (136)	45.6 (215)	70.1 (318)	53.2 (669)
Total	14.1 (799)	28.2 (791)	53.0 (655)	30.4 (2245)

TABLE 6. Percentage with College Plans, by Neighborhood Status, Socioeconomic Status, and Intelligence, for Male and Female Milwaukee Public High School Seniors

NEIGHBOR-HOOD STATUS	LOW SOCIOECONOMIC STATUS			MIDDLE SOCIOECONOMIC STATUS			HIGH SOCIOECONOMIC STATUS			Total
	Low Intelligence	Middle Intelligence	High Intelligence	Low Intelligence	Middle Intelligence	High Intelligence	Low Intelligence	Middle Intelligence	High Intelligence	
Males										
Low	13.0 (92)	23.8 (84)	41.5 (41)	13.3 (75)	36.5 (74)	46.2 (39)	32.1 (28)	36.7 (49)	69.1 (42)	30.5 (524)
Middle	11.9 (84)	18.3 (71)	33.8 (77)	25.9 (85)	40.3 (72)	53.9 (102)	46.5 (43)	54.2 (48)	79.0 (76)	39.7 (658)
High	27.3 (33)	25.0 (44)	57.1 (35)	31.6 (38)	54.8 (62)	69.8 (63)	52.6 (38)	71.6 (116)	86.0 (143)	62.2 (572)
Total	14.8 (209)	22.1 (199)	41.2 (153)	22.2 (198)	43.3 (208)	57.4 (204)	45.0 (109)	59.6 (213)	81.2 (261)	44.3 (1754)
Females										
Low	4.8 (167)	17.1 (105)	21.2 (66)	9.5 (116)	30.0 (90)	39.6 (53)	22.2 (45)	37.7 (61)	47.5 (40)	20.3 (743)
Middle	4.8 (168)	17.4 (86)	21.1 (71)	6.5 (123)	17.5 (97)	42.3 (97)	21.4 (56)	35.1 (57)	51.3 (78)	21.1 (833)
High	13.8 (58)	30.0 (40)	39.5 (38)	25.4 (71)	47.7 (86)	67.2 (58)	50.9 (59)	69.8 (119)	78.6 (140)	53.2 (669)
Total	6.1 (393)	19.5 (231)	25.1 (175)	11.9 (310)	31.1 (273)	48.6 (208)	32.5 (160)	53.2 (237)	65.5 (258)	30.4 (2245)

status category. In this instance, living in a higher status neighborhood is clearly related to college plans.

For the girls, the influence of neighborhood context is also reduced in all subpopulations except for those from high socioeconomic status families where the effects are about the same regardless of intelligence. In other words, girls living in higher status neighborhoods tend to have high educational aspirations, regardless of their measured ability, if they come from high socioeconomic status families. There continues to be some relationship between neighborhood context for girls from middle socioeconomic status families in the middle and high intelligence groups, and for highly intelligent girls from low-status families, but the association is not as large as in the preceding instances.

The results of this analysis suggest that neighborhood context is associated more with the educational aspirations of girls than boys and is strongest for girls from high socioeconomic status families. Why this should be true is not readily apparent from the analysis but deserves some speculation. One possible explanation is that those high socioeconomic status parents who place a high value on college education for their daughters are likely to insist on living in high status neighborhoods where their daughters can attend superior high schools, while those high status parents who do not emphasize college education for their daughters are more likely to remain in lower status neighborhoods. This explanation, of course, shifts the causal emphasis from the neighborhood back to the family, and is essentially a straight ecological argument which cannot be tested directly with the data of this study because no information is available on residential mobility. A second and somewhat more social-psychological speculation would be that, since high educational aspirations are generally less common for girls than for boys and are less salient in terms of future

occupational careers, girls are more susceptible to the influences of the social milieu than boys.[16] This might help to account for the apparently greater influence of neighborhood context on girls than on boys but would not explain why high socioeconomic status girls are particularly responsive to neighborhood context. Possibly the explanation is that the high status girls in the lower status neighborhood, who find themselves among associates with low aspirations, tend to reduce their own aspirations to the normative level of the group in order to be popular and possibly to improve their potential marriage opportunities with the boys in their neighborhood. The high status boys are less likely to be influenced by the desire for popularity and marriage prospects within the neighborhood group because of the salience of college education to their later career plans and because in any event they probably intend to defer marriage until they finish college. For girls from low and middle status families, college aspirations are not high, in any case, because of lack of encouragement and support from parents; consequently, even a favorable neighborhood context is not likely to have much effect on their educational aspirations. It should be emphasized again that this is only speculation—data are not available from our study to test this line of reasoning.

The results of partialling out the influence of sex, socioeconomic status, and intelligence indicate that neighborhood context—although it apparently has special significance for some subpopulations—probably does not make a large contribution to the explanation of differences in the educational plans of this group of high-school seniors. Actually the magnitude of its contribution has not been assessed either in the above tables or in other relevant studies. To provide a more accurate estimate of its contribution, the data have been analyzed using correlation techniques. The results of this analysis are as follows: The zero-order correlation (r) of neighborhood status with college plans is +0.299.[17] The multiple correlation (R) · of sex, socioeconomic status, and intelligence with college plans is +0.479 and the coefficient of determination (R^2) is 0.229, which means that these three background factors account for 22.9 per cent of the variance in college plans. The addition of neighborhood status as a predictor variable increases the multiple correlation (R) to +0.497 and the coefficient of determination (R^2) to 0.247. Thus, neighborhood status results in an absolute increase of 1.8 per cent in the explained variance of college plans beyond the effects of sex, socioeconomic status, and intelligence (.247 − .229 = .018 or 1.8 per cent). Consequently, it may be concluded that although neighborhood context makes some contribution to the explained variance in college plans over and above that made by the traditional variables, its added contribution is indeed small.[18]

These results should not be interpreted to mean that neighborhood context can be dismissed as a factor in educational aspirations of youth. Even the small amount of variance accounted for by neighborhood status over and above that accounted for by sex, socioeconomic status, and intelligence makes some contribution to the understanding of educational aspirations. This contribution is important when the traditional variables leave a large proportion of the variance unexplained. Moreover, as the cross-tabular analysis indicates, the effect of neighborhood context is considerably more important in some subpopulations than in others—a fact that is not revealed by the multiple correlation analysis. Nevertheless, the results of the analysis reported in this paper indicate that past claims for the importance of neighborhood context in the development of educational aspirations may have been considerably overstated.[19] Whether more direct measures of normative climates than the socioeconomic level of the neighborhood

or school, or other measures of neighborhood or school climates, would reveal a closer relationship with educational aspirations must await new evidence based on actual assessments of these climates. Such evidence was not available in this study, nor has it been presented in any of the past studies. Whatever the prospects for future research, the present study clearly casts doubt on the popular notion that the socioeconomic status of the neighborhood in which the youth resides has a substantial influence on his educational aspirations that cannot be explained in terms of his sex, ability, and socioeconomic status.

Notes

1. The research literature on these influences is vast and need not be detailed here. Numerous references are given in William H. Sewell, A. O. Haller, and M. A. Straus, "Social Status and Educational and Occupational Aspirations," *American Sociological Review,* 22 (February 1957), pp. 67–73.

2. Educational aspirations of rural and urban youth are examined in William H. Sewell, "Community of Residence and College Plans," *American Sociological Review,* 29 (February 1964), pp. 24–38. This paper also includes references to many earlier studies. Peer group influences are examined in the studies by Archie Haller and C. E. Butterworth, "Peer Influences on Levels of Occupational and Educational Aspiration," *Social Forces,* 38 (May 1960), pp. 289–95; Harold H. Punke, "Factors Affecting the Proportion of High School Graduates Who Enter College," *Bulletin of the National Association of Secondary School Principals,* 38 (November 1954), pp. 6–27; James S. Coleman, "Academic Achievement and the Structure of Competition," *Harvard Educational Review,* 29 (Fall 1959), pp. 330–51; and Robert E. Herriot, "Some Social Determinants of Educational Aspiration," *Harvard Educational Review,* 33 (1963), pp. 157–77. Studies dealing with the influence of socioeconomic composition of school, neighborhood, and community on educational plans include: Alan B. Wilson, "Residential Segregation of Social Classes and Aspirations of High School Boys," *American*

Sociological Review, 24 (December 1959), pp. 843–44; Robert J. Havighurst and Bernice L. Neugarten, *Society and Education* (Boston: Allyn and Bacon, Inc., 1962), p. 155; Natalie Rogoff, "Local Social Structure and Educational Selection," in A. H. Halsey, Jean Floud, and C. Arnold Anderson (eds.), *Education, Economy, and Society* (New York: The Free Press, 1961), pp. 242–43; John A. Michael, "High School Climates and Plans for Entering College," *Public Opinion Quarterly,* 24 (Winter 1961), pp. 585–95; Carolyn W. Sherif, "Self-Radius and Goals of Youth in Different Urban Areas," *Southwestern Social Science Quarterly,* 42 (December 1961), pp. 259–70; Stuart Cleveland, "A Tardy Look at Stouffer's Findings in the Harvard Mobility Project," *Public Opinion Quarterly,* 26 (Fall 1962), pp. 453–54; James S. Coleman, *The Adolescent Society* (New York: The Free Press, 1962); and Ralph H. Turner, *The Social Context of Ambition* (San Francisco: Chandler, 1964).

3. James Bryant Conant, *Slums and Suburbs* (New York: McGraw-Hill, 1961), p. 12.

4. *Op. cit.,* pp. 242–43.

5. William H. Sewell, *op. cit.,* and William H. Sewell and Alan M. Orenstein, "Community of Residence and Occupational Choice," *American Journal of Sociology,* 70 (March 1965), pp. 551–63.

6. Wilson presents evidence of a high degree of concordance between the patterns of school and residential segregation (Wilson, *op. cit.,* p. 837). Rhodes, Reiss, and Duncan have also shown that the residential segregation pattern is reflected in the school segregation pattern. A. L. Rhodes, A. J. Reiss, Jr., and O. D. Duncan, "Occupational Segregation in a Metropolitan School System," *American Journal of Sociology,* 70 (May 1965), p. 690.

7. *Op. cit.*

8. *Op. cit.*

9. Sherif, *op. cit.*

10. Since this paper was submitted for publication, Campbell and Alexander have reported a study in which the correlations between school status and college plans of boys in various family-status categories ranged from $r = +0.07$ to $r = +0.16$. They attempted to explain this relationship in terms of interpersonal influences of the boys' significant others, as measured by average score of friends' statuses. Ernest Q. Campbell and C. Norman Alexander, "Structural Effects and Interpersonal Relationships," *American Journal of Sociology,* 71 (November 1965), pp. 284–89.

11. Rhodes, Reiss, and Duncan, *op. cit.,* pp. 682–94.

12. Elaboration technique is fully described in Herbert Hyman, *Survey Design and Analysis* (New York: The Free Press, 1955), Chapters vi and vii.

13. For further details about how the original survey was conducted, see J. Kenneth Little, *op. cit.*

14. V. A. C. Henmon and M. J. Nelson, *The Henmon-Nelson Test of Mental Ability* (Boston: Houghton Mifflin Co., 1942).

15. The five indicators were factor-analyzed using the principal-components method, and were orthogonally rotated according to the varimax criterion. This produced a two-factor structure composed of a factor on which the three economic items were most heavily loaded, and a factor on which the two educational items were most heavily loaded. The composite socioeconomic status index was developed by squaring the loadings of the principal items of each factor as weights, multiplying student scores on the items by the respective weights, and summing the weighted scores within each factor to obtain factor scores. Then the two factors were combined into a composite socioeconomic status score by multiplying the factor scores of all students by constants which would produce approximately equal variances for both and then summing the weighted factor scores for each student. The resulting composite socioeconomic status scores of all the students were then multiplied by a constant to produce a theoretical range of scores between 0 and 99.

16. Coleman, *op. cit.,* pp. 97–143, presents evidence in support of this assertion. Attention is called to the apparent disagreement between these findings and the higher correlations of neighborhood status with boys' ambitions than with girls' ambitions in Turner's study, *op. cit.,* pp. 58–59.

17. All correlation coefficients discussed in this analysis are based on actual scores on the indexes of family socioeconomic status, intelligence, and neighborhood status, and not on the three-category system used in the tables. Sex and college plans are treated as dichotomous variables. The zero-order correlations of sex, socioeconomic status, and intelligence with college plans are $+0.143$, $+0.383$, and $+0.362$, respectively.

18. Some measure of the occupational status of the fathers of the high school senior class has customarily been used to represent community, neighborhood, or school socioeconomic status. Occupational composition of the employed males in the school district was used in this study because it was believed to be

conceptually better and more independent of the student's socioeconomic status. Because some readers will wish to know whether the results would have been more favorable to the hypothesis had the usual measure been used, the correlations were also computed using the percentage of fathers in white-collar occupations for each senior class (school status) in place of the neighborhood-status variable. The results were as follows: $r = 0.184$ (school status and college plans), $R = +0.485$ (multiple correlation of school status, sex, socioeconomic status, and intelligence with college plans), and $R^2 = 0.235$. Subtracting 0.229 (the R^2 for sex, socioeconomic status, and intelligence with college plans) from 0.235 (the above R^2), results in an increase of 0.006 or 0.6 per cent in the explained vari-

ance. In other words, school status added less than one per cent to the explained variance in college plans, over and above the contribution of sex, socioeconomic status, and intelligence. Thus, if school status rather than neighborhood status had been used in the analysis, the results would have provided even less support for the thesis.

19. Although the problem to which this paper is addressed logically requires that sex, intelligence, and socioeconomic status be put into the multiple regression equation before neighborhood status, some readers may also wish to know what additional contribution intelligence and socioeconomic status would have made had each of these variables been entered last in the equation. The results would have been as follows:

		DEPENDENT VARIABLE: COLLEGE PLANS		
INDEPENDENT VARIABLES	R	Per Cent of Variance Explained	Per Cent Increase in Explained Variance Due to:	
Sex, intelligence, socioeconomic status, and neighborhood status	0.497	24.70	—	
Sex, intelligence, and socioeconomic status	0.479	22.94	Neighborhood status:	1.75
Sex, neighborhood status, and intelligence	0.438	19.18	Socioeconomic status:	5.52
Sex, neighborhood status, and socioeconomic status	0.430	18.49	Intelligence:	6.21

32. Structural Effects and Interpersonal Relationships

ERNEST Q. CAMPBELL AND
C. NORMAN ALEXANDER

EVER SINCE Durkheim pointed out the importance of social facts, sociologists have generally felt justified in asserting that the social climate exerts influence upon the behaviors of individuals. Frequently, how-

ever, problems that arise with the attribution of causal influence to these structural and contextual variables have been ignored or dealt with casually. Just as we oppose a reductionist tendency to make inferential

Reprinted with permission from the *American Journal of Sociology*, LXXI (November 1965), pp. 284–89 (copyright 1965 by the University of Chicago).

leaps from the traits or characteristics of individuals to the behavior of larger groups, and even whole societies, so must we take care to avoid any simplistic notions of direct, unmediated "structural effects."

The value systems and normative milieus of the larger social structure typically influence the behaviors of individuals through transmission and enforcement by certain *specific* others for any given individual. In Inkeles' cogent comment, "All institutional arrangements are ultimately mediated through individual human action." [2] In short, it is necessary to consider the position of the individual within the social structure—defined in terms of his specific relationships to other members of the collectivity—before attributing causal relevance to characteristics of the total collectivity. While this general statement may appear rather obvious, the implications that follow from it are sometimes overlooked.

Rather than proceed directly from characteristics of the larger system to the behavioral responses of individuals, it is more appropriate to apply a two-step model for the purposes of causal inference. This involves, first, social-psychological theory, which deals with the individual's response to a *given* social situation, and, second, theory at the structural level, which deals with the determination of that given social situation by characteristics of the larger social system. We must keep in mind the fact that the actor responds to that segment of the total system which, for him, is perceptually important and salient; rarely does he (inter-) act with reference to the system as a whole.

Thus, more sophisticated analyses of "structural effects" must take into account *both* steps in this causal chain—moving from the characteristics of the total system to the situation faced by the individual due to the effects of these characteristics and then from the social situation confronting the individual to his responses to it. In this manner we hope to achieve greater

theoretical understanding of the causal processes involved and, perhaps, contribute to the integration of social-psychological and structural theory. It is the purpose of this paper, then, to interpret the nature of certain structural effects by linking them to a systematic social-psychological theory.

Social-Psychological and Structural Levels

A number of theorists have developed relatively similar and systematic theories to account for interpersonal influences among the members of a collectivity and to explain how consensus emerges through interpersonal attractions.[3] Since the basic propositions are common to the theories of Festinger, Heider, Homans, and Newcomb,[4] we shall assume a sufficient familiarity with them to justify the following statement of only those hypotheses specific to our immediate purposes: (1) The greater the attraction of a person, P, to another, O, the more likely he is to come to be similar to O, with regard to X— where X represents those values, behaviors, and attitudes that are perceived to be of importance and common relevance. (2) The greater the similarity of a person, P, to another, O, with regard to X, the more likely he is to come to be highly attracted to O.

Blau, on the other hand, has dealt with structural effects, demonstrating that an individual with attribute X may manifest different behaviors—in behavioral areas related to X—as a function of the distribution of X in the collectivity.[5] However, Blau shows only that this analytic variable, the distribution of X, *may* influence the behaviors of the individual independently of his own value on X; he does not provide a rationale for predicting the direction or nature of differences nor specify when and under what conditions these effects are likely to occur. The question of how it comes about that structural characteristics lead to an accurate prediction of personal response inconsistent with predictions based on personal attributes is unexplored.

Two recent studies by Simpson and Wilson [6] find interpersonal and structural influences on the aspirations of high-school students. Simpson shows that the higher the reported socioeconomic status of an individual's best friends, the higher his own aspirations are likely to be, holding parental influence constant. Wilson finds that the larger the proportion of middle class students in a high school, the greater the likelihood that students of a given socioeconomic stratum have high educational aspirations.

Although Wilson's emphasis is structural and Simpson's interpersonal, both of these studies may be interpreted in terms of balance-theory predictions based on interpersonal influences. At the social-psychological level, it has been shown that the educational aspirations and attainments of an individual's friends influence his own aspirations and achievements apart from the status of his parents.[7] Since mobility

and educational aspirations are directly related to the socioeconomic status of a student, we should observe that the educational aspirations of an individual are directly related to the status of his friendship choices, holding his own status constant. This is precisely the relationship found by Simpson.

In order to explain Wilson's findings at the structural level in these terms, it is necessary to assume only that friendship choices are randomly distributed in the system. As the average socioeconomic status in a school rises, the more often will individuals at each status level choose friends of high status—simply because there are proportionately more of them available to be chosen. We can then explain the observed association between the average status of a school and the educational aspirations of its students in terms of the intervening variable of interpersonal influence by an individual's friends. Whether we regard the relationship between average school status and student aspirations as spurious will depend, of course, on the theoretical assumptions we make about the nature of these relationships. Before discussing these possibilities, how-

TABLE 1.   Correlations among School Status, Friends' Status, and College Plans of High-School Seniors—By Parental Educational Level

| | *ZERO-ORDER CORRELATIONS* | | | *PARTIAL CORRELATIONS* | | |
PARENTAL EDUCATIONAL LEVEL	*School Status with College Plans* (1)	*Friends' Status with College Plans* (2)	*School Status with Friends' Status* (3)	* (4)	† (5)	*N* (6)
Both parents college	.10	.15	.49	.03	.12	172
One parent college	.16	.29	.36	.06	.26	183
Both parents high-school graduates	.15	.28	.50	.01	.24	147
One parent high-school graduate	.07	.19	.34	.01	.18	178
Neither parent high-school graduate	.14	.31	.40	.02	.28	295

* School status with college plans, holding friends' status constant.
† Friends' status with college plans, holding school status constant.

ever, we will present certain data relevant to the points being raised.

Data Analysis

In connection with a larger study,[8] questionnaires were administered to 1,410 male seniors in thirty high schools in the eastern and Piedmont sections of North Carolina. Each respondent was asked the following question: "What students here in school of your own sex do you go around with most often?" Up to two choices were coded for each case, a choice being considered codable if directed to another member of the high-school senior class who returned a signed questionnaire.[9]

Students were divided into five status levels according to the educational attainment of their parents.[10] Next, each of the thirty schools in the sample was assigned the average status of its students, that is, we arbitrarily assigned weights (from 1 to 5) to the five status levels and, treating this as an interval scale, computed a mean value for each school. For convenience, we shall refer to this measure as "school status." Finally, the average (mean) status of friends was determined for each respondent by this same arbitrary weighting of parental educational levels. Thus, we have three measures for each respondent: his personal status, his friends' status, and the status of his school. In addition, his college plans were determined by his response to the question: "Realistically, do you expect to go to college this coming fall?"

First, we shall examine the correlation between the status of the school and the proportion of individuals at each status level who plan to attend college. A positive value will be consistent with the structural effect reported by Wilson. Second, we shall examine the association between the status of an individual's friends at each personal-status level and the percentage who plan to go to college. A positive re-

lationship will support Simpson's findings. When both of these expectations are confirmed, we shall determine whether there is a direct association between the average status of a school and the tendency of individuals at each status level to choose friends of high status. Confirmation of this hypothesis would suggest that the influence of friends may be an intervening variable that mediates the association between average school status and college expectations. Then we will examine at each of the five personal status levels the partial correlations between (a) friends' status and college plans with school status controlled and (b) college plans and school status with friends' status controlled. We expect the relationship between school status and college plans to disappear in this analysis; but the relationship between college plans and friends' status should remain strong despite controls on school status. If this is the case, we shall argue that a two-step model is required for proper interpretation of structural effects phenomena, and we shall present this model.

The correlation coefficients pertaining to these expectations are presented in Table 1. It is apparent from inspection of column (1) of this table that, following the conceptions of Blau and Wilson, there *is* a structural effect: at each of five personal-status levels, the association between average school status and college plans is positive. Similarly, column (2) supports Simpson's findings: within each personal-status level there is a positive association between college plans and the status level of friendship choices. And in column (3) we see that persons at every status level are more likely to choose high-status friends when there are relatively large numbers of high-status persons in the system. Thus, school status is related to the individual's college plans; so is the status of his friends; and the status of friends chosen by those at each status level is related to the status of the school.

We come now to the basic question of

interest: Is there a relationship between school status and the college plans of individuals at each status level apart from the effects of interpersonal influence that are indicated by the status of friends? The answer to this question should be negative if our hypothesized two-step model is correct. In other words, we expect only negligible variation to be explained by school status when friendship status is held constant. The partial correlations presented in column (4) of the table show that this is precisely what occurs. By contrast, when school status is held constant, the relationship between college plans and friends' status remains strong, as revealed in the partial correlations in column (5) of Table 1. These two sets of partial-correlation coefficients support the inference that the structural effects of school status are best conceived of as due to the interpersonal influences of an individual's significant others.

Discussion

Given knowledge of an individual's immediate interpersonal influences, the characteristics of the total collectivity provide no additional contribution to the prediction of his behaviors in these data. Thus we have no indication that an important structural effect exists independently of interpersonal influences. So little additional variation is explained by school status that we could easily regard the remainder as due to our inability to involve in the analysis *all* of the relevant interpersonal influences (e.g., the individual's additional friends of the same sex, his friends of the opposite sex, his "ideal" referents in the system, etc.).

On the other hand, we would support as reasonable the expectation that there are structural factors that determine the orientations of individuals to others having particular characteristics. This is why we

want to stress the use of a two-step analytical model. Social-psychological theories specify the conditions under which individuals respond to *given* characteristics of their social environments. But research on "structural effects" is required to permit a specification of the conditions under which certain structural variables produce these relevant characteristics of an individual's social environment, the characteristics that furnish the "givens" in social-psychological theories. Then, with knowledge of structural variables, we should be able to specify when individuals will orient themselves toward specific types of others, and then use the characteristics of their significant others to predict their behaviors.

It is well established that the values and attitudes of individuals are shaped by and emerge from their continued interaction in social situations and that significant others are particularly influential in these processes. We are also convinced that there are certain regularities in the frequency with which particular types of individuals are chosen as focuses of interaction in certain social situations; and we believe that these regularities could be predicted from knowledge of relevant characteristics of the collectivity as a whole. However, until there is specification of the correspondence between structural variables and the proclivity to relate to particular types of persons in the collectivity, it is not possible to speak in causally relevant terms of structural effects on individual behaviors—inasmuch as these seem due to intervening interpersonal influences.

We must raise also the possibility of a direct causal link between individual behaviors and characteristics of the total collectivity. Here we are asking whether it may be that values of the total collectivity constitute behaviorally relevant expectations toward which the individual orients himself. The crucial question, but one to which our data cannot provide an answer, is this: Is there a school-wide value system toward which the individual is oriented and upon which he bases his behaviors apart from the immediate influences of his particular significant others? That is, measures of the values held by individuals in a given system neither confirm nor deny the independent existence of a collective value system. In order to say that X is an influential system value, we have to know that people in the system perceive it as such and act accordingly. Lacking evidence that participants perceive the existence of system-wide values and norms, researchers cannot draw firm conclusions about their effects; and we do not establish the existence of such perceived value systems with analytic structural variables. We therefore are not prepared to deny the potential influence of collectivity value systems, though we do assert the necessity for their independent measurement.

Summary

We have worked toward the integration of social-psychological and structural theory, and we believe that this has important implications for research dealing with structural effects. We have argued that the normative influences of the distribution of an attribute within a collectivity are best explained by a two-step model. This perspective suggests a research strategy that first employs structural variables to account for the psychologically relevant characteristics of an individual's social environment and then explains his behaviors in terms of a social-psychological theory whose predictions are based on given conditions of the social environment. It also argues that the norms and value systems of collectivities are not appropriately assessed by analytic measures.

Notes

1. Based on data secured during conduct of Grants M-04302 and MH-08489, National Institute of Mental Health, Ernest Q. Campbell,

Principal Investigator. The Graduate Fellowship Program, National Science Foundation, freed the time of the second author for work on this paper, an assistance gratefully acknowledged. We are indebted to Charles Federspiel for statistical consultation.

2. Alex Inkeles, "Personality and Social Structure," in R. K. Merton, Leonard Broom, and L. S. Cottrell, Jr. (eds.), *Sociology Today: Problems and Prospects* (New York: Basic Books, 1959), p. 251.

3. C. Norman Alexander, Jr., and Richard L. Simpson, "Balance Theory and Distributive Justice," *Sociological Inquiry*, XXXIV (Spring 1964), pp. 182–92.

4. Leon Festinger, *Theory of Cognitive Dissonance* (Chicago: Row Peterson & Co., 1957); Fritz Heider, *The Psychology of Interpersonal Relations* (New York: John Wiley & Sons, 1958); George Homans, *Social Behavior: Its Elementary Forms* (New York: Harcourt, Brace, & Co., 1961); Theodore M. Newcomb, *The Acquaintance Process* (New York: Holt, Rinehart & Winston, 1961).

5. Peter M. Blau, "Structural Effects," *American Sociological Review*, XXV (April 1960), pp. 178–93.

6. Richard L. Simpson, "Parental Influence, Anticipatory Socialization, and Social Mobility," *American Sociological Review*, XXVII (August 1962), pp. 517–22; Alan B. Wilson, "Residential Segregation of Social Classes and Aspirations of High School Boys," *American Sociological Review*, XXIV (December 1959), pp. 836–45.

7. C. Norman Alexander, Jr., and Ernest Q. Campbell, "Peer Influences on Adolescent Aspirations and Attainments," *American Sociological Review*, XXIX (August 1964), pp. 568–75.

8. "Normative Controls and the Social Use of Alcohol," National Institute of Mental Health Grants M-4302 and MH-08489. Questionnaires were administered to 5,115 seniors of both sexes in sixty-two high schools. The sample in this paper includes only males in the thirty high schools that met the following criteria: (1) more than 15 males responded; (2) more than 95 per cent of the males gave their names; (3) more than 90 per cent of the males completed the questionnaire; (4) more than one-third of the males planned to go to college. The fourth criterion resulted in the elimination of only one school which would otherwise not have been eliminated. The criterion was included because there are certain data available only for those adolescents who plan to attend college.

9. We coded only two choices per case in

order to maximize information about the respondent's interpersonal relationships and to minimize the loss of cases who selected a limited number of friends.

10. The status levels and their arbitrary weights were as follows: (5) both parents went to college; (4) only one parent went to college; (3) neither parent went to college, but both graduated from high school; (2) neither parent went to college, and only one graduated from high school; (1) neither parent graduated from high school.

C. Contextual Analysis

33. A Contextual Analysis of Academic Failure[1]

DAVID NASATIR

THE RISING tide of enrollment and increased pressure for admission to limited facilities have created a critical need for means by which to select those students who will be able to complete a college or university career. Admission to institutions of higher education comes to be more and more the result of testing programs designed to identify the academic failures among the surplus of candidates. But the costs of errors in such attempts are high. Thousands who were mistakenly thought to be good risks needlessly drain these institutions' limited resources, while training is consequently denied to many students who might well have gained more from it. Data which illuminate the process of failure are consequently pertinent to the growing problem of selection.

It is generally recognized that an explanation of failure must rely upon more than the simple assessment of intelligence. Over the past ten years studies of failure and withdrawal have appeared, on the average, about once a month and have examined failure in light of personality, social class, and many other variables in addition to intellect. However, the search for an explanation solely in terms of variables antecedent to the experience of education, no matter how complex, oversimplifies the problem. It is also necessary to explore the milieu in which students gain their formal education.

Today's universities are often as large as small cities and as complex in their social life. The undergraduate community in such a setting is neither a collection of atomized individuals in a "mass" society nor a homogeneous village; it is instead divided into many subgroups whose members interact far more with each other than they do with members of the larger community. The standards and conduct of these groups are often disparate; the years spent at the university may encompass quite different experiences for members of different groups.

The most important, visible, permanent, and manipulable basis for student subcultures is the set of organized residence groups—dormitories, fraternities and sororities, cooperative houses, private boarding houses, and the like. It is within these settings that students take on the attitudes and values, the work habits and play orientations that shape their activities and temper their entire university careers. Though the effect upon individual students

Reprinted with permission from *The School Review*, 71 (Autumn 1963), pp. 290–98.

differs, the consequences of a particular group attribute in the process of failure—say a favorable orientation to academic standards—can be seen simply by comparing the rate of failure of its members with the rate for otherwise similar groups lacking such an orientation.

In order to explore such effects systematically, all students entering Berkeley campus of the University of California in the fall of 1959 were given a battery of psychological tests and a detailed questionnaire about their expectations, anticipations, values and attitudes.[2] In all, 2,782 students participated. By the time two academic years had passed—in the spring of 1961—940 of these students had dropped out of the university. Six hundred and thirty-six of the "dropouts" (about 23 per cent of the class as a whole) had been dismissed because of academic failure.

More than 420, or 66 per cent, of the dropout students and some 70 per cent of the students who had remained in school replied to questionnaires similar to those of 1959. In addition, some 2,500 other students representing the various groups to which the study subjects belonged also filled out questionnaires. The combined responses provided a description of the social contexts in which the failures had lived, worked, and played and provided comparable information on their academically more successful peers.

There are pronounced differences in the social backgrounds of students living in different types of residence groups, but among the groups within one type, the uni-versity dormitories, the distributions of backgrounds appear to be roughly comparable.[3] The assignment of entering freshmen to dormitories is done on the basis of the order in which the applications are postmarked. Since there is a perpetual housing shortage at the university, many students simply state "dormitory" on their application without expressing a preference, in the hope of increasing their chances of getting accommodations. As a result, differences among entering students tend to be distributed throughout the dorms in a nonsystematic fashion. Similar as their entering students might be, however, each group achieves a more or less distinct character; the selective migration after admission, house mothers, graduate residents, and faculty fellows, and the traditions associated with particular domitories are only some of the factors which contribute to their cultural differences.

Table 1 shows the distribution of the failure rate among these dorms. The range—from 0 to 56 per cent—is large, but it might be explained to some extent by differences in physical facilities and location. Yet considering only four dormitories which are identical in all physical aspects, there is still a range of from 0 to 33 per cent in the failure rates. Differences among buildings need not reflect the distinct style of life, however, or the value systems of the groups which dwell within their walls.

In an analysis of responses by students to a question concerning the main purposes of a college education, it is possible to characterize these groups by the proportion of

TABLE 1.   Failure Rate by Residence

	RESIDENCE					
	1	*2*	*3*	*4*	*5*	*6*
Per cent failing	33	23	56	22	0	19
Number of students in dorm from entering class of '59	(48)	(74)	(43)	(47)	(48)	(50)

members expressing agreement with a statement that the most important reason for attending college is to obtain a basic general education and appreciation of ideas. This will be referred to as the "academic" orientation. Although other reasons (such as development of the ability to get along with people, development of moral capacities, or preparation for marriage) are put forth, those who are not "academics" are overwhelmingly "vocational" in their orientation. To distinguish between academic and non-academic contexts, the six dormitory groups have been dichotomized into those above and those below the mean of the distribution proportions of group members choosing the academic response as the purpose of a college education. Examination of Table 2—failure rate by type of context—reveals an unexpected result:

TABLE 2. Failure Rate by
Type of Residence

	TYPE OF RESIDENCE	
	Academic	Non-academic
Per cent failing	21	14
Bases of percentages	(162)	(148)

TABLE 3. Failure Rate by
Type of Individual

	TYPE OF INDIVIDUAL	
	Academic	Non-academic
Per cent failing	10	20
Bases of percentages	(84)	(226)

a higher proportion of the students in academic contexts fail than in non-academic contexts.[4] While only 14 per cent of the students who entered in 1959 and lived in the nonacademic dorms failed, 21 per cent of the students living in what would have

seemed the more retentive type of context failed during the same period.

It is surprising that those contexts characterized by a high proportion of members with an academic orientation have a higher rate of academic failure than their less academic counterparts. But it is even more surprising that the rate of failure for academically oriented or non-academically oriented *individuals* (see Table 3) is the reverse of that for groups; among the academically oriented members the failure rate is half that among the non-academically oriented members. While 10 per cent of the academics have failed, 20 per cent of the non-academics have done so.

The apparent anomaly of Tables 2 and 3 taken together, showing a higher failure rate in academic contexts but a lower rate among academic individuals, suggests that there is more in the process of failure than can be explained by either individual attitudes or contextual atmosphere alone. The *relation* of the individual to his milieu is an essential ingredient as well. Table 4

TABLE 4. Failure Rate by Type of
Residence for Types of Individuals

	TYPE OF RESIDENCE	
TYPE OF INDIVIDUAL	Academic	Non-academic
Academic (per cent)	7	12
Bases of percentages	(42)	(42)
Non-academic	26	14
Bases of percentages	(120)	(106)

shows the combined effect of attitudes and atmosphere upon the failure rate. Examination of the first cell of this table reveals the lowest failure rate. This is what might have been expected; the academically oriented students in an academic context tend to stay in school. The surprising results come with an examination of the cell diagonally opposite. Here it is seen that for the non-academic students in a non-academic atmosphere, the failure rate, although twice as high as for academics, is still low by comparison to one other cell. In the lower left corner the highest failure rate of all is seen for those non-academic students dwelling in academic contexts. Finally, the out-of-place academics—individuals with an academic orientation living in non-academic dorms—have a higher failure rate than their more harmoniously situated academic peers, but the rate is still lower than that of the non-academics, regardless of context.

Apparently the harmony which students maintain with their surroundings has a great deal to do with the proportion of students that fail. Even for the non-academics, the failure rate is reduced in a sympathetic context. This can be understood more easily perhaps when the nature of dormitory life is considered. It is in such settings of aimless and carefree camaraderie in the student rooms, where talk is free and opinions and sentiments are unguardedly expressed, that the mainstream of student intellectual life flows, rather than in the course of the instrumental contacts of the lecture hall. Yet for the out-of-place academic, there remains the larger culture of the university to support him in his scholarly pursuits. Respected faculty and successful graduates can symbolically reaffirm his efforts if necessarily at a physical remove. But the out-of-place non-academic finds much less support from informal relations in the general atmosphere of his surroundings and has no alternative culture so readily available—and so legitimate—within the university at large.

Contexts do not exist by themselves, however; they are manifested in social interaction. The extent to which the informal life of the individual is spent with other members of his group partaking of their interpretations of life, affects his risk of failure. He shares with his colleagues patterns of expectation and behavior—expectations of scholarly judgment, patterns of preparing for classes—elements central to academic failure and success. Variation in the degree to which individuals are truly a part of the residential context should effect some variation in the relation of individual orientation, context and rate of failure.

To examine this aspect, students were asked what proportion of their time they spent in the company of other members of their residence groups. Answers ranged from all to none. Those answering that they spent all of their time, or at least more than half of their time with other members were considered to be "integrated" into their groups. Table 5 shows that integra-

TABLE 5.   Failure Rate by Degree of Integration

	DEGREE OF INTEGRATION	
	Integrated	Non-integrated
Percentage	11	20
Bases of percentages	(97)	(213)

tion is itself a factor in reducing the failure rate. While 11 per cent of the integrated students failed, 20 per cent of the non-integrated ones did. As Durkheim noted some sixty-five years ago, "there is . . . in a cohesive and animated society a constant interchange of ideas and feelings from all to each and each to all, something like a mutual moral support, which instead of throwing the individual on his own resources, leads him to share in the collective energy and supports his own when exhausted." [5]

This study reports a case where context and individual orientation affect the failure rate of students. It appears that although an academic individual orientation is effective in retaining students, a similar contextual orientation serves to raise the failure rate. Analysis of both variables simultaneously leads to the conclusion that this effect is due largely to the non-academically oriented in academic groups, since over 90 per cent of all of the failures from academic contexts are themselves non-academically oriented. But as suggested earlier, the non-integrated academic, regardless of his immediate context, can draw some support for his intellectual activities from the university culture at large. Thus, as seen in Table 6, the difference in the failure rate

TABLE 6. Failure Rate by Type of Individual and Degree of Integration

	DEGREE OF INTEGRATION (PER CENT)	
TYPE OF INDIVIDUAL	Integrated	Non-integrated
Academic	10	9
Bases of percentages	(30)	(54)
Non-academic	12	24
Bases of percentages	(67)	(159)

for integrated versus non-integrated dormitory men with an academic orientation is negligible. The story is quite different, however, among the men not having an academic orientation. There, the failure rate of the non-integrated students is twice that of the integrated. These men are not

only out of joint with their larger surroundings, but also are denied many of the supports that group membership can provide. Without an academic orientation, and without a supportive context, students manifest a high rate of failure.

This all suggests that an important variable in the understanding of failure rates is to be found not solely at the level of individual orientation, nor solely at the level of contextual factors, but instead in the relation of the individual to his context. Integration does, in fact, make a considerable difference. The question now becomes the interaction of these three levels of variables: the individual, the contextual, and the relational. Table 7 reveals that within levels of integration, the initial relation of failure rates to harmonious surroundings does remain. The overall level of failure is affected, however. In general, the rate is about 10 percentage points higher for the non-integrated students in any given category than similarly situated integrated students. Even so, the lowest failure rates within each level of integration are to be found among those who are in harmony with their context, the highest among those who are not. Among the integrated, for example, none of the academic individuals in academic dorms failed and only 7 per cent of the non-academics in non-academic dorms. But 16 per cent of the non-academics in academic contexts and 19 per cent of the academics in non-academic con-

TABLE 7. Failure Rate by Type of Individual, Degree of Integration, and Context

	INTEGRATED INDIVIDUALS		NON-INTEGRATED INDIVIDUALS	
TYPE OF INDIVIDUAL	Academic Context	Non-academic Context	Academic Context	Non-academic Context
Academic (per cent)	0	19	11	29
Bases of percentages	(14)	(16)	(28)	(26)
Non-academic (per cent)	16	7	30	17
Bases of percentages	(38)	(29)	(82)	(77)

texts failed. Among the non-integrated individuals, the smallest rate is again found in the upper left-hand corner cell, among the academically oriented in academic contexts. The rate for non-academics in non-academic contexts (lower right-hand corner cell) is higher, but still much lower than the rate for those out of harmony with their surroundings (29 per cent and 30 percent failure, respectively, for the academics in non-academic contexts and the non-academics in academic contexts).

Many factors bear on the success or failure of students in college; only three have been examined here. Yet even this simple analysis becomes complex for it is the combination of variables that best explains the differences in failure rates. Traditionally, the approach to this problem has been through a study of the characteristics of individuals, or of contexts. It is hoped that by examining variables of a different order —the relations of individuals to social contexts—a fruitful alternative has been suggested for future research.

Notes

1. Revised version of a paper read at the annual meeting of the American Sociological Association, August 1962. Data were gathered as part of a larger project directed by Hanan C. Selvin and Thomas R. McConnell sponsored by the National Institute of Mental Health Grant Number USPHS-MH 3734. Acknowledgment is gratefully given for the advice of John Finley Scott on matters of prose style.

2. The data were gathered under the auspices of the Center for the Study of Higher Education as part of a larger study of selected institutions.

3. To simplify the analysis, only the failure rate for the six men's dormitories at Cal is explored in this paper.

4. Although this statement is in a form well known for its logical and statistical inaccuracies (see W. S. Robinson, "Ecological Correlations and the Behavior of Individuals," *American Sociological Review*, XV (June 1950), pp. 351–57), it is in fact true for the individual dormitories studied as well as for the aggregation of these groups.

5. Émile Durkheim, *Suicide*, trans. G. Simpson (New York: The Free Press, 1962), p. 210.

34. The Social Context of Apprehension

PAUL F. LAZARSFELD AND
WAGNER THIELENS, JR.

[Ed. Note: During the decade following the end of World War II, many American colleges and universities came under suspicion and attack on political grounds. Since these attacks were frequently directed at the social sciences, the authors, in 1955, undertook a study of a sample of 2451 social science teachers in 165 colleges throughout the nation. The aim was to investigate the restrictions on academic freedom generated by these events.

The following selection examines the bearing of the college context on the professor's "apprehension" about expressing his views openly. In order to follow the discussion, several terms must be clarified. "Apprehension" refers to the teacher's concern that his political opinions may affect his professional reputation or job security. The terms "permissive" or "conservative" refer to the faculty member's support of freedom of expression for leftist political views on campus. "Productivity" deals with the professor's professional contributions. "Incidents" mean events on campus in which professors had been subject to attack or pressure by virtue of deviant views.]

IN THIS LAST chapter we would like to examine more fully some of the determinants and consequences of apprehension. The full complexity of the situation we set out to study is still bound to elude us in one single inquiry. And yet, we can indicate some lines for future work by discussing two sets of data in more detail.

To begin with, there is a marked difference in apprehension between younger and older teachers. This finding, if not a particularly surprsing one, nevertheless turns out not to be simply explained. Quite an array of data will be introduced in order to interpret it. Our conclusion from this discussion will be renewed and more precise emphasis on . . . the mutual support which creates a common climate of opinion and morale among social scientists. This emphasis will be further justified by returning to age differences, this time in terms of permissiveness.

Next, we will watch the interplay between the incidents occurring on a campus, the extent to which they are perceived by various kinds of teachers, and their resultant bearing on the spread of apprehension.

In short, this chapter directs special attention to the social context of apprehension.

Age and Apprehension

Younger teachers are likely to be more permissive than older ones. We would expect, because of this, that they are also more apprehensive. This is indeed the case: 53 per cent of the teachers aged forty or younger are apprehensive, compared to 46 per cent of those between 41 and 50, and 31 per cent of those over 50. However, even when the factor of permissiveness is eliminated, age continues to play a role. The three parts of Table 1 show this, for

Reprinted in part with permission from Chapter X of *The Academic Mind* (copyright 1958 by The Free Press, a division of the Macmillan Company, New York).

they reveal that among the professors on each level of permissiveness, the younger respondents are more often apprehensive.

Why do younger teachers show more apprehension? Because they lack the security of tenure, will be the first answer which comes to mind. But surprisingly enough, this is not the correct explanation. Table 2 compares the proportions of apprehensive respondents for those who have and who do not have tenure. Within each age group the differences are small and inconsistent. Among both those with and without tenure, however, the younger teachers remain more apprehensive than the older ones.

Thus the role of tenure should not be overrated. It is true that ousting a teacher is legally more difficult for a school if he has tenure. But on the one hand, life can be made unpleasant for a professor even though he does not lose his job; on the other, flagrant discrimination, if brought to light, is not easily defended even when directed against a person without tenure.

Another possibility deserves exploration. As a professor grows older he is likely to have published more, he becomes better known, and so might feel more secure because he can count on the support of his academic public. Also, his publications sometimes provide him with independent income, and thus perhaps with a cushion against temporary unemployment. . . .

Our questionnaire asks: "Do you have any outside sources of income besides your salary?" Since outside income can, of course, come from other sources, such as consultations or investment, this more general formulation of the question permits an additional test of whether economic security affected professorial apprehension during the difficult years. The results of Figure 1 are quite surprising in one respect.

Looking first along the two lines, in each case the most apprehension is found among the professors of medium productivity. This makes intuitive sense: quite likely these

TABLE 1.   On Each Level of Permissiveness, Older Teachers Are Less Apprehensive than Younger Ones

	PROPORTION APPREHENSIVE		
	Clearly Permissive	*Somewhat Permissive*	*Conservative*
Age:			
40 or less	62%	52%	34%
41–50	56%	47%	29%
51 or older	36%	30%	29%

TABLE 2.   Tenure Does Not Account for the Lower Frequency of Apprehension Among Older Professors

	PROPORTION APPREHENSIVE	
	Teachers With Tenure	*Teachers Without Tenure*
Age:		
40 or less	52%	54%
41–50	45%	50%
51 or older	31%	30%

individuals have expressed themselves enough in public to become controversial, but have not acquired enough status to take attacks with relative equanimity. The surprise comes when, on each productivity level, it develops that respondents with outside income in no way show a lower frequency of apprehension, but in most cases a slightly higher one. Outside income is often derived from consultations. We have noticed before that men and women who do such outside work are likely to be more permissive. We took this as a sign of their greater sensitivity to a diversity of demands; it would also make them more alert to civil liberties problems, overbalancing

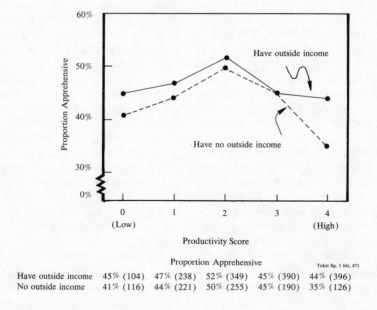

Tekst fig. 1 blz. 471

Have outside income	45% (104)	47% (238)	52% (349)	45% (390)	44% (396)
No outside income	41% (116)	44% (221)	50% (255)	45% (190)	35% (126)

FIGURE 1.   Apprehension as Related to Productivity and the Availability of Outside Income.

whatever security they might derive from their additional income. In their net effect, then, none of the elements of objective security—tenure, professional status, outside income—which come with higher age are noticeably related to apprehension. These factors, therefore, cannot explain why it declines so markedly with age.

The Role of Integration

Rather, we submit, it is a special kind of psychological security that plays a role here. Sociologists might call it a sense of social integration. The newcomer at a school, unacquainted with the traditions of his profession or of his college, feels insecure. He doesn't quite know what is expected of him, and even if he is told, can't judge what latitude he has for individual variations. The older a man gets and the longer he has taught at the same place, the more at home he is likely to feel. It is

the difference between the well-known apprehension of the first-time weekend guest and the experienced visitor who, as the saying goes, "knows the ropes."

While tightly knit proof of this idea is not possible with the data on hand, two questionnaire items are suggestive indicators of this integration: the number of years a respondent has taught at his present college, and the way he feels about the relations among faculty members. We can use them to make several points. First, let us notice that the longer a professor teaches at a college, the more satisfied he is with the social climate in the faculty. Among those on a campus for five years or less, 20 per cent considered faculty relations fair at best; this proportion diminishes to 10 per cent among teachers with more than ten years' residence. Doubtless this is partly a question of self-selection; teachers who feel especially uneasy are likely to leave or to be forced out by conflict. And for those who remain on the campus, it is probably also a matter of personal adjustment.

In any case, apprehension is related to both of these integration factors. Figure 2 classifies all respondents by their length of residence at the present college and their judgment of faculty relationships, and reports the proportion of apprehensive teachers for the nine resulting combinations.

The separation of three lines shows that apprehension is more frequent among respondents who consider relations among faculty members less satisfactory. Undoubtedly, this works both ways: A satisfying personal environment puts a man more at ease; this enables him to look at other people with more trust and he thus encourages their good will. And inversely, apprehension and interpersonal difficulties can reinforce each other.

Reading along the two lower lines of Figure 2, we find that the longer teachers have taught at a school, the less apprehensive they are. The top line is interesting: for the minority of 369 respondents in whose judgment faculty relations are not good at all, apprehension is about equally high, regardless of the length of time they have taught at their colleges.

This is, then, how we think the more widespread apprehension of younger teachers can be explained. They were newcomers at their schools, inexperienced in the rules of the game, and uncertain about the support they could count on, and so the events of the difficult years were bound to appear more threatening to them than to their older colleagues.

Since the uncertainties of a beginning career are in themselves something of a trial for young teachers, it can only be regrettable if these teachers are put under additional stress by outside forces. Under such circumstances it would seem important that the American Association of University Professors, as the major professional organization of college teachers, pay special attention to the newcomers. We found . . . that permissive social scientists are more likely to belong to the A.A.U.P.; because younger teachers are more permissive, one might expect that they are, therefore, more often A.A.U.P. members, and that this would help alleviate their apprehension. Actually, the opposite is true. . . . Memberships is more frequent among older teachers; and it is especially rare exactly among the younger people who have not yet been able to achieve attention through professional activities. The question arises whether the A.A.U.P. has not missed out in attracting the very social scientists who need help most.

The importance to teachers of a sense of social belonging is reinforced by one more finding. . . . Social scientists have what we call a feeling of occupational inferiority: they think that the community

TABLE 3.   Social Scientists Who Have a Greater Occupational Inferiority Feeling Are More Frequently Apprehensive

	Low Imputed Esteem for Profession	High Imputed Esteem for Profession
	PROPORTION APPREHENSIVE	
Clearly permissive	58%	51%
Somewhat permissive	48%	41%
Conservative	33%	29%
Average	46%	40%

leaders, especially businessmen and politicians, attribute little prestige to the professor when he is put beside three comparable occupations. Apprehension is the greater, the more pronounced this feeling of low standing. Table 3 selects as an example the image professors have of how businessmen judge them. The respondents are

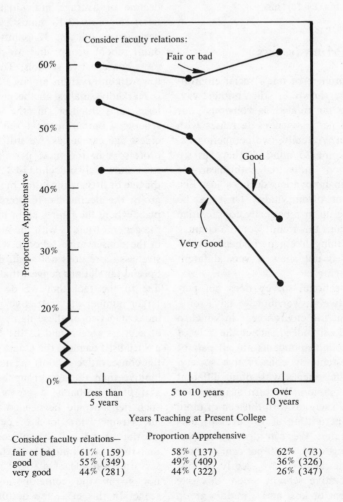

Consider faculty relations:

Fair or bad

Good

Very Good

Proportion Apprehensive

60%
50%
40%
30%
20%
0%

| Less than 5 years | 5 to 10 years | Over 10 years |

Years Teaching at Present College

Consider faculty relations—	Proportion Apprehensive		
fair or bad	61% (159)	58% (137)	62% (73)
good	55% (349)	49% (409)	36% (326)
very good	44% (281)	44% (322)	26% (347)

FIGURE 2. The Longer Social Scientists Have Taught at a College, and the Better They Feel about Faculty Relations, the Less Apprehension They Experience.

divided according to the prestige they attribute to themselves: they may expect high esteem (first or second rank) or low (third or fourth).

We know that the more permissive professors are most pessimistic about their prestige; now . . . on each level of permissiveness apprehension is more frequent among teachers for whom this occupational inferiority feeling is pronounced. . . .

The meaning of integration, it is true, has now changed. Earlier, we talked about respondents' integration among their peers. Now we talk about the way they feel their profession is integrated in the larger community. Still, in this more general way, Table 3 shows again the socio-psychological determination of apprehension. Mutual support within the college makes for less apprehension, just as lack of support by the larger community (or teachers' doubts to this effect) makes for more.

Age and Permissiveness

The importance of one's social environment can be shown in still another way. We have so far treated as "obvious" our finding that permissiveness decreases with age. But is it? Actually, two competing explanations come to mind. Perhaps as we grow older our individual enthusiasm for and belief in innovation declines just like other elements of our vitality. Or it may be that growing up in a basically conservative society explains this trend; would a country where something like a permanent revolution prevailed not show a very different "effect" of aging?

A cross-sectional survey does not permit a definitive answer, but we have some evidence that the environment in which a man lives does, indeed, affect the role of age. While our respondents are all part of the same essentially conservative society, they work in colleges with quite different climates of opinion. We turn again to our seventy-seven schools with thirteen or more interviews, permitting us to develop characterizing rates. We can distinguish permissive colleges, where 60 per cent or more of the social scientists are clearly permissive; conservative schools where this rate is 39 per cent or less; and a middle group where the permissive sector is from 40 to 59 per cent. Figure 3 reports the relation between age and permissiveness in these three groups of institutions.

In order to summarize the information in a compact way, the figure presents, for each type of school, the average permissiveness score for each age level. . . . These averages may provide a more sensitive measure of differences than percentages.

Let us begin by comparing the first two age groups. Between the youngest and the middle age categories we find the following decline of average individual permissiveness: 15 points (3.13 minus 2.98) in highly permissive colleges, 32 points in the medium school group, and 36 points in the most conservative schools. Thus the trend toward conservatism among older teachers is markedly smallest in the permissive colleges and highest in the conservative schools. Comparing next the middle and oldest age categories, we still find that the professors in the most permissive institutions show only a decline of 12 points after the age of fifty, while in the medium college group the decline is 36 points. The only place where the figures seem to run against the general trend is with the oldest teachers in the conservative schools, whose permissiveness score does not again drop sharply. Special tabulations suggest that this may be due to the fact that we do not have a larger number of "restrictive" items in our index. On two of these items (disapproval of a guest speech and of the formation of a Socialist League), the oldest professors in the conservative schools are not more prohibitive than the age group between forty and fifty. Probably a greater variety of such items would be needed to bring out an extremely low level of permissiveness. On the other hand, it is of course possible that there is a limit below which the conservative attitude of a social scientist cannot go in the contemporary American scene. In this case, the bottom right percentage of Figure 3 might not be a statistical artifact, but the measure of a cultural ceiling which limits the degree to which age and social environment may induce a conservative position. Only future studies can clarify this point. However, apart from this one exception, Figure 3 shows again that the social context in which these social scientists work has a pronounced influence on their attitudes. The proverbial conservative trend of age is much smaller in a highly permissive environment. . . .

So far the notion of social context has

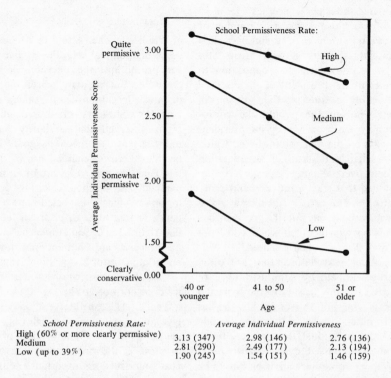

School Permissiveness Rate:	Average Individual Permissiveness		
High (60% or more clearly permissive)	3.13 (347)	2.98 (146)	2.76 (136)
Medium	2.81 (290)	2.49 (177)	2.13 (194)
Low (up to 39%)	1.90 (245)	1.54 (151)	1.46 (159)

FIGURE 3.   The Average Level of Permissiveness According to Age, in Three Groups of Colleges.

meant relationships with other people: how long one has worked with them, the way one gets along with them, and the influence of the prevailing climate of opinion. But during the difficult years another element was bound to be important and therefore deserves special attention: the series of attacks and accusations against teachers which beset a number of campuses. How were these episodes perceived and what effect did they have on our respondents' apprehension?

The Experience of Pressure

Preceding our statistical evidence, some preliminary observations are called for.

. . . We wish to describe more fully the way [actual incidents of threats to freedom of speech] reach the "ultimate consumer," the professor himself. Rather than review all types of incidents in this light, we can concentrate on cases of pressures from the school administration. The reports are essentially of two kinds. Some tell of crude interferences; a few examples will quickly give a picture of such cases. Second, and more interesting perhaps, are the descriptions of relatively gentle pressures.

HARSH PRESSURES

Our interviews contain reports of abrupt dismissals for such things as taking the Fifth Amendment, for "speaking too freely in class on the subjects of race and sex," for "having too liberal politics," and so on.[8] Professors also described a number of instances in which they themselves had been directly threatened with firing. Still others were convinced that opposition to the wishes of the president of their school could readily result in their dismissal. Teachers who said they would like to protest strongly against a ban by the president of a debate on the admission of Red China to the United Nations or of an invitation to a controversial guest speaker, sometimes added that such a move would probably bring them instant dismissal. As a Southern respondent put it, "A vigorous protest is not worth much when you can't get an audience, you just get fired."

Promotions and tenure, too, are often arbitrarily withheld by administrations. In many cases, nothing is said to the bypassed teacher, leaving him to wonder how he has erred. In others, the administration frankly informs the individual that he has fallen short or been passed over because he is controversial, sometimes advising him to be more careful so that it will be possible to advance him in the future. . . .

At some schools, presidents and administrative officials take it upon themselves to monitor the research produced by their faculty. Our interviews contain instances in which research reports had been significantly delayed for publication; one Southern school president, for instance, postponed publication of a survey showing that the community predominantly opposed the local dual school system until after the election in which the issue was voted upon. Some school presidents do not hesitate to request that certain research topics be completely avoided, that important passages be deleted, etc. Sometimes, in fact, research reports are edited in advance by teachers, in anticipation of adverse administration reactions. . . . Finally, our records show that a few college administrations have dropped controversial courses, usually in a social science, from the curriculum. . . .

GENTLE PRESSURES

When a teacher is told that he can either cease his political activities or give up hope for promotion, the decision he faces is clear-cut. But in many cases the exercise of power by administrative officials is more complex. Students of organization have often observed that authority has many indirect ways to reach its goal. The subordinate believes that he has to obey certain rules. But the rules are often not made explicit. The teacher feels it is up to him to sense what is expected, and often expends a great deal of effort in looking for the right clues. Sometimes he may even misinterpret an unintentional remark by an administrator as a hint fraught with danger. In such situations a man in authority does not need to be explicit to influence a teacher. He can intervene so deftly as to give no appearance of interfering, and still get things his way. The yielding of teachers to these gentle pressures is a problem of academic freedom important enough to deserve detailed examples.

The "request" is a favorable device of many administrative officials. Teachers are requested to avoid controversial topics, to refrain from poltical activity, to make contributions to the "right" political activities, to avoid unfavorable references to school benefactors, to increase their contacts with students, to decrease their contacts with students, and so on. Typically, the request is accomplished by a disclaimer, to show it is not an order. . . .

Sometimes the request is implicit. Teachers frequently describe how a matter was "called to their attention." In a typical instance, a Midwestern economist, to illustrate a general discussion of social class, cited fraternities and sororities as examples of social distinction. The story was carried to an official of the university, who phoned the teacher simply to "remind" him of it, going on to say that of course the professor had the right to say whatever he wanted. Nevertheless, the call was taken by the respondent as a veiled threat to his academic freedom. Another form of the implicit request might called the "nudge." A respondent who has made frequent speeches in recent years says that whenever he talks on a noncontroversial subject, no comment at all is forthcoming from the administration, but when he deals with a topic like the admission of Communist China into the United Nations, the dean of the school invariably remarks casually to him, "Oh, I hear you've been urging Red China's admission to the U.N." [10] . . .

The Impact of Incidents

We know that a teacher who had himself been the target of an incident was especially likely to be apprehensive. But how did his colleagues react to the episode? Did they know of it at all? And if so, did they too become more apprehensive? . . .

Table 4 shows that permissive teachers notice more incidents than conservative respondents. For instance, at all schools where there were from one to three corroborated incidents, an average of .67 incidents was reported by clearly permissive respondents (two reports for every three teachers), compared to an average of .36 for conservative professors (about one for every three).

Does the number of incidents which come to a professor's attention increase his apprehension even if he is not himself involved? The matter is not easy to resolve. Even if apprehension and the number of perceived incidents turn out to be correlated, we can not be sure how this connection comes about; the apprehensive teacher is more sensitive to academic freedom problems and therefore undoubtedly is quicker to notice if a colleague encounters difficulties. But we can take account of this, at least to a considerable degree, by a separate study of professors on different levels of permissiveness. This should help to discount their selective perception. If, then, the number of incidents is still related to increased apprehension, we can well argue that a threat to colleagues spreads apprehension among all social scientists. The facts are summarized in Figure 4, which is again restricted to corroborated incidents and excludes all respondents who were accused or attacked themselves.

Looking at the separation between the three lines, we see again our familiar finding that permissiveness is strongly associated with apprehension. The new information is to be found reading across each line. Regardless of teachers' own ideological position, and despite the fact that none of the individuals considered here has personally experienced difficulties, the more that incidents involving colleagues occur around them, the more apprehensive they are.

TABLE 4. Within the Same Objective Situation,
Permissive Teachers Noticed More Incidents

	AVERAGE NUMBER OF INCIDENTS NOTED		
PERMISSIVENESS LEVEL OF INDIVIDUAL TEACHERS	Schools with 1–3 Corroborated Incidents	Schools with 4–6 Incidents	Schools with 7 or More Incidents
Clearly permissive	.67	1.16	2.42
Somewhat permissive	.57	.96	2.24
Conservative	.36	.89	1.58

But Figure 4 also tells an unexpected story. The effect of campus events is greatest, not upon the more permissive, but upon the more conservative professors. In the top line the figures increase by 9 per cent, in the bottom one by 23 per cent. The most probable explanation is as follows: A highly permissive teacher is concerned with civil liberties in general; he pays attention to events in other colleges and to discussion on the national level. His apprehension is considerable even if nothing especially dramatic happens on his own campus; local events increase his apprehension only slightly. But a conservative professor is less alert to civil liberties issues. If his own college is quiet, then his apprehension is low. Only if casualties occur nearby does he begin to worry, and then his attitude comes to resemble that of his highly permissive colleagues.

This differential effect of the objective campus environment has considerable implications, and needs to be documented as well as our data permit. We shall, therefore, show that the administration's performance

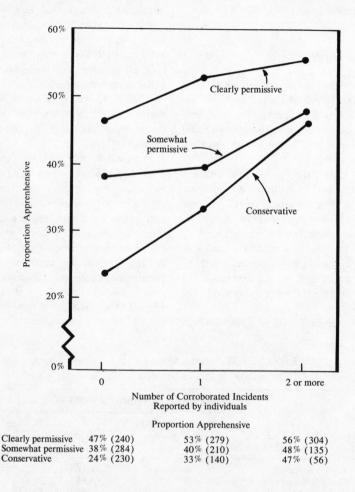

	Proportion Apprehensive	
Clearly permissive	47% (240)	53% (279)	56% (304)
Somewhat permissive	38% (284)	40% (210)	48% (135)
Conservative	24% (230)	33% (140)	47% (56)

FIGURE 4. The More Incidents Professors Learn About, the More Apprehensive They Are.

also affects the conservative more than it does the permissive professors.

For each of the seventy-seven schools in which we conducted thirteen or more interviews, we can report what we previously called the protection rate: the proportion of respondents who feel that their administration would support them wholeheartedly in the event they were accused of being leftists. Thus these colleges can be classified into four groups, ranging from poorly protected to highly protected schools.

One would expect that the more protected a faculty, the lower the apprehension felt by its members. And in general this is indeed the case. But it is not true for our two most permissive categories of teachers (who together make up what we have called "clearly permissive" teachers). In Figure 5 their apprehension is practically unaffected by the protectiveness of the administration; but among the remainder the proportion of apprehensive professors decreases markedly.

In general, then, apprehension increases with the number of incidents on the campus and is relieved by an administration's protective performance. . . . The new and important aspect of the last two tables is the differential reactions of professors with varying degrees of permissiveness. Conservative teachers are quite strongly affected by local events. Permissive social scientists, on the other hand, show a high apprehension which is little influenced by events on their own campuses. Several previous findings make highly plausible our surmise that the reaction of these men and women is more affected by what happens in their profession at large. Permissive social scientists are more interested in following civil liberties news; they put much more emphasis on general professional privileges than on the public relations problems of their own college; their publication record shows that they are more oriented toward a nationwide audience. All this fits in with a way of looking at the world which has been given considerable attention by social analysts.

The World Around Us

It has repeatedly been found that people living under the same conditions do not always view them the same way and are differently affected by them. Reviewing the pertinent literature, one is struck by a recurring distinction which is not easily spelled out. First of all, there is no established term to describe it. Even more than in other parts of this report, we share here T. S. Eliot's concern for the right word:

> the word neither diffident nor ostentatious,
> an easy commerce of the old and the new,
> the common word exact without vulgarity,
> the formal word precise but not pedantic.

We propose to say that people's meaningful worlds are of varying *effective scope.* For some this scope is relatively bounded—it includes as events of psychological importance only those that are close to them. Others' effective scope is considerably more extended.

The earliest systematic observations on this were probably made in the study of social stratification, when working-class persons were compared with members of the middle class. For example, the mere physical distance within which friendships develop is more compressed in the lower socio-economic strata. The topics about which such individuals talk and the items they read in newspapers are also centered more on local matters. But effective scope goes beyond literal distance. Social research has directed attention to variations in individuals' level of aspiration. The wishes and fantasies of working-class youths have repeatedly been found to be more restricted than those of their middle-class age peers, even when realistic monetary considerations are excluded. Moreover, criticism of existing conditions, when it occurs at all,

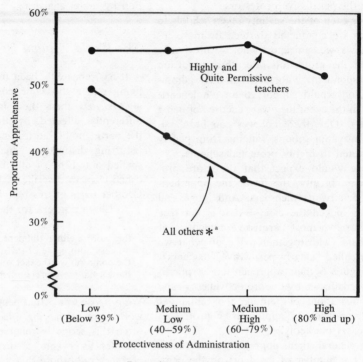

FIGURE 5. How Administrative Protectiveness Affects the Frequency of Apprehension.

Proportion Apprenhensive

	Low (Below 39%)	Medium Low (40–59%)	Medium High (60–79%)	High (80% and up)
Highly and quite permissive	55 (117)	55% (268)	56% (366)	52% (151)
All others	50% (143)	43% (315)	37% (336)	33% (158)

*In these 77 larger schools, the number of conservative professors is rather small, to get reliable figures they were combined with the somewhat permissive group. Figure 5 is based on all respondents in these seventy-seven schools.

is more timid in these lower economic strata. This has been found in diversified fields—in criticism of radio programs as well as of one's commanding officer in the army. As a matter of fact, it has occasionally been said that the problem of the underdog is not so much that he does not get his share of the world's goods as that he has been kept from developing a strong enough drive to want them. The man with an environment of limited effective scope does not notice many things which are more distant; and even if they are pointed out to him, he thinks that they are quite out of his reach.

Socio-economic position is by no means the only factor related to the effective scope of individuals' worlds. Differences in personality and in the public role one is expected to play make for similar variations. . . . Studies have shown that some professionals working for industry or for government agencies are oriented mainly toward their employer, while others are more concerned with the reactions of their profession. A corresponding observation has been made in studies of community leadership. Some leaders are primarily interested in helping to solve strictly local problems, while others feel called upon more to bring the larger world, say of art or music, to their community. The apt terminology of "local" and "cosmopolitan" leaders has been suggested for these two orientations. Clearly, what is meant is a difference in the effective scope of the environment: the cosmopolitan type has a relatively extended scope; the local type is more limited—he knows less and cares less about what is going on in the world at large.

External circumstances can restrict or widen an individual's effective scope. Studies carried out during the depression of the 1930's indicated that long-lasting unemployment made the effective scope of workers and their families even more limited than before. Paradoxically, the longer workers were unemployed, the less they kept track of employment opportunities outside of their communities; the unemployment of parents also led to an impoverishment of their children's fantasy world. Conversely, it has been found that if businessmen happen to travel abroad, not only do they develop more interest in international affairs, but they also become more hospitable to ideas of international solidarity, such as approval of the United Nations or a free-trade policy.

What we call the effective scope of a man's world characterizes, thus, what he perceives, what he has contact with, and what he reaches for through his interest or his expectations. Partly still a metaphor and partly a step toward a precise concept, the term is backed by a broad array of empirical data. It greatly facilitates the summary of our own findings regarding the permissive social scientist: on the average, his occupational world has a more extended effective scope than that of his conservative colleague. But the difficult years have threatened to restrict this scope. As a matter of fact, as we have seen, this has some-times already happened: a number of social scientists, for instance, have withdrawn from participation in community activities, and some have confined themselves to a narrower sphere of teaching and research. *In these respects, then, the effective scope of higher education in America was threatened.*

One must look at this in the light of the history of higher education in this country. A new and rapidly expanding country needed colleges in order to train ministers and school teachers. It was only at the turn of the century that a group of far-sighted men realized how provincial American college education had remained. Basic research, the teaching of world history, the social sciences—in short, most of the topics concerning the world at large—were neglected until the first graduate schools were created, barely sixty years ago. In an amazingly rapid development, American universities became the equal of European institutions, and, since the end of World War II, have even passed them on many fronts.

It would be dangerous to have the effective scope of the American college campus restricted again. Experience in other fields suggests that this danger may not be easily visible to an outsider. For example, before World War I, people knew dimly about slum conditions in big cities and the ravages of child labor, and yet it took many surveys concretely describing these conditions before the demand for social legislation became articulate and strong. And so with questions of academic freedom. We are concerned here again with an issue raised once before. Many citizens who believed they were serving the security of their country by attacking college professors probably did not realize that, in doing so, they endangered an important development in American higher education.

Auxiliary Readings

A. Group Characteristics and Their Interrelations

R. B. Cattell, "New Concepts for Measuring Leadership, in Terms of Group Syntality," *Human Relations,* 4 (1951), pp. 161–84.
Cattell has developed the concept of *syntality* to define for groups what the concept of personality does for the individual. Since factor analysis has been employed to clarify personality traits, the author suggests that it be similarly employed for syntality traits. Groups may be characterized by *population* variables (deriving parametric indices from aggregates); *structural* variables (based on interrelations among members); and *syntality* variables (which are primarily global CC's). The concept of leadership is defined not in terms of the individual, but in terms of its influence upon group syntality.

C. R. Pace and G. G. Stern, "An Approach to the Measurement of Psychological Characteristics of College Environments," *Journal of Educational Psychology,* 49 (1958), pp. 269–77.
An attempt to develop measures of "college environment," deriving from Murray's "need" and "press" categories. A College Characteristics Index is developed, dealing with various aspects of college life (teaching, rules and regulations, student organizations, etc.). These characteristics of the college are classified according to whether they are harmonious with the Murray needs. The instrument was employed in five colleges and its reliability and validity assessed. Athough itemized indices are employed, the items refer to characteristics of the entire institution, not of its constituent members.

P. M. Blau, "Formal Organization: Dimensions of Analysis," *American Journal of Sociology,* LXIII (July 1957), pp. 58–69.
Distinguishes three major dimensions of formal organization: the structural, organizational, and developmental. The structural dimension is based on aggregate CC's, such as proportion of members identifying with the group, the average number of sociometric choices, homogeneity of interests, etc. The organizational dimension derives primarily from global CC's, such as personnel policies, supervisory practices, hierarchy of offices, official rules, etc. The developmental dimension deals with change and adjustment. The panel technique, used primarily in the study of individual change, is recommended as a procedure for investigating organizational dynamics.

H. C. Selvin and W. O. Hagstrom, "The Empirical Classification of Formal Groups," *American Sociological Review,* 28 (1963), pp. 399–411.
A sophisticated attempt to reveal the major underlying dimensions of groups through the use of aggregative indices. Twenty women's residence groups were studied in terms of sixty-one aggregative characteristics. A factor analysis of these group characteristics reveal five major orthogonal factors, isolating the major dimensions along which these groups can be ranked. The groups are found to fall into a small number of empirical types. The authors suggest that such a procedure is applicable to even broader levels of group analysis, such as secondary groups and even total societies.

J. Coleman, *et. al., Macrosociology* (Boston: Allyn and Bacon, 1971).

Coleman reviews the use of global indicators in small group research, community studies, and anthropological work. What kind of performances, collective products, institutional arrangements, tribal costumes, etc. are used to make inferences as to the social structure or the norms of the collective? What is the nature of the inference from the indicators to the underlying reality?

M. F. Nimkoff and R. Middleton, "Types of Family and Types of Economy," *American Journal of Sociology,* LXVI (November 1960), pp. 215–25.

A multivariate analysis of global characteristics, treating the society as the unit of analysis. A study of the 549 cultures included in Murdock's "World Ethnographic Sample" shows that in societies dominated by agriculture, fishing, and animal husbandry, the extended family system prevails; hunting and gathering societies, on the other hand, tend to have an independent family system. Geographically mobile societies also tend to have independent families, but this is entirely due to the nature of the economic system; "when general subsistence patterns are partialled out in the analysis, there is no significant relationship between mobility and family type."

G. P. Murdock, *Social Structure* (New York: Macmillan Company, 1949), pp. 75–90.

The classical work employing the community as the unit of analysis and examining relations among community variates. Building upon the original crosscultural area files, and supplementing these data with additional information from other societies, the author is able to show relationships between migration and political independence, slavery and stratification, migration and stratification, etc. An important tradition of anthropological investigation has since developed from this work.

C. Ackerman, "Affiliations: Structural Determinants of Differential Divorce Rates," *American Journal of Sociology,* LXIX (July 1963), pp. 13–20.

Advances the notion that the pattern of the network of affiliations is a structural determinant of the probability of divorce in societies. Sixty-two societies meeting certain criteria were selected from the Human Relations Area Files. Community endogamy is treated as an ordinal variate. The more endogamous the community, the lower the divorce rate; the more exogamous, the higher the rate. The same holds true for consanguine endogamy. Communities permitting marriage with first cousins show low divorce rates, whereas communities forbidding marriage with second degree cousins are high in divorce. Employing fundamentally global CC's, the author presents some interesting conditional relationships.

W. V. Heydebrand, "The Study of Organizations," *Information. International Social Science Council,* VI, No. 5 (October 1967), pp. 59–86.

An exhaustive examination of the literature on organizations. Suggests how organizational characteristics can be classified by aggregate statistics or global properties, and points to potentialities for multivariate analysis of such data. The author offers a set of criteria for the future development of organizational research.

P. M. Blau, W. V. Heydebrand and R. E. Stauffer, "The Structure of Small Bureaucracies," *American Sociological Review,* 31 (April 1966), pp. 179–91.

An investigation of 156 public personnel agencies, employing aggregate and global CC's exclusively as variates. Each agency is characterized in terms of degree of division of labor (reflected in distinct occupational titles), professionalization (proportion of staff with college degrees), managerial hierarchy (ratio of managerial to nonsupervisory staff); and administrative staff (proportion of clerks to total staff). A sophisticated multivariate analysis leads to a number of valuable generalizations about the nature of bureaucracy.

E. Harvey, "Technology and the Structure of Organizations," *American Sociological Review,* 33 (April 1968), pp. 247–59.

A study of forty-three industrial organizations, examining the relationship between organizational technology and various aspects of organizational structure. The more "technically diffuse" the organization, the fewer the number of sub-units of the organizational structure, the fewer the levels of authority, the smaller the ratio of managers and supervisors to total personnel, and the lower the program specification. Technically diffuse organizations are shown to have a "low" organizational structure even when size, location, form of ownership, etc. are controlled.

B. The Weight of Collective Characteristics

L. Meltzer, "Comparing Relationships of Individual and Average Variables to Individual Response," *American Sociological Review,* 28 (1963), pp. 117–23.

The attitudes of individuals, and the average attitudes of the groups of which they are members, are related to a number of dependent variables. The relationship of the group attitude (even though based on individual responses to the dependent variable) is generally stronger than that of the individual attitude itself. Where the dependent variable refers to group process, the average group attitude shows the stronger relationship; where the dependent variable refers to the respondent himself, the individual independent variable is more powerful.

P. M. Blau, "Structural Effects," *American Sociological Review,* 25 (April 1963), pp. 178–92.

Caseworkers in a public assistance agency were studied with regard to attitudes and behavior toward clients and work. These caseworkers were organized into units of five or six under a supervisor. It was thus possible to consider the individual caseworker's pro-client orientation and the aggregate pro-client orientation of each group. The data show that the caseworker's attitudes and behavior are affected by the group norms independently of the individual's attitude, even though the group norms are based on the individual's attitudes. Blau calls the group influences "structural effects" as distinguished from "individual effects." The structural and individual effects are about equally powerful.

R. L. Simpson, "Parental Influence, Anticipatory Socialization, and Social Mobility," *American Sociological Review,* 27 (August 1962), pp. 517–22.

An attempt to assess peer and parent influences on mobility aspirations. Parental advice to enter professions was the indicator of parental influence; the occupations of the fathers of the three best friends indicated peer influence. The results showed that both parent and peer influences had an effect on mobility aspirations independent of one another (particularly in the working class). Overall, parental influence was more strongly related to aspirations than peer influence.

M. L. Levin, "Social Climates and Political Socialization," *Public Opinion Quarterly,* 25 (1961), pp. 596–606.

Demonstrates that various environments—the family, the high-school climate, and the national political scene—influence adolescent political preferences. Both social status and family environment influence these preferences. But while family environment continues to exercise a powerful influence when social status is controlled, status has almost no impact when family environment is controlled. Family environment is an "intervening variate."

M. Pinard, "Structural Attachments and Political Support in Urban Politics: The Case of Fluoridation Referendums," *American Journal of Sociology,* LXVIII (1963), pp. 513–26.

The thesis is advanced that behavior on fluoridation referendums is influenced by degree of community integration. A total of 262 communities is studied, based on aggregate statistics. Community integration is indexed by diverse measures: turnout at the polls, population size, level of unemployment, community growth, and ethnic and status structures. An ingenious multivariate analysis enables the investigator to determine the significance of these structural variates. The mode of analysis is essentially comparative.

C. Contextual Analysis

J. A. Davis, J. L. Spaeth and C. Huson, "A Technique for Analyzing the Effects of Group Composition," *American Sociological Review*, 26 (April 1961), pp. 215–225.

Suggests a technique for assessing the effects of a given attribute, both as a characteristic of individuals and of aggregates. The authors classify a number of types of relationships which may appear, and offer empirical examples of the procedure.

M. Rosenberg, *Society and the Adolescent Self-Image* (Princeton: Princeton University Press, 1965), chapter 4.

Contextual dissonance refers to a situation in which the individual's social characteristics differ from those of the population by which he is surrounded. The data indicate that young people reared in a dissonant religious context manifest more symptoms of emotional disturbance. Among those in dissonant contexts, pupils raised in "culturally dissimilar" neighborhoods appear more likely to show these symptoms.

A. B. Wilson, "Residential Segregation of Social Classes and Aspirations of High-School Boys," *American Sociological Review*, 24 (December 1959), pp. 836–45.

Does the socioeconomic context of the high school affect the educational aspirations of boys, independently of their own socioeconomic status? Within the same socioeconomic level, boys in the higher status schools are more likely to aspire to college than those in lower status schools. This relationship is maintained even when a number of relevant variables is controlled. Other values, such as political party preference, are also shown to be affected by the school context.

L. I. Pearlin and M. Rosenberg, "Nurse-Patient Social Distance and the Structural Context of a Mental Hospital," *American Sociological Review*, 27 (February 1967), pp. 56–65.

A study of the social distance between nursing staff and patients in a mental hospital. The status distance attitudes of nursing personnel working on predominantly Negro, mixed, or predominantly white wards are compared. Among the lower level nursing personnel, the racial composition of the ward does not influence status distance, but among higher level nursing staff, the effect of the ward composition is considerable. Similarly, among those highly "obeisant to authority," the racial context has a much greater effect than on those low in obeisance. Other examples show how the contextual effect is conditioned by individual characteristics.

S. A. Stouffer, *et al*. The American Soldier: Combat and Its Aftermath (*Studies in Social Psychology in World War II*, Vol. II) (Princeton: Princeton University Press, 1949), pp. 250–52.

This massive sociological study of American fighting men contained one of the early examples of contextual analysis. Three groups were distinguished: green troops in green outfits; green troops in veteran outfits (replacements); and veterans in these divisions. The green troops were more likely to feel ready to go into battle than the equally inexperienced replacements, who were surrounded by veterans. Conversely, the replacements were less likely than the green troops to feel that they could take charge of men in combat; contact with the veterans reduced their feelings of competence.

P. H. Ennis, "The Contextual Dimension in Voting." In W. McPhee and W. A. Glaser (eds.), *Public Opinion and Congressional Elections* (New York: The Free Press, 1962), pp. 180–211.

An article illustrating both comparative studies (in which the relative impact of different contexts is assessed) and contextual studies (in which the relationships between variates are found to be conditional upon the contexts). The contextual variates are communities, characterized in terms of demographic structure, party preponderance, and local climates of opinion. For example, the impact of occupational position on vote is much stronger in metropolitan than in rural areas. Numerous illustrations of such contectual effects are presented.

Panel Analysis

Introduction

SOCIAL LIFE IS an ever-changing, ever-moving process, and the development of techniques for the study of change stands as one of the foremost challenges of social science methodology.

Not that we have been indifferent to the issue of time in our earlier sections. The discussion of multivariate analysis sought to alert the reader to the essential distinction between antecedent and intervening variables, the former being temporally prior to the independent variable, the latter entering at a point in time between the independent and dependent variables. Similarly, in the discussion of conditional relationships, we have seen how the use of the age variable may enable us to approximate the study of time; the younger the individual, the stronger the relationship between his social class and voting behavior, thus suggesting an increasing level of class consciousness in recent decades. Finally, of course, the fundamental distinction between the independent and dependent variable implies that the former is temporally prior, since an assumed cause can never come after its effect.

Many readers will be familiar with two types of studies that deal directly with time: the trend study and the prediction study. But neither of these is a very forceful tool in the study of causation. Prediction studies by definition are not concerned with causation; trend studies permit some interpretive inferences, but such studies are only concerned with net change. Thus, the popularity of a politician may remain constant over time, but this may result from the fact that some people begin to admire him while others turn away. If we really want to explore causal relationships in such a situation, we will profit greatly by repeated observations on each sample in the study. Such a panel study [1] allows us to observe the sequencing of variates rather than merely to rely upon assumptions about their time order.

Note the similarity to a field like econometrics. There, the introduction of difference equations represented great progress over the analysis of supply and demand; there were always such problems as whether a swelling of demand made for an increase in supply or whether an overabundant supply decreased demand. Once demand and supply could be ascertained at different time periods, the problems were reduced. As a matter of fact, panel analysis originated from a parallel dilemma. In early mass communications research, it was often observed that people who listened to a specific program were more likely to use the product it advertised. This was seized upon as evidence of the persuasive power of the program. But equally plausibly, people might have begun to listen *after* they bought the product in order to be assured that they had made the correct choice. As we shall see at the end of this section, panel analysis permits us to separate these two sequences.

General Principles of Panel Studies

The logical nucleus of any panel study derives from a question which can be answered in two ways and which is asked of the same people twice. The total information so acquired can be represented in a fourfold table such as that below, where we have inserted arbitrary figures. When

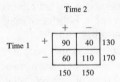

we look only at the marginals (the figures outside the four central cells) the only thing we can say is that the table shows a trend toward a small increase in positive replies. But inside the fourfold table we see that this net increase reflects a considerable change of position within the sample: one hundred respondents have played a game of musical chairs.

The student must realize that the same set of marginals is compatible with any number of "inside figures." In one extreme situation, 130 positives could maintain the same position; then by necessity, if the same marginals were to be kept, the twenty changers would be those who switched from minus to plus. The + − cell would be zero. On the other hand, it is possible to find a complete reversal of position where scarcely any cases fall in the + + or − − cells. (The Lazarsfeld 1939 article in the annotated bibliography documents such

a shift in public opinion when it was discovered that a liberal senator had once been a member of the Ku Klux Klan.)

The movement of observations taken on each individual from one time to the next is usually called turnover. From a single such table, one can proceed to more complex forms of analysis by subdividing the data. For example, one can study men and women separately and hence the question of whether women are more likely to change than men. This would give a table with eight entries. Once such a table is established, it can lead to a surprisingly large number of interpretations according to the type of qualifying variates introduced. We can proceed even further by studying several variates and the fashion in which they change over more than two periods.

The basic tenets of panel analysis are described systematically in the initial selection. In 1946, the Philadelphia Philosophical Society called a meeting to review the significant recent advances in empirical research. Selection 35 is the report given at that occasion to introduce the main precepts of panel analysis. Ten years later, there were sufficient applications to the study of voting behavior to introduce a standard presentation in the *Handbook of Social Psychology*.[2] There, Lipset *et al.* reported on the psychology of the voting decision. Lazarsfeld contributed a "doctrine" on panel analysis, and the following set of selections is guided by his 1954 outline.

Turnover

The dichotomous turnover table mentioned above was deceptively simple. With a specific set of marginals, the inside of the table was fixed as soon as the entry in one cell is given. Therefore, the entire process of turnover could be described by a single index. Many such indices have been debated. But when each observation falls into more than two categories the matter becomes far more complex. Take as an example the following table:

Scientific Majors at the Undergraduate and Graduate Levels *

| B.S. MAJOR | Ph.D. MAJOR | | |
	Physics	Chemistry	Biology
Physics	108	5	—	113
Chemistry	5	486	16	507
Biology	—	6	223	229
	113	497	239	

* Occupational Mobility of Scientists, Bulletin No. 1121, Bureau of Labor Statistics, 1953, pp. 27–8.

On even such a simple 3×3 table one can demonstrate turnover as a conceptual idea.

Thus, like the concepts we discussed in Section I, we must develop the imagery of turnover before it can be measured. How should we think of it? Is it the proportion of people who change position, that is, the thirty-two majors who are outside the main diagonal in the table above? Perhaps so. But we might also be interested in how far people change. Physics, chemistry, and biology represent three substantive steps in the scientific discipline. Do changers move as far away from their original position as possible, or do they tend to take smaller steps? Thus, for example, do physicists shift to chemistry (nearby) or to biology (far away)? Conversely, how far do biologists move?

Any measure of turnover would correspond to what was called a parametric index in Section I. The student should carry out a variety of numerical experiments with the tables. For example, take the previous table, and let the marginal distributions stay fixed. How many cells can be filled arbitrarily? The student will discover that only four of the cells can be filled in this way.

This is usually expressed by saying that such a table has four degrees of freedom. Suppose then that the number of stable people, those in the main diagonal, is also fixed in advance. Again, this means that only one of the remaining six cells can be filled arbitrarily. Somehow, this is psychologically surprising. If the two marginal distributions are not fixed (always counting the total sample as 100 percent), the number of degrees of freedom doubles.

Once this numerical possibility has sunk in it becomes clear that the notion of turnover can require quite a variety of indices for proper description. Clearly, the situation becomes more complex with a large number of subcategories. Thus, it might be useful to add one more exercise with a 4×4 turnover table. Remember that what we are trying to establish are ways of characterizing the shape of the turnover where two variables are involved simultaneously. Even when one seeks to describe the shape of a single variate, for example, the scores on a scale of political liberalism, the imagery of "shape" can be broken down into many "dimensions." Where are the bulk of the scores? (The modes.) How widespread is the distribution? (The standard deviation.) Is the distribution skewed or symmetrical? (Even the beginner should know that this is expressed essentially by the third moment.) A turnover table is more complex only because it is a simultaneous distribution of two variates.

Only with specific kinds of data do turnover tables seem to be studied for their own sake. Mobility is one of these areas. Has there been a significant change in social class or occupational choice from one generation to another? A typical turnover table is provided in Selection 36. Rogoff relates occupation of father to the occupation of son in a large sample. She does not develop a specific index but analyzes the total structure of the table. Her technique happens to be identical with the one used in the Radermacher-Smith selection in the first edition.

The student might ponder the fact that sometimes seemingly different notions, like affinity and turnover, can be expressed by the same type of quantification.

One aspect of the turnover phenomenon has stirred up debate: how does one know whether change is due to measurement error or true shifts? Every classification is subject to technical error—carelessness of interviewers, faulty coding, etc. Approximately 5 per cent of all questionnaires if repeated at two intervals show changes in sex, age, and other items that should be constant. There are other changes which everyone will agree reflect reality. In Selection 37 Kendall shows that if people are asked about their moods at two different times, 30 per cent change their answer. It is at this point that an argument is possible. Has the mood truly changed or has the meaning of the adjectives shifted from one time to the next? Words are only indicators of an underlying state of mind and the relation between the observed data and the intended classification is not necessarily stable. But oscillations are of substantive interest and to think of them as errors seems unjustified. Still the problem of distinguishing different sources of change remains unsolved. The best one can do at the moment is to make sure that the notion of measurement error taken over from test theory does not confuse the substantive problems of social research. Kendall's way of doing this is to show that turnover can be substantively predicted. In the original monograph from which our selection is taken she develops a variety of methods by which one can ask people to make choices of varying degrees of difficulty. The closer the resemblance between the two alternatives of a choice, the more likely it is that the turnover will be larger when the choice has to be made twice.

It is only fair to represent the opposite position which Maccoby and Hyman take in Selection 38. Their main point is that a simple mathematical model can be developed which would explain some findings of voting panels as results of error. It seems to us that they are mistaken because their mathematical model can as well be interpreted substantively. To permit the student to form his own judgment, Lazarsfeld has added a discussion (Selection 39) permitting a direct comparison of findings with other selections in this volume. By more than a coincidence this selection also explains the index of turnover which Kendall uses.

Qualified Change

It was mentioned above that in most cases one is not only interested in one turnover table, but wants to compare a number of such tables. These comparisons deal with the same people under different conditions. Kendall exposes the same group of students to a variety of questions, and Rogoff compares the population of Indianapolis at two points in history.

By contrast, in the analysis of qualified change, we start with a population which is then subdivided into two more groups by some essential characteristic. It is the effect of this characteristic on the turnover in which we are interested. It will turn out that this more complex approach provides considerable flexibility to what at first seems a simple array of figures. Such qualified change can be of interest in a variety of ways.

Suppose we take two observations on prospective voters during an electoral campaign. Between these two observations, the respondents could have been exposed to the influence of listening to a radio speech or talking to a political canvasser. What was the effect of this exposure? The net effect of this exposure as glimpsed by a trend study of voter preferences might be very small. But a more detailed study of the structure of change could reveal that the people who were exposed to these propaganda events changed quite markedly in the direction of the influence while other respondents switched in the opposite direction, presumably because of other unidentified influences. A panel analysis is especially useful in the case of self-selection where people themselves choose whether they want to be exposed. (The relationship of panels to laboratory experiments will be discussed in Selection 47.)

A similar problem arises when the qualifier is a basic disposition or environmental factor which is related to the original observation. Sons of Republicans are more likely to express Republican intentions the first time than are sons of Democrats. Are they also more likely to persist in these intentions? The problem is similar to the modes of causal analysis discussed in Section II, but we are now on safer ground. The time sequence of the three variates is clearly established.

Let us discuss the procedure by drawing upon hypothetical data. We would start out with a turnover table relating vote intention at the beginning of a campaign to intention at a later phase of the campaign. The qualifier is the political attitude of the father. Suppose we have a number of male voters, some of whom are sons of Republicans and some of whom have Democrat fathers. We ask our sample about their voting plans and then divide the group into those who intend to vote Republican and those who say they will choose Democrat. We shall make the reasonable assumption that sons are more likely to express the

same voting intent as their fathers than the opposite intent. Some time later we establish again how the respondents intend to vote. For simplicity's sake we shall assume that both groups of respondents show the same amount of turnover. The numerical schema below then represents this situation.

This looks like an uninteresting exercise because we have introduced so many restrictions: same turnover in both types of families, which means that the "correlation" between the intentions at two different points in time is the same for both groups. And we have also assumed constant marginals: the "correlation" between the political climate of the family and the individual intentions of our respondents remains unchanged as far as the sample as a whole is concerned.

Still, the figures of Schema I can produce some additional information. It is technically and substantively important to bring this point out clearly. To facilitate the explanation we have attached letters to the four rows of Schema I. We now rearrange the rows by shifting to a different qualifier. We begin by dividing the respondents according to their first vote intention. Then we relate in each subgroup the family background to the second vote intention. This leads to Schema II, where the old rows (A) and (C) now form the fourfold table to the left and rows (B) and (D) the one to the right.

The new layout forces a new perspective because each row tells its own story: thus,

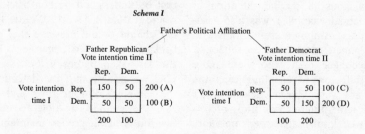

Schema I

Father's Political Affiliation

		Father Republican Vote intention time II					Father Democrat Vote intention time II		
		Rep.	Dem.				Rep.	Dem.	
Vote intention time I	Rep.	150	50	200 (A)	Vote intention time I	Rep.	50	50	100 (C)
	Dem.	50	50	100 (B)		Dem.	50	150	200 (D)
		200	100				100	200	

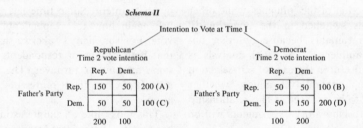

Schema II

Intention to Vote at Time I

		Republican Time 2 vote intention					Democrat Time 2 vote intention		
		Rep.	Dem.				Rep.	Dem.	
Father's Party	Rep.	150	50	200 (A)	Father's Party	Rep.	50	50	100 (B)
	Dem.	50	50	100 (C)		Dem.	50	150	200 (D)
		200	100				100	200	

row A says that of the people who come from a Republican background and intended to vote Republican the first time, 75 per cent maintained this intention at the second interview while 25 per cent defected to the other party. The other three rows can be easily read in an analogous way.

Taking the new arrangement as a whole we notice that family background plays a double role: sons of Republicans who intend to vote Republican (A) maintain this intention much more frequently than sons of Democrats who intend to vote Republican (C); corresponding results arise from comparing rows (B) and (D). This is a finding which makes much sociological sense. If people come from social backgrounds favorable to a decision they are much more likely to maintain their plan than those whose intentions might be undermined by conflicting cross-pressures.

Two selections illustrate the application of the general idea. Clausen (Selection 40) shows that soldiers' plans to return to school were more frequent among younger men; but in addition, implementation of plans (analogous to second intention in our hypothetical example) was also associated with age. Among those veterans who had *not* planned to go back to school, it was the younger men who were more likely to shift toward enrolling than the older veterans were. Glaser (Selection 41) reports the same findings in a study of voting. It is well known that men are more likely to have a vote intention than women

are. But if one interviews the two groups a second time to ascertain actual voting, it turns out that men have more often carried through their intentions than women have.

At first one might consider this a finding of great generality. If a background factor favors an intention, it has the additional effect of stabilizing this intention. And yet one might feel that here is another statistical trick, because the result could be derived as a numerical necessity from the assumptions of stable marginals and equal turnover built into Schema I. Actually the situation is as follows. We deal here with situations where a background factor maintains its relationship with some criterion (choosing an occupation, voting, etc.) over a long period of time. Generally speaking, it is necessary that this equilibrium be maintained by some social mechanism. This mechanism is represented by the double role of the background factor: it is related to the original position as well as to the probability that it remains unchanged.

The implication of this mechanism can best be understood by constructing a case where it does *not* work. We use the layout of Schema II and preserve the figures for background and first interview. This gives the asterisked figures in Schema III. But now we assume that the defection rate is the same in all four rows and the same as in the sample as a whole. In other words, two-thirds of all groups maintain their intention and one-third defect the next time.

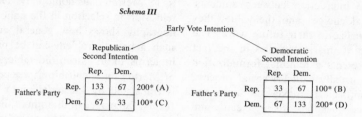

Schema III

This gives the figures *within* the two contingent tables. But now one of the assumptions built into Schema I cannot be maintained. *The relation between family background and second intent is now lower than the initial one.* The student should check this by adding the two contingent tables of Schema III.

This is the reverse of the Schema II example. If the mechanisms of conditional effects are not operative, then the *original association between background and intention gets corroded.* The student is urged to study other possibilities by numerical examples, e.g., if a Republican family background loses its maintaining effect, while the Democratic family keeps it. The teacher might also discuss what happens to the relation between first and second vote intentions in Schema III as compared to Schema I. Incidentally, the whole story can be put into general form by applying dichotomous algebra (see Selection 23). The student should relate all these numerical examples to the notion of a dichotomous cube developed there. He should notice especially that the difference between Schemas I and II consists in cutting the dichotomous cube into different directions. The selection by Glaser provides many additional examples which permit us to compare various conditional effects. Selection 42 by Pasanella describes the amazing similarity between the study of these conditional effects in sociology and the use of moderator variables in psychological research.

Concurrent Changes

So far we have assumed that we are coping with one criterion established twice and with a qualifying factor. We reach an additional level of complexity if we turn to the study of two variates, both of which may change between the two time periods. In the article by Lipset *et al.*, listed in the Notes on page 329, we have a typical example. Respondents were asked in August and again in October what party they intended to vote for and how they felt about Willkie's candidacy. Willkie had just emerged as a Republican candidate; he was hitherto unknown and people only slowly formed an opinion about him. While usually vote intention and opinions of a candidate are highly related, there was an initial uncertainty in the reaction. Only at the second interview was the usual high association between the two variates reestablished. But how did it come about? Did people change their vote intent to fit their impression of the new candidate, or did the sequence work in reverse?

The minimum data to describe this mode of analysis requires a table with 16 cells. The observation on the two variates at the first point in time consists of the four cells of the fourfold table which are now listed in serial order. For these four groups, the same combination of four responses is available at the second observation. The full information therefore requires a 4 × 4 tabulation. A typical example of such a sixteenfold table is discussed in a study by Morris

Rosenberg (first edition) where he examined the interaction between students' occupational choices and the values they hoped to realize in their future work. The importance of this system lies in the fact that it represents a minimal formalization of what is usually called a social process. In this approach it makes no sense any more to raise questions of simple cause and effect. The variates at one time are related to the same variates the next time and the whole schema provides a first approach to problems which are usually called feedbacks or loops or interactions. Such processes are crucial for empirical social research, and it is therefore not surprising that they have been analyzed in a variety of ways. Selection 43 reproduces an unpublished paper by Lazarsfeld which raised the issue and originally proposed one kind of index to assess the relative effect of one factor upon the other. Several others had been suggested since, based on a variety of considerations. We have singled out in Selection 44 a procedure developed by Coleman. It is based on the idea that people move from one combination of positions to another, partly by random shocks and partly due to the attraction which the two factors exercise. The mathematics by which Coleman separates these parameters is too difficult to reproduce but Selection 44 provides interesting examples of the results. It has also the merit of introducing additional elements into a sixteenfold table.

One has to take seriously the relation between the seemingly simple scheme of a sixteenfold table and the general notion of social process. The latter theme requires the idea of continuous interaction between at least two variates, an idea which goes beyond the simple notion of unidirectional causation. If we find that people who are friends are likely to share the same values, we do not even stop to raise the question of which "causes" which. We take it for granted that association favors similarity of seeing the world, which in turn facilitates

friendship, which in turn strengthens what R. K. Merton calls homophily. The Lazarsfeld-Merton selection in the annotated bibliography shows how general analysis of such a broad problem can be reproduced in terms of a sixteenfold table. An essay of Merton on friendship as a social process is translated by Lazarsfeld into this more formal language. Both authors then discuss what is gained and lost by such a translation.

Repeated Observations on Collectives

For the sake of simple exposition, we talked about panels in terms of observations on individuals. But collectives can also be the object of panel analysis. A startling example is Lipset's study of voting records of Southern counties just prior to the Civil War. At the regular presidential election of 1860 the voters had a choice between an antislavery and a proslavery party. A few months later a referendum was held on secession. There was a considerable turnover between the two events. Many counties which had voted for the Republicans (antislavery candidates) voted for secession and the other way around. Lipset uses as a qualifier economic information on the actual slave-holding situation in all the counties. His interpretation is as follows. In the usual political election, people are strongly influenced by party and personal loyalties; these have been shaped by many factors. But in the vote on secession, economic interests took priority and these shifts of salience account for many changes. This analysis stays within panel procedures already described but shows its explanatory value in an unusual context. One should expect that many other users of historical data could profit from Lipset's pioneering idea as expressed in Selection 45.

Levenson, in Selection 46, deals with another kind of collective: small groups where each member made a sociometric choice among the other members. His units of analysis are pairs of people between which there could be reciprocal, unilateral or no choices. A repeated observation would show which of the prior choices broke up and which new ones were created. The patterns of constantly changing relationships provide interesting ideas on the paths along which friendships might be sought and dissolved.

Relation Between Panels and Experiments

There is an obvious connection between these study designs. Like the panel, the experiment permits a clear time sequence between stimulus and response. The experiment has the added advantage that the experimental and the control group can be made comparable by proper randomization procedures whereas in the panel study, the people who choose to listen to a speech, for example, are not comparable to those who did not tune in to the same speech. The qualifier procedure can greatly improve the comparability but can rarely achieve the precision of a controlled experiment. On the other hand, the experiment can lead to fallacious application as the following examples show. When educational radio became available, much optimism was aroused because laboratory experiments had shown how much people learned from such programs. In fact, however, educational radio was rather ineffective. Those people who were most likely to profit from it just selected not to listen. Such a finding could only be brought out by a qualified turnover study. For example, one could use an index of educational level as a qualifier and then study all possible interrelations between it, listening and learning.

The whole question is lucidly explained by Hovland in Selection 47. Hovland presented his paper in a seminar on panel analysis sponsored by the nascent Ford Center for the Behavioral Sciences. The present selection was his presidential address to the Eastern Sociological Association, and it is one of the last publications of this creative colleague.

In Selection 48 Kendall applies panel analysis to the evaluation of an instructional program in a medical school. The problem was whether a one-semester course on comprehensive medical care would affect the attitudes of medical students. It was not possible to get strict control, but it was possible to schedule the course so that for some of the students, the experimental course preceded a course in obstetrics whereas for other students, the course order was reversed. Panel analysis enabled Kendall to distinguish the more permanent from the more transitory effects of the comprehensive care lectures.

Interestingly enough this section has to have an open end. Attention to panel research has continuously increased; the sixteenfold table has especially intrigued various writers because of the surprising richness of data it provides. In recent years a number of authors, such as Raymond Boudon, James Coleman, David Heise, Otis Duncan, have proposed mathematical models to better understand the mutual interaction process underlying such material. The senior editor, whose original paper is one of our selections, has also extended this analysis in monographs available from the Bureau of Applied Social Research. From there also, a bibliography of these recent publications can be obtained; their content goes beyond the scope of the present collection.

Notes

1. At this point, the majority of these inquiries have been conducted in connection with political campaigns. The introduction to *The People's Choice*, cited in the annotated bibliography, gives an account of how such studies developed and spread to other countries.
2. Seymour M. Lipset *et al.*, "The Psychology of Voting," *Handbook of Social Psychology*, Vol. II (Reading, Mass.: Addison-Wesley, 1954), pp. 1150–63.

A. General Statements

35. The Use of Panels in Social Research

PAUL F. LAZARSFELD

THE FOLLOWING remarks are designed to draw attention to a fairly recent development in social research. In its bare essentials, the type of study to be discussed consists of repeated interviews made with the same group of persons. The people participating as subjects in such studies are commonly known as panel members and the whole procedure has become widely known under the name of panel technique.

There are two main types of research problems to which the panel technique is likely to be applied. If the effect of some specific event or series of events is to be studied, then we have the first type of situation in which the panel technique may be used. In one such case, a sample of voters in an Ohio county was kept under observation for six months during the 1940 Presidential campaign, the purpose being to study what effect the propaganda of the two parties had upon the way people made up their minds.[1] In another case, the American Association for the United Nations wanted to find out the best way of getting Americans more interested in the progress of U.N. activities. A sample of persons in a mid-West city of about 800,000 was inter-

viewed about their attitudes towards the United Nations and the actions of the United States in foreign affairs. An intensive informational campaign was conducted by this organization and after the campaign was over the same sample was interviewed again.[2] In a similar way, advertising agencies sometimes use panels to study the effectiveness of their promotional efforts.[3]

The other main type of panel study is somewhat more difficult to describe because no major findings are yet available in the literature. In a society as complex and changing as our own, the individual is continually placed in a situation where he must reconcile the different and variant elements of his experience. A Quaker who is a convinced pacifist sees the country endangered by an enemy. How will he resolve the conflict between his pacifism and his patriotism? A convinced Communist sees the Soviet Union making moves which he considers imperialistic. How will he reconcile his party loyalty and his intellectual judgment on a specific political issue? But we don't need to remain in the area of big issues to look for problems of this kind. In everyday life almost everyone is con-

Reprinted with permission from *Proceedings of the American Philosophical Society*, 92, No. 5 (November 1948) (copyright 1948 by the American Philosophical Society).

tinuously under cross-pressures of some kind. People belong to different social groups which may have conflicting interests. The individual must make all sorts of choices among his needs, desires, and situational demands, some of which are relatively important, others relatively insignificant.

The study of people under cross-pressures is one of the major concerns of social science today. In going through recent social science literature one often comes across statements of the following sort, "In getting higher education the English Catholic must choose between ethnic affiliation and religion; he generally chooses to study with his Protestant ethnic fellows at McGill University. . . . "[4] The application of the panel technique to problems of this sort allows a greater degree of analytical precision. It would allow us to state, for example, the proportion of English Catholics who go to McGill for their higher education and the proportion who go to Catholic institutions, and to compare intensively those who resolve the conflict between their ethnic affiliation and their religion in one way with those who resolve this conflict in another.

The understanding of what actually transpires in such situations will make for tremendous gains in the understanding of social change. The application of the panel technique to this area of social science interest will be one of its major contributions. By keeping sets of people under repeated observation, we can register the changes they make in their attitudes, affiliations, habits, and expectations. We can learn which of the various attitudes, affiliations, etc., are more basic and hence more constant and which are more superficial and changeable. We hope to determine, if elements change, which element in a psychological or social situation is the more dominant one controlling the changes in the other factors.

The outstanding example of such a study is that undertaken by Theodore Newcomb of the students of a "progressive" college attended by the daughters of well-to-do families. The faculty of this college was quite liberal but the background of the girls quite conservative. For four years the investigators observed the various ways in which one group of girls resolved this conflict.[5]

The reader who is somewhat acquainted with social science literature will at this point raise a justified question especially with reference to the first type of study. If we want to know the effect of a political campaign or a similar event, why do we have to reinterview the same people? Couldn't we interview one group of respondents before the event and a similar one after the event. By comparing the two, the argument runs, we would get a fairly good idea as to the influence which the event had. Numerous examples of this kind come to mind. Many of us have seen public opinion polls taken, for instance, before and after the President made a major public announcement. If people think better of him after the speech then we are sure the speech was a success. Poll data are available which show that the attitude of the average American to the Russians improved every time they were victorious in a battle during the war and slumped every time the Russians, after the war, made a move against one of their neighboring countries. This type of study is undoubtedly of very great value and is usually called a trend study.[6]

It is important to consider the differences between such trend studies and the panel technique. A considerable amount of additional information is obtained by reinterviewing the same people. The most important difference is our ability to single out in a panel study exactly who are the people who change. Once singled out, the changers can be subjected to more intensive study to determine the psychological and social-psychological elements which operated to produce the changes in question. A trend study may show us the net impact of events on opinion. A panel study can allow us to single out the individuals who changed their opinion in the course of the repeated interviewing, to probe for the psychological meaning of the event, and the role played by the various mass media of communication in the change. By interviewing the same people at least twice, we can answer questions such as the following: Are people more likely to change when they are very interested in an event and follow it in great detail; or when they are only slightly concerned and know of it only in a casual way? Some preliminary evidence seems to show that the latter is more likely to be the case. There are many proverbs which claim that men are more apt to shift than women and many others which claim the exact opposite. The panel technique permits us to say whether men or women are more likely to shift their opinions. Incidentally, the results so far do not seem to point to any sex differences.

The study of actual changes often leads to unexpected results. At the time that Senator Black was appointed a judge of the Supreme Court, he was accused of having been at one time a member of the Klu Klux Klan. It happens that there is some information available on who was affected by this allegation which suddenly threatened to change the image of a liberal into that of a reactionary. Although Senator Black received about the same amount of approval before and after the allegation, a kind of game of musical chairs took place. Jews and Catholics turned against him while about an equivalent number of Protestants were more in favor of his appointment than before the storm broke.[7]

The last example points to a second value of the panel technique. Trend studies often indicate that an event has not brought about any net change in opinion. But it might very well be that underneath this apparent constancy, there is a great amount of shift-ing of positions which can only be found out if the same people and their attitudes are traced over a period of time. At the beginning of the present 1948 presidential campaign, there is some indication of a new development in American politics. As long as Roosevelt was alive, there was a strong feeling in the population that the Democratic Party was the party of the common man whereas the Republicans represented more the interests of the wealthier sections of the population. There are indications that this appraisal of the two parties has changed somewhat and that voters, especially among the working class, are less sure than before which of the two parties represents their interests better.

Suppose that one further development takes place (for which there is no evidence but which we bring in to make our example more dramatic); some sections of the business community might feel that their interest in an active recovery program in Europe is better served by a Democratic administration. Then we might have at this moment an internal shift in the social stratification of the two parties which might go beyond any net change in both which polls or the election might show up. Such a social restratification of the major parties has taken place several times in the political history of this country. The historian looking back over this period many decades hence will not miss such a development. But if we want to know and understand it at the time it happens, we have to make studies of repeated interviews with the same people.

This is not the place to go further into detail on the comparison of panel and trend studies.[8] We shall turn rather to the other type of panel study in order to show briefly some of its considerably more complex technical aspects. The following table (Table 1) exemplifies some of the technical difficulties. It is taken from a small group of people who were interviewed twice during a presidential election. Each respondent was asked two questions: How he intended to vote and whether he felt that the Republican candidate if elected would make a good President. Because both questions were each answered on two different occasions by each respondent we have four pieces of information about each member of the panel. Table 1 classifies these replies first according to whether they were obtained at the first interview or at the second. For each interview we can then sub-classify the respondents into four groups: those who wanted to vote Democratic and who were also personally opposed to the Republican candidate; those who wanted to vote Democratic but personally respected the opposing candidate; those with Republican vote intentions who, however, disapproved of their party's candidate; and those with Republican vote intentions who also approved of the candidate.

All the information which can be obtained from two questions and two interviews with the same respondents can be represented in the following type of table.

TABLE 1

SECOND INTERVIEW

FIRST INTERVIEW	Dem. Ag.	Dem. For	Rep. Ag.	Rep. For	Total
Dem. Against	68	2	1	1	72
Dem. For	11	12	0	1	24
Rep. Against	1	0	23	11	35
Rep. For	2	1	3	129	135
Totals	82	15	27	142	266

Let us first look at the last column. Most Democrats are against the person of the Republican candidate and most Republicans are for him. But 59 of the 266 respondents have a kind of personal attachment. Twenty-four Democrats think that the opposing candidate is all right while 35 Republicans, although they intend to vote for their party, obviously wish that another candidate had been put up.

Now let us look at the bottom row of figures which come from the second interview. The number of people with such detached views has decreased. Obviously, what the campaign has done is to intensify partisan feeling. Only 15 Democrats now have a good word to say about the Republican candidate and only 27 Republicans have any doubts left about him.

But that is not all that we would like to know from this table. How do people reconcile their vote intention and their opinion on a specific issue? Do the Democrats who like the opposing candidate shift to him or do they remain Democrats and start to see him in a darker light? The answer is given in the second row of our table. There is only one case of the former, but 11 cases of the latter type. And it so happens that similar figures prevail for the Republicans. Let us look at the third row where we find the respondents who at the first interview intended to vote Republican but didn't like their candidate. One of them switched to the Democrats but 11 now feel better towards their candidate. In this one case there is no doubt that most people adjust their cross-pressures in a one-sided direction. If their party loyalties are in conflict with a specific opinion of their own they are rather more likely to maintain their party loyalties and change their opinion.

This is of course just one example from which no general conclusion should be drawn. But it shows the type of problem and the type of procedures which derive from the use of the panel technique. Just for the record it might be mentioned that the statistical analysis of tables like the preceding one is quite difficult and proper procedures are still in the process of development. It can easily be seen how many more problems would arise if we had more than two interviews and more than two questionnaire items to deal with.

Besides the difficulties in analysis discussed above, there is one other drawback of the panel technique. There is a danger that we may change our respondents' attitudes by the very fact that we reinterview them repeatedly. In some cases the danger is obvious. Suppose, for example, we interview people during a vaccination campaign. If we repeatedly ask people whether they have been vaccinated, our interviewers will probably act as reminders and speed up the success of the campaign in our panel beyond the performance of the population at large. In this case, then, the results of our study will be quite misleading. It could of course happen that our interviewers antagonize the respondents and as a result they might be less likely to get vaccinated. In other cases the panel bias is not likely to be marked. If interest in an election is high and everyone talks about it, the fact that a respondent has been asked about his vote intentions is not going to influence him very much. In any case this is a matter for concrete study. We cannot tell in advance when bias is likely to exist or not.

Actually, a few such studies of bias have been made. The technique used is fairly simple. At the time the panel is picked out a second group of respondents known as a "control group" is set up as closely matched to the panel as possible. This second group, however, is not interviewed until the whole panel study nears its end. At the time the last interview is made with the panel, the control group is also interviewed. From a statistical point of view the two groups were originally alike and should therefore at the end of the study show the same distribution of attitudes were it not that the panel group was interviewed repeatedly. Whatever significant differences show up between the two groups can be attributed to the effect of the panel bias.

Two examples should give an idea of how much work there is still to be done in this direction. During a presidential campaign it was found that the distribution of opinions in the panel was no different than in the control group. But the panel made up its mind somewhat quicker. Under the

impact of the repeated interviews the "Don't Knows" in the end were less numerous in the panel than in the control group. This is a very encouraging result. On the other hand it was found that if people were repeatedly interviewed about their newspaper reading habits the panel group was likely to do more newspaper reading than the control group. The reappearance of the interviewer obviously stimulated the reading interests of the panel members. There was some indication, however, that approximately from the third interview on this effect became less and less marked. It might very well be that if the panel had gone on longer, the panel bias would have disappeared in the end.

TABLE 2

	2nd INTERVIEW		
	Yes	No	Totals
1st INTERVIEW			
Yes	50	50	100
No	50	850	900
Totals	100	900	1000

TABLE 3

	2nd INTERVIEW		
	Yes	No	Totals
1st INTERVIEW			
Yes	400	100	500
No	100	400	500
Totals	500	500	1000

There are many operational problems involved in panel studies just as in any other large-scale research operation. How can we get people to participate in a panel and to stick to it? How do we substitute for unavoidable losses? Is it sometimes possible to correspond with panel members by mail rather than to make personal contacts?

Should we handle a panel as the American Senate is handled, always substituting part of it by new members?

Finally, there are a number of serious statistical problems to be dealt with. They all center around the concept of turnover. The following two tables exemplify the problem. They each represent one question on which people have been interviewed twice.

In the first question (Table 2) 100 people changed their minds one way or another. On the second question (Table 3) 200 people did so. One might feel that the turnover on the second question is therefore greater. But one must consider that many fewer people said "Yes" to the first question at the time of the first interview. One therefore cannot expect as many people to change as in the second case. It might be more advisable to compute the turnover as percentage of the people who said "Yes" both times. This would give a turnover of 200 per cent for the first and 50 per cent for the second table and now we would have to say that the first question has the larger turnover. There are obviously still many other ways in which turnover can be described. What index we can use to describe best the turnover in such tables is a very vexing problem, especially because most all of the statistical treatment of panel data goes back to this one point. But this is not the place to deal with such technical matters at length. It is preferable to end up with some more general theoretical considerations which will show the place panel studies are likely to hold in the social sciences in the coming years.

Basically, what we do in a panel study is relate information obtained at one time to information obtained at a subsequent time. We are in the center of what has come to be called dynamic social research. We study changes and we want to explain these changes. We know who changed and we have information on people prior to their change. Explaining the change necessarily

means to relate this previous information to the subsequent change. Everything will depend therefore upon how ingenious we are in deciding what information we should gather at different time periods. To exemplify the problem more clearly, let us assume that we are dealing with a panel of people who are about to move into a public housing project where Negroes and whites will live together.[9] If we center our attention on the whites then we know in advance that some of them will get along with their Negro fellow tenants and some will not. Some will improve their ability to get along with people of other races and some will not. What information should we collect from all these prospective tenants prior to the time they move into the housing project to help us explain what shifts in racial attitudes will take place?

We will obviously want to know their race attitudes prior to their entrance into the housing project. But it will also be important to know their *expectations*. It may turn out that the greater their initial uneasiness the more will they be pleasantly surprised by reality. On the other hand we know that some people have a hard time experiencing "reality," and if they enter a situation with apprehension they behave nervously and start trouble. Some sort of index of psychological flexibility is needed.

Pieces of information about the psychological predisposition of the respondents have been called *intervening variables* because they intervene, as it were, between the individual's reaction and the situation in which he is placed.[10] In the example given above, where a group of individuals are about to enter a public housing project, we have people who will be subject to the same external experience. They will, however, react differently. Between the external situation and the individual response there intervene certain psychological and social characteristics which channel the response in an individually characteristic fashion.

Social psychologists in recent years have developed out of their experience many hypotheses as to which intervening variables are of importance. We talk of a person's *level of aspiration* or of a person's *expectations,* indicating that we consider that such information will be of value in interpreting how the individuals will react to the situations in which they are placed.

The important intervening variables have to be ascertained before expected changes take place. To follow through with the example given above, we should know as much as we can about the panel members before they move into the inter-racial housing project. Once they have been living there it is too late to look for such information, for we can never know then whether what we have found has not already been influenced by their new experience. This is, of course, exactly where the importance of the panel technique lies. We periodically study people's attitudes, expectations and aspirations. We find out what has happened to them between interviews: what they read, with whom they talked, what external events impressed them, etc. Both the situational factors and the intervening variables change continuously. Our analysis would weave back and forth from these two series of data, expressing, in one case, reaction to the situation as a function of some psychological predisposition, and, in another, the psychological predisposition as a function of the changing situation. We would want to know how people's expectations affect the way they react to changes in their environment; and how the environment experienced changes their hopes and concerns.

On more than one occasion it has been said that one of the difficulties which impede the progress of social science is the fact that we cannot experiment with human beings in the same way that the agricultural station experiments with animals and plants. It should not be overlooked, however, that life itself is in a very real sense a continuous series of experiments. In the course of time, almost everything conceivable and sometimes things previously inconceivable happen to one group of persons or another. Although many of these events are, as yet, unpredictable, some events, fortunately for our purpose, occur with sufficient regularity or frequency so that if we know just what sort of persons will be subject to them, we can observe the various ways in which they will respond. Panel studies are conducted, usually, on the impact of events of a given predictable regularity such as voting in a presidential election, exposure to certain advertising, etc. If we find the right statistical technique we will be able to interrelate "stimulus, predisposition, and response" and with time and experience our hope is to understand, predict, and control human behavior more successfully.

The panel technique discussed here is an expensive and rather slow research operation. A social science, unfortunately, will not develop overnight, and, if we want to develop one, we will have to pay for it in time and money. We cannot prefer mere speculation because it comes to us quickly or simpler methods like cross-sectional polls and artificial laboratory experiments because they are cheap. The panel technique is just in its beginnings—we have just begun to explore some of the implications of its use—and most of its future development will require long and arduous work. Among the many lines along which the methods of the social sciences are developing, the panel technique seems to be one of the most promising for the future of a fuller understanding of human behavior.

Notes

1. P. F. Lazarsfeld, B. Berelson, and H. Gaudet, *The People's Choice* (N. Y.: Duell, Sloan and Pearce, 1944).

2. National Opinion Research Center, Report No. 37a, Cincinnati Looks Again.

3. A. R. Root, and A. C. Welch, "The continuing consumer study: a basic method for the engineering of advertising," *Journal of Marketing* 7 (July 1942).

4. E. C. Hughes, *French Canada in Transition* (University of Chicago Press, 1943), p. 86.

5. T. Newcomb, *Personality and Social Change* (N. Y.: Dryden Press, 1942).

6. Jerome S. Bruner, *Mandate From the People* (N. Y.: Duell, Sloan and Pearce, 1944); Cantril, Hadley, *Gauging Public Opinion* (Princeton: Princeton University Press, 1944).

7. P. F. Lazarsfeld, "The Change of Opinion During a Political Discussion," *Journal of Applied Psychology,* 23 (1939), pp. 131–47.

8. Interested readers will find such a discussion and concrete examples in Chapter 10, "The Panel," in *Say It With Figures* by H. Zeisel (N. Y.: Harpers, 1946).

9. An especially rich source for such explanatory variables will be found in a housing study organized by the Lavanburg Foundation under the direction of Robert K. Merton.

10. The interested reader will find a thoroughgoing discussion of important intervening variables in M. Sherif, *An Outline of Social Psychology* (N. Y.: Harpers, 1948).

B. Turnover

36. The Measurement of Mobility

NATALIE ROGOFF

MOBILITY DATA in this study, and in most other studies, are presented in the form of tables which cross-classify father's occupation by son's occupation. These tables indicate the frequency of movement from any position to any other position in the occupational structure. The usual procedure in previous mobility research has been to consider primarily the diagonal cells, where father's and son's occupational position coincide. The frequency, or usually the proportion of cases in these cells, is primarily used as the measure of occupational inheritance or immobility. The remaining proportion of cases, those where the son's occupational position differs from that of his father, is taken as the amount of mobility experienced by the population. Thus, if 60 per cent of the sons of professional fathers are professionals, the remaining 40 per cent have experienced mobility; while if only 20 per cent of the sons of clerical workers are themselves clerks, 80 per cent of this group have been mobile. Therefore, the description runs, son of clerks are twice as mobile as sons of professionals.

The inadequacy of these procedures has been demonstrated for systematic mobility research, especially for studies which compare social structures that differ from one another in place or time.[1]

The source of the difficulty is that no account is taken of the total number of positions available in each occupational class. Movement into and out of each occupational class needs to be considered in relation to this availability or demand factor. For example, this study will show that in the period from 1905 to 1912, in the community studied, the number of positions available in unskilled work outnumbered the positions available in professional work by more than three to one. In studying the amount of movement into these two occupational classes, the three-to-one ratio of available positions should be taken into account. Irrespective of his father's occupational position a son was three times as likely to become an unskilled worker as a professional worker. If, in fact, there was three times as much mobility into unskilled work as into professional work by a given group of sons, then, relative to the availability of positions, these sons experienced equal "units" of mobility into the two occupational classes.

However, availability of positions is not

Reprinted in part with permission from Chapter 2 of Natalie Rogoff, *Recent Trends in Occupational Mobility* (copyright 1953 by The Free Press, a division of the Macmillan Company).

the sole determinant of mobility. In addition, there are "factors that are variable for the individual members of groups within the society (education, ambition, 'pull,' race, etc.) and determine variations in the chances of movement to a given class; these factors are, of course, various social characteristics of the individual." [2] It is due to the operation of these factors that sons of the same and different social origins (as measured by father's occupation) differ in their occupational mobility.

Therefore, we may speak of total mobility as the resultant of general availability factors and of personal or group factors. Changes in either of these sets of factors will normally bring about corresponding changes in the total amount of mobility. Trends in the demand (availability) factors in our society are easily observed in the shifting occupational composition of the American labor force. For example, the rapid growth of the professions has resulted in the entry into the professions of many sons from other occupational classes, since professional fathers alone could not supply the increased demand. The great increases in white collar and semi-skilled occupations, and the decline in the proportion of farmers, have also resulted in large amounts of demand mobility.

Demand mobility is, of course, an important aspect of many social structures. However, when mobility data are used as an index of the relative openness of a society, the influence of personal and group factors on occupational movement is of greater concern. If movement within the occupational structure is more restricted for some social groups than for others, this can be seen only by controlling the effect of mobility changes due to changes in the occupational structure. If the actual mobility experienced by one group is shown to fall short of the demands of the occupational structure, while another group exceeds its share of opportunities, we are then in a position to discuss barriers, restrictions, and rigidity in the social structure. [3]

This becomes especially important when comparisons are made between different societies or the same society at different times. Our interest in these comparisons is in whether or not the different social groups in each society or at each time occupy positions in proportion to their size and to the number of available positions. Such information will remain hidden unless the effect of differences in availability are ruled out. For example, this study will show that a larger proportion of unskilled workers' sons became clerks in 1940 than in 1910. Without further analysis, this might be interpreted solely as an indication of a weakening of the barriers between blue-collar and white-collar occupations, brought about by better educational facilities, raising of levels of aspiration, decreasing discrimination in hiring policies, and so forth. However, the *demand* for clerical workers also increased between 1910 and 1940; this increase was exactly proportional to the increase of mobility into clerical work experienced by the sons of unskilled workers. Relative to the demand factor, the sons in 1940 made the move into clerical work no more frequently than the sons thirty years earlier. It must therefore be inferred that personal and group factors operated to exactly the same degree in 1910 as in 1940 in hindering or inducing this type of occupational mobility. This is the form in which information concerning mobility is of greatest theoretical use. Unless the two sources of mobility are separated, we do not know if occupational movement results from changing demands of the occupational structure, or from changes in the degree of freedom to move within limits set by demand, or both.

Accordingly, this study will use a relatively simple procedure and an unambiguous definition of the type of mobility to be measured. Following Goldhamer, ". . . we wish to isolate an expression for social dis-

Table 1. Actual Mobility of All Sons, 1910

SONS' OCCUPATIONAL CLASS

FATHERS' OCCUPATIONAL CLASS	Professional	Semi-Professional	Proprietors, Managers and Officials	Clerical and Sales	Skilled	Semi-Skilled	Unskilled	Protective Service	Personal Service	Farming	All Classes
Professional	79	14	46	91	82	41	12	2	8	2	377
Semiprofessional	3	20	7	16	10	10	4	2	2	—	74
Proprietors, managers and officials	91	35	264	345	253	131	62	12	48	12	1,253
Clerical and sales	37	19	49	288	145	70	24	3	16	8	659
Skilled	51	43	111	414	1,323	460	190	22	87	19	2,720
Semi-skilled	23	14	34	129	299	297	97	7	31	9	940
Unskilled	10	9	35	137	336	238	430	11	42	8	1,256
Protective service	2	1	17	34	52	31	14	4	5	—	160
Personal service	1	4	5	23	34	27	15	1	19	—	129
Farming	92	31	163	392	746	448	377	34	116	286	2,685
All classes	389	190	731	1,869	3,280	1,753	1,225	98	374	344	10,253

Table 2. Actual Mobility of All Sons, 1940

SONS' OCCUPATIONAL CLASS

FATHERS' OCCUPATIONAL CLASS	Professional	Semi-Professional	Proprietors, Managers and Officials	Clerical and Sales	Skilled	Semi-Skilled	Unskilled	Protective Service	Personal Service	Farming	All Classes
Professional	134	30	36	132	73	45	12	4	7	1	474
Semi-Professional	18	22	4	20	27	14	3	2	4	—	114
Proprietors, managers and officials	92	41	212	368	172	238	30	19	25	6	1,203
Clerical and sales	84	57	83	461	165	179	26	14	21	2	1,092
Skilled	89	78	117	520	880	734	154	58	83	16	2,729
Semi-skilled	38	32	63	262	279	657	81	34	65	9	1,520
Unskilled	17	11	20	94	111	216	206	17	26	2	720
Protective service	6	2	16	55	41	76	21	20	3	1	241
Personal service	8	7	9	28	37	49	6	3	17	—	164
Farmers	62	27	96	248	378	470	145	58	83	68	1,635
All classes	548	307	656	2,188	2,163	2,678	684	229	334	105	9,892

tance mobility alone, in which variation in the demand factor is ruled out for all the expressions that we compare. Or stated otherwise, we wish to compare amounts of mobility between various positions for a fixed unit of demand. This can be accomplished very simply by *defining social distance mobility as total mobility divided by the demand factor*." [4]

Using standard notation, this definition can be expressed as follows:

Let x_{ij} = number of sons moving from father's occupational class i to occupational class j

Let R_i = number of fathers in occupational class i

C_j = number of positions (sons) in occupational class j

N = total number of positions (or sons or fathers)

Total mobility = $\dfrac{x_{ij}}{R_i}$, the proportion of sons with i fathers who move to j

Demand factor = $\dfrac{C_j}{N}$, the proportion of total positions available in class j

Social distance mobility = $\dfrac{x_{ij}}{R_i} \div \dfrac{C_j}{N}$

$$= \frac{x_{ij}N}{R_iC_j} = \frac{x_{ij}}{R_iC_j/N} \ .$$

In the last form, the denominator of the definition of social distance mobility corresponds exactly to the definition of expected values as they are used in conventional contingency analysis. The whole expression is then seen as the ratio of the actual cell value to its expected value. In this form, social distance mobility is defined as the ratio between actual mobility and the amount of mobility we would expect were there no relation between the son's occupational class and the occupational class of his father. The expected

mobility values represent the amount of movement that would occur if social distance factors did *not* operate, in other words, if only availability factors influenced occupational movement.

When the actual amount of mobility coincides with the expected amount, the ratio will, of course, be unity. When twice as many sons as expected enter an occupational class, the ratio will be two. The difference in these two ratios, whether they be based on data from the same table or different tables, is in no way attributable to variations in the availability of occupational positions, since these variations have been accounted for in the definition of social distance mobility. A ratio of one has the same meaning in a highly diversified and changing occupational structure as it does in a simple and stable structure. "One unit is that amount of mobility that is to be expected were there no relation between sons' and fathers' occupational class position. . . . This means that all comparisons . . . have a common basis that enables us to attach precise and readily interpretable numbers that are fully comparable and express the essential ideas involved in the study of 'open' and 'closed' or 'mobile' and 'rigid' social structures." [5]

Notes

1. The discussion presented in this chapter is based on the work of Herbert Goldhamer. The quotations that follow are taken from a manuscript by Herbert Goldhamer in which the technique used in this study is set forth. This manuscript was read before a meeting of the Society for Social Research in Chicago, Illinois, in May, 1948.

2. Goldhamer, *op. cit.,* p. 5.

3. Restrictions on mobility are usually considered only when they reduce the opportunities for "upward" mobility. But such restrictions also operate to hinder "downward" movement. For example, when a doctor's son limits his occupational choice to a business or professional career, self-imposed barriers prevent him from engaging in unskilled work.

4. Goldhamer, *op. cit.,* p. 8.

5. Goldhamer, *op. cit.,* pp. 9–10.

37. The Nature and Determinants of Turnover

PATRICIA KENDALL

WHENEVER REPEATED or comparable measures are made, changes are observed. The sons of tall men tend to be shorter than their fathers; students who earn top scores on an intelligence test at one time do less well on a repetition; individuals who measure high on the F-scale appear to be less authoritarian if they fill in the same questionnaire a few months later. The term "regression effect" has been applied indiscriminately to such observations. But mechanisms involved may be quite different. Some tall men marry small women, and so, for generic reasons, their sons may be shorter than the fathers. The I.Q. test has limited reliability: many students get different scores upon re-testing, and because of the so-called ceiling effect, high scorers can only go down; the same is true for the F-scale, although actual experience may account for changes rather than the "error" built into the intelligence test.[1]

The study which is condensed here deals with the difference between the last two cases. Are all such changes due to the shortcomings of the classificatory instrument, or can a case be made that some changes are "true" in the sense that they can be accounted for by substantive considerations? While errors exist, of course, the emphasis in the following pages is on evidence that turnover is a phenomenon which reflects concrete change in the triple sense that it is experienced, that it can be understood, and that it can be manipulated by experimental procedures.

For the present purpose, two parts of the original study have been selected. In the first, we concentrate on the experience of mood. Everyone knows that moods change. The problem was to find a quantitative index of mood, to compare it on two occasions, and to understand the meaning of such change. The second part deals with the determinants of another type of change: there, attitude questions requiring choices of varying difficulties are introduced; it is shown that by varying the "closeness" of the choice, the turnover between two observations could be predictably affected.

I. Turnover in Mood

Mood was measured by four rating scales on which college students were asked to locate themselves. These "mood barometers" dealt with overall good spirits as well as with the specific dimensions of irritability-placidity, optimism-pessimism, and expansiveness-contraction. Each student was asked to reanswer the same four questions one month later. The evidence at our disposal suggested that our subjects had no difficulty expressing their moods in terms of graphic scales.

One of the most striking features of answers to the four mood barometers is the similarity of the marginal distributions obtained in the two interviews. Despite the month's interval between the two questionnaires, roughly the same proportion of sub-

Reprinted in part with permission from *Conflict and Mood: Factors Affecting Stability of Response* by Patricia Kendall (copyright 1954 by The Free Press, a division of the Macmillan Company, New York).

TABLE 1.   Marginals of the Mood Barometers Are Constant

SCALE VALUES	GOOD SPIRITS		IRRITABILITY		OPTIMISM		WELL-BEING	
	Int. I	Int. II	Int. I	Int. II	Int. I	Int. II	Int. I	Int. II
0–15	1%	3%	4%	4%	2%	4%	2%	3%
16–25	2	3	3	4	4	3	5	2
26–35	5	5	6	7	5	3	5	6
36–45	9	7	8	9	7	9	8	10
40–55	14	15	18	14	20	20	18	16
56–65	12	10	12	14	15	14	10	12
66–75	26	21	15	15	17	17	18	19
76–85	20	25	16	18	17	17	19	19
86–100	11	11	18	15	13	13	15	13
Total	512	512	512	512	512	512	512	512

jects assumed the same scale positions on the four questions. Table 1 shows how the sample distributed itself on the four questions at the two interviews. Each of the scales has been divided into nine segments.

From these several distributions, it is apparent that few students claimed to be in really bad moods (values of 0–25). Each distribution is negatively skewed, with the median point far toward the upper end of the scale. To put it somewhat differently, in each case, more than two-thirds of the subjects placed themselves above the half-way mark in mood.

Without further information we can only speculate as to why this is the case. One possible explanation is that the answers reflect traditional American beliefs that it is "wrong" to be pessimistic and irritable. A second possible explanation, and one which has interesting implications, is that in a college population such as that studied, individuals are indeed as well adjusted, on the average, as their answers suggest. Our subjects were young, they were well enough off to attend college; there is little reason, therefore, why they should not feel in good spirits generally.

But constant marginals rarely imply the absence of internal variations. Indeed,

when first and second interviews are compared, we find rather wide fluctuations on each of the four questions. Consider, for example, the way in which our subjects evaluated their good spirits in the two interviews in Table 1 at the top of the page. While there is a positive correlation between first and second interview responses, there is great internal variation. This same pattern holds for all the questions. It is these fluctuations in mood which interest us especially. We must have some way of classifying respondents who have and have not experienced a shift in mood. We might, of course, have made use of the type of material presented in Table 2 but this would clearly prove to be unwieldy. What we did was dichotomize each of the four mood items, combine them for each individual and characterize the total mood as positive or negative, depending on how many of the questions the individual had answered favorably. With such a dichotomy at two time periods, we could distinguish those whose mood was positive both times, those who shifted from good to bad moods, those who changed from bad to good, and those whose mood remained consistently bad.

As Table 3 on page 344 indicates, even

TABLE 2.   There Is Considerable Fluctuation Between the First and Second
Interview in Evaluations of Good Spirits

Interview *II*		*Distribution of Scale Values*						
86–100	—	—	2	2	8	5	14	11	15
76–85	—	2	4	13	13	14	38	28	15
66–75	—	3	5	15	13	12	33	21	6
56–65	—	1	4	4	8	9	13	10	5
46–55	—	2	6	5	17	7	16	16	7
36–45	—	—	2	1	3	9	9	10	3
26–35	—	—	—	4	4	4	9	4	2
16–25	—	1	—	—	2	1	6	2	1
0–15	3	1	1	1	2	1	3	1	—
	0– 15	16– 25	26– 35	36– 45	46– 55	56– 65	66– 75	76– 85	86– 100
					Interview I				

though the change classes are well populated, the marginal distribution of mood is
constant from one interview to the next.

Almost half the respondents had changed
from good to bad moods. Is this chance or
has it a substantive foundation? To find out
we used the following technique. All of the
subjects were asked whether "anything particular happened in the last few days which
put you in a good or bad mood." At the
time of the second interview, 55 per cent
said "No, nothing special has happened,"
22 per cent said something had occurred
which put them in a good mood; and 23
per cent reported incidents which placed
them in a bad mood. From the way in
which our respondents described what had
happened to them, only "special events"
were considered influential. For example,

TABLE 3.

Interview II	*Interview I*		
	Good Mood	*Bad Mood*	*Total*
Good mood	171	103	274
Bad mood	114	126	240
Total	285	229	514

one girl who reported that she was in an
especially good mood, explained:

A special gentleman is coming for the
weekend after saying he couldn't come.

Another of our subjects explained that
he was in a bad mood because "A Ror-
schach (test), self-scored, indicates an im-
mature personality." Still other respondents reported accidents which had put them
in especially bad moods. However general
these incidents may be in the population
as a whole, all of them were unexpected
and of a special nature for the particular
individuals who reported them.

Individuals are clearly aware of influences making for changes in mood. In the
(+ −) group of Table 4, where mood
deteriorated between the first and second
interviews, most of the respondents who
reported that something had happened indicated that it was an event which led them
to develop a bad mood; exactly the reverse
is true in the (− +) group. The trend is
clear: The mood changers spoke of pressures conducive to their present mood
states. One should not underrate the importance of this result. The classification of
changers is based on descriptive ratings one

TABLE 4.

	Mood Class	
Report of Special Event Preceding Second Interview	$(+\,-)$	$(-\,+)$
"Something happened which put me in a *bad* mood"	45	3
"Something happened which put me in a *good* mood"	12	35
Total cases	57	38

month apart. Most likely the respondents did not remember their previous position. The stories told at the second interview referred to recent experiences to which causal impact was imputed. The correspondence between the two sets of data does indeed certify to the reality of change.

II. Determinants of Turnover

Recent work on causal analysis has greatly clarified the notion of "random elements." Take the simple equation between two variables with a random term introduced: $y = ax + e$. The e can either mean that y was unreliably measured or that a number of other factors influencing y are not considered in the model. Considerable work on separating the two meanings has been done by model builders. Here we pursue a more direct way. We are able to demonstrate that the random element may have substantive meaning because we can manipulate it experimentally.

The factor we are introducing is the element of conflict due to the necessity of making choices. If people are asked twice to choose between two alternatives they often change sides. The more similar the two alternatives the more difficult the decision. Further—so goes our hypothesis—the greater the difficulty, the greater the turnover if the choice has to be made twice.[2]

The relevance of this general proposition for a study of turnover is not obvious until its implications are considered. What are the consequences of being asked to choose between two equally desirable (or equally weighted) alternatives? One solution of the dilemma is not to make the decision at all. If the individual cannot decide whether to vote for Candidate *X* or Candidate *Y*, he may not vote at all.

Running out of the field, so to speak, provides one possible escape from the dilemma. It is a solution which is probably adopted more frequently than is generally recognized. But what if this escape is blocked for one reason or another; what happens when the individual is *required* to choose between equivalent alternatives? It is our hypothesis that when forced to select in this situation, the decision will be an unstable one and the individual will waver back and forth between one alternative and another.

Had there been a general interest in the problem of what happens when persons are forced to choose between equivalent alternatives, a variety of experimental situations might have been constructed. But we chose to limit ourselves to experimentation within the context of a questionnaire; in addition, the questions which have been used correspond, by and large, to those which are asked in public opinion surveys. Even within these restrictions, there is still considerable latitude, of course.

Our study focused almost entirely on goal dilemmas with 18 questions calling for a choice between competing needs, conflicting ideals or distinct preferences. Thus, for example, the following question about needs:

When we think of the ideal kind of job, most of us would probably agree that we want a secure job which is important and well-paying at the same time. But some time during their lives many people have to choose between a *secure* job which would *never* be well paying or a *well-paying* job which is not, and never will be secure. If

you were offered two jobs, *equally interesting and important,* which do you think you would choose? '
  —I would choose the *secure* job, even though it does not and never will pay well.
  —I would choose the *well-paying* job, even though it is not and never will be secure.

Since it was our expectation that the most severe dilemma would occur when the two alternatives were equally desirable, we set up a procedure for offering the questions in three versions: where both options were equally desirable, where the first was more appealing, and where the second was stronger. The variations were constructed on the basis of the judgments of three experts. Their expectations of the relative attractiveness of the different alternatives was clearly reflected in the marginal distributions. That is, when the two alternatives were set up as being equally appealing, they were selected with almost equal frequency. In the two modified versions, where one alternative was constructed to be more attractive, the marginal distributions of choices were noticeably assymmetrical.

Once we were able to set up decision conflicts, three basic relationships were explored: (1) First of all, was *equivalence* of the alternatives in fact related to experience difficulties in choosing between them? (2) Was this same equivalence related to instability of response? (3) Finally, did those who said they had experienced difficulties make less stable choices?

1. According to our original proposition, the more nearly equivalent the alternatives, the more difficulty the subjects would experience in choosing between them. A special "difficulty question" was asked in conjunction with each of the decision questions so that the respondent reported whether he had great, some, or little difficulty in reaching the decisions. By examining the three versions of each question, we found that, indeed, those respond-

TABLE 5.   There are Few and Slight Deviations from the Expected Pattern That the Set of Alternatives With Most Symmetrical Marginals Is Most Difficult to Answer and the Set of Alternatives With Least Symmetrical Marginals Easiest to Answer.

Deviations From Pattern of Complete Correspondence	Number of Questions
0	5
1	5
2	1
3	1
Total questions	12

ents faced with the most nearly equivalent set of alternatives did experience the most severe dilemma in choosing between them. That is, as seen in Table 5 above, the questions where each of the alternatives was chosen by an equal number of people (a sign that the two options had equal attractiveness) the respondents reported greater difficulty in making a choice than where the relative strength of the alternatives was unbalanced. This finding confirmed our proposition.

2. We found evidence of a fairly close relationship between equivalence of alternatives and turnover in response. In Table 6,

TABLE 6.   Those Presented With the Set of Most Nearly Equivalent Alternatives Are Slightly Less Stable in Their Choices Than Are Those Presented With Alternatives Differing More in Relative Attractiveness.

Relative Attractiveness of the Alternatives	Index Value	Number of Cases
The two are equally attractive	.06	179
"Well paying" is more attractive	.04	181
"Secure" is more attractive	.03	189

TABLE 7. There Are Few and Slight Deviations from the Expected Pattern That the Set of Alternatives With Most Symmetrical Marginals Receives Most Unstable Answers and the Set of Alternatives With Least Symmetrical Marginals Receives Most

Deviations From Pattern of Complete Correspondence	Number of Questions
0	6
1	8
2	1
3	—
Total questions	15

the job question is used to illustrate the analytic procedure. First of all, a turnover index was calculated for groups answering the different sets of alternatives.[3] Then, the turnover index was examined in the light of the relative attractiveness of the choices. The procedure is illustrated for the job question. In Table 6, the index value is only slightly larger when the two alternatives are stated as being equally attractive.

But the total picture for the fifteen questions confirmed our hypothesis that when the choices were more equivalent, turnover was greatest. Table 7 presents the overall relationship between equivalence and turnover.

3. Turning from items to individuals, we examined the relationship between experienced difficulties and the dependent variable, turnover. Individual respondents were classified according to the amount of difficulty which they reported having experienced. In Table 8, we see that those who said they had greater difficulties with the

TABLE 8.

Reported Difficulties	Turnover Index	Number of Cases
Some of great	.07	64
Little	.03	64

job questions gave more unstable answers —that is the turnover index was higher.

Comparable analysis of the other sets of alternatives revealed the same result for most of the cases, as seen in Table 9 below. While in five cases the respondents who experienced a dilemma revealed as much instability as those reporting a lack of difficulty, in *no* case did they show a greater

TABLE 9. In Most Questions Those Who Report Some or Great Difficulty Are Less Stable in Their Responses Than Those Reporting Little Difficulty.

	Number of Questions
Respondents reporting some or great difficulty show *less* stability than do those reporting little difficulty	32
Respondents reporting some or great difficulty show *as much* stability as do those reporting little difficulty	5
Respondents reporting some or great difficulty show *more* stability than do those reporting little difficulty	—
Total questions	37

degree of consistency. In other words, while our expectation was not always confirmed, it was never refuted.

The three relationships which have been investigated in these sections can be related to each other in the following way:

Equivalence—Experienced difficulties—
Instability

There is a fourth type of relationship which might be explored: that between equivalence and stability for groups reporting different degrees of difficulty. If experienced difficulties really do interpret the relationship between equivalence and stability, then these "partial relationships," as they are called, should vanish. We were unable to carry out this kind of analysis in any systematic fashion, because there were not enough cases. Tentatively, however, it appears that the relationship between equivalence and stability does indeed decrease when experienced difficulties are introduced as the intervening variable.

We conclude with a somewhat more complex finding which, however, can be considered a kind of experimentum crucis. Equivalence was established so far either statistically by looking at marginals or by directly asking respondents about the difficulty of choices. It occurred to us that the judgment of the people involved could be tapped without their being too aware of the issue involved. The opportunity to express the equivalence of alternatives was provided by asking all of our respondents to rank certain qualities:

> We know that a friend generally has many desirable qualities, but we would like to know which in the following list seem *most* important to you. Place a "1" in front of the quality which you consider most important for a friend to have, a "2" beside the next most important quality, and so on for all five in our list.

> —— Loyalty
> —— Generosity
> —— Brilliance
> —— Sense of humor
> ——Good appearance

Our assumption was that those qualities which were assigned *adjacent* ranks would be most nearly equivalent in perceived importance. That is, those qualities ranked first and second by an individual are more nearly equivalent for him than are those which he ranked first and fifth, let us say.

Data on stability were obtained in the following way. Each of the qualities was paired with every other, resulting in a list of ten combinations. The respondents were then instructed in both interviews:

> We would like you to circle the quality in *each* of the ten pairs which you would be most likely to look for in a friend. (You will draw ten circles in all.)

At the conclusion of the second interview it was possible to determine, for each pair, how many subjects had shifted from one quality to the other.

The question was whether stability of response was related to equivalence of the alternatives. For example, did those who ranked "loyalty" and "generosity" first and second show less stability than those who ranked them first and fifth? [4]

It required a somewhat complicated analysis to answer such a question. By referring back to the first part of the question, in which the several qualities had been ranked, it was possible to isolate those for whom loyalty and generosity, for example, differed by one rank, by two ranks, or by three or four ranks. These procedures furnished three different groups of respondents, one in which the two qualities were perceived as being *almost equal* in attractiveness, a second in which there was *some difference* in attractiveness, and a final one in which there was a *great difference* in the relative importance attached to the two qualities.

The second and crucial step in the analysis was to determine the stability of decision between those qualities within each of the three groups. Making use of the second part of the questions, where the respondents were asked twice to choose between loyalty and generosity, it was possible to study the turnover in these choices among those for whom the two qualities differed by one rank, among those for whom they differed by two ranks, and among those for whom they differed by three and four ranks.

The same procedures were repeated for the other nine pairs of qualities. Table 10 reports the results for each of the pairs separately, and for all combined. The figures in Table 10 are the values of the turnover index. By and large, the questions

TABLE 10. Those Who Believe That the Qualities Differ in Importance By One Rank Are Less Stable in Their Choices Than Those Who Believe That the Qualities Differ More.

Qualities	Difference of One Rank	Difference of Two Ranks	Difference of Three or Four Ranks
Loyalty or generosity	.05	.03	.00
Sense of humor or brilliance	.10	.02	.01
Good appearance or loyalty	.02	.04	.03
Brilliance or good appearance	.13	.06	.04
Loyalty or sense of humor	.06	.03	.00
Good appearance or sense of humor	.11	.01	.03
Generosity or brilliance	.10	.06	.02
Loyalty or brilliance	.12	.04	.00
Sense of humor or generosity	.16	.08	.00
Generosity or good appearance	.16	.06	.03
All pairs	.10	.04	.02

which we raised initially find affirmative answers, for qualities which were assigned adjacent rankings generally were selected with less stability than were qualities assigned very different rankings. That is, greater instability is generally associated with greater equivalence of the alternatives. These findings suggest, further, that when equivalence is established by the respondents themselves it bears the same relationship to instability of response as it does when it is established by expert opinion, by inferences from marginal symmetry, or by some other means.

The table is really quite startling. With only one exception, those individuals who saw the widest differences between the characteristics (column 3) were the most stable in their choices. Where there was least distinction in the qualities (column 1), choices were most changeable. In terms of our study, conflict was a factor contributing to turnover.

Notes

1. Consider, for example, the statement by Robert L. Thorndike: "Reliability or the consistency in a measurement procedure is a matter of degree and not an all-or-none matter. Whenever we measure anything, whether in the physical, the biological, or the social sciences, that measurement contains a certain amount of chance error. The amount of chance error may be large or small, but it is always present to some extent. If the chance errors are small in size, relative to the variation from person to person, the reliability or consistency of the measure is high. If the chance errors become large in proportion to the variation from person to person, the reliability of the measure is low." (*Personnel Selection: Tests and Measurement Techniques*, New York: John Wiley & Sons, 1949, pp. 68–9.)

2. This same proposition appears, under somewhat different guise, in both economics and psychology. In studies of economic demand we encounter it in the concept of "indifference," a state of equilibrium in which the prospective consumer finds alternative combinations of commodities equally desirable and hence interchangeable. He is "indifferent" to which combination he receives, and therefore cannot choose between them. The same notion is met, in slightly different form, in psycho-physics. The well-known Weber-Fechner law deals with the difficulties of discriminating between objects which weigh very nearly the same amount. By generalization, the law has also been found applicable to other sensory discriminations.

3. The construction of the index is described in Appendix A of *Conflict and Mood*. We can interpret the index values intuitively as the probability that an individual will change his response. The index has a lower

limit of 0, when there are no cases in one or both of the turnover cells, and an upper limit of .50, when the cross-tabulation of answers obtained from the repeated question reveals no relationship at all. As we shall see, the index value usually varies between .50 and .10, although occasionally it is as high as .30. See also paper by P. F. Lazarsfeld in Section IV of this reader.

Because the sampling distribution of the index has not yet been worked out, it is not possible to determine when one value is significantly different from another. What we have done instead is to make use of a technique which has gained acceptance in recent years. When we compare the relative stability of two tables, we first of all make a somewhat arbitrary and impressionistic judgment as to which has a greater degree of turnover, based on the difference between the two index values. We then accumulate a large number of such comparisons and note the frequency with which tables characterized in one way have greater turnover than those characterized in another way. In other words, our results are based generally on the *consistency* of a variety of differences, some of them large and others of them small, rather than on the significance of any one difference. For other examples of this kind, see S. A. Stouffer et al., *The American Soldier*, I, p. 157.

4. This is a slightly different version of the question asked previously. Originally we asked whether the *same individual* is more unstable in his decision between qualities to which he assigns adjacent rankings than he is in his decision between qualities to which he assigns very different rankings. The question which we have just raised is whether the *same set of alternatives* is answered with less consistency by those who consider the qualities equivalent than it is by those who do not consider them equally important.

38. Measurement Problems in Panel Studies

E L E A N O R   E.   M A C C O B Y   A N D   R A Y   H Y M A N

THE PROBLEM of how to measure change is important for all the social sciences. At first thought it might seem that, relative to other measurements, the measurement of change presents no new problems. But, in fact, the simple questions "Has a change occurred?" and "Has group A changed more than group B?" stir up many difficulties. Many of these difficulties cannot be resolved with current measurement procedures.

The major advantage of a "panel" design over a series of cross-section surveys is presumed to be that it is more sensitive to change—that it can give more informa-

tion about *who* changed, how much, in what direction, and why. It is especially important, therefore; to consider the measurement problems inherent in "change analysis" in any effort to evaluate the panel method in general or any selected panel study in particular.

A first difficulty seems to be one of scale units. At best, scaling in the social sciences, especially attitude scaling, gives us ordinal scales. To answer many questions of attitude change, it seems at least an equal-interval scale is needed. Let us look at a typical problem. We want to see whether a certain instructional film has a

Reprinted with permission from Chapter 3 of *American Voting Behavior*, Eugene Burdick and Arthur Brodbeck, eds. (copyright 1959 by The Free Press, a division of the Macmillan Company, New York).

greater effect upon an extreme group than it has upon a moderate group on some attitude continuum. We observe changes on the attitude scale for each group. We want to be able to say that group A changed by a different amount than did group B. But this assumes that a change of x scale units at the high end of the scale is equivalent to a change of x scale units at the lower end of the scale. Clearly we cannot say this unless we have an equal-interval scale.

A further limitation in comparing changes between groups who are at different initial levels is imposed by ceiling effects. An individual who is at the top of the scale has little room to improve relative to someone who is much lower on the scale. . . .[1] An equal-interval scale is necessary if we are to compare the differential change between two groups; a ratio scale is necessary if we are to have an index of amount of change which is to have any absolute meaning.

A second kind of measurement problem is introduced by errors of measurement—by unreliability in the measuring instruments. Perhaps we should raise first the question of what kinds of response variability are to be regarded as error. If a child's I.Q. is measured once, and then measured again a week later with a parallel form of the test, and the two scores differ by ten points, we say that the difference is due to measurement errors. We do not believe that the I.Q. has actually changed ten points in a week. Our reason for calling the change "error" arises partly out of our definition of I.Q.—we are trying to measure something stable enough, something basic enough, that it could not change so much in such a short period. (Of course, those who define I.Q. simply as what I.Q. tests test, can regard the change as *real* change—as real as any other change.)

In studying changes in voting intentions, response instability is the very center of our interest. We would obviously be throwing out the baby with the bath water if we

labeled all changes in response, from one measurement to another, as "error." Kendall, in her book *Conflict and Mood,* has focused her attention on the characteristics of people who change their minds on public opinion issues, and for her this group is of interest not because it includes the cases concerning which an interviewer or a coder made a mistake, but because the members of this group demonstrably have something in common in their life situations and in their personalities which leads them to vacillate. Let us attempt, then, to classify the different sources of response instability, and point out which ones we propose to consider "error" and which ones are the kinds of changes that we feel deserve study in their own right.

Let us assume that interview questions concerning an individual's candidate preferences are intended to tell us how the individual would actually vote if the election were held the day of the interview. The ballot he would cast if he actually went into a voting booth we shall call the criterion. If we interview the individual repeatedly over time, the criterion itself may be unstable. That is, we interview some people who would actually vote differently at Time 1 than they would at Time 2. Some of this "criterion instability" is predictable, in that it is related to specific characteristics of the individual or his environment which are subject to study by a social scientist. These specific characteristics may be dealt with as *variables* and are assumed to have comparable effects on the different people who share a similar score on the variable. Thus, people who are subject to persuasive efforts from proponents of both candidates during a campaign share a high score on the "cross-pressures" variable, and one can ask whether they are more alike in their "criterion instability" than people who share a low score.

There is criterion instability that is highly idiosyncratic, however. The writers know of an instance of a young wife, reared in a

Republican family, who was persuaded to her husband's Democratic views and voted as a Democrat in several elections. Then her father, to whom she was very close, died just before a presidential election. She voted Republican because she knew how much her father had wanted to cast a Republican vote in this particular election, and she decided to cast her vote in his place, as a kind of last gesture of loyalty. The fact that this young woman had a Republican father and a Democratic husband meant, of course, that she was subject to cross-pressures, and her voting instability might be predicted on that basis. The fact that the cross-pressures showed up in her voting behavior only upon her father's death, however, was more idiosyncratic. Another woman, under similar cross-pressures, might vote with her father while he was alive and feel freer to vote with her husband after her father's death. For purposes of studying the effects of cross-pressures alone (without reference to interaction with personality variables), these individual situational factors which determine whether cross-pressures will be effective may be regarded as a source of error. So may the momentary headache, the recovery of a loved one from sickness, the arrival in the mail of a heavy insurance bill—any one of which, occurring on the day before rather than on the day after the casting of a vote, may make a difference in the vote, and a difference which varies from one individual to another.

In addition to what we have called "criterion instability," there is instability in voting intentions owing to measurement errors. By measurement error we mean any deviation of our measurement from the criterion. Such deviations could arise from deliberate misstatements by the respondents. In addition, they may occur when the interviewer makes a mistake in reading the question or recording the respondent's answer, or when the coder in the home office miscodes, or when the IBM clerk punches the wrong number in a punch card. Occasionally such errors are systematic (as when an interviewer anticipates that most respondents in a particular part of town will belong to the same party, and therefore over-records the votes for that party). More often, they have as great a probability of occurring in one direction as in the other. When such errors are made on one measurement and no error is made on an earlier or later measurement, then the respondent is recorded as a person who changed his mind, even though his voting intentions were actually stable.

To summarize, then, instability in response to a question about voting intentions may be classified as follows:

Type A. Criterion instability
    1. Idiosyncratic—uncorrelated with other variables of interest
    2. Systematic—related to a variable which affects numbers of people alike
Type B. Instability due to measurement errors
    1. Systematic (biased)
    2. Random

Berelson et al.[2] are interested primarily in Type A-2 instability. The problem is to sort out this variety of instability from the rest. There are instances in which errors of Type B-2 could produce the kinds of shifts in response which are reported in *Voting,* and there are of course serious difficulties, when this is the case, in attributing the changes to anything other than measurement error. Specifically, this is true when statistical regression is involved. When errors of measurement exist, then on remeasurement the extreme groups will be less extreme. Hovland et al. in their Appendix illustrate such effects and how they may mislead the unwary into unwarranted conclusions.

Maccoby in her review of *Voting* illustrates how errors of Type B-2 might vitiate some of the conclusions made by

Berelson *et al.* Let us examine the reconstruction of Chart LVIII which she presents. We will deal only with those people who state they are going to vote the same as, or opposite to, their families. The measurements are taken at two different times—intentions in June are compared with how respondents said they actually voted in November. We are interested in the kind of shifts that take place in voting intentions as illustrated by Table 1.

TABLE 1.   Respondents' Voting Intentions in June in Relation to Family Preference Compared to November Vote * (Number)

| NOVEMBER VOTE | VOTING INTENTIONS IN JUNE | | |
	Same as Family	Opposite to Family	Marginals
Same as intention in June	273	25	298
Changed to other party	22	13	35
Total	295	38	333

* Data from Berelson *et al.*, *Voting,* Chart LVIII, p. 121.

Before we proceed to discuss the implications of this table, we should carefully note two features of the data. The proportion of people who intend to vote the same as their families is overwhelmingly large both in June and in November, being approximately 89 per cent and 86 per cent respectively. Secondly, the proportion of people who show any shift in voting intention from June to November is slightly more than 10 per cent of the total. In evaluating marginal changes, it is only these 35 individuals who can provide us with useful information.

Now what kinds of inferences do we want to make from the data in such a table? We will follow Berelson *et al.* and arbitrarily assume that these 333 people constitute the complete population concerning which we want to make conclusions about attitude shifts. Such a restriction eliminates the problem of sampling error. For the moment we are only concerned with the question: Did these 333 people show a shift in either direction? Such a question, however, is trivial. It is obvious that we would ask such a question only because we are interested in generalizing to a larger population from which these 333 people are only a sample. But for the sake of simplicity, we will start by assuming no sampling error.

But the removal of sampling errors does not remove all the sources of error in the table. If there were no errors in the table, we could look at it and say whether a change took place and in what direction. And we could say this with probability 1.00. But we can expect that we will have mistakes, errors of recording, and other errors which we can classify as errors of measurement. The existence of such errors of measurement means that we are still dealing with a sampling problem. We can imagine that our table is one of a large set of possible tables that we could have obtained on these 333 panelists. If we assume that these errors are random and nonsystematic, then this one table can be used as an unbiased estimate of what the "true" population table looks like. Because our one table is one sample of an indefinitely large number of possible tables, any inferences must be of a statistical nature. This means, contrary to the position of Berelson *et al.*, that we cannot avoid making statistical inferences, even if we wish to restrict our inferences to changes exhibited by only these 333 people.

Berelson *et al.* want to use such a table to say something about the direction of shifts in voting intentions. Let us construct a dummy table (Table 2) to correspond to Table 1 to illustrate their argument.

Berelson *et al.* point out that only 7 per

TABLE 2.   Voting Intentions in June in Relation to Family Preference Compared to November Vote (Generalized Form)

NOVEMBER VOTE	VOTING INTENTIONS IN JUNE		
	Same as Family	Oppo- site to Family	Mar- ginals
Same as intention in June	a	b	a + b
Changed to other party	c	d	c + d
Total	a + c	b + d	N

cent of those who intended to vote the same as their families in June defected from this position in November; whereas 34 per cent of those who intended to vote differently from their families in June returned to the fold. Such a result is interpreted as implying a greater shift toward conforming with the family than toward defecting. The comparisons are based on the proportions $c/(a$ plus $c)$ versus $d/(b$ plus $d)$.

But, as Maccoby points out, such a comparison is misleading if errors of measurement exist. The first thing to note in Table 1 is that if we look at the total proportion who tend to vote with their families in June as compared with the same proportion in November, there is a slight decrease in the proportion of people who stick with family intentions (89 per cent in June versus 86 per cent in November). And we should further note that we have a statistical test by which we can detect whether a systematic shift has taken place in either direction (we can use either the chi-square test for correlated proportions, or its equivalent, the sign test). The test is based on the number of people who change in either direction; therefore its sensitivity is proportional to the total number who shift and not to the total number in the panel.

For the 35 cases in Table 1 who show a change, the probability of finding a deviation this great or greater from a hypothetical split of 0.50 is between 0.25 and 0.10. This would not lead us to conclude that a change has taken place, but note that if we did conclude a change had taken place, we would have concluded that it took place in a direction opposite that suggested by Berelson et al.

Note that we have suggested that the appropriate comparison is between the frequencies d versus c rather than the proportions $c/(a$ plus $c)$ versus $d/(b$ plus $d)$. And note further that two procedures tend to give opposite results for this table. Why is this so? And why do we maintain that the appropriate comparison is between d and c? We can illustrate our point with a hypothetical example. Let P equal the proportion of results which are accurately reported and let Q equal $1-P$ or the probability of making an error in measurement. Further, let us assume a dichotomous scale that P and Q are the same for all the individuals.

Now let us imagine a situation wherein the "true" number of people who intend to vote the same way as their family is S and the "true" number who intend to vote opposite their family is O. We will assume that S and O do not change, i.e., remain constant over the time period in which we are interested. To make our illustration concrete, let us assign the following numbers to P, Q, S and O.

Let $P = 0.90$
  $Q = 0.10$
  $S = 200$
  $O = 100.$ $N = S + O = 300$

In other words, the probability of misclassifying each of our panelists is 0.10. We assume that the probability of misclassifying an individual is independent of how another individual was classified. Now imagine that we measure these 300 individuals at time $t1$ and again at time $t2$.

The observed number of Sames and Opposites at time $t1$ will be:

Observed number of Sames $= PS + QO$
$$= 0.9(200) + 0.1(100) = 190.$$
Observed number of Opposites $= QS$
$$+ PO = 0.1(200) + 0.9(100) = 110.$$

Note that the errors of measurement tend to make us underestimate the number of panelists who are Sames (in the majority) and overestimate the number of panelists who are Opposites (in the minority). As unreliability increases the estimates of the proportions of Sames and Opposites will regress toward 0.50 regardless of the true split. This is one effect of unreliability.

Now let us examine the effect of regression as we study the changes on remeasurement at time $t2$. We can predict the following numbers of observations in each of our four categories:

Observed number of Sames who stay
Same on second measurement $= P^2S$
$+ Q^2O = 0.81(200) + 0.01(100) = 163$
Observed number of Sames who change
to Opposite $= PQS + PQO$
$$= 0.09(200) + 0.09(100) = 27$$
Observed number of Opposites who
change to Same $= PQS + PQO$
$$= 0.09(200) + 0.09(100) = 27$$
Observed number of Opposites who stay
Opposites $= Q^2S + P^2O$
$$= 0.01(200) + 0.81(100) = 83$$

These observations can be placed into a 2 by 2 table analogous to Table 1 and Table 2. Note that Table 3 is what we would expect the observations to look like on times $t1$ and $t2$ under the assumptions that no change has taken place, but that errors of measurement which are equally probable for all individuals have occurred.

Note that if we estimate the proportion of each group that has changed from $t1$ to $t2$, as do Berelson et al., we find that 27/190 or approximately 14 per cent of those

TABLE 3. Hypothetical Observations on Respondents at Time 1 Compared to Those at Time 2 (Number)

OBSER-VATIONS AT T2	OBSERVATIONS AT T1		
	Same as Family	Opposite to Family	Mar-ginals
Same as at $t1$	163	83	246
Opposite to those at $t1$	27	27	54
Total	190	110	300

who originally intended to vote the same as their families have defected and now intend to vote opposite to their families. But 27/110 or approximately 24 per cent of these who intended to vote opposite to their families have come back into the fold. If we followed Berelson et al., we would use such information to conclude that pressures are stronger to change toward voting with family than vice versa. But we have constructed our problem so that this is not the case. We have estimated changes on the basis of unreliability of measurement alone.

If we wish to find out whether this sample is becoming more homogeneous (more voters agreeing with their families' political positions), the correct procedure is to compare the marginals. We note that the proportion of Sames is exactly the same at $t1$ as it is at $t2$. The correct statistical comparison is between the frequencies of those who changed from Same to Opposite versus those who changed from Opposite to Same. We see that these are identical as we would expect them to be if only errors in measurement are involved. The differences in the *proportions* of changers in each group are due to the fact that the groups are unequal in size to begin with.

So far we have considered only whether a systematic change has occurred over the whole sample in a particular direction.

There is another question. It is possible that although the marginals remain the same at $t1$ and $t2$, a large number of counterbalancing "real" changes have taken place. In other words, is the total of 54/300 changers greater than we should expect on the basis of unreliability of measurement alone? Clearly, we cannot answer such a question unless we have a control comparison or independent knowledge of the reliability of measurement. One possible way in which such a question might be answered is in terms of the model for attitude change developed by Anderson. Here we would measure our panelists at times $t1$, $t2$, $t3$. Times $t1$ and $t2$ would be separated by a very short interval in time, say one day or a week, whereas $t2$ and $t3$ might be separated by a much longer period—say several months. Following Anderson's model we would test the hypothesis that the same matrix of transitional probabilities fits changes from $t1$ to $t2$ and those from $t2$ to $t3$. If such an hypothesis were rejected it might suggest that a real change occurred between times $t2$ and $t3$ which could not be explained by changes occurring due to unreliability between times $t1$ and $t2$. One difficulty with this procedure would be the acceptability of using the changes from $t1$ to $t2$ as a measure of unreliability. Also the memory factor and the effects of a recently preceding measurement may produce a spurious stability.

The primary concern in most panel studies is not to detect whether a change in marginals has occurred over the whole sample. This question could be answered by comparing the marginals of two successive cross-section studies. A panel design is employed in the hope that it will permit the study of *internal* changes within the sample—showing how some groups change differently from other groups. Even some of these questions can be answered without reinterviewing the same respondents. Using two successive cross-section studies, one can see, within the limits of sampling error, whether white-collar union members have changed more than blue-collar union people, for example. A panel design is primarily useful to determine whether people change differentially who have different initial positions on a variable (such as an attitude variable) which is itself subject to change.

A panel analysis often involves the comparison of two or more groups in the direction and amount of their shift. Let us take for illustration a reconstruction of Chart LXII from *Voting*. The "don't knows" have been omitted from both groups in Table 4.

Looking at the marginals, we see that

TABLE 4.   Comparison Between Shifts in Voting Intentions of Two Groups at Two Times * (Number)

	Nonunion white collar			Union labor		
	VOTING INTENTIONS IN JUNE			VOTING INTENTIONS IN JUNE		
AUGUST INTENTION:	Rep	Dem	Marginals	Rep	Dem	Marginals
Same as intention in June	174	28	202	104	69	173
Changed to opposite party	7	7	14	13	11	24
Total	181	35	216	117	80	197

* Data from Berelson *et al.*, *Voting*, Chart LXII, p. 125.

neither group showed an overall shift in political preference. And on the basis of our earlier analysis, it is evident that one can *not* conclude (as Berelson *et al.* did) that "within social strata with unambiguous political preferences, the political majority is more stable than the political minority." This conclusion was derived from the fact that, among non-union white-collar people, a higher *proportion* of June Democrats changed party by August than was true among June Republicans. But as we have seen, if equal numbers changed in the two white-collar groups (as they did), this fact could be explained on the basis of Type B-2 errors alone, and cannot therefore be attributed to the "criterion instability" in which the authors of *Voting* are interested.

There is another interesting question which may be asked of the data in Tables 3–4, however. This question concerns whether there was more instability among union labor than among nonunion white-collar people. We have seen that the number of shifts from one position to another upon remeasurement that can be attributed to measurement error depends on (*a*) the error rate and (*b*) the total number of cases to whom this error rate is applied. If measurement errors are random, there is no reason to expect that more errors would be made in measuring the political preferences of union people than in measuring nonunion white-collar people. Tables 3–4 show that among the nonunion white-collar group, there were 14 "changers" out of a total of 216 people. Among union labor, there were 24 "changers" out of 197 people—a somewhat higher proportion. There should be no difference in these proportions if errors of measurement alone were involved, so that if the difference between the proportions is greater than we would expect by chance, there is evidence for greater criterion instability among union labor.

We believe that there are a number of questions that may be answered by comparing groups such as the two groups described in Table 3–4, questions which are not made indeterminate by the problem of errors of Type B-2. One can determine, on the basis of the reasoning above, whether there is a greater total amount of counterbalancing changes (not reflected in marginal change) in one group than in the other. One can also determine whether the marginal changes of the two groups differ in amount or direction. What one cannot determine without a control group (or some other source of an estimate of the amount of measurement error) is how much of the internal shifts within any one group may be attributed to Type B error and how much to the "real" Type A changes which the panel analyst would like to study.

Notes

1. Patricia L. Kendall, *Conflict and Mood* (New York: The Free Press, 1954).

2. Bernard Berelson, Paul Lazarsfeld, and William McPhee, *Voting* (Chicago: The University of Chicago Press, 1954).

39. The Problem of Measuring Turnover

PAUL F. LAZARSFELD

MANY INDICES have been proposed as measures of association in fourfold tables. Now turnover as a concept is something like the reverse of a "correlation." However, in the turnover case one can be more explicit as to where one wants to go. If we consider various models by which change may come about, the appropriate index develops almost "naturally." We shall restrict ourselves to the case where the two marginals are the same. This is usually called an equilibrium pattern. While individuals may move back and forth, the distribution of observations remains the same for the whole group.

Our main interest is in what we shall call an oscillation model. It is implicitly used in Selections 37 and 38 included in this section, Maccoby and Kendall. I shall add comments on two other models to stress the point that turnover measures should be related to substantive ideas about the nature of change. The main model will be described so that it becomes understandable to the mathematically untrained reader. For the other two, the substantive assumptions will be clear, but the mathematical treatment will be more condensed.

The oscillation model assumes that people have a basic position from which they stray occasionally but to which they are continuously pulled back again. As an example take two interviews in two subsequent weeks where the same people are asked whether they bought magazine M at a newstand. The model assumes that people have a "true" position—say, they are or are not "regular" readers of the magazine. And yet they do not always act accordingly. Occasionally the "nonreaders" buy a copy and the "readers" do not; mathematically, this means that the probability of a reader buying a copy is not $p_r = 1$ but somewhat smaller, say $(1 - x)$.

TABLE 1.

	PROPORTION IN EACH POSITION	PROPORTIONS IN EACH "TRUE" GROUP WHO BOUGHT MAGAZINE M IN A SUCCESSION OF 2 WEEKS	
		Week (1)	Week (2)
True Readers	p_r	$1 - x$	$1 - x$
True Nonreaders	$p_{\bar{r}}$	x	x
	$p_r + p_{\bar{r}} = 1$		

Unpublished manuscript, 1968.

Inversely, the "nonreader" has a reading probability somewhat higher than zero, say $p_{\bar{r}} = x$. (For simplicity's sake we assume that the two deviations from one and zero are alike; this will suffice to present the general idea.) We now interview a sample of people on two successive weeks to find out whether or not they had bought the weekly issue. What answers should we expect? We put our verbal assumptions into the form of a scheme (see Table 1).

Of course, we do not know the proportion of "true" readers and the degree x of their oscillation. But we can compute these two "parameters" by linking the model to actual observations. Suppose that our interviews had yielded the following turnover table:

TABLE 2.

Second week

		+	−	
	+	.2	.1	.3
First week	−	.1	.6	.7
		.3	.7	

Actual readers and nonreaders are designated by (+) and (−) respectively. Frequencies are converted into proportions of the sample. If 1000 people were interviewed, the table would say that in each week 10 per cent or one hundred were found to buy M that week but not the other week.

It is easy to see what proportion of people in each week would have reported a purchase according to the model: $(1 - x)$ per cent of the "true readers" and x per cent of the "true-nonreaders." Thus

$$.3 = p_r(1 - x) + p_{\bar{r}}x = p_r + x(p_{\bar{r}} - p_r)$$
$$= p_r + x(1 - 2p_r) \quad (1)$$

Since this is one equation with two unknowns, we need a second equation. It is simplest to look at the people who bought M in one week but not in the next. Here a new aspect of the model enters. The random elements which force both groups to deviate from their "normal" behavior, e.g., being on a trip, no magazine available, are supposed to be unrelated from one week to the next. The probability of buying one week but not the other is therefore simply the product of the two independent probabilities. In consulting the scheme one will find that it is the same for the two "true" groups: $(1 - x) \cdot x$. The total observed proportion therefore will be:

$$p_{\bar{1}2} = p_{1\bar{2}} = x(1 - x)(p_r + p_{\bar{r}})$$
$$= x(1 - x) = .1$$

The proportions $p_{\bar{1}2} = p_{1\bar{2}}$ are observed data: people who bought M in one but only one of two weeks. Thus the last equation permits us to compute x. The equation $x^2 - x + .10$ has one solution

$$x = 1 - \frac{\sqrt{1 - 4(1)}}{2} = .12 \quad (2)$$

Thus 12 per cent of "true readers" do not buy the magazine in an average week and 12 per cent of "true-nonreaders" do buy it. Incidentally now we can also compute the proportion of "true" readers p_r. We know this is linked to the proportion of observed readers by the equation

$$.3 = p_r + (.1)(1 - 2p_r)$$

Thus, $p_r = .25$. In this case the proportion of "true" readers is smaller than the proportion of readers actually observed in any one week.

In this model x would be an appropriate index of turnover. The greater x is, the more do people deviate from their true position at each observation, thus creating larger figures in the "deviant" cells.

The oscillation model has implications for Selections 37 and 38. Kendall uses a turnover index that is identical with the x in our scheme. Thus, if she says that a more difficult choice increases turnover from .03 to .06, this is what is meant: In a choice between close alternatives (White Label versus Ballantine Scotch) after equilibrium is reached, 94 per cent stick to a basic position, and 6 per cent shift around because random influences affect their vote, e.g., advertisements. In a choice between more distant objects (milk versus wine at lunch), preferences are more definite, and only 3 per cent would at a specific occasion (e.g., a foreign guest) shift from their "true" position. Kendall shows that this x can be experimentally manipulated in a variety of ways.

Maccoby constructs a hypothetical situation in which a turnover table is created by errors of measurement (Selection 38, Table 2). It is easy to see that her story is identical with the oscillation mode. Our x is her error. But why adopt this idea from a psychometric tradition? Certainly if a man changes his vote intention it does not mean that the interview is ambiguous; much more likely a multiplicity of influences make him oscillate around his "true" position from one interview to the next. And in the case of mood, where x is quite large, every reader knows only too well how realistic change is. Mood shifts would manifest themselves irrespective of the way they are "measured."

Obviously this does not settle everything. In many situations there is measurement error superimposed upon oscillation. And in others there are permanent changes for which a different model is appropriate. In order to decide on a measure of turnover, the mathemaical models must express a substantive theory as to the mechanism by which turnover comes about.

We add briefly two other models which would lead to different turnover measures. In the previous case, the oscillation model, the probabilities of change were, so to say, attached to each person irrespective of the size of the group to which he belonged. This could be called a "psychological model." But one might construct

a "sociological model" where the distribution of attitudes in the whole group affects the stability of the individual member. The simplest assumption is as follows: A person's attitude is the more stable the more other people share it with him. Let us combine this idea with the basic principles of the oscillation model which seems to correspond best with our general empirical observations. The simplest oscillation model in this sense would look as follows:

TABLE 3.

Time

%		I	II
Class A	v_A	$1 - kv_B$	$1 - kv_B$
Class B	v_B	kv_A	kv_A
$v_A + v_B = 1$			

The difference between Table 3 and Table 1 is obvious. The earlier oscillation x, which was the same for both classes, is now substituted by an oscillation which is the smaller the larger the class to which it applies. It can be shown easily that in this case the class frequencies v_A and v_B are the same as the observed frequencies p and $q = 1 - p$, respectively. By a computation which is similar to the one which leads to equation 2, we find the value of k by solving equation 3.

$$k^2 - 2k + \frac{p_{1\bar{2}}}{pq} = 0 \qquad (3)$$

Interestingly enough the solution turns out to be $1 - \sqrt{\phi}$, where ϕ is the well known Pearson correlation coefficient applied to a four-fold table.

Finally we shall look at our main example in a different light. Take the respondents who were observed readers the first time. What proportion stick to their first behavior? ⅔ = 67 per cent. The proportion of shifters is 23 per cent. The values .67 and .23 are called transition probabilities. They indicate the probability that an observed reader will remain one the next week (.67) or that he will become an observed nonreader (.23). The non-readers in the first observation also have two transition probabilities: $6/7 = .86$ for staying, .14 for shifting. These figures can be entered into a socalled transition matrix

$$\begin{pmatrix} .67 & .23 \\ .14 & .86 \end{pmatrix} = T$$

The model assumes that this transition matrix remains the same from week to week. Mathematically, this means that the transition probabilities between the first and the third week can be obtained by squaring T. Over n weeks the transition matrix is T^n. (See Bartos in annotated bibliography for details.) The substantive meaning of this model is as follows. If an observed reader has become a nonreader one week he would move into the second row of T; he will act the third week like all other nonreaders irrespective of how long they have been nonreaders. In this model there is no "true" position. Everyone's action at time $(t + 1)$ is determined by where he is at time t.

Suppose now that a sample starts at a state where p_0 per cent are observed readers and $(1-p_0)$ per cent are observed nonreaders. The probabilities of shifting are a for readers and b for nonreaders. Then it can be shown mathematically: (1) an equilibrium state will be reached with

$$\frac{b}{a + b} \%$$

readers, (2) from week to week the proportion of readers will be:

$$p_t = \alpha f^t + \gamma \tag{4}$$

where p_t is the proportion of readers in week t, while

$$\alpha = p_0 \text{ and } \gamma = \frac{b}{a + b}$$

(3) The term f determines the speed with which the process approaches equilibrium, the state when the marginal distribution remains constant in spite of internal shifts. The smaller the f, the more speedily the equilibrium state is reached. Mathematically $f = a + b$, the sum of the two shift probabilities. Intuitively also large shifts mean big turnovers. Thus f would be the "natural" turnover index in this model.

It happens to be possible to distinguish this model from the two oscillation models. There the proportion of shifters between any two observations remains the same irrespective of the time distance between them. In the present model this proportion increases the longer the lapse between two interviews.

Each model has its own turnover index and they will be numerically different from each other for one given turnover table. But this is irrelevant. The difference becomes crucial when *two* tables (A and B) are compared. Then it can happen that one model declares that A has the greater turnover and another model asserts this for B. Which is right can only be decided by turning to the substantive assumptions of the models.

In the Introduction to this section it was shown how much more complex the notion of turnover becomes if the repeated observation is a polytomy, that is, if it consists of more than two categories. We shall now add another generalization. Suppose we are not interested in the turnover of one dichotomy alone, but rather, we have several such items which are all considered indicators of one underlying (latent) dichotomy. A typical example for our purposes can be found in *The American Soldier* (Volume IV, pp. 448 ff.), where the problem was to gauge the attitudes of enlisted men toward their officers. Three questions were asked of enlisted men and were repeated within a few months. There was a sharp drop in their positive replies: 79% found their officers fair the first time, whereas only 59% did the second time; for the question of whether the officers were good leaders, the positive answers dropped from 65% to 36%; for "Do they share hardships with you?" the decline was from 65% to 49%. Thus the average dip was about 20%. But on each question there was internal turnover. An average of 8% had improved their opinions, and the proportion of disillusioned soldiers (28%) was actually larger than the net change. (p. 452)

A computation similar to the "oscillation model" was carried out. It was assumed that each single question expressed the basic attitude but with an overlay of change due to the particular wording of the item. (In terms of Table 1, each had its own x.) But the basic attitude could also change and, in principle, have its own turnover. The computations showed, however, that this was not the case. The oscillations of the specific questions cancelled each other. On the basic attitude, 30% deteriorated, and only 1% improved.

Now that we have given the general idea of this procedure, we can be somewhat more specific about its advantages. For one, it does not presuppose any statistical equilibrium—the marginal frequencies may be different from one wave to the next. Secondly, it brings out the probabilistic character of the indicators. Thus the computations reported in *The American Soldier* show that the question on leadership was negatively answered by 13% of the "truly" satisfied respondents, and positively by 12% of the "truly" dissatisfied ones. Incidentally, this also demonstrates that this is more flexible than the simple oscillation model. In Table 1 the two latent probabilities are not necessarily related now. In the first row $(1 - x)$ would be .87, and the probability in the second row could be computed in its own right. (It happens to be .12.) Finally, since the publication of *The American Soldier,* it has been found that two items per wave are sufficient to compute all the "latent parameters."

No more than these general hints can be given here. For more detailed information, one of the several available texts on latent structure analysis will have to be consulted. The reader should also examine some of the recent papers by Hubert Blalock and his collaborators on the measurement of unobserved variables. The two approaches are quite closely related.

C. Qualified Change

40. Studies of the Postwar Plans of Soldiers

JOHN A. CLAUSEN

[Ed. Note: This is a brief excerpt from Clausen's account of his work on the prediction of postwar occupational and educational decisions from the intentions of soldiers as expressed when they were in the army. Clausen utilized both stated intent as well as background characteristics to predict the number of soldiers who could be expected to enter various kinds of postwar positions. In this selection, he is focusing upon enrollment in schools and colleges.]

Population Characteristics and Prediction of Enrollment

THE GREAT majority of soldiers who expressed plans to attend school after discharge were young single men who had been out of school a relatively short time when they were inducted into the service. Even among men discharged from the Army in December 1945, although single men under twenty-five years of age and out of high school a year or less before induction numbered only 10 per cent, they contributed 56 per cent of the group with definite plans to attend school and 31 per cent of those with tentative plans.

A question much discussed in attempting to arrive at estimates of veteran enrollment was whether older married men and those longer out of school at the time of discharge were at all likely to return to school, even if they did have plans to go. It might be expected that those lacking the usual characteristics of a school population would run into more problems and difficulties in attempting to become students than would the young single group differing only by a few years of age from the normal college population. Such reasoning apparently resulted in limiting educational benefits of the original Servicemen's Readjustment Act of 1944 to veterans under twenty-five and those whose education was interrupted by the war. On the other hand, it seemed possible that the older or married men and those longer out of school might well be more strongly motivated toward further education if they formulated plans for enrollment in the face of the difficulties to be anticipated.

Examination of the results of the follow-up of December separatees indicates

Reprinted in part with permission from "Studies of the Postwar Plans of Soldiers: A Problem in Prediction" in *Measurement and Prediction*. Studies in Social Psychology in World War II, Vol. IV, by Samuel A. Stouffer *et al.* (copyright 1950 by Princeton University Press), pp. 568–622.

that, among the older or married men and those out of school more than a year before they entered the service, the proportion carrying out or sustaining their plans in the first few months after discharge was less than that of the younger single group more recently from school when inducted. It will be seen in Table 1 that for each category of school plans, the group having the characteristics usually associated with student status was more likely to return to school. Nevertheless, because they comprised so large a proportion of the total sample, the group less likely to return did contribute a majority of the students from among December separatees. (The data are contained in the bottom line of Table 1.)

One reason for the higher predictive value of plans expressed by the December separatees as compared with July separatees seems to have been the differential proportion of men having the characteristics usually associated with school performance. Among the July separatees only about 5 per cent were single, under twenty-five, and out of school less than a year before induction, and of these, a considerable number had entered the Army during peacetime so that their education had not in any sense been interrupted by the war.

In summary, it appears that plans for post-separation school enrollment were more highly predictive of enrollment of veterans having characteristics most similar to those of a school population than of enrollment of older veterans, married veterans, or those who had left school more than a year before they entered the service. On the other hand, among the younger, unmarried veterans out of school only a short time before they entered the service, those who had not planned to return to school after discharge were more likely to shift in the direction of enrolling, so that the overall accuracy of prediction from plans alone was not appreciably different from that obtaining for the older men, those married and those longer out of school. It would appear that those having the char-

TABLE 1. Postseparation Returns to School by Plans Expressed at Separation among Single Men under Age Twenty-five out of School a Year or Less, and Among Other Separatees (December 1945 Separatees) (Per cent)

STATUS THREE TO FOUR MONTHS AFTER DISCHARGE	SINGLE MEN UNDER 25, OUT OF SCHOOL ONE YEAR OR LESS				ALL OTHERS			
	Total	Definite Plans	Tentative Plans	Other	Total	Definite Plans	Tentative Plans	Other
Total	100	100	100	100	100	100	100	100
In school or college	25	54	21	8	2	35	14	1
Planning to enroll	20	29	32	13	4	36	35	2
Had applied for aid	(9)	(16)	(16)	(3)	(2)	(13)	(19)	(1)
Had not applied	(11)	(13)	(16)	(10)	(2)	(23)	(16)	(1)
Not planning to enroll	55	17	47	79	94	29	51	97
Number of cases	211	70	19	122	1,887	55	43	1,789
Percentage constituted among all veterans in school or planning to enroll	45	28	5	12	55	18	10	27

acteristics most similar to a school population were, upon discharge, most likely to encounter a situation which they defined as favorable to enrollment.

The Situation Encountered After Discharge

We know that implicit in the plans expressed by soldiers and separatees was an evaluation of various contingencies relating to the situation to be encountered after discharge. Plans expressed in the summer of 1944 on the basis of an assessment of future contingencies as they appeared at that date might readily be shifted as a result of a continuing reassessment of those contingencies. Specifically, the man whose plans for school in the summer of 1944 rested on the conviction that he would be demobilized within a year and could start college in the fall of 1945 might well decide to go to work upon learning a year later that he would be in service well into 1946. This would be particularly true if in that intervening year he acquired a wife or a prospective wife.

The surveys of separatees indicated that there had not been any major change from July 1944 to December 1945 in the proportion of soldiers planning to enroll in school, although there had been a slight increase. Nevertheless it must be assumed that a number of soldiers decided not to attend and a slightly larger number decided to attend school as a result of changed evaluations of the situation to be encountered after discharge. Since the follow-up studies were conducted only among separatees, they do not afford adequate data on the magnitude of such changes. Among men discharged in July 1945, however, there is a clear indication that within two months after discharge a considerable number of veterans reevaluated the opportunities available to them and shifted their

plans accordingly. When they first learned that they would be among the first men demobilized, many veterans discharged at this time resolved to work in war industry, in order to get a chance at some of the high wages they had heard so much about while in service, and others decided to seek a good permanent job while the labor market still made great demands for workers. With the surrender of Japan, however, a number of these men decided to go to school instead. It is quite possible that such men would have expressed plans for school if surveyed a year earlier, and that the termination of the war thus resulted in a return to plans previously modified by prospects of war industry employment. The fact remains that the changed situation seems to have resulted in a more serious underestimate of school enrollment of July separatees than was true of December separatees.

It has already been mentioned that the increase in allowances to veterans attending schools, provided by amendment in December 1945 to the earlier Readjustment Act, probably increased slightly the number of veterans actually enrolling in schools and colleges, and the fact that many veterans had inflated notions of the sort of jobs available to them may also, after deflation of such notions, have resulted in some increase in enrollment. Countering this, crowding in the colleges, which absorbed about two thirds of the full-time enrollees, has probably limited somewhat the proportion of later separatees who were able to carry out their plans to enroll in school.

In concluding this review of the attempt to predict the enrollment of veterans in schools and colleges from a knowledge of plans expressed while in service, brief consideration is given to the relationship between plans to enroll in school on a part-time basis, and actual part-time enrollment within a few months after discharge. Slightly over 11 per cent of the December separatees had reported that they would like to attend part-time school and that they thought they actually would attend after discharge. . . . The men planning to attend part-time school comprised nearly half of those who were enrolled or expected to enroll at the time of the follow-up. But, as will be seen in Table 2, less than a fourth of the men who had expressed plans for part-time school had actually carried out or sustained their plans. Further, those who had not carried out plans for part-time school were not counterbalanced by any substantial enrollment by men who had not expressed plans to enroll. This situation had early been foreseen in reporting soldiers' plans. The fact that plans for part-time school might be compatible with almost any other activity meant that a considerable number of men might report their own wishful thinking. There was nothing in the questionnaire to force the soldier to evaluate his own plans for part-time school.

Table 2 also indicates that of those veterans who did not sustain their plans for part-time school, an appreciable proportion shifted either to full-time school or to on-the-job training. Thus, it is to be noted that either an intensified interest in education, leading to full-time enrollment, or a reevaluation of training opportunities, leading to a choice of on-the-job training, would result in wrong prediction just as would a decline in interest leading to a discarding of all plans for education.

To soldiers interested in further education there was available aid for full-time school, for part-time school, or for on-the-job training. Full-time school was most often chosen by young single men, particularly by those who had been in school just before they entered the service. Part-time school appealed more often to the married men who felt they could not afford to return to school full-time, and to single men who had been working before entering the service. Relatively few soldiers knew about the possibilities of on-the-job training until

TABLE 2. Relationship Between Various Categories of Soldiers' Educational Plans and Educational or Job-Training Status Three to Four Months After Discharge (December 1945 Separatees) (Per cent)

EDUCATIONAL STATUS AT TIME OF FOLLOW UP	PLANS FOR EDUCATION EXPRESSED AT DISCHARGE				
	Total	Full-time School*	Part-time School	Vague Interest, No Plans†	No Interest
Total	100.0	13.8	11.4	25.5	49.3
Full-time school	10.0	7.6	0.9	0.8	0.7
In school	(4.7)	(3.6)	(0.3)	(0.4)	(0.4)
Planning to enroll	(5.3)	(4.0)	(0.6)	(0.4)	(0.3)
Part-time school	5.5	1.1	2.6	1.0	0.8
In school	(1.2)	(0.5)	(0.5)	(0.1)	(0.1)
Planning to enroll	(4.3)	(0.6)	(2.1)	(0.9)	(0.7)
On-the-job training	11.6	1.2	1.9	3.3	5.2
In training	(4.6)	(0.4)	(0.8)	(1.0)	(2.4)
Planning to enter	(7.0)	(0.8)	(1.1)	(2.3)	(2.8)
All others	72.9	3.9	6.0	20.4	42.6

* Includes those with definite and tentative plans plus those considering enrolling full-time.
† Includes those who said they would like to enroll but did not plan to do so.

well along in the demobilization period. While the types of training for which aid was available are in some respects quite dissimilar, they did apparently serve in some instances as adequate substitutions, one for another, so that no real change of plans would be involved. This would be particularly true in the case of on-the-job training as a substitute for business or trade school, and part-time college as a substitute for full-time enrollment.

One further note is relevant: the 1944 cross-sectional survey found that of soldiers definitely planning to enroll in full-time school, two thirds planned to enroll in college, about a fourth planned to enroll in trade and business school courses and less than 5 per cent planned to complete standard high school courses. Veterans Administration operating statistics as of summer 1946 showed veterans enrolled in educational institutions to have almost identical distribution by type of school with that predicted on the basis of soldiers' plans.

41. Intention and Voting Turnout

WILLIAM A. GLASER

PAST VOTING turnout studies almost always have been static analyses. Usually they have described the relationship between participation rates and the demographic attributes, attitudes, and social experiences of members of the electorate. Since each such study ordinarily is based on a single cross-sectional survey or on statistics referring to the Election Day period alone, both turnout and its determinants are derived at the same point of time, only simultaneous correlations are possible, and the analyst cannot show how turnout is affected by temporally prior conditions.

The development of multi-wave panel interviews in modern social research permits the study of attitude change, decision-making, and action over time. By reinterviewing the same respondents at intervals, political sociologists already have discovered much about how voters decide their candidate choices during the course of an election campaign. A panel design permits such process analysis not only of candidate preference but also of turnout and non-voting. Elsewhere I have reported certain basic patterns by which voters' pre-election attitudes, social influences, and role prescriptions determine their turnout rates on Election Day.[1] In this paper I shall describe certain conditions under which pre-election intention to vote is subsequently executed at various turnout rates.

This paper is one of the publications of the Regional Panels Project. The data were gathered in 1950 by cooperating regional survey organizations, under the sponsorship of the American Association of Pub-

Reprinted with permission from the *American Political Science Review,* 52 (1958), pp. 1030–40 (copyright 1958 by the American Political Science Association).

lic Opinion Research. Before the midterm election in that year, respondents were interviewed in Colorado, Iowa, Minnesota, and Washington. Most of them were reinterviewed after Election Day. The results subsequently were analyzed and now are being published by the Bureau of Applied Social Research, Columbia University.[2] Since it is a two-wave panel study, this project can yield information on the dynamics of translating intention into turnout, which no single-wave survey can. The Regional Panels Project has additional advantages arising from the use of a common questionnaire with four independent samples. If we claim discovery of a relationship, we can test its existence in four independent samples and need not await future replication to gain confirmation. For simplicity in presentation, our tables will combine data from all available states, but most of the findings occur independently in each sample. Since our samples do not perfectly represent the populations of the United States or of specific regions, we do not claim that the numbers in our tables are perfectly accurate estimates of the numerical rates of American voting behavior; but our data can demonstrate the existence of systems of relationships among variables.

I. The Execution of Turnout Intention

Some general principles about intention can be inferred from the over-all picture of how the Regional Panels respondents acted upon their pre-election plans. Table I combines all four states, but the same pattern appears in each state individually.

As a comparison of the absolute numbers in the cells of the turnover table shows, the number of persons who defect from a positive intention to vote greatly exceeds the number of those who turned out without expecting to beforehand—i.e., 192 as against 29. A comparison of the marginal

frequencies shows that the aggregate turnout rate in November is lower than the intention rate in October. This negative trend appears commonly in other political panel studies, where intention to vote is overstated at the beginning of the campaign and steadily erodes thereafter.[3]

The discrepancy between turnout intention and execution is not in itself surprising and follows from the very nature of the act. In America voting is expected, and so most persons can establish tentative self-perceptions of themselves as "good citizens" by telling pre-election interviewers that they intend to vote. But for the individual, turnout is conducted with almost no publicity and is enforced by few sanctions; all such kinds of social action are unstable in execution. Another reason for the net loss in turnout intention is that most Americans perceive voting as a kind of semi-spectator activity rather than a serious involvement of their interests. In other sorts of social behavior, as an act involves more obvious and serious consequences for the individual, his expression of intention becomes more realistic and more stable.[4] Throughout this paper, we shall find that the greater the feeling of involvement in the election campaign, the more likely the voter will fulfill a positive intention to vote.

Any analysis in social research aims to uncover relationships and then to elaborate them by discovering the specifying conditions under which they differently occur. Consequently we search next for some of the conditions associated with differential rates of turnout. Section II will examine intergroup differences in execution, and the two subsequent sections will investigate how different degrees of social influence and psychological involvement produce different rates.

Ideally, any special sector of social action —such as political behavior—should be explicable by deduction from generally applicable principles of sociology and psychology. Elsewhere I have summarized the

TABLE I.   Fewer People Vote than Intended to Vote Earlier in the Campaign

INTENTION IN OCTOBER	TURNOUT BEHAVIOR ON ELECTION DAY		
	Voted	Did Not Vote	October Totals
	%	%	%
Will go	67	14	81
Undecided	2	3	5
Probably won't go	2	12	14
Election day totals	71	29	100

various relationships which have been found to exist between intention and action in different areas of behavior. The characteristics of people relate in systematic fashion to their intentions at one time, the trends between intention and action at two successive times, the total amount of instability in their fulfillment of their intentions, the rates at which they execute an intention to act, and the rates at which they deviate from an intention not to act.

On the basis of our data, the execution of turnout intention consistently falls into certain types among all the various possible relationships between intention and action. The voting behavior described in the succeeding sections of this paper adheres to the following rules:

A. *Intention.* Voters with the strongest motivations, social influences, and role prescriptions express the highest rates of turnout intention before the election.

B. *Trend.* All categories of voters decline from their aggregate intention rates to some extent, but some do so more than others. The strongest motivation, social stimuli, and role prescriptions—which are associated with the highest intention rates—also exercise greater "braking" influence on this tendency to decline. The largest declines characterize the voters with the weakest predispositions.

C. *Turnover.* The aggregate amount of instability in executing intention is a sum of individual deviations from positive intentions to vote plus individual reversals of intentions to abstain. Systematic differences in turnover fail to appear in our data. Some-

times the more strongly motivated and influenced type of voter reveals the greatest amount of change, sometimes the most weakly predisposed groups have the highest turnover.

D. *Executing a positive intention to vote.* The stronger the motivations, social stimuli, and role prescriptions, the more likely the voter will carry out a previously expressed intention to participate. Types of voters with the weakest predispositions are most likely to desert such an intention.

E. *Reversing an intention to abstain.* According to Tables II and III the social categories of voters possessing the strongest systems of predispositions are the persons most likely to desert prior abstention plans. Some exceptions occur in Table IV, when individual attitudes are singled out. In these special cases, sometimes reversals of abstention plans occur most frequently among the weakly predisposed, usually as a consequence of a larger amount of instability among them.

F. *Turnout.* People with the strongest motivations, social influences, and role prescriptions not only have the highest pre-election intention rates, but also they reveal the highest turnout frequencies. As a result of the differential execution of positive intentions to vote, the intergroup differences in turnout are larger than the earlier differences in intention.

II. Demographic Background Variables

Tables II, III, and IV present the relevant data for respondents classified according to the social statuses, social influences,

TABLE II.   Social Statuses, Intention, and Turnout

DEMOGRAPHIC GROUP	% WHO EXPRESSED INTENTION TO VOTE IN OCTOBER	% TREND[5]	% TURN-OVER[6]	TOTAL % WHO VOTED IN NOV.	% WHO VOTED IN NOVEMBER Among Those Who Intended To Vote	% WHO VOTED IN NOVEMBER Among Those Who Did Not Intend To Vote
Sex:						
Men	84 (641)	− 9	43	76	86 (536)	29 (105)
Women	78 (707)	−16	38	66	79 (554)	17 (153)
Age:						
40 and over	86 (767)	− 5	40	78	87 (656)	27 (111)
30–39	81 (333)	−15	44	60	80 (270)	24 (63)
21–29	67 (245)	−26	46	49	67 (163)	13 (82)
Socio-economic status:						
A and B	92 (115)	− 9	45	83	88 (106)	(3/9)
C	84 (642)	−13	44	73	82 (538)	26 (104)
D	71 (214)	−22	43	55	72 (152)	15 (62)
Money income of respondent's family:						
$3,000 and over	78 (213)	− 6	36	73	87 (166)	23 (47)
Less than $3,000	77 (140)	− 8	23	69	86 (108)	9 (32)
Occupation of respondent or his breadwinner:						
White collar	86 (195)	− 9	44	78	86 (168)	30 (27)
Business and farm	85 (447)	−10	44	77	85 (378)	29 (69)
Skilled labor	73 (242)	−16	32	62	80 (177)	12 (65)
Labor	76 (365)	−14	37	65	81 (277)	18 (88)
Social Class:						
Upper	88 (336)	− 8	46	81	87 (297)	33 (39)
Middle	81 (567)	−12	40	71	83 (381)	23 (106)
Lower	75 (445)	−17	39	62	78 (332)	17 (113)
Education:						
College	84 (293)	− 7	25	78	90 (246)	15 (47)
Completed high school	83 (405)	−15	48	71	80 (337)	28 (68)
Some high school	81 (221)	−21	36	64	76 (179)	12 (42)
Grade school, none	77 (425)	−10	41	69	83 (326)	24 (99)
Marital status:						
Married	81 (505)	− 7	40	76	87 (411)	27 (94)
Not married	79 (103)	−14	43	68	80 (81)	23 (22)
Religion:						
Protestant	81 (718)	−12	43	72	82 (584)	25 (134)
Catholic	85 (203)	−22	34	67	76 (173)	10 (30)
Party Identification:						
Republicans	87 (407)	− 9	39	79	87 (353)	26 (54)
Democrats	79 (584)	−16	43	66	78 (461)	21 (123)
Independents	78 (339)	−10	37	79	84 (264)	21 (75)

and attitudes elicited by our questionnaire. . . .

Certain consistent patterns in the execution of intention are manifested in some of the social statuses in Table II. Men, older people, and higher status voters have the highest intention rates, the smallest negative trends, and the highest turnout frequencies. In addition, these social categories are most likely to carry out an intention to vote, and they are most likely to reverse an intention to abstain. Conversely, women, the young, and lower class people have the lowest intention rates, show the largest declines in aggregate voting intention, register the weakest executions of positive intentions, maintain most firmly their intentions to abstain, and have the lowest final turnout rates. Cross-sectional surveys have previously demonstrated such social differences in final turnout behavior on Election Day, and our data show that such relationships are the final outcome of a systematic pattern which prevails throughout the campaign.

As a direct consequence of the social differences in turnout behavior, Republicans and Democrats express intentions and carry them out differently. Since party identification is associated with class and age in most regions of America, parties vary in the turnout behavior of their adherents. The entry at the bottom of Table II shows that in contrast to Democrats, Republicans have higher rates of intention and of final turnout. Republicans have a smaller negative trend and a smaller turnover, and at each level of intention Republicans vote more often.

All these differences are part of a differential involvement in American politics which demographic categories exhibit. This involvement is determined by a series of motivations, social stimuli, and role prescriptions which men, persons over forty, and the upper class possess to a greater extent than do women, the young, and the lower class. The former more strongly than the latter are expected to vote and to think about politics as part of the behavior prescribed for their social statuses. In addition, later sections of this paper will show how the strongest values of such motives and social stimuli consistently exercise the greatest preserving effects on a positive intention to vote and often generate the greatest change in plans not to vote. Among the Regional Panels respondents, men, persons over forty, and the upper class translate intentions into turnout at the highest rates because they tend to possess the stronger values; while the lower rates of performance by women, the young, and the lower class are the reflections of the effects which weaker motives and social stimuli exercise upon intention.

III. Social Influences

Table III describes the relationships and effects which various social influences exercise on the expression and execution of turnout intention. Nearly all cases follow the identical pattern.

The process may be understood clearly by intensive examination of mass media exposure as a paradigm case. The higher the exposure, the higher the intention rate in October, the higher the final turnout rate in November, and the smaller the negative trend between October and November. Among those who intended to vote, the differences in turnout rates between the persons standing at the low value and at each successively higher value on the index of mass media exposure represent the "preserving effects" which increments of exposure exercise upon a positive intention to vote. Among those who did not intend to vote, the differences in turnout rates between the low and higher index positions represent the "generating effects" by which increments of exposure induce change in a negative intention. The last two columns of Table III show that the

TABLE III.   Social Influences, Intention, and Turnout

SOCIAL INFLUENCES	% WHO EXPRESSED INTENTION TO VOTE IN OCTOBER	% TREND	% TURN-OVER	TOTAL % WHO VOTED IN NOV.	% WHO VOTED IN NOVEMBER	
					Among Those Who Intended to Vote	Among Those Who Did Not Intend to Vote
Turnout of the rest of the respondent's household:						
All others voted	93 (229)	− 7	42	87	91 (214)	(5/15)
Others divided between voting and nonvoting	85 (26)	−27	57	62	68 (22)	(1/4)
All others failed to vote	66 (97)	−52	65	32	44 (64)	9 (33)
Turnout of the respondent's spouse:						
Spouse voted	86 (139)	+ 1	54	87	93 (120)	47 (19)
Spouse failed to vote	79 (48)	−26	64	58	66 (38)	(3/10)
Turnout of the respondent's friends:						
Most friends voted	83 (299)	− 7	35	77	88 (247)	23 (52)
Some or few friends voted	58 (65)	−11	43	52	76 (38)	19 (27)
Amount of exposure to mass media:						
High	93 (138)	− 4	58	89	92 (128)	(5/10)
Medium high	88 (252)	− 7	40	81	89 (221)	29 (31)
Medium low	87 (247)	−18	42	71	79 (215)	22 (32)
Low	70 (337)	−23	49	54	69 (235)	18 (102)
Participation in political conversations:						
Actively participated	90 (589)	−10	29	81	88 (528)	20 (61)
Did not actively participate	74 (753)	−15	44	63	78 (557)	22 (196)
Contacted by party representatives:	88 (214)	−12	44	78	84 (189)	28 (25)
Not contacted	80 (758)	−15	41	68	80 (608)	21 (150)

higher the mass media exposure, the larger the preserving effects upon an intention to vote and the larger the generating effects inducing reversals of intentions not to vote.

These patterns occur in nearly every part of Table III. The stronger the social influences which might arouse an individual respondent's political awareness, then the higher the intention rate in October, the higher the turnout rate in November, the smaller the decline during the campaign, the stronger the preserving effects upon an intention to vote, and the stronger the generating effects arousing change in an intention not to vote. The only exception is a possible reversal in the generating effects associated with exposure to political conversations; and this may result from the fact that non-participants are generally far more unstable than are those persons who participate in conversations.

IV. Attitudes

Nearly the same patterns govern attitudes as well as social influences. However, as Table IV shows, variations in attitudes often are associated with eccentric fluctuations in the amount of turnover, and systematic generating effects fail to appear.

But for this irregularity, a consistent process can be found in Table V. The stronger the attitudes denoting awareness of the campaign, then the higher the intention rate in October, the higher the turnout rate in November, generally the lower the decline between October and November, and the stronger the preserving effects upon an intention to vote.

TABLE IV.   Attitude, Intention, and Turnout

| | | | | | % WHO VOTED IN NOVEMBER | |
ATTITUDE	% WHO EXPRESSED INTENTION TO VOTE IN OCTOBER	% TREND	% TURN-OVER	TOTAL % WHO VOTED IN NOV.	Among Those Who Intended to Vote	Among Those Who Did Not Intend to Vote
Amount of interest in the campaign:						
Great deal	94 (371)	− 8	27	86	91 (349)	18 (22)
Quite a lot	89 (463)	−13	56	77	82 (411)	38 (52)
Not much, none	70 (464)	−16	49	59	74 (324)	23 (140)
Amount of issue involvement:						
High	91 (181)	− 2	57	89	93 (165)	50 (16)
Medium high	85 (299)	−11	32	76	86 (255)	18 (44)
Medium	81 (362)	−16	39	69	80 (295)	19 (67)
Medium low	77 (323)	−18	38	63	78 (249)	16 (74)
Low	69 (182)	−13	49	60	76 (126)	25 (56)
Amount of candidate involvement:						
High	90 (245)	− 8	48	83	88 (220)	36 (25)
Medium high	91 (154)	−20	35	73	79 (140)	(2/14)
Medium	85 (274)	−16	38	71	81 (232)	19 (42)
Medium low	72 (115)	−12	51	63	77 (83)	28 (32)
Low	67 (184)	−19	44	55	73 (124)	17 (60)
Knowledge about the campaign:						
Knew name of one or both candidates	86 (211)	− 4	29	82	92 (182)	21 (29)
Knew name of neither candidate	66 (158)	−13	45	58	76 (105)	21 (53)

V. Conclusion

Panel analysis has enabled us to extend past knowledge about voting behavior in certain ways. We have long known that when pre-election turnout intentions or Election Day turnout are studied in separate cross-sectional surveys, men, persons over forty, the upper class and Republicans have higher rates for both intentions and for turnout than do women, the young, persons of lower status and Democrats. Panel analysis now has shown that men, persons over forty, the upper class and Republicans have the highest rates in translating their intentions into action, thus demonstrating that a consistent and continuous social process operates over time to produce differential final turnout rates among the categories in the population.

We have long known that the unequal turnout rates by sex, age, class and party identification are associated with the distributions of motivations, social stimuli, and role prescriptions among these groups. Panel analysis has shown that the strong stimuli and motivations possessed by the high-turnout group are associated with high pre-election intention rates; these stimuli and attitudes exercise strong preserving effects on a positive intention to vote; and they have effects generating change upon intentions not to vote. We have also found that the weaker predispositions possessed by the low-turnout group are associated with lower intention rates, and they exercise weaker preserving and generating effects upon intentions. Consequently the differences in turnout behavior which exist over time among persons categorized by sex, age, class and party identification can be explained by the unequal distribution of certain predispositions and experiences, and further explained by the different effects of these upon the development of turnout behavior over time.

Our findings also bear upon the familiar problem of turnout prediction, which long has interested pollsters and social scientists. Our analysis suggests certain new approaches. First of all, as section II of this paper shows, when a respondent expresses any sort of a turnout intention in a pre-election interview, the predictive significance of that intention depends on the social identity of the person. As a rough beginning, a positive intention to vote is a more accurate predictor for men, persons over forty, upper class persons and Republicans, than it is for others. An intention not to vote will be followed more consistently by the women, the young, the lower class, and Democrats, than it will by others. An intention expressed by any person so identified will have a different likelihood of resulting in turnout, according to the level of motivation and interpersonal experiences which support it. Some social influences (such as the turnout plans of the rest of the family and the respondent's exposure to mass media) may be especially useful in turnout prediction. A comparison of Tables III and IV suggests that certain social influences exercise a more consistent patterning upon the expression and execution of intention than do the attitudes which survey analysts ordinarily examine. Pollsters' turnout scales until now usually have been weighted cross-tabulations of intention with interest and with a few other attitudes which are so similar to interest that they are redundant. Perhaps more efficient prediction can be achieved by weighted cross-tabulations involving intention, demographic identity, interest, any other attitudes essentially different from interest, and exposure to certain crucial social influences.

The results of this paper also have practical implications for the most economical use of canvassing by political parties and by civic organizations. A scarce service like the efforts of party workers—so far as they can be freely deployed—will be used wastefully if it is directed at the diligent kinds of persons who intend to vote, since very likely they will vote any way. This scarce service also will be used uneconomically if it is invested in the non-diligent types of persons who don't intend to vote, unless they can be taken bodily to the polls, since a great deal of stimulation is needed before they can be aroused.

Canvassing will be used most economically when it is aimed at those persons who are most variable in translating their intentions into action. Among people who originally plan to vote (as evidenced by registration or by responsiveness exhibited in preliminary conversations with party workers), follow-up contacts should concentrate on those who have the highest probability of defecting from their plans—i.e., women, the young, the lower class, persons from all demographic groups who combine positive intentions with weak motivations, or with exposure to few social stimuli which reinforce turnout. Among people who plan not to vote, follow-up contacts should concentrate on those who have the highest probability of changing their minds—i.e., legally eligible men, those over forty, upper status persons, members of all demographic groups who combine negative intentions with strong motivations, or with exposure to many politically relevant social stimuli. In practice, as is well known, canvassing is often used wastefully, since much superfluous effort is directed at members of high turnout social categories who intend to vote and who are already certain to carry out these intentions because of social pressures and their own motivations.

Notes

1. My chapter in a book on Congressional voting behavior edited by William N. McPhee and William A. Glaser (eds.) *Public Opinion and Congressional Elections* (New York: The Free Press, 1962). (footnote added later)

2. The principal publication is McPhee and Glaser. Earlier findings appear in the Free-

man and Showel articles and in an A.A.P.O.R. roundtable, all in *Public Opinion Quarterly,* 15, pp. 703–14 and 805–7; and 17, pp. 288–92. See also W. A. Glaser, "The Family and Voting Turnout," *Public Opinion Quarterly,* 23 (1959–60), pp. 563–70.

3. Bernard Berelson, *et al., Voting* (Chicago: Univ. of Chi. Press, 1954), p. 31.

4. For example, in rough proportion to the relative prices of their various desired purchases, consumers tend to plan their shopping more soberly, and their expressed intentions more clearly predict their behavior. George Katona, *Psychological Analysis of Economic Behavior* (New York: McGraw-Hill Book Company, 1951), pp. 82–3. For an act as serious as moving one's residence, the intention to move diverges greatly from the desire to move, and the former predicts mobility far more accurately than the latter. Peter H. Rossi, *Why Families Move* (New York: The Free Press, 1955), Chapter VI. In the case of electoral participation, obviously people make no such clearcut distinction between "intention to vote" and "desire to vote." All such findings corroborate the familiar principle in psychology that the more an intention corresponds to a central need of the organism, the less likely it will be forgotten. For a development of this idea, see Kurt Lewin, *Intention, Will and Need,* in David Rapaport (ed.), *Organization and Pathology of Thought* (New York: Columbia University Press, 1951), Chapter 5. Our questionnaire items asking about intention did not remind the respondent about the barriers which might subsequently confront him, and voting turnout is the kind of action where the penalties for acting (resulting from neglect of some rival commitment) often exceed the penalties against abstention. On the weakness of questionnaire items which fail to confront the respondent with future dilemmas, see John Dollard, "Under What Conditions Do Opinions Predict Behavior?," *Public Opinion Quarterly,* Volume 12 (Winter 1948–1949), p. 632.

5. TREND shows amount of change undergone by an aggregate group relative to the number of members who intended to vote. It is computed as:

$$\frac{\text{No. voting in Nov.} - \text{No. intending to vote}}{\text{No. intending to vote}}$$

6. TURNOVER shows total deviation from early intention in aggregate group between pre-election interview and Election Day. It is the sum of the proportions of defectors and of converts to voting.

42. Moderators, Suppressors, and Other Stratifying Devices

ANN K. PASANELLA

EDUCATIONAL RESEARCH has been roundly criticized for dancing along its merry way with nary a glance at survey research methodology.[1] Today, the charge may be somewhat unjust. But whether fair or not, there are some striking parallels between prediction research in education and multivariate research in sociology. This paper will take a look at some of these similarities.

What Do We Mean by Multivariate Research?

We are talking about the analysis of dichotomies in the *Language of Social Research* tradition. Since it has been explained by Lazarsfeld and others,[2] we shall not attempt a fullblown exposition here. Just a flashing look at the principles, particularly the processes of stratifying and slicing.

Rarely does the analyst find much to say about a single dichotomous variable. To know there are more men than women in the state of Utah may be of interest to husband hunters or sporting goods dealers, but it is not a large step forward in the analysis of social processes. Even with the cross-tabulation of two variables, statements of cause and effect are difficult. How does one know what other factors should be considered?

What survey research does is to introduce a third variable to elaborate the meaning of the relationship between the original two variables. Most often, in social research, the first variable is an attribute or characteristic of a social grouping or collective; the second attribute, or dependent variable is an attitude or action or decision. The test variable is usually a social attribute or social context. Thus, in an early study of radio listening according to the age of the listeners, education was introduced to elaborate upon the original relationship. As it happened, in the case of classical music programs, though it first seemed that age had no relevance to listening habits, it turned out that among the highly educated, older people tuned in more frequently, among the poorly educated, it was the young who listened.

This is an unadorned example and conveys none of the richness of social research, but it illustrates what we mean by introducing a *test factor or qualifier*. In our example, the test factor was education. It is still left to the analyst to explain the new relationship involving the test factor, and he might choose to pull in other test variables to explore the connections between education and listening. Or he might leave the matter alone. But each time, what he does is to break up a two-variable relationship into sections or subgroups according to a third variable. By specifying the conditions under which relationships do or do not exist, or by finding the variables which intervene in relationships, or by finding the

Unpublished manuscript, 1969, begun as a staff paper when the author was assistant director of research for the College Entrance Examination Board.

spurious associations, he tries to learn something about causes and effects. Thus, he takes one fourfold table containing two variates (Table 1):

TABLE 1.   Classical Music Listeners in Two Age Groups

		AGE		
		Young	Old	
LISTENING		+	−	
Listen	+	304	380	684
Don't Listen	−	696	920	1616
		1000	1300	2300

and transforms it into *two contingent tables* arranged according to a third variate (Table 2). This third variate is the test factor or stratifying factor. Here is the example we mentioned earlier where the relationship between listening and age was illuminated by introducing education as a qualifier.

All three variables are expressed as dichotomies. Either a subgroup possesses the attribute or does not or has a high "score" or a low "score." Lazarsfeld[3] has suggested that the two original variables and the test variable can be envisioned together as a "dichotomous cube," where instead of two contingent tables representing three attributes as in Table 2, we have an eight-compartmented cube where each cell represents a combination of three attributes. But whether we talk of cutting cubes or splitting bricks or slicing cheese, the point is that we can cut in any direction depending upon what vantage point we want to choose. In the preceding example, we might have divided our total listeners by age and then looked at the relationship between education and listening or, for that matter, we could have used listening-nonlistening as the stratifier for examining the connections between age and education. The point is that the analyst must decide for himself what makes sense. This point should become clearer below when we give other examples from educational research.

One more word about social research before we turn to cutting devices. Sometimes in social research, we look at change over time. Not just net changes like the trend from rural to urban living, but an examination of components of change. Which groups remain the same when studied twice? How many switch from Democrat to Republican as compared to those who change from Republican to Democrat? Once again, we look at the position in two points of time by introducing a qualifier; we subdivide the total sample by some seemingly important characteristic and look at the effect of this characteristic on the movement from one place to another. One might, for example, ask the effects of viewing or not viewing a propaganda film on attitudes toward the

TABLE 2.   Relation Between Age and Listening to Classical Music, By Education

	HIGH EDUCATION			LOW EDUCATION		
	Young	Old		Young	Old	
Listen	192	212	404	112	168	280
Don't Listen	408	188	596	288	732	1020
	600	400	1000	400	900	1300

war. Attitudes would be measured before and after the film. And, indeed, this has been done.

In a true experiment, though, we are apt to make sure that seeing the film is not related to any prior characteristics of our sample. The situation is denser where we select a qualifier and suspect that it is related to our independent variable. Thus we could subdivide our sample according to father's education (high or low) and then see to what extent high scholastic ability is related to plans to attend college. This, too, has been done—it was found that wealthy students plan to go to college no matter what their ability; less fortunate students make college plans only when they are highly able.[4]

What Is Educational Prediction?

For a number of years, educational psychologists have sought to predict academic success on the basis of past performance in school and various background and ability variables. The search has to some degree been rewarded. In situations where selection and rejection are necessary because of limits in available positions, particularly in the entrance to higher education, the psychologist's prediction studies have enabled the admissions officer to make individual forecasts of college performance for each applicant. This may sound like crystal-gazing. But what the officer does is to decide upon his criterion of performance (most frequently he resorts to college grades), collect criterion data on some group of enrolled students (e.g., freshmen), go back to their admissions folders, and retrieve some common data (ability scores and high-school record win by an overwhelming majority). With the same type of information for each student, he can plot the statistical relationship of these variables to college success. Because the admissions officer receives test scores and high school grades—these are continuous or quantitative variables—he computes the correlation between the predictors and the criterion. If he has several measures, it is often advantageous to combine the information through a standard statistical procedure known as multiple regression analysis which selects the one best combination of several predictors for estimating future success. Thus, for example, in women's liberal arts colleges, it may be found that a verbal ability score will be given four times the weight of a mathematical score, but high school record will receive most emphasis of all. For each college situation, there is one combination of the predictors that is optimal. When the several measures are combined, the appropriate measure of effectiveness is called the multiple correlation coefficient. It must be emphasized once again that this correlation is derived from quantitative data, not from the dischotomies we have mentioned earlier in this paper.

Today, there are literally hundreds of such studies, but they seemed to have reached some sort of prediction barrier.[5] In technical terms, the multiple correlations rarely go beyond .70; the psychometrician would say that such predictors explain only about half the variance in grades achieved.

And because we are dealing with individuals in real-life situations where consequences are nonreversible, there has been a relentless search for ways of improving these predictions. The predictors are frail in themselves; they are subject to what the psychologist calls errors of measurement. No one is enchanted with grades as an indicator of all that a college hopes to accomplish with its students. So, psychologists have looked for new predictors (new kinds of abilities), other types of predictors (personality tests, interest inventories, creativity measures, ratings from teachers, samples of work) and even new kinds of criteria—(teachers' nominations, success in later life, etc.) But the cumulation of predictors has not helped much.

The Search for Moderator Variables

What the researchers have realized is that individuals are best described as possessing constellations of variables and such constellations can differ from person to person. The emphasis must be on what combinations of predictors are valid for what types of people in what situations.[6] In line with this attitude is the research that seeks to find out if a particular set of predictors is more valid for one subgroup than another. Such subgroups are formed by our old friend, the stratifier variable. We look for those conditions under which a relationship between predictor and criterion is especially strong or especially weak. In terms of Lazarsfeld's elaboration procedure, we examine the *differences* in contingent relationships with the practical goal of improving the prediction process.

A good deal of work has been done in this vein. For example, demographic qualifiers such as sex have proven to be useful in separating out predictable from unpredictable students. Indeed, in study after study, women have proven to be more predictable than men in terms of college grades as estimated from ability test scores. Schematically, this could look as follows (Table 3):

(a) and (d) is higher than the proportion in (1) and (4). Ability and grades do not necessarily go hand in men's glove.

Why? One conditional analysis cannot tell us. Are men in general less geared to grade getting in college? Are there differing rates of growth for men and women in the period between high school and college? In fact, another study of contingent relationships does shed some light on these questions. It was found [7] that male students who express a preference for a major field achieve higher grades than those who do not. That is, where men have a specific goal, they work at grades. On the other hand, a later study revealed that girls performed equally well in college whether or not they had clearly defined goals. Thus it was suggested that women come to college to get an education no matter what the specific content, whereas men come for more focused purposes, primarily in terms of occupations. Although differences in predictability between men and women do not necessarily entail differences in the absolute level of scores or college grades, one study,[8] at any rate, has discovered just such differences in favor of girls.

Another demographic variable that has been used as a stratifier is type of secondary school, whether public or private. McArthur found [9] that public school boys were more predictable than private school boys. One explanation may be that private

TABLE 3.

		Sex						
		Men College Grades				Women College Grades		
		High	Low				High	Low
Ability scores	High	(1)	(2)		Ability scores	High	(a)	(b)
	Low	(3)	(4)			Low	(c)	(d)

Figuratively speaking, since one would have to select an appropriate turnover index, the proportions of people falling in cells

school graduates have a tradition of the gentlemanly C; public school boys have a more achievement-oriented set of values.

Sometimes a personality attribute is used to qualify the correlation between two other tests. In one of the earliest studies of this type, Stagner [10] classified freshmen into two groups by using subscales of the Bernreuter Personality Inventory and then, for each group, he correlated an aptitude test with grades. Correlations followed an amazingly regular pattern:

TABLE 4.

	CORRELATIONS OF APTITUDE SCORE WITH GRADES	
	Poorly Adjusted Group	*Better Adjusted Group*
1. Neuroticism scale	.45	.60
2. Self-sufficiency scale	.37	.50
3. Dominance scale	.44	.71

In each case, better adjusted students were more predictable. Their personality test was used as a qualifier of the correlation between predictor and criterion.

Similarly, but some 30 years later, Hoyt and Norman [11] found that normal students (as determined by MMPI scores) were markedly more predictable than maladjusted students.

Frederiksen and Melville [12] found that a compulsiveness scale could be used as a qualifier of the correlation between interest test scores and grades at Princeton. As a matter of fact, they used a very ingenious measure of compulsiveness—high scores on the accountant scale of the Strong Vocational Interest Blank. They found that in the total group, the correlation of interest and grades was .10. When the groups were stratified, compulsive students were far less predictable than non-compulsive ones (*r* of −.01 compared to *r* of .25). This stands to reason. Compulsive individuals will compensate for lack of interest with diligence.

Non-compulsive individuals will be more selective as to the areas in which they will strive for achievement and will allow interterest some rein.[13]

Had these personality test scores been plugged into the regular regression equations, they would have obscured the stratified correlations such as Stagner gave us. Once we know that we have high correlations for normal students we are still left with the question of improving the predictions for less adjusted students. Fulkerson [14] has gone so far as to suggest that such analyses imply that one should only make a decision for those for whom the test is valid. In fact, this position is not so extreme as it sounds. Think of the clinician who uses his private methods of assessment and prediction because he sometimes feels that tests do not adequately reflect the patient's personality structure. (Even the clinician depends upon statistical assumptions, though; he has his own "private correlations" of variables drawn from his professional experience with patients.) [15]

Prediction studies incorporating demographic characteristics such as age, sex, socioeconomic background, urban or rural origin have used the stratified relationship with the social category *as a moderator* of the relationship between ability or high school grades and college achievement. In other words, for some types of individuals, the relationship between indicators of ability or achievement and college performance is different than for others. Some authors have termed this the interaction of test and individual.[16]

In 1956, Saunders [17] reviewed some of the existing studies of the stratified correlation type and used the term moderator variable for those situations where the predictive validity of a psychological measure varies systematically in accord with another independent variable. Where the third variable is a dichotomous one, the statistical technique of analysis of covariance will suffice for separating each distinct group. But the modifier can be a continuous variable that divides the sample into a large number of ordered subsets. Thus, Saunders took the Frederiksen and Melville data on compulsiveness but used the full compulsiveness scale as a new "modifier" variable. How did he do this?

One approach could have been ordinary multiple regression: how well does the combination of engineering interest scores and compulsiveness scores predict freshman engineering grades? But Saunders adds as a third predictor the product of the two scales, thus increasing what he calls the "moderated multiple regression coefficient." Actually this is a somewhat simplified form of a problem which survey analysts have recently studied.[18] The solution lies in the use of the triple correlation xyz, but a discussion of this procedure is beyond the scope of the present paper.

Anastasi[19] has called the use of moderator variables a promising development in the interpretation of test validity. She raises an intriguing idea. Not only can we stratify groups in terms of those who are predictable versus those who are unpredictable, but she suggests that even when the predictor is equally valid for the subgroups, the subgroups as identified by the stratifier may be qualitatively different in important ways and the validity coefficient may in a sense mean something different for each.

Though it may sound as if we have wandered far afield of qualified contingent tables, we have not. Any of these moderator variable studies could be put in the schematic form of Table 5. In this hypothetical example, we are making the extreme assumptions that mental health correlates neither with aptitude scores nor grades. In the empirical situation, this might be quite false.

Some of these moderator studies have revealed findings that have implications far beyond the sheer matter of prediction. Thus, a study by Beach on the relationship

TABLE 5. Relation Between Aptitude and Grades for Two Types of Students

		NORMAL STUDENTS			MAL-ADJUSTED STUDENTS	
		College Grades			College Grades	
		+	−		+	−
Aptitude	+	80	20	100	50	50	100
	−	20	80	100	50	50	100
		100	100	200	100	100	200

between sociability, type of teaching, and performance showed that sociability was negatively associated with achievement in lecture and discussion classes but positively related in leaderless groups. This matter of the possible interaction between personality characteristics and aspects of the teaching situation is of great interest to educational researchers today, and there is promising work on the possibility of modifying the classroom structure in accordance with these findings. That is, the teaching would vary according to types of students.[20] This willingness to modify the teaching rather than to insist upon the adjustment of student to teaching represents a welcome change in education.

Notice another development here. Classroom setting is a contextual variable, in the sociological sense. Thus, when Lazarsfeld and Thielens carried out their study of McCarthyism in American colleges, they found that the differences between teacher apprehension and teacher judgment of colleagues' fears varied in accordance with the college climate, that is, the actual number of academic freedom confrontations.

Current research at the Center for the Study of Higher Education in Berkeley is along these lines: the study of the relationship between individual student characteristics as moderated by the college setting. So is George Stern's work on the consonance or dissonance of student attributes and college characteristics.

Suppressor-Releasor Variables

A special case of the moderator variable is the so-called suppressor variable. Once again, it can be placed in the now-familiar contingent table form. The problem about the suppressor variable is its seeming illogicality. But we shall try to make it comprehensible.

An example is put forth by McNemar.[21] Suppose a predictor correlates moderately with a criterion, say .400, but one wishes to raise the correlation to a more dependable level. A second test is introduced as the qualifier, a test that correlates .000 with the criterion! But it overlaps the first variable quite significantly; the correlation is .707. Lo and behold, the multiple correlation including our new variable rises to .566, a respectable increase over our original correlation of .400.

First, how can this happen? During the war, a test of mechanical ability correlated fairly well with a criterion of success in pilot training. A test of verbal ability did not, although it was related to scores on the spatial test. It is true that some verbal ability is needed to read and understand the mechanical test items. When the verbal score was included in the regression equation, it was allowed to "subtract" out that portion of verbal ability that was really irrelevant to success as a pilot.

Schematically, this could be represented as the change between Tables 6 and 7, were we to think in terms of dichotomies. In Table 7, the subgroup on the right is more predictable than the one on the left. But what a strange business. If a potential pilot doesn't have verbal ability but does have mechanical ability he will have a greater likelihood of success (20 out of

TABLE 6.   Unstratified Relationship

		Pilot Performance for Total Group		
		+	−	
Mechanical Aptitude for total group	+	60	40	100
	−	50	50	100
		110	90	200

25) than if he has high verbal ability and high mechanical aptitude (40 out of 75)!

The name that has been given to such a variable with a low correlation with the criterion (grades) but a very high intercorrelation with the predictor (ability) is a suppressor variable. It might be equally appropriate to call it a *releasor* variable, since it frees the predictor from encumbering elements and allows it to function effectively as a forecaster.

Deviator Studies

We come now to a somewhat different case although we shall once again put forth our analogy to contingent analysis. Up to now, we have seen how an original relationship between predictor and criterion is refined in the light of a stratifying factor. In the group thus stratified, relationships are different from the original, undifferentiated one and may also be quite divergent from one another. In the latter case, we say that one subgroup is more predictable than the other. (Except in those cases, where one contingent relationship is positive, the other negative. There, we would not conclude that the groups were unlike in predictability.)

Sometimes, though, we want to attempt to understand something about the process by which our predictor is associated or not associated with the criterion. Once again,

TABLE 7.   Relationship of Table 6 Stratified by Verbal Ability

		High Verbal Pilot Performance					Low Verbal Pilot Performance		
		+	−				+	−	
Mechanical Aptitude	+	40	35	75	Mechanical Aptitude	+	20	5	25
	−	15	10	25		−	35	40	75
		55	45	100			55	45	100

we introduce a new variate. But this time, we use the original predictor as the stratifier. What then is the relationship between the new variate and the criterion for those who are grouped according to the original predictor? Such a table will not help us to improve our prediction directly, but it will help us to sort out the contexts under which the original predictor operates and its role in the phenomenon of turnover.

We might take just a minute to explain this notion of turnover. If a group of respondents are asked a political question in May and again in September before an election, they could conceivably show the following pattern of association between responses (Table 8). Each time, there were 200 pluses and 100 minuses; the situation seems stable. But by looking inside the table, note how much movement there was. Two hundred out of the total 300 actually remained the same. The remaining 100 exchanged positions—50 going in one direction, 50 in the other.

If we looked at Table 8 in terms of a prediction table, we would say that though

TABLE 8.   A Turnover Table

		Second Response		
		+	−	Total
First Response	+	150	50	200
	−	50	50	100
	Total	200	100	300

first response (or test score or high school grades) did bear a positive relationship to second response (or college grades), still 100 people were severely mispredicted. Why? Was there something that distinguished the 50 high-ability-low grade students from the 50 high-ability-high grade students? And the same for low-ability students?

It is a tempting question and has been pursued with avidity by various educational researchers. The troublesome group are the so-called underachievers. Why do they fail to utilize their capacities, the admissions officers will ask? One answer— and it is not the one usually sought—is that the college environment is so different from the high school setting as to create discontinuity for the student. Fishman has analyzed the implications of such disbalances between school and college contexts in an article entitled "A Social-Psychological Approach to College-Going." [22]

Flaugher and Rock [23] did find that small-town origin seemed to be characteristic of those high-ability students who failed to do well in college. The authors hypothesized that a sort of culture shock accounted for the difficulties of small-town students on large campuses. Should one call these studies deviator studies because they deal with the components of inconsistency? Flaugher and Rock compared those students who performed worse or better than the rest with their particular ability score. This is wise. Back in 1958,

Lazarsfeld cautioned about a conceptual difficulty with many over and under-achiever studies. That is, since over and underachievment are defined in terms of distance from the regression line for predicting grades from test scores, what one may be comparing are not different types of achievers, but different types of ability, that is, high- and low-ability students. Only when original level of ability is taken into account can one call the studies analyses of over and underachievement. Lavin [24] seconded the warning in his review of academic prediction studies.

A typical "deviator" study would run as follows: A relationship is found between ability and grades, but it is noted that there is some "turnover." That is, some students of high ability do not do well in college; the reverse is true for students of low ability. In order to learn more about this turnover, we try to decompose the turnover groups in some fashion by looking at them in the light of another predictor. *We stratify by the first predictor,* unlike the moderator studies which stratify by a new variable.

Thus it has been found that underachievers were characterized by dependency whereas overachievers were not; [25] or that low-ability students, who were low on "autonomy" performed more poorly than low-ability students who were more independent. Another study found that overachievers were lower than underachievers in the need for affiliation. Aside from measures of independence, need for achievement or introversion, there have been studies of the relationship of self-image to achievement, overachievers exhibiting greater self-confidence than underachievers.

Before we give a numerical example in contingent table form, a few more comments about the general framework.

Some of these studies have failed to avoid the pitfall of compounding differences in ability with differences in achievement; they merely lined up ability test scores against grades and noted relative discrepancies in accomplishment. Since prediction is always imperfect, there are bound to be "deviant cases" or off-quadrant cases, as Marks has called them. [26] In statistical regression analysis, there will be as many prediction errors at the upper end of the ability test scale as at the lower end. (The skeptical reader may well ask whether capacity is indeed indicated by scores on an aptitude test. Some of the same factors that negate the importance of grade-getting in college may also impede performance on a multiple-choice test. And, of course, there are many critics of the multiple-choice test in principle because they feel it standardizes response possibilities to such an extent that true intelligence is masked. We shall not try to explore this here.)

The mention of "deviant cases" is a term borrowed from sociological analysis. Thus in any multivariate analysis, some cases do not fit the predominant patterns. It is sometimes necessary to add other variables the investigator had not thought of in the beginning. For example, in the famous study of the "Invasion from Mars" radio program, [27] it was found that in general, listeners who tuned in at the beginning of the program realized it was a drama rather than a news broadcast. But 15 per cent of the early listeners missed this entirely and still believed the program was indeed a news warning of an invasion from outer space. A closer scrutiny of these deviant cases revealed that ever since the Munich crisis, some listeners expected regular programs to be interrupted by special news bulletins and thus interpreted the invasion as another of these. Therefore, the basic analysis was refined by looking at the "peculiar" cases. In a sense, this is what the over-underachiever analyst is doing.

Once one has begun to explore the methodology of these studies, it is apparent that more work is needed to clarify the boundaries between what we have called moderator variable studies, suppressor variable studies, and deviator variable studies. Sometimes, they seem exceedingly close to merging. Thus Marks,[28] in asking for attention to off-quadrant cases, gives an example of what he calls a moderator variable, a variable that is correlated with the correlation between two other variables. His substantive example is one that we have described in overachiever-underachiever terms. It will be a good subject for a numerical example.

Marks states that in a study at the University of Rochester, when the sample was stratified on undergraduate grades, the relationship between test scores and graduate grades was quite high where undergraduate grades were high but quite low where undergraduate grades were low. The actual correlations were:

1. Correlations for the total group
aptitude test and undergraduate grades $r_{13} = .40$
undergraduate grades and graduate grades $r_{23} = .50$
multiple correlation of two predictors with graduate grades $R_{3.12} = .61$

as contrasted with

2. Correlations for two groups stratified by undergraduate grades (variable 2)

High on 2, aptitude test and college grades $r = .70$ (r_{13} for high on 2)
Low on 2, aptitude test and graduate grades $r = .20$ (r_{13} for low on 2)

His interpretation is that where undergraduate grades are high, one can assume high motivation toward college work. Ability is applied to college performance. But where grades in college are low, the students probably lacked motivation to achieve. Thus, the aptitude test had predictive power for the strongly motivated group, but not for the other group.

But how is ability tied in? Can motivation account for the high ability students who do not achieve as compared to the high ability students who "live up" to their own capacities? And what is going on in the low ability group? To find out, we shall stratify the groups by the original predictor, variable 1, academic ability. It must be remembered that aptitude test score is the index of ability, and that undergraduate grades are taken as the index of motivation (Table 9).

Here, when we use ability as the stratifying variable, we can say that motivation (remember this means undergraduate grades) has a preserving effect but not a generating effect. By that we mean that if

TABLE 9.

	ABILITY						
	HIGH				LOW		
	Graduate Grades				*Graduate Grades*		
Motivation	High	Low	Total	*Motivation*	High	Low	Total
High	170	30	200	High	70	80	150
Low	75	75	150	Low	100	100	200
Total	245	105	350	Total	170	180	350

a student has high ability in the first place, strong motivation will keep him geared toward graduate ' school performance. There is a positive relationship between motivation and graduate school marks for highly able students. Note that if a student possesses high aptitude but low motivation, he has only a 50–50 chance of doing well in graduate school.

But the stratified relationship is very low for the poor ability students. (Of course we are talking in comparative terms. We assume that a really low ability student would not bother with graduate school!) That is, even high motivation does not produce good grades for the low ability students. This is what we mean by the lack of generating effect. Whether powerfully or weakly motivated, lower ability students just do poorly in graduate school.

Incidentally, the marginal figures in the "totals" cells show us that ability and motivation are related and that the association between motivation and graduate grades is also positive and slightly stronger.

In our contingent fourfold tables, we treated this study as a "deviator" analysis; we focused upon comparisons between those who were similar in original ability, but turned out differently, in terms of graduate school accomplishment. There would be nothing to prevent us from treating this as a moderator study, just as Marks did. The moderator would be motivation as expressed by college grades. Our aim is simply to portray the varieties of stratification, by transforming prediction studies into contingent analyses.

There are certainly many other interesting points of similarity or convergence between the psychometric tradition and the multivariate one; current work on the comparison of attribute and quantitative statistics in the analysis of causality is one. Others that come to mind are construct validity; the measurement of change as distinct from error; path analysis; and elaboration methods.

Notes

1. Martin Trow, "Education and Survey Research," in Charles Glock (ed.) *Survey Research in the Social Sciences* (New York: Russell Sage Foundation, 1967), pp. 315–75.

2. Aside from papers in Sections II and III of this volume, see for example, Paul F. Lazarsfeld, "Survey Analysis: The Analysis of Attribute Data" in *International Encyclopedia of the Social Sciences* (New York: The Macmillan Co., and the Free Press, 1968). Also Morris Rosenberg, *The Logic of Survey Analysis* (New York: Basic Books, 1968).

3. Paul F. Lazarsfeld, "The Algebra of Dichotomous Systems," in Herbert Solomon (ed.) *Item Analysis and Prediction* (Stanford: Stanford University Press, 1961), pp. 111–57.

4. For example, see William Sewell and Vimal Shah, "Social Class, Parental Encouragement, and Educational Aspirations," *American Journal of Sociology,* 73 (March 1968), pp. 559–72.

5. Joshua A. Fishman and Ann K. Pasanella, "College Admission-Selection Studies," *Review of Educational Research,* 30 (February 1960), pp. 298–310.

6. Such a viewpoint is espoused by Morris I. Stein, *Personality Measures in Admissions* (New York: College Entrance Examination Board, 1963).

7. Henry Weitz, Mary Clark, and Ora Jones, "The Relationship Between Choice of a Major Field and Performance," *Educational and Psychological Measurement,* 15 (1955), pp. 28–38.

8. Leo A. Munday, "A Note on Sex Differences in Achievement and Predictability of College-Bound Students," a speech prepared for the 1967 annual meeting of the Illinois College Testing Commission, Joliet, Illinois, December 8, 1967.

9. Charles McArthur, "Subculture and Personality During the College Years," *Journal of Educational Sociology,* 33 (1960), pp. 260–68.

10. Ross Stagner, "The Relation of Personality to Academic Aptitude and Achievement," *Journal of Educational Research,* XXVI (May 1933), pp. 648–60.

11. Donald P. Hoyt and Warren T. Norman, "Adjustment and Academic Predictability," *Journal of Counseling Psychology,* I (Summer 1954), pp. 96–9.

12. N. Frederiksen and D. Melville, "Differential Predictability in the Use of Test Scores," *Educational and Psychological Measurement,* 14 (1954), pp. 647–56.

13. Note that this line of reasoning sounds like the direct opposite of that used in the sex difference studies. There, the fact that women were *more predictable* was explained on the basis that they worked hard at everything whereas men were more selective in their approach to course achievement.

14. Samuel Fulkerson, "Individual Differences in Response Validity," *Journal of Clinical Psychology,* 15 (1959), pp. 169–73.

15. A point expressed by Henry S. Dyer in "Actuarial vs. Clinical Prediction in College Admissions" (unpublished manuscript, 1962).

16. A comprehensive review of this and other literature in the educational research field can be found in James V. Mitchell, Jr. "Education's Challenge to Psychology: The Prediction of Behavior from Person-Environment Interactions," *Review of Educational Research,* 39 (December 1969), pp. 695–721.

17. David R. Saunders, "Moderator Variables in Prediction," *Educational and Psychological Measurement,* 16 (Summer 1956), pp. 209–22.

18. See, for example, R. Boudon, " A New Look at Correlation Analysis," in Blalock and Blalock (eds.), *Methodology in Social Research* (New York: McGraw-Hill, 1968). Also, P. Lazarsfeld, "A Memoir in Honor of Professor Wold," in T. Dalenius *et. al.,* (eds.), *Scientists at Work* (Stockholm: Almquist and Wiksell, 1970).

19. Anne Anastasi, "Some Current Developments in the Measurement and Interpretation of Test Validity," *Invitational Conference on Testing Problems,* 1963 (Princeton: Educational Testing Service, 1964). A good deal of research on moderators has been reported by E. Ghiselli, for one.

20. Lee J. Cronbach, "How can Instruction Be Adapted to Individual Differences?" in Robert M. Gagné (ed.), *Learning and Individual Differences* (Columbus, Ohio: Charles E. Merrill, 1967), Chapter 2.

21. Quinn McNemar, *Psychological Statistics* (New York: John Wiley & Sons, 1955).

22. In N. Sanford (ed.), *The American College* (New York: John Wiley, 1962.)

23. Ronald Flaugher and Donald Rock, "A Multiple Moderator Approach to the Identification of Over- and Underachievers," *Educational Testing Service Research Bulletin* (April 1969), No. 26.

24. Paul F. Lazarsfeld, "On a Project to Map Out the General Area of Non-Intellectual Factors in the Prediction of College Success," Unpublished manuscript submitted to College Entrance Examination Board, May 1959. Also David E. Lavin, *The Prediction of Academic Performance* (New York: Russell Sage Foundation, 1965).

25. Elva Burgess, "Personality Factors of Over- and Under-Achievers in Engineering," *Journal of Educational Psychology,* 45 (1956), pp. 89–99.

26. Melvin Marks, "How to Build Better Theories, Tests and Therapies: The Off-Quadrant Approach," *American Psychologist,* 19 (October 1964), pp. 793–98.

27. Hadley Cantril, Hazel Gaudet, and Herta Herzog, *The Invasion from Mars* (Princeton: Princeton University Press, 1940), pp. 76–9.

28. Marks, *op. cit.,* p. 797.

43. Mutual Effects of Statistical Variables

PAUL F. LAZARSFELD

[Ed. Note: While the following paper is an old one, having been written in 1946, it is included because it presented an approach which has given rise to a good deal of recent work and discussion. Some of these more recent discussions are presented in the annotated bibliography.]

THE SOCIAL scientist frequently deals with tables containing data where the direction of any causal link between two correlated variables is not only ambiguous, but the two variables may even each have an effect on the other. For instance, in a study of the 1940 presidential campaign conducted by the Bureau of Applied Social Research the following relation was found to exist between the respondents' vote intention and their opinion of Willkie:

TABLE 1. Opinion of Willkie

Vote Intention	Dislike Willkie	Like Willkie	Total
Democrat	72	24	96
Republican	35	135	170
Total	107	159	266

The two variables were highly correlated ($r = .53$), but we could not say a priori which was the "cause" and which the "effect." Were people going to vote Republican because they liked Willkie, or did they

Unpublished manuscript, 1946.

388

approve of Willkie because they were Republicans? As a matter of fact, both types of causal relation will occur; with some people the personality of the candidate will determine their vote-choice, and with others party loyalty will determine their attitude toward the candidate. However, it is still important to determine which of the two variables is "stronger," that is, which has the greater effect on the other, which was the "cause" in the majority of cases. When we know the answer to this question, we shall know whether Willkie's candidacy was a decisive factor in determining the 1940 vote, or whether it was simply one of the many questions on which people make up their minds in accordance with their already established political preferences.

It would be helpful if, before entering into the statistical details of our problem, we first sketch the general trend of the argument to follow. If we have two variables A and B, then one minimum condition for A being the cause of B is, of course, that A precede B in time. It is exactly the lack of such information which makes it impossible in Table 1 to make any statement about the direction of the causal relationship if it exists at all. It is suggested in this paper that the problem be solved by making two interviews and so getting for A as well as for B two pieces of information at two different times.

Suppose then that between the first and the second interview certain changes have come about in the variable A. To be more concrete, let us assume that this variable A is opinion on Willkie as a candidate. The factors which account for such changes in A can be divided into three groups. The first group we might call "trend factors." Willkie had good publicity or some historical events made him appear to be a more suitable candidate and, therefore, opinion on Willkie improved. In addition to these trend factors, we have "chance factors." Here we would classify perfunctory changes brought about by the usual conglomerate of untraceable reasons which make people change. Finally, we have the variable B. Obviously, some people will change their opinion between the first and the second interview because, in the meantime, their affiliations as prospective Republican voters have convinced them that Willkie is the right candidate.

If we look at variable B the same division can be made. Trend factors will have caused a number of people to shift their allegiance from the Democratic to the Republican party. Chance factors will also account for some of the shifts and finally variable A, the appraisal of Wilkie as a candidate, might account for some of the party shifts.

The problem we propose to discuss here is how one could eliminate the trend factors and the chance factors and so center on the extent to which variable A accounts for shifts in variable B and the other way around. To put it more precisely: if for the purpose of this discussion we call trend and chance factors irrelevant factors, can we eliminate them and determine which of the two variables has a greater influence upon change in the other? In order to answer this problem, we have now to proceed with a somewhat more rigorous formulation.

By reinterviewing the respondents we divide each of the categories appearing in Table 1 into four subgroups according to the opinions expressed at the second interview; thus, the total sample is subdivided into 16 categories. The results are expressed in a so-called sixteen-fold panel table (Table 2).

TABLE 2 [a]

FIRST INTER-VIEW	SECOND INTERVIEW			
	Dem. Ag.	Dem. For	Rep. Ag.	Rep. For
Dem. Ag.	(11)	(12)**	(13)**	(14)
Dem. For	(21)*	(22)	(23)	(24)*
Rep. Ag.	(31)*	(32)	(33)	(34)*
Rep. For	(41)	(42)**	(43)**	(44)

[a] The figures in the scheme (Table 2) are not, of course, meant to stand for actual numbers but they simply serve to identify each particular cell in the table.

Now let us consider for a moment what we mean by saying that the attitude A has an "effect" on, or is the "cause" of the attitude B. We mean two things: First of all, the attitude A will tend to *generate* the attitude B; that is, if a person has the attitude A but not the attitude B, he will tend to acquire the attitude B: the attitude pattern $A\overline{B}$ (where $\overline{B}$ denotes the lack of B, or non-B) will tend to change to AB, and conversely, the pattern $\overline{A}B$ will tend to change to $\overline{A}\overline{B}$; secondly, the attitude A will tend to *preserve* the attitude B; that is, there will be fewer changes from $A\overline{B}$ to AB than we would expect from chance variations in the attitude B. Thus, the attitude pattern

AB will tend to be stable; and conversely, the attitude pattern $\overline{AB}$ will also tend to be stable. An example from the field of medicine will clarify what we mean: Let us assume that consumption of vitamin preparations (variable A) has a positive effect on a person's health (variable B).[1] This means, first of all, that people who are in bad health and who take vitamin preparations will tend to improve in health ($A\overline{B}$ changes to AB) and that people who originally were in good health but who consume an insufficient amount of vitamins will tend to lose their good health ($\overline{A}B$ changes to $\overline{AB}$). Secondly, people in good health who take vitamin preparations will tend to retain their good health (AB is stable), and people in bad health who do not take vitamin preparations will tend to remain in bad health ($\overline{AB}$ is stable).

The question, which of two variables is "stronger," which has the greater effect on the other, then, is equivalent to the question, which of the two variables has a greater tendency to *generate* and to *preserve* the other. Assume for the moment that "vote intention" is stronger than "opinion on Willkie." From what has gone before we see that this would influence the distribution among two types of respondents appearing in the sixteen-fold panel table (Table 2). Consider first those respondents whose attitudes were "maladjusted" (i.e., Democrats liking or Republicans disliking Willkie) at the first interview but had become adjusted by the time of the second interview. These respondents are represented in Table 2 by the four subclasses marked with an asterisk [i.e. (21), (24), (31), and (34)]. If "vote intention" is stronger than "Willkie opinion," the majority of adjustments will occur by way of "Willkie opinion" adjusting itself to "vote intention": Democrats who originally liked Willkie will come to disapprove of him rather than change their vote to Republican, and, similarly, Republicans who disliked Willkie will come to approve of him

rather than change their vote to Democratic. That is, in terms of the sixteen-fold table, (21) and (34) will tend to be greater than (24) and (31).

Secondly, consider those respondents whose attitudes, while adjusted at the first interview, had become maladjusted at the second interview [the groups marked with double asterisks in the table: (12), (13), (42), and (43)]. If, again, "vote intention" is stronger than "Willkie opinion," the loss of adjustment will be caused, in the majority of cases, by "vote intention" moving away from the adjustment with "Willkie opinion," since the weaker variable ("Willkie opinion") will be *preserved* by the stronger variable ("vote intention") more effectively than the stronger variable by the weaker. Thus the losses of adjustment will, in the majority of cases, be of two types: Democrats disliking Willkie changing to Republicans disliking him, or Republicans approving of Willkie changing to Democrats approving of him. There will be fewer cases of Democrats against Willkie changing to Democrats for Willkie, or Republicans against him. In Table 2, then, (13) and (42) will tend to be greater than (12) and (43).

It is clear that the relative strength of the two variables will not affect the distribution among the other groups of respondents appearing in the sixteen-fold table, since those groups consist of people who either changed both of their attitudes [(14), (23), (32), and (41)] or who changed neither of their attitudes [(11), (22), (33), and (44)].

A good measure of the relative strength of the two attitudes, then, will be the number of adjustments toward "vote intention" beyond the expected chance value, plus the excess beyond the expected chance value of losses of adjustment away from "Willkie opinion." It is shown in any treatise on statistical theory [2] that this sum is given by

$$2\left(\frac{\Delta_H}{N_H} + \frac{\Delta_V}{N_V}\right)$$

where the determinant

$$\Delta_H = \begin{vmatrix} (21) & (24) \\ (31) & (34) \end{vmatrix}$$
$$= (21)(34) - (31)(24),$$

and N_H is the sum of the elements of Δ_H, that is, the total number of adjustment cases. Similarly,

$$\Delta_V = - \begin{vmatrix} (12) & (13) \\ (42) & (43) \end{vmatrix}$$
$$= - [(13)(42) - (12)(43)]$$

and N_V is the sum of the elements of Δ_V, that is, the total number of loss-of-adjustment cases.[3]

In the ideal case

$$\frac{\Delta_H}{N_H} \text{ and } \frac{\Delta_V}{N_V}$$

will have the same sign: they will both be positive if the first variable (in the present example "vote intention") is stronger, and both negative if the second variable (in the present example "Willkie opinion") is stronger. Their relative magnitude will depend on the comparative frequency of adjustment and maladjustment cases, that is, on whether the correlation between the two variables has been increasing or decreasing in the interval between the two interviews.

The absolute magnitude of

$$\frac{\Delta_H}{N_H} \text{ and } \frac{\Delta_V}{N_V}$$

for any two given variables will depend on two factors beside the relative strength of the two variables: the time interval between the two interviews and the total number of cases in the sample (the sixteen-fold table). The dependence on the total number, N, of cases in the sample is linear: It can be shown easily that $\dfrac{\Delta_H}{N_H}$ ranges from $\tfrac{1}{4} N_H$ to $- \tfrac{1}{4} N_H$; and similarly

$$\frac{\Delta_V}{N_V}$$

ranges from $\tfrac{1}{4} N_V$ to $- \tfrac{1}{4} N_V$.

Obviously, the maximum value of $N_H + N_V = N$. Thus, the limits of

$$\frac{\Delta_H}{N_H} + \frac{\Delta_V}{N_V}$$

are $\tfrac{1}{4} N$ and $- \tfrac{1}{4} N$. In order to eliminate the effect of sample-size on our measure we divide it by $\tfrac{1}{4} N$, thus arriving at the final index for the relative strength of two variables A and B:

$$I_{A,B} = \frac{8 \left(\dfrac{\Delta_H}{N_H} + \dfrac{\Delta_V}{N_V} \right)}{N}$$

It is clear that the magnitude of N_H and N_V for any given sample size and for any given time interval will also depend on an independent characteristic of the variables involved: their variability in time. For instance, such a variable as a person's "economic status" will not, normally, change in the interval between two interviews; on the other hand, for instance, a person's use of a particular brand of toothpaste will be much more likely to change in such an interval. Since N_H and N_V are numbers of people who changed one of their attitudes between the two interviews, their magnitude, and thus the magnitude of

$$\frac{\Delta_H}{N_H} + \frac{\Delta_V}{N_V}$$

will vary with the "turnover" between the two interviews of the variables appearing in the sixteen-fold table (by "turnover" of a variable we mean the number of people who changed in this variable between the two interviews. For instance, the turnover of "vote intention" would be the number of people who changed from Democratic to Republican plus the number of people who changed from Republican to Democratic). It might be considered desirable to correct the index $I_{A,B}$ to eliminate the effect of the magnitude of the turnover; however, this cannot be done properly, since the turnover of each variable is at least partly caused by the effect of the other variable: if the variable A has a strong generating effect on the variable B, the latter will tend to "adjust" to A, and thus its turnover will be increased, etc. It is impossible to determine from the sixteen-fold table just to what extent the turnover of each variable is caused by the effect of the other variable, and to what extent it is independent of this effect. We, therefore, have to keep in mind that the magnitude (*but not the sign*) of $I_{A,B}$ may depend, to some extent, on the variability of the two attitudes A and B.

We have stated above that in the ideal case Δ_H and Δ_V will both be positive or both negative depending only on the relative strength of the two variables in the sixteen-fold panel table. However, it happens frequently that one of the variables has a much higher turnover than the other. This is partly independent of the relative strength of the two variables, but it will affect the distribution among the sixteen groups in the panel table. For instance, in the example we have been discussing "Willkie opinion" is a much less stable attitude than "vote intention," which usually changes very little, even from year to year. Thus, there will be between the two interviews a greater "turnover" in "Willkie opinion" than in "vote intention." In Table 2, therefore, (21) and (34), which are groups of "Willkie-opinion" changers, will tend to be greater than (31) and (24), which are groups of "vote intention" changers. Hence, the greater variability of "Willkie opinion" will tend to increase the algebraic magnitude of $\dfrac{\Delta_H}{N_H}$. However, at the same time this great variability will tend to decrease the algebraic value of $\dfrac{\Delta_V}{N_V}$, since (12) and (43) ("Willkie opinion" changers) will tend to be greater than (13) and (42) ("vote intention" changers). Thus, it may happen that the two determinants Δ_H and Δ_V have opposite signs; but the total value of $I_{A,B}$

will not be affected by the relative variability since the two biases, being opposite in sign, cancel each other.

We are now equipped to determine the relative strength of "vote intention" and "Willkie opinion" from the data found in the 1940 Bureau of Applied Social Research study. Table 3 presents the numerical data.

TABLE 3.   Vote Intention and Willkie Opinion

FIRST INTER-VIEW	SECOND INTERVIEW				
	Dem. Ag.	Dem. For	Rep. Ag.	Rep. For	Total
Dem. Ag.	68	2	1	1	72
Dem. For	11	12	0	1	24
Rep. Ag.	1	0	23	11	35
Rep. For	2	1	3	129	135
Total	82	15	27	142	266

Here the distribution at the first interview is given in the *Total* column (this is, of course, identical with the distribution in Table 1), and the distribution at the second interview is given in the *Total* row. We see that the correlation between the two variables increased considerably between the two interviews ($r = .53$ at the first, $r = .67$ at the second interview), and in fact there were considerably more adjustment cases than cases of loss of adjustment: $N_H = 11 + 1 + 1 + 11 = 24$, $N_V = 2 + 1 + 1 + 3 = 7$. "Willkie opinion" was considerably more unstable than "vote intention": the turnover of "Willkie opinion" $T_W = 30$, the turnover of "vote intention" $T_V = 7$. Hence, we should expect the two determinants Δ_H and Δ_V, to have opposite signs. We have:

$$\Delta_H = \begin{vmatrix} 11 & 1 \\ 1 & 11 \end{vmatrix} = 120;$$

$$\Delta_V = - \begin{vmatrix} 2 & 1 \\ 1 & 3 \end{vmatrix} = -5$$

Thus:

$$I_{A,B} = \frac{8\left(\dfrac{120}{24} - \dfrac{5}{7}\right)}{266} = .129$$

We see that "vote intention" is actually considerably stronger than "Willkie opinion," and thus Willkie's candidacy in itself was not a decisive factor in determining the 1940 vote.

We have now completed the discussion of the index $I_{A,B}$ for the relative strength of two statistical variables.[4] In the remaining part of this paper we shall discuss

lesser extent—with every other attitude in the group.

It was also found that all the correlations were higher at the second than at the first interview.[6] As the campaign progressed, the voters developed increasingly consistent attitude patterns, adjusting any conflicting opinions to the general pattern. By evaluating the mutual effect indices $(I_{A,B})$ between the various attitudes, we could determine the relative importance of each of the attitudes in establishing the final pattern. Table 4 gives the relative strength for each pair of attitudes in the group:

TABLE 4.   Relative Strength of Attitudes $(I_{A,B})$

STRENGTH OF: (A)		*WITH RESPECT TO:* (B)			
In Order of Strength Relative to Vote Intention	*Vote Intention*	*Roosevelt Opinion*	*Third Term Opinion*	*Willkie Opinion*	*Gov. vs. Bus. Exp.*
Vote Intention	**	+.029	+.037	+.129	+.144
Roosevelt Opinion	−.029	**	+.052	+.067	+.101
Third Term Opinion	−.037	−.052	**	+.025	+.090
Willkie Opinion	−.129	−.067	−.025	**	+.079
Government vs. Business Exp.	−.144	−.101	−.090	−.079	**

briefly several examples for the use of this measure in actual research.

"Willkie opinion" was only one of a number of political attitudes which played a part in shaping the pattern of the 1940 presidential election. The Sandusky repeated interview study gave us an opportunity to analyze the causal interrelations among a group of these attitudes and to discover their relative importance in influencing the vote-decisions of the electorate. At each of two interviews the following five attitudes were ascertained for each respondent: *Vote Intention; Roosevelt Opinion; Third Term Opinion; Willkie Opinion; Importance of Government versus Business Experience in a President.* A sixteen-fold panel table was set up for every set of two attitudes in the group.[5]

As was to be expected, each attitude was found to be correlated—to a greater or

We see that a definite rank order of importance emerges for the attitudes: each variable is stronger than every variable below it in the chain and weaker than every variable above it. The complex aggregate of attitudes making up party loyalty, and thus *vote intention,* is stronger than any single campaign issue. That is, in the 1940 campaign a person's vote was not determined by his opinion on any one of the specific campaign issues, but his opinions on these issues were rather determined by his party loyalty. This does not mean, of course, that the sum total of the various issues did not have an important effect on the final vote. It simply means that there was no single outstanding issue which determined the outcome of the election.

Of all the various issues those connected more or less directly with the person of President Roosevelt were the most important. *Roosevelt Opinion* was the strongest of any of the various attitudes.

Next comes *Third Term Opinion,* which was itself determined largely by both *Vote Intention* (i.e., party loyalty) and *Roosevelt Opinion.*

Willkie Opinion was much less important, as we should expect, since Willkie was comparatively unknown. The *Government versus Business Experience* question is shown to be a trumped-up issue: it is by far the weakest of all the attitudes analyzed; nevertheless, it is highly correlated with *Vote Intention* ($r = .60$ at the first interview and $r = .73$ at the second interview), and thus people make up their minds on this issue almost entirely on the basis of their previously established party loyalty.

One other fact emerges clearly from the rank order of importance of the various attitudes: definite, specific attitudes of satisfaction or dissatisfaction with the actions of the administration (as expressed, e.g., in *Roosevelt Opinion*) are more important than more general theoretical "principles," which apparently are usually projected largely to rationalize already existing attitudes. We see this, first from the fact that the more theoretical *Third Term* attitude is weaker than the more specific *Roosevelt Opinion* and again from the unimportance of the *Government versus Business Experience* question. One

might generalize from this that people derive their ideologies from their specific needs rather than adapting their specific action to their ideology.

Another mutual effects problem that occurred in the 1940 political study was the question of the interdependence of *Vote Intention* and *Expectation on Outcome of Election.* The data show that the two variables were highly correlated (at the two interviews we are considering here $r = .64$): People who were going to vote Republican generally expected Willkie to win the election, and people who were going to vote Democratic generally expected Roosevelt to win. Since Roosevelt actually did win, one might draw the conclusion from this that Democrats were generally more accurate than Republicans, but it seems very doubtful whether that is a correct interpretation of the data. Actually the interdependence between the two variables appears to be more directly causal. The question is only in which direction the causal chain usually goes. Do people usually decide how they will vote, and then, either because of wishful thinking pure and simple, or because they assume that the arguments that convinced them will convince everybody, or because of some other reason connected with what they would *like to happen,* they come to the conclusion that their candidate will win? Or do

TABLE 5. Vote Intention and Expectation

FIRST INTERVIEW Vote;Expec.	SECOND INTERVIEW Vote;Expec.				
	R;R	R;D	D;R	D;D	Total
R;R	59	10	1	0	70
R;D	13	14	0	4	31
D;R	3	0	1	3	7
D;D	6	3	7	69	85
Total	81	27	9	76	193

people usually, because of a desire to be on the winning side or for similar reasons, decide to vote for the candidate whom they expect to win the election? The first type of causation we may designate by the general term "wishful thinking," and the second we may call "bandwagon effect." The question, then, is: Which was more important in the 1940 campaign: wishful thinking or the bankwagon effect? The answer will depend on the value of the mutual effect index $I_{A,B}$ for a sixteen-fold panel table of the two variables.

Table 5 is such a panel table, the first interview taken in June 1940, and the second in August. We see that Democratic expectation is considerably higher than Democratic vote at both interviews; that is, while practically no Democrats expected a Republican victory, quite a few Republicans expected a Democratic victory. We further see that *Expectation* is considerably more unstable than *Vote Intention:* $T_E = 39$, $T_V = 17$. For the mutual effect index we have:

$$\Delta_H = \begin{vmatrix} 13 & 4 \\ 3 & 3 \end{vmatrix} = 27, N_H = 23;$$

$$\Delta_V = - \begin{vmatrix} 10 & 1 \\ 3 & 7 \end{vmatrix} = -67, N_V = 21$$

The two determinants have opposite signs, since the turnover of expectation is so much larger than that of vote. However, $\dfrac{\Delta_V}{N_V}$ is numerically much larger than $\dfrac{\Delta_H}{N_H}$. We have

$$I_{A,B} = \frac{8\left(\dfrac{27}{23} - \dfrac{67}{21}\right)}{193} = -.084$$

Thus we see that the "bandwagon effect" predominates. The respondents were more likely to base their vote on their expecta-

tion than to base their expectation on who they decide to vote for.

Our third example comes from a very different field, that of advertising research. After an advertising campaign we usually find a correlation between "seeing" the ads and "buying" the product advertised. The naive interpretation would be to interpret the correlation entirely as an effect of the advertising. However, it frequently happens that the observed correlation is at least partly spurious, due to the fact that those groups which, because of their characteristics are most likely to buy the product, are also frequently most likely to be exposed to the advertising campaign. Even after the spurious part of the correlation is removed by controlling the sample, the remaining nonspurious part cannot be interpreted *a priori* as being due only to the effect of "seeing" on "buying." There will generally also be an effect of "buying" on "seeing": people may look at an advertisement because they already bought the product and are therefore interested in it. Thus, here again we have a problem in mutual effects. The answer to the question whether, for any particular advertising campaign "seeing" or "buying" is the stronger variable will have an important bearing on the question whether the advertising campaign was successful or not. If an observed correlation, no matter how high, is found to be due almost completely to the effect of "buying" on "seeing," the campaign can hardly be regarded as successful. On the other hand, even a smaller correlation, if due primarily to the effect of "seeing" on "buying" will indicate a more or less successful campaign.

An example of a sixteen-fold panel table constructed from two interviews about such a campaign is Table 6.

We see that most respondents neither saw the ads nor used the product; however there were somewhat more "users" than "seers." There was a comparatively high

TABLE 6.   Seeing and Buying

FIRST INTERVIEW	SECOND INTERVIEW See;Buy				
See;Buy	+;+	+;−	−;+	−;−	Total
+;+	83	8	35	7	133
+;−	22	68	11	28	129
−;+	25	10	95	15	145
−;−	8	32	6	493	539
Total	138	118	147	543	946

correlation between buying and seeing at both interviews ($r = .23$ at the first, $r = .26$ at the second interview), and seeing was considerably less stable than buying: $T_S = 156$, $T_B = 87$.

We have:

$$\Delta_H = \begin{vmatrix} 22 & 28 \\ 25 & 15 \end{vmatrix} = -370, N_H = 90$$

$$\Delta_V = - \begin{vmatrix} 8 & 35 \\ 32 & 6 \end{vmatrix} = 1072, N_V = 81$$

Hence:

$$I_{A,B} = \frac{8\left(-\dfrac{370}{90} + \dfrac{1072}{81}\right)}{946} = +.077$$

Thus we see that in this case "seeing" was the stronger variable, and the advertising campaign can be regarded as successful.

Appendix A

We have arrived at a measure for the relative strength of two variables by considering in what way the effect of one variable on the other will manifest itself in a sixteen-fold table. The measure can also be derived rigorously. Here we can only give a brief indication of the trend of thought followed in this derivation.

From the sixteen-fold table (Table 2) we can derive two four-fold tables, the first of which gives the interrelation between "vote intentions" at the first interview and "Willkie opinion" at the second interview, thus:

TABLE A-1

VOTE INTENTION AT FIRST INTERVIEW	WILLKIE OPINION AT SECOND INTERVIEW	
	Dislike	Like
Democratic	(11)+(13) +(21)+(23)	(12)+(14) +(22)+(24)
Republican	(31)+(33) +(41)+(43)	(32)+(34) +(42)+(44)

The second four-fold table gives the interrelation between "Willkie opinion" at the first interview and "vote intention" at the second interview.

TABLE A-2

WILLKIE OPINION AT FIRST INTERVIEW	VOTE INTENTION AT SECOND INTERVIEW	
	Democrats	Republicans
Dislike	(11)+(12) +(31)+(32)	(13)+(14) +(33)+(34)
Like	(21)+(22) +(41)+(42)	(23)+(24) +(43)+(44)

Now the correlation, if any, in Table A-1 will be the apparent effect of "vote intention" on "Willkie opinion." There cannot, here, be a causal chain from "Willkie opinion" to "vote intention," because of the time-relationship of the variables: "vote intention" precedes "Willkie opinion." Correspondingly, the correlation in Table A-2 will give the apparent effect of "Willkie opinion" on "vote intention." The "total" of each fourfold table (i.e. Tables A-1 and A-2) is N, the total sample.

If we denote the determinant of Table A-1 by $\Delta_{A,B}$ and the determinant of Table A-2 by $\Delta_{B,A}$, the sign of

$$\frac{\Delta_{A,B}}{N} - \frac{\Delta_{B,A}}{N}$$

will be a rough indication of which of the two variables is the stronger, since $\frac{\Delta_{A,B}}{N}$ is a measure of the apparent effect of the first on the second variable, and $\frac{\Delta_{B,A}}{N}$ is a measure of the apparent effect of the second on the first variable. From Table 2 in the text we get:

$$\frac{\Delta_{A,B}}{N} = \begin{vmatrix} 80 & 16 \\ 29 & 141 \end{vmatrix} \times \frac{1}{266} = \frac{10816}{266}$$
$$= 40.6$$

and

$$\frac{\Delta_{B,A}}{N} = \begin{vmatrix} 71 & 36 \\ 26 & 133 \end{vmatrix} \times \frac{1}{266} = \frac{8507}{266}$$
$$= 31.9$$

We see that this rough measure already indicates that "vote intention" is stronger than "Willkie opinion." However, this measure contains a number of spurious factors, and it sometimes happens that even its sign is wrong (even though it happens to be correct in the present case). Note that we have been speaking of "apparent effects" in connection with $\Delta_{A,B}$ and $\Delta_{B,A}$: the original distribution of the two variables, the correlation between them, any shifts in the distributions between the first and second interview, and the relative variability of the two variables will all affect these two determinants; sometimes these spurious factors will completely overshadow the actual difference in strength of the two variables.

The spurious factors can be separated algebraically, and the structure of

$$\frac{\Delta_{A,B}}{N} - \frac{\Delta_{B,A}}{N}$$

then turns out to be the following:

$$\frac{\Delta_{A,B}}{N} - \frac{\Delta_{B,A}}{N} = 2\left(\frac{\Delta_H}{N_H} + \frac{\Delta_V}{N_V}\right) + Q$$

where Q is the sum of the spurious factors. Thus we see that the measure $I_{A,B}$ is the non-spurious part of the difference in apparent effects corrected for the sample size.

Appendix B

(By William S. Robinson)

THE STATISTICAL SIGNIFICANCE OF $I_{A,B}$:

Let us denote the general second order determinant by

$$\Delta = \begin{vmatrix} P_{11} & P_{12} \\ P_{21} & P_{22} \end{vmatrix}$$

and the sum of its elements by $N = P_{11} + P_{12} + P_{21} + P_{22}$.

The variance of $\dfrac{\Delta}{N}$ is then given by:

$$\delta^2\left(\frac{\Delta}{N}\right) = \frac{(N-1)(N-2)}{N^4} \times$$

$$[(P_{11}P_{22}(P_{11} + P_{22}) + P_{12}P_{21}(P_{12} + P_{21})]$$

$$+ \frac{(N-1)}{N^3} \times (P_{11}P_{22} + P_{12}P_{21})$$

$$- \frac{2(N-1)(2N-3)}{N^5} \Delta^2$$

Now

$$\delta^2\left(\frac{\Delta_1}{N_1} + \frac{\Delta_2}{N_2}\right) = \delta^2\left(\frac{\Delta_1}{N_1}\right) + \delta^2\left(\frac{\Delta_2}{N_2}\right)$$

and, therefore, the mean deviation of $I_{A,B}$ is given by:

$$\delta(I_{A,B}) = \frac{8}{N} \times \sqrt{\delta^2\left(\frac{\Delta_H}{N_H}\right) + \delta^2\left(\frac{\Delta_V}{N_V}\right)}$$

$I_{A,B}$ will, in general be considered significant if it is numerically greater than twice its mean deviation (significant on the 5 per cent level). If it is numerically greater than three times its mean deviation, it is significant on the 1 per cent level.

As an example let us test the significance of $I_{A,B}$ in the "vote intention" "Willkie opinion" table (Table 2).

We have:

$$\frac{\Delta_H}{N_H} = \begin{vmatrix} 11 & 1 \\ 1 & 11 \end{vmatrix} \times \frac{1}{24}, \text{ and } \frac{\Delta_V}{N_V}$$

$$= \begin{vmatrix} 3 & 1 \\ 1 & 2 \end{vmatrix} \frac{1}{7}$$

Hence:

$$\delta^2\left(\frac{\Delta_H}{N_H}\right) = \frac{(23 \times 22)}{24^4}$$

$$\times (121 \times 22 + 2) +$$

$$\left(\frac{23}{24^3}\right) \times 122 - \frac{(2 \times 23 \times 45)}{24^5}$$

$$\times 120^2 = .70$$

$$\delta^2\left(\frac{\Delta_V}{N_V}\right) = \left(\frac{6 \times 5}{7^4}\right) \times (6 \times 5 + 2) + \frac{6}{7^3}$$

$$\times 7 - \left(\frac{2 \times 6 \times 11}{7^5}\right) \times 5^2 = .33$$

Thus:

$$\delta(I_{A,B}) = \frac{8}{266}(\sqrt{.7 + .33}) = .031$$

Since:

$$I_{A,B} = .129 > 3 \times .031$$

$I_{A,B}$ is highly significant.

Notes

1. These variables cannot very well be designated as "Attitudes," but the principle is the same.

2. Cf., e.g., Yule and Kendall, *Theory of Statistics*, 11th Ed. (1937), paragraph 3.13, pp. 43–4.

3. The scheme for computing the two determinants from the sixteen-fold table may be summarized graphically as follows:

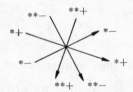

The group designated by * enter into Δ_N, those designated by ** into Δ_V.

The groups designated by + enter into the positive term of their determinant, those designated by − enter into the negative term.

4. Appendix A, part of the original paper, discusses the possible shortcomings of other indices which later were called "cross-lagged correlations." (Footnote added 1972.)

5. Because of lack of space we have to omit the original sixteen-fold tables and their characteristics. A detailed memorandum is on file at the Bureau of Applied Social Research.

6. The only exception was the correlation between "vote intention" and "third term opinion," which remained constant, as it was exceptionally high ($r = .93$) already at the first interview.

44. High-School Social Status, College Plans, and Interest in Academic Achievement: A Panel Analysis *

EDWARD L. MCDILL AND JAMES S. COLEMAN

IN THE PAST two decades, sociologists have been increasingly concerned with academic achievement and aspiration and with the adolescent subculture. Although these concerns have resulted in a plethora of research in these two areas,[1] little systematic research has been conducted on the relation of the adolescent subculture to academic achievement and aspiration.[2] As Haller and Butterworth point out,[3] this is true despite recognition by sociologists that the values of youth which shape their aspirations develop largely as a consequence of interaction with one another.

In previously reported research, one of the authors began an examination of this relationship.[4] Since the present investigation is a further development of this work, a review of relevant findings is in order here.[5]

In each of the ten schools studied in the work cited above, it was found that scholastic achievement was less valued than other activities. For boys, athletics were most highly valued and for girls a premium was placed on "being popular" and "being a leader in extra-curricular activities." Even more important is the finding that students with high status in the eyes of their peers

(termed the "elites" in that work) chose the brilliant student image less frequently than did the various student bodies as a whole, even though these elites *came from higher socio-economic backgrounds and were more likely to plan to go to college.* Other important differences between cities and non-elites were the following. Boy elites were more likely to participate in athletics, to prefer to be a nationally famous athlete and be remembered in school as a star athlete, and less likely to want to be remembered as a brilliant student. Girl elites were more likely to participate in extra-curricular activities and less likely to choose the brilliant student image. In short, the elites placed less value on scholastic success than did the non-elites.

Values held by the elites correspond to the status of those who had achieved in these areas. Boys who had achieved as athletes were much more likely to be among the elites than were those who had achieved as scholars; similarly, girls who were seen as popular with boys were much more likely to have high status than were those who had achieved as scholars.

These findings indicate that adolescent

Reprinted with permission from the *American Sociological Review*, 28 (December 1963), pp. 905–918 (copyright 1963 by the American Sociological Association).

* The first wave of data used in this panel analysis was gathered under a contract from the United States Office of Education. The first-mentioned author was on a Social Science Research Council Fellowship at Johns Hopkins University during the time the present analysis was conducted. The authors wish to express their appreciation to S.S.R.C. for making the analysis possible.

social systems channel the energy of teen-agers in certain directions, divert it from others. In many schools, these social systems apply sanctions that support athletics and social activities and discourage scholastic achievement. Yet there is the paradoxical fact, noted above, that students with high status in these adolescent social systems more often intended to go to college than did the student bodies as a whole. Thus students with high status were more likely to want to go to college than others, yet they seemed to place *less* value on academic achievement than did their peers with lower status. Furthermore, in the earlier research it was found that the higher frequency of college plans among those with high status was not merely a result of the higher socio-economic backgrounds from which some of them came— for status among peers was more highly related to intention to go to college than to socio-economic background. Thus it appeared that high status in the school led to both a greater interest in college and a lesser interest in scholarly achievement. Is this apparent paradox genuine, and if so, what accounts for it?

Data presented here allow further examination of this paradox. In the spring of 1961, students who had been freshmen in the original study were graduating seniors. In six of the original ten schools, these seniors completed questionnaires similar to the ones they had filled out as freshmen, constituting a four-year panel. Such a panel study is of considerable importance because with the proper techniques of analysis, it enables one to scrutinize inferences based on cross-sectional data from the perspective of changes over time. Correlation of two attributes in a cross-sectional study gives no evidence about the sequence of changes through time.

In the present case, the freshman-to-senior panel makes it possible to investigate the effect of school status on college orientation and on achievement orientation

over the four years of school. It allows as well an examination of the reverse question: What about the effect of these attitudes on status in the adolescent social system? Does a desire to go to college help increase a boy's or girl's status? If one is highly oriented to scholastic achievement does it hurt his status?

Method

Data for the first wave of the panel were obtained in the fall of 1957 from the population of ten high schools located in northern Illinois. Questionnaires were administered to approximately 8,900 male and female students in classroom situations.[6] The same questionnaire data for the second wave were obtained in the spring of 1961 from the 612 *seniors* (i.e., those who were freshmen in 1957) in six of the original ten schools.[7]

Table 1 presents information on the general background characteristics of the schools. As can be seen, the ten schools analyzed in *The Adolescent Society* cover a variety of social contexts, though they are not a representative sample of U.S. high schools. But the six schools included in the present study tend to be more homogeneous in terms of socioeconomic background, size of community, and location (all six are located in small towns except number six, which is in a rapidly growing suburb of a large metropolitan area). The six schools also show less variation in size because the three largest schools of the ten are excluded from the analysis. Thus, the only large school remaining in the present analysis is number six.

Students planning to go to college are undoubtedly overrepresented, since there were dropouts between the freshman and senior years. Finally, the geographical mobility of students between 1957 and 1961 probably introduces some bias.[8]

TABLE 1.   Selected Characteristics of the High Schools *

GENERAL CHARAC-TERISTICS	SCHOOLS									
	0	1	2	3	4	5°	6	7°	8°	9°
Number of Students in 1957	169	364	513	421	538	733	1,053	1,383	1,935	1,862
Location	town	town	town	town	town	city	suburb	city	city	suburb
Average Family Income in 1957**	6,000	6,400	6,400	6,400	5,800	5,100	6,200	5,400	7,200	11,400
Community Population	1,000	4,000	7,000	6,000	5,000	3,600,000	9,000	25,000	10,000	17,000
Number of Students to Whom Questionnaires Were Administered in Both 1957 *and* 1961	30	75	111	87	117	. . .	192			

* All schools except number 5 are public schools. School 5 is a Catholic boys' school.
° Data from these schools were not obtained in 1961.
** Given to the nearest hundred dollars.

Results

Students were asked the following question: "If a boy (girl) came here to school and wanted to get in with the leading crowd, what boys (girls) should he (she) get to be friends with?" The number of times an individual was mentioned as a member of the leading crowd was used to compute his index of change in status in the adolescent social system. Those students receiving no choice or only one choice either in 1957 or in 1961 were classified as having *low* status, and those receiving two or more choices were classified as having *high* status.[9] This procedure yields four status change types: high-high, high-low, low-high, low-low.

An index of change in intention to go to college was obtained from the following question, asked in both the freshman and senior years: "Are you planning to go to college after high school?" Those giving an affirmative response at either point in time were classified as *yes,* and those giving a negative or undecided response were classified as *no,* yielding four college-intention change types: yes-yes, yes-no, no-yes, no-no.

Finally, an index of change in value placed on scholastic achievement was obtained from responses to the question "If you could be remembered here at school for one of the three things below which would you want it to be?" Boys: Brilliant student, Athletic star, Most popular. Girls: Brilliant student, Leader in activities, Most popular.[10] Those giving the "brilliant student" response at either point in time were classified as placing *high* value on scholastic achievement, and those giving either of the other two responses, as placing low value on achievement.

A first step in the analysis is to examine changes in the marginals and the correlations over time. Table 2 shows the relation between social status and college intentions, and between social status and achievement orientation, at the beginning of the freshman year and at the end of the senior year.

TABLE 2. Relations of Social Status in Adolescent Social Systems to College Intentions and to Value Placed on Academic Achievement in Freshman and Senior Years

		Freshmen					Seniors		
		Social Status					Social Status		
		High	Low				High	Low	
College Plans	Yes	85	206	291	College Plans	Yes	112	155	267
	No	59	252	311		No	57	278	335
		144	458	602			169	433	602

$$\varphi = .12$$
$$\frac{\varphi}{\varphi \max} = \frac{.12}{.58} = .21*$$
$$.01 > P > .001$$

$$\varphi = .28$$
$$\frac{\varphi}{\varphi \max} = \frac{.28}{.69} = .41*$$
$$.001 > P$$

		Freshmen					Seniors		
		Social Status					Social Status		
		High	Low				High	Low	
Achievement Orientation	High	34	151	185	Achievement Orientation	High	36	125	161
	Low	102	267	369		Low	124	269	393
		136	418	554°			160	394	554°

$$\varphi = -.10$$
$$\frac{\varphi}{\varphi \max} = \frac{-.10}{.80} = -.13*$$
$$.02 > P > .01$$

$$\varphi = -.10$$
$$\frac{\varphi}{\varphi \max} = \frac{-.10}{1.00} = -.10*$$
$$.05 > P > .02$$

* Each phi coefficient is expressed as a proportion of its maximum value.

° The smaller number of respondents answering the achievement orientation item is due to the fact that it was near the end of the questionnaire in the first wave, and a number of questionnaires in all ten schools were not completed. In the second wave, the item was near the beginning, and the response rate was 97%.

Examining changes in marginals, it is evident that both the number planning to attend college and the number with high achievement orientation declined. It should be remembered that this is a selected group of students, those who *continued* in high school. Those who dropped out of school were considerably less likely either to report college plans or to place a high value on achievement.

The correlation between social status and college intentions is positive at both points in time.[11] In addition, the correlation increases over the four years of school. Apparently the factors that were operative early in high school to create a relation between adolescent social status and college plans continued to operate *even more strongly* during the four years in school to increase the relationship. This does not tell us whether college plans shifted to come in line with status, or vice versa. The decrease in the number of students of low status having college plans together with the increases in both those of high status with college plans and those of low status without college plans suggests that those of low status who had college plans moved in *both* directions—some toward high status and some toward non-college plans. The actual shifts will be shown in a table showing the position of each person at the two points.

Achievement orientation is negatively related to social status at both times.[12] Here, however, the negative relation *declines* slightly over the four years, indicating that whatever factors produced the negative relation in the first place weakened slightly over the four years of high school.[13]

For both the relationships shown in Table 2, the underlying process remains unclear. Does membership in the social elite of the school make a student hold to his college plans more than he otherwise would? Does it make him more likely to gain an interest in college than if he were not in the leading crowd? Or do college plans help put a person in the leading crowd or maintain his position if he's there already? The sixteen-fold tables relevant to these questions and the comparable questions for achievement orientation are shown as Tables 3 and 4.

A mere inspection of the sizes of various cells is not enough to indicate the processes represented in these complex tables. For this purpose, we have employed a mathematical model. The substantively simplest mathematical model that can be used to show changes over time in an attribute is one that predicates this change purely on the basis of the person's present state on this attribute itself. This is of little use in studying change and effects of variables on

TABLE 3.   Changes in Social Status in Adolescent Social Systems
and in College Intentions between 1957 and 1961 *

			TIME II: SPRING 1961				
Social Status°	*College Intentions°*	*Social Status:* * *College Intentions:°*	+ +	+ −	− +	− −	*Total*
+	+		50	10	13	12	85
+	−		12	23	6	18	59
−	+		41	8	96	61	206
−	−		9	16	40	187	252
	Total		112	57	155	278	(602)

* Cell entries are frequencies, not percentages.
° A plus sign indicates high social status or intending to go to college. A minus sign indicates low status or not intending to go to college.

TABLE 4.   Changes in Social Status in Adolescent Social Systems and in Value
Placed on Scholastic Achievement between 1957 and 1961 *

		TIME II: SPRING 1961				
	Value	*Social Status:*° +	+	−	−	
	Placed on	*Value Placed on*				
Social	*Scholastic*	*Scholastic*				
Status°	*Achievement*°	*Achievement:*° +	−	+	−	*Total*
+	+	4	18	6	6	34
+	−	14	54	8	26	102
−	+	9	10	74	58	151
−	−	9	42	37	179	267
Total		36	124	125	269	(554)

* Cell entries are frequencies, not percentages.
° A plus sign indicates high social status or high value placed on academic achievement. A minus sign indicates low status or value placed on academic achievement.

one another, but a slight complication, the one we have made, is useful: we have let the change be a function of the person's present state on *another* attribute as well as this one. Thus by estimating the *amount* that it depends on this other attribute (as estimated from the data), we can make inferences about effects of variables on one another. These are considerably stronger than the inferences usually made from cross-sectional data.

The mathematical model is a four-state continuous-time Markov process in which the individual has a certain small probability of change on either variable in any small increment of time. Labeling $++$ state 1, $+-$ state 2, $-+$ state 3, and $--$ state 4, then the changes in social status are changes between states 1 and 3, and and between states 2 and 4. The changes on college plans or on scholastic achievement orientation are changes between states 1 and 2, and between states 3 and 4. The probability of change from state 1 to state 3 in an infinitesmally small increment of time, *dt*, is p_{13}, or $q_{13} \, dt$, where q_{13} is a transition rate in a continuous-time process. The transition rates may be thought of as rates of "flow" across the boundaries. They are nonnegative numbers, with no upper

bound. These q_{ij}'s, or transition rates, make possible inferences about effects of these attributes on one another. The equations governing this continuous-time process are:

$$\frac{dp_i}{dt} = -(q_{12} + q_{13}) \, p_1 + q_{21}p_2 + q_{31}p_3$$

and similarly for the other three states (where p_i is the probability of being in state i).

The processes described by the four equations are portrayed graphically in Figure 1.

Estimates of the q_{ij}'s allow comparisons among them—and such comparisons are necessary to answer the questions posed above. For example, if q_{31} is greater than q_{42}, this implies that college plans make a boy or girl more likely to become a member of the leading crowd. For q_{31} is the transition rate toward membership in the leading crowd for those individuals planning to go to college, and q_{42} is the transition rate toward membership in the leading crowd for those who are not planning to attend college. Thus if $q_{31} > q_{42}$, this means that the probability per unit time of gaining entrance into the leading crowd is greater for those who plan to attend college than for those who do not.

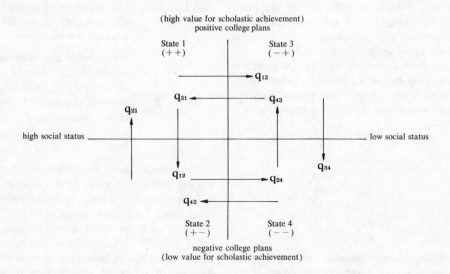

FIGURE 1. The relations among college plans, social status, and valuation of scholastic achievement.

Using Table 3 to estimate the value of q_{ij}'s we obtain: [14]

$$q_{12} = .227$$
$$q_{13} = .284$$
$$q_{21} = .388$$
$$q_{24} = .548$$
$$q_{31} = .373$$
$$q_{34} = .522$$
$$q_{42} = .112$$
$$q_{43} = .282$$

Comparisons between the horizontal rates in Figure 1 indicate the effect of college plans on adolescent social status. The relevant comparisons are: [15]

$q_{31} > q_{42}$
.373 > .112

Those with positive college plans are more likely to get into the leading crowd than those with negative plans.

$q_{24} > q_{13}$
.548 > .284

Those with negative college plans are more likely to move out of the leading crowd than those with positive plans.

Thus in both directions, the data indicate that college plans have a positive effect on membership in the leading crowd.

Comparisons of the vertical rates indicate the effect of membership in the leading crowd on college plans.

$q_{21} > q_{43}$
.388 > .282

Those who are in the leading crowd but do not plan to attend college are more likely to formulate such plans than are those who are not members.

$q_{34} > q_{12}$
.522 > .227

Those who are outside the leading crowd and plan to attend college are more likely to abandon such plans than are those in the leading crowd.

Here also, in both directions, the data indicate that membership in the leading crowd has a positive effect on plans to attend college, both by inducing such plans and by protecting the plans already made.

What about the relative sizes of these effects? Which variable affects the other more strongly? The effects seem to be rather equally balanced—both variables exert approximately equal influence.

A similar analysis of Table 4 gives the following values for the q_{ij}'s (where states 1 and 3 are a high value placed on scholastic achievement, and 4, a low value):

$$q_{12} = 2.817$$
$$q_{13} = .791$$
$$q_{21} = .733$$
$$q_{24} = .430$$
$$q_{31} = .259$$
$$q_{34} = .730$$
$$q_{42} = .271$$
$$q_{43} = .260$$

Comparisons between the horizontal rates in Figure 1 indicate the effect of the student's valuation of scholastic achievement on his social status:

$q_{42} > q_{31}$
.271 > .259

Those who place a low value on scholastic achievement are very slightly more likely to gain entrance to the leading crowd than are those who highly value such achievement.

$q_{13} > q_{24}$
.791 > .430

Those who place a high value on scholastic achievement are more likely to move out of the leading crowd than. are those who place a low value on such achievement.

Thus in both directions, the data indicate that a student's valuation of scholastic achievement has a negative effect on membership in the leading crowd.[16]

Comparisons of the vertical rates indicate the effect of membership in the leading crowd on valuation of scholastic achievement.

Those who are members of the leading crowd are

$q_{21} > q_{43}$
.733 > .260

more likely to gain a positive valuation of scholastic achievement than those who are not members.

$q_{12} > q_{34}$
2.817 > .730

Those who are members of the leading crowd are more likely to abandon a positive valuation of scholastic achievement than those who are not members.

These rates show that members of the leading crowd are more likely to change in *both* attitudinal directions. However, the effect toward a positive value is .473 (.733 − .260), while the effect toward a negative value is 2.087 (2.817 − .730), the highest yet found. Thus in balance it is clear that the overall effect of membership in the leading crowd is to create a low valuation of scholastic achievement.[17]

How are these results to be interpreted? How is it that membership in the leading crowd can simultaneously bring about a positive orientation to college and a negative orientation to scholastic achievement? How is it that college plans can make a boy or girl more likely to become or remain a member of the leading crowd, while a positive orientation to scholastic achievement means that he is less likely to remain in the leading crowd?

Interpretation is facilitated by direct examination of the relation between college plans and orientation to achievement. Table 5 shows that both in the freshman year and in the senior year, there is a positive relation between the two attributes. Furthermore, this relation has increased over the period of high school, principally because lack of college plans decreases achievement orientation and low achievement orientation destroys college plans.[18]

Thus despite their opposite relations to elite status in the school social system, college plans and achievement orientation are related to one another—and increasingly

TABLE 5.   Relation Between College Intentions and Value Placed on
Academic Achievement in Freshman and Senior Years

		Freshmen					Seniors		
		Achievement Orientation					Achievement Orientation		
		High	Low				High	Low	
College Plans	Yes	96	173	269	College Plans	Yes	91	156	247
	No	89	194	283		No	70	235	305
		185	367	552			161	391	552

$$\varphi = .04$$

$$\frac{\varphi}{\varphi \max} = \frac{.04}{.72} = .06*$$

$$.30 > P > .20$$

$$\varphi = .14$$

$$\frac{\varphi}{\varphi \max} = \frac{.14}{.72} = .19*$$

$$.001 > P$$

* Each phi coefficient is expressed as a proportion of its maximum value.

so through high school. The structure of relations becomes more puzzling still and suggests that the relation between college plans and achievement orientation among those of high status and those of low status should be examined separately. Table 6 shows that among freshmen with low status there is a positive relation between college plans and achievement orientation. Among those with high status no such relation exists; furthermore, they had, overall, a lower level of achievement orientation. Table 7 shows that by the senior year, the relation had sharpened among the low-status students and a slight positive relation had developed among the high-status. The level of achievement orientation, however, is still lower among the latter than among the former, particularly among those planning to go to college.

This examination suggests that a rather complex set of processes relates these three attributes. First, considering only the positive relation between college plans and status, the mutual effects of these attributes suggest two processes: a boy or girl in the leading crowd is in a group in which the majority are going to college. This fact, true from the beginning of the freshman year, certainly stems in part from the somewhat ascriptive nature of these leading crowds. Membership is greatly facilitated by coming from a "good" family in town, a family likely to plan to send its children to college. Thus for those who gain entrance to the leading crowd during high school, socialization toward college intentions presumably occurs. Similarly, outside the leading crowd, most of the cliques have a majority of non-college members. Socialization here works the other way: toward plans and activities that preclude college, often toward short-range goals that divert interest from college.

The other process, by which college plans or their absence lead a person into or out of the leading crowd apparently proceeds according to the maxim "birds of a feather flock together." This is especially true in high school, where the curricula differ for college and non-college students. Those with college plans have courses, activities, and interests in common with many members of the leading crowd, while

TABLE 6. Relation Between College Intentions and Value Placed on Academic Achievement in Freshman Year Holding Constant Status in Adolescent Social Systems

	Freshmen			
	LOW STATUS		HIGH STATUS	
	College	Non-college	College	Non-college
Per cent with High Value Placed on Achievement	41%	33%	22%	28%
Number of Cases	(194)	(234)	(81)	(57)

those without such plans have courses, activities and interests in common with more people outside the leading crowd. These commonalities lead to association and thus movement into or out of the leading crowd.

Scholastic achievement orientation in relation to high status obviously does not work the same way. It is not a value held by most members of the leading crowd and in fact is held less frequently by them than by those outside. Thus there is no tendency to socialize leading crowd members into holding this value, but rather the opposite. (The transition rate away from achievement orientation among members of the leading crowd is 2.817, the highest of all those computed, and 2.087 higher than among non-leading crowd members.) This process is counter to the general tendency for college plans and achievement orientation to affect each other positively.

All indications point to socialization *away from* scholastic achievement orientation in the leading crowd, simultaneous with socialization toward college.

Examination of Tables 6 and 7, showing that the association between college intentions and scholastic achievement is higher outside the leading crowd than inside, suggests that the path to college is somewhat different for the two groups. For those outside the leading crowd, college plans more often stem from (and lead to) achievement orientation than is true for those inside the leading crowd. To put it simply (and, of course, oversimplying in order to state the dominant process), college plans apparently derive from parent or peer socialization for those in the leading crowd but more often derive from an interest in the scholastic content of college for those outside the leading crowd.

TABLE 7. Relation Between College Intentions and Value Placed on Academic Achievement in Senior Year Holding Constant Status in Adolescent Social Systems

	Seniors			
	LOW STATUS		HIGH STATUS	
	College	Non-college	College	Non-college
Per cent with High Value Placed on Achievement	45%	23%	24%	18%
Number of Cases	(150)	(269)	(111)	(56)

The Effects of Sex on the Relations Among Status, College Plans, and Achievement Orientation

In *The Adolescent Society* important sex differences were found concerning the relation of social status in the schools to college plans and achievement orientation.

First, status was more strongly related to such plans for boys in the school-by-school comparisons than it was for girls, and there was less interschool variation for boys.[19]

Secondly, for all schools combined, boys named as "best scholars" by the students were more likely to want to be remembered as "brilliant students" than were the girl "best scholars." Furthermore, grade-by-grade comparisons (for all schools combined) revealed that in all grades except freshman, girl "scholars" were progressively *less* likely to want to be remembered for brilliance while boy scholars were progressively *more* likely to want to be remembered for brilliance.[20]

These differences strongly suggest that the adolescent culture has a differential impact upon the educational orientation of boys and girls and thus necessitate the introduction of sex as a control variable. In Table 8 and 9 the relations of status to college plans and to achievement orientation are presented separately by sex. Comparisons of these results with those in

TABLE 8. Relations of Social Status in Adolescent Social Systems to College Intentions and to Value Placed on Academic Achievement in Freshman and Senior Years for Boys

		Freshmen					Seniors		
		Social Status					Social Status		
		High	Low				High	Low	
College Plans	Yes	32	116	148	College Plans	Yes	63	88	151
	No	22	143	165		No	18	144	162
		54	259	313			81	232	313

$$\varphi = .11$$

$$\frac{\varphi}{\varphi \max} = \frac{.11}{.48} = .23^*$$

$$\varphi = .34$$

$$\frac{\varphi}{\varphi \max} = \frac{.34}{.62} = .55^*$$

		Freshmen					Seniors		
		Social Status					Social Status		
		High	Low				High	Low	
Achievement Orientation	High	14	81	95	Achievement Orientation	High	20	61	81
	Low	34	152	186		Low	55	145	200
		48	233	281			75	206	281

$$\varphi = -.04$$

$$\frac{\varphi}{\varphi \max} = \frac{-.04}{.63} = -.06^*$$

$$\varphi = -.03$$

$$\frac{\varphi}{\varphi \max} = \frac{-.03}{.93} = -.04^*$$

* Each phi coefficient is expressed as a proportion of its maximum value.

TABLE 9. Relations of Status in Adolescent Social Systems to College Intentions and to Value Placed on Academic Achievement in Freshman and Senior Years for Girls

		Freshmen					Seniors		
		Social Status					Social Status		
		High	Low				High	Low	
College Plans	Yes	53	90	143	College Plans	Yes	49	67	116
	No	37	109	146		No	39	134	173
		90	199	289			88	201	289

$$\varphi = .12$$

$$\frac{\varphi}{\varphi \max} = \frac{.12}{.68} = .18*$$

$$\varphi = .20$$

$$\frac{\varphi}{\varphi \max} = \frac{.20}{.82} = .24*$$

		Freshmen					Seniors		
		Social Status					Social Status		
		High	Low				High	Low	
Achievement Orientation	High	20	70	90	Achievement Orientation	High	16	64	80
	Low	68	115	183		Low	69	124	193
		88	185	273			85	188	273

$$\varphi = -.16$$

$$\frac{\varphi}{\varphi \max} = \frac{-.16}{.99} = -.16*$$

$$\varphi = -.15$$

$$\frac{\varphi}{\varphi \max} = \frac{-.15}{.99} = -.15*$$

* Each phi coefficient is expressed as a proportion of its maximum value.

Table 2 and with each other reveal several noteworthy findings.

Looking at college plans by sex at the two points in time reveals that the overall decrease in college plans in Table 2 is accounted for entirely by girls; in fact, there is a slight increase in such intentions for boys. Further examination shows that sex specifies the original relation between status and such plans. That is, the relation is more pronounced among boys than among girls at both points in time, and the increase in the size of the relationship over the four years is considerably greater for boys. These two findings clearly demonstrate that the school status system has greater impact on boy's college plans than on girls'.

One plausible explanation for this sex difference is that girls' college intentions are more a function of family influences than of peer influences, while the opposite is true for boys.[21] Among boy cliques, college attendance undoubtedly becomes more salient during the high school years than among girl cliques because a college education is more important in preparing males for a desirable occupation. That is, boys with high status are more likely to realize the importance of a college education in maintaining prestige than are high-status girls. Conversely, given the greater value placed on college attendance among boys, those who conform to such a value are more likely to be accorded high status than are their female counterparts.[22]

The overall decrease in achievement orientations over the four years shown in Table 2 occurs for both boys and girls, but the negative relation between status and achievement orientation is more pronounced among girls at both points in time. This stronger negative relationship shows that girls are more constrained by the status system not to value scholastic achievement highly. A consistent finding of the original research was noted above: girl "scholars" were less likely to want to be remembered as brilliant students than were boy "scholars," both in the overall comparisons and in the year-in-school comparisons. Both sets of results reflect the lack of social rewards in the girls' status systems for having an intellectual orientation.[23]

The relation between college plans and achievement orientation in both the freshman and senior years for boys and girls separately is shown in Table 10. These results are consistent with those in Table 5 in that the size of the relationship for both sexes increases from the freshman to the senior year. However, the relationship is stronger for boys at each point, and the

TABLE 10.   Relation Between College Intentions and Value Placed on Academic Achievement in Freshman and Senior Years Holding Constant Sex

BOYS

		Freshmen						Seniors		
		Achievement Orientation						Achievement Orientation		
		High	Low					High	Low	
College Plans	Yes	50	85	135	College Plans		Yes	54	84	138
	No	45	100	145			No	27	115	142
								81	199	280

$$\varphi = .07$$
$$\frac{\varphi}{\varphi \max} = \frac{.07}{.75} = .09^*$$

$$\varphi = .21$$
$$\frac{\varphi}{\varphi \max} = \frac{.21}{.65} = .32^*$$

GIRLS

		Freshmen						Seniors		
		Achievement Orientation						Achievement Orientation		
		High	Low					High	Low	
College Plans	Yes	46	88	134	College Plans		Yes	37	72	109
	No	44	94	138			No	43	120	163
		90	182	272				80	192	272

$$\varphi = .04$$
$$\frac{\varphi}{\varphi \max} = \frac{.04}{.72} = .06^*$$

$$\varphi = .09$$
$$\frac{\varphi}{\varphi \max} = \frac{.09}{.80} = .11^*$$

* Each phi coefficient is expressed as a proportion of its maximum value.

increase is considerably greater for boys. Since advanced education is more important to males and the attainment of a college degree requires some degree of intellectual orientation, this difference is to be expected. In fact, what is more surprising is that the relation between these two variables is not stronger. The relative lack of association reflects the discrepancy between adolescent and adult norms concerning the coincidence of intellectual orientation with going to college.[24]

Discussion and Conclusion

To return to the combination of college plans and negative achievement orientation in the leading crowds, the question still remains, how can this occur? A general orientation, widely held and widely admired by teen-agers, may account for the paradoxical combination of college plans and a negative evaluation of achievement: an orientation toward "sophisticated," "adult" activities. For a teen-ager in a generally middle class environment, college holds promise of such activities—campus social life, freedom from parental control, a shift to new friends, and all the other social attributes of college. But being a brilliant student promises none of these. Rather, it is associated with childhood, with good grades and gold stars dispensed by teachers.

In short, to teen-agers the image of scholastic achievement is largely an image of a subordinate status relative to adults that they are trying to escape. The source of this may well be that scholastic achievement in elementary and high school is largely gained by conformity and not by intellectual ferment. Thus socialization by a set of peers, unless these peers be themselves scholastically oriented, is likely to be away from scholastic achievement orientation while at the same time toward college. Whatever the association that

adults see between college and intellectualism, adolescents who are at the center of their high school social systems see the two as quite distinct entities: college promises adult status, but scholastic achievement carries the connotation of acquiescence and subordination to adults.[25]

Notes

1. As noted by John C. Ball, in "The Effect of Educational and Community Factors Upon Academic Achievement in Kentucky High Schools" (unpublished), studies of academic achievement have usually followed one of two lines of inquiry: (1) an analysis of characterestics possessed by persons of high performance, such as I.Q. or certain personality traits, or (2) a focus on such social background factors as race, ethnicity, social class, and subcultural values. See, for example, Kenneth Eells, *et al., Intelligence and Cultural Differences* (Chicago: University of Chicago Press, 1951), Joseph A. Kahl, "Educational and Occupational Aspirations of Common Man Boys," *Harvard Educational Review,* 18 (June 1953), pp. 233–42; David C. McClelland, *et al., The Achievement Motive* (New York: Appleton-Century-Crofts, 1953); William H. Sewell, Archie O. Haller, and Murray A. Straus, "Social Status and Educational and Occupational Aspirations," *American Sociological Review,* 22 (February 1957), pp. 67–73; David C. McClelland, *et al.,* (eds.), *Talent and Society* (Princeton: Van Nostrand, 1958); Albert J. Reiss, Jr., and Albert L. Rhodes, "Are Educational Norms and Goals of Conforming, Truant, and Delinquent Adolescents Influenced by Group Position in American Society?" *Journal of Negro Education,* (Summer 1959), pp. 252–67; Bernard C. Rosen, "Race, Ethnicity, and the Achievement Syndrome," *American Sociological Review,* 24 (February 1959), pp. 47–60; and David C. McClelland, *The Achieving Society* (Princeton: Van Nostrand, 1961).

In the area of the adolescent subculture, see A. B. Hollingshead, *Elmtown's Youth* (New York: John Wiley & Sons, 1949); Wayne Gordon, *The Social System of the High School* (New York: The Free Press, 1957); H. H. Remmers and D. H. Radler, *The American Teenager* (Indianapolis and New York: Bobbs-Merrill, 1957); Eli Ginzberg (ed.), *Values and Ideals of American Youth* (New York: Columbia University Press, 1961).

2. Some of the more important of the limited number of studies are Hollingshead, *op. cit.;* Gordon, *op. cit.;* A. O. Haller and C. E. Butterworth, "Peer Influences on Levels of Occupational and Educational Aspiration," *Social Forces,* 38 (May 1960), pp. 289–95; Walter L. Wallace, "A Study of College Student Peer-Group Interpersonal Environments" (unpublished); Alan B. Wilson, "Residential Segregation of Social Classes and Aspirations of High School Boys," *American Sociological Review,* 24 (December 1959), pp. 836–45; and the following works by James Coleman: "Academic Achievement and the Structure of Competition," *Harvard Educational Review,* 29 (Fall 1959), pp. 330–51; "The Adolescent Subculture and Academic Achievement," *American Journal of Sociology,* 65 (January 1960), pp. 337–47; and *The Adolescent Society* (New York: The Free Press, 1961).

3. *Op. cit.,* p. 290.

4. See footnote 2, *supra.*

5. The research was conducted in the Midwest in 1957 and 1958. Data were obtained from the student bodies of ten high schools in communities ranging in size from 1,000 to that of Chicago and varying in socioeconomic level from working class to executive and professional. School size ranged from 150 to 1,950.

6. In order to maximize the reliability of responses to the questionnaires, they were administered at both points in time by members of the research staff in the absence of the teacher and with guaranteed anonymity.

7. Permission to readminister the questionnaires was not granted by two of the schools; a third was a three-year school; and no request was made to the single non-public school in the sample.

8. There were 961 freshmen in the 1957 wave and 612 seniors in the 1961 wave, representing a loss of 26 per cent. The overwhelming majority of this loss may be attributed to three factors: school dropouts, geographical mobility, and absenteeism. The relative contribution of each is not known.

9. This arbitary cutting point is the same as that used in *The Adolescent Society,* p. 102, permitting comparison of the present results with those of the original research. In the following analysis the terms "high status" and "membership in the leading crowd" are used interchangeably.

10. As a check on the validity of this item as a measure of the value placed on scholastic achievement, another measure of this phenomenon was analyzed, and the results were essentially the same as those presented here.

Reference is made to these findings at appropriate places in the discussion below. The item was "Different people strive for different things. Here are some things that you have probably thought about. Among the things you strive for during your high school days, just how important is each of these? (Rank from 1 to 4: 1 for the highest in importance to you, 2 for the second highest, 3 for the third highest, and 4 for the lowest.)

___pleasing my parents

___learning as much as possible in school

___living up to my religious ideals

___being accepted and liked by other students"

Respondents giving a rank of either 1 or 2 to "learning as much as possible in school" at either point in time were categorized as placing *high* value on scholastic achievement; those giving a rank of 3 or 4 were classified as placing *low* value on achievement.

11. If the *total* freshmen classes for the six schools are examined rather than only those who continued in school, the relation is slightly stronger:

		Social Status		
		High	Low	
College Plans	Yes	103	281	384
	No	89	467	556
		192	748	940

This gives a $\frac{\varphi}{\varphi \max.}$ of 23

12. If the *total* freshmen classes are examined rather than solely those who continued in school, the relation is somewhat stronger:

		Social Status		
		High	Low	
Achievement Orientation	High	41	256	297
	Low	149	473	622
		190	729	919

$$\frac{\varphi}{\varphi \max.} = -.24$$

13. Using the other item for achievement orientation presented in footnote 10, the negative relation to social status was quite weak for freshmen; however, it increased over the four years in school. This suggests that caution should be used in drawing inferences from the *decline* in the relation of social status to the item used in the text.

14. The equation used for estimating the value of q_{ij} is an iterative one, deriving from the fact that in a continuous-time markov process the values of n_{ijt} (the number who started in state i and were in state j at time t) relative to n_i (the row marginals) are given by the following infinite series:

$$\frac{n_{ijt}}{n_i} = tq_{ij} + t^2 \sum_{k=1}^{4} \frac{q_{ik}q_{kj}}{2} + t^3 \frac{\Sigma\Sigma q_{ik}q_{kh}q_{hj}}{2 \times 3}$$
$$+ \dots$$

for all states $j \neq i$.

Letting $t = 1$, and transposing, an iterative procedure can be set up:

$$q_{ij}^{(m+1)} = \frac{n_{ij}}{n_i} - \sum_{k=1}^{4} \frac{q_{ik}^{(m)}q_{kj}^{(m)}}{2}$$

$$- \sum \frac{q_{ik}^{(m)}q_{kh}^{(m)}q_{hj}^{(m)}}{6}$$

$- \dots$ using values of q_{ij} from the mth iteration to calculate the $m + 1$ value of q_{ij} on the left, and using as many terms in the infinite series as are greater than some threshhold value of accuracy. For these purposes

$$q_{ii} = - \sum_{j \neq 1} q_{ij}$$

and in accord with the model, $q_{i,5-i}$ is arbitrarily zero. In Table 4, the iteration does not converge, and the iteration equation was truncated after 11 terms to force convergence.

A simplified calculation that will give approximate values is

$$q_{ij} = \frac{-n_{ijt}}{n_i - n_{ijt}} 1n \frac{n_{ijt}}{n_i}$$

This latter formula assumes that no more than one jump is made, while the iterative formula makes no such assumption. Ordinarily, the principal difference between the approximate values and the exact ones is that the latter are somewhat larger. Some values, however, are underestimated more than others by the approximate procedure. However, none of the substantive results would be altered if the approximate procedure, assuming one jump only, were used.

That the model does fit the data in Tables 3 and 4 can be shown by putting values of q_{ij} in the first equation of this footnote and estimating values of $\frac{n_{ij}}{n_i}$. The resulting frequencies, which can be compared with the actual data in Tables 3 and 4, are

For Table 3

55.4	10.0	13.0	6.6
12.0	25.2	3.8	18.0
40.9	7.2	97.0	60.9
10.6	16.0	40.0	185.4
119.0	58.4	153.7	270.9

For Table 4

4.5	16.3	5.5	7.6
12.7	54.7	8.8	25.8
8.3	18.5	66.3	57.9
8.8	41.7	36.9	179.5
34.4	131.2	117.6	270.8

15. Another comparison shows that regardless of college plans, the rates out of the leading crowd (.548, .284) are greater than those into it (.373, .112). This may seem incompatible with the fact that the leading crowd gains in size over the four years, but it is not. Since it is a minority, the probability of dropping out per unit time must be larger than the probability of coming in, if statistical equilibrium is to be maintained. The discrepancy in rates in and out is not large enough to maintain the minority size that the leading crowd had, and as a consequence, it increased in size.

16. Use of the other item for achievement orientation reveals essentially the same effect of achievement orientation on social status.

17. Introduction of the other item for achievement orientation shows comparable results.

18. The 16-fold table is
    (achievement orientation $= x$)
    (college plans $= y$)

	x y	$x +$ $y +$	$+$ $-$	$-$ $+$	$-$ $-$	Total
	$+$ $+$	48	7	27	14	96
Fall	$+$ $-$	11	27	9	42	89
1957	$-$ $+$	24	16	86	47	173
	$-$ $-$	8	20	34	132	194
	Total	91	70	156	235	552

Spring 1961

The transition rates are

	+ +	+ −	− +	− −
+ +		.179	.541	
+ −	.307			1.109
− +	.266			.465
− −		.243	.299	

Comparisons among these transition rates show that the principal effects are those of low achievement orientation bringing about abandonment of college plans (.465 compared to .179) and lack of college plans leading to low achievement orientation (1.109 compared to .541).

19. Coleman, *The Adolescent Society,* p. 116.

20. *Ibid.,* p. 251.

21. This is the case in both the freshman and senior years. A simultaneous control of the effects of status in school and family background (as measured by father's education) reveals the following differences:

(a) In both the freshman and senior years, family background accounts for more variation in college plans of girls than it does in the plans of boys. On the other hand, at both points in time, social status accounts for more of the variation in college plans of boys than of girls.

(b) For girls, at both points in time, family background accounts for more of the variation in college plans than does status in school. For boys, in the freshman year, family background is more strongly related to college plans than is school status, but in the senior year the reverse is true.

(c) The relation of social status to college plans increases for both sexes from the freshman to the senior year; however, the increase is greater for boys than for girls. It is also important to remember that these schools are either small-town (0, 1, 2, 3, 4) or working-class suburban (6). As the original research shows (p. 115), in such contexts, college-going is less salient to the future of girls and in the girls' leading crowds than it is in middle-class urban and suburban schools.

The full implications of these results are being explored in a separate paper.

22. A comparison of the transition rates for the sexes based on panel data revealed that this is the case.

23. As emphasized in the original research (pp. 252–54), girls are under a second restraint: to conform to adult demands to achieve higher grades in school, which they uniformly attained. (This difference in achievement has become commonplace knowledge in research in this area. See, for example, Alan B. Wilson, "Social Stratification and Academic Achievement" in A. Harry Passow (ed.), *Education in Depressed Areas* (New York: Bureau of Publications, Teachers College, Columbia University, 1963). In the present instance the girls appear to solve the conflicting demands of adults and peers by achieving good grades but not performing in an outstanding manner nor appearing aggressively bright. They do not perform as well as the best boy students nor as poorly as the worst boy students. The fact that the girls' intra-individual variance for grades was lower than the boys' in nine of the ten schools reflects their effort to minimize deviation from these double constraints.

24. Limitations of space preclude the presentation separately by sex of the 16-fold turnover tables and transition rates (q_{ij}'s) for the data presented in Tables 8, 9, and 10. The patterns of transition rates are generally consistent with the overall combined patterns of transition rates presented in pages 911–913 above and with the relationships based on the cross-sectional data presented in Tables 8, 9, and 10. These 16-fold tables and q_{ij}'s are available from the authors on request.

25. This statement of course overlooks the variation among high school social systems. In some, the leading crowds disdain not only an achievement orientation but college as well. At the other extreme, in some leading crowds there is a broad interest in scholastic achievement as well as in college. However, it is likely that social systems similar to those found in the schools studied here are more common than either of the other two cases in contemporary United States.

E. Repeated Observations on Collectives

45. The Emergence of the One-Party South —The Election of 1860

SEYMOUR M. LIPSET

THE continued allegiance of the South to the Democratic party stands out as the largest single deviation from a class conflict view of the American party struggle. Though some suggest that the Democratic loyalties of the South are reinforced by its position as an economically relatively depressed section of the country, it seems somewhat preposterous to view the southern planters and small-town businessmen as a depressed stratum. But there is no denying that some of the most conservative, if not reactionary, segments of the American body politic are southern Democrats. Some of the variables underlying this fact have already been discussed . . .[1] However, an analysis of the link between the post-Civil War identification with the Democratic party and class cleavage within the *ante bellum* South may illustrate how the diverse interests and values of different strata are affected by such confusing and emotion-laden issues as slavery and Negro rights, and supply some of the reasons for the long-term continuation of a seemingly non-logical pattern. This chapter deals briefly with these issues by a survey of the last real two-party election in the South—that of 1860.

The election of 1860 stands out decisively as the presidential election which most affected American life. Its controversies culminated in the Civil War. The formal party system has not changed much since then, and the regional loyalties and antagonisms formed in that period have continued to affect party allegiancies down to the present day. The election itself took place as the end to a great national debate on the place of slavery in American life— a debate which had grown in intensity during the entire first half of the nineteenth century. As one reads over the story of the period, it is difficult to avoid the feeling that if there was ever an election with a salient issue, in which voters made a fundamental choice, it was this one.

However, an examination of the sources of support of the four presidential candidates in this election suggests that issues associated with slavery of the rise of the Republican party were not the decisive ones affecting the vote of *most* Americans, although they may have changed the vote

Reprinted with permission from Chapter XI of *Political Man: The Social Bases of Politics* (copyright 1959 by Doubleday & Co., New York).

of important minorities. There were four candidates: Lincoln representing the Republicans; Douglas, the northern Democrats; Breckenridge, the southern Democrats; and Bell, the Constitutional Union party. Lincoln and Bell, seemingly, were nominees of new parties, but in fact they represented the northern and southern Whig parties, which had split along regional lines earlier than the Democrats. Although there were four candidates in the race, the contest in each region of the country was largely a two-party affair. In the southern states it was a contest between the secessionist Democrats supporting Breckenridge and the old Whig Constitutional Unionists who advocated remaining in the Union. In the North it was the Democrat, Douglas, who opposed slavery but favored saving the Union by giving the southern states various guarantees for their "peculiar institution." The northern Whig-Republicans under Lincoln also hoped to save the Union but vigorously opposed the extension of slavery in the territories or new states and included a number of prominent abolitionists in their ranks. Thus the northern Whig-Republicans and the southern Democrats represented the two extremes, while the northern Democrats and the southern Whig-Constitutional Unionists represented the groups in each section of the country who were seeking to compromise the cleavage.

The four-candidate race of 1860 succeeded a three-party fight in 1856, when the American, or Know-Nothing, party contested the election against the Democrats and Republicans. Any attempt to understand the results of the 1860 election must begin with an examination of the social composition and ultimate political destination of the Know-Nothing voters. Both their leadership and voting strength suggest that the bulk of their vote came from former Whigs. This was particularly true in the South where their presidential candidate, Millard Fillmore, secured 45 per cent of the vote in 1856, essentially the strength of the Whig party. In the North, most former Whigs voted for the Republican party, which won 45 per cent of the total sectional vote, while Fillmore secured only 13 per cent of the votes of the northern electorate.

In 1860, the now divided Democrats increased their vote in both the North and the South, but the Republicans, absorbing the bulk of Fillmore's vote in the North, obtained approximately 54 per cent of the vote in that section and a majority in the Electoral College. The Republican victory in 1860 cannot be credited to any drastic shift away from the Democrats, but rather to the fact that all northern anti-Democratic votes were gathered together under one party for the first time since the Whig victory of 1848. As a matter of fact the Democrats actually *gained* five congressional seats in the North in 1860. In the South, the Constitutional Unionist and former Whig, Bell, secured 41 per cent of the vote, only 4 per cent less than the 1856 vote of the candidate of the Know-Nothing party, the former Whig, Fillmore.

A cursory analysis of the county election returns, North and South, indicates that for the most part men continued to vote in 1860 for the same party they had always voted for, although a shift to the Democrats in the South and to the Whig-Republicans in the North continued. If one compares the results of the elections from 1840 to 1860, one finds that in each of them, in both North and South, the Democrats were disproportionately backed by the lower strata—the poorer farmers, the foreign born, the non-Anglo-Saxons, the Catholics, and the nonslaveholders in the South; while the Whigs were based on the more privileged classes—the merchants, the more well-to-do farmers, the native-born Protestants of Anglo-Saxon ancestry, and the large slave-holding plantation owners.[2] These relationships obtained during this entire period, although, as indicated above, the southern Democrats gained considerably in Whig areas, while the Republicans absorbed a group of Free Soil (Van Buren) Democrats as well as some anti-Catholic groups who had supported the American party.

These results—particularly in the South—present some interesting problems for the student of elections. It is clear that Bell, the southern candidate opposing secession and seeking to keep the South in the Union even under Republican control, was disproportionately backed by slaveowners, while Breckenridge, the candidate of the "red-hots" who saw little future for the South and its institutions in the Union, received the bulk of the votes of the men who did not own slaves and who had often opposed the conservative well-to-do plantation owners in intrastate political controversies.

The correlations between party vote and various social characteristics in 1860 are understandable only if we make the assumption that most voters in that year voted along traditional lines. The more deprived social groups remained loyal to their regional Democratic candidates, Breckenridge and Douglas, while the more privileged voted for the regional candidates of the old Whig party, Bell and Lincoln. For example, the straw votes cast for President in 1860 at St. Paul's School were divided almost entirely between the two Whig candidates, with Bell receiving 46 per cent and Lincoln 37 per cent.[3] The election of 1860, like every election since 1828, was fought out between the supporters and opponents of Andrew Jackson. Table I, which shows the variation in voting patterns of southern counties according to the ratio of slaves in the county, clearly demonstrates that the strength of the secessionist Democrat Breckenridge lay with the whites living in areas in which there were few slaves. The table seems to suggest that the fewer the slaves in a county, the greater the support for secession, since Breckenridge car-

TABLE I.   Proportion of Counties Voting for Breckenridge in Seven Southern States —Virginia, Alabama, Georgia, Mississippi, North Carolina, Tennessee and Louisiana *

Relative Position of County in Proportion of Slaves within Its State	Total	Number for Brecken-ridge	Per cent for Brecken-ridge
High	181	94	52%
Medium	153	87	56
Low	203	130	64

* Douglas, the northern Democrat, secured 13 per cent of the southern vote. Since he, like Bell, supported the Union his votes have been considered together with Bell's as anti-Breckenridge. In locating counties as high, medium, or low in proportion of slaves, it was necessary to use different classifications for each state. This was done in part because the sources employed to secure the data differed among themselves in the way in which they reported percentage of slaves in the population. More important than this reason, however, was the fact that states varied greatly in the proportion of slaves so that the plantation states had many slaves in most counties, while some of the border states had few counties in which slaves were a majority. In all the southern states, however, the proportion of slaves in the population served to differentiate the wealthier from the poorer counties, and in general, whether a county was high or low in proportion of slaves within a state was highly correlated with its voting patterns.

The data for this and succeeding tables have been calculated from information reported in the following works: Joseph Carlyle Sitterson, *The Secession Movement in North Carolina* (Chapel Hill: University of North Carolina Press, 1939); Henry T. Shanks, *The Secession Movement in Virginia, 1847–1861* (Richmond: Garrett and Massie, 1934); Lewy Dorman, *Party Politics in Alabama from 1850–1860* (Augusta: Alabama State Department of Archives and History, 1935); Percy Lee Rainwater, *Mississippi Storm Center of Secession, 1856–1861* (Baton Rouge, La.: Otto Claitor, 1938); Thomas P. Abernethy, *From Frontier to Plantation in Tennessee* (Chapel Hill: University of North Carolina Press, 1932); and Ulrich B. Phillips, *Georgia and State Rights* (Washington: Government Printing Office, 1902).

ried almost two thirds of the counties which were low in slaves, while almost half the counties that were high in slaves voted against him.

Whether a Breckenridge vote actually meant a vote for secession, however, was tested directly three to six months after the presidential election when the same states held referenda (or elections to conventions) in which voters were called upon to express directly their sentiments for or against secession from the Union. The situation had changed, of course, since Lincoln had been elected President, and it was clear that a large group in the South had decided on secession. These convention-delegate elections were hotly contested in most southern states, and the results were closer than many realize, with the Union forces getting over 40 per cent of the vote in many states. Although no one has done a detailed study of the leaders of the secession and Union forces in these elections, historical works on the struggle in different states indicate that most of the antisecession leaders had been leaders of the Whig and Constitutional Union parties, while the secessionist leadership was largely, though far from exclusively, in the hands of Democrats. This fact, together with the results of the presidential election presented in Table I, might lead one to expect that the Whig slaveholders who backed Bell in the presidential election would be the principal source of Unionist sentiment, while the low-slave counties would back secession, following up their vote for Breckenridge.

In fact, however, the relationship between slave-ownership and voting Unionist shown in the presidential election was completely reversed in the referenda. In these elections, the counties with many slaves supported secession, and those with few slaves backed the Union.

A comparison of Table I and Table II reveals about as drastic a shift in identification with an issue as it is possible to imagine in elections occurring within a

TABLE II. Proportion of Counties with Different Ratios of Slaves Voting for Secession in Seven Southern States

Relative Position of County in Proportion of Slaves within Its State	Secession	Union		(N)
High	72	28	100%	(181)
Medium	60	40	100%	(153)
Low	37	63	100%	(203)

three- to six-month period. A majority of the voters in 64 per cent of the counties having few or no slaves voted for the secessionist Democrat Breckenridge in the fall of 1860, and a majority in 63 per cent of the same counties voted for the Union in the subsequent referenda held in the winter of 1860–61. Conversely, a majority of the voters in almost half the counties with plantation farming and many slaves voted against Breckenridge in the election, but the secessionist position carried 72 per cent of them a short time later. The factors underlying this astonishing change can be partially clarified by looking at the vote of counties in the same way that panel studies of voting analyze changes of decision in individuals who are reinterviewed over a period of time. That is, we can differentiate among these counties in terms of the shifts in the two votes, and see where the shifts took place.

The data in Table III make clear what happened in 1860–61. In the presidential election, men continued to vote along traditional party lines. When, however, party labels vanished and the issue became one of secession versus Union, the class or economic factors previously inhibited by party loyalties broke through. The slaveholders voted for secession in the referenda, while those living in areas with few slaves voted for the Union.[4] Party loyalties and issues linked to parties did, however, continue to

TABLE III.   Relationship Between Vote in Presidential Election in 1860 and
Subsequent Vote for Secession or Union in Seven Southern States in Counties with
Different Proportions of Slaves

			Relative Proportion of Slaves in County			
	HIGH		MEDIUM		LOW	
			Presidential Vote—1860			
Vote on Secession	Brecken-ridge	Bell-Douglas	Brecken-ridge	Bell-Douglas	Brecken-ridge	Bell-Douglas
Pro-Secession	82%	61%	82%	30%	50%	14%
Pro-Union	18	39	18	70	50	86
(N)	(94)	(87)	(87)	(66)	(130)	(73)

have some effect on voting behavior and attitudes toward secession in the referenda. This is clear from the fact that two fifths of the high slave counties which were predominantly Whig in the presidential voting followed Whig policy and the advice of many of their leaders by voting to remain in the Union. Among low-slave counties, half of those which had voted for Breckenridge shifted to vote for the Union, while over four fifths of the low-slave counties which opposed Breckenridge voted for the Union. Party tradition was most decisive among the group of counties which were in the middle group in the proportion of slaves in the population. On the whole, they voted in the referenda as they had voted in the election. If they were Democratic, they went for secession; if Whig, they were for the Union.

Thus the heavily Democratic counties which had a large slave population were much more likely to support secession. A tradition of Whig voting and the presence of few or no slaves increased support for the Union. The Democratic party, however, received its support from the group which was most predisposed to favor the Union—the voters in nonslave areas—while the pro-Unionist Whigs were backed by whites living in plantation areas with many slaves.

It must, of course, be kept in mind that the conclusions presented here are subject to all the pitfalls of ecological analysis, particularly the fact that the imputation from the voting of areas to the voting of individuals within those areas does not necessarily follow.[5] It is possible, though not likely, that the vote of the high slave areas for the Unionist candidate in 1860 came from the non-slaveowners in plantation districts and that the slaveholders actually voted for Breckenridge. Many variables besides traditional party loyalty and the proportion of slaves in a given area affected the voting picture.

Nevertheless, viewing the 1860–61 elections and referenda in the South in terms of the characteristics of the counties which changed their votes sharply illuminates what occurred in that crucial year among the southern electorate. The old well-to-do Whig slaveowners and their followers continued in 1860 to oppose the southern demagogues from the lower nonslave-owning strata of the white population, and the latter remained loyal to the party of Jackson even after it became the party of slavery and secession. But once the die was cast and the vote represented an issue rather than a party, enough of the Breckenridge supporters opposed secession and enough backers of Bell, the Constitutional Unionist, supported it to make it accurate to say that, in proportionate terms, the slaveowners voted for secession and the nonslave-owning whites opposed it.

Although the data are unsystematic and incomplete, an examination of election returns by county for the South suggests that the two major parties, Whig and Democratic, divided the electorate more or less along economic and status lines from the 1830s on.[6] The major deviation from this tendency occurred in mountain areas, where poor nonslave-owning white farmers voted for the Whigs, reputedly because the party supported government payment for internal improvements such as roads. The Democrats were traditionally opposed to internal improvements on the grounds that these benefited the mercantile classes of the cities who should properly pay for them.

With the rise of the slavery issue, the Whigs lost some strength in the plantation areas but still remained the dominant party there. The fact that the northern Whigs, who were predominantly middle-class Protestants, were the strongest antislavery group in either major party made the existence of the Whigs as a national party impossible, and the southern Whigs floundered while their northern compatriots formed the Republican party.

After the Civil War and the end of Reconstruction, the Democratic party retained the old centers of Jacksonianism—the areas which did not have a plantation economy and which were low in Negro population—and also gained the support of, was in fact captured by, the old Whig-supporting plantation owners and businessmen of the cities. The Republican party maintained some continuity with the old southern Whigs by retaining the votes of the poor whites in the mountains who backed the Whigs in the '30s and '40s because they wanted roads. It was this group which voted Constitutional Union in 1860, for the Union in the referenda of 1860–61, fought in the Union army against the Confederacy, and remained loyal to the Republican party

all during Reconstruction, the later era of white supremacy, and the age of Roosevelt and Truman.

An ecological panel analysis among southern whites which focused on the shifting counties and areas over a long period would probably show that the two groups which were unstable in 1860–61 have been a potential source of change in the one-party South ever since Reconstruction. The old Whig classes became Democratic as a result of the Civil War, but they are miscast outside of the legitimate inheritor of the Whig tradition, the Republican party. The well-to-do strata and areas which were most loyal to the Constitutional Unionists in the election and to the Union in the referendum seem to be the same ones that today have a propensity to shift to the Republicans. On the other side, the counties which were traditionally nonplantation Democratic and which shifted to vote for the Union in 1860–61, appear to be the same counties which, after the Civil War, backed agrarian third parties or "populist" factions within the Democratic party, and which remain in the party now while the old Whig strata bolted to the Republicans as a reaction to the restored liberalism of the national Democratic party.[7]

Notes

1. For detailed analyses of the one-party South, see V. O. Key, Jr., *Southern Politics* (New York: Alfred A. Knopf, 1949); Alexander Heard, *A Two-Party South* (Chapel Hill: University of North Carolina Press, 1952); and J. B. Shannon, *Towards a New Politics in the South* (Knoxville: University of Tennessee Press, 1949).

2. The basic research to demonstrate the continuity of voting choices within the Whig-Democratic framework has not been fully done although there are a number of local studies which indicate that the Whigs, Americans, and Republicans drew their votes from the same sources, while the Democrats, united or cleaved, retained the loyalties of the strata and sections which had backed Jackson and Van Buren from 1828–1840.

3. Arthur Stanwood Pier, *St. Paul's School* (New York: Charles Scribner's Sons, 1934), p. 60; also quoted in E. Digby Baltzell, *Philadelphia Gentlemen* (Glencoe: The Free Press, 1958), p. 316.

4. A study of German settlements in Texas suggests that some of the non-Anglo-Saxon minority ethnic groups among the whites may have followed similar patterns to those of the poor white farmers. Analysis of the voting patterns of German towns in Texas before 1860 indicates that most of them voted overwhelmingly for the Democratic party, although their organizations and publications were anti-slavery. This pattern of loyalty to the Democratic party continued in the election of 1860 when they voted for Breckenridge. In the secession referendum in 1861 they voted against secession. See Rudolph L. Biesele, *The History of German Settlements in Texas* (Austin: Von Boechmann-Jones Co., 1930).

5. For discussions of the limitations of the application of ecological correlations to individual attributes, see W. S. Robinson, "Ecological Correlations and the Behavior of Individuals," *American Sociological Review*, 15 (1956), pp. 351–57; Leo A. Goodman, "Ecological Regressions and Behavior of Individuals," *American Sociological Review*, 18 (1953), pp. 663–64; and O. D. Duncan, "An Alternative to Ecological Correlation," *American Sociological Review*, 18 (1953), pp. 665–66.

6. "The line of social cleavage that separated the Whig planters from the toiling but prosperous hill farmers and from the indolent 'poor whites' was a severely distinct one, enough to engender political antagonism. In their stately mansions, surrounded with almost every comfort of the day and with many luxuries, and educated in the polished manners of their class, the planters regarded as social necessities what to others were symbols of effeminacy and dandyism, or at least of foolish extravagance. . . .

"The origin of this social line which so nearly coincided with the party line can be traced, in the southern Atlantic states at least, well back into the eighteenth century. But it was in connection with the developments which culminated in the triumph of Jacksonian Democracy that the real tightening of these lines was begun . . . the Jackson party was met by a powerful opposition in which the southern planters played a conspicuous part. Social distinctions between the people of the black belt and the people of the back country were then able to reassert themselves and the social unity of each class had the inevitable effect of furthering and cementing their political unity.

"The Whig party in the South, then, contrary to the prevailing notion that it drew its chief support from the non-slave-holding whites above the 'mean-white' class was from its origin, and continued to be throughout its history, the party of the planter and the slaveholder—the aristocrat of the fertile black belt. The Democratic party, on the other hand, drew upon the opposite side of the social scale—especially upon the small farmer of the back hill-country who could always be reached by the party's appeal to the agrarian spirit." A. C. Cole, *The Whig Party in the South* (Washington: The American Historical Society, 1913), pp. 69–72; an important addition to this generally held view has been presented by the historian Charles Sellers, who points out that the southern Whigs were formed and led by "business and professional men of the towns," that 74 per cent of their Congressional representatives were lawyers, that almost all southern bankers were Whigs. "The Whig party in the South was controlled by urban commercial and banking interests, supported by a majority of the planters, who were economically dependent on banking and commercial facilities." Charles G. Sellers, "Who Were the Southern Whigs?" *American Historical Review*, 59 (1954), pp. 335–46.

7. A recently published study of Louisiana elections from the beginning of statehood to the present suggests some of the potential untapped resources for a study of electoral continuity and discontinuity. It clearly indicates continuities in Louisiana politics from the pre-Civil War period down to the present. See Perry H. Howard, *Political Tendencies in Louisiana, 1812–1952* (Baton Rouge: Louisiana State University Press, 1957); see also Allan P. Sindler, *Huey Long's Louisiana* (Baltimore: The Johns Hopkins Press, 1956).

46. Sociometric Panels

BERNARD LEVENSON

IN THIS PAPER we shall discuss some of the insights into group processes and friendship changes which the sociometric panel yields and which other techniques misinterpret or fail to detect.

We will begin with a discussion of the unit of analysis in the sociometric panel. Then we shall consider some examples from the literature of sociometric turnover. Finally, we will discuss the analysis of qualified sociometric turnover tables. In that discussion we shall point out that sociometric data impel us to introduce a type of qualifier not encountered in conventional panels. The number of studies with repeated sociometric data so far undertaken are few. Consequently, in some sections we will only be able to speculate about the questions that are raised when traditional substantive problems of sociometry are considered in panel terms.

Unit of Sociometric Analysis

Suppose that each member of an interacting group was asked to respond to some sociometric item, then the designations can be registered in a $N \times N$ sociometric matrix (Table 1).

The sociomatrix has been arranged so as to reveal two cliques. A, B, and C, who choose each other, are in one clique; D, E, and F, who also choose each other, form the second clique. There are no choices between cliques.

Now suppose that at some subsequent time the six people were reinterviewed, and reported their closest associates as in Table 2.

Although inspection reveals that the time 2 sociomatrix is different from the time 1, it is not immediately evident what changes occurred. At time 1 each individual received and conferred two choices, and again at time 2 each received and conferred two choices. If we study the two tables, we will discover what has changed: B and D have switched clique membership.

Inspection of successive sociomatrices may be sufficient for studying interpersonal change in small groups such as this, but for groups large enough to provide interesting sociological problems more systematic methods for studying sociometric change are necessary.

But how can this be done? With sociometric data there is no unique way of transforming repeated responses into a turnover table. A turnover table can be formed only after we settle upon the unit of analysis. Each individual can be characterized by combining all of his choices into some index; or all of the choices designating him can be indexed; or both sets of designations can be combined. Thus sociometric turnover can be studied, using the individual as the unit of analysis.

We can also study sociometric turnover using the dyad as the unit. This is what will be used in the ensuing exposition. Operationally, the dyad as a unit of analysis means that in a group with N individuals there will be $\dfrac{N(N-1)}{2}$ dyads.

This is a previously unpublished paper. The author wishes to acknowledge the ideas and other help given him by David Caplovitz and by Valerie Moolman.

TABLE 1. Hypothetical Sociomatrix (time 1)

CHOOSERS	A	B	C	D	E	F	Choices Made	
A	–	c	c				(2)	
B	c	–	c				(2)	
C	c	c	–				(2)	c = close associate
D				–	c	c	(2)	
E				c	–	c	(2)	
F				c	c	–	(2)	
Choices received:	(2)	(2)	(2)	(2)	(2)	(2)	(12)	

With a simple sociometric criterion involving only choice or nonchoice, dyadic relationships can be classified into three categories: mutual, unilateral, and nonconnected. Since each relationship is observed at two time points, the data are entered in a nine-fold sociometric turnover table (Table 3).

One curious situation arises immediately. Although nine cells are shown in Table 3, there are actually ten. The cell U_1U_2 covers both stable and oscillatory unilateral relationships. In one case A chooses B at time 1 and time 2; in the other, A chooses B at time 1 whereas B chooses A at time 2.

In the following pages the number of oscillatory U_1U_2 relationships in each table will be specified, since they have substantive meaning.[1]

Now that we have presented the formal framework, let us turn to some empirical examples of dyadic sociometric turnover.

Sociometric Turnover

The first example of a sociometric turnover table is derived from data appearing in a book by J. L. Moreno.[2] He administered sociometric tests to girls who were housed in the same cottage at a correctional

TABLE 2. Hypothetical Sociomatrix (time 2)

CHOOSERS	A	B	C	D	E	F	Choices Made	
A	–		c	c			(2)	
B		–			c	c	(2)	
C	c		–	c			(2)	c = close associate
D	c		c	–			(2)	
E		c			–	c	(2)	
F		c			c	–	(2)	
Choices received:	(2)	(2)	(2)	(2)	(2)	(2)	(12)	

TABLE 3.   Sociometric Turnover Table

	TIME 2 *RELATIONSHIPS*		
TIME 1 *RELATION-* *SHIPS*	*Mutual*	*Uni-* *lateral*	*Non-* *con-* *nected*
Mutual	M_1M_2	M_1U_2	M_1N_2
Unilateral	U_1M_2	U_1U_2	U_1N_2
Nonconnected	N_1M_2	N_1U_2	N_1N_2

institution. The purpose of his study was to use sociometry as a basis for "reconstructing" the group so as to increase group harmony. At the time of the first sociometric test the girls in the cottage had known each other for about two years. After studying the initial sociometric data and interviewing the girls, Moreno transferred three girls to other cottages and moved one new girl into the cottage. Eighteen months later Moreno administered another sociometric test to see whether the changes had increased group harmony. Later we shall examine these changes in more detail and critically evaluate Moreno's interpretation of the data. For our present purposes, however, we shall deal only with the twenty-seven

girls who were in the cottage at both sociometric tests.

It should be noted that Moreno presented his data in the form of two sociograms. Short of dramatic changes in group structure, the successive states of a large number of dyadic relationships are not apt to be detected by a diagrammatic technique. Moreno's two sociograms have been converted into a dyadic turnover table which allows us to assess in a systematic way the changes in relationships. Since the girls were asked to indicate not only whom they would like to have in their cottage but also whom they would not want to have, there are six types of relationships in Table 4 instead of three as in Table 3.

Study of the turnover table reveals that in a period of eighteen months, less than 4 per cent of the 351 relationships underwent any change, a rather small percentage. Of the twelve relationships which did change, ten apparently contributed to greater group harmony: three pairs switched from mutual indifference to mutual acceptance; six pairs moved from rejection–indifference to mutual indifference; and one pair changed from acceptance–rejection to mutual indifference. Two pairs, which switched from mutual acceptance to

TABLE 4.   Turnover in Sociometric Relations *

	RELATIONSHIPS AFTER RECONSTRUCTION OF COTTAGE						
RELATIONSHIPS BEFORE RECON-STRUCTION OF COTTAGE	*Mutual Accept-ance*	*Accept-ance; Indif-ference*	*Mutual Indif-ference*	*Accept-ance; Re-jection*	*Indif-ference; Re-jection*	*Mutual Re-jection*	*Time 1 Totals*
Mutual Acceptance	15		2				(17)
Acceptance; Indifference		27					(27)
Mutual Indifference	3		275				(278)
Acceptance; Rejection			1	5			(6)
Indifference; Rejection			6		15		(21)
Mutual Rejection						2	(2)
Time 2 Totals	(18)	(27)	(284)	(5)	(15)	(2)	(351)

* Source: J. L. Moreno, *Who Shall Survive?* (Beacon, New York: Beacon House, 1955). Data refer to Cottage #16.

TABLE 5.   Turnover in Sociometric Relationships

| RELATIONSHIPS AT TIME 1 | RELATIONSHIPS AT TIME 2 | | | |
	Mutual	Unilateral	Non-connected	Time 1 Totals
Mutual	14	1	0	(15)
Unilateral	4	10*	3	(17)
Non-connected	0	6	40	(46)
Time 2 Totals	(18)	(17)	(43)	(78)

* Direction of choice changed in 2 of the 10 unilaterals.

mutual indifference, apparently decreased group harmony.

To illustrate the utility of sociometric turnover analysis in shedding light on the evolution of group structure, we shall contrast the Moreno data with data from another study. Table 5 was computed from two sociograms appearing in an educational journal.[3] The sociograms represented the interpersonal networks of a group of thirteen school children, and the interval between tests was about six weeks.

If we had relied on the marginal proportions we might conclude that three pairs, unconnected at the first test, became friends by the second test. We might also conclude that the unilateral relations were exceedingly stable. But the internal entries tell a different story. Instead of six changes, as the marginals might suggest, there were sixteen, which amounts to 21 per cent or about six times the turnover in the Moreno table.[4] And there too, remember, the sociometric criterion was more refined; the turnover table consisted of 36 cells, whereas the table above contains only 9 cells. Moreover, instead of being most stable, the unilaterals were least stable. More than half of the 17 unilaterals underwent some change. Four pairs advanced to mutuality, three unilateral choices were withdrawn, and two unilaterals underwent a change in the direction of choice.

Contrast the volatility of the unilaterals in this group with the stability of the unilaterals in the Moreno group (Table 4, line 2). There were 27 unilaterals in that group at time 1; eighteen months later, these same girls were still making unilateral choices. The turnover table of the second group (Table 5) suggests that the process of friendship is still going on: some individuals are making overtures to others; where overtures have already been made, some evoke responses while others are apparently rebuffed and consequently withdrawn. The fact that two unilaterals oscillated suggests relationships that are still in equivocal or uncertain states: an overture may have been made—perhaps not too affirmatively —but by the time the target individual has responded, the initiator's interest has subsided.

In sum, sociometric panel analysis calls attention to substantive problems that go undetected in static analysis. In sociometric literature, "unilateral" choices usually connote interpersonal maladjustment. Individuals making unilateral choices are assumed to be hungering for friendship with an unresponsive peer. But as the turnover tables suggest we have to distinguish between a unilateral choice in a group that has reached some sort of equilibrium from a unilateral choice in a group where relationships are crystallizing. In the Moreno group, of the 27 acceptance–indifference relationships, *100* per cent were in the same state *18 months later,* whereas in the second group, *53* per cent of the unilaterals changed in *one and a half months.* Obviously a unilateral choice in the second group means something quite different from such choice in the first: it may be an indicator of "overture-making" and quite adequate interpersonal adjustment. In the former group the unilateral choice apparently represents some type of "love at a distance" or an indication of superiority–inferiority or leadership followership. Short of those rare cases where two people's fancies are simultaneously ignited upon confronting each other, there must be a point in all relationships where one member of the pair makes an initial overture of friendship.

The concept of "overture-making," suggested by the panel analysis, has far-reaching implications for research on the problem of interpersonal adequacy. In the field of mental health and in educational sociology efforts are frequently made, through sociometric tests, to identify "social isolates" and to uncover their characteristics. By observing individuals over time, it might well turn out that in some cases isolation results from inability to make affirmative overtures, or inability to perceive overtures made by others, or inability to communicate affirmative responses to overtures. The dynamics of overture-making and overture-response can be explored more deeply by means of qualifiers, to which we now turn.

Qualified Sociometric Turnover

Two kinds of qualifiers will be discussed. When the pair is the unit of analysis, we may use as qualifiers some characteristic of the pair—for example, whether the two are similar in race, sex, or rank, or whether they share the same opinion on some subject. This type will be called an "attribute qualifier" to differentiate it from the "sociometric qualifier." In the latter, a qualifier is constructed from sociometric data on the relationship between each pair member and others in the group. In the discussion below, the sociometric qualifier will be whether the pair members share a common relationship with some third person in the group.

Attribute Qualifiers

Here we will illustrate the notion of attribute qualifiers in sociometric panel data by discussion of two examples. These examples are intended to be illustrative of qualifier analysis in sociometric panels; no attempt is made to be exhaustive or to present a unified theory of friendship formation.

NEGRO-WHITE FRIENDSHIPS

Data from a sociometric panel have been re-analyzed to show turnover in white–white, Negro–Negro, and Negro–white subgroups.[5] Table 6 shows how relationships

TABLE 6. Sociometric Turnover of White–White Subgroup

	TIME 2			
TIME 1	*Mutual*	*Unilateral*	*Non-connected*	*Time 1 Totals*
Mutual	6	1	–	(7)
Unilateral	2	3*	3	(8)
Nonconnected	1	1	11	(13)
Time 2 Totals:	(9)	(5)	(14)	(28)

* No changes in direction of choice.

among the white–white dyads changed from the first to second interviews. The figures reveal eight changes: one mutual went to unilateral while three unilateral choices were withdrawn; one new unilateral choice was made; and three mutual choices developed. Note, too, that five of the eight changes involved time 1 unilaterals. The reduction in the unilateral category increases both the mutuals and non-connections and appears to show polarization of relationships at time 2.

Overall, the Negro–Negro turnover table shows a small increase and a slight polarization. The withdrawal of two unilateral choices is compensated by one new unilateral and one mutual (Table 7).

The Negro–white subgroup reveals a different pattern. Altogether there were twenty-one sociometric changes, as Table 8 below exhibits.

None of the eleven unilaterals at time 1 was converted into mutuals. And in place of the seven unilaterals which were with-drawn, eleven new ones were initiated. In other words, the within–white and the within–Negro subgroups both showed slight increases in friendship; in the Negro–white subgroup the mutuals decrease somewhat, although paradoxically, the volume of overture-making increases. Note, too, the greater instability of relationships in the Negro–white subgroup compared to the other two subgroups.

Among the Negro–white relationships, who were the "rebuffed" unilaterals and who were the new aspirants? When the members of the dyad can be distinguished by some characteristic, the 3×3 turnover table can be expanded into a 4×4 table. Table 9 below classifies the unilaterals according to the race of the chooser. Of the eleven time 1 unilaterals, three were white choosers, and eight were Negro. Of the new unilaterals, two are white unilaterals compared to nine Negro unilaterals. Thus, the Negroes, though slightly in the minority (8 whites, 6 Negroes), initially made most

TABLE 7. Sociometric Turnover of Negro-Negro Subgroup

	TIME 2			
TIME 1	Mutual	Unilateral	Non-connected	Time 1 Totals
Mutual	1	–	–	(1)
Unilateral	–	–	2	(2)
Nonconnected	1	1	10	(12)
Time 2 Totals:	(2)	(1)	(12)	(15)

TABLE 8. Sociometric Turnover of Negro-White Subgroup

	TIME 2			
TIME 1	Mutual	Unilateral	Non-connected	Time 1 Totals
Mutual	4	1	1	(6)
Unilateral	–	4*	7	(11)
Nonconnected	–	11	20	(31)
Time 2 Totals:	(4)	(16)	(28)	(48)

* One change in direction of choice.

TABLE 9.   Sociometric Turnover of Negro-White Subgroup

			TIME 2		
			Unilateral		
TIME 1	*Mutual*	*White Chooser*	*Negro Chooser*	*Non-connected*	*Time 1 Totals*
Mutual	4	1	–	1	(6)
Unilateral:					
White Chooser	–	2	–	1	(3)
Negro Chooser	–	1	1	6	(8)
Nonconnected	–	2	9	20	(31)
Time 2 Totals:	(4)	(6)	(10)	(28)	(48)

of the overtures, received the most rebuffs, but nevertheless at time 2 increased their number of overtures.

It is of note, too, that the Negroes were quicker to withdraw a unilateral choice. Of the three white unilaterals only one resulted in withdrawal of the overture to the Negro; whereas of the eight Negro unilaterals seven resulted in withdrawal of the overture to whites.

We cannot of course make generalizations about Negro–white interpersonal relations on the basis of these tables. But the method of analysis does suggest a line of future research, namely, duration of overture.

In static sociometry, unilateral choices are often considered indicators of interpersonal inadequacy or as a sign of incohesiveness in the group, although what evidence we can marshal shows that often they are anticipatory friendships. Sociometric panels direct us to look at different types of unilateral choice, according to their persistence:

1. Long continued unreciprocated choices;
2. Overtures which are neither too defensive nor too persistent—maintained long enough to test possibility of friendship;
3. Rapidly-withdrawn overtures.

The analysis of unilateral relationships among Negroes and whites in terms of the time-factor raises many interesting questions. What are the consequences of rebuffed Negro overtures for the Negroes? Which Negroes abandon the possibility of developing such friendships, and which increase their aspiration to secure such friendships? Does the Negro aspirant for white friendship manifest his aspiration by increasing the number of overtures while reducing their duration? Does the defensive overture intrude into within–Negro relationships? And how does relatively higher volume of overture-making to whites by some Negroes (if this is actually the tendency) affect the whites' attitudes toward Negroes? These are the sorts of questions which sociometric panels can answer not only for Negro–white relationships but for relationships in other ethnic groups.

ACADEMIC STANDING

In the previous discussion, we used *race* as a qualifier, a characteristic which is clearly visible on initial contact. Let us turn to a qualifier which ordinarily is not known until a relationship has progressed somewhat. Here we are examining the impact of academic standing upon pair relationships where the standing is not evident at the intial encounter. Do those equal in academic standing develop more stable

TABLE 10.   Sociometric Turnover of Equal Pairs

| | TIME 2 | | | |
TIME 1	Mutual	Unilateral	Non-connected	Time 1 Totals
Mutual	7	–	1	(8)
Unilateral	1	3*	1	(5)
Nonconnected	8	12	63	(83)
Time 2 Totals:	(16)	(15)	(65)	(96)

* No changes in direction

relationships than those who are unequal? In the study from which the data are taken, members of student pairs were compared with respect to the number of college credits.[6] Those within fifteen credits of each other were classified as "equal"; differences in excess of fifteen were classified "unequal." Greeting were used as the sociometric criterion—that is, each panel member was asked to name the others in his class to whom he had occasion to say "hello" or some equivalent greeting. It can be seen that equals (Table 10) were more successful than unequals (Table 11) both in maintaining and in increasing the number of interactions. There are different ways of comparing the changes in the two sub-tables: (a) new mutuals versus dissolved mutuals; (b) new mutuals and new unilaterals versus dissolved mutuals and withdrawn unilaterals; (c) new choices versus withdrawn choices. All of the comparisons show that the equal pairs were both more likely to make new friendships and much more likely to preserve friendships already made.

The greeting criterion is relatively superficial and requires only minimal acquaintance. On a criterion involving more interaction, discussion of course work, the same study revealed that similarity of academic status appeared to be more influential in initiating and sustaining involvement between pairs than it was in affecting the stability of the more superficial relationship involving greetings. The results suggest that with closer acquaintance, awareness of differences in status is greater and greater awareness of differences in status lessens association across status lines.

This interpretation raises the question of what aspects of a relatively "invisible" status distinction—such as rank within a group—new members, or members unacquainted with each other, are responding to. For as we saw, even students having

TABLE 11.   Sociometric Turnover of Unequal Pairs

| | TIME 2 | | | |
TIME 1	Mutual	Unilateral	Non-connected	Time 1 Totals
Mutual	26	5	1	(32)
Unilateral	7	19*	12	(38)
Nonconnected	24	41	335	(400)
Time 2 Totals:	(57)	(65)	(348)	(470)

* Five changes in direction of choice.

a minimal greeting acquaintance interacted less with those of different academic standing, even though the standing was stipulated independently by the researcher. Such students were presumably responding to some visible cues or correlate (such as age) of academic level. This raises the problem of false attribution—for example, one student may incorrectly assume that a younger student, who in fact has an equal number of course credits, is not his peer.

SOCIOMETRIC QUALIFIERS

As we have noted, sociometric turnover tables can be qualified by an attribute shared by the members of the dyad. They can also be qualified by the relationship of the dyad to others in the group. Sociometric relationships qualified by other relationships are designated as "sociometric qualifiers." Essentially, this type of qualification recognizes the fact that dyads are not two-person societies in a social vacuum but are imbedded in larger interpersonal networks. The relative stability of triads has received attention in the sociological literature since Simmel's initial analysis.[7] And in recent years, investigations have burgeoned, usually in experimental settings. The main drawback to this type of study is that the triads are treated as if they are atomized three-person societies. The conclusions of such experiments cannot necessarily be extrapolated to triads embedded in larger on-going groups. The sociometric panel enables this problem to

be investigated in its natural setting. The method by which this analysis can be carried out is by means of sociometric qualifiers.

The notion of sociometric qualifiers was first pointed up by re-analysis of the sociometric changes in the Moreno group. To appreciate its importance, the re-analysis will be described in detail. As will be recalled, Moreno made four changes in the composition of the group—changes which he concluded contributed toward increased group harmony. Three changes involved the transfer of girls to other cottages.

As the inventory of their relationships at the first sociometric test shows, none of the three girls was integrated in the life of the group (Table 12). Girl #1 was a complete isolate insofar as the other girls in her cottage were concerned. Girl #2 was not chosen by 22 of the 26 other girls in her cottage, was rejected by 3 of them, and rejected the one girl who accepted her. Girl #3, the most popular of the trio, was the recipient of two choices. Clearly, the three girls were not solar figures in the cottage. Though their transfer might install them in a more congenial environment, it could hardly be expected to produce significant realignments in the interpersonal life of the cottage.

The fourth change involved an addition. Judging by girl No. 4's relationships at the second sociometric test, we can only assume that she had low interpersonal

TABLE 12.

TRANSFERS FROM COTTAGE				TRANSFERS TO COTTAGE	
Time 1 Relationships	Girl #1	Girl #2	Girl #3	Time 2 Relationships	Girl #4
Mutual Acceptance	0	0	0	Mutual Acceptance	0
Acceptance-Indifference	0	0	2	Acceptance-Indifference	0
Mutual Indifference	26	22	23	Mutual Indifference	24
Acceptance-Rejection	0	1	0	Acceptance-Rejection	1
Indifference-Rejection	0	3	1	Indifference-Rejection	1
Mutual Rejection	0	0	0	Mutual Rejection	0

"penetrability" (Table 12). Since our data are limited to sociograms, no inference can be made why girl No. 4 failed to achieve assimilation. But it is reasonable to assume that her impact on the cottage was negligible.

Despite the scant data, some inferences can be made about the changes which did occur. They revolve around three situations: two of these, it is surmised, are prototypes of interpersonal role conflict situations. Let us look at the two situations which suggest plausible explanations.

Situation 1: At time 1, MY, DA and KL are related in this way:

views about her, ignited a chain of interpersonal changes. Of the 12 changes during the 18 months, girl MY accounts for 10 of them; it is hard to see how Moreno's "reconstruction" of the group was connected with MY's behavior.[8]

Situation 2: The sociograms involved in this change suggest another cross-pressure situation (Figure 3).

We observe that GT and TH are mutual friends, but they differ with respect to their opinion of SP. At time 2, TH no longer rejects SP nor does SP accept TH. One would have guessed that the time 1 pattern was not stable. Why GT still chooses SP

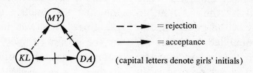

FIGURE 1.

That is, *KL and DA are mutual friends, but have opposite opinions of MY.* Also, DA is MY's only friend.

At time 2, MY is no longer a friend of DA nor does KL reject her. And MY, by switching to another subgroup within the cottage, accounts for 10 relational changes. MY's constellation at time 1 and time 2 are depicted in Figure 2 below.

Apparently, MY is thoroughly accepted in the new clique, for her relationship with MR, SP, and CL is one of mutual acceptance. Moreover, various people who rejected her the first time no longer do so; and similarly, she withdraws all of her rejections. Without more information we cannot infer much about the cross-pressure situation that impelled MY into the new clique: Did she join it first and then withdraw her friendship with DA, or did DA withdraw her friendship with MY, thus impelling MY to look for new friends? But it does seem that the cross-pressure situation, where two friends held incompatible

is puzzling and probably could be understood by post-panel interviewing.

The third situation, a change from mutual acceptance to mutual indifference, cannot be explained from the bare sociograms. Nonetheless, two of the three foci of change revolved around interpersonal crosspressure situations *where two friends held conflicting attitudes toward a third person in their milieu.* One might conjecture that this type of situation produces strain on the three people involved and hence is unstable.

It would seem that situations where relationships are in the process of crystallizing provide an especially fruitful context for observing the preserving and generating functions of third persons. To show this we shall subject the data on the 13 school children presented earlier in Table 5 to further analysis.

Each of the 78 pairs was examined to see whether or not both members shared a common friendship with a third person in

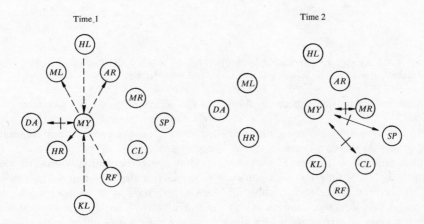

FIGURE 2.

the group. "Common friendship" was defined by any of the patterns depicted in Figure 4.

In future research, a stronger criterion of "common friendship" might be adopted. Moreover pairs might be classified by the number of common friendships they share. And conceivably, one-step common friendships might be distinguished from two-step friendships.

Of the seventy-eight pairs comprising the group, fifty-six pairs shared a common friendship; that is, A and B chose or were chosen by some person in the group. The remaining 22 pairs were unconnected with any common third person.

Table 13 exhibits the sociometric turnover of the 22 pairs which at time 1 did *not* share any common friendships. The striking thing to be noted in this table is that almost 80 per cent of the pairs are in the unconnected category at time 1 and remain so at time 2. This suggests that dyadic relationships in this type of peer situation do not tend to arise in isolation from larger networks of social relations. Furthermore, it will be noted that no new interpersonal ties evoved between time 1 and time 2. The two changes that did occur were both in the direction of friendship deterioration: one of the four mutuals became a unilateral relationship and the

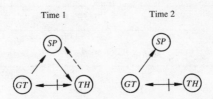

FIGURE 3.

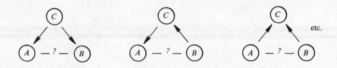

FIGURE 4. Examples of common friendships (A and 8 are pair-wise relationships which can be mutual, unilateral, or nonconnected; C is "common friendship").

one unilateral relationship became non-connected.

Table 14 shows the sociometric turnover among those who shared a common friendship. In contrast it will be noted that the unconnected pairs at time 1 now constitute about 50 per cent of the total number of relationships. As for the changes which occurred, no mutual relationships were dissolved while 4 new mutual relationships developed. Of the 16 unilateral choices, 4 were reciprocated by the second observation, with only 2 overtures being withdrawn. And of the 29 non-connected relationships, 6 new friendship overtures were made. Thus, among pairs interconnected with a third group member, relationships already existent tended to become more viable while pairs that were initially unacquainted tended to become acquainted.

VALUE HOMOPHILY AND THE RULE OF
THIRD PERSONS

In his investigations of a bi-racial community, Robert K. Merton introduced the term "value homophily" to characterize the tendency for friends to hold similar values.

In the following pages we will attempt to relate value homophily with the interpersonal cross-pressure pattern elaborated above.

Underlying the tendency toward value homophily is the idea that value conflicts are experienced as strain by friends; as a result of this strain, friends are pressured to make their values more harmonious or to terminate their relationship. Observing that some conflicts do persist, Merton accounts for their incidence with this explanation:

. . . It is not at all inevitable that a particular value will be expressed, by one or the other, in the *early* stages of a developing friendship. In some proportion of the cases, personal attachments will form in the course of repeated contact long before either partner to the relationship is aware they are sharply at odds in this one particular respect—say, with respect to racial values. Once the relationship has become firmly established . . . it can, in some instances, tolerate a larger load of disagreement. . . .[9]

In other words, when value conflicts come to the surface only after a friendship

TABLE 13. Sociometric Turnover among Pairs Which Had
No Common Friendship at Time 1

| TIME 1 | TIME 2 | | | |
	Mutual	Unilateral	Non-connected	Time 1 Totals
Mutual	3	1	0	(4)
Unilateral	0	0	1	(1)
Nonconnected	0	0	17	(17)
Time 2 Totals:	(3)	(1)	(18)	(22)

TABLE 14.   Pairs Which Shared a Common Friendship at Time 1

| | TIME 2 | | | |
TIME 1	Mutual	Unilateral	Non-connected	Time 1 Totals
Mutual	11	0	0	(11)
Unilateral	4	10*	2	(16)
Nonconnected	0	6	23	(29)
Time 2 Totals:	(15)	(16)	(25)	(56)

* Two changed direction.

has solidified, the relationship is not so easily eroded by value conflict. In this situation friends can evolve a tacit agreement to curb discussion of controversial topics.

The previous discussion on interpersonal cross-pressure suggests conditions when value conflicts are subject to continual confrontations. A conflict of values which is embodied in third persons interacting with the dyad cannot remain covert. Interaction acts as a periodic irritant. Two whites who are not friends with any Negroes, for example, may have different values concerning integration of schools or mixed residential neighborhoods. If neither is intensely partisan, they might avoid open controversy. But when one white is friendly with a Negro in the group and the other white is unfriendly toward him, then it may prove virtually impossible to avoid controversy. Figure 5 depicts a conflict of attitudes between White No. 1 and White No. 2, where No. 1 is friendly with Negro No. 3 and White No. 2 is unfriendly toward him, causing a continual strain on the White No. 1–White No. 2 relationship.

In short, when values are anchored in third persons in the milieu, the effort required to segregate relationships will only increase the saliency of the conflict and the continuous caution required to avoid references to the third person will attenuate the spontaneity of the relationship. In these circumstances, the values of the one or both members of the dyad will need to change to preserve the friendship or the friendship will deteriorate. Conversely, where the value conflict is not concretized in third persons, we can expect it to be less of a barrier in the formation or maintenance of friendships.

STRUCTURAL SOURCES OF STATUS HETEROPHILY

The conception of the intermediary is certainly not a new idea. For instance, an anthropologist employs the concept in mate selection:

Although the networks of husband and wife are distinct, it is very likely, even at the time of marriage, that there will be

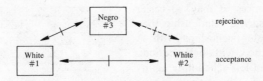

FIGURE 5.   Cross-pressure situation where value conflicts are likely to be salient.

overlapping between them. Judging by the Newbolts' account of their genealogy, one of the common ways for husband and wife to meet is through the introduction by a person who is simultaneously a friend of one and a relative of the other. Male relatives of the wife are likely to be friends or colleagues of the husband, and, after a marriage has continued for some time, the husbands of a set of sisters are likely to become friends.[10]

And William J. Goode suggests that one factor contributing to higher divorce rates among lower-class couples is that the spouses do not share numerous common friends; consequently there are fewer third parties motivated to bolster a deteriorating relationship.[11]

The remainder of this paper will be devoted to discussing two types of heterophily: (1) where a single dimension is involved, such as age, education, or socioeconomic status; (2) where dichotomous attributes are involved but each individual is characterized by two, such as sex and marital status.

Type 1. Heterophily with respect to a single dimension. One of the outstanding empirical generalizations in studies of interpersonal contact is that propinquity correlates highly with friendship. How might the conception of the intermediary explain how *distantly located* individuals become friends?

Friendship might arise as two-stage social process. Consider three individuals, A, B, and C. A and B are unacquainted with each other and live relatively far apart; C, however, knows both A and B and is also located between the two, and thus is in a position to play the role of intermediary. In many circumstances, it may be easier for him to create such a relationship than to maintain separate friendships with A and B. If he interacts with both periodically, it will demand less scheduling agility if all three are friends. C's relationship with respect to A and B may be said to be geographically homophilous: the heterophily is

conjectured to arise as a subsequent stage through C's "closure of the triad." Without an interpersonal bridge such as C, it may be exceedingly unlikely that A and B will become friends.

Similarly, with other variables, such as age, rank, education, socio-economic status. In general, with continuous variables or with ordered characteristics, the individuals in the middle of the social spectrum can play the role of social node and bridge distantly located individuals.

Type 2. Multi-attribute heterophily. Type 2 is a more interesting, though perhaps less obvious, bridging mechanism. In this type, instead of characterizing people by positions on a continuous variable, we characterize them by more than one attribute.

Consider, for example, a group where each member is classified by marital status and sex. The interpersonal process by which *single males* and *married females* may become acquainted is depicted in Figure 6.

In some circumstances the type of relationship between i and k (Figure 6) tends to exist only as a triad; if j should leave the group or break his relationship with i or with k, the i-k relationship dissolves. In other circumstances, i and k might through some chance encounter develop a congenial

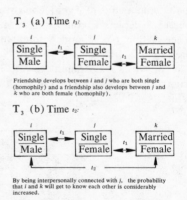

T_3 (a) Time t_1:

Friendship develops between i and j who are both single (homophily) and a friendship also develops between j and k who are both female (homophily).

T_3 (b) Time t_2:

By being interpersonally connected with j, the probability that i and k will get to know each other is considerably increased.

FIGURE 6.   Illustration of process whereby heterophily arises.

relationship and then *seek* a social node to provide the relationship with more stability and legitimacy.

In sum the process that we have conjectured to generate heterophilous relationships operates in stages through social nodes. The process illustrated by Figure 6 might be expressed by this qualitative formula: Homophily on attribute A (between i and j) + Homophily on attribute B (between j and k) → Heterophily on both attributes AB (between i and k).

By now, perhaps, the discussion may ring a bell, for it brushes against some deep problems in sociological theory. The social node connecting individuals with disparate characteristics has been elaborated by a number of sociologists: usually, the individuals who do the connecting straddle two groups and are presumed to experience role-conflict.

For example, Robert K. Merton has stated that

> . . . what is conflict between the multiple statuses of individuals can be from the standpoint of social structure an important type of stable interdependence . . .[12]

And Berelson, Lazarsfeld, and McPhee, in the following passage suggest the cohesive functions of overlapping memberships:

> . . . curiously, the voters least admirable when measured against individual requirements contribute most when measured against the aggregate requirement for flexibility. For those who change political preferences most readily are those who are least interested, who are subject to conflicting social pressures, who have inconsistent beliefs and erratic voting histories. Without them —if the decision were left to only the deeply concerned, well integrated, consistently principled ideal citizens—the political system might easily prove too rigid to adapt to changing domestic and international relations . . . the people exposed to membership in overlapping strata . . . may be the least partisan and the least interested voters for the entire system. Here again is an instance in which individual inadequacy provides a positive service for the society . . .[13]

Two concluding observations deserve mention: (1) although heterophily involves more people and requires more time to evolve, such relationships should be studied in their own right and not merely written off as "deviant cases"; (2) what has been theorized "in the large" by many sociologists can be formalized and systematically investigated "in the small" by means of the sociometric panel.

Notes

1. It should be mentioned that dyadic turnover has been studied by at least two other researchers. Leo Katz and Charles H. Proctor, in an article "The Concept of Configuration of Interpersonal Relations in a Group as a Time Dependent Stochastic Process," *Psychometrika,* XXIV No. 4 (December 1959), attempt to test whether a Markov chain model can be applied to pairwise relations over time.

2. J. L. Moreno, *Who Shall Survive?* (Beacon, New York: Beacon House, 1955). Data refer to Cottage #16.

3. Margaret L. Hayes and Mary Elizabeth Conklin, "Intergroup Attitudes and Experimental Change," *Journal of Experimental Education* (September 1953), pp. 26–27.

4. The percentage change as an index of stability is extremely crude when one compares groups of different size, as in the present instance. The discerning reader will note that in both tables the cell which makes the largest contribution to the stable relationships contains the pairs which were unconnected at both time points. The size of this cell tends to increase geometrically with the number of members in the group. Since the Moreno group consists of 27 members and this group of only 13, the proportion of stable unconnected pairs must necessarily be larger in the Moreno group, which in turn means that other things being equal, the Moreno group will be characterized by more stability. We point this out as a problem of index construction which must be solved if groups of different size are to be compared. Since our purpose here is primarily illustrative, the statement suggested by the data need not wait upon a solution of the index problem.

It should be noted that sociometric turnover tables cannot be considered in the same way as ordinary contingency tables. Each of the N individuals in the group contribute to $(N-1)/2$ relationships. For work concerning the statistical significance of such tables, see Philip J. Runkel, J. E. Keith Smith, and Theodore Newcomb, "Estimating Interaction Effects among Overlapping Pairs," *Psychological Bulletin,* 54, No. 12 (March 1957), pp. 152–58.

5. Sumner Cohen, "Group Structural Changes as Affected by Age and Passage of Time" (unpublished Honors Thesis, Harvard University, April 1, 1952). The subjects were 8-year-old boys who belonged to a Boston settlement house play group.

6. The data are from a sociometric panel conducted by the writer. The group was an Introductory Sociology class in the School of General Studies at Columbia University, 1957. The first wave was administered about one month after the start of the semester and the second wave about five weeks later.

7. Kurt H. Wolff (trans. and ed.), *The Sociology of Georg Simmel* (Glencoe, Ill.: The Free Press, 1950), pp. 118–62.

8. This is not intended as deprecation of Moreno's important work but only to underscore the utility of panel analysis.

9. Paul F. Lazarsfeld and Robert K. Merton, "Friendship as Social Process: A Substantive and Methodological Analysis," in Morroe Berger, Theodore Abel and Charles H. Page (eds.), *Freedom and Control in Modern Society* (New York: D. Van Nostrand Co., Inc., 1954).

10. Elizabeth Bott, *Family and Social Network* (London: Tavistock Publications Ltd., 1957), p. 140.

11. William J. Goode, *After Divorce* (New York: The Free Press, 1956), pp. 66–7.

12. Lecture on social theory, Graduate Dept. of Sociology, Columbia University, April 22, 1957. See also, Lewis A. Coser, *The Functions of Social Conflict* (New York: The Free Press, 1956), p. 80.

13. Bernard R. Berelson, Paul F. Lazarsfeld, and William N. McPhee, *Voting* (Chicago: University of Chicago Press, 1954), p. 316.

F. Relationship Between Panels and Experiments

47. Reconciling Conflicting Results Derived from Experimental and Survey Studies of Attitude Change

CARL I. HOVLAND

TWO QUITE different types of research design are characteristically used to study the modification of attitudes through communication. In the first type, the *experiment,* individuals are given a controlled exposure to a communication and the effects evaluated in terms of the amount of change in attitude or opinion produced. A base line is provided by means of a control group not exposed to the communication. The study of Gosnell (1927) on the influence of leaflets designed to get voters to the polls is a classic example of the controlled experiment.

In the alternative research design, the *sample survey,* information is secured through interviews or questionnaires both concerning the respondent's exposure to various communications and his attitudes and opinions on various issues. Generalizations are then derived from the correlations obtained between reports of exposure and measurements of attitude. In a variant of this method, measurements of attitude and of exposure to communication are obtained during repeated interviews with the same individual over a period of weeks or months. This is the "panel method" extensively utilized in studying the impact of various mass media on political attitudes and on voting behavior (cf., e.g., Kendall and Lazarsfeld, 1950).

Generalizations derived from experimental and from correlational studies of communication effects are usually both reported in chapters on the effects of mass media and in other summaries of research on attitude, typically without much stress on the type of study from which the conclusion was derived. Close scrutiny of the results obtained from the two methods, however, suggests a marked difference in the picture of communication effects obtained from each. The object of my paper is to consider the conclusions derived from these two types of design, to suggest some of the factors responsible for the frequent divergence in results, and then to formulate principles aimed at reconciling some of the apparent conflicts.

Reprinted with permission from *American Psychologist,* 14 (1959), pp. 8–17 (copyright 1959 by American Psychological Association).

Divergence

The picture of mass communication effects which emerges from correlational studies is one in which few individuals are seen as being affected by communications. One of the most thorough correlational studies of the effects of mass media on attitudes is that of Lazarsfeld, Berelson, and Gaudet published in *The People's Choice* (1944). In this report there is an extensive chapter devoted to the effects of various media, particularly radio, newspapers, and magazines. The authors conclude that few changes in attitudes were produced. They estimate that the political positions of only about 5 per cent of their respondents were changed by the election campaign, and they are inclined to attribute even this small amount of change more to personal influence than to the mass media. A similar evaluation of mass media is made in the recent chapter in the *Handbook of Social Psychology* by Lipset and his collaborators (1954).

Research using experimental procedures, on the other hand, indicates the possibility of considerable modifiability of attitudes through exposure to communication. In both Klapper's survey (1949) and in my chapter in the *Handbook of Social Psychology* (Hovland, 1954) a number of experimental studies are discussed in which the opinions of a third to a half or more of the audience are changed.

The discrepancy between the results derived from these two methodologies raises some fascinating problems for analysis. This divergence in outcome appears to me to be largely attributable to two kinds of factors: one, the difference in research design itself; and, two, the historical and traditional differences in general approach to evaluation characteristic of researchers using the experimental as contrasted with the correlational or survey method. I would like to discuss, first, the influence these

factors have on the estimation of overall effects of communications and, then, turn to other divergences in outcome characteristically found by the use of the experimental and survey methodology.

Undoubtedly the most critical and interesting variation in the research *design* involved in the two procedures is that resulting from differences in definition of exposure. In an experiment the audience on whom the effects are being evaluated is one which is fully exposed to the communication. On the other hand, in naturalistic situations with which surveys are typically concerned, the outstanding phenomenon is the limitation of the audience to those who *expose themselves* to the communication. Some of the individuals in a captive audience experiment would, of course, expose themselves in the course of natural events to a communication of the type studied; but many others would not. The group which does expose itself is usually a highly biased one, since most individuals "expose themselves most of the time to the kind of material with which they agree to begin with" (Lipset *et al.,* 1954, p. 1158). Thus one reason for the difference in results between experiments and correlational studies is that experiments describe the effects of exposure on the whole range of individuals studied, some of whom are initially in favor of the position being advocated and some who are opposed, whereas surveys primarily describe the effects produced on those already in favor of the point of view advocated in the communication. The amount of change is thus, of course, much smaller in surveys. Lipset and his collaborators make this same evaluation, stating that:

> As long as we test a program in the laboratory we always find that it has great effect on the attitudes and interests of the experimental subjects. But when we put the program on as a regular broadcast, we then note that the people who are most influenced in the laboratory tests are those who, in a realistic situation, do not listen to the program. The controlled experiment always

greatly overrates effects, as compared with those that really occur, because of the self-selection of audiences (Lipset *et al.*, 1954, p. 1158).

Differences in the second category are not inherent in the design of the two alternatives, but are characteristic of the way researchers using the two methods typically proceed.

The first difference within this class is in the size of the communication unit typically studied. In the majority of survey studies the unit evaluated is an entire program of communication. For example, in studies of political behavior an attempt is made to assess the effects of all newspaper reading and television viewing on attitudes toward the major parties. In the typical experiment, on the other hand, the interest is usually in some particular variation in the content of the communications, and experimental evaluations much more frequently involve single communications. On this point results are thus not directly comparable.

Another characteristic difference between the two methods is in the time interval used in evaluation. In the typical experiment the time at which the effect is observed is usually rather soon after exposure to the communication. In the survey study, on the other hand, the time perspective is such that much more remote effects are usually evaluated. When effects decline with the passage of time, the net outcome will, of course, be that of accentuating the effect obtained in experimental studies as compared with those obtained in survey researches. Again it must be stressed that the difference is not inherent in the designs as such. Several experiments, including our own on the effects of motion pictures (Hovland, Lumsdaine, and Sheffield, 1949) and later studies on the "sleeper effect" (Hovland and Weiss, 1951; Kelman and Hovland, 1953), have studied retention over considerable periods of time.

Some of the difference in outcome may be attributable to the types of communica-tors characteristically used and to the motive-incentive conditions operative in the two situations. In experimental studies communications are frequently presented in a classroom situation. This may involve quite different types of factors from those operative in the more naturalistic communication situation with which the survey researchers are concerned. In the classroom there may be some implicit sponsorship of the communication by the teacher and the school administration. In the survey studies the communicators may often be remote individuals either unfamiliar to the recipients, or out-groupers clearly known to espouse a point of view opposed to that held by many members of the audience. Thus there may be real differences in communicator credibility in laboratory and survey researches. The net effect of the differences will typically be in the direction of increasing the likelihood of change in the experimental as compared with the survey study.

There is sometimes an additional situational difference. Communications of the type studied by survey researchers usually involve reaching the individual in his natural habitat, with consequent supplementary effects produced by discussion with friends and family. In the laboratory studies a classroom situation with low postcommunication interaction is more typically involved. Several studies, including one by Harold Kelley reported in our volume on *Communication and Persuasion* (Hovland, Janis, and Kelley, 1953), indicate that, when a communication is presented in a situation which makes group membership salient, the individual is typically more resistant to counternorm influence than when the communication is presented under conditions of low salience of group membership (cf. also, Katz and Lazarsfeld, 1955, pp. 48–133).

A difference which is almost wholly adventitious is in the types of populations utilized. In the survey design there is, typically, considerable emphasis on a random sample of the entire population. In the typical experiment, on the other hand, there is a consistent over-representation of high school students and college sophomores, primarily on the basis of their greater accessibility. But as Tolman has said: "College sophomores may not be people." Whether differences in the type of audience studied contribute to the differences in effect obtained with the two methods is not known.

Finally, there is an extremely important difference in the studies of the experimental and correlational variety with respect to the type of issue discussed in the communications. In the typical experiment we are interested in studying a set of factors or conditions which are expected on the basis of theory to influence the extent of effect of the communication. We usually deliberately try to find types of issues involving attitudes which are susceptible to modification through communication. Otherwise, we run the risk of no measurable effects, particularly with small-scale experiments. In the survey procedures, on the other hand, socially significant attitudes which are deeply rooted in prior experience and involve much personal commitment are typically involved. This is especially true in voting studies which have provided us with so many of our present results on social influence. I shall have considerably more to say about this problem a little later.

The differences so far discussed have primarily concerned the extent of overall effectiveness indicated by the two methods: why survey results typically show little modification of attitudes by communication while experiments indicate marked changes. Let me now turn to some of the other differences in generalizations derived from the two alternative designs. Let me take as the second main area of disparate results the research on the effect of varying distances between the position taken by the communicator and that held by the recipi-

ent of the communication. Here it is a matter of comparing changes for persons who at the outset closely agree with the communicator with those for others who are mildly or strongly in disagreement with him. In the naturalistic situation studied in surveys the typical procedure is to determine changes in opinion following reported exposure to communication for individuals differing from the communicator by varying amounts. This gives rise to two possible artifacts. When the communication is at one end of a continuum, there is little room for improvement for those who differ from the communication by small amounts, but a great deal of room for movement among those with large discrepancies. This gives rise to a spurious degree of positive relationship between the degree of discrepancy and the amount of change. Regression effects will also operate in the direction of increasing the correlation. What is needed is a situation in which the distance factor can be manipulated independently of the subject's initial position. An attempt to set up these conditions experimentally was made in a study by Pritzker and the writer (1957). The method involved preparing individual communications presented in booklet form so that the position of the communicator could be set at any desired distance from the subject's initial position. Communicators highly acceptable to the subjects were used. A number of different topics were employed, including the likelihood of a cure for cancer within five years, the desirability of compulsory voting, and the adequacy of five hours of sleep per night.

The amount of change for each degree of advocated change is shown in Figure 1. It will be seen that there is a fairly clear progression, such that the greater the amount of change advocated the greater the average amount of opinion change produced. Similar results have been reported by Goldberg (1954) and by French 1956).

But these results are not in line with our

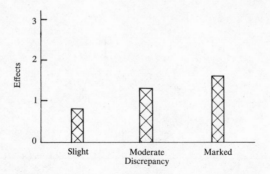

FIGURE 1.   Mean opinion change score with three degrees of discrepancy (deviation between subject's position and position advocated in communication). [From Hovland & Pritzker, 1957]

hunches as to what would happen in a naturalistic situation with important social issues. We felt that here other types of response than change in attitude would occur. So Muzafer Sherif, O. J. Harvey, and the writer (1957) set up a situation to simulate as closely as possible the conditions typically involved when individuals are exposed to major social issue communications at differing distances from their own position. The issue used was the desirability of prohibition. The study was done in two states (Oklahoma and Texas) where there is prohibition or local option, so that the wet-dry issue is hotly debated. We concetrated on three aspects of the problem: How favorably will the communicator be received when his position is at varying distances from that of the recipient? How will what the communicator says be perceived and interpreted by individuals at varying distances from his position? What will be the amount of opinion change produced when small and large deviations in position of communication and recipient are involved?

Three communications, one strongly wet, one strongly dry, and one moderately wet, were employed. The results bearing on the first problem, of *reception,* are presented in Figure 2. The positions of the subjects are indicated on the abscissa in letters from *A* (extreme dry) to *H* (strongly wet). The positions of the communication are also indicated in the same letters, *B* indicating a strongly dry communication, *H* a strongly wet, and *F* a moderately wet. Along the ordinate there is plotted the percentage of subjects with each position on the issue who described the communication as "fair" and "unbiased." It will be seen that the degree of distance between the recipient and the communicator greatly influences the evaluation of the fairness of the communication. When a communication is directed at the pro-dry position, nearly all of the dry subjects consider it fair and impartial, but only a few per cent of the wet subjects consider the identical communication fair. The reverse is true at the other end of the scale. When an intermediate position is adopted, the percentages fall off sharply on each side. Thus under the present conditions with a relatively ambiguous communicator one of the ways of dealing with strongly discrepant positions is to *discredit* the communicator, considering him unfair and biased.

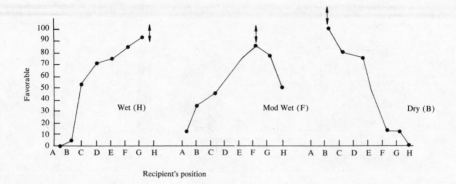

FIGURE 2.   Percentage of favorable evaluations ("fair," "unbiased," etc.) of wet (*H*), moderately wet (*F*), and dry (*B*) communications for subjects holding various positions on prohibition. Recipients position range from *A* (very dry) to *H* (very wet). Position of communications indicated by arrow. [From Hovland, Harvey, & Sherif, 1957]

A second way in which an individual can deal with discrepancy is by distortion of what is said by the communicator. This is a phenomenon extensively studied by Cooper and Jahoda (1947). In the present study, subjects were asked to state what position they thought was taken by the communicator on the prohibition question. Their evaluation of his position could then be analyzed in relation to their own position. These results are shown in Figure 3 for the moderately wet communication. It will be observed that there is a tendency for individuals whose position is close to that of the communicator to report on the communicator's position quite accurately, for individuals a little bit removed to report his position to be substantially more like their own (which we call an "assimilation effect"), and for those with more discrepant positions to report the communicator's position as more extreme than it really was. This we refer to as a "contrast effect."

Now to our primary results on opinion change. It was found that individuals whose position was only slightly discrepant from the communicator's were influenced to a greater extent than those whose positions

deviated to a larger extent. When a wet position was espoused, 28 per cent of the middle-of-the-road subjects were changed in the direction of the communicator, as compared with only 4 per cent of the drys. With the dry communication 14 per cent of the middle-of-the-roaders were changed, while only 4 per cent of the wets were changed. Thus, more of the subjects with small discrepancies were changed than were those with large discrepancies.

These results appear to indicate that, under conditions when there is some ambiguity about the credibility of the communicator and when the subject is deeply involved with the issue, the greater the attempt at change the higher the resistance. On the other hand, with highly respected communicators, as in the previous study with Pritzker using issues of lower involvement, the greater the discrepancy the greater the effect. A study related to ours has just been completed by Zimbardo (1959) which indicates that, when an influence attempt is made by a strongly positive communicator (i.e., a close personal friend), the greater the discrepancy the greater the opinion change, even when the

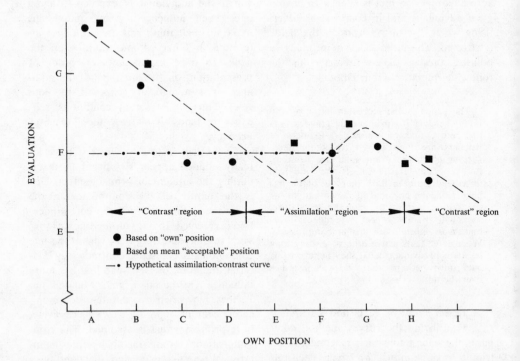

FIGURE 3. Average placement of position of moderately wet communication (F) by subjects holding various positions on the issue, plotted against hyopthetical assimilation-contrast curve. [From Hovland, Harvey, & Sherif, 1957]

experimenter made a point of stressing the great importance of the subject's opinion.

The implication of these results for our primary problem of conflicting results is clear. The types of issues with which most experiments deal are relatively uninvolving and are often of the variety where expert opinion is highly relevant, as for example, on topics of health, science, and the like. Here we should expect that opinion would be considerably affected by communications and furthermore that advocacy of positions quite discrepant from the individual's own position would have a marked effect. On the other hand, the types of issues most often utilized in survey studies are ones which are very basic and involve

deep commitment. As a consequence small changes in opinion due to communication would be expected. Here communication may have little effect on those who disagree at the outset and function merely to strengthen the position already held, in line with survey findings.

A third area of research in which somewhat discrepant results are obtained by the experimental and survey methods is in the role of order of presentation. From naturalistic studies the generalization has been widely adopted that primacy is an extremely important factor in persuasion. Numerous writers have reported that what we experience first has a critical role in what we believe. This is particularly stressed in studies of propaganda effects in various countries when the nation getting across its message first is alleged to have a great advantage and in commercial advertising where "getting a beat on the field" is stressed. The importance of primacy in political propaganda is indicated in the following quotation from Doob:

> The propagandist scores an initial advantage whenever his propaganda reaches people before that of his rivals. Readers or listeners are then biased to comprehend, forever after, the event as it has been initially portrayed to them. If they are told in a headline or a flash that the battle has been won, the criminal has been caught, or the bill is certain to pass the legislature, they will usually expect subsequent information to substantiate this first impression. When later facts prove otherwise, they may be loath to abandon what they believe to be true until perhaps the evidence becomes overwhelming (Doob, 1948, pp. 421–22).

A recent study by Katz and Lazarsfeld (1955) utilizing the survey method compares the extent to which respondents attribute major impact on their decisions about fashions and movie attendance to the presentations to which they were first exposed. Strong primacy effects are shown in their analyses of the data.

We have ourselves recently completed a series of experiments oriented toward this problem. These are reported in our new monograph on *Order of Presentation in Persuasion* (Hovland, Mandell, Campbell, Brock, Luchins, Cohen, McGuire, Janis, Feierabend, and Anderson, 1957). We find that primacy is often *not* a very significant factor when the relative effectiveness of the first side of an issue is compared experimentally with that of the second. The research suggests that differences in design may account for much of the discrepancy. A key variable is whether there is exposure to both sides or whether only one side is actually received. In naturalistic studies the advantage of the first side is

often not only that it is first but that it is often then the only side of the issue to which the individual is exposed. Having once been influenced, many individuals make up their mind and are no longer interested in other communications on the issue. In most experiments on order of presentation, on the other hand, the audience is systematically exposed to both sides. Thus, under survey conditions, self-exposure tends to increase the impact of primacy.

Two other factors to which I have already alluded appear significant in determining the amount of primacy effect. One is the nature of the communicator, the other the setting in which the communication is received. In our volume Luchins presents results indicating that, when the same communicator presents contradictory material, the point of view read first has more influence. On the other hand, Mandell and I show that, when two different communicators present opposing views successively, little primacy effect is obtained. The communications setting factor operates similarly. When the issue and the conditions of presentation make clear that the points of view are controversial, little primacy is obtained.

Thus in many of the situations with which there had been great concern as to undesirable effects of primacy, such as in legal trials, election campaigns, and political debate, the role of primacy appears to have been exaggerated, since the conditions there are those least conducive to primacy effects: the issue is clearly defined as controversial, the partisanship of the communicator is usually established, and different communicators present the opposing sides.

Time does not permit me to discuss other divergences in results obtained in survey and experimental studies, such as those concerned with the effects of repetition of presentation, the relationship between level of intelligence and susceptibility to attitude change, or the relative impact of mass media and personal influence. Again, however, I am sure that detailed analysis will reveal differential factors at work which can account for the apparent disparity in the generalizations derived.

Integration

On the basis of the foregoing survey of results I reach the conclusion that no contradiction has been established between the data provided by experimental and correlational studies. Instead it appears that the seeming divergence can be satisfactorily accounted for on the basis of a different definition of the communication situation (including the phenomenon of self-selection) and differences in the type of communicator, audience, and kind of issue utilized.

But there remains the task of better integrating the findings associated with the two methodologies. This is a problem closely akin to that considered by the members of the recent Social Science Research Council summer seminar on *Narrowing the Gap Between Field Studies and Laboratory Studies in Social Psychology* (Riecken, 1954). Many of their recommendations are pertinent to our present problem.

What seems to me quite apparent is that a genuine understanding of the effects of communications on attitudes requires both the survey and the experimental methodologies. At the same time there appear to be certain inherent limitations of each method which must be understood by the researcher if he is not to be blinded by his preoccupation with one or the other type of design. Integration of the two methodologies will require on the part of the experimentalist an awareness of the narrowness of the laboratory in interpreting the larger and more comprehensive effects of communication. It will require on the part of the survey researcher a greater awareness of the limitations of the correlational method as a basis for establishing relationships.

The framework within which survey research operates is most adequately and explicitly dealt with by Berelson, Lazarsfeld, and McPhee in their book on *Voting* (1954). The model which they use, taken over by them from the economist Tinbergen, is reproduced in the top half of Figure 4. For comparison, the model used by experimentalists is presented in the lower half of the figure. It will be seen that the model used by the survey researcher, particularly when he employs the "panel" method, stresses the large number of simultaneous and interacting influences affecting attitudes and opinions. Even more significant is its provision for a variety of "feedback" phenomena in which consequences wrought by previous influences affect processes normally considered as occurring earlier in the sequence. The various types of interaction are indicated by the placement of arrows showing direction of effect. In contrast, the experimentalist frequently tends to view the communication process as one in which some single manipulative variable is the primary determinant of the subsequent attitude change. He is, of course, aware in a general way of the importance of context, and he frequently studies interaction effects as well as main effects; but he still is less attentive than he might be to the complexity of the influence situation and the numerous possibilities for feedback loops. Undoubtedly the real life communication situation is better described in terms of the survey type of model. We are all familiar, for example, with the interactions in which attitudes predispose one to acquire certain types of information, that this often leads to changes in attitude which may result in further acquisition of knowledge, which in turn produces more attitude change, and so on. Certainly the narrow question sometimes posed by experiments as to the effect

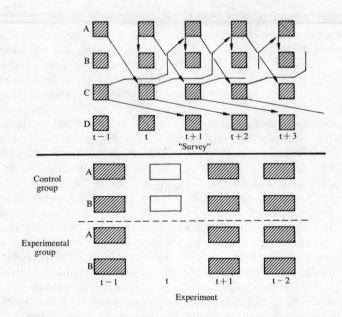

FIGURE 4. *Top half:* "Process analysis" schema used in panel research. (Successive time intervals are indicated along abscissa. Letters
indicate the variables under observation. Arrows represent relations
between the variables.) [From Berelson, Lazarsfeld, and McPhee, 1954]
  Bottom half: Design of experimental research. (Letters on vertical
axis again indicate variables being measured. Unshaded box indicates
experimentally manipulated treatment and blank, absence of such treatment. Time periods indicated as in top half of chart.)

of knowledge on attitudes greatly underestimates these interactive effects.

But while the conceptualization of the
survey researcher is often very valuable,
his correlational research design leaves
much to be desired. Advocates of correlational analysis often cite the example of a
science built on observation exclusively
without experiment: astronomy. But here
a very limited number of space-time concepts are involved and the number of competing theoretical formulations is relatively small so that it is possible to limit
alternative theories rather drastically
through correlational evidence. But in the
area of communication effects and social
psychology generally the variables are so

numerous and so intertwined that the correlational methodology is primarily useful
to suggest hypotheses and not to establish
causal relationships (Hovland *et al.,* 1949,
pp. 329–40; Maccoby, 1956). Even with
the much simpler relationships involved
in biological systems there are grave difficulties of which we are all aware these
days when we realize how difficult it is to
establish through correlation whether eat-
ing of fats is or is not a cause of heart
disease or whether or not smoking is a
cause of lung cancer. In communications
research the complexity of the problem
makes it inherently difficult to derive causal
relationships from correlational analysis
where experimental control of exposure is

not possible. And I do not agree with my friends the Lazarsfelds (Kendall and Lazarsfeld, 1950) concerning the effectiveness of the panel method in circumventing this problem since parallel difficulties are raised when the relationships occur over a time span.

These difficulties constitute a challenge to the experimentalist in this area of research to utilize the broad framework for studying communication effects suggested by the survey researcher, but to employ well-controlled experimental design to work on those aspects of the field which are amenable to experimental manipulation and control. It is, of course, apparent that there are important communication problems which cannot be attacked directly by experimental methods. It is not, for example, feasible to modify voting behavior by manipulation of the issues discussed by the opposed parties during a particular campaign. It is not feasible to assess the effects of communications over a very long span of time. For example, one cannot visualize experimental procedures for answering the question of what has been the impact of the reading of *Das Kapital* or *Uncle Tom's Cabin*. These are questions which can be illuminated by historical and sociological study but cannot be evaluated in any rigorous experimental fashion.

But the scope of problems which do lend themselves to experimental attack is very broad. Even complex interactions can be fruitfully attacked by experiment. The possibilities are clearly shown in studies like that of Sherif and Sherif (1953) on factors influencing cooperative and competitive behavior in a camp for adolescent boys. They were able to bring under manipulative control many of the types of interpersonal relationships ordinarily considered impossible to modify experimentally, and to develop motivations of an intensity characterestic of real-life situations. It should be possible to do similar studies in the communication area with a number of the variables heretofore only investigated in uncontrolled naturalistic settings by survey procedures.

In any case it appears eminently practical to minimize many of the differences which were discussed above as being not inherent in design but more or less adventitiously linked with one or the other method. Thus there is no reason why more complex and deeply involving social issues cannot be employed in experiments rather than the more superficial ones more commonly used. The resistance to change of socially important issues may be a handicap in studying certain types of attitude change; but, on the other hand, it is important to understand the lack of modifiability of opinion with highly involving issues. Greater representation of the diverse types of communicators found in naturalistic situations can also be achieved. In addition, it should be possible to do experiments with a wider range of populations to reduce the possibility that many of our present generalizations from experiments are unduly affected by their heavy weighting of college student characteristics, including high literacy, alertness, and rationality.

A more difficult task is that of experimentally evaluating communications under conditions of self-selection of exposure. But this is not at all impossible in theory. It should be possible to assess what demographic and personality factors predispose one to expose oneself to particular communications and then to utilize experimental and control groups having these characteristics. Under some circumstances the evaluation could be made on only those who select themselves, with both experimental and control groups coming from the self-selected audience.

Undoubtedly many of the types of experiments which could be set up involving or simulating naturalistic conditions will be too ambitious and costly to be feasible even if possible in principle. This suggests the continued use of small-scale experiments which seek to isolate some of the key variables operative in complex situations. From synthesis of component factors, prediction of complex outcomes may be practicable. It is to this analytic procedure for narrowing the gap between laboratory and field research that we have devoted major attention in our research program. I will merely indicate briefly here some of the ties between our past work and the present problem.

We have attempted to assess the influence of the communicator by varying his expertness and attractiveness, as in the studies by Kelman, Weiss, and the writer (Hovland and Weiss, 1951; Kelman and Hovland, 1953). Further data on this topic were presented earlier in this paper.

We have also been concerned with evaluating social interaction effects. Some of the experiments on group affiliation as a factor affecting resistance to counternorm communication and the role of salience of group membership by Hal Kelley and others are reported in *Communication and Persuasion* (Hovland et al., 1953).

Starting with the studies carried out during the war on orientation films by Art Lumsdaine, Fred Sheffield, and the writer (1949), we have had a strong interest in the duration of communication effects. Investigation of effects at various time intervals has helped to bridge the gap between assessment of immediate changes with those of longer duration like those involved in survey studies. More recent extensions of this work have indicated the close relationship between the credibility of the communicator and the extent of postcommunication increments, or "sleeper effects" (Hovland and Weiss, 1951; Kelman and Hovland, 1953).

The nature of individual differences in susceptibility to persuasion via communication has been the subject of a number of our recent studies. The generality of persuasibility has been investigated by Janis

and collaborators and the development of persuasibility in children has been studied by Abelson and Lesser. A volume concerned with these audience factors to which Janis, Abelson, Lesser, Field, Rife, King, Cohen, Linton, Graham, and the writer have contributed will appear under the title *Personality and Persuasibility* (1959).

Lastly, there remains the question of how the nature of the issues used in the communication affects the extent of change in attitude. We have only made a small beginning on these problems. In the research reported in *Experiments on Mass Communication,* we showed that the magnitude of effects was directly related to the type of attitude involved: film communications had a significant effect on opinions related to straightforward interpretations of policies and events, but had little or no effect on more deeply intrenched attitudes and motivations. Further work on the nature of issues is represented in the study by Sherif, Harvey, and the writer (1957) which was discussed above. There we found a marked contrast between susceptibility to influence and the amount of ego-involvement in the issue. But the whole concept of ego-involvement is a fuzzy one, and here is an excellent area for further work seeking to determine the theoretical factors involved in different types of issues.

With this brief survey of possible ways to bridge the gap between experiment and survey I must close. I should like to stress in summary the mutual importance of the two approaches to the problem of communication effectiveness. Neither is a royal road to wisdom, but each represents an important emphasis. The challenge of future work is one of fruitfully combining their virtues so that we may develop a social psychology of communication with the conceptual breadth provided by correlational study of process and with the rigorous but more delimited methodology of the experiment.

References

B. R. Berelson, P. F. Lazarsfeld, and W. N. McPhee, *Voting: A Study of Opinion Formation in a Presidential Campaign* (Chicago: University of Chicago Press, 1954).

Eunice Cooper and Marie Jahoda, "The Evasion of Propaganda: How Prejudiced People Respond to Antiprejudice Propaganda," *Journal of Psychology,* 23 (1947), pp. 15–25.

L. W. Doob, *Public Opinion and Propaganda* (New York: Holt, 1948).

J. R. P. French, Jr., "A Formal Theory of Social Power," *Psychological Review,* 63 (1956), pp. 181–94.

S. C. Goldberg, "Three Situational Determinants of Conformity to Social Norms," *Journal of Abnormal Social Psychology,* 49 (1954), pp. 325–29.

H. F. Gosnell, *Getting Out the Vote: An Experiment in the Stimulation of Voting* (Chicago: University of Chicago Press, 1927).

C. I. Hovland, "Effects of the Mass Media of Communication," in G. Lindzey (ed.), *Handbook of Social Psychology,* Vol. II. *Special Fields and Applications* (Cambridge, Mass.: Addison-Wesley, 1954), pp. 1062–1103.

C. I. Hovland, O. J. Harvey, and M. Sherif, "Assimilation and Contrast Effects in Reactions to Communication and Attitude Change," *Journal of Abnormal Social Psychology,* 55 (1957), pp. 244–52.

C. I. Hovland, I. L. Janis, and H. A. Kelley, *Communication and Persuasion* (New Haven: Yale University Press, 1953).

C. I. Hovland, W. Mandell, Enid H. Campbell, T. Brock, A. S. Cohen, A. R. McGuire, W. J. Janis, I. L. Feierabend, L. Rosalind, and N. H. Anderson, *The Order of Presentation in Persuasion* (New Haven: Yale University Press, 1957).

C. I. Hovland and H. A. Pritzker, "Extent of Opinion Change as a Function of Amount of Change Advocated," *Journal of Abnormal Social Psychology,* 54 (1957), pp. 257–61.

C. I. Hovland and W. Weiss, "The Influence of Source Credibility on Communication Effectiveness," *Public Opinion Quarterly,* 15 (1951), pp. 635–50.

I. L. Janis, C. I. Hovland, P. B. Field, Harriett Linton, Elaine Graham, A. R. Cohen, D. Rife, R. P. Abelson, G. S. Lesser, and B. T. King, *Personality and Persuasibility* (New Haven: Yale University Press, 1959).

E. Katz and P. F. Lazarsfeld, *Personal Influence* (New York: The Free Press, 1955).

H. C. Kelman and C. I. Hovland, "Reinstatement of the Communicator in Delayed Measurement of Opinion Change," *Journal of Abnormal Social Psychology,* 48 (1953), pp. 327–35.

Patricia L. Kendall and P. F. Lazarsfeld, "Problems of Survey Analysis," in R. K. Merton and P. F. Lazarsfeld (eds.), *Continuities in Social Research: Studies in the Scope and Method of the American Soldier* (New York: The Free Press, 1950), pp. 133–96.

J. T. Klapper, *The Effects of Mass Media* (New York: Columbia University Bureau of Applied Social Research, 1959, mimeo).

P. F. Lazarsfeld, B. Berelson, and Hazel Gaudet, *The People's Choice* (New York: Duell, Sloan and Pearce, 1944).

S. M. Lipset, P. F. Lazarsfeld, A. H. Barton, and J. Linz, "The Psychology of Voting: An Analysis of Political Behavior," in G. Lindzey (ed.), *Handbook of Social Psychology,* Vol. II. *Special Fields and Applications* (Cambridge, Mass.: Addison-Wesley, 1954), pp. 1124–75.

Eleanor E. Maccoby, "Pitfalls in the Analysis of Panel Data: A Research Note on Some

Technical Aspects of Voting," *American Journal of Sociology,* 59 (1956), pp. 359–62.
H. W. Riecken (Chairman), "Narrowing the Gap between Field Studies and Laboratory
Experiments in Social Psychology: A Statement by the Summer Seminar," *Items, Social
Science Research Council,* 8 (1954), pp. 37–42.
M. Sherif and Carolyn W. Sherif, *Groups in Harmony and Tension: An Integration of
Studies on Intergroup Relations* (New York: Harper, 1953).
P. G. Zimbardo, *Involvement and Communication Discrepancy as Determinants of Opin-
ion Change* (Unpublished doctoral dissertation, Yale University, 1959).

48. Evaluating an Experimental Program in Medical Education

PATRICIA KENDALL

SINCE the end of World War II, there is
probably no medical school in the United
States which has entirely escaped experimentation in its educational methods and
program. In some instances, such experimentation has been fairly limited in its
objectives; for example, new teaching approaches have been tried in particular
courses. In other cases, the modifications
have been more extensive and the goals
more all-embracing. The best example is
provided by the School of Medicine of
Western Reserve University, which undertook a complete revision of its curriculum
in 1956, along somewhat radical and still
controversial lines.[1]

The existence—and, indeed, proliferation
—of such experimental programs implies
the parallel need for evaluation studies
aimed at determining the extent to which
the modified courses have produced desired
changes in attitudes or increases in knowledge. Perhaps the most ambitious and systematic evaluation study was that carried

out by Hammond and Kern at the University of Colorado. More usually, however,
evaluations (when they are made at all)
tend to remain on a rather impressionistic
level. The educators in charge of the experimental programs talk in terms of how well
the courses were "liked" by the students
taking them, or whether they seemed to
have the desired effects.

There are probably several ways of accounting for the fact that such experimental
programs in medical education have not
regularly been submitted to systematic
evaluation. First of all, an evaluation study
worthy of the name requires time and
money. It is not always easy to convince
the executive faculty of a medical school
that available funds or student time should
be devoted to rigorous study of a new
course. Secondly, the creators of experimental programs often impress one as being
men of conviction who have little question
about the efficacy of the changes they have
introduced. They *know* that the courses

Reprinted with permission from Chapter 15 of *Innovation in Education,* Matthew B. Miles
(ed.) (copyright 1964 by Teachers College Press, Columbia University; all rights reserved).

they have developed are the best possible under existing conditions; and in the light of this assumed fact, systematic evaluation seems superfluous.

But there is an additional explanation for the fact that such a relatively small number of evaluation studies has been undertaken. Even when there is no reluctance regarding them, actually carrying them out presents certain problems. The present chapter, by means of a case study of an evaluation program carried out over several years, indicates what some of these problems are and clarifies how they were handled in one instance. We shall start with the difficulties one encounters at the beginning of an evaluation study, and then proceed to those which develop later.

The Evaluation Study

THE SPECIFICATION OF OBJECTIVES

Obviously, the evaluation of an experimental program presupposes fairly precise knowledge of the objectives of the program. Without such knowledge, it is manifestly impossible to say whether or not the program has been successful. Often the objectives of an experimental course in medical education are stated in rather general terms—"to overcome resistance to psychiatry," "to improve the quality of teaching in a department of anatomy," and so on.

A first step in any evaluation study is therefore a specification of the objectives of the program being investigated. This case was no exception. The program was a newly designed course in medicine, pediatrics, and psychiatry offered fourth-year students in an Eastern medical school. At first the aims of the program were stated in fairly broad terms. It was hoped that through this course in comprehensive medicine, as it was called, students would learn the relevance of social and psychological factors in the diagnosis and treatment of disease, would

develop more humanistic attitudes toward patients, and would gain experience in operating as members of a medical team. When we were asked to assist in the evaluation of the program, our first concern was to help the directors of the course define their purposes more concretely, so that these could be translated into testable dimensions, for which suitable indicators could in turn be found.[2]

After interviewing the medical educators who developed the course, and carefully studying all written documents pertaining to it, it was possible to spell out some of the main changes which were hoped for. We were then able to develop attitude questions through which the existence or nonexistence of such changes could be assessed. Space limitations make it impossible to indicate all of these, but a few representative examples can be given.

Attention to Social and Psychological Problems. One of the general objectives of the program was to teach students the importance of taking into account the social and psychological problems of their patients. But, upon further clarification, it turned out that the program's directors did not mean this to be taken literally or applied universally. They recognized that there are some patients who can be treated more routinely than others. Accordingly, they desired more specifically that their students develop an appropriate degree of clinical judgment—the ability to know when attention to social and psychological problems is called for, and when it is not. To measure the degree to which students possessed such judgment before and after their course in comprehensive medicine, we devised the following question:

Assume that you, as a doctor in a hospital ward or clinic, are caring for the patients described below. In each of the cases, how important—for the kind of care you might give—would extensive knowledge of the patient's *family and social surroundings* be to you?

20-year old man with pneumonia
12-year old boy with broken leg
17-year old girl with menstrual cramps
60-year old man with heart attack
30-year old woman with headache
 5-year old girl with measles
10-year old boy with bedwetting
40-year old woman with acute appendicitis
35-year old man with rheumatic heart disease
75-year old man with cancer of the large
 bowel

For some of the cases described, it clearly would be imperative to have extensive knowledge of the patient's family and social surroundings; in other cases, such knowledge, while perhaps useful, would be less urgent. In the evaluation study, we investigated whether students were better able to make this distinction after participation in the program.

Attitudes Toward Patients. The directors of the program also hoped for changes in attitudes toward patients. They felt that, all too often, advanced medical students viewed the patients whom they saw solely as specimen cases from whom to learn medicine, and were only secondarily concerned with what they were able to accomplish for the patients. Those in charge of the course considered this attitude incompatible with the kind of medicine they were trying to teach their students; they therefore hoped to engender student interest in the welfare of patients. Again, the specification of this desired effect of the program led to the development of several questions. One of them read:

> Do you look upon your contact with patients while in medical school primarily as an opportunity to learn medicine? primarily as an opportunity to help patients? as presenting equal opportunities to learn medicine and to help patients?

In the evaluation study, we examined changes in responses to this question to determine whether students had become more interested in patients as a result of the course.

Professional Relationship. At the same time, however, the directors of the program believed that the students should not become overly involved with their patients. They contended that a physician who becomes too friendly with patients may endanger his ability to provide optimal medical care: his sympathy for the patient may prevent him from ordering painful or dangerous procedures when these are indicated. Accordingly, it was hoped that the students would learn that a strictly professional relationship with patients is most appropriate. To ascertain whether or not this was the case, the following question was devised:

> Would you prefer a patient who wants to know you only on a doctor-patient basis? wants to know you also on a friend-to-friend basis? it makes no difference?

Quality of Medical Care. Finally, those responsible for the program wanted students to learn how to provide medical care of high quality. Once again, however, this objective needed specification. Indicators were found for many of the dimensions which were ultimately spelled out, and these were included in the questionnaire administered periodically to the students. One obvious dimension, for example, is the amount of time allocated to each patient. If a patient is to receive optimal medical care, his physician must be prepared to devote a lot of time to him, if this is called for on a particular occasion. This means in turn that the physician should not regularly schedule a large number of patients each day. To see whether this aspect of comprehensive care had been learned through the program, the following question was developed:

> Dr. W is a general practitioner who, at the age of 50, is financially well off, respected and admired in the middle-class suburban community in which he lives. Each day Dr. W sees thirty to forty patients whose illness range from measles to cancer of the cervix. To you, does the fact that

Dr. W sees thirty to forty patients a day suggest:

    that he is a very competent doctor to be able to care for so many people

    that he can hardly provide competent care if he treats so many people

    neither

The specification of the objectives of any experimental program is a preparatory phase. Once it is accomplished, the investigator is ready to undertake the evaluation proper.

EVALUATION

Ideally, an evaluation study is modeled after a classical controlled experiment. As in any experiment, one wants to eliminate the possibility that observed changes in attitude and behavior are caused by extraneous factors, and not by the program being evaluated.[3]

The Classical Design. To eliminate this possibility, one introduces controls. Parallel to the group being exposed to the experimental program, one sets up a control group exactly similar in all essential respects; the only difference is that the experimental program is withheld from this control group.

In the case of the educational program which we studied, this would have meant dividing the fourth-year class into two more or less equal groups, matched according to such characteristics as class standing and initial attitudes toward patients, and then exposing one of the groups to the new course in comprehensive medicine while the other group studied the traditional course in fourth-year medicine. Schematically, this would have looked as follows:

Experimental group	*Control group*
Pretest	Pretest
Exposure to course in comprehensive medicine	Exposure to traditional course in fourth-year medicine
Posttest	Posttest

If the experimental group experienced more change than the controls in the directions hoped for by the directors of the program, then these shifts could be attributed to the program.

This arrangement would have been the simplest and safest for evaluation of the new course in comprehensive medicine. However, the executive faculty of the medical school refused to sanction it. Their argument was that if the new course were really superior to the old one, it would be unfair to students in the control group to deprive them of participation in it; they therefore decided that all fourth-year students should pursue the new course.

A Revised Design. This decision by the executive faculty forced a modification in the design of the evaluation study. Each fourth-year class was still split into two groups. The A groups, as we designated them, took the course in comprehensive medicine in the first semester of their final year, and then studied surgery, obstetrics-gynecology and an elective subject in the second semester. The so-called B groups reversed this process: they studied surgery (etc.) in the first semester and comprehensive medicine in the second.

Even though each class was thus composed of two groups, there was no assurance that they would be matched to each other. Indeed, there was good reason to fear that they would not be. For example, once the course in comprehensive medicine got under way, students were allowed to indicate whether they would prefer to take it in the first or second semester of their final year. Over 80 per cent of the students queried on this score told us they had received the semester assignments they had asked for. And there was always the strong possibility that their decision had been motivated by their internship plans. Fourth-year medical students have to apply for the internships of their choice at about the first of the year; to be favorably considered their applications should be accompanied by a letter of recommendation from a faculty member in the medical school. Thus, it could have developed that all of the prospective interns in internal medicine, hoping to obtain strong letters of recommendation from the Department of Medicine, would elect to take the course in comprehensive medicine in the first semester, in order to become known to members of the Department before the application deadline. In contrast, all of the prospective surgical interns, similarly motivated, might have elected to take surgery in the first semester.

In actual fact, it turned out that there were no such systematic differences between those taking the course in compre-

later, just as the first term was drawing to a close, the students answered the same questions a second time. In addition, those who had spent the first term in the course in comprehensive medicine were asked a supplementary set of questions about their experiences during the term. (3) Then, at the end of the fourth year, shortly before their graduation from medical school, the students answered our questions for a third time. And now it was the students who had participated in the experimental program during the second semester who were asked about their experiences.

Again, let us represent this design schematically so that it can be contrasted with a classical experimental design.

	End of third year	Middle of fourth year	End of fourth year
A groups	Course in comprehensive medicine	Courses in surgery, ob-gyn and elective	
B groups	Courses in surgery, ob-gyn and elective	Course in comprehensive medicine	
	Test 1	Test 2	Test 3

hensive medicine in the first semester and those taking it in the second. But because we had had no hand in the groups' composition, and because we could not be absolutely certain that there were no initial differences between them (even though none were apparent), we decided to adopt a design in which each student would serve as his own control.

This was made possible by the use of a so-called "panel design." Repeated observations were made of the same individual, on the same criteria: (1) At the end of the third year, just before starting their final year, the students were given a self-administered questionnaire; it asked about their attitudes toward patients, their standards of medical care, experiences they had had in medical school, their career plans, and so on. The responses they gave at this time formed the baseline for studying subsequent changes in attitude. (2) Six months

ASSESSING PROGRAM EFFECTS

Let us present an actual finding to show how this design permitted evaluation of the effects of the course in comprehensive medicine. The example is based on a question considered earlier, that dealing with the value of patient contacts. It will be recalled that the students were asked whether they viewed such contacts primarily as an opportunity to learn medicine, primarily as an opportunity to help patients, or as an opportunity to do both. Virtually none of the students said they looked on contacts with patients mainly as an occasion to help them. Instead, they said either that they looked upon patient contacts as an opportunity to learn medicine, or as an occasion both to help patients and to learn medicine. From the point of view of the directors of the program, who wanted to see students develop more concern with the welfare of their patients, the latter response is the "correct" one. The question, then, is whether students were more likely to give this response after participation in the program. The results are shown in Table 1.

TABLE 1. Effect of Program on Attitude Toward Patient Contacts

TIME POINTS	PER CENT SAYING THEY VIEW PATIENT CONTACTS AS OPPORTUNITY BOTH TO LEARN AND TO HELP PATIENTS	
	A Groups	*B Groups*
End of third year (T_1)	59	52
Middle of fourth year (T_2)	79	53
End of fourth year (T_3)	64	72

N = approx. 165 for all percentages

Before reviewing the substantive conclusions to be drawn from Table 1, let us consider the reasoning by which we shall arrive at these conclusions. A table like this one contains three comparisons of immediate relevance to evaluation of the course in comprehensive medicine. Quite obviously, we should compare the behavior and attitudes of the A and B groups before and after their participation in the program; if the program was effective, both groups should shift in the desired direction during their term in the course. At the same time, however, in order to attribute such shifts to the program and not to some other factors, we must be able to show that the B groups, which only entered the program at the beginning of the second semester, had not experienced a comparable change during the first semester. We can express these conditions in the following way:

$(T_2 - T_1)$A groups and $(T_3 - T_2)$B groups should show shift in desired direction; but

$(T_2 - T_1)$B groups should be zero, or in opposite direction from that desired.

An examination of the figures in Table 1 shows that these conditions are exactly met.[4] Between the end of the third year and the middle of the fourth, while they were participating in the course in comprehensive care, students in the A groups developed a greater orientation to the welfare of their patients. A similar change occurred with the B groups between the middle and end of the fourth year, the period they spent in the program; during this time they too came to be more concerned with the welfare of their patients. But previously, during the first semester, these same students in the B groups had been completely unaffected in their attitudes. On the basis of these three comparisons, made singly and in combination, we can conclude that the course in comprehensive medicine was quite effective in enlarging students" views regarding the value of patient contacts.

DISTINGUISHING SHORT- AND LONG-TERM EFFECTS

But there is still more to a table like this one. In evaluating an educational program, it is often desirable to differentiate between its short- and long-term effects. A classical controlled experiment does not usually provide data relevant to this question. However, a fourth comparison in tables of this kind yields a first approximation to the differentiation of short- and long-term effects, an unexpected bonus of the design used here. This is the comparison of responses given by the A groups at the middle and end of the fourth year—the period when they had already completed their term in comprehensive medicine and had gone on to study other fourth-year courses. If the effects of the program are long-term,[5] then any shift observed at the end of the first semester should be maintained at the end of the second. If, on the other hand, the program has only a short-term effect with respect to a particular attitude or mode of behavior, then we shall observe a reversal during the course of the second semester.

Referring again to Table 1, we see that, although the program seemed to have a fairly marked effect on judgments of the value of patient contacts, this effect was short-lived. At the end of the fourth year, the number of students in A groups saying that they looked on such contacts primarily as an opportunity to learn medicine was very nearly as high as it had been at the end of the third year.

In broad outline, then, this is the mode of analysis employed in evaluating a course in comprehensive medicine. Basing conclusions on the four comparisons just specified, we were able to identify the main effects of the program, and to distinguish which of these seemed to be long-lasting and which more ephemeral.

Additional Features of the Study

We have completed our essential task of indicating how, in one case, a program in medical education was evaluated, and so might conclude here. But it may be of some interest to review certain additional features of this evaluation study.

A first addition was suggested by the fact that the program under **Study of Trends** consideration was a *fourth*-year course; it is a program to which students are exposed quite late in their medical school careers. Some students, as a matter of fact, participate in the program almost up to the day of graduation. In view of this, it might be misleading to study the effects of the course without at the same time examining the processes of change taking place in the first three years of medical school. For example, one effect of the program was to

increase interest in the social and emotional problems which patients present. Quite different meanings should be attached to this finding, according to the nature of the changes taking place in earlier years. Suppose that in the first three years, before coming into personal contact with the experimental program, students had become progressively less interested in these social and emotional problems. Then the effect of the program would have been a reversal of a previously existing trend, and we would feel that the course had accomplished more than if there had been no trend at all over the first three years, or if the previously existing trend had been toward increasing interest.

Let us provide two examples of differing contexts for the effects of the program. Earlier, we quoted a question having to do with the competence of a general practitioner who sees from thirty to forty patients a day; one of the program's objectives was to impress upon students that a habitually heavy patient load is incompatible with the provision of comprehensive care. The trend of responses over the first three years of medical school suggests that recognition of this fact developed even before the students came in contact with the course in comprehensive medicine. This is shown in Table 2.

TABLE 2. Class Judgments on Dr. W's Competence

Class	Per Cent Saying That Dr. W Cannot Provide Competent Care	Number of Students
First year	52	(309)
Second year	62	(310)
Third year	66	(325)

There is thus a clear-cut trend over the course of medical school, one with which the directors of the experimental program in comprehensive care would be sympathetic. Does the course add anything to this trend? Again we resort to the kind of format used in Table 1. The relevant data are shown in Table 3.

TABLE 3.   Effect of Program on Judgments of Dr. W's Competence

TIME POINTS	PER CENT SAYING THAT DR. W CANNOT PROVIDE COMPETENT CARE	
	A Groups	B Groups
End of third year	67	72
Middle of fourth year	75	60
End of fourth year	63	66

The two most obvious comparisons—those involving the behavior of the A and B groups before and after their participation in the program—lead to the conclusion that the program did have an effect on the students' standards of medical care. But in this instance the really crucial piece of evidence is provided by the behavior of the B groups during the first semester, before they entered the program. During that time, under the influence of the courses in surgery, obstetrics-gynecology, and an elective subject, the students' appreciation of the need to spend time with patients—fairly high at the start—suffered considerably. Aside from its substantive interest, this reversal is convincing evidence that the effects attributed to the program were real, and not just the continuation of a previously existing trend.

But there is a second set of findings which provides quite a different context, and suggests correspondingly different conclusions about the effectiveness of the program. To show this we turn to a new question. It is a well-known fact that many medical students prefer to work with patients who have well-defined physical illnesses. There are several reasons for

this: it is easier to learn medicine from patients in whom it is possible to find an organic disturbance; patients with no apparent positive findings present a particular challenge, and are sometimes considered threatening; finally, patients who do not have easily identified illnesses offer little opportunity to apply therapeutic measures and to study their effects on disease processes.

To find out the extent to which students did in fact have these preferences, they were asked the following question:

Would you prefer a patient whose illness is entirely physical? whose illness is chiefly emotional in origin? it makes no difference?

Since almost no students expressed a preference for patients with illnesses which were chiefly emotional in origin, we are dealing once again with a dichotomy.

Table 4 indicates that from the end of the first year to the end of the third year there is a fairly marked trend in answers to this question.

TABLE 4.   Class Preferences for Patients with Physical Illness

Class	Per Cent Preferring Patients With Physical Illness	Per Cent Saying It Makes No Difference	Number of Students
First year	27	66	(245)
Second year	39	58	(241)
Third year	45	52	(253)

Two-thirds of the freshmen students, but only about half of the third-year students, said that it made no difference to them whether they saw a patient with a physical or an emotional illness. On the other hand, only about a quarter of the first-year students, but nearly half of those in their third year, expressed a definite preference for a patient with a physical illness.

From the point of view of those directing the experimental program being evaluated, the trend recorded in Table 4 was an undesirable one. It is the objective of the program to teach students how to provide adequate care for all patients, not just those who present "interesting" problems. What effect did the program have on this trend? The relevant data are shown in Table 5.

TABLE 5.   Effect of Program on Preferences for Patients with Physical Illness

TIME POINTS	PER CENT SAYING THEY PREFER PATIENTS WITH PHYSICAL ILLNESS	
	A Groups	*B Groups*
End of third year	47	46
Middle of fourth year	46	57
End of fourth year	54	58

The effects of the program are quite different here than in the previous instance. During their term in the program, both the A and the B groups remained stationary in their attitudes toward patients with physical illness. But both prior to and following participation in the experimental course, the trend which had been noted in earlier phases of medical school continued. To put it somewhat differently, the course succeeded in checking a trend considered undesirable, although it was not able to counteract the trend. This, too, of course, was a positive accomplishment of the program, even though it may not seem so striking at first glance.

To sum up, if one views the effects of the program in the context of what has happened prior to the fourth year, one is better able to assess their meaning.

SPECIFICATION OF EFFECTIVE FACTORS

Even though one may feel some satisfaction in identifying the effects of an experimental program, thus being able to judge the extent of its success or failure, an evaluation study is more complete if one can at the same time specify what accounts for program effectiveness. One may be interested in this from a theoretical point of view, perhaps in order to classify the kinds of factors associated with attitude change. But the specification of effective factors also has practical implications. To strengthen an experimental educational program, or to duplicate it in another setting, it is essential to know just which features of the program account for its effectiveness, and with what type of student it is most likely to succeed. This is a problem more easily posed than solved, for in order to test these helpful dispositions and effective features, they must be introduced into the questionnaire. And it requires a certain amount of systematic analysis to think of them at the time the questionnaire is being prepared. It is one thing to ask students to introspect about what they consider particularly effective in the program; it is quite another to test the effectiveness of such factors by the statistical method to be exemplified presently. We do not want to deprecate the value of retrospective studies, but wish rather to show the special aspects of a panel analysis.

To think of relevant factors, one must consider the dimensions along which the experimental program can vary. In this case, for example, some students may have had the good fortune of being exposed to unusually attractive patients, while less lucky colleagues saw a disproportionately high number of unpleasant patients. In some instances, students may have encountered medical problems of special interest, while other students may have seen only routine problems. And the instructors who helped the students interpret their experiences may have had different degrees of skill.

In addition to these intrinsic variations, external factors may affect the success of the program. The students may be overworked; the routine of the appointment system in the clinic may break down; and so on.

Finally, students can differ considerably in their attitudes. As we have already seen, some approach a patient wanting only to learn from him; others want also to help the patient. Students may also differ in the degree to which they feel involved with the patient. This latter item is used here to exemplify our analysis.

Shortly after entering the program, each student was assigned to a family, for whose medical welfare he was to be responsible for the following six months. Whenever a member of the family needed medical care, he was seen by "his" student-physician; if the patient needed hospitalization, this was arranged by the student, who then followed the course of the patient's illness in the hospital. After the patient's discharge from the hospital, his recuperation and rehabilitation were supervised by the student responsible for his care. As one can imagine, some students became very involved with their Family Care families. To find out the extent to which this happened—and to which students it happened—we asked the following question:

> Compared with most of the patients you've seen this term, do you think you were emotionally involved with your Family Care family to a greater extent? to about the same extent? to a lesser extent? [6]

Our central concern at the moment is not with the phenomenon of involvement itself, but rather with its contribution to the observed effects of the program. One of these effects, it will be recalled, was that students were more likely to view their contacts with patients as an opportunity to learn medicine *and* to help the patients, rather than simply as an occasion to learn medicine. To what extent did this effect come about because of the students' involvement with their Family Care patients? The relevant data are provided in Table 6.

TABLE 6. Change in Attitude Toward Value of Patient Contacts, as Result of Emotional Involvement with Family

	Per Cent Saying AFTER *Program They View Patient Contacts as Opportunity Both to Learn and to Help Patients*	
	Attitude before	
Emotional Involvement With Family	*Program:*	
	Learn Medicine	*Both Learn and Help*
Greater extent	62 (21)*	94 (33)
Same extent	60 (67)	93 (96)
Lesser extent	48 (31)	90 (38)

* The figures in parentheses refer to the number of cases in each group.

It is important to understand the format of this table. As in Table 1, the numerical entries are once more the percentages of students saying that they looked on their contacts with patients as an opportunity to learn medicine and help the patients as well. But in Table 1, the responses were given at different points in time. The figures in Table 6 refer to responses made immediately after the students had completed their term in the program: at the middle of the fourth year for the A groups, and at the end of that year for the B groups.

As was suggested earlier, experiences in the course in comprehensive medicine might have had differential effects on students, depending on the attitudes with which they entered the program. If students were patient-oriented to begin with, those who had experiences compatible with these attitudes would presumably be more likely to have the attitudes reinforced. If students were originally learning-oriented, then exposure to such experiences would presumably lead to more frequent conversions. Therefore, in Table 6 it was necessary to separate students according to the attitudes they had expressed immediately prior to participation in the program.

Table 6 shows that students' emotional

involvement with families did indeed have differential effects, according to their initial attitudes. Among those who entered the program already expressing the attitude considered desirable, the experience of involvement had little effect: in the main, their already patient-oriented attitudes were merely reinforced. But among those who felt initially that patient contacts primarily enabled them to learn medicine, the experience of involvement did have an effect: the greater the degree of involvement, the more likely their conversion toward a patient-oriented attitude.

Through a series of analyses such as this one, we were able to arrive at some tentative conclusions about the factors contributing most to observed program effects.

THE NEED FOR REPLICATION

Our final point can be stated briefly. When one evaluates an educational program—whether in a medical school, a high school, or a kindergarten—the number of cases available for study is obviously limited by the sizes of the classes. The investigator may have the feeling that these are not large enough for sound statistical analysis. This was true in the present case. Each fourth-year class in the medical school numbered about 80 students. But since these were divided into two groups, the conclusions would have been based on only 40 students, had the analysis been confined to only one fourth-year class. One might have felt uneasy about results deriving from such a small number; in addition, more complicated analyses of the kind reported in Table 6 would have been precluded. The solution, then, was to cumulate fourth-year classes until we had a large enough number of cases. Instead of basing the evaluation on only one fourth-year class, we assembled data from four. This gave us a total of about 330 students, half of them in A groups and the other half in B groups.

Such replication has an additional advantage. There is always a possibility that particular findings, even when statistically significant, have come about by chance. But this possibility is reduced if one can show —as we actually did in our preliminary analyses—that the same phenomenon has occurred independently in four instances. Replication can therefore increase our confidence in our results.

Notes

1. For a description of the thinking behind this revision, see J. T. Wearn, T. H. Ham, J. W. Patterson, and J. L. Caughey, Jr., "Report on an Experiment in Medical Education," *Journal of Medical Education,* 31 (1956), pp. 516–29, 530 ff.

2. It is interesting to note that, partly as a result of the evaluation study, the directors did clarify their objectives. Today, some ten years after the research was begun, they talk in precise terms.

3. This danger is always particularly prominent in the evaluation of educational programs; as students grow older and gain experience, their attitudes are likely to be modified by the very fact of maturation.

4. A comparison of the responses given by the A and B groups at the end of the third year (T_1) shows how closely the two groups resembled each other initially, even though they were largely in the program on a self-selected rather than randomly assigned basis. This comparability was generally found in other aspects of the study. But even when groups were noncomparable on some aspect, it made little difference, since each student was serving as his own control.

5. Of course, "long-term" is used here in a relative sense. In the evaluation study, we were only able to follow the students for six months after their completion of the course in comprehensive care. In a subsequent study of the same students during their internships and residencies, many of the same questions were repeated. It will therefore be possible to investigate which of the shifts found in the present study were maintained for longer periods of time.

6. The relative nature of this question should be noted. It would have been quite meaningless to ask the students how involved they had been with their families; what seemed like a high degree of involvement to one student might have been considered moderate by another. Asking the question in relative terms circumvented this difficulty.

Auxiliary Readings

A. General Statements

S. M. Lipset, P. F. Lazarsfeld, A. H. Barton, and J. Linz, "The Psychology of Voting: An Analysis of Political Behavior," pp. 1150–64 in G. Lindzey (ed.), *Handbook of Social Psychology*, Vol. II (Cambridge, Mass.: Addison-Wesley, 1954).

The panel technique has generally been applied in studies of short-term change, particularly election campaigns. Drawing upon voting studies, this selection discusses the fundamental elements of panel analysis: the turnover table; qualified change (distinguishing constant qualifiers and time-bound qualifiers); and concurrent change and mutual interaction. The nature of the panel study is further clarified by comparing it with experimental studies, on the one hand, and trend studies, on the other.

H. Zeisel, *Say It With Figures* (New York: Harper and Bros., 1947), Chapter X.

One of the earliest and clearest expositions of the panel technique in the literature. The panel is compared with other procedures for measuring change, and its usefulness as an instrument of causal analysis is assessed. This chapter also contains a good discussion of some of the pitfalls in panel analysis. Subsequent editions have brought the book up to date.

J. Tinbergen, "Economic Business Cycle Research," pp. 61–86 in *The American Economic Association, Readings in Business Cycle Analysis*, Part I (Philadelphia: Blakiston Co., 1944).

Shows how the economist approaches process analysis. The parallels with panel analysis deserve careful study and discussion.

B. Turnover

P. F. Lazarsfeld, 1939, "The Change of Opinion During a Political Discussion," *Journal of Applied Psychology*, XXIII (February 1939), pp. 131–47.

When President Roosevelt nominated Hugo Black for the Supreme Court, the early opinion polls showed that Protestants tended to oppose him, non-Protestants to support him. It was then publicly alleged that Black had formerly been a member of the Ku Klux Klan. The later poll showed about the same total proportion favoring Black, but the Protestants now tended to support him, the non-Protestants to oppose him. Reverse trends in the subgroups produced an absence of change for the total population, even though the turnover was very large.

Otto Bartos, *Mathematics of Small Group Research* (New York: Columbia University Press, 1969).

This text offers much more than the title indicates. It is the best elementary introduction to matrix algebra and its application to mobility and panel studies as well as to sociometry. The connection between formulae and substantive topics should be helpful for any beginner. A section on game theory is equally valuable.

N. M. Bradburn and D. Caplovitz, *Reports on Happiness* (Chicago: Aldine, 1965), Chapter 4.

In 1962 the National Opinion Research Center conducted a study of various aspects of mental health (worries, anxiety, positive and negative feelings, etc.). In October 1962 the Cuban missile crisis, threatening war between the nuclear superpowers, erupted. The NORC immediately conducted an additional interview with a portion of the sample, and was able to assess the impact of this international crisis on several different aspects of mental health.

G. Katona, "Attitude Change: Instability of Response and Acquisition of Experience," *Psychological Monographs,* No. 463 (1958).

The author was especially concerned with the turnover of trichotomies. Many of his own studies deal with expectations where people are classified as optimists, pessimists or undecideds. Katona develops indices which help to distinguish general trends from individual change in attitude. Turnover data is related to conventional business cycle research. Then in his final sections, the author moves into a general theory of the relation between information and behavior. The monograph provides an important link between the University of Michigan work on psychological economics and the Columbia University studies of voting behavior.

R. K. Goldsen, M. Rosenberg, R. M. Williams, Jr., and E. A. Suchman, 1960. *What College Students Think* (Princeton: Van Nostrand, 1960), Chapter I.

A discussion of how college students' educational values changed over a two-year period. During this time span, there was a decreased emphasis on the importance of college education for providing vocational training or developing career skills and an increased emphasis on providing a basic general education and appreciation of ideas, developing interest in community and world problems, and developing ethical standards and values. Illustrates the high level of "turnover" in educational values during the college years.

F. Modigliani and F. E. Balderston, "Economic Analysis and Forecasting: Recent Developments in Use of Panel and Other Survey Techniques," pp. 372–98 in E. Burdick and A. J. Brodbeck, *American Voting Behavior* (New York: The Free Press, 1959).

Reports a number of useful panel studies, particularly in the area of consumer behavior. A familiar problem is: how well can one predict purchasing behavior from intention? The panel results reveal considerable turnover. Fifty-six per cent of people planning to buy a car in 1952 did so compared with 15 per cent who originally did not have this intention. But since seven-eighths did not plan to buy, about two-thirds of the actual purchases were made by those who originally did not intend to buy.

C. Qualified Change

P. H. Ennis, "The Contextual Dimension in Voting," pp. 180–211 in W. McPhee and W. Glaser (eds.), *Public Opinion and Congressional Elections* (New York: The Free Press, 1962).

This study includes a panel analysis, treating the social context as a qualifier variable. Respondents are classified as "majority" voters if their political affiliation agrees with that dominant in their communities, and as "minority" voters if it does not. While the amount of total change (turnover) differs little for these two types of voters, the majority voters show a strong tendency to shift to their "own" party whereas the minority voters are just as likely to shift away from, as toward, their party. Many other examples of change appear in this perceptive article.

T. M. Newcomb, *Personality and Social Change* (New York: Dryden Press, 1943).

The first major study based on repeated interviews, it is very rich in the psychological interpretation of the findings. The first part presents statistical results, while the latter sections are based on case studies. A unique follow-up study of Newcomb's sample twenty-five years later is reported in T. M. Newcomb, K. E. Koenig, R. Flacks, and D. P. Warwick, *Persistence and Change: Bennington College and Its Students After Twenty-five Years* (New York: Wiley, 1967).

E. A. Suchman, 1949. "Factors Determining Which Men Got Promoted," Chapter 6, Section II in S. A. Stouffer, *et al., The American Soldier: Adjustment During Army Life,* Vol. I (Princeton: Princeton University Press, 1949).

A panel of about five hundred soldiers was interviewed twice within a period of six months on attitudes toward various aspects of army life. Soldiers who are more conformist are shown to be more likely to be subsequently promoted, and, conversely, promotion has the effect of making soldiers at all levels of criticism more favorable toward army life.

D. Concurrent Change

D. C. Pelz and F. M. Andrews, "Detecting Causal Priorities in Panel Study Data," *American Sociological Review,* 29 (December 1964), pp. 836–48.

A procedure is suggested for the study of the mutual interaction of variables using continuous, rather than dichotomous, data; it is called the "cross-lagged panel correlation." Assume variables A and B are measured at time 1 and 2. If the correlation between A at time 1 and B at time 2 is greater than the correlation of B at time 1 and A at time 2, then A may be said to have "causal priority" over B. The authors present empirical applications and point to certain conditions which must be met if the procedure is to work satisfactorily.

P. F. Lazarsfeld and R. K. Merton, "Friendship as a Social Process: a Substantive and Methodological Analysis," pp. 18–66 in M. Berger, T. Abel, and C. H. Page (eds.), *Freedom and Control in Modern Society* (New York: Van Nostrand, 1954).

In the first part of the article, Merton presents a theoretical analysis "of the social processes involved in the formation, maintenance, and disruption of friendship"; in the second part, Lazarsfeld presents a formal framework encompassing the research operations required for testing the theoretical ideas. He stipulates a series of "sequence rules" in a 16-fold table which test the statements of process. Further refinement in process analysis is introduced by extension of the time dimension (three or more points in time); increase in the number of variables considered (three or more variables); and finer subdivisions of variables (three or more categories). Theories of social process can be encompassed by the 16-fold table or its refinements.

A. H. Barton and B. Anderson, "Change in an Organizational System: Formalization of a Qualitative Study," in A. Etzioni (ed.), *Complex Organizations* (New York: Holt, Rinehart and Winston, 1961).

In a study by McCleery as reported in the preceding chapter, the effects of a policy change on the management of a prison were described. Barton and Anderson recast the qualitative narrative in terms of the variables and time periods involved. Flow charts are constructed which show the interaction system implied in the McCleery paper. Finally, these charts are translated into systems of difference equations. For the mathematically untrained reader, numerical examples are provided to make the solutions intuitively understandable.

P. Lazarsfeld, B. Berelson and H. Gaudet, *The People's Choice,* 3rd Ed. (New York: Columbia University Press, 1969).

The series of introductions to this early panel study provide a good history of the development of the panel method. Based on a review by the French sociologist François Chazel, panel studies of elections in France and England are summarized.

Raymond Boudon, "A New Look at Correlation Analysis," Chapter 6 in H. Blalock and A. Blalock (eds.), *Methodology in Social Research* (New York: McGraw-Hill, 1968).

The author shows the identity of path analysis and the Simon-Blalock method. He suggests the term dependence analysis and relates it to dichotomous algebra. His ideas on the linear decomposition of conditional probabilities also provide the link to work by James Coleman on panel analysis.

D. Heise, "A Model for Causal Inference from Panel Data," Chapter 3 in E. Borgatta (ed.), *Sociological Methodology 1970* (San Francisco: Jossey-Bass, 1970).
The author applies path analysis to repeated observations. He emphasizes the relation between true causal lag and the time distance between the panel waves. The linear assumptions of path analysis prohibit the use of joint frequencies of higher than second level. Within its limitations, this paper gives interesting results which are corroborated by a simulation experiment reported in the same volume.

E. Repeated Observations on Collectives

No additional references could be located. However, material from such studies as Project Talent would lend itself to this type of analysis because of the double sampling of schools and students.

F. Relationship Between Panels and Experiments

D. T. Campbell, "From Description to Experimentation: Interpreting Trends as Quasi-experiments," pp. 212–42 in C. W. Harris (ed.), *Problems in Measuring Change* (Madison: University of Wisconsin Press, 1963).
The author discusses a number of research designs in terms of their distance from controlled experiments. He pays substantial attention to panel analysis and especially to sixteen-fold tables. He assumes that the "cross-lagged correlations" of interaction studies would give results similar to the "mutual effects" index; but the examples in the text prove the point only by numerical coincidence.

Index